The Handbook of
Family Psychology
and Therapy

Volume I

The Handbook of Family Psychology and Therapy

Volume I

Edited by

Luciano L'Abate

Georgia State University

THE DORSEY PRESS
Homewood, Illinois 60430

ISBN 0-256-03487-7

Library of Congress Catalog Card No. 84–73505

Printed in the United States of America

1 2 3 4 5 6 7 8 9 0 K 2 1 0 9 8 7 6 5

Foreword

Historically, psychologists have been largely concerned with the individual and only in the recent past have begun to consider the significance of family members as agents of influence on the individual. In developmental psychology, for instance, the subject of study first of all was the child himself, and then the mother/child dyad. Later, theorists and practitioners began to consider the role of the father as an important determinant in the development of the child. Still later, other family members, most notably siblings and grandparents, were added to this influential triad. So the system known as the family has become increasingly more differentiated and, as a totality, has become a primary focus of investigation.

As we deal with the complexity of the family, we must utilize a systems approach in the development of models on which to build our theories. We must also keep in mind that as complex as the family system is, it does not exist in isolation but at the intersect of all of our other societal institutions—the schools, the media, the health system, the world of work, and government at all levels—and is therefore influenced by them. The social ecology of the family has been increasingly noted as a major determinant of family concerns and problems. One of the most dramatic of these problems is that of child abuse, which (as all figures indicate) is increasing at an alarming rate, indicative of both a dramatic breakdown of the nurturant function of the family in this country and rapidly growing social stresses (poverty and rising unemployment, for instance). Underlying such problems are breakdowns in, or difficulties with, the links between family members and between families and society.

These connections and their dynamics constitute the central theme in family psychology. The underlying assumption is that people must be viewed and, where necessary, treated with regard to their roles as family members. The family must be seen as a dynamic and multi-faceted whole. Family psychology also recognizes a lifespan approach to psychology; the examination of family relationships as they change over time is essential to this field. Finally, a systems approach demands that the family continually be conceptualized as a part of a larger system, namely, the society in which the family is embedded.

This *Handbook* appears at a time when demand for such a text is becoming increasingly apparent. The striking change in the demographics of our society underline the need for attention to a family psychology. Almost 20 percent of all American families (and 50 percent of black American families) are headed by single parents. Future thinking concerning the family must increasingly deal with family forms other than the conventional nuclear family. Similarly, the rising rate of divorce and subsequent increase in the number of issues related to remarriage, custody, and the roles of family members affected by divorce ("custody" issues for grandparents, for example) are not fully recognized by traditional psychology or sociology texts. The growing number of mothers in the work force and of two-income families and the impact of the workplace on family life are all phenomena with which the social sciences must be concerned. An expanding need for, and reliance on, day care in America, a new mobility that may separate family members by great distances, changing housing patterns, and the splitting of families along generational lines all affect the interactions of family members with one another and with their communities.

The importance of family-related issues to many professionals and the need to address these issues have outstripped the availability of thoughtfully produced resources. Academicians, service providers, clinicians, and social policy analysts, among others, should find *The Handbook of Family Psychology and Therapy* a useful contribution to our understanding of the family. Such a comprehensive publication as this will have widespread appeal, being appropriate for established professionals as well as new adherents to family psychology. Many of the chapters combine the practical with the theoretical, and these volumes will be immediately useful to social psychologists, developmental psychologists, and family counselors.

The relationship of the individual to the family has been too long neglected as a subject of study for psychologists. Generally considered the domain of sociology, family studies in psychology have for the most part been confined to the field of child development. To undertake the task of making this the subject of a psychological text is admirable, and Luciano L'Abate has done a laudable job of choosing topics and subtopics pertinent to this theme. The book represents a novel conjoining of issues that are inherently related, distilling information from the great amount of research already completed. The contributors to this book succeed in covering a wide range of topics concerning both normal and pathological family functions.

A final aim of the editor and authors of this publication is the integration of knowledge from many disciplines. If we are to maximize our accomplishments in the field of family psychology, it must be through the cooperation and efforts of a broad array of workers in the fields of psychology, sociology, education, medicine, and law. We must be willing to work towards an ever greater convergence of these disciplines around family-related issues and to take an interdisciplinary approach to the study of families.

The principal functions served by this *Handbook* seem to be fourfold. First, it serves to circumscribe an emerging field of study. Secondly, these volumes highlight the role of the family as a source of developmental influence, an agent of change, and an appropriate and necessary unit of preventive and remedial intervention. Thirdly, students of the field and those for whom the concept of family psychology is a new one will find in this work a splendid introduction to the field. Finally, this text, with its wide scope of focus, has considerable value as a source of new inquiry and theorizing.

As in the evolution of all thought, fields of study within psychology are born, mature, and sometimes vanish. This *Handbook* may well constitute the formal birth of the field of family psychology. It is a movement of the present that can only increase in importance over the coming decades. Future thinking will be characterized by an ecological approach in which the individual is characterized as behaving within a family which in turn is embedded in a broad social environment. This *Handbook* points us towards the future of psychological thought, and as such is a seminal work.

Edward Zigler
Sterling Professor of Psychology
Yale University

Preface

The purpose of this reference work is to put together under one cover information about the relationship of the individual to the family. The branch of psychology that deals with this relationship is called *family psychology,* linking concern for the individual, which has been the task of psychology, with concern for the family, which as a whole has been a task of sociology.

A recent survey by Burr and Leigh (1982) pointed out that, according to titles, at least 25 different names were being used to designate family-oriented departments. By contrast, the title and the definition of family psychology are clear enough. To paraphrase a cliché, it's the name—without the game.

The lack of an academic and professional field of family psychology is an anachronism when we consider that at least two thirds of our waking and sleeping time is usually spent with someone we care about or who cares for us. Psychology and psychoanalysis have paid lip service to the family's early influence on the individual. Yet, family references in psychology textbooks (except for child development textbooks, where such references may reach up to 15 percent of the total) may be totally absent in textbooks representing the fields of personality, theories of personality, and especially social psychology—as if personality and social psychology originated and are being maintained in a vacuum (Dunne & L'Abate, 1978).

It is the recognition of the importance of the family context *throughout the life span* (L'Abate, 1976) that makes such bypassing unbelievable to commonsense readers, even those who know nothing about psychology. The family, as an aggregate of individual members, has been relatively neglected by psychology as a science and as a profession (L'Abate, 1983). Fortunately, there are many signs that this neglect is decreasing considerably. *The Handbook of Family Psychology and Therapy* demonstrates that interest does indeed exist. Yet, in collaborating on this manuscript, we have been aware that family psychology as an academic discipline is practically nonexistent. As a clinical profession, family psychology remains ill-defined, except perhaps for the Academy of Psychologists Interested in Sex, Marital, and Family Therapy (now called the Academy of Family Psychology). The *Handbook*, then, has at least two functions: first, to collect under one cover what we know about the relationship of the individual with the family; second, to serve as a springboard for a more effective and clearly defined discipline of family psychology by summarizing past findings, theories, and applications.

The *Handbook* thus describes a field that is academically nonexistent and professionally ill-defined. Its purpose is to define this field in ways that show the continuity if not the congruence of individual psychology and family psychology. Contributors to the *Handbook* were asked to rely as much as possible on studies in which the relationships of family members (e.g., parents, sibs) have been investigated.

The field of family psychology is so undeservedly unrecognized and ignored by psychology that it has nowhere to go but up! The family does need recognition as a legitimate unit of psychological study and practice (Thaxton & L'Abate, 1982), and the *Handbook* represents such recognition.

Conger's (1981) article was an articulate and much needed summary of the state of the American family. Although this important and relevant statement included the family as a unit of psychological study and practice, Conger did not go far enough in the implications of what the family field means to psychology as a science and as a profession.

In the first place, psychologists are not prepared, conceptually or practically, to deal with families. As already noted, a recent survey (Dunne & L'Abate, 1978) showed that most textbooks in general, social, personality, and abnormal psychology have had very few or no references to family concepts (e.g., parents, marriage, parent-child interaction). The only exception was developmental psychology.

In the second place, with the exception of the AAMFT-approved Georgia State University clinical program (L'Abate, Berger, Wright, & O'Shea, 1979), no institutions grant a Ph.D. in family psychology. In fact, the term *family psychology* is relatively new (L'Abate, 1983). Contrast this state of affairs to the number of programs in social psychology, which as a whole has been extremely uninterested in dealing with marriage and the family. If there is a field of family psychology, it is still a clinically applied one. As far as I know, there is no academic program in family psychology.

In the third place, most clinical programs remain stuck at the individual level of training, along with whatever the level may imply (i.e., linear, noncontextual approaches that use outmoded clinical tests and procedures). In other words, most clinical training is still very traditional, clinging to World War II models and ignoring most of the advances that have been made in the past quarter of a century in mental health services (L'Abate & Thaxton, 1981).

In the fourth place, the current status of the family, which Conger (1981) aptly described as changed and still changing, requires the application of new educational tools for educators as well as trainers. We need preventive rather than solely therapeutic models which will allow us to deal with families in toto, not in parts as we have done thus far.

The jump that is required in order to move from the individual to the family might be described as a quantum leap. Although that description may seem an exaggeration, the process does require thinking in circular, contextual, and dialectical fashions that most of us are neither trained for nor accustomed to (Weeks & L'Abate, 1982). The jump is not an easy one. It will be resisted mostly by those whose linearity and rigidity in thinking do not permit alternatives. The family is an alternative that has caught psychology with its pants down, so to speak. We'd better hurry and pull them up, along with our bootstraps. We are singularly unprepared, academically and clinically, to deal with families. More than Conger's thoughtful address will be needed to move psychologists toward different models of thinking and training.

Fortunately, psychologists are becoming increasingly more involved in the field of family therapy (Thaxton & L'Abate, 1982). Despite the shortcomings already mentioned, we, as latecomers to this relatively new field, can learn from errors made by other disciplines and add a dimension that is still in short supply, that is, rigor both in theory and in research.

Even the respected critics of psychological trends and theories (Sarason, 1981) who have recently decried psychology's focus on the individual without historical and cultural contexts, have failed to mention the family as the vital nexus between the individual and society. Although this connection was recognized early by Murphy (1947), the recognition within the field of personality development remained unheeded in theory and practice.

The *Handbook* is an attempt to fill a large gap that the science and profession of psychology has allowed: the relationship of the individual with the family. By no means as comprehensive as it might be, the *Handbook* is nevertheless an attempt to represent, as much as possible, the field of family psychology. Psychologists of all persuasions and specialties will, we hope, concede that the attempt was needed.

Luciano L'Abate

REFERENCES

Burr, W. R., & Leigh, G. K. *Newsletter: National Council for Family Relations,* 1982, *27,* 1–5.

Conger, J. J. Freedom and commitment: Families, youth, and social change. *American Psychologist,* 1981, *36,* 1475–1484.

Dunne, E. E., & L'Abate, L. The family taboo in psychology textbooks. *Teaching of Psychology,* 1978, *5,* 115–117.

L'Abate, L. *Understanding and helping the individual in the family.* New York: Grune & Stratton, 1976.

L'Abate, L. *Family psychology: Theory, therapy, and training.* Washington, D.C.: University Press of America, 1983.

L'Abate, L., Berger, M., Wright, L., & O'Shea, M. Training in family studies: The program at Georgia State University. *Professional Psychology,* 1979, *10,* 58–64.

L'Abate, L., & Thaxton, M. L. Differentiation of resources in mental health delivery: Implications for training. *Professional Psychology,* 1981, *12,* 761–768.

Murphy, G. *Personality.* New York: Harper & Row, 1947.

Sarason, S. B. *Psychology misdirected.* New York: Free Press, 1981.

Thaxton, M. L., & L'Abate, L. The second wave and the second generation: Characteristics of new leaders in family therapy. *Family Process,* 1982, *21,* 359–362.

Weeks, G. R., & L'Abate, L. *Paradoxical psychotherapy: Theory and practice with individuals, couples, and families.* New York: Brunner/Mazel, 1982.

Acknowledgments

Lucy Rau Ferguson is responsible for helping to change the title of the training program at Georgia State University from *Family Studies* to *Family Psychology*. At the first Mailman Center Conference on Applied Child Psychology in January 1980 in Miami, her questioning led me to assert that, indeed, *family psychology* was not an empty term (the term had not, to my knowledge, been used until then). Despite that historical acknowledgment, I cannot believe that we waited until 1980 to coin the term. Surely, someone must have used it earlier— I would like to know who that someone is so that his or her contribution can be acknowledged.

A former Dorsey Press editor deserves the credit for conceiving the idea of this *Handbook*. A matter of being in the right place at the right time: He suggested it to me, and by return mail, I sent him an outline of possible topics. From that initial, rather skimpy outline, a larger one grew, and potential contributors were contacted. Originally, we thought about a board of consultants; however, many persons, approached with a fait accompli, begged off. Among the many who helped with their support and ideas were George Levinger at the University of Massachusetts, Norma Radin at the University of Michigan, Bernard Murstein at Connecticut College, Robert Woody at the University of Nebraska at Omaha, Norman Garmezy at the University of Minnesota, Gerald Zuk of New Orleans, as well as many other colleagues and students whose response to the idea of *The Handbook of Family Psychology and Therapy* was "Why not? Other, less-relevant fields are receiving much more recognition than this one." I cannot cite all of them—the list would be too long. The strong support of contributors, colleagues, and consultants kept me going throughout the writing and editing of the manuscript. Their support has meant, and continues to mean, a great deal to me. I hope that any whom I have failed to name will not feel slighted.

I am grateful to Amy Alexander, Billy Sue Groutas, Leila L'Abate, and Lisa Reddy for their help with the Author and Subject Indexes.

Marie Morgan deserves credit for *really* editing many of the chapters that my associates and I wrote and for suggesting improvements in all of them. The *Handbook* would have not materialized without her careful typing, proofing, and improving.

L. L.

LIST OF CONTRIBUTORS

Stephen I. Abramowitz
Division of Clinical Psychology
Department of Psychiatry
Davis Medical Center
University of California
Sacramento, California

James F. Alexander
Department of Psychology
University of Utah
Salt Lake City, Utah

Dennis A. Bagarozzi
School of Social Work
East Carolina University
Greenville, North Carolina

Cole Barton
Department of Psychology
Davidson College
Davidson, North Carolina

Steven R. H. Beach
Department of Psychology
State University of New York at
Stony Brook
Stony Brook, New York

Kathryn Beckham
Department of Child and
Family Development
College of Home Economics
University of Georgia
Athens, Georgia

Jay Belsky
College of Human Development
The Pennsylvania State University
University Park, Pennsylvania

Audrey Berger
Rochester Regional Forensic Unit
Rochester, New York

Michael Berger
Department of Psychology
Georgia State University
Atlanta, Georgia

Stephen D. Berger
School of Human Services
New Hampshire College
Manchester, New Hampshire

Andrew Christensen
Department of Psychology
University of California at Los
Angeles
Los Angeles, California

Victor G. Cicirelli
Department of Psychological
Sciences
Purdue University
West Lafayette, Indiana

Teresa Cooney
College of Human Development
The Pennsylvania State University
University Park, Pennsylvania

Mary Crawford
Department of Psychology
Michigan State University
East Lansing, Michigan

Jeri A. Doane
Yale Psychiatric Institute
Yale University of Medicine
New Haven, Connecticut

Bernice T. Eiduson
Family Styles Project
Neuropsychiatric Institute
Center for the Health Sciences
Los Angeles, California

Doris R. Entwisle
Department of Psychology
The Johns Hopkins University
Baltimore, Maryland

Beverley Fehr
Psychology Department
The University of British Columbia
Vancouver, British Columbia,
   Canada

Lucy Rau Ferguson
Private Practice
Berkeley, California

Hiram E. Fitzgerald
Department of Psychology
Michigan State University
East Lansing, Michigan

Martha Foster
Department of Psychology
Georgia State University
Atlanta, Georgia

Joseph Frey III
Department of Psychiatry
Medical College of Georgia
Augusta, Georgia

Gary F. Ganahl
Department of Psychiatry
West Virginia University Medical
   Center
Morgantown, West Virginia

Richard Gilbert
Department of Psychology
University of California at Los
   Angeles
Los Angeles, California

Jeffrey A. Giordano
Gerontology Department
University of South Florida
Tampa, Florida

Frances K. Grossman
Department of Psychology
Boston University
Boston, Massachusetts

Bernard G. Guerney, Jr.
College of Human Development
The Pennsylvania State University
University Park, Pennsylvania

Louise Guerney
College of Human Development
The Pennsylvania State University
University Park, Pennsylvania

Russell W. Irvine
Department of Educational
   Foundations
Georgia State University
Atlanta, Georgia

Edgar H. Jessee
St. Mary's Hospital
Knoxville, Tennessee

Gregory J. Jurkovic
Department of Psychology
Georgia State University
Atlanta, Georgia

Kenneth Kaye
Department of Psychiatry
Northwestern University
Chicago, Illinois

Luciano L'Abate
Department of Psychology
Georgia State University
Atlanta, Georgia

Robert A. Lewis
Department of Child Development
   and Family Studies
Purdue University
West Lafayette, Indiana

Robert M. Milardo
Human Development
University of Maine at Orono
Orono, Maine

Daniel R. Miller
Department of Psychology
Wesleyan University
Middletown, Connecticut

Nancy E. Moss
Division of Clinical Psychology
Department of Psychiatry
Davis Medical Center
University of California
Sacramento, California

Clifford I. Notarius
Department of Psychology
The Catholic University of America
Washington, D.C.

K. Daniel O'Leary
Department of Psychology
State University of New York at
Stony Brook
Stony Brook, New York

Gerald R. Patterson
Oregon Social Learning Institute
Eugene, Oregon

Daniel Perlman
Department of Family Studies
The University of British Columbia
Vancouver, British Columbia,
Canada

William S. Pollack
McLean Hospital
Harvard Medical School
Boston, Massachusetts

Gary R. Racusin
Yale Child Study Center
New Haven, Connecticut

Mark W. Roosa
Center for Family Studies
Arizona State University
Tempe, Arizona

R. Barry Ruback
Department of Psychology
Georgia State University
Atlanta, Georgia

Jennifer E. Sade
Department of Psychology
The Catholic University of America
Washington, D.C.

Jill D. Sanders
Department of Psychology
University of Utah
Salt Lake City, Utah

Victor D. Sanua
Department of Psychology
St. John's University
Jamaica, New York

Sadell Sloan
Private Practice
Atlanta, Georgia

Michael T. Smith
Department of Psychology
Georgia State University
Atlanta, Georgia

Monta P. Smith
Associate School Psychologist
Walton County Public Schools
Monroe, Georgia

George Sobelman
Rechovot, Israel

Joseph Stevens
Early Childhood Education
Georgia State University
Atlanta, Georgia

Barbara Strudler-Wallston
Department of Psychology and
   Human Development
George Peabody College for Teachers
Vanderbilt University
Nashville, Tennessee

Clifford H. Swenson, Jr.
Department of Psychological Sciences
Purdue University
West Lafayette, Indiana

Lynda D. Talmadge
Department of Psychology
Georgia State University
Atlanta, Georgia

William C. Talmadge
Private Practice
Atlanta, Georgia

Lyn Thaxton
William Russell Pullen Library
Georgia State University
Atlanta, Georgia

Donna Ulrici
Private Practice
New York, New York

Joan Vondra
College of Human Development
The Pennsylvania State University
University Park, Pennsylvania

Victor Wagner
Private Practice
New York, New York

Lynn S. Walker
Department of Pediatrics
School of Medicine
Institute for Public Policy Studies
Vanderbilt University
Nashville, Tennessee

Janet Warburton
Western States Family Institution
Salt Lake City, Utah

Donald J. Wendorf
Family Therapy Associates
Birmingham, Alabama

Edward Zigler
Department of Psychology
Yale University
New Haven, Connecticut

Irla L. Zimmerman
Family Styles Project
Neuropsychiatric Institute
Center for the Health Sciences
Los Angeles, California

Contents

Volume I

Section Three
Affect and the Family

Section Five
Parenthood and Parenting

Volume II

Section Six
Nontraditional Family Styles and Groups

Section Seven
Psychopathology and the Family

exchange conceptions of marital and family behavior and clinical
evaluation. Additional considerations.

Section Nine
Therapeutic and Preventive Interventions

Section Ten
Issues in Training

Section One

Historical and Theoretical Background

Chapter 1

Models of the Family: A Critical Review of Alternatives*

DANIEL R. MILLER
GEORGE SOBELMAN

This *Handbook* represents a pioneering effort to establish a psychological specialty that is virtually nonexistent. The paucity of research on the family as such is surprising in view of the tremendous public interest in the universal familial problems. Changes in sexual mores, the increasing rate of divorce, the possible demise of the family in its present form, and methods of rearing children are a few examples. Then why so little *psychological* research on topics that are uniquely familial? We trace the problem to a particular methodological preoccupation. As researchers, psychologists have reversed the usual sequence of steps in planning research, in which one specifies the questions to be studied and then determines the best methods for finding answers. Instead, they first committed themselves to a scientific model for conducting inquiries, developed appropriate instruments and statistics, and then looked for questions that would fit the methods. Moreover, the model they selected is a very specialized one; it was borrowed from constructs developed to explain mechanical and astronomical phenomena. Often, the questions about familial relationships do not fit the model and are ignored on the grounds that they are "unscientific." Since the rejected issues constitute some of the most fundamental ones pertaining to the family, it is small wonder that much of the field has been ignored.

This chapter, then, is devoted to premises and questions—the ones that have created the current impasse and some alternatives that seem

---

* We wish to thank Norman Miller and Karl Scheibe for their helpful criticisms.

more viable for certain familial problems. The chapter begins with some current views of research and the problems they raise, continues with a survey of alternatives developed in a discipline that is devoted to helping families with practical problems, reviews some historical trends that led to the current formulations of the alternatives, and concludes with a critical examination of contradictory viewpoints.

THE CURRENT PSYCHOLOGICAL MODEL

Psychologists are certainly sophisticated about the significance of models. They appreciate the fact that premises about scientific inquiry define the boundaries of a discipline, set limits on possible subjects and methods, and consequently predetermine possible answers. Hence, though the issues are abstract and there are no right or wrong positions, the choice of a model (say, to be used for research on the family) generates much controversy, particularly among sophisticated theorists, who tend to have the strongest commitments. Often their criticisms of one another become heated because they are keenly aware of how significant the resolution of their disagreements can be for themselves and the profession. Criteria accepted by the profession define the boundaries of the field, are applied by editors in evaluating articles and books submitted for publication, and determine the content of academic texts. In recent years, a group of theorists who regard themselves as a protesting minority have published papers in the *American Psychologist* in which they take strong exception to the premises they attribute to the establishment, questioning them in terms of principles derived from current writings in the philosophy of science. Their viewpoints will be highlighted, starting with the status quo and examining some of the criticisms.

Psychology as a science: Objectivity and determinism

In many introductory texts, psychology is defined as a science of behavior. The "science" label refers to premises borrowed from astronomy and physics, British empiricism, and positivism. According to the current position, psychology is empirical above all. It is crucial that hard data be collected, preferably by means of controlled experiments, either in the laboratory or the field. The concept of control is derived from Mill's method of difference, which requires the comparison of two situations alike in all respects but the one identified as the cause or the effect, depending on the hypothesis being investigated. Hypotheses must be formulated beforehand and tested by the data. Theoretical terms must be connected with facts or with terms supported by facts.

It is necessary that the procedures be reliable and unbiased in the sense of being value free.

Only by satisfying such criteria, many psychologists feel, is it possible to arrive at the general laws (like those developed by the physicists) that are needed for dependable prediction. By "law," the physicists refer to an invariable, functionally dependent relationship that is universal in the sense of being independent of the society or the historical period. The determinism underlying such principles was most enthusiastically described by LaPlace (Nagel, 1961, p. 281):

> An intelligence knowing all the forces acting in nature at a given instant, as well as the momentary positions of all things in the universe, would be able to comprehend in one single formula the motions of the largest bodies as well as of the lightest atoms in the world. . . . To it nothing would be uncertain, the future as well as the past would be present to its eyes. Discoveries in [physics] have brought the mind within reach of comprehending in the same analytical formula the past and future state of the system of the world.

The partiality to physical models probably accounts for the strong influence that behaviorism has had on psychologists' methods. As a theoretical movement that is most concerned with the explanation of human reactions without appealing to experience, behaviorism has diversified to such an extent that the various proponents seem to agree only on the original methodical insistence on the use of publicly observable data. This criterion seems to have been inscribed indelibly on the thinking of psychologists, who are consequently uncomfortable with old-fashioned, subjective concepts like mind and will and, until recently, were inclined to favor behavioral constructs. Compatible with this bias is the advocacy by some psychologists of a form of operationism that restricts them to constructs which are defined in terms of empirical procedures.

Reductionism and individualism

Probably the most debatable of the current criteria for arriving at constructs and methods, reductionism has been borrowed from physical scientists who, in their quests for universal principles, have been very successful in reducing what seemed like relatively autonomous theories at one level of complexity to other, more inclusive, theories at a simpler level: chemistry has been reduced to physical theory, and thermodynamics to statistical mechanics. Accordingly, some social scientists feel that scientific progress requires a reduction of concepts at the higher levels to the simpler or smaller units at lower levels and ultimately to the science of mechanics. In practice, this view leads to two types of conversion. One is the attempt to account for the properties of complex constructs in terms of the properties of their constituents: society, family, and relationships should, according to the reductionist, be explained with reference to the psychological properties of their members. The other type of conversion is the translation of principles and concepts of one theory to the principles and concepts of another which is presumed to be more basic: reducing psychoanalytic principles to learning theory. One means of achieving reduction is by applying the criterion of parsimony: Given alternate theories which seem equally effective in accounting for a particular phenomenon, the superior of the two is the one that entails the fewest assumptions and is most appealing to common sense. Parsimonious explanations tend to be tied to observable data and to involve few postulates about internal states or collective arrangements.

Reducing the complex to the simple has a special implication for defining empirical psychological problems: "From its inception . . . American psychology has been quintessentially a psychology of the individual organism" (Sarason, 1981, p. 827). Investigators who are unhappy with fuzzy concepts like group mind and group boundaries can take comfort from a view of groups as aggregates of individuals, physical entities with attributes that are easier to measure. Committed to reduction, these researchers hew to the line taken by Allport (1924) in his influential text: "There is no psychology of groups which is not essentially and entirely a psychology of the individual" (p. 4). This is a position that dominates the field to this day. The profession has tended to downplay the study of groups as entities and of teleologically organized activities. Despite important theoretical contributions (particularly by Lewin and his followers) to the study of the group as a system, the topic is neither theoretically nor empirically in the center of contemporary social psychology (Pepitone, 1981). Moreover, the quest for general laws that apply to individuals regardless of the context has lead most social psychologists to conceive of individuals apart from the specific conditions of their ecology, culture, and historical period. Small wonder that psychologists tend to make short shrift of the family, the understanding of which (some specialists feel) requires descriptions of interpersonal patterns and cultural influences.

OBJECTIONS TO THE TRADITIONAL MODEL

There is much appeal in a system of principles the elements of which are logically related to one another and linked to objective observations obtained while unrelated variables are held constant. Unfortunately, critics have discerned many flaws in this model of a brave new world of theorizing, particularly as it applies to topics such as the family.

Objectivity and determinism

The possibility of being truly objective has been questioned by many. As observed by Kant, there can be no preinterpreted givens. Our values determine which segments of reality become significant to us, which ones we choose to study, and how we study them. Like everyone else, scientists are members of a society which, at a particular place and time, has many values about research (Kuhn, 1962). The knowledge of science is accumulated by professional groups whose members are in constant communication about desirable problems, philosophies of science, and sources of funds. An investigator's quest for objectivity can be tempered, then, by knowledge that the results will be judged by peers and may affect the flow of funds. Certain shared values can even result in significant topics being ignored. Instances in point are the virtual neglect of the biological superiority of women and the genetic sources of antisocial behavior, both topics that run counter to the prevailing values about desirable research (Hager, 1982).

The strong faith that physicists placed in determinism during the 19th century wavered once questions were raised about predictability in quantum mechanics. Just how much determinism is applicable to the social sciences is a moot point. The experimenter is faced with many complex, interacting, and special variables. Unlike the inanimate objects of physics, humans have conceptions and opinions about the investigative process, a fact that creates unpredictable changes in findings (Nagel, 1961). An interviewee's response may be affected by reactions to the interviewer's membership in a different social class, impressions of the purpose of the interview, perceived pressures, or the social significance of the topic. Given another interviewer or a different conception of the procedure, the results are different. It has thus far not been possible to ascertain all the variables affecting such differential responses. Moreover, once the results of a study are disseminated, this information creates changes, thus invalidating hypotheses that were valid before the results were made public. Word that a particular method of childrearing, say feeding on demand, is having adverse effects on the infants may prompt mothers to abandon the practice, thus invalidating a finding that people in two social classes differ significantly in their use of the method.

Excessive faith in the ability of experimental psychologists to predict social behavior has drawn the fire of a number of psychologists. The artificiality of experimental conditions is a common target. "In order to behave as scientists," complains Bannister (1966), "we must construct situations in which our subjects . . . can behave as little like human beings as possible and we do this in order to allow ourselves to make statements about the nature of their humanity" (p. 24). Another target is unwarranted generalization from the experimental setting to many other settings:

> Some particular set of conditions in an experiment is generally taken to be representative of all possible conditions of a similar type. . . . The social psychologist as experimenter is content to let a particular situation stand for an indefinite range of possible . . . situations in a vague and unspecified way. (Deese, 1972, pp. 56–60)

Such objections might be dismissed as a misuse of experiments rather than flaws in the deterministic outlook. It is more difficult to disregard the claim that social phenomena can never be the objects of universal laws, since their meanings are inextricably linked with their culture and history. Most social institutions have been organized with respect to specific environments and are products of special cultural traditions. If this is true, then psychological and sociological generalizations, unlike those in physics, are likely to be limited to the phenomena of a historical period and to special social groups. Taking issue with the universalism of Piaget, Freud, and Skinner, Scheibe (1979) states that psychology is a science only as an extension of biology. He thinks that there is another part of psychology that is akin to history and biography. There, essential unpredictability prevails, and events need to be clarified by means of the narrative. Manicas and Secord (1983) also argue most persuasively against "the mistaken assumption that it is the aim of a scientific psychology to explain our everyday actions by showing that they can be derived from a single set of laws . . . as discovered in the experimental laboratory" (p. 405). These authors think that a wide variety of physical, biological, psychological, and sociological systems and structures may be needed to explain specific behaviors. They view experimentation as a valuable means of clarifying processes underlying behavior, but think it is misused when it is applied to the explanation of actual events, which may be products of the subjects' unique traits, history, setting, and culture.

Reductionism

Usually ignored in the literature on reductionism is the fact that the most frequently cited examples in physics have involved homogeneous systems: Both systems contained descriptive terms with approximately the same meanings. Valuable reductions of the heterogeneous type have also been made, but under special conditions: Both systems contained terms with unambiguous meanings, and all principles could be formulated in explicit statements; both systems shared many expressions with the same meanings, so that logical or empirical linkages could be made; the reduction contained significant new insights (Nagel, 1961). In making reductions, no psychologist has attempted to satisfy the criteria for either homogeneous or heterogeneous systems. Often the attempt is justified solely by a faith in the superiority of the encompassing, presumably simpler, system. Some recent examples are the reduction of social altruism to biological constructs and of schizophrenia to a biochemical pathology.

Sometimes the reduction entails an oversimplification that does violence to the facts. Differences between men and women have often been explained in biological terms even when the variables were intrapsychic characteristics and sex roles. Although alternative social hypotheses about gender could be supported by previous findings, interpretations were favored which entailed simplistic reductions of psychological and social attributes to presumed neurological structures and unsupported assumptions about associations between gonads and the brain (Unger, 1979).

In the study of psychopathology, the appeal of reductionist thinking has led to the proliferation of research in psychophysiology, psychopharmacology, behavior genetics, and biological psychiatry, it being presumed that explanations in the language of such scientific specialties are more meaningful than explanations in the language of personality, social relationships, and culture. A review of reductionists' attempts to clarify psychopathological states gives Peele (1981) the impression that many investigators devise "convoluted and secondary biological formulations for phenomena that can already be understood in social-psychological terms" (p. 815). The exercise provides no evident gains in insight and may even pervert meaning.

Individualism and the ahistorical orientation

Sometimes oversimplification is the product of an attempt at universality, which precludes the use of information about culture, society, or history. In fact, culture, society, and history tend to be neglected because they are taken to be scientifically less meaningful than biochemistry or genetics (Peele, 1981). Those who, like Mead (1934) or Vygotsky (1962), think that the interpsychological precedes the intrapersonal, are concerned that psychologists tend to take the social world as a given and fail to examine the ways in which psychological functions are the social and historical products of collective endeavor. "By reducing conflicts to individual subjective processes," Sampson (1981) feels, "we overlook those questions of social structure that are necessary to ground both our understanding and our recommendations for their resolution" (p. 737). Illustrating this point is the criticism by McLemore and Benjamin (1979) of DSM III, the system the American Psychiatric Association uses to classify mental disorders. Clinical utility, they feel, requires a psychosocial nosology focusing on interpersonal behavior and social psychological variables, not the reduction to static, individual, often subjective, symptoms akin to those of physical illness.

These complaints suggest that the elegance of the traditional scientific model often makes it so appealing that some practitioners apply it in a doctrinal manner, whether or not it is appropriate. In such instances, it is used as a Procrustean bed. It eliminates from the research those elements of the problem that do not lend themselves to reduction, even though they are theoretically important, and devotes excessive attention to trivial topics because they can be reduced. Such eliminations and distortions explain the relative paucity of research on the family as an entity; on the contents and organization of environments, which are often dismissed as abstract stimuli; and on members of American subcultures, including rural residents, women, the working class, and immigrants.

"There is a creeping sense of malaise about psychology," Sarason (1981) thinks; a malaise whose source he illustrates with reference to addresses of past presidents of the American Psychological Association. With one notable exception, John Dewey, "one would hardly know that psychology existed in a particular society having a distinctive social order deriving from a very distinctive past. . . . Instead one finds a riveting on the individual organism" (p. 827). It is difficult to take cognizance of culture and history when groups are reduced to aggregates of individuals and their attitudes, motives, and attractions, and families are reduced to inner conflicts, learned responses, and cognitive misperceptions. Moreover, the quest for fundamental laws is bound to restrict the permissible object of study to the one universal unit, the individual, who does have some universal psychological attributes.

No one denies the significant contributions that individual psychology has made to the understanding of human behavior. It is the omissions and distortions produced by doctrinal individualism that elicit criticism because they preclude the study of important social questions. Interestingly, it is the specialists who apply psychological theory to practical, everyday problems who are most unhappy about the oversimplifications and distortions produced by individualism. Successful application of theory requires an acknowledgment of the "manifold contexts in which (people) live and work interdependently—role systems, communications networks, status and power hierarchies, economic structures, and normative cultures" (Pepitone, 1981, pp. 976–977). Billig (1976) decries the tendencies of social psychologists to reduce social conflicts to individuals' misperceptions, implying that resolution requires only a clarification of the misunderstandings. This psychologizing of conflict, he feels, ignores the actual social contradictions which are the source of the misconceptions.

The experiment (in which the professional investigator manipulates the conditions to which naive subjects respond) may, in conjunction with the traditional medical models of treatment, have contributed to the prevalent tendency of service-oriented psychologists to exert unidirectional influence on their clients. This asymmetry, say Tyler, Pargament, and Gatz (1983), creates incongruities between methods and goals: The therapist makes the patient dependent in order to foster independence; the teacher communicates expertise to passive listeners in order to create autonomous thinkers; the consultant assumes the identity of "expert" in order to create a collaborative relationship with the consultee. Eschewing individualism, these authors feel that service will be more effective if viewed as part of an interaction between peers, both of whom are expected to change their special perspectives and skills. The service-oriented psychologist cannot escape the social standpoints of the society or the historical period any more than the experimenter can.

Concentration on the individual instead of the relationship between client and consultant results in dysfunctional activities that are anti-democratic. Cronbach (1982) thinks the consultant's values are crucial to the establishment of a democratic relationship. Designing the evaluations of social problems, he thinks, requires an understanding of the pluralism of values, democratic governance, and accommodation to conflicting interests which prevail in American organizations at this time.

FORMULATING A PARADIGM

What paradigms of inquiry are available to the investigator or practitioner, say someone who works with families and for whom the traditional paradigm is too limiting? The remainder of this chapter is devoted to a consideration of alternatives. The founders of family therapy decided on a paradigm that is quite different from the one used in academic psychology. Since they were one of the groups who thought seriously about philosophy of science and the issues they raise are important to anyone who aspires to study or change families, their thinking and its origins are presented next in some detail. Underlying the discussion is a conception of the paradigm as a group of principles which sets limits on the definition of constructs and the development of methods in order to clarify the problem to be investigated. The paradigm, in other words, is a framework for understanding data. Data may be conceived in terms of reductionistic or holistic, ahistorical or historical, universalistic or cultural categories.

Each paradigm provides latitude for a delimited range of models, which are representations of theoretical structure showing how the parts are systemically interrelated. In some models, the family has been viewed in such varied terms as systems of communication, behavioral interaction, distribution of power, and cognitive orientation.

A model is not good or bad in an absolute sense. The same model can be very helpful in the study of one type of topic and less helpful in the study of another. Even that choice is not always clear-cut, because models overlap. Since people often act as members of groups, psychological models have to include some mechanisms which pertain to the social structure. And since families are made up of people, collectivistic models have to take cognizance of the psychological makeup of individuals.

The choice between alternates depends on their comparative fruitfulness for the topic under investigation. In a study of the reasons why couples are attracted to one another, the investigator might well use a psychological model—starting with people's needs and analyzing the extent to which a pairing offers mutual gratification. Such a model seems inadequate if the topic is the shift in psychotic symptoms from one member of the family to another. For such problems, we need premises pertaining to the overall structure of the family.

An understanding of the paradigm which was formulated by the movement's founders, and their reasons for eschewing almost all the premises dear to the hearts of experimental psychologists, requires an introductory description of the field. As a movement, family therapy is relatively young; approximately 30 years old. At its inception, it was an oppositional movement. Some of the founders were psychiatrists who were disillusioned with medicine and the efficacy of psychoanalysis; some were socially conscious practitioners who were concerned with the social welfare of the poor and worked in marginal urban districts; some were sophisticated social scientists who were critical of the physicians' and psychologists' models and were eager to formulate alternatives.

An idealistic group, the founders chose to concentrate their attention on schizophrenia, a disorder that occupies approximately one fourth of the hospital beds in the country, is common among the poor, occurs primarily during the most productive periods of the patients' lives, often deprives the patients of their freedom, and about which there is no consensus as to causes or treatment (Jackson, 1960). In the first issue of *Family Process*, the official journal of the movement, 12 of the 15 articles and 9 of the 15 books reviewed were devoted to schizophrenia.

Unlike academic psychologists, family therapists first tried to clarify their questions and then to formulate suitable models. From the first, they were impressed by a striking phenomenon: the rotation of symptoms among members of families with a psychotic patient. If one member of a marital pair improves as a result of psychotherapy, the spouse often gets worse. As a child begins to shed symptoms, the parents' marriage begins to break down or one parent becomes very disturbed. The founders were also struck by the conditions under which symptoms fluctuate. After improving in the hospital, patients who return to their families, even for a short period, often relapse and have to be readmitted. Sometimes, even the visit by a close relative to the hospital exacerbates the symptoms. Such observations suggest that the symptoms express difficulties in the relationships between the patients and their relatives. Moreover, the disorder seems to be transmitted from one generation to the next in a manner that makes sense if examined in terms of interdependence and communication among family members rather than in terms of genetics. In fact, early findings (Bateson, Jackson, Haley, & Weakland, 1956; Bowen, 1959; Jackson, 1959; and Lidz, Cornelison, Fleck, & Terry, 1957) led the nascent family therapists to conceive of the family as an interacting, socially coordinated group and of the schizophrenic's symptoms as meaningful attempts to communicate with others.

The double bind

Insights generated by clinical work with schizophrenics pushed early family therapists into formulating a model of the family in which it was conceived as a collective entity with its own unique traits that could not be reduced to the attributes of its members; as a system of dynamically changing interrelated elements, not a collection of individuals with static traits; as activated by the communications and distributions of power among members, not their motivational states. Characteristics of the initial model and its application to familial problems are best summarized by a review of a paper that arguably is the most consequential for the history of the movement and is a watershed in therapies of the 20th century. Entitled "Toward a theory of schizophrenia" (Bateson et al., 1956), it defined the basic components of the model that is the dominant one in the field and the standard by which subsequent models have been judged.

Written by Gregory Bateson, the director of a project, and his coworkers, the paper contained the results of an extensive study of live and filmed clinical observations of interactions between hospitalized schizophrenic patients and their mothers. It is devoted to the "double bind," a type of communication that is presumed to be characteristic of families with schizophrenic members. As described by the authors, the double bind has six ingredients: (1) two or more persons; (2) repeated experience; (3) a primary negative injunction; (4) a secondary injunction conflicting with the first at a more abstract level and, like the first, enforced by punishment or signals which threaten survival; (5) a tertiary negative injunction prohibiting the victim from escaping from the field; and (6) learning by the victim to perceive relationships in terms of the double bind, so that only some of the components may be sufficient to precipitate panic or rage.

Underlying these criteria are a number of premises pertaining to methods of inquiry. Presumed in the combination of the first, third, and fourth criteria is an interaction in which one person is giving conflicting message to the second; the writers are defining schizophrenia as interpersonal. By explaining it in terms of a relationship *between* the designated patient and another person, they are rejecting the reductionism inherent in the psychiatric definition of schizophrenia as a disease contained *within* the individual.

Using a homeostatic conception, Jackson (1959), one of the original authors, later explained the persistence of symptoms by postulating that familial interaction creates pressure on the patient to stay the same. Adapting Ashby's cybernetic model (1956), Jackson defined symptoms as one kind of input into the family as a homeostatic system (Jackson, Beavin, & Watzlawick, 1967). This conception is patterned after biological models, which are applied to systems of constantly changing components, the relationships among which are organized to maintain a relatively steady state, or homeostasis, in the face of marked environmental changes. Analogously, his model is aimed at explaining how the members' relationships, of which the patient's symptoms are requisite components, help the family to maintain its stability as a system.

An understanding of homeostasis requires information about interaction among elements of the system and the surroundings to which it must make continuous adjustments. Hence, the significance of the fifth criterion of the double bind, the negative injunction preventing the patient from leaving the field. The injunction is typically enforced by illness, parental authority, and youth, all of which can make the patient dependent on others' cooperation. Rather than following the behaviorists' lead in dismissing the social field as a collection of unidentified stimuli, writers in *Family Process* have identified such components as values, morals, differential obligations of males and females, and the social networks that tie family members to groups in the community.

The double bind highlights the importance of communication in defining the interpersonal relationship. The third and fourth premises—the negative injunction and the conflicting, more abstract, secondary injunction, both enforced by threat—portray a particular pattern of communication; in this case, multichanneled, contradictory, and bound to create confusion and anxiety.

When people do anything together, it is impossible for them to avoid communication (Ruesch & Bateson, 1951); even silence or indifference conveys vivid messages. The double bind is created by contradictory messages: a mother lovingly offers to hold her child, expresses distaste and discomfort nonverbally when the child starts to comply, continues to express affection verbally, and hints that she is disappointed by the child's hesitancy and fear. What can the child do? Approaching her, withdrawing, even commenting on the contradictory pressures, are likely to have unpleasant consequences. Yet there is no leaving the field. Escape entails recourse to nonrational behavior: possibly confusion, misinterpreting the message, changing one's picture of self.

Viewed in the context of social and familial systems, then, the symptoms of schizophrenics are no longer the obscure, bizarre components of clinical syndromes, the recognition of which requires the expertise of an "alienist." On the contrary, symptoms make sense when decoded as communications designed to promote the patient's adaptation to ongoing social relationships, thus contributing to the family's homeostasis. As indicated by the second and sixth premises, repetition of the patterns of communication causes them to be learned and generalized to similar settings outside the family, at which time they are often far less adjustive than they were in intrafamilial relationships.

CLINICAL PRESSURES CREATE THE NEED FOR A NEW PARADIGM

It was practical considerations and social events, not theoretical interests, that led to the questioning of traditional assumptions about the nature of psychotherapy. Many clinicians were discouraged by the results of individual therapy. Moreover, they did not think that their patients' pathologies were sufficiently clarified by the reductionistic and deterministic theories favored by medical and psychoanalytic thinkers.

Social developments were also creating pressures to abandon the long-term treatment of individuals. An America that had long thought of itself as child centered and future oriented was shocked by the increasing numbers of divorces and concerned with repairing the fragmented family. There was also a strengthening of the American commitment to increasing social welfare for the public at large and, among clinicians, to developing short-term methods that could be made available to the poor.

In response to these pressures, clinicians expanded their efforts in two directions. They gradually shifted their attentions from individual to dyad to triad to group to community. And they explored many new methods with all four. Of particular interest here are the techniques of replicating familial relationships—in play therapy with dolls representing members of the family, in psychodramatic reenactment of familial events, in the equivalents of familial experiences that occur in groups. Limitations of space confine us primarily to a chronicle of the increasing number of patients treated simultaneously as revealed in the literature on dyads, groups, and families.

Dyads

In the 1930s and 1940s, clinical researchers became interested in their patients' mothers and other relatives. Attention was focused particularly on mothers, whose problems seemed inseparable from those of their offspring. Early studies revealed that mothers of schizophrenics were rejecting (Kasanin, Knight, & Sage, 1934; Tietze, 1949) or overprotective (Despert, 1938; Kasanin et al., 1934). Examining dyadic relationships in the marriage and between the child and both parents, Levy (1943), a pioneer in the study of maternal overprotection, demonstrated how disturbed marriages create the context for overprotection. It was common, for example, for a dominant mother to forgo her commitment to a failing marriage by forming an alliance with the son and against her passive husband. Levy found that certain relationships between members of different generations create conditions under which pathology flourishes: overprotecting mothers are themselves often the offspring of unloving parents. The inclusion of both parents and of intergenerational relationships in the picture are practices that are common in current publications of family therapists.

The study of the dyad was an important theoretical breakthrough. It demonstrated the value of working on supraindividual systems, motivated clinicians to propose theoretical models of relationships, and made practitioners more sensitive to the importance of social norms and positions connected with the patients' places in society. Moreover, experience in conducting dyadic research enabled clinicians to become increasingly sophisticated in their analyses of interactional patterns. Using psychoanalytic constructs, Johnson and Szurek (1952) showed how a child can use symptoms to express a parent's unconscious wishes. But the child is not simply a victim of the parent's pathogenic influence; the acting out is often reflexively oriented to exposing parental disturbances.

Although it helped to initiate family therapy as a movement, the historic paper on the double bind by Bateson et al. (1956) pertains to a dyadic relationship, between mother and child, not to the family. This is probably because Bateson was very influenced by Fromm-Reichmann's conception (1948) of the schizophrenogenic mother, which received wide currency in the early 1950s. According to that conception, the schizophrenic is distrustful and resentful of others because of warp and rejection in infancy and childhood, mainly by a dominant mother. Fromm-Reichmann does not explain the father's contribution to the child's difficulties except to observe that he is unable to be supportive because he is submissive and inadequate.

Groups

It is probably experiences with groups that helped clinicians to formulate the principles that underlie current thinking in family therapy. Although work with groups can be traced to Greek concepts about the engendering of catharsis by Greek tragedy, the modern movement had one acknowledged founder, Moreno (1937), who coined the term *group psychotherapy.* Influenced by developments in the theater, Moreno was primarily concerned with spontaneity, role, and play. In fact, he combined the last two into the concept of role-playing, which entails the member of a group taking the role of another and is almost synonymous with the parallel concept used by Mead (1934) as part of his theory of socialization. In Moreno's groups, a member played the role of another to gain insight into that person's inner world and to provide a contrast to the manner in which the latter played the problematic role.

During World War II, the armed services became interested in group psychotherapy because so many military personnel needed assistance. Bion (1961), who helped to organize therapeutic services in the British army, lists three assumptions underlying his procedures: The group is to be treated as an entity, and interpretations made of the actions of the collectivity or its subgroups; only current events within the group are relevant to its characteristics; problems of the group are concerned with relations between them and overarching organizations. One example of the latter is his interpretation of neurotic behavior on a military ward as an unconscious alliance among inmates in response to the hospital and military authorities. The categories thus pertain to contemporaneous events, not history; to relationships within and between groups, not to attributes of individuals; and to linkages with outside groups identified by their forms of social organization, not to universal principles of behavior which the members share with subhuman species. These are assumptions that underlie the methods of many current group therapists.

Psychotherapy with groups provided the needed impetus for a movement devoted to work with the family. To begin with, the family is a special type of group, with many of the same problems—struggles over power, relationships with other groups in the community, barriers to communication—as the nonfamilial groups whose functions were being analyzed in psychotherapy. In addition, events in groups often recapitulate familial relationships (Yalom, 1970). Members react to leaders as though they are fathers or mothers, idealizing them, resenting them, and competing for their favors. But such experiences are still not the real thing, and sometimes they must yield to other activities. As Yalom points out, the working through of unfinished business from the past is not the primary purpose of group therapy, which is to clarify current sequences in the group process.

Families

Various individuals conducted psychotherapy with the family from the beginning of the century, including people as prominent as Adler and Moreno, but they had little influence on practitioners outside their schools. Ackerman (1954), who is credited with initiating the modern movement, was intrigued by the fluctuation of symptoms in response to familial interactions, a theme that was echoed in the findings of nearly simultaneously published reports by other clinicians who were treating families (Bateson et al., 1956; Jackson, 1957; Johnson & Szurek, 1952; Wynne, Ryckoff, Day, & Hirsch, 1958). Most of the beginners thought of the family as a system and of pathology as contributing to the maintenance of the system. The problem had finally been located—not in the schizophrenic patient, not in the mother or parents, but in the family.

The hypothesis of the double bind was then extended to interactions within triads (Weakland, 1960) and was elaborated into the "perverse triangle" (Haley, 1973), in which there is a denial of the coalition between members of two generations against the third member. There followed "triadic-based" family therapy (Zuk, 1971), multiple family therapy (Laquer, 1970), and therapy with family networks (Speck & Attneave, 1973). By this time, all constraints created by reductionistic standards about the importance of working with small social units, preferably individuals, had been abandoned.

EXPLORING ALTERNATIVES

Once clinicians had broken with the individualistic premises of astronomical models, they turned to other disciplines for models that would be more suited to the study of familial interaction. Two authors of the paper on the double bind, Gregory Bateson and Don Jackson, were particularly influential in introducing their colleagues to a nonclinical climate of opinion which provided the wellsprings for current clinical thinking. Current models of the family are ultimately products of trends in biology, physics, sociology, and linguistics which created specific positions concerning determinism, reductionism, and the historical view of causality. These trends were integrated into the social sciences and psychiatry by two writers: psychologist Kurt Lewin and psychiatrist Harry Stack Sullivan, who had profound effects on the intellectual climate in the two decades before family therapy became a movement and who served as the conduits, through the writings of Bateson and Jackson, of the holistic and teleological traditions to the field of family therapy. In a book written with Ruesch and published five years before the paper on the double bind, Bateson acknowledges his indebtedness to the Gestalt (Lewinian) school and to Sullivan (Ruesch & Bateson, 1951). Sullivan, as editor of *Psychiatry*, promoted the collaborative research that Bateson and Ruesch conducted on communication (Cottrell & Foote, 1952); Bateson and Lewin attended a number of meetings sponsored by the Macy Foundation, where they had many opportunities to exchange ideas (Lipset, 1980).

In this section, we begin with a very short summary of the thinking in other disciplines that affected the models of Lewin and Sullivan and then describe the conceptions of these writers that helped therapists to formulate their models of the family.

Functions and systems

Biological. The study of systems is a product of trends in biology, physics, sociology, and linguistics which originated in the last century. Biologists study organisms that engage in goal-directed activities. They conceive of a living thing as being a system of components which work together to produce the integrated whole. They think of a bodily organ, for example, as having functions that are designed to facilitate the activities of the whole body and its other parts. The analysis of functions from the perspective of integrated systems is required, biologists think, to answer the questions that are distinctly biological. Some phenomena can be reduced to simpler chemical and physical components, but this does not help to answer the questions that interest members of the profession.

Physical field theories. Social scientists have also been influenced by field theories in physics: Maxwell's electromagnetic theory, the Fourier theory of heat flow, and especially Einstein's general theory of relativity. In electrodynamics, the force on a charged body due to the presence of other such bodies is determined by the condition of the electromagnetic field in its vicinity, not by the positions and velocities of other bodies. The field cannot be regarded as a sum of partial fields, each created by a distinct, charged particle.

Intrigued by the heuristic value of gravitational and electromagnetic force fields, social scientists began to phrase questions in terms of systems. They also began to question their faith in determinism in view of Heisenberg's conceptions of uncertainty (1930): When the equations of quantum theory are defined in customary spatiotemporal terms, they do not conform to deterministic explanations of the processes. Although some physicists have been critical of Heisenberg's reasoning, it has created skepticism about causality as a universally valid principle. Some philosophers (Nagel, 1961) now assume, in fact, that causality refers to a general objective to obtain deterministic explanations and that it does not require the adoption of any particular premises about methodology. Investigators in the social sciences are, consequently, less concerned than they used to be with satisfying strict criteria for making operational definitions, establishing mathematico-deductive systems, and identifying causal chains; many are more inclined to indulge in imaginative speculations about phenomenology and dynamic systems.

Functionalism. The homeostatic familial model would be unthinkable were it not for the work of anthropologists and sociologists on the functional analyses of social systems. Functionalism pertains to social institutions: principles that govern individuals' activities. The regulation is aimed at resolving perennial, basic societal problems such as the organization of procreative and biological relations and the socialization of the members of each new generation.

Underlying functional analysis are the assumptions that different parts of the society are interdependent and that their activities are regulated by various equilibrating mechanisms. Specific practices are interpreted in terms of the contributions they make or can make towards the maintenance of some stated characteristic or conditions of the social structure, which is constantly adjusted in response to changing internal or external environments.

Since maintenance entails the monitoring of external and internal changes, systemic thinking requires attention to environments and the larger systems of the society. Often the analysis is devoted to relationships between subsystems and encompassing systems. It is assumed that no one system is sufficient, by itself, to explain social stability. The family alone, for example, cannot generate the common culture which ensures the possibility of meaningful and stable familial action. To understand familial operations, one must analyze them in the context of the culture, the historical period, and the encompassing societal systems.

Aversive to individualistic thinking, advocates of systemic thinking stress the collective characteristics of social organization. Most of the family's functions cannot be deduced solely from the characteristics of its individual members. On the contrary, the individuals can often be ignored in many types of social analysis. The replacement of an employee in a large organization usually does not affect the operations of the organization; the structures of social networks can be analyzed without reference to the members' attributes; language, art, and philosophy can be discussed in virtual abstraction from concrete human behavior. If the systemic explanation of a family, for example, could be reduced analytically to intrapsychic characteristics of its individual components, the functionalist would reject the results because they would change the meaning of topics under study—topics such as integration among parts of the system, maintenance of the stability of a designated state, reaction of the family to change.

Even when individuals must be taken into account, the sociologist classifies them with respect to their roles and social categories, paying little heed to individual differences concerning physical characteristics or psychological attributes. Roles and categories identify individuals with various groups, indicating how they will be expected to participate in the complementary fulfillment of shared goals and how they will be evaluated by others. Such are the conceptions that Simmel, Durkheim, and Mannheim have in mind when they state that culture and social structure transcend the individual.

Structuralism in linguistics and anthropology. The emphasis that family therapists place both on communication and on systems can be traced to developments in linguistics which, in the opinion of the philosopher Ernst Cassirer (1945), have had so revolutionary an effect on modern intellectual life that they are comparable to the investigations of Galileo, which in the 17th century changed scientists' conceptions of the physical world. To explain the nature of these developments, we have only sufficient space to sketch a few features in the complex systems of two of the most influential thinkers, Saussure and Levi-Strauss, emphasizing those features that have affected clinicians' premises about the family.

Swiss linguist Ferdinand de Saussure (Culler, 1977), who worked mostly in the latter part of the 19th century, broke with the European philological tradition by proposing two dichotomies. In the first, he distinguished between language, the corpus of linguistic rules needed for communication, and speech, the everyday use made of the linguistic system. It is the former, he thought, that provides the key to the functions of language.

In the second dichotomy, he divided language along synchronic and diachronic axes. Synchronic, or structural, linguistics creates a revolutionary shift in perspective. It is ahistoric. Concerned with the understanding of functions, it is concentrated on particular systems or structures apart from the systems from which they emerged. Diachronic refers to evolution over time: studies of the histories of languages, etymologies, and phonetic changes. Saussure advocated the synchronic study of language, in contrast to the diachronic studies by his predecessors.

Another facet of Saussure's linguistics marks him as one of the pioneers of systems theory. He observed that the linguistic sign is arbitrary: there is no natural link between it and the object it signifies, only a conventional one. Language is, then, a system of relations among its units, not a collection of fixed and unchangeable essences. By itself, a unit has no absolute meaning. Its value is determined by the place it occupies within the linguistic system. Saussure's famous summation of this fundamental insight: "Language is a form and not a substance."

During the same period, studies of Indian languages by American anthropologists could not follow the diachronic European philological tradition because Indians had no historical documentation. Extrapolations from other, related languages proved to be unhelpful. The circumstances, then, required a new approach: language was studied with respect to culture. Ethnographic studies of this sort led to an appreciation of the ways in which language molds styles of perception and cognition.

This synchronic tradition helps to account for the Americans' receptivity to the anthropological writings of Levi-Strauss (1963), whose structuralism (like that of Saussure's) is founded on studies of relations among the elements of a system. Levi-Strauss investigated cultural phenomena such as systems of kinship, totemism, and myth. His studies of the changing relationships among the different components of a system reveal that what appears at first to be a unit with constant properties actually varies with the context of relationships. An example is provided by the interpretation of symbols in myth. It seems like common sense to assume that a symbol has a fixed meaning regardless of where it occurs. In fact, its meaning varies with the place it occupies within a myth and with the ecology of the cultural transmission. The total system determines the meaning. This principle is basic to structural analysis. An understanding of cultural phenomena requires a reconstruction of the underlying system of which they are manifestations.

Levi-Strauss, more than anyone else, has been responsible for the extension of structuralism into fields other than linguistics. His emphases on relationship and context have contributed to a climate of opinion that made family therapists receptive to theories like the double bind. This concentration on abstract symbolic order stands for a way of thinking that is opposed to the individualistic tradition in psychology. So diminished is the role of intentional human agency in Levi-Strauss's system that he has been criticized as picturing the individual as nothing more than a replaceable unit within a soulless system. His view is not far from the picture of the human actor in cybernetics, in which the individual is regarded as a "nodal point in a communicational system" (Shands, 1971).

What struck Cassirer as being so revolutionary about structuralism was the primacy granted to relations among parts of systems. This orientation has four major implications for conceptions of the family within the social sciences. First, structuralists substitute an ahistorical interpretation for analyses in terms of historical antecedents. Next, they explain phenomena by locating them within total, underlying systems instead of dissecting them into components. Third, in their descriptions of system, structuralists use communicational rather than social, motivational, or behavioral units. Finally, their drift away from reductionism is so strong that they sacrifice interest in the individual in favor of the familial relationship, an abstract symbolic organization.

LEWIN AND SULLIVAN

The systems of Lewin and Sullivan represent fusions of work in a number of disciplines. Lewin, a social psychologist, transposed field theory from physics and adapted the mathematics of topology to the study of personality and groups. Sullivan, a specialist in the treatment of schizophrenia, was associated with the anthropologist Edward Sapir in the study of language and communication. A strong interest in sociology, particularly the works of Cooley and Mead, explains Sullivan's concentration on interpersonal relationships and the self in his analysis of social relationships.

Lewin was connected with the Gestalt school, which specialized in the empirical investigation of Kant's thesis that the mind imposes its organization on perceived objects. As the Gestaltists expanded this viewpoint, the mind organizes the elements of a field into a configuration with an aggregate significance that is both larger and different from the characteristics or sum of its individual parts. Assuming an innate capacity on the part of mind to create meaning by organizing incomplete data into configurations, they demonstrated how figure and ground, which were viewed epistemologically as interdependent parts of a perceptual field, would be organized differently under various experimental conditions. Although Lewin's theories were very influential, a partiality to the definition of psychology as a natural science caused his colleagues to be relatively unsympathetic to his interest in systems, his emphasis on culture, his analysis of the nature of groups, and his strong antireductionistic bias (Pepitone, 1981).

Sullivan's theoretical position is harder to classify. It is easy to recognize the influences of Meyer, Sapir, Dewey, and especially Freud and Mead on his writing, but his integration of their ideas with his own is unique. Critical of schools of thought, a gadfly to psychoanalysts and Kraepelinian classifiers, he insisted that pathology is a disturbance of relationships, not an individual disease. In the remainder of this chapter, we consider each of the philosophical issues bearing on the paradigm of the family, first summarizing Lewin's and Sullivan's positions and then reviewing criticisms of their positions by some current practitioners.

Objectivity and cognition

Lewin included the structures of both individual and group in his theory. He aspired to create a scientific system even though his data were derived from the life space, which is a cognitive organization of self and environment. Lewin emphasized that life space is to be distinguished from the actual processes in the physical or social world, some of which do not affect the life space. The system is nonteleological. It is the cognitive organization of time—the totality of people's views of psychological present, past, and future—that affects behavior. Learning entails a change in cognitive structure.

Sullivan was sympathetic with Bridgman's conditions for operational definitions and for scientific validation, and he regreted that they cannot be met by the psychiatrist, especially in the case of mental operations and speculations about the early stages of personality development. Vowing to meet the spirit of Bridgman's criteria, Sullivan blithely proceeded to postulate cognitive states that could not possibly be operationalized: the uncanny, dissociated systems unconnected with awareness or unrepresented in focal awareness, and the relaxing of security operations during sleep. Like Lewin, he found that the understanding of pathological relationships requires the collection of cognitive data.

One product of the cognitive orientation is the use of the self. Lewin's conception of the person's life space would have permitted a systematic analysis of self, but though he used terms such as *self-regulation,* he restricted his systematic attention to the "person." Profoundly influenced by Mead, Sullivan made the "self-system" a cornerstone of his theory, dividing it into the "good me," "bad me," and "not me." He postulated that self is the collection of security operations for reestablishing equilibrium when there is an excess of anxiety, that it is the integrator of all zones of interaction and physiological apparatus that are meaningful in interaction, and that it is an internal representative of societal norms and of the distorted personifications which are keys to certain pathological states.

Reduction: Field and group

The "field" is Lewin's most fundamental construct (1951). He conceived of all behavior as a change of some state of the field in a given unit of time. The field of a group such as the family is its life space, which he defined as the group's conception of itself in its environment. Basic to the conception of field is the assumption that its various parts, people and environment, are interdependent. Research of his associates reveals that the same environment may vary in meaning, depending on a group's goals, ideologies, leadership, and internal tensions. Groups also have their special structural properties, which differ from the properties of subgroups and of individual members. Structural properties are defined by relations between parts and are not parts themselves.

Like Simmel before him, Lewin asserted that size contributes to the properties of a social unit. Some properties of the group as a whole which cannot be reduced to the properties of the members are degree of cohesiveness, homogeneity of ideology, and atmospheres. Lewin analyzed social events by studying social entities in the context of a social field. The analysis of the structures of group and subgroup within their ecological setting was designed to estimate the possibility of change as a product of forces throughout the field.

For Sullivan, like Lewin, field theory in physical science is the source of an interpersonal model. The interdependent forces characteristic of a field are used to conceptualize the situation, which includes people's internal structures and their patterns of interaction within a given context (1948). In psychotherapy, the situation consists of a two-way relationship between psychiatrist and patient in a specific context. Dismissing static conceptions of personality, Sullivan said that it is an amalgam of relationships which he inferred from "patterns of processes which characterize the interaction of personalities in particular recurrent situations or fields which include the observer" (1953, p. 111).

As a clinician, Sullivan needed a two-person relationship and its ongoing processes in the interpersonal field in order to understand schizophrenia. He divided these processes into conjunctive ones, which reduce tension between participants, and disjunctive ones, which by producing anxiety contribute to a disintegration of the relationship. In his analyses of families, he concentrated on the disjunctive forces which block integration with other groups in the community whose cooperation is necessary for the family to do its work. It should be emphasized that disjunction is an attribute of relationships and cannot readily be derived from the members' individual traits.

Society and culture

As noted earlier, the aim of formulating universal laws akin to those governing the solar system precludes the study of society, culture, and history. An interest in field theory, in contrast, prompts the investigator to obtain all the information about the field that may affect the subjects' behavior. Not surprisingly, Lewin studied topics like the changing of food habits, the self-esteem of people in minority groups, and the rate of production in a factory, all of which entail a conception of social groups as systems within their society, culture, and historical period. His deep interest in social organization and culture is indicated by a comment on food habits:

> They are part and parcel of the daily rhythm of . . . being alone and in a group; of earning a living and playing; of being a member of a town, a family, a social class, a religious group, a nation; . . . of living . . . in a rural area or a city, in a district with good groceries and restaurants or in an area of poor and irregular food supply. (1951, p. 173)

Sullivan was equally emphatic about the importance of taking societal and cultural facts into account. Citing sources in anthropology and sociology (1953), he stressed that people are bound together by the various tasks they carry out in common and the social norms that regulate those activities. Sullivan wrote on a variety of social issues: antisemitism, organizing national defense, the comparative stress faced by adolescents in different societies, and culture and the preservation of mental health. He conceived of mental disorders as attributes of people's interactions as they are integrated with others' interactions within the society. His use of the "dynamism" of self was modeled after the conception of Mead, who observed that interchange with others must occur before a person becomes a self.

Temporality

Field theory requires an ahistorical view of causality. It is only the properties of the field at a particular time that can affect behavior at that time. As a field theorist, Lewin took account of past and future events, but as part of a time perspective; the psychological past, present, and future are all simultaneous parts of the psychological field at a given time. This view is incompatible with teleological assumptions that future goals cause present behavior or with the psychoanalytic assumption that past events cause present ones.

Sullivan also took an ahistorical position, using the interpersonal field as his basis for explaining behavior. He was very interested, however, in recurrent past experiences which may explain how the patient learned pathological habits of adapting to others in the family. Such habits, especially those acquired before the advent of speech, operate in what Sullivan called the "prototaxic" or nonconscious mode, which is why they create difficulties in relationships outside the family. Sullivan said that clinicians have to reach very much further back than the presenting situation to comprehend the meaning of psychoses, but his conception of the reaching back refers to logical priority, not causes. Like Lewin, he assumed that given the sequence of many conflicting messages over time, the past of the patient must be represented in the present in order to influence contemporaneous behavior; his primary concern was with "current patterns of relationships."

System

Lewin was, above all, a systematist who analyzed groups like the family as part of a "social field." This includes the totality of social entities and their interrelationships as defined by barriers, channels of communication, and positions in the field. The relative positions constitute the group's structure, its ecological setting, and possibilities of locomotion within the field. Lewin presumed that forces affecting behavior within a field are constantly changing, and that what happens depends on the distribution of the forces, their strengths, and their directions.

When he attempted to understand social states such as the production level of a work team or the rate of production in an autocratically run group, Lewin analyzed them as "quasi-stationary processes," which, like a river, continuously change their elements while velocity and direction remain the same. The rate of production remains relatively constant if there is a balance of opposing forces, such as pace and the strain of work versus incentive systems and the pay scale. Rate of aggression remains relatively constant if there is a balance of forces such as the pressure of autocratic control, aggression afforded by the type of activity, degree of inner tension, and strength of the "we feeling."

Sullivan studied the interpersonal field defined by the interaction of two or more people's dynamisms. Dynamism refers to "the relatively enduring patterns of energy transformation." Patterns are interpersonal; they are means of self-expression through use of certain physical zones and modes in the satisfaction of needs with particular people in given environments. An individual's dynamism can be nonoperative if the corresponding dynamism is lacking in the other person. By his field theory, Sullivan referred to the patterns of processes which characterize the interaction of personalities in particular recurrent situations or fields which include the observer. Sullivan thought that all observations can be reduced to four categories: tensions, energy transformations, observable actions, and mental activities.

Both Lewin and Sullivan anticipated all the currents in modern family therapy. Lewin formulated the philosophical premises: the structuralist emphasis on the here and now, interdependence in the social field (where any change echoes through the system), the principle that the whole is more than the sum of the parts, and homeostasis. In addition to taking similar positions on these issues, Sullivan developed current conceptions of the nature of pathology. He thought that pathology is inherently adaptive; that symptoms are integral to the adaptations the patient made to disfunctional relationships when young. Hence the data used to arrive at a diagnosis must be relational, not solely individual. He stressed the importance of communicational patterns. In fact, 30 years before the paper on double bind, he anticipated the theme of conflicting communicational channels when he stated that there is a difference in what the schizophrenic thinks and what he feels called upon to say to others he feels he must accommodate (Sullivan, 1927). These observations were noted later by Jackson (1961), one of the authors of the paper on the double bind. Sullivan's emphasis on anxiety as a primary, disjunctive influence is echoed in the many references to anxiety in the paper on the double bind; his postulate that, under the impact of anxiety, tenderness is replaced by malevolent behavior is virtually paraphrased in the description by Bateson et al. (1956) of the primary and secondary conflicting injunctions.[1]

SOME CRITICISMS OF COLLECTIVIST POSITIONS

As might be expected in a thriving new movement, family therapists take divergent positions with regard to most of the premises that enter into models of the family. In fact, a vociferous and sophisticated minority has begun to criticize the commonly accepted premises of the new establishment, using arguments that are redolent of the positions of academic individualists. Since such criticisms are of interest to anyone who studies the family, we review them in this final section, beginning with criticisms of holism and homeostasis, which are hard to separate from one another.

Reduction

The reductionists' position is passionately expressed by L'Abate (in press), who characterizes current family therapy as being overly holistic and antianalytic and is concerned about the extent to which work

---

[1] It will interest historians of science to note that despite the easily traced and profound influences of Sullivan on the theories of family therapists, he receives little acknowledgment in the literature. Apart from Jackson's many appreciative comments, we have found only two subsequent references in hundreds of publications. Lewin fares even worse. We found not one reference to Lewin in any of the publications on family therapy. It seems that even when they borrow copiously from the ideas of others, members of new movements (especially ones which represent sharp breaks from established thinking) need to convince themselves that the movements arose by means of spontaneous generation.

with families is done without taking the personalities of individual members into account. It is true that family therapists have generally employed cybernetic and sociological models in which individual differences are ignored in favor of relationships and institutional arrangements. This does not mean, however, that collective and individual concepts cannot be integrated into the same system. This has, in fact, been done in Bowen's (1966) model of familial relationships. In addition to analyzing the family as a system in terms of equilibrium, flexibility, triangles, and overfunction, he also thinks of the individual in terms of differentiation of self, ego boundaries, and pseudo self.

Another criticism leveled against holistic theories is that there is no way of reducing them to testable formats because the systemic structure is incompatible with a linear style of causal reasoning (Gurman & Kniskern, 1981). There are certainly clinicians who espouse systems that are too vague to be examined empirically and who are satisfied with testimonials. It does not follow, however, that models of social systems must be reduced to the properties of individual members to permit the design of empirical studies. We are surprised that psychologists have less faith in the possibility of testing a social theory containing collective concepts than they would in the possibility of testing the law of gravitation or the electromagnetic field theory.

It should be kept in mind that theoretical systems are not tested directly: It is not possible to evaluate the theory of relativity by means of one simple design. Instead, one derives implications as a basis for formulating testable hypotheses. One example of how this can be done with respect to theories of homeostasis is provided by Miller and Westman (1966), who derived a number of hypotheses from current models and then did the necessary empirical work. In their research, they concentrated on the assumption that the designated patient's symptoms are part of a repertory of interpersonal responses aimed at safeguarding the family's stability. If this is true, they reasoned, then the family should cooperate in maintaining the symptoms or, failing in such attempts, show signs of decreased stability. Patients in the study were preadolescent boys who were seriously retarded in reading even though their nonverbal IQs were above average; they lacked any physical pathology that would account for retardation and had had considerable competent individual instruction in reading. Miller and Westman derived four testable propositions from the assumption that families endeavor to maintain the patients' symptoms: The families resist seeking psychotherapy when it is recommended; some of those who do seek it are prompted by reasons other than the plight of the patient; they misinterpret diagnostic statements which conflict with beliefs that contribute to homeostasis; they sabotage therapeutic procedures, particularly those that threaten equilibrium.

These deductions are supported by the clinical findings. On the average, families with boys who are severely retarded in reading either do not seek psychotherapy or, if they do, the delay is longer than that of families with other types of patients. Quite a few of the families who finally ask for consultation are prompted by a new crisis, not by the problem in reading. In one such instance, the father had installed a female friend in the bedroom and forced his wife to sleep in the living room. The latter coerced the family to seek help for the son's problem in reading, at which time everyone discussed the impending breakup of the marriage.

Many parents whose offspring cannot read think of them as being mentally retarded or brain injured. When informed that diagnostic procedures have ruled out either pathology, some parents continue to label their children as intellectually handicapped, acting as though they have not received the contradictory information. The sabotage of therapy takes many forms. Some parents privately give their children reading drills after being asked to desist because such drills are associated with long years of failure and boredom. Others find new difficulties in meeting their appointments once the patients begin to improve. Almost all families use teamwork to create confusion during therapy when topics arise that might threaten the status quo. Finally, as commonly reported in the literature, improvement of the official patient is often followed by deterioration in familial stability; talk of divorce and signs of psychosis in a parent are not unusual.

Findings of this sort indicate that systemic propositions need not be reduced to individualistic terms in order to be subject to empirical research. First, they help the skeptic to visualize how holistic propositions can be tested. Next, they suggest that if a holistic proposition has sufficient clarity, it should be possible to make deductions that can be investigated empirically. Third, the findings show how the derivation of deductions expands the implications of the original principle. Finally the results of testing make it possible to invalidate a principle, which is an important asset of the procedure.

Lack of parsimony is another criticism of systemic theories that requires attention, mostly because it is made so often. According to this principle, when two models are both logically and empirically acceptable, the preferable one has the fewest assumptions. Sometimes this is combined with the additional principle that the choice be the one that appeals most to common sense.

The criterion of parsimony is founded on a mistaken premise that has been accepted by some social scientists: that collective entities in the natural sciences have a lower empirical status than do concepts referring to the objects of direct observation. Constructs such as galaxies, the earth's magnetic field, and the earth's atmospheric envelope demonstrate that this is not so. The best argument against the criterion is provided by Bogdan (in press), one of its advocates: There are no clear-cut means of comparing two theories with respect to numbers of assumptions, or of assessing appeal to common sense. It is not surprising, then, that principles which are dismissed as unparsimonious in one decade or in one group are judged to be parsimonious in another decade or in another group.

According to a related claim, the meanings of collective terms can only be clarified by means of individualistic terms. Sometimes this position is supported by the assertion that the individual is a real, palpable being—unlike social systems, which are abstract entities. At other times it is supported by the contention that groups consist of individuals and need to be explained in terms of individuals' subjective states.

One cannot help but be sympathetic to people who are unhappy about collective entities in view of the past popularity of terms like *group mind* and *general will,* which are too unclear to permit speculations about their underlying assumptions or implications for behavior. Such concepts are also misleading; each is a hypostatic transformation of a complex system of social relations into an autonomous entity with influence over its components, as though the system were thinking like a person. But such unsound terms do not necessarily demonstrate that all collective concepts are necessarily vague or reified like group mind. Nor does the fact that social groups consist of individuals indicate that all collective terms either can or have to be derived from their members' attributes any more than the physical properties of a table can or have to be derived from the properties of its atomic constituents. Moreover, the apparent objectivity with which the corporeal being can be identified can create the mistaken impression that the citizen in the community is a unit comparable to the biological organism. Contrary to the mistaken impression created by a conflation of the biological organism and the socially relevant person, the unity of the latter is split into many components, each representing roles, social categories, social positions, and components of self which connect the individual with different systems and subsystems in the community.

While empirically minded, Framo (1981) is justifiably concerned about the tendency of empirical investigators to define problems in terms that are most convenient to research. He fears that when theory is converted to operational definitions, the experimenter often ends up measuring something that bears little resemblance to the original. All humanity has been distilled from the investigation, which is devoted to pallid, trivial variables. Such distortions are likely, we think, when collective terms are reduced as a prelude to operational definition. In our opinion, a family has characteristics, like stability and flexibility, which cannot be reduced without distorting their meanings and which are needed for the definition of other collective terms. Just as it is the obligation of the systematists to use clear terms and suggest testable propositions, it is the obligation of the reductionists to demonstrate that translation is possible without altering the meanings of collective terms and, more important, that their translation is not a trivial exercise. Finally, the doctrinal reductionists must show by examples that they can create a theoretical system with premises that pertain only to individuals and still be capable of answering all the theoretical questions that are being addressed by the systematists. We are not impressed by the readiness of reductionist critics to accept these challenges.

Homeostasis

The collective concept of homeostatic systems has been a frequent target of criticism because many systems in the past have been reified in a manner that attributed to social groups human properties that they did not have. This kind of reification need not occur if we follow the biologists' practice and conceive of the functions of an activity in terms of the contributions it makes toward the maintenance of some stated condition in the system of which the activity is a part. It is necessary that the system be delimited and that the possible variations of the state be clearly identified.

Homeostatic models have been justifiably criticized as being limited in value, first by sociologists and then by family therapists (Hoffman, 1980; Speer, 1970): They can be helpful in explaining functions that promote constancy, but they are useless in accounting for change, even in the therapeutic relationship. What good are they to the therapist, who is trying to induce change? Early systems theorists concentrated their efforts on accounting for the maintenance of steady states; some even restricted their conception of structure to components relevant to constancy, ignoring the many deliberate and accidental changes that become permanent. Such versions appealed to the founders of family therapy because they were intrigued by the idea that symptoms contribute to familial stability.

The possibility of accounting for different types of change seems perfectly compatible with the nature of homeostatic models. The systems of Lewin (1951) and of Mead (1934) contain provocative suggestions of the types of change, and mechanisms for inducing it, that can be included in a homeostatic model. The apparent constancy of Lewin's quasi-stationary equilibrium, for example, is a product of a specified balance between oppositional forces for and against change. If an individual is tempted to behave in new ways, this is prevented by commitment to the group. If the group alters its standards, the same force field facilitates the member's adaptation of the new standards and stabilizes conduct at the new level of the group. Change requires "unfreezing" the present level of the group, raising the level, and then "freezing" it at the new level. These processes entail alterations both in the forces that affect equilibrium and of related components of the social field.

Objectivity and individualism

Family therapists are in serious disagreement about the criterion that data should be limited to what is publicly observable. A negative position regarding this criterion is evident in the article on the double bind, which contains many references to the subjective states of hostility and anxiety. Bateson (1972) subsequently expanded his cognitive position, stressing that behavior is affected by the meaning of events in addition to the events themselves. He thus took issue with strict behaviorists, who in their explanations of behavior restrict their attention to the stimulus properties of the environment, ignoring the fact that such properties are organized cognitively. Reverting to an individualistic position, Bateson begins with individuals who have ideas and can learn. He then postulates that the ideas of each member lead to behavior that confirms or supports the ideas of every other member, thus creating the patterns of familial behavior.

In contrast, Jackson's cybernetic version of systems theory led him to adopt the model of the individual as a black box that cannot be opened but which permits the observer to supply it with information and to observe responses. As he says in his last book with Beavin and Watzlawick (1967), this model eliminates the necessity of invoking intrapsychic hypotheses, which he feels are ultimately unverifiable. It is sufficient, he thinks, to work with observable relationships between input and output, his phrase for communication.

The slack created by the downplaying of the individual's internal dynamics is taken up by the emphasis on interaction. Haley (1977) elaborated on Jackson's position, adding power, coalitions, and control to his framework. As Haley (1971) conceives of therapy, "Change really comes about through interactional processes set off when a therapist intervenes actively and directively in particular ways in a family system, and quite independently of the awareness of the participants about how they have been behaving" (p. 7). There is no necessity to cultivate insight, he thinks, since it cannot affect the patient's symptoms. Instead he recommends that the therapist initiate action by offering a reinforcement program or directives for the family to follow.

Strongly disapproving of the exertion of power over people who do not understand what is happening, Bateson ascribes the therapists' need for control to anxiety that we all have about our imperfect understanding of the world. He condemns the manipulation of power, which in his opinion corrupts the therapists. In the expression of his moral position, he joins others (Feshbach, 1978) who believe that the proliferation of social policies has been shifting the goals of clinicians away from individual characteristics such as insight, choice, and responsibility and toward compliance, capacity to contribute to the group's stability, and economic productivity. This shift has, in turn, led to a deemphasis on theories in which internal psychological states, processes, and insight are major components and to a prominence of biochemical and reinforcement methods aimed at eliminating the symptoms that prevent patients from meeting their obligations to society. Bateson takes strong stands in opposition to manipulation and in favor of investigating internal states and helping patients to regain autonomy through increased understanding.

CONCLUSION

We began with the thesis that the philosophy of science currently favored by a majority of psychologists is one reason why the family has been neglected as a subject of research by psychologists. The concept of the family is suspect when reductionism requires that it be redefined in terms of the properties of individual members in order to be comprehensible; when standards of objectivity require that the abstract principles pertaining to its social organization be analyzed in terms of publicly observable data; and when the quest for universal laws rules out the consideration of cultural norms which tie the family to other organizations in the society. Hence, problems pertaining to the family tend to be dissected into childrearing practices, the life cycle, mate selection, and the like, the over-all family processes being left to the sociologists, anthropologists, and psychiatrists. Much of this chapter has been devoted to questioning the adequacy of the current paradigm and to describing a holistic alternative: the ways in which it differs from individualistic paradigms, its historic roots, its use in family therapy, and some criticisms of it.

The impressive capacity of academicians to generate theories and collect significant data bears vivid testimony to the great value of individualistic models for certain types of research. The purposes in writing this chapter have been to question the assumption that this type of "scientific" paradigm is sufficient for all types of research, to show how another type might be preferable in conducting research on the family, and to highlight the importance of selecting models with the same care that one selects methods.

REFERENCES

Ackerman, N. W. Interpersonal disturbances in the family. *Psychiatry,* 1954, *17,* 359.

Allport, F. *Social psychology.* Boston: Houghton Mifflin, 1924.

Ashby, W. K. *An introduction to cybernetics.* New York: John Wiley & Sons, 1956.

Bannister, D. Psychology as an exercise in paradox. *Bulletin of the British Psychological Society,* 1966, *19,* 21–26.

Bateson, G. *Steps to an ecology of mind.* New York: Chandler, 1972.

Bateson, G., Jackson, D. D., Haley, J., & Weakland, J. H. Toward a theory of schizophrenia. *Behavioral Science,* 1956, *1,* 251–264.

Billig, M. *Social psychology and intergroup relations.* New York: Academic Press, 1976.

Bion, W. *Experiences in groups.* London: Tavistock Publications, 1961.

Bogdan, J. L. Family organization as an ecology of ideas: An alternative to the reification of family systems. *Family Process,* 1984, *23,* 375–388.

Bowen, M. Family relationships in schizophrenia. In A. Auerback (Ed.), *Schizophrenia—An integrated approach.* New York: Ronald Press, 1959. Pp. 147–178.

Bowen, M. Family: The use of family theory in clinical practice. *Comprehensive Psychiatry,* 1966, *7,* 345–374.

Cassirer, E. Structuralism in modern linguistics. *Word,* 1945, *1,* 99.

Cronbach, L. J. *Designing evaluations of educational and social programs.* San Francisco: Jossey-Bass, 1982.

Cottrell, L. S., & Foote, N. N. Sullivan's contribution to social psychology. In P. Mullahy (Ed.), *The contributions of Harry Stack Sullivan.* New York: Hermitage House, 1952. Pp. 181–206.

Culler, J. *Ferdinand de Saussure.* New York: Penguin Books, 1977.

Deese, J. *Psychology as science and as art.* New York: Harcourt Brace Jovanovich, 1972.

Despert, J. L. Schizophrenia in children. *Psychiatric Quarterly,* 1938, *12,* 366–371.

Feshbach, S. The environment of personality. *American Psychologist,* 1978, *33,* 447–455.

Framo, J. L. The integration of marital therapy with sessions with families of origin. In A. S. Gurman & D. P. Kniskern (Eds.), *Handbook of family therapy.* New York: Brunner/Mazel, 1981. Pp. 133–158.

Fromm-Reichmann, F. Notes on the development of treatment of schizophrenics by psychoanalytic psychotherapy. *Psychiatry,* 1948, *11,* 263–273.

Gurman, A. S., & Kniskern, D. P. (Eds.). *Handbook of family therapy.* New York: Brunner/Mazel, 1981.

Hager, M. G. The myth of objectivity. *American Psychologist,* 1982, *37,* 576–579.

Haley, J. (Ed.). *Changing families.* New York: Grune & Stratton, 1971.

Haley, J. Toward a theory of pathological systems. In G. Zuk & I. Boszormenyi-Nagy (Eds.), *Family therapy and disturbed families.* Palo Alto, Calif.: Science and Behavior Books, 1973. Pp. 11–27.

Haley, J. *Problem solving therapy.* San Francisco: Jossey-Bass, 1977.

Heisenberg, W. *The physical principles of the quantum theory.* New York: Dover, 1930.

Hoffman, L. The family life-cycle and discontinuous change. In B. Carter & M. McGoldrick (Eds.), *The family life cycle.* New York: Gardner Press, 1980.

Jackson, D. D. The question of family homeostasis. *Psychiatric Quarterly,* 1957, *31,* 79–90.

Jackson, D. D. (Ed.). *The etiology of schizophrenia.* New York: Basic Books, 1960.

Jackson, D. D. The monad, the dyad, and the family therapy of schizophrenics. In A. Burton (Ed.), *Psychotherapy of the psychoses.* New York: Basic Books, 1961.

Jackson, D. D., Beavin, J. H., & Watzlawick, P. *Pragmatics of human communication.* New York: W. W. Norton, 1967.

Johnson, A., & Szurek, S. A. The genesis of antisocial acting out in children and adults. *Psychoanalytic Quarterly,* 1952, *21,* 323–343.

Kasanin, J., Knight, E., & Sage, P. The parent-child relationship in schizophrenia. *Journal of Nervous and Mental Disease,* 1934, *79,* 249–263.

Kuhn, T. S. *The structure of scientific revolutions.* Chicago: University of Chicago Press, 1962.

L'Abate, L. *Systematic family therapy.* New York: Brunner/Mazel, in press.

Laquer, H. P. Multiple family therapy and general systems theory. In N. W. Ackerman (Ed.), Family therapy in transition. *International Psychiatry Clinics,* 1970, *7,* 99–124.

Levi-Strauss, C. *Structural anthropology.* New York: Basic Books, 1963.

Levy, D. *Maternal overprotection.* New York: Columbia University Press, 1943.

Lewin, K. *Field theory in social science.* Westport, Conn.: Greenwood Press, 1951.

Lidz, T., Cornelison, A., Fleck, S., & Terry, D. The interfamilial environments of schizophrenic patients: II. Marital schism and marital skew. *American Journal of Psychiatry,* 1957, *114,* 241–248.

Lipset, D. *Gregory Bateson: The legacy of a scientist.* Englewood Cliffs, N.J.: Prentice-Hall, 1980.

Manicas, P. T., & Secord, P. F. Implications for psychology of the new philosophy of science. *American Psychologist,* 1983, *38,* 399–413.

McLemore, C. W., & Benjamin, L. S. Whatever happened to interpersonal diagnosis? *American Psychologist,* 1979, *34,* 17–34.

Mead, G. H. *Mind, self, and society.* Chicago: University of Chicago, 1934.

Miller, D. R., & Westman, J. C. Family teamwork and psychotherapy. *Family Process,* 1966, *5,* 49–59.

Moreno, J. L. Interpersonal therapy and the psychopathology of interpersonal relations. *Sociometry,* 1937, *1,* 9–76.

Nagel, E. *The structure of science.* New York: Harcourt Brace Jovanovich, 1961.

Peele, S. Reductionism in the psychology of the eighties. *American Psychologist,* 1981, *36,* 807–818.

Pepitone, A. Lessons from the history of social psychology, *American Psychologist,* 1981, *36,* 972–985.

Ruesch, J., & Bateson, G. *Communication: The social matrix of psychiatry.* New York: W. W. Norton, 1951.

Sampson, E. A. Cognitive psychology as ideology. *American Psychologist*, 1981, *36*, 730–743.

Sarason, S. B. An asocial psychology and a misdirected clinical psychology. *American Psychologist*, 1981, *8*, 827–836.

Scheibe, K. E. *Mirrors, masks, lies, and secrets: The limits of human predictability.* New York: Praeger Publishers, 1979.

Shands, H. C. *The war with words: Structure and transcendence.* The Hague: Mouton, 1971.

Speck, R., & Attneave, C. *Family networks.* New York: Vintage Books, 1973.

Speer, D. Family systems: Morphostasis and morphogenesis, or 'Is homeostasis enough?' *Family Process*, 1970, *9*, 25–278.

Sullivan, H. S. Affective experience in early schizophrenia. *American Journal of Psychiatry*, 1927, *6*, 468–483.

Sullivan, H. S. The meaning of anxiety in psychiatry and in life. *Psychiatry*, 1948, *11*, 1–13.

Sullivan, H. S. *The interpersonal theory of psychiatry.* New York: W. W. Norton, 1953.

Tietze, T. A study of mothers of schizophrenic patients. *Psychiatry*, 1949, *12*, 55–65.

Tyler, F. B., Pargament, K. I., & Gatz, M. The resource collaborator role. *American Psychologist*, 1983, *38*, 388–398.

Unger, R. K. Toward a redefinition of sex and gender. *American Psychologist*, 1979, *34*, 1085–1094.

Vygotsky, L. *Thought and language.* Cambridge, Mass.: MIT Press, 1962.

Weakland, J. H. The "double bind" hypothesis of schizophrenia and three-party interaction. In D. D. Jackson (Ed.), *The etiology of schizophrenia.* New York: Basic Books, 1960. Pp. 373–388.

Wynne, L., Ryckoff, I., Day, J., & Hirsch, S. H. Pseudo-mutuality in schizophrenia. *Psychiatry*, 1958, *21*, 205–220.

Yalom, J. D. *The theory and practice of group psychotherapy.* New York: Basic Books, 1970.

Zuk, G. *Family therapy: A triadic based approach.* New York: Behavioral Publications, 1971.

Chapter 2

Toward a Developmental Psychology of the Family*

KENNETH KAYE

Family psychology has to be more than a *part* of the study of human development. It will be viewed here as a conceptual *revolution* in developmental psychology, demanding the overthrow of some cherished traditional assumptions. The problem addressed in this chapter is how to begin replacing the old, inadequate concepts—about knowledge, about action, about motivation—with concepts at the level of the social system instead of the individual, without the new concepts turning out to be even less adequate than the old.

The principal question to be wrestled with will be referred to as the Locus question: How can knowledge, action, and other psychological constructs be located in an entity larger and more diffuse than an individual nervous system? Part of the answer will be hinted at in two ideas: the incompleteness, or "dove-tailing," of all human skills and the externality rather than internality of one's sense of self. Before we can make any attempt at answers, however, we need to explore the kinds of phenomena that a psychology of the family should be expected to explain.

The worst fate that could befall the movement toward a psychology of the family would be for that phrase to mean different things to all its proponents, hence to have no real meaning. To some, it would mean nothing more than the study of how family members interact with each other. To others, it might mean nothing more than acknowledging that children are not the only people in families who develop;

* I am grateful to Dr. Charles H. Kramer and to Professor L'Abate for their comments on the first draft of this chapter.

so do their parents, grandparents, aunts, and uncles. Or it might mean nothing more than a certain ideological stance with respect to psychological theorizing—for example, the attitude that explanations should be bidirectional, circular, or "systemic" rather than linear or "cause-and-effect." Carried to extremes, it might mean the abandonment of science in favor of epistemological obfuscations.

All of those views are bound to be represented in a book of this scope at this primitive stage (notwithstanding about 30 years of work) in the development of our science. At the outset, therefore, I must state my own view: *A psychology of the family means a science whose unit of study is no longer the individual mind/body/person but a developing social system of physically separate people.* Studying a fundamentally different kind of creature—the social system—will require a revolution in the way psychologists think. Many of the investigators who have been responsible for the birth and infancy of family psychology have recognized the difficulty of the required conceptual shift, but the field still remains at a preconceptual stage in this respect: We know a few things about the "behavior" of family systems, but have yet to explain how it is that a system of organisms can "behave" in an organized fashion.

For reasons to be discussed in this chapter, a systems psychology must be a different enterprise from the study of individuals. It is not the same as studying interaction among people, where the individuals are still the units of analysis. A family psychology means that the family becomes the subject unit, with its own character and own course of development. If families were merely the algebraic sums of their members, we would not need a special analysis at this level. Hence, to view the family as an entity with its own psychology is to assume that it is different from the sum of its parts.

Yet a science that is still psychology, not sociology, must concern itself with explaining the actual processes of communication, decision making, learning, and development. To explain such processes at the family level instead of at the individual level amounts to a new paradigm because traditional psychology is based on the assumption that knowledge, action, and motivation are properties of individual *organisms.* Those concepts cannot simply be shifted out to refer to social systems.

A psychology of the family must be a *developmental* psychology, because the concept of adaptation is essential to our very definition of a social system. Conversely, developmental psychology is always implicitly, and should be explicitly, a psychology of the family. The mildest argument for that proposition is that human beings develop in the context of their families; the stronger and more interesting argument is that families themselves are the entities whose development really has to be explained. Hopefully, the latter view will soon be more widely held. The family approach will invade, dominate, and irreversibly alter developmental psychology, rather than being an ancillary field of study.

Traditional developmental psychology takes the individual as its unit of analysis; the child's parents and other family members are conceptualized as potential influences upon the child's development. Instead, we can see that each family member's individual development is an aspect of larger processes of change in their system. This is an idea to which most of us developmental psychologists are willing to give lip service; yet until now, it has really been the individual in whose development we were interested. And it will continue to be so, unless we either cease to be psychologists or address the problem of how knowledge, action, and motivation exist in the interfaces between organisms.

To illustrate the questions that await investigation in this virtual *terra incognita* beyond the conceptually safe Old World of individual psychology, this chapter will make use of excerpts from a contemporary novel about a family.[1] I quote the comments of a fictional narrator, partly in order to offset the unabashedly theoretical contents of this chapter and partly because the novelist achieves greater coherence, clarity, and truth-to-life than any anecdotal case study could offer. For example, his protagonist contemplates the impossibility of separating his existence and self from his roles as son, husband, and father:

> *Excerpt 1:* I have this unfading picture in my mind . . . of this festive, family birthday celebration in honor of my little girl at which my old mother and my infant daughter are joyful together for perhaps the very last time. And there I am between them, sturdy, youthful, prospering, virile (fossilized and immobilized between them as though between book-ends, without knowing how I got there, without knowing how I will ever get out), saddled already with the grinding responsibility of making them, and others, happy, when it has been all I can do from my beginning to hold my own head up straight enough to look existence squarely in the eye without making guileful wisecracks about it or sobbing out loud for help. (Heller, 1974, pp. 194–195)

The chapter is in three parts. The first part argues that the mystery about how it is possible for several distinct individuals to comprise a developing system is the most important problem psychology can now address. Psychologists, sociologists, and anthropologists understand the functioning of interpersonal systems about as well as biologists under-

---

[1] The excerpts throughout the chapter are from *Something Happened* by Joseph Heller, 1974. New York: Alfred A. Knopf, Inc. Copyright 1974 by Alfred A. Knopf, Inc. Reprinted by permission.

stood the functioning of the organism before Harvey traced the circula-
tion of the blood, nearly four centuries ago. Theories about how systems
operate are as primitive, vague, and mystical as were the medieval
theories based on blood, phlegm, lymph, and bile.

The second part of the chapter discusses some conceptual and methodological obstacles in the way of the revolution many of us would
like to see. The foremost problem is that the notion of a social system,
seen as having a life of its own like an organism, is merely a metaphor.
It is not a theory. It does not explain anything, and it is not testable.
It has been around for at least 150 years without answering the most
essential questions about the interaction and concerted action of people
in social systems.

The third part of the chapter presents 10 essential questions, all
beginning with the word *how*. All 10 questions have to do with processes of behavior, not just with structural descriptions of the family,
and with causal mechanisms, not just with correlations. In other words,
they are questions that can only be answered by psychology—not sociology, not anthropology, not epistemology. The questions and my tentative gropings toward answers will be restricted to *families: units of
two or more persons related by kinship or marriage and by the economics of sharing a household over a significant period of their lives.*
However, at a broader level, the questions apply to all social systems.

SOCIAL SYSTEMS AND THE SOCIAL SCIENCES

It could be argued that government should stop supporting research
in every field *except* the psychology of social systems. Science and
industry are well equipped to accomplish any constructive purpose
that people can manage to agree upon. It is the process of settling
upon common purposes and collaborating in common endeavors that
still eludes mankind. Dimly we realize that failures in social relations
can now at any time trigger destruction beyond comprehension. Our
challenge—to explore the interpersonal mysteries and bring our understanding of social systems to a par with our understanding of the physical universe and of biological organisms—has an 11th-hour urgency.

The ignorance of social scientists—our ignorance—is comparable
to that of physiologists four centuries ago. It was known that air was
somehow necessary to animal life and that blood moved through veins,
but not that blood is pumped by the heart in a continuous loop carrying
oxygen from the lungs out to every cell and returning to the lungs.
Sixteenth-century physicians were as helpless in the face of physiological problems as we are today in the face of social problems. After
Harvey presented a model of the circulatory system, everything fell
into place for physicians and biologists. They could begin to trace which

organs put things into the blood and which took things out; within a few scientific generations, they could fight infection and disease, anesthetize against pain, transplant organs.

When we theorize about social systems, we sound more like physicians before Harvey, with their vague notions about the four "humours." Consider the following state-of-the-art account of family therapy:

> People are always functioning with a portion of their possibilities. There are many possibilities, only some of which are elicited or constrained by the contextual structure. Therefore, breaking or expanding contexts can allow new possibilities to emerge. The therapist, an expander of contexts, creates a context in which exploration of the unfamiliar is possible. She confirms family members and encourages them to experiment with behavior that has previously been constrained by the family system. As new possibilities emerge, the family organism becomes more complex and develops more acceptable alternatives for problem solving. (Minuchin & Fishman, 1981, pp. 15–16)

Does this not make therapy, and the family's development itself, sound like magic? Indeed, there are those who use that very word; not a promising basis for research.

Within this century, we ought to be capable of seeing the essential processes of social interaction—including human development and group dynamics—with clarity, certainty, and revolutionary impact comparable to Harvey's discovery.

An emerging view of interaction. The potentially apocalyptic consequence of our continued ignorance about social systems is only one argument for pushing beyond metaphors to a serious science of interpersonal dynamics. A second argument comes from the field of developmental psychology itself. Two trends have made our individually oriented theories seem less and less adequate in the past decade or two.

One trend is toward a lifespan conception of human development. We no longer think of development as something that happens to children and ceases at the end of adolescence. The other trend is toward the study of interaction—between parent and child, among children, between parents, between child and teacher. Obviously, these two trends are closely related. Criticizing the research up to 1972 on parent-child attachment behavior, Hartup and Lempers concluded that "an interactional phenomenon has been reduced to a set of individual differences and attachment characterized as an appendage of the organism rather than as a dimension of the social intercourse in which the organism is engaged" (1973, p. 238).

Once one stops thinking of development as the effect of adults upon children and sees the adults too as continuing to develop through the course of parenthood, one necessarily finds parent-child interaction a more interesting and complex affair. For example, a decade of intensive work by students of parent-infant interaction has erased the model of an infant who consisted partly of an autonomously maturing intelligence and partly of attachment bonds responding to maternal nurturance. We now see the infant as eliciting certain kinds of parental behavior that are preadapted to pull him through a kind of universal curriculum, or "apprenticeship" (Kaye, 1982). Thus human infants and human parents are designed for a joint function. Their function is to ensure that infants are transformed, over the first year of life, from mere organisms into members of family systems: self-conscious, language-using persons.

Now we can look at adolescence the same way. Instead of just asking what goes on inside the minds and bodies of children from the time they reach puberty until they (hopefully) leave their parents' homes, we can ask how parents and children normally collaborate in the development of a less-dependent relationship.

> *Excerpt 2:* I do not talk to my daughter as I should to a child, or would if she were somebody else's. I'm not nice to her. If my little boy misbehaves, I respond to him dotingly as a careless, mischievous, or overtired little boy who needs a kiss and a hug and the mildest of reprimands; it is a normal, predictable, endearing mistake, and I correct him tolerantly in an almost deferential way. If my teen-age daughter does something wrong, it is something *wrong:* it is an insulting, intentional, inexcusable attack against me that requires swift and severe retribution. (I do not treat them the same.) I wonder why. Is it because she's a daughter? Or a first child, for whom my aspirations were too high, and in whom I am now therefore disappointed? Or is it that she is already in her teens, growing up and away from me, slipping free from my authority, already preparing to live without me, to challenge frontally my wisdom, morality, and ability, and threatening to dislodge me, if she can, from my shaky stronghold of dictatorial self-esteem? (Heller, 1974, p. 178)

The first step is to see parent-child interaction (and all interpersonal interaction) as bidirectional, and the next step is to realize that it is *more* than bidirectional: It is a relationship organized to achieve certain goals that the members could not achieve singly. This is one of the criteria for calling a group or organization a social system: Its members demonstrate *shared purpose.* Furthermore, they could not come together ad hoc to function in this way; the relationship depends upon a *shared history.* In other words, the system undergoes its own development, over and above (but somehow entailing) the development of its members, each of whom is also, separately, an open system.

The concept of *open systems* requires some background. System theory originated in the late 19th-century revolt against reductionist, molecular, mechanistic theories in physics. The science of cybernetics grew out of that movement. Later, when general systems theory (von Bertalanffy, 1968) emphasized the distinction between closed and open systems, it was part of another revolt: a revolt within cybernetics against using physical theories as models of the mind and of human society. A system is open, as opposed to closed, if it functions as a unit so as to exchange energy and information with its environment. The functioning of the parts is subordinated (organized) to a goal or direction of the whole. By virtue of this organization, the second law of thermodynamics (entropy) is violated. Over the lifetime of the system, there is an increasing organization. Energy is brought into the system to counteract entropy, and information is created in the system. An important part of the theory is that this occurs at a decreasing cost: The system develops so as to function more efficiently vis-à-vis the outside world. An automobile engine, which tends toward entropy, is a closed system. As the interacting parts wear down and lose precision, the performance of the whole declines. A horse, over the same period of time, grows internally more complex—i.e., gains information—and performs more efficiently. It is an open system.

The concept of system in developmental psychology. The word *system* means organization and adaptation; but of course *individual development* also means organization and adaptation. The criteria of shared purpose and shared development, in adaptation to the outside world, are inherent in the concept of a social system. But the same criteria are also inherent in the concept of *organism* as an open system or in the concept of an organized intelligence or an organized self. Hence it would appear easy for developmental psychologists, used to thinking about those types of organization, to think in terms of the family system. In fact, developmental psychologists would recognize as important all of the "how" questions to be discussed later in this paper:

How does a family adapt over time while retaining its identity?

How do differences among families come about?

How is the development of a family constrained by the community and culture, and vice versa?

How does the need for the family to develop affect individual development, and vice versa?

How do families create, recruit, and indoctrinate new members?

How do families mediate between the community (or society at large) and their individual members?

How do families act through their individual members' encounters with the world?

How does an individual bring about changes in other individual members and in the family as a whole?

How does the individual mind internalize the workings of the whole family system?

How do families equip their members for participation in other systems?

Yet developmental psychologists have barely addressed these questions. Nor have they addressed many other questions that require thinking in terms of families as opposed to individuals. A survey of three different volumes of *Developmental Psychology* (1972, 1977, and 1982) revealed that fewer than 10 per cent of the studies published had anything to do with interaction. In more than 9 out of 10 studies, the subjects were individuals (for example, 25 four-year-old children), and the measures were of individual behavior (for example, a learning task). The remaining 9 to 10 per cent of the studies also nearly always involved individual subjects as the unit of analysis. Although social interaction was measured, it was measured as an independent or dependent variable on each subject, in order to test hypotheses about, for example, differences in some aspect of social behavior according to age, gender, or socioeconomic status.

About 1 study in 100 published in *Developmental Psychology* actually studies interaction between people (*behavioral* interaction rather than statistical interaction between variables). I made this survey originally to document an increase in studies of parent-child interaction (my view of the field having been distorted by several edited volumes, especially on mothers and infants), but in fact there was no such increase.

What *has* increased is the use of systems rhetoric to describe interactions within the family. Now we have to progress beyond that rhetoric to operational concepts and methods. Indeed, a few investigators have recently laid the groundwork for doing so. As we shall see when the questions listed above are discussed later in this paper, the notion of family systems is a heuristic device for helping us to formulate good questions. At the same time, it may be one of the obstacles in the way of answering them.

OBSTACLES TO A PSYCHOLOGY OF THE FAMILY

We know remarkably little about the actual processes of family life. We know *what* happens in families, at a general level, but we really know nothing about *how* it happens. Perhaps our situation is like that of the proverbial fish who, it is said, has no concept of water. We are so thoroughly immersed in these processes that we cannot see them. However, we may think we understand them better than we do. In the next section, examples of routine interactions will be used to illustrate the kinds of questions that have to be asked. This section prepares the way for that by discussing some obstacles to the investigation of those topics.

Metaphors are not theories.   One such obstacle is confusion between metaphors and theories. The idea that a social system is like an organism, for example, is only a metaphor. A metaphor is not testable; it cannot be disproved. It becomes a theory only when stated in a form that generates hypotheses. Consider the following seminal statement, one of the first suggestions that the concept of homeostasis could be applied to social systems:

> It seems not impossible that the means employed by more highly evolved animals for preserving uniform and stable their economy (i.e., for preserving homeostasis) may present some general principles for the establishment, regulation, and control of steady states that would be suggestive of other organizations, even social and industrial, which suffer from distressing perturbations. (Cannon, 1938, p. 305)

This conjecture was not a theory, it was a suggestion that there might be a useful analogy between the ways organisms regulate themselves in response to perturbations and the ways "organizations," or (as we would now say) social systems, do so. Why *should* there be general principles that apply to both levels of organization? Structuralists like Piaget (1967) argue that there must be similarity across all forms of adaptation, because adaptation is an inherent principle of biology. (Piaget goes even further, finding the ultimate laws not in biology but in mathematics.) But there is no reason to assume such broad generality of explanatory principles, other than to simplify man's quest for order in the universe. It is perfectly plausible that family systems arise and function through processes uniquely their own. Any similarities to other forms of organization—human intelligence, group behavior, international relations—may come about in several ways:

1. Human intelligence reflects the discourse frame in which it is acquired during infants' apprenticeship to adults.
2. Decision-making processes, by groups as well as by individuals, reflect the basic organization of human intelligence.
3. Skills learned within the family transfer to people's behavior as members of other systems.
4. Similarities may also be due to coincidence.

5.   Apparent similarities can result from distorted perceptions of phenomena by social scientists, in their quest for order.

There are reasons to believe that the similarities are due to the
first three causes more than to the last two. The important point here,
however, is that there is no scientific basis for considering the similarities to be due to guiding principles of the universe—structuralist, sys-
tems-ist, or otherwise. Furthermore, as Cannon made clear, whatever
general principles we can find are merely the starting point for research. If we use a metaphor—for example, "a family is like an organism"—it is only so as to be able to proceed toward an understanding
of all the ways the metaphor is inadequate. "A family is like an organism, except that its parts all have separate lives; how can that be?"
(We shall return to this question several times.)

Two kinds of description are necessary to psychological theory building: P-models and C-models (Kaye, 1977, 1982). Both are perpetually
incomplete. A P-model (P for *process*) has the virtue of describing
how a system seems to work in real time; for example, one possible
P-model of the situation Heller captured in Excerpt 2 would be "adolescents' questioning of parents' values leads the parents to feel rejected
and frustrated, which makes them impatient and defensively deprecat-
ing, which elicits a defensive reaction from the adolescent." A psychologist would then push toward a more detailed P-model by investigating
each of those actions and reactions in further detail. The aim of explanatory theories is to be as specific as possible about actual mechanisms
while still remaining simple and general enough to be useful.

C-models (C for *competence*, in Chomsky's, 1965, sense) describe
the results a system is capable of producing, without attempting to
specify the causal chain by which those results come about. A C-model
of the parent-child relationship during adolescence might be "mutual
alienation plus mutual defensiveness." This refers to the same phenomenon as the P-model, again from a systems perspective, but it makes
no attempt to specify what causes what. Like metaphors, C-models
are a necessary step in labeling the processes that are most worth
understanding, but only P-models express those as processes and articulate them schematically.

Unfortunately, P-models are complicated, often inelegant, usually
boring. C-models, by virtue of their reductionism, tend to be elegant
and impressive. Also unfortunately, P-models often suggest a linear
causal sequence, especially in developmental psychology, where until
recently the parent was seen as cause and the child as effect. Hence,
the lack of causal sequence in C-models may make them more attractive to theorists who try to go beyond simplistic linear causation models.
But the sample P-model presented above is *not* linear; it is, in fact,

systemic. It is a fallacy to regard causal models and systems approaches as antithetical. One can (and should) still seek theories about how things work in real time (L'Abate, 1976), about what leads to what, even when one knows that the direction of effects in open systems is not linear.

A family is not an organism. The organic analogy, as a scientific heuristic device, dates back at least as far as Comte, who christened sociology 150 years ago. The metaphor itself is as ancient as literature (someone is head of the family, or is his father's right arm, or relaxes in the bosom of his family, etc.). Although, as suggested above, the similarities between social systems and organisms are probably not coincidental, it may be more useful now to emphasize the *differences* between social systems and organism systems. Because of those differences, the statement "families are systems" does not explain anything.

An organism is a physical entity, its parts all mechanically connected and all with fixed specialized functions. Its memory resides in an identifiable organ, its actions are directed by that same organ, and communication among the organs is conducted through fixed pathways. We are still ignorant about much of that organization, particularly within the brain, which apparently does not reflect the "fixed pathway" structure found in the organism as a whole. Nonetheless, we have a physical basis upon which to map the processes of perception, memory, emotion, action. We have no such physical basis for an analogous discussion of *family* processes. Where is the family's memory? What does it mean to say a family "has energy," "is motivated to change," "struggles to maintain its identity," "acts to restore its equilibrium"? This is the Locus question. In reality, it is not families that perceive, act, remember, or possess energy, motivation, or identity; it is people who do so. Yet they do so in a concerted way. And they "read each other's minds." What does that mean? It is the only way we can express the fact that family members correctly predict one another's reactions, know what each other is feeling at various times. Yet it is hardly an explanation.

Family members are *each* intact organisms. They are practically identical to one another in structure—compared with, say, the differences between a heart and a liver. The members replicate, rather than being differentially assigned, the capacities for perception, memory, emotion, action, and communication. Their specialized roles are learned, not fixed. This needs no more evidence than the fact that those roles vary across families and even more so across cultures.

Not only are the members of the system physically detached from one another, they are also detached in time. All parts of an organism begin and end their life together. All family members enter the system and leave it at different times. Children move into adult roles and form new families, yet also perpetuate their old family identity; so long as offspring continue to be produced and to identify with the family name, we can speak of a family existing for many generations: the Adamses, the Batesons, or the Hatfields and McCoys. Continuity of identity requires the young to be able to read and internalize the previous generation's minds, find mates compatible with the family patterns they have acquired, and produce a new generation in their turn.

All these mysterious processes are ignored if we interpret the organic analogy too narrowly. Certainly, a family is a biological phenomenon. It does have certain structural similarities to other levels of biological organization. It has the properties of goal directedness, coordination, feedback, adaptation. But those properties are not necessarily achieved through the same processes that account for them at the organism level. And the analogy does not necessarily generate any sensible hypotheses about family functioning.

Sociology is not psychology; family therapy is not family psychology. A third potential obstacle to a psychology of the family is the fact that developmental psychologists are relative latecomers to the field. Concepts and issues already seem to have been staked out by sociologists, anthropologists, and clinicians, often on territory that we psychologists must also share. This would not be a problem, since the same ground can be mined for different minerals, except that the first explorers of a field tend to chart roads through it that inevitably affect the way later explorers see it.

Sociology obviously has much to teach us; but it cannot answer our questions, because it *assumes* a social entity. In that science, C-models pass for explanation. Never having had the possibility of tracing real-time processes as psychology can (sometimes) do, sociology has depended upon the very structural/descriptive/metaphorical models we hope to go beyond. Sociology, like systems theory, provides some C-models of the family; psychology has yet to provide the corresponding P-models.

Furthermore, the methods of statistical regression, which (besides anecdote) are sociologists' chief methods of research, may not be sufficient for the psychologists who would embrace the questions to be discussed below. We do, of course, use correlation coefficients, factor analysis, and path analysis to test hypotheses. Ultimately, however, we may also have to use experimental designs. In the same way that individuals can be observed under laboratory conditions, assigned to intervention versus control groups or to pretest-training-posttest designs, so can dyads and whole families. The sociologist may be more concerned with what actually happens, in all its complexity, under real-world conditions; whereas our contribution to an understanding of the processes involved under those conditions may require us to control, standardize, and simplify the conditions under which we make our observations (see, for example, Gottman, 1979; Reiss, 1981; Strodtbeck, 1954; Wynne & Singer, 1963).

If the relation between psychology and sociology is complementary in this respect, the relation between developmental psychology and the clinicians (psychologists, psychiatrists, social workers, and others) to whom we owe most of our current literature on the family may be more problematic. Clinicians have different goals: to develop better methods of intervention, to improve diagnosis so as to know when a given type of intervention is indicated, and to waste as little time as possible probing any family processes more deeply than necessary to meet those first two goals. Family therapists focus directly on dysfunctional processes in the types of families who seek professional help. In principle, we know that an understanding of the specieswide and culturewide processes through which all families develop would be of approximately the same value to the study of dysfunctional families as the knowledge of human physiology is to the study of disease. In practice, however, the basic questions are harder to get funded. Research money and time are invested directly on applications of inadequate theories, on ways of intervening with dysfunctional families before we understand family processes in general. (Should cancer research funds be spent testing every combination of chemotherapy and radiation therapy, or should they be spent on basic cell biology, immunology, genetics?)

At this point, we do not even know what dysfunctional families represent in terms of universal family processes. Are their problems due to the absence of normal functions? Are they due to normal processes being carried to extremes, without adequate regulation or counterbalancing actions? Or do functional and dysfunctional families simply differ in goals, using substantially the same interaction and developmental processes to achieve them? The question is not whether families with serious problems are normal (they are) or whether normal families have problems (they do). The question is whether families seen clinically provide an adequate data base for investigating normal family processes. We might spend 100 years studying what goes on in the types of families we come into contact with as therapists, without learning much about the processes that are missing or impaired in those families. The latter may be what we most need to know in order to help them. So the observation of well-functioning (effective, adaptive) families is a crucial part of developmental psychology's task (Kantor & Lehr, 1975), and the vision of family interaction that one gets from a clinical sample may be as much an obstacle as an aid.

Finally, the family therapy literature happens to have distorted several of the most important concepts pertaining to systems. Two examples will suffice. One is the concept of open versus closed systems. As explained above, all organic systems are open, which means that they exchange resources with their environments without dissipating their energy and organization. In fact, they continually adapt so as to avoid such dissipation. Closed systems, such as river systems and solar systems, lack the ability to adapt so as to preserve their relationship to their surroundings. They may survive for millions of years, but their inexorable course is one of decay (entropy). Open systems may be seen as brief anomalies along that course, when complex organization and coordination processes stave off the decay.

The words *open* and *closed* are not the best ones to convey this important distinction, but they are the words we must use if we are to profit from what general systems theory can teach us about open systems. *All* families are open systems, including those that appear "closed" in the sense of rigid, insular, and enmeshed (Kantor & Lehr, 1975; Olson, Sprenkle, & Russell, 1979). In fact, the latter type of family displays the characteristics of an open system (coordination of the parts to stave off entropy) more intensely than the looser, disengaged type of family. Dysfunctional families *do* adapt constantly to outside perturbations; the problem is that they adapt only so as to perpetuate their rules of interaction rather than to survive and thrive in a changed environment. These adaptations are *mal*adaptive for the members as individuals. Either they must sacrifice themselves, or the family structure as a whole must eventually collapse.

The words *open* and *closed* are frequently applied intuitively by clinicians, suggesting that some families are closed systems. This confounding of the metaphor only makes it more difficult to ask the most important theoretical questions about families, for the idea of systems changing from closed to open and vice versa has no meaning in terms of the broader theory of social systems.

A second misunderstood concept is homeostasis, which in systems theory means the ability to restore a steady state—in an open system, by a purposive organized direction. For example, our metabolic rate increases if our body temperature falls below 98.6°F. It decreases whenever our temperature rises above that level. By analogy, families are usually described in the clinical literature as trying to restore homeostasis when they resist therapeutic change. (Like the metabolic system, they slow down when things get too hot.) The therapist's lament, that identified patients' families frequently strive to maintain them in the "sick" role, is encountered by the student of family therapy as the essence of "systems thinking." Yet, as Ackerman pointed out long ago: "It is a misconception to consider as 'homeostatic' the strivings toward a state of static equilibrium that we observe clinically in certain patients. This is not homeostasis; this is psychopathology" (Ackerman, 1958, p. 71).

The semantic problem is that homeostatic does not mean static. It means adapting, as when a family successfully launches its adolescents and develops new forms of communication, affection, interdependence, and autonomy. (*Equilibration* is a better word than *homeostasis* because it does not imply that the end state will be the same as the old state. Technically, homeostasis means the continual restoration of a steady state, such as an optimal body temperature, whereas *equilibration* means achieving a balance between opposing forces, not necessarily returning to any given state.) Specific patterns are adjusted, new patterns are evolved, so that the social system's identity and broader functions are preserved. However, giving the process a name does not constitute an explanation. It is merely the first step toward asking good "how" questions.

TEN GOOD QUESTIONS FOR A PSYCHOLOGY OF THE FAMILY

The following list of unanswered questions is an attempt to lay the foundation for a developmental psychology that takes the family system as its subject. All 10 questions begin with the word *how*, to emphasize that we need to investigate the actual processes, working toward more adequate P-models. In each case, important work has already been done; but progress will be limited until we confront the Locus question—the problem of where a family's knowledge, beliefs, values, goals, actions, and patterns of interaction actually reside.

How does a family adapt over time, while retaining its identity? Precisely what adapts? Consider the major adaptation that must occur when parents learn, for example, that something is wrong with one of their children. Is it a matter of adaptation in the two people? Or does the narrator here speak for "we" in a more complicated sense?

> *Excerpt 3:* By now, my wife and I have had our fill—are sick and glutted to the teeth—of psychologists, psychiatrists, neurologists, neurosurgeons, speech therapists, psychiatric social workers, and any of all the others we've been to that I may have left out, with their inability to help and their lofty, patronizing platitudes that we are not to blame, ought not to let ourselves feel guilty, and have nothing to be ashamed of. . . . Why can't the simpleminded fools understand that we *want* to feel guilty, *must* feel guilty if we're to do the things we have to? . . .

We hate them all, the ones who were wrong and the ones who were right. After awhile, that made no difference. The cause didn't matter. The prognosis was absolute. . . .

"If only we hadn't had him," my wife used to lament. "He'd be so much better off if he'd never been born."

"Let's kill the kid," I used to joke jauntily when I thought he was just innately fractious (I used to carry color snapshots of all three of my children in my wallet. Now I carry none), before I began to guess there might be something drastically wrong.

I don't say that anymore. (Heller, 1974, pp. 497–499)

The couple has to adjust, but they have to do so in a way that allows them to remain the same "we." By analogy with other kinds of open systems, we say that a family must constantly reorganize and differentiate new specialized subsystems—in this case, the doctor-hating subsystem—if it is to go on functioning as a unit. Differentiation, which means creating the new patterns from within the old repertoire, is what ensures the continuity in the family's sense of identity—as opposed to having the solution tacked on by an external authority. But when we call it *differentiation,* we are merely drawing an analogy to embryogenesis without explaining anything: How does it really occur, in the action schemas of individuals and in such a coordinated way that their whole family can be said to have adapted yet remain the same family?

Suppose that one were to attempt a P-model of family adaptation in response to the severe trauma alluded to in Excerpt 3: cerebral palsy in one of the children. Assuming such a task were undertaken by investigators who had observed many such families over a period of years, what would their task involve? How would it be different from the kind of systems analysis we are already familiar with? It would be specific enough to be tested against new cases, which means specifying operationally the observable events that would confirm or disconfirm the model. If we were to hypothesize, for example, that both parents' guilt provides their motivation for coping (as Heller's protagonist claims), then families against whom the model is tested had better display first guilt and then coping—but not the latter without the former, or the P-model must be revised.

To use a more everyday example, when mother takes a new job, it requires every other member of the family to adapt, both in their relations with mother and in their relations with each other. Without this mutual adaptation and consequent development of the family as a whole, individual transactions with the environment would lead toward dissolution of the family (entropy). The function of adaptation is to preserve the family's identity despite those individual transactions. (Identity means the members' sense of belonging to an enduring, distinct unit.) But we need to go beyond this broad level of generalization to models of the specific communication processes that occur in response to such events. Can we predict the flow of effects from mother through the other family members? Does it depend upon certain aspects of the structure of that particular family? Upon their history? Is there a set of adaptations that might occur prior to the new job, to prepare the members to cope with its later consequences? How does the system as a whole, through each member, place limits on the extent of deviation from family patterns that will be tolerated? (Obviously, all of the questions to be discussed in the remainder of this chapter overlap with one another.)

Central to the problem of adaptation with continuity, and essential to the definition of open systems, is the notion of homeostasis or self-regulation. Observers of families, regardless of theoretical persuasion—from Freud (1920/1963) to Bateson (1949) to Haley (1976) and Bronfenbrenner (1979)—discuss the regulating sequences by which systems resist significant change. In therapy, this resistance means one has to convince the patient system (whether an individual or a family) that giving up its symptoms will be a relatively minor adjustment for the sake of preserving its ego or its family integrity. In well-functioning families, when a particular member appropriately ceases to perform some function (for example, by growing up and moving out of the home), that role will have to be taken over by someone else or compensated for in other ways.

We know what homeostasis means at the level of the individual organism. We can spell out some homeostatic mechanisms in specific terms. Thermoregulation is the classic example; oxygenation of the blood is another. In these cases, P-models indicate what leads to what, in a time sequence and in actual physical pathways. Although the models are inevitably incomplete at many points, they correspond to real mechanisms, and they are subject to revision the more those mechanisms are understood in detail.

When homeostasis is invoked to account for a *family's* behavior, there is no such model of pathways and step-by-step mechanisms. To predict that "something will happen to restore the parental hierarchy (or the absence of a hierarchy)," for example, is like saying "the body's temperature will return to 98.6°" without having the vaguest notion of how that regulation occurs. Family therapists are interested in filling in the steps of homeostasis in each particular family with which they work, but this field has not progressed to the point where anyone has undertaken a general P-model of homeostasis in all families, or even in all families of a particular type.

How do differences among families come about?   This question is inseparable from the previous question. If we say, "although they have changed, they are still the same family," we do not simply mean that the same people are still living together. We mean that they continue to be different, in certain ways, from other types of families: more religious, perhaps, or more competitive or more intellectual or more affectionate.

A subset of all the characteristics that make a family unique, only those characteristics the members are aware of, are included in their identity as a family. In fact, their identity may also include *false* beliefs about being different. More important than any objective comparison that might be made between this family and others is the family's own *consciousness* of being different. Their beliefs about what makes their family unique are, in fact, part of each one's individual identity. "We are . . ." is inevitably defined in terms of "others are not."

> *Excerpt 4:* Some melting pot. If all of us in this vast, fabulous land of ours could come together and take time to exchange a few words with our neighbors and fellow countrymen, those words would be *Bastard! Wop! Nigger! Whitey! Kike! Spic!* (Heller, 1974, p. 284)

The beliefs that family members hold about their family's merits, deficiencies, values, and rules partially determine how they behave. How does that work? And where does that consciousness reside? It can only be in the minds of the individual family members, yet it is somehow shared. Reiss (1981) expresses the Locus question when he considers how a family can be said to have an idea: "Despite the charms of the concept of shared construct, however, it is immediately apparent that there are problems with it. The first problem is the concept of 'shared.' Constructs or beliefs or conceptions are entities ordinarily residing in the heads of single individuals" (Reiss, 1981, p. 66).

Do shared concepts come about through verbal instruction, through conscious discussion of family traits, or by each member analyzing patterns of interaction, comparing them with those observed outside the family, and translating them into a set of generalizations about their family? It is reasonable to assume that the sense of identity is based on some real characteristics of the family; but at the same time, the members' beliefs about their family identity affect their behavior and thus create many of those differentiating characteristics.

When we ask about the origins of differences among families—differences of either kind, externally validated or internally believed—we are asking about causal processes. It is not a question of estimating the relative importance of nature (heritability plus assortative mating) versus nurture (learning), or even of how much of each. It is a question of *how* all the variance develops over the life cycles of all the individuals who become parts of the family. If we were to be satisfied with correlations (e.g., less-educated parents tend to be more authoritarian) or with generalizations (e.g., Italian-American families tend to be more enmeshed than Anglo-American families), we would be retreating at least one scientific generation. What we need are P-models of the *processes* by which a family becomes uniquely itself.

How is the development of a family constrained by the community and culture, and vice versa?

> *Excerpt 5:*   And I sometimes feel that I would not spend so much time and money and energy chasing around after girls and other women if I were not so frequently in the company of other men who do, or talk as though they wanted to. (Heller, 1974, p. 65)

> *Excerpt 6:*   "Listen," I exclaim to my children frantically, "you don't have to do what everybody else does. You can be whatever you want to be. I'll help. You don't have to join the Cub Scouts or play baseball or go to Sunday school or even to college. What do you want to do?
> "Join the Cub Scouts and play baseball," says my boy.
> "Go into my room and play my records now," says my daughter.
> (Heller, 1974, p. 165)

It is clear that a developmental psychology of the family must be a cross-cultural enterprise in the same way that an individual psychology must be at least a cross-family enterprise. We need to understand the extent and limits of cultural effects upon family development. That means the effect of cultural and subcultural *differences* upon differences among families in their adaptation. For example, why and how do Anglo-Saxon Protestant families typically develop much more interpersonal differentiation and intergenerational autonomy than do Chinese-American families?

We can think of the family as the middle level of three basic levels addressed by the social sciences: the individual, the family, and the tribe. When speculating about the evolution of man, scientists have paid too little attention to this middle level. For other species, it may be appropriate to jump, as modern genetics has, from the organism to the population (tribe) level. For human genotypes, however, evolutionary adaptation has probably depended less on the success of phenotypes—individual carriers of the genotype, each of whom is either more or less fit to survive—than on the success of their families in equipping them for survival. For example, a newborn infant's "innate" endowment includes not only intrinsic behavioral processes but behavioral processes built into parents as well (Kaye, 1982). In fact, it is not only the human organism or the human mind that has evolved in our species; family *processes* had to be specially adapted for the transformation of human offspring into full-fledged family members.

At the macro, or cultural level, it is also true that cultural evolution has depended to a large degree upon the abilities of families to pass down skills and traditions from each generation to the next. And just as the evolution of our species has depended on the evolution of family processes, so have different cultures required their own cultural adaptations in family structure and dynamics.

However, we should not assume, as traditional models of the family and society do, that the effects are all in the direction

$$SOCIETY \rightarrow FAMILY.$$

An evolutionary perspective suggests that the nature of human families has constrained the development of societies more than the other way around. Laws, religions, languages were not free to evolve in any direction that might have been adaptive for a particular population. They were constrained by the fact that they had to be transmissible from adults to children. Every natural language reflects constraints of the human brain, its cognitive capacity and its learning capacity, but also constraints of interpersonal interaction processes that have evolved for parents and children (demonstration and imitation, for example), without which any linguistic invention would have expired within a generation.

Those family processes are therefore more than just a missing level of analysis in the social sciences. They are what we must understand if we are to progress any further in explaining development at either the individual level or the societal level.

Let us hypothesize that there are certain features of family process that are indispensable to individual development and certain features that are indispensable to the adaptation and survival of any larger community. As evidence for this general proposition, one can cite the radical attempts to disrupt family bonds that followed both the French and the Russian revolutions. In both cases, these attempts failed utterly and were soon reversed. However, we know relatively little of what the specific psychological processes within the family are upon which the nature of man and society depend—not to mention how those processes evolved or how they are rediscovered by every family.

How does the need for the family to develop affect individual development, and vice versa? We say that both the individual and the family are open systems and that all open systems adapt to their environments in order to survive. Yet the individual and the family each constitute part of the environment to which the other must adapt; that is, individuals' development necessitates adaptations in their families, but the development of the family system as a whole depends upon—indeed, consists of—adaptations in its individual members.

It might be the case empirically that one of these levels of development is prior to the other: for example, that the only reason family systems develop is because they consist of members who are changing over time.[2] A family of *closed* systems (a network of computers, for example) would not develop; and the reason is to be found not in its structure but in the fact that its constituent hardware cannot adapt. (Software can adapt, but only to the extent that it is programmed to do so—by humans.) One could postulate that any system of closed systems must be a closed system (with the miraculous exception of the amino acid molecules that compose life itself) and any system of open systems must be an open system. Therefore, families undergo development simply because their individual members do.

On the other hand, we could entertain the opposite hypothesis. Family development could be the dominant process, and individual development mainly a consequence. Perhaps the idea of an intrinsic (within the individual person) motive to develop is a myth. It could be that the tendency of individuals is to remain the same, as much as possible, and that any long-term course of psychological development is actually in the service of the continual adaptation of the family. This would explain why individuals have to die and be replaced by new individuals; the organism is too conservative to go on changing and changing.

> *Excerpt 7:* I suppose it is just about impossible for someone like me to rebel anymore and produce any kind of lasting effect. I have lost the power to upset things that I had as a child; I can no longer change my environment or even disturb it seriously. They would simply fire and forget me as soon as I tried. They would file me away. (Heller, 1974, p. 15)

> *Excerpt 8:* I know at last what I want to be when I grow up.
> When I grow up I want to be a little boy. (Heller, 1974, p. 319)

In terms of Hofstadter's (1979) generalization of Gödel's Proof, the family is the higher frame that gives meaning to the individual developing within. Yet such a recourse to mathematics remains a "metaphorical fugue," in Hofstadter's words.[3] To what sort of plausible causal model might it lead? What does it mean to say that families have an intrinsic need to develop?

What it might mean is that equilibration is inevitable wherever organisms are required to interact with one another. In other words, perhaps a relationship between people can never just *be;* it must always

---

[2] We can reject the idea that families develop *because* they are open systems. In reality, we describe families as systems because we find that they do develop; what motivates them to do so is neither their "nature," as Aristotle would have it, nor the definition of an open system, but some mechanisms as yet unspecified.

[3] We need feel no hesitation about inverting the fugue, so far as the relation between family and society is concerned. We need not see society as a higher, or outer, frame. As suggested in the preceding section, families are the internal frame that give meaning to the cultures developing around them.

become and continue to become. Looked at in this way, the very existence of a family (or any social system) would be conceived of as dynamics rather than as structure. Just as atoms are really motion and energy rather than particles, perhaps families have to be defined as continuously changing relationships rather than as sets of people. If permanent equilibrium among the members were ever achieved, the family would vanish.

At the individual level, Piaget (1967) refers to equilibration between assimilation and accommodation. (Assimilation means responding to new events by imposing one's familiar skills and perceptual categories upon them; accommodation means modifying one's skills and perceptual categories as new conditions require.) Criticisms of his general theory (Haroutunian, 1983; Kaye, 1982) center on its being a metaphor rather than an explanation. However, a similar theory can be applied to the equilibrium between individuals and their families in a way that is neither circular nor untestable. The individual has to adapt to a changing system without changing himself so much as to lose his identity. This, too, leads to deeper questions—for example, how does the person know how much change is too much? Nonetheless, this approach, seeing the individual as driven by the family's development (and by other systems' development), would come closer to being a testable causal theory of human development than Piaget's, which reduces equilibration to a universal (structuralist) property of all biological systems.

How do families create, recruit, and indoctrinate new members?

If we think of schemas (skills or pieces of knowledge) as programs complete unto themselves and as having to be somehow inserted into the brains of new system members so that they can perform their roles properly, then it is extremely difficult to imagine how such learning ever takes place. The action schemas about which people receive direct instruction are a relatively small proportion of all the things they learn how to do—and even those actions are composed of hundreds of subroutines, few of which are ever discussed explicitly with instructors or receive any direct reinforcement. The analogy between skills and computer programs (e.g., Kaye, 1977) falls flat when we realize that older family members do not behave like programmers, in the sense of writing and debugging.

Instead, suppose we focus on the fact that most human skills are incomplete. They consist of links which only form a chain when linked to the actions of others.[4] Even so solitary an act as walking along the

---

[4] This idea could easily be expressed within the programming metaphor in terms of READ or INPUT statements, but that might be misleading. The way programs are written has nothing to do with the way skills develop.

sidewalk depends upon unconscious expectations about the behavior of other people—for example, knowing that you will avoid bumping into one another by each stepping to the right. A recently arrived visitor to England causes a few collisions or near-collisions until he realizes that the other pedestrians expect him to step to his left, as they do. The more uniquely human the skill, the more its execution is a matter of anticipating the responses of someone else. There could not be writing without reading, selling without buying, decorating without admiring. This fact will be referred to as the dovetailed nature of human skills. (Yes, this too is merely a metaphor, but it may lead to a theory.)

Sears (1951), in a neglected paper worth resurrecting today, emphasized the importance of this dovetailing of action schemas: "These anticipatory reactions to [another's] behavior are the *expectancies* that make the behavior of the two people truly interdependent" (p. 480; italics in the original). The most promising lead we have toward an answer to the Locus question remains his still-untested theory that mutual expectations are the behavioral mechanism maintaining cohesion and stability in groups of two or more individuals.

To account for the fact that possessors of skills are able to entrain novices into their patterns of interaction—hook them onto the chain— we must add a second concept. Some forms of interaction seem to have the special function of socializing new members of systems. I refer to these forms of behavior as *parental frames*, because they are most obviously manifested in parent-child interaction. They appear to be species-universal in their general forms, culturally institutionalized in particular forms. Ubiquitous frames include: demonstration, discourse turn-taking, feedback, completing a learner's apparent intentions (including the intention to speak), and serving as an extension or backup memory (Kaye, 1982). These and other parental frames make it possible for individuals who are less skilled (in the rules of a particular family and, often, in general) to extend their competence step by step. The system members who provide frames tend to fill in the missing links in a learner's current competence, which makes it possible for the system to function despite the learner's inadequacies while at the same time it presents repeated demonstrations and feedback to guide the learning process.

Many of the same framing processes are used throughout life, when a new member enters any system.

> *Excerpt 9:* There is this wretched habit I have of acquiring the characteristics of other people. I acquire these characteristics indiscriminately, even from people I don't like. If I am with someone who talks loud and fast and assertively, I will begin talking loud and fast right along with him (but by no means always assertively). If I am with someone

who drawls lazily and is from the South or West, I will drawl lazily too and begin speaking almost as though I were from the South or West, employing authentic regional idioms as though they were part of my own upbringing and not of someone else's. (Heller, 1974, p. 64)

Imitation is a special genius possessed by our species, from which all of our "higher" cognitive processes are derived. It remains a great mystery to which this chapter cannot do justice.[5] But theories of imitation are at least beginning to be couched in terms of interaction between learner and demonstrator. Someday perhaps all forms of socialization will be seen thus.

There are at least three fundamentally different routes through which people enter families: birth, marriage, and adoption. These three cases differ primarily in terms of how much the new member knows about the rules of the system at the outset. The way the old members socialize the new depends on that initial knowledge.

Newborns are the only ones who do not have to unlearn any prior interaction patterns as they learn to be members of the family; but they do not have the benefit of all the transferable skills, including language, that an older recruit brings to the learning task. The process of creating a system member—in fact, a person—out of the raw material offered by a human infant is a process of apprenticeship, during which adults and older children co-opt the infant's limited skills. They create frames within which a very little bit of competence can make the infant appear, to himself as well as to them, to perform cognitive and social actions of which he is not yet really capable on his own. Performing those actions within the parental frames guarantees the infant optimal feedback to use in developing his skills. Little by little, the adults loosen the frames, expecting more links from the infant as his skills increase. The process is simultaneously cognitive (sensorimotor development), linguistic, and affective (individuation of the self). At all three levels, it is a dialectical process.

When a family incorporates an older child (older than nine months or so) through adoption or fostering, the child's prior experiences are bound to make a difference in the kind of substrate they provide for socialization into the new system. This fact suggests that research on the process of adoption should consider the problem of transferring into the new system social interaction patterns learned in prior systems, not merely the effects of traumatic early experiences or of the fact of adoption itself. (Almost all the research to date deals with apparent effects of the fact of adoption, or of knowledge of the fact, rather than with adoption as a developmental process over time.) Of course,

---

[5] For a discussion of the large literature on infants' imitation of adults' acts, gestures, and language, see Kaye (1982).

when infants are adopted at birth, their cognitive status is like any other newborn. But their apprenticeship may be affected by their parents' expectations, hopes, and fears (Kaye, 1982).

When a new member enters by marriage, imitation of the family patterns certainly plays a large role; but the process does not have to start from scratch as with an infant. Nor does it have the benefit of the child's flexibility and genius for imitation. Joining a family would be difficult indeed if mates were assigned at random. Fortunately, people usually select mates on the basis of a commonality in their assumptions about family roles, goals, and patterns of interaction. In societies where marriage choices are made by the heads of the young adults' families rather than by the prospective spouses themselves, these arranged marriages are probably even more culturally endogamous than romantic ones are. So the mutual socialization of the new partners normally takes place on a foundation of experience in similar families. The process is bound to go more smoothly the better the new spouses fit into the joints and seams of social schemas developed with the partners' original others—their families of origin. This is a familiar truth about mutual expectations in the course of interaction sequences; but it is also true at the intrapsychic level of object relations (Ackerman, 1958; Boszormenyi-Nagy, 1965).

At this point, a third new concept must be introduced along with dovetailed skills and parental frames. It is the idea that the whole self is dovetailed. The self is not a constituent of a given individual, but one of those "shared" constructs to which we have been alluding. This means only that Person A's self is constructed, at least in part, of elements that appear in B's, C's, and D's (for example, his parents', siblings', or spouse's) constructs of who A is. The self is constructed and internalized, but not by the individual alone. It is a matter of mutual projection and introjection between significant others (Boszormenyi-Nagy, 1965). When we speak of validating the self within one's family, we are referring to interactions akin to those in more mundane forms of social behavior—for example, in constructing a sentence or a meal. Perhaps the links have a broader time frame and a more abstract expression, but the process is no less a social one.

We can represent the self in a P-model as a real-time process: "a special kind of loop or detour taken by consciousness in the course of action, whenever our attention falls upon some aspect of our situation to which we anticipate a social response" (Kaye, 1982, p. 209). For example, a toddler manifests self-consciousness when, after falling down, he looks around to see if anyone was watching. This is where Gödelian conceptualizations become relevant (Hofstadter, 1979): The self can only be referred to in the context of a larger frame. "This behavior I am experiencing is observable by some *other* experiencer/

behavior, which is not-I"—and that awareness is what, recursively, defines "I." I am aware (i.e., the person who wrote the sentence you are reading was aware, when he wrote it, that you might be aware) that the definition of self quoted in the first sentence of this paragraph is inadequate. It does not deal with "thinking about the self" as a form of action, nor at the other extreme does it suggest how the self can affect one's actions unconsciously. If the definition has any heuristic value, it is to remind us that the self is behavior, rather than a thing somewhere, and that our selves derive from the fact that so much of what we do requires us to anticipate how the responses of others will coordinate with our own.

This chapter is not the place for an extended discussion of selves and family systems, but there is one more point to be made. It is a mistake to consider an individual person (whether one means by that the person's self or simply the sum total of the person's skills, values, goals, etc.) as a "subsystem" of the family. Perhaps the marital dyad or the mother-child dyad is a subsystem, but the individual person is *more* than a member of the family. While the family is making the infant one of its members, it is also making him a member of the community. He will share its language and culture, soon acquiring teachers and other significant investors in his self outside the family. An adult who marries into the family also remains a member of other systems, and the new family only dovetails into a part of that person's self. As the self is not entirely within the person, so the person is not entirely within the family—nor is it the function of parental frames to try to swallow the person up.

How do families mediate between the community (or society at large) and their individual members?   Consider, for example, the effects of communities upon child development. Obviously, the family enters the picture as an intervening variable—but how? Bronfenbrenner (1983) has recently reviewed the research on community effects upon childrearing. He found two serious flaws in the research to date. One flaw was the tendency to conclude that differences in childrearing in different kinds of communities (e.g., urban or rural) were *results* of living in those communities rather than, equally plausibly, part of the reason different families choose to live where they do. The second problem, central to our present discussion, was "the now-familiar failure to distinguish between immediate and direct effects—those community features that influence children directly versus those that operate through the family" (Bronfenbrenner, 1983, p. 45).

The family system, with its rules, its shared knowledge, and its shared purposes, is a buffer between the individual and the wider world. One way in which families serve as buffers is that information is literally filtered through family members—for example, the child's knowledge about the world of work or the parent's knowledge about the adolescent drug culture. Reiss (1981) describes an extreme example of a family whose mother was the sole source of news. But actually, in every family, *all* shared constructs are products of the information-gathering and cognitive processing of individuals. Then the shared constructs come into play in each individual's subsequent cognitive activity and in their communication with one another.

Even more important than the filtering of facts may be the muting or intensifying of the emotional impact of outside events. For example, the personal significance of a war, an assassination, an economic depression, or a sporting event is a function of how the event is perceived and reacted to by one's family.

Another sense in which families mediate between the world and their individual members is through shared perceptions and assumptions that each member internalizes and hence carries into his or her life outside the home. We are familiar with some of the ways language (Whorf, 1956) and other aspects of culture (Berger & Luckmann, 1966) bias perception, thought, and action in members of one society as compared to another. We can hypothesize that family systems have their own microcultures, determining what their members see and believe.

> *Excerpt 10:* I don't want my wife ever to find out she drinks too much at parties and sometimes behaves very badly with other people and makes an extremely poor impression when she thinks she is making a very good one! . . . As neatly and promptly as I can, before much damage is done, I will move in to rescue her, to guide her away smoothly with a quip and a smile. I never rebuke her (although I am often furious and ashamed); I humor her, praise her, flatter. I want her to feel pleased with herself. (I don't know why.) (Heller, 1974, pp. 98–99)

> *Excerpt 11:* One of my children—I forget which one—had a bad dream years ago about snapping fishes swimming in the bed, and I remembered instantly I had suffered those too.
> "There were fishes in my bed," I sobbed, shivering. "Swimming around on the blankets."
> "They aren't there now," my brother comforted me patiently. "Keep looking and you'll see." (Heller, 1974, p. 514)

Although we can point to instances of family members shaping one another's world views both consciously (Excerpt 10) and unconsciously (Excerpt 11), we have no idea what cognitive processes are involved, to what extent they are different from those due to the larger culture or pave the way for the latter, at what ages and through what interactive mechanisms they operate.

How do families act through their individual members' encounters with the world? This turns the previous question inside out. There we asked about the family as mediator between the individual and the world; here we acknowledge that individuals are the mediators between social systems.

Reiss (1981) offers a P-model called the cycle hypothesis to explain how families form links (through individual members) to their communities while being selective about which of the community's subsystems they choose to link with. Like any model, it needs to be filled in. One part in particular cries to be filled in, for this model begs the Locus question: Where are the decisions about selectivity made? It is fine to conceive of the family as a unit, but the fact remains that it is *individuals* who do the acting, speaking, observing, and thinking.

A sociologist who analyzes the relations between family and community makes the simplifying assumption that the whole family's interests are involved whenever one member spends money, disseminates information, or obtains resources or information for the family as a whole. Yet such processes obviously require a flow of information, within the family to a liaison member who interacts with the external system, back through one or more liaisons, and among the family members again. It is up to psychologists to characterize those intersystem transactions in terms of intrasystem, intermember communication patterns.

> *Excerpt 12:* "Will you have to travel more than you have to travel now?"
> "No. Probably less."
> "Will you make more money?" my daughter asks.
> "Yes. Maybe a lot more."
> "Will we be rich?"
> "No." . . .
> "I don't want you to be a salesman," my daughter exclaims with unexpected emotion, almost in tears. "I don't want you to have to go around to other people's fathers and beg them to buy things from you." (Heller, 1974, pp. 106–107)

We can see such intrasystem communication processes at work on any particular occasion; but we know virtually nothing about what sort of regular patterns occur across occasions and/or across families.

How does an individual bring about changes in other individual members and in the family as a whole? Because the individual is only one member of a larger system, it is easier to think of him or her as subject to being changed by the family than as having a significant influence upon it. Systems are extremely powerful. On the other hand, since they consist of nothing other than their members, their memory (that is, their stable identity) consists only in the memories of the individual members. Whatever a family is like, its individual members make it that way, each in varying degrees. What makes some husbands, fathers, mothers, or siblings more significantly influential than others?

> *Excerpt 13:* Someday soon someone may be dropping bombs on us.
> I will scream:
> *"The sky is falling! They are dropping bombs!* People are on fire!
> The world is over! It's coming to an end!"
> And my wife will reply:
> "You don't have to raise your voice to me." (Heller, 1974, p. 109)

Under the heading of parents' influence upon children falls what Piaget called "the American question": How can parents motivate and facilitate the optimum development of their children? Rejecting its implicit linear-effects assumption should not lead us to dismiss the question itself. It can be expressed systemically: How do parents' expectations translate into patterns of family interaction? How does each different child come away from those interactions with his or her own set of skills, values, goals, expectations—with a distinct self—and in turn maintain or modify the parents' expectations? The theory toward which this chapter is groping would answer the question in terms of the dovetailed nature of skills: Parental frames entrain children's skills when the latter are still quite rudimentary. The parents and older siblings therefore do not have to teach the child to do things their way; for the most part, they just have to do so themselves.

These ideas lead directly to our last two questions: how individuals internalize family routines and how families equip their members to join other systems. The adequacy of children's cognitive and social skills (there is really no difference) depends upon the children having learned to anticipate how their significant others will interact with them. And it also depends upon how well all that they have learned with those "others of origin" generalizes to the community in which they find themselves.

How does the individual mind internalize the workings of the whole family system? This question can be asked about any social system: Any systemic process that psychologists can identify must be known, at some level, by the members of the system.

> *Excerpt 14:* My mother . . . had merely lifted a glass to her lips
> and drained it of some strawberry punch. But my daughter was watching
> her. And when my daughter, who was herself being trained then by
> my wife and me to drink from a glass and faithfully rewarded with
> handclaps of delight and cries of "Good girl!" whenever she succeeded,

saw my mother drink from a glass, she banged her own hands down
with delight and approval and called out:
"Good girl, grandma!" (Heller, 1974, p. 193)

At least, all must know how to perform their own roles and must
possess enough understanding of other members' roles to be able to
anticipate the others' significant behavior and fit their own behavior
into it properly. Every actor in a play needs to know his own lines
plus all his cues in the other players' lines. In fact, he comes to know
the whole of any scene in which he appears. What form does that
knowledge take in the case of a family member, who acts in a repertory
company that never plays the same scene exactly the same way, yet
follows its own unique and binding set of rules?

This question is complicated further. Some but not all of the individual's internalized knowledge of how the family works will be conscious.
Some will be common to every member, some unique to each. Some
will be learnable by any person who joins the system; some will vary
with age, sex, biological relationship, and previous history.

Perhaps some of the members' knowledge about intrafamily transactions is preadapted in the nature of individual human skills and in
universal social processes. However, to the extent each family has its
own rules, these have to be learned by the individual members. Furthermore, since we know that new members retain their individuality,
we need to explain not only how they accommodate to the family's
patterns but also how they assimilate those patterns to their own individual skills and styles.

Part of the explanation of our ability to internalize social scripts
and rules is the fact that so much of our so-called individual behavior
is inherently designed to fit together with someone else's action. Most
of what we do would be impossible, pointless, or delusional if we did
it in isolation. The same can be said about a good deal of the behavior
of lower organisms, including human infants, but in those cases it is
a matter of dovetailed evolution rather than of learning. The simplest
and most universal example is the way an organism's sexual behavior
fits the behavior of members of the opposite sex of its own species.
The behavioral fit is as critical to reproduction as is the anatomical
fit, and equally a product of evolution. Another illustration, restricted
to mammals, involves the fit between lactation and sucking. But there
is no species to compare with our own, in which dependence upon
others transcends so many domains of behavior, including acquired,
not just innate, patterns.

For example, our ability to imitate, without which we would be
able to learn none of the skills that distinguish us from lower species,

depends upon the way other people provide models for us. We do not simply observe how human skills are performed and then privately imitate them; from early infancy, we engage in a complex interaction through which our parents and other elders analyze what parts of their demonstrations need to be made salient to us, while we analyze what parts of our existing schemas need to be modified (Kaye, 1982).

Given that kind of active apprenticeship, which normally begins within the family, there is ample opportunity for individual members to learn to give and receive signals about taking turns and sharing intentions, two processes essential to the dovetailed nature of human action. In fact, that is the first agenda for infants and their parents. It begins at birth, is "second nature," and is rarely accessible to conscious description. (All three of these facts suggest that the way the system's rules are internalized by members must be quite different from the logical, complete, and schematic way they are likely to appear in our P-models. But P-models can at least express, as C-models cannot, the extent to which we understand the psychological processes involved.)

How do families equip their members for participation in other systems? The family is the only social system that creates some of its members from scratch (infants). Every other system's members come in with prior training in how to be a member of at least one system, their family of origin. This original training in how to participate in a social system must be one of the family's most important functions for our species. It is also the principal means by which the family ensures its own ability to adapt and survive; for, as pointed out above, its transactions with other systems are nothing other than the successful simultaneous membership of its own members in other systems.

The most obvious family training for participation in the community is training in the community's language. Language has been and will continue to be an active field of research. Studies of language learning only began to multiply when Bellugi and Brown (1964) and others made use of Chomsky's (1965) transformational grammar to characterize the levels of language ability demonstrated by young children. These were C-models, not P-models, but they were the kind of descriptive tool that students of other developing skills still lack. Hence we know far less about the acquisition of those skills.

Nonetheless, we can make a few general observations about parental frames and the process of socialization. Families seem to do little or no direct training in the interaction rules of other systems. So it must be in learning how to be members of the family itself—with its own processes, some of which are fairly universal and some of which are idiosyncratic—that children learn how to accommodate themselves to social systems in general. The rules themselves need not be universal; but it may be that the processes for co-opting new members and the processes for learning how to become a new member are common across systems.

We have recently had a great deal of research on how parents initiate infants in the communication skills and other expectations of the family. This, however, is only the preliminary step in making the child a member of the community. What about adolescence—the period of preparation for leaving home? Our theories about development in that stage still largely ignore the parents' role. They focus either psychoanalytically on the adolescent's inner emotional turmoil or sociologically on the peer group. Parents themselves are often blind to their own role. They sometimes experience sadness or frustration at the healthy outcome of normal family processes, their children's entry into other systems.

> *Excerpt 15:*   She is trying to establish some position with us or provoke some reaction, but my wife and I don't know what or why. She wants to become a part, too, I guess, of what she sees is her environment, and she is, I fear, already merging with, dissolving into, her surroundings right before my eyes. She wants to be like other people her age. I cannot stop her; I cannot save her. (Heller, 1974, p. 66)

As suggested earlier in this chapter, it is reasonable to assume that family developmental processes in every society include parental prods for separation at puberty. It is even possible that this prodding may occur within interactive frames derived from those the parents used for their infants' socialization into the family in the first place. This area of inquiry may be the next frontier for a developmental psychology of the family.

SUMMARY: THE END OF AN ILLUSION

We have touched upon many of the same questions that developmental psychology has traditionally addressed. A psychology of the family need not look beyond those questions for its substantive focus. It should be an attempt to reformulate those traditional questions in terms of a social system, yet in a way that allows them to be answered with scientific explanations, not merely with metaphors.

The concepts of dovetailed skills, parental frames, the locus of self outside the individual, and family as a dynamic rather than structural entity are not necessarily the concepts of greatest importance to the reader's own work. Growing out of this author's research on parent-infant interaction, they were used here as illustrations of a way of thinking. They were also suggested as possible beginnings of a solution to the problem of how knowledge, action, and motivation can reside in a social system.

The questions discussed above are more than theoretically intriguing. Although it may seem grandiose to hope that a better understanding of family processes can prevent a nuclear holocaust, the arms race is, after all, a problem of social interaction. The foregoing questions about how one learns what to expect of one's fellow system members, about the dovetailing of many of our action patterns into the anticipated actions of other people, and about the boundaries and differences between families, can be translated into parallel questions about trust and distrust at the global level of interaction. We cannot expect to solve our most urgent social problems, either at the level of families or at the level of nations, without an adequate theory of social systems.

The principal obstacle is the very metaphor that provides our starting point: the idea that a family is an organic (open) system. If that truth is taken as an explanation, then it is a primitive, almost mystic one. In reality, it should merely be taken as a statement of our ignorance. P-models, theories about processes, are what we must work toward if we are to understand how it is possible for families and other social systems to function as if they were unified creatures.

The questions discussed in this chapter all involve how individual human beings perform as agents for a larger system. The locus of a family's *memory*—the knowledge it possesses, including its sense of identity and awareness of its own interaction rules—is nowhere other than in the memories of its individual members. Similarly, the family's *actions* are nothing but the actions of its individual members. Hence, family processes are communication processes. Psychologists know a good deal about communication at the level of how one person encodes a message and another decodes it—that is, about language, its development, and its relation to thought. Yet we know virtually nothing about what determines the pattern of messages from the moment certain kinds of events impinge upon the family until various members have been informed, decisions reached, actions taken. If that pattern were nothing but the summation of individual messages, then we would have no need to talk about the system. We use the systems metaphor because we believe that these communication patterns are organized and coordinated at the level of the family as a whole.

The questions that have been raised also involve family *development.* This does not mean listing the obvious stages that families pass through as their members grow older. It means investigating the causal relations between the development of individual members and the development of the family system. It is possible that one level of development (individual or family) may account for the other. It is also possible that both levels of development depend upon one another. In any case,

the problems to be investigated include how families create and indoctrinate new members, then give them autonomy while retaining them
as members who need not live under the same roof. (The power of
families is even more remarkable when we see it operating across
vast distances, even transcending death.)

Individual persons are not simply building blocks out of which social
organizations are composed. Social processes are fundamental and are
the building blocks out of which persons are composed. Our subjective
sense of individual autonomy is an illusion.

> *Excerpt 16:*   "If it doesn't work out," I kept assuring myself right
> up to the day of the ceremony, "I can always get a divorce."
> I *can't* always get a divorce.
> I don't know how it's done.
> Maybe I attach too much importance to a shirt.
> I'll have undershorts at the laundry. Will she let me come for them?
> Or will she burn them, hide them? Will she tell me my little boy is
> upset when he isn't? That she cannot live without me when she can? I
> know she'll tell me she's thinking of killing herself. The obstacles appear
> insurmountable. In the summer my winter clothes are in mothballs; in
> the winter, my summer suits are hanging somewhere else and my sneak-
> ers are packed away. How will I ever get them all together? I'd need
> weeks. I don't have time to get a divorce. There's so much packing to
> be done (she won't help). (Heller, 1974, p. 484)

Perhaps psychology, "the science of the mind," had to begin with
the illusion of an autonomous mind and person inhabiting each individual body. To get started on a scientific basis, psychologists needed a
clear unit of analysis. (Even social psychology drifted away from its
original subject, group behavior and the "group mind," and became
the experimental study of social feelings and social behavior in individuals.) Now, however, it is time to go beyond that illusion, to attempt
psychological analyses of sociological processes. Although we are benefiting from a surge of clinical attention to the family, our scientific
progress will not be easy.

REFERENCES

Ackerman, N. *The psychodynamics of family life.* New York: Basic Books, 1958.

Bateson, G. Bali: The value system of a steady state. In M. Fortes (Ed.), *Social structure.*
Oxford: Clarendon Press, 1949.

Bellugi, U., & Brown, R. (Eds.). The acquisition of language. *Monographs of the Society
for Research in Child Development,* 1964, *29* (No. 92).

Berger, P., & Luckmann, T. *The social construction of reality.* Garden City, N.Y.: Doubleday
Publishing, 1966.

Boszormenyi-Nagy, I. A theory of relationships: Experience and transaction. In I. Boszormenyi-Nagy & J. Framo (Eds.), *Intensive family therapy.* New York: Harper & Row, 1965.

Bronfenbrenner, U. *The ecology of human development.* Cambridge, Mass.: Harvard University Press, 1979.

Bronfenbrenner, U. *The ecology of the family as a context for human development.* Unpublished manuscript prepared for the Five-Year Plan of the Institute for Child Health and Human Development, Washington, D.C. 1983.

Cannon, W. *Wisdom of the body* (Rev. ed.). New York: W. W. Norton, 1938.

Chomsky, N. *Syntactic structures.* The Hague: Mouton, 1965.

Freud, S. The psychogenesis of a case of homosexuality in a woman. In *Sexuality and the psychology of love.* New York: Collier, 1963. (First published in German, 1920.)

Gottman, J. *Marital interactions: Experimental investigations.* New York: Academic Press, 1979.

Haley, J. *Problem-solving therapy.* New York: Harper & Row, 1976.

Haroutunian, S. *Equilibrium in the balance: A study of psychological explanation.* New York: Springer-Verlag, 1983.

Hartup, W., & Lempers, J. A problem in life-span development: The interactional analysis of family attachments. In P. Baltes and K. Schaie (Eds.), *Life-span developmental psychology: Personality and socialization.* New York: Academic Press, 1973.

Heller, J. *Something happened.* New York: Alfred A. Knopf, 1974.

Hofstadter, D. *Gödel, Escher, Bach: An eternal golden braid.* New York: Basic Books, 1979.

Kantor, D., & Lehr, W. *Inside the family.* New York: Harper & Row, 1975.

Kaye, K. The development of skills. In G. Whitehurst & B. Zimmerman (Eds.), *The functions of language and cognition.* New York: Academic Press, 1977.

Kaye, K. *The mental and social life of babies: How parents create persons.* Chicago: University of Chicago Press, 1982.

L'Abate, L. *Understanding and helping the individual in the family.* New York: Grune & Stratton, 1976.

Minuchin, S., & Fishman, C. *Family therapy techniques.* Cambridge, Mass.: Harvard University Press, 1981.

Olson, D., Sprenkle, D., & Russell, C. Circumplex model of marital and family systems: I. Cohesion and adaptability dimensions, family types, and clinical applications. *Family Process,* 1979, *18,* 3–28.

Piaget, J. *Six psychological studies.* New York: Random House, 1967.

Reiss, D. *The family's construction of reality.* Cambridge, Mass.: Harvard University Press, 1981.

Sears, R. A theoretical framework for personality and social behavior. *American Psychologist,* 1951, *6,* 476–483.

Strodtbeck, F. The family as a three-person group. *American Sociological Review,* 1954, *19,* 23–29.

von Bertalanffy, L. *General system theory.* New York: Braziller, 1968.

Whorf, B. *Language, thought, and reality.* Cambridge, Mass.: MIT Press, 1956.

Wynne, L., & Singer, M. Thought disorder and family relations of schizophrenics: A research strategy. *Archives of General Psychiatry,* 1963, *9,* 191–198.

Chapter 3

Personality Development in the Family

CLIFFORD H. SWENSEN, JR.

A useful structure for considering personality development in the family derives from Lewin's (1951) formula, $B = f(P,E)$, which states that behavior is a function of the person and the environment. Expanding this formula to state that a relationship is a function of the persons involved in the relationship and of the environment or situation within which the relationship exists produces the following formula (Swensen, 1977):

$$R = f(P_1 P_2 \cdots P_n)E$$

or

Relationship $= f$(Person 1, Person 2, $\cdots$ Person n) Environment

One obvious consequence of this formula is that the relationship changes when any person in the relationship or the environment of the relationship changes. In family relationships, which are maintained over long periods of time, the individuals in the family change and so does the environment.

People change. Not only do babies grow up and leave home, thus altering their relationships to their parents, but adults also change, thus altering the relationship between the parents. The factors that affect personality development in the family must then include the personality development of each member of the family.

The environment within which a family lives also changes. Some changes are obvious, such as moving from one community to another. However, the culture also changes, and cultural changes have an impact upon the family and affect the relationships among family members. At one time, the family was primarily an economic unit. Today, the family has little economic utility but has great significance for the life satisfaction of its members.

The family, usually thought of as the nuclear family—father, mother, and children—does not live in a vacuum. The family is connected to, and typically maintains a connection with, a wider network of relatives, including grandparents, aunts, uncles, cousins, and often even more distant kin. This larger network also affects the relationships among the members.

No variable acts alone in affecting relationships; the variables interact with one another. If, for example, an older daughter graduates from high school and leaves home to attend college or takes a job and moves into her own apartment, her relationships with the other family members change. The relationships among family members who remain at home also readjust. If she later returns home for summer vacation or loses her job and must return home, she will not find waiting for her the same home that she left but will find that her relationship to the other family members has changed. She will probably find the family far more confining than she remembered, and the other family members will probably discover that she takes up more space and creates more disruption in the family tranquillity than she did before she left home.

PERSONALITY DEVELOPMENT

Personality development in a family is a function of the persons within that family (i.e., a function of the personalities of the members of the family). As personalities develop, relationships change and the balance throughout the family changes; thus, as one person within the family changes, the relationships throughout the family change.

The pattern of change is not confined to the members of the family who happen to be physically present. A grown child who has left home continues to affect the family members left behind, and the parents who are left behind continue to affect the children who have left home. The effect extends beyond death. Anderson (1980), in his play *I Never Sang for My Father,* depicted a son still grappling with his inability to resolve the tensions of his relationship with his dead father. Anderson wrote, "Death ends a life, but it does not end a relationship, which struggles on in the survivor's mind toward some final resolution, some clear meaning, which it perhaps never finds" (p. 55). We continue, perhaps as long as we live, to seek resolution, to work on our relationships with our parents.

Because the patterns of relationships repeat themselves through generations, a family's dynamic balance today is not composed simply of the interaction of the personalities of those now present but includes members of the family who are no longer present or who have died long ago. Boszormenyi-Nagy and Spark (1973) wrote that "the basic structure of our existence and of our children's existence remains at least partially determined by the unsettled accounts of past generations" (p. 24). The family is a system of relationships determined by the interactions among living members and containing echoes of past relationships and of members who died before some of the living family members were born. Our relationships with our parents and our grandparents live on in our relationships with our children and our grandchildren. As we develop as persons, our relationships with those who went before us change, just as our relationships with our children change.

People do of course pass through stages of personality change as they mature from infancy through adulthood to old age. In adulthood, stable periods that last for six to eight years alternate with transition periods that last for three to five years. People appear most likely to fall in love during the transition periods (Friedlander & Morrison, 1980; Geller & Howenstine, 1980). Men tend to marry during the early adult transition and tend to divorce during the midlife transition (Geller & Howenstine, 1980). A love relationship is part of the individual's effort to meet the challenges of the next stage of personal development. Love, throughout life, is an integral part of personal development, both a cause and a consequence of that development (see Chapter 11).

The stages of life, particularly adult life, develop as a process of differentiation and integration, a development in the direction of an increased sense of inner freedom (Gould, 1980). The main themes of life center on work and love. When either area presents a problem, the individual faces a challenge to grow (Smelser, 1980a, 1980b). For example, problems in a marriage are a sign that one or both of the partners are growing. One may avoid, deny, and repress the problem (in effect, fixating at a particular stage of development), or one may develop a more complex and appropriate cognitive structure (i.e., differentiate) and thus move on to another, more complex stage. Because the family is the main focus of love, problems in the intimate relationships of family life precipitate fixation or growth (Jourard, 1975).

Development is a dialectical process (Hogan, 1976; Riegel, 1975, 1976) produced by the interaction among the biological, psychological, and social factors (Riegel, 1975) in a person's life. When one factor changes, all of the others must readjust to reestablish harmony, and from this interaction emerge the stages of life. The dialectical process is an interaction between the two poles of differentiation and integration (Giele, 1980). Differentiation emphasizes the autonomy that one must have to cope with the changing circumstances of life; integration is the process of unification with other people, which is also necessary for a satisfactory life. Development is differentiation and growth in the face of new challenge, and the integration of the growth with the total life structure. We are motivated to develop our yearning for inclusion and our yearning for distinctness, twin yearnings that are in constant tension (Kegan, 1982). Each stage represents a swing toward integration or toward differentiation. Another way to look at stages is that differentiation represents the transition from one stage to another, and the establishment of a new stage represents integration at a new and more complex level of development.

Development toward complexity gives one greater internal control over behavior, providing greater flexibility and therefore greater choice in determining how life will go. For example, those who work at more complex tasks develop a more complex cognitive structure (Kohn, 1969, 1980). The complexity of a job is determined by the amount of thought and independent judgment the job requires. In general, work with people and work with data are more complex than work with things or work that is closely supervised. This, of course, is a description of the difference between white-collar work and blue-collar work. Dealing with a more complex life situation produces a more complex cognitive structure, which is expressed in relationships within the family as well as in other areas of life.

Erikson's stages

The best-known system of stages of development that cover the life span is that of Erikson (1950), who described each stage as presenting a developmental task that must be solved before the person can grow to the next stage. Erikson described eight stages which essentially extend the Freudian stages of adult development.

Stage I. Oral sensory: trust versus mistrust (learning to trust other people).

Stage II. Muscular-anal: autonomy versus shame or doubt (the period in which a child learns self-control).

Stage III. Locomotor-genital: initiative versus guilt (Erikson's equivalent to the Freudian oedipal stage).

Stage IV. Latency: industry versus inferiority (the school age, during which a child learns many new skills and is exposed to comparing the performances of self and peers).

Stage V. Puberty and adolescence: identity versus role confusion (developing a clear sense of personal identity, a stable sense of self as an individual apart from the family).

Stage VI. Young adulthood: intimacy versus isolation. (The previous stage, in which the person develops a stable sense of self, must be completed successfully before one can form an intimate relationship with another person.)

Stage VII. Adulthood: generativity versus stagnation and self-absorption (producing and assuming responsibility for helping younger persons to develop).

Stage VIII. Maturity: ego integrity versus despair (old age, in which one who has successfully weathered life can look back and see life as having value and significance).

The tasks of the stages are not met at one time in life and solved once and for all. Each task continues throughout life, but at particular times, each becomes the paramount task that must be solved before the person can move on to the task of the next stage.

Levinson's eras

In Erikson's scheme, only one stage, adulthood, lies between adult courtship and old age. Recent investigators have observed more than one stage in adult life. Levinson (1980; Levinson, Darrow, Klein, Levinson, & McKee, 1978) described adult development as a sequence of alternating periods in which the person builds a life structure and then changes the life structure:

1. *Preadulthood.* The first era, preadulthood, covers the period from birth to age 22.

2. *Early adulthood.* Early adulthood, from age 17 to 45, is a period for forming and pursuing youthful aspirations, establishing a niche in society, raising a family, and reaching a senior position in the adult world. It is the period in which people are most pressured by inner ambitions and passions and by the outside demands of family, work, and the community. This era is divided into subperiods:

    a. From age 17 to age 22 is the early adult transition in which the person must alter existing relationships with other persons and institutions and take the first step into the adult world.

    b. From age 22 to age 28 is the period of entering the adult world, during which the person must shift the center of attention from the family of origin to a new home base and establish him- or herself in the world.

    c. The age-30 transition, from age 28 to age 33, is for most persons a time of crisis in which they must work on the flaws in their first adult life structure.

    d. Ages 33 to 40 are a time for settling down to build a second life structure and to work toward the realization of dreams.

It is in this period that work and family demands reach a peak.

    e.   Age 36 to age 40 is a period for accomplishing goals and becoming a senior member of the world.

    f.   From age 40 to age 45 is the period of midlife transition.

3. *Middle adulthood.* The third era, middle adulthood, spans the time from around age 40 to age 65. This group forms the dominant cohort in every society. In middle adulthood, the passions of youth and early adulthood are tempered by increased compassion, reflectiveness, and judiciousness. In this era, one is less tyrannized by inner conflicts and external demands and is able to love self and others more genuinely. This era begins with the midlife transition (age 40 to age 45) in which the person reappraises life, integrates the polarities between young-old, destruction-creation, masculine-feminine, and attachment-separateness. During the ages from 45 to 50, one enters middle age. From 50 to 55, one builds a new life structure for middle age. The culmination of middle adulthood is from ages 55 to 60, in which one builds a second life structure to work toward the major goals of this era. The late adult transition from ages 60 to 65 completes middle adulthood.

4. *Late adulthood.* At age 65, one enters late adulthood.

Gould's transformations

Gould (1975, 1978, 1980) described a process of adult development that, as an expansion of self-definition, is in many respects similar to that described by Levinson. The process of growth is a dialectical alternation between growth and intimacy. Love relationships are always in one position or another in the alternation between periods of relative estrangement, in which the partners are not growing in the same way at the same time, and periods in which they are at the same stage of growth and are intimate.

1.   Persons in their 20s, while becoming established as adults, establish love-life bonds that consist of contracts, collusions, and conspiracies that temporarily support the sense of identity. One is deeply dependent on the other and needs to keep the terms of the original contract, although many of the terms may have been agreed upon unconsciously.

2.   In a person's late 20s and early 30s, collusions and conspiracies begin to unravel, and the contracts no longer seem appropriate. The marital relationship becomes confused and uncertain, and as the partners become more complex, their relationship becomes more complex. Often, there are young children to care for, which adds to the complexity.

3.   In the midlife period, a need for a clearer and fuller self-defini-

tion emerges. We become aware of limited time and feel a need for deeper authenticity in our lives, placing further stress on the original conspiracies and contracts. To the extent that the partner insists on maintaining the original contract, growth is inhibited, and the response is withdrawal. Midlife men and women who are trying to recapture functions that they sacrificed in early adulthood so that they can reestablish the original relationship are often traveling in opposite directions. Men become more concerned with inward sensations, emotional sensitivity, and intimate relationships; women are working toward developing more independence and power. The process may create conflict in the relationship: The husband's desire for greater intimacy is perceived by the wife as a demand for regression; the wife's drive for greater independence and power is perceived by the husband as rejection.

Life stages and ego development of the individual

Note that the described life stages all end with a rather sketchy description of the years after age 50. With a steadily increasing life expectancy and changes in childbearing customs, new stages of adult life are probably emerging (e.g., Swensen, 1983a, 1983b). Note also that the descriptions of Levinson and Gould are more extensive than those described almost 30 years earlier by Erikson. Adult life stages, then, are not a fixed phenomenon: The stages are changing, and the adult personality is also changing. Longitudinal studies covering a quarter of a century seem to indicate that a personality shift is occurring in adult Americans (Fiske, 1980). Recent studies have found fewer autonomous, self-generating people and more outer-directed people, who need to be told how to think, feel, and behave. If adult development is toward growth and greater inner freedom, these findings suggest that adult development is, on the average, less advanced in adults today than it was 25 years ago. On the other hand, if adult development is an alternation between autonomy and intimacy, a new level of average adult development may be emerging in our society. In any case, adults continue to develop through life, and the course of individual development changes in response to changing biological, psychological, and social factors. Current descriptions of adult life stages should be considered nothing more than an interim report.

Stages of personality development can be described in terms of ego functioning. The ego is not a thing, but the organization of the totality of one's personality (Loevinger, 1976). It organizes our perception of our experience and our attempts to cope with the problems presented by that experience. Personality develops through alternating periods of differentiation and integration, an increasingly more complex personality structure. The more differentiated and integrated our personalities are, the more we can accommodate to others, the more accurately we can perceive others, and the more appropriately we can react to others (Raush, Barry, Hertel, & Swain, 1974).

Loevinger's ego development

Personality development moves from a simple, undifferentiated, unintegrated personality structure toward a complex, highly differentiated, well-integrated personality structure. The consequences of this development for relationships with other persons have been described (e.g., Kegan, 1982; Raush et al., 1974), but the concept of ego development that is perhaps best and most useful in the study of interpersonal relationships is that of Loevinger (1976). Her development of the concept, which comprises six stages and three main transitional levels (Loevinger, 1976; Swensen, 1977, 1980a, 1980b), represents an effort to integrate several developmental concepts, including those of Freud, Erikson, and Piaget.

The stages and the main levels of ego development are as follows:

I-1   Presocial stage

As a newborn, one is unable to differentiate from other people or the environment.

a.   *Symbiotic stage:*   The baby has differentiated from other people but experiences other persons as existing only to satisfy its needs.

I-2   Impulsive stage

The impulsive stage begins with the development of language. Other persons are differentiated, but primarily as sources of reward and punishment. The expression of impulses often leads to punishment, so the child is concerned with controlling impulses to avoid punishment. Because other persons are seen primarily as sources of reward and punishment, gaining reward and avoiding punishment are the primary focus of relationships.

I-Delta   Self-protective stage

The child begins to anticipate short-term rewards and punishment. At this stage, the person's primary concern in relationships is what can be obtained from other persons. Interaction with others is a zero-sum game: What one person gets, the other person loses. Relationships are a competition in which there are winners and losers. Problems and punishment are blamed on the environment and other people. The focus of concern in a relationship is the rewards obtained from the relationship. If the rewards decline, the relationship is broken off for another relationship that promises to be more rewarding. The likelihood is quite small that persons at the impulsive or the self-protective stages of development will maintain a relationship for an extensive period unless external, environmental factors keep them in the relationship. For children, the obvious external factor is physical dependence upon parents.

(Persons at stages I-1 through I-Delta are quite self-centered in their relationships.)

I-3 Conformist stage

The person at this stage experiences relationships for the first time from a vantage point outside the self and perceives that certain rules govern relationships with other persons. The rules are obeyed because they are the rules. The needs and desires of other persons are recognized, but only in stereotypes. The person is particularly concerned with prestige, status, and what other people think. There is an awareness of values, but the punishment for failing to meet certain values is the disapproval of others. Relationships are governed by what the person thinks "should" or "should not" be done.

I-3/4 Self-aware level (called a level because it is a transition between two stages, although it is the modal level of American adults)

At this level, the persons has begun to perceive that, although there are rules, the rules do not always seem to apply; some rules conflict with other rules; and, further, the person does not agree with all of the rules. People at this level perceive that other groups have different rules that seem to work just as well as the familiar ones. Persons at this level, aware that their opinions do not entirely agree with what they perceive to be the opinions of the groups to which they belong, keep dissenting opinions to themselves, except in the company of trusted intimates.

I-4 Conscientious stage

The person's values are internalized. The person is often acutely self-critical because of awareness of internal feelings, needs, and motivations as well as the feelings, needs, and motivations of others. At this stage, both self and others are perceived in greater complexity. The person is not likely to feel so much concern with what other people think but is more concerned with whether or not personal behavior is meeting internal standards. If, however, the person's behavior hurts another, he or she will feel guilt.

I-4/5   Individualistic level (a transition level)

One perceives behavior in terms of psychological motivation and is aware that, although one may be financially and physically independent of others, one is still emotionally dependent. The moralism of earlier stages begins to be replaced with an awareness of the inner conflicts of self and others and with a greater tolerance for self and others.

I-5   Autonomous stage

The person is aware of the individuality of others, accepts them for who they are, and is willing to allow them to be who they are. There is an awareness that inner conflict is inherent in human life, and an acceptance of that conflict. The person values personal autonomy and is willing to grant autonomy to others. Parents at this stage are willing to let children make their own mistakes, only trying to prevent their making disastrous mistakes. Personal relationships are especially cherished.

I-6   Integrated stage (similar to Maslow's description of the self-actualized person)

The person not only accepts individuality in others but values it, encouraging and helping others to develop their own unique personalities. Developing from the first to the last stages of ego development, one develops from an inability to perceive other persons at all toward being able to perceive others accurately and to relate to them intimately and harmoniously, promoting the growth of self and others.

Ego development and the family life cycle

Obviously, children as well as parents continue their personal development throughout the life cycle; thus the stages of ego development of the family members change during the family life cycle. The stages of ego development that may be represented within the family at different stages of the family life cycle are presented in Table 1.

When the family begins (the stage of "beginning families"), the only persons in the family are the husband and the wife, who most likely are at either the conformist or the conscientious stage of ego development. They may be at the self-protective stage; if they are, the marriage

Table 1

Stages of ego development that may be present in family members at different stages of the family life cycle

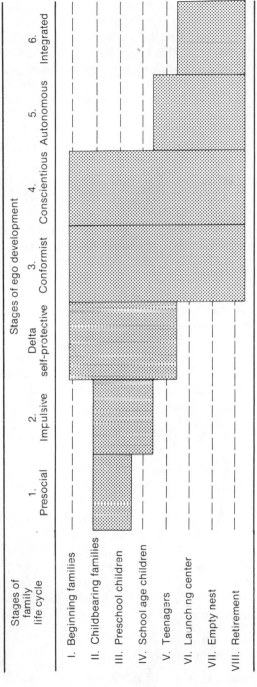

Stages of ego development

Stages of family life cycle	1. Presocial	2. Impulsive	Delta self-protective	3. Conformist	4. Conscientious	5. Autonomous	6. Integrated

I. Beginning families

II. Childbearing families

III. Preschool children

IV. School age children

V. Teenagers

VI. Launching center

VII. Empty nest

VIII. Retirement

will probably be an unstable one (unless a strong, supportive social structure keeps them in the relationship). My own research, as well as that of others (Nettles, 1978), indicates that husbands and wives are overwhelmingly at the same stage of ego development. When a couple begins to have children, persons at the presocial stage of development (the infants) enter the family. As the children grow up, they pass through the presocial, the impulsive, and probably the self-protective stages, reaching the conformist stage before they leave the family. Meanwhile, the parents have continued their own development. If both they and the children are lucky, the parents may have reached the autonomous stage by the time the children are teenagers. If the parents continue to develop, they may in their later years achieve the integrated stage, although it is unlikely that parents will achieve this stage before the children leave home. Not more than 10 percent of older persons have reached the autonomous or the integrated stage of development (Swensen, Eskew, & Kohlhepp, 1977; Swensen & Moore, 1979; Swensen & Trahaug, 1979). For example, a typical family (e.g., parents aged 36 and 33; children aged 6, 3, and 6 months) would probably include persons at the conformist stage (the parents), the self-protective, the impulsive, and the presocial stages.

This development shifts the nature and the balance of family relationships. The bonds between people weaken the longer they are related (Levinger, 1977a, 1977b); and as persons age, they prefer more autonomy (Cohler, 1983), partly because they tire of meeting the dependency needs of younger family members. The shift does not mean that older persons do not want and need the support of the family's social structure—satisfying, intimate relationships with other members of the family—but that they need relief from the demands of dependent children. Childrearing, with or without love, is a tiring business. Most married couples report that life and marriage are much more enjoyable after the children leave home (J. G. Turner, 1975; Swensen, 1983a, 1983b).

The power relationships change also, with the children gaining more power as they get older. As parents age, children eventually emerge as the center of power in the extended family. This process of change produces strains (Beavers, 1977; Beavers & Voeller, 1983; Lewis, Beavers, Gossett, & Phillips, 1976) that are best managed by healthy, or optimal, families (i.e., families headed by parents who have reached the autonomous stage).

Vaillant's longitudinal study

In a longitudinal study of adult development, Vaillant (1977) observed that as the subjects aged, they developed more mature psychological defenses and that this course of development both affected and was affected by their intimate relationships. He described four levels of defenses:

Level I consisted of psychotic defenses, such as delusional projection, denial, and distortion.
Level II defenses were immature mechanisms, such as projection, schizoid fantasy, hypochondriasis, passive-aggressive behavior, and acting out.
Level III consisted of neurotic defenses, such as intellectualization, repression, displacement, reaction formation, and dissociation.
Level IV (mature) defenses included altruism, humor, suppression, sublimation, and anticipation.

Those who used primarily mature defenses were physically healthier, earned more money, had more friends, had progressed further in their occupations, reported themselves as happier, had fewer divorces, gave more money to charity, and were more active in their communities. The subjects whose lives had the worst outcomes had had unloving childhoods. Of those whose outcomes were best, most had achieved a stable marriage before the age of 30, had had supportive mentors during their early careers, and had been able to come to terms with their adolescent children. As the more successful ones aged, they worried more about their children and less about themselves. Most of them had stayed married to their first wives.

The most successful subjects were described as persons who had enjoyed loving, supportive relationships early in life and who had been able to provide loving, supportive relationships later in life. Vaillant noted that "there was probably no single longitudinal variable that predicted mental health as clearly as a man's capacity to remain happily married over time" (p. 320).

Personality development, then, continues throughout the life span, including the adult years. The development goes through periods of transition and stability, but the general direction of development is toward greater complexity and a greater ability to integrate more phenomena and experiences, both in time and in space. The individual who more accurately perceives self and others, can anticipate more accurately the outcome of present behavior and can understand present behavior in terms of past events. The growth of the individual, which is toward a greater understanding and appreciation of self and others, is reflected in the ability to form more intimate, satisfying, and harmonious relationships. One is more successful not only in intimate relationships but in other areas of life as well, such as being a better care giver to children. In adult life, one seeks relationships with others who are at one's own level of development (Swensen & Moore, 1979). Personality development, which continues throughout life, is a process that is both a cause and a consequence of the kinds of intimate relationships that people develop.

THE FAMILY

Putting together two observations—that a relationship is a function of the persons in the relationship and of the situation within which the relationship exists, and that people develop throughout their lives—we see family relationships as a function of the family members' levels of personal development and of the situation within which the family exists. Because a family of several members will include persons at different stages of personal development, a family should encompass several different kinds of relationships. Further, as the individuals within the family develop personally through various stages, the relationships within the family will change. Within a family, then, a variety of kinds of relationships will exist, and the relationships themselves will exhibit a course of development.

The Latin word from which the English *family* is derived refers to a household consisting of all the members who live together, whether or not they are related. This chapter, however, refers to what might be considered the typical American family—the modified extended family (Clayton, 1975, chap. 5; Cohler, 1983; R. H. Turner, 1970). A modified extended family is one in which a single unit may consist of a father, a mother, and dependent children, but the unit maintains continuous contact and communications with grandparents, aunts and uncles, cousins, and other family members. Family members show a continuous interest in each other and give each other help when help is needed. The larger clan gathers from time to time for special occasions, such as Christmas and birthdays, and if the members are separated by some distance, they visit with some regularity.

Much has been made of recent census data showing that only a minority of households consist of the "standard" nuclear family—father, mother, and dependent children. In charting trends, Naisbitt (1982) concluded that by the year 2000 only 14 percent of U.S. households will constitute such units. The statistic does not consider that the increasing life span and continued improvement in older persons' economic situations may dictate an even smaller percentage. Reflecting upon my own family, for example, I observe that my immediate family—my parents, my wife's parents, my wife and I, and our children—encompass eight separate household units. A year ago, not one of these household units consisted of husband, wife, and dependent children. Today, only one of them does. Our family statistic is 12 percent, which is below the national average. Yet, every person in the eight household units grew up in a household consisting of husband, wife, and dependent children. The proportion of households that is typical nuclear families fails to reflect an accurate picture of family structure and integration. The fact of the matter is that the eight household units in my family maintain continuous contact, and we consider ourselves part of a larger, single-family structure.

Structure, dynamics, and types of families

How is the family—an intimate group of people—put together, and how does the family function? Dimensions are the basic variables in which groups or persons within a group may differ. The dynamics of the group concerns how persons within the group interact. Although the dimensions suggested for the ordering of families can in theory produce an infinite number of different kinds of families, most families can in fact be classified into a limited number of types.

For a better understanding of the family—a group of persons in a long-term, intimate relationship, a special kind of group—let us begin with the dimensions that have been useful in describing groups.

Figure 1
A schematic diagram of Bales's three-dimensional model of interpersonal behavior

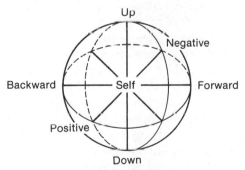

Source: From C. H. Swensen, *Introduction to interpersonal relations* (Glenview, Ill.: Scott, Foresman, 1973), p. 197.

How persons interact in groups is the basis for a system that Bales (1970) developed for diagnosing personality (see Figure 1). The system has three dimensions: up-down, positive-negative, and forward-backward. The up-down dimension represents dominance and submissiveness (the person in the up direction is more dominant). The positive-negative dimension includes positive associations, such as love and satisfying interpersonal relationships, and negative associations, such as hostility and anxiety. In the forward-backward dimension, forward implies offering an item for group acceptance, moving the group toward some united action; backward is dissociating the item from authority.

Each person tends to move the group toward the part of the space where he or she is. For example, a person in the up-positive-forward section of the space tends to be ascendant, friendly, and takes the initiative in leading the group to accomplish tasks. A person in the up-negative-forward direction also tends to be dominant and to urge the group to get tasks done, but is less concerned with relationships within the group and appears to be authoritarian. A person in the down-backward position is submissive and noncooperative in helping the group accomplish tasks.

Bales (Bales & Cohen, 1979, chap. 33) applied this system in analyzing a family who was presented in a television series. This particular family eventually disintegrated and did not solve problems very effectively before the disintegration. In Bales's analysis, this family had no member who was particularly strong in the forward sector (i.e., one who was particularly concerned with moving the family to get tasks accepted and accomplished). The only member of the family in the forward sector was the mother, who was not particularly dominant when compared with other members of the family and who, because she tended to be negative rather than positive, was not effective in getting the family members to work together.

Any group must perform two kinds of functions—the integrative and the instrumental. The integrative has to do with the members of the group working together. The instrumental has to do with getting certain essential jobs finished. Although a family in our present society exists primarily to meet emotional needs for nurturance and love, tasks must still be done, such as cooking the meals, washing the dishes, carrying out the garbage, paying the bills, and deciding where to go on vacation. Meeting the emotional needs of the members of the family also presents instrumental problems. Christmas may be a time for reexpressing family solidarity and love, but it requires a lot of shopping, decorating, baking, and bill paying if it is to come off as an emotionally successful occasion. A family, to function successfully as a group, must have members who are dominant, serving as leaders in getting the jobs done, and who also integrate the group and care for the feelings of the members, fostering the positive relationships among them. That is, a functioning family requires members who are up-forward and up-positive. There is nothing sacred about Bales's dimensions, but they do relate to the dimensions that have emerged repeatedly in studies of the dimensions that underlie interpersonal relationships (e.g., Swensen, 1973, chap. 7), and they are applicable to the dimensions that others have applied to the structure of the family.

Bales's dimensions relate to the stages of ego development. There should be no direct correspondence between the two, because Bales's dimensions underlie the interaction of persons in a group; the stages of ego development describe the complexity of the personality organization of individuals. The factor that distinguishes persons at the more complex stages of development from those at the simpler stages is how effectively they promote the welfare of the family and its individual members, not how effectively they perform a particular role within the family. To function adequately, however, a family needs persons to perform certain functions. Somebody must lead the group, somebody must move the group forward to do the tasks that are necessary for the group's success, and somebody must integrate the personal relationships in the group so that the group members' emotional needs are met and so that the group has interpersonal cohesion.

Because persons at the more complex levels of ego development perceive reality more accurately, form more satisfying relationships with others, and are generally more competent at the various tasks of life, we expect them to perceive the roles that need to be filled if the family is to function successfully and to perform those roles. That is, persons at the more complex levels of ego development are flexible enough to function in different parts of the space defined by Bales's dimensions. In the family, however, the parents (who are older and more powerful) are likely to be the ones who guide and urge the family to fulfill its necessary functions. The parents are also likely to have grown to the most complex levels of ego development, and persons at the more complex levels of ego development would tend to be toward the dominant forward directions of Bales's space. Sensitive to, and concerned about, interpersonal needs, persons at the more complex stages of ego development would also tend toward the positive of the positive-negative dimension. Persons at the more complex levels of ego development may, however, oppose and resist the family's moving in directions of which they disapprove, may passively allow others to lead, and may be distinctly antisocial.

From a study of 19 families (Kantor & Lehr, 1975), 9 of which had produced a schizophrenic, emerged three dimensions that appear to be the same as Bales's. Kantor and Lehr analyzed the interactions among the family members' efforts to regulate space. Using a complex system, they viewed family interaction as an attempt to obtain a goal—affect, power, or meaning. These dimensions underlie the targets of the family—or, in Bales's terms, the attempts to move the group toward some goal. If what a family considers important to accomplish reflects what is most meaningful to the family, the power dimension corresponds to up-down, the affect dimension corresponds to positive-negative, and the meaning dimension is similar to forward-backward. Meaningfulness has to do with an integrated sense of direction and destination; even the minor goals that a family elects to pursue ultimately end up at some destination.

Kantor and Lehr described four players in the family: the mover, the opposer, the follower, and the bystander. The mover, who tries to gain access to a target, would be in the forward part of Bales's space; the opposer, who reacts with dissent to the mover, would be in the backward sector; the follower would be less dominant, would be down, and supports either the mover or the opposer, depending upon whether the follower were in the forward or the backward space. The bystander, somewhere in the middle, would be less dominant than the mover and the opposer and, therefore, down.

Kantor and Lehr also described three basic types of families: *(a)* the closed family, which is run by an authority and in which the members must follow the rules (stability is the core purpose of the closed family); *(b)* the open family, which is flexible and in which each member is free to establish movements within the family guidelines (the open family's purpose is to be attentive to the needs of the individual and the family); *(c)* the random family, in which members develop their own systems of space, time, and energy usage and in which conflicts are frequent and may or may not be resolved (the random family's purpose is free exploration).

If we apply Bales's dimensions to these family types and speculate about the levels of ego development, who would lead these family types? The closed family would be led by a person who is probably somewhat up (or dominant) and forward, but on the negative side of the positive-negative dimension. This family is concerned with following rules, so the members who set the tone for the family would probably be at the conformist stage of ego development, the stage at which concern with rules is at a maximum. The open family would probably be led by parents who are somewhat dominant, but forward and positive, and who are able to maintain the family functioning while integrating the needs of the family as a whole with the individual needs of the family members. Leading an open family is a rather demanding task, one that requires a person who can perceive the needs and motives of others and who can perceive and deal constructively with conflict. Such a person(s) should be at a stage beyond the conformist stage, probably at the autonomous stage, because of the required ability to perceive and deal constructively with potential conflict. The random family, although given a purpose by Kantor and Lehr, appears from the description to be more a collection of persons who occupy the same space at the same time than a functioning family. Perhaps the parents in such a family would not be very dominant, not forward, and probably not particularly positive. Such parents would probably be at a stage of ego development less complex than the conformist stage, perhaps the self-protective stage. Such a family might be rather chaotic and ineffectual in identifying and achieving goals.

Beavers (1977; Beavers & Voeller, 1983; Lewis et al., 1976) described families along two dimensions: disturbed-healthy and centripetal-centrifugal. The main dimension ranges from the disturbed, or dysfunctional, family to the healthy, or optimal, family. Family systems develop from chaos to rigidity to flexibility. Out of the chaos arises a leader who takes charge and organizes a rigid structure. Only after a structure has been established and accepted can a flexible structure emerge. As a family becomes more able, excessively centripetal or centrifugal styles diminish.

As described also in Chapters 4 and 5, there are three main types of families: healthy (optimal), adequate (midrange), and disturbed (dysfunctional).

1.   Healthy families have a clear and flexible structure, but function is their main concern. They have a clear hierarchy of power, with the father leading; but the children are able to influence family decisions. The members of the healthy family are able to have meaningful encounters and relationships with the broader social environment and with persons outside the family. As the family members age, the family becomes a loosely connected, lovingly respectful group of equal adults.

2.   The midrange, or adequate, families tend to have a rigid authority structure that discourages the development of autonomy in the children. These families may be either centrifugal or centripetal. Because such families do not offer a clear model for negotiation or compromise, they tend to have either overt or covert conflict.

3.   Dysfunctional, or disturbed, families have a chaotic structure. In disturbed families, every member is isolated and alone. These families have no effective leadership, no tolerance for the clear and responsible expression of opinion, and little ability to reach consensual solutions.

Within the preceding three broad types, Beavers (Beavers & Voeller, 1983) more specifically described nine family types:

1.   Optimal families are those whose members seek and find intimacy; the hierarchical structure of the family is well defined and accepted; and the family adjusts well to its evolution.

2.   Adequate families are more control oriented, often attempt to resolve conflict by intimidation and direct force, exhibit role stereotyping, and are usually led by conventional, powerful males who are not emotionally expressive.

3. Midrange centripetal families are those in which authority rules (the family members are greatly concerned with rules and authority) and in which sex role stereotyping is maximal.

4. Midrange centrifugal families are those in which control by intimidation is less successful, open hostility is expressed, blame and attack are frequent, and manipulation is used by all family members.

5. Midrange mixed families are a mixture of the two preceding types.

6. Borderline centripetal families are those in which control battles are intense, but open rebellion is not expected.

7. Borderline centrifugal families are those in which anger is more openly expressed, the parental coalition is poor, and stormy battles occur regularly.

8. Severely disturbed centripetal families have little ability to resolve ambivalence or to choose and pursue goals; they are unable to focus attention on any topic in a discussion; and their functioning is chaotic.

9. Severely disturbed centrifugal families express much open hostility and great contempt for any show of dependency; family members exhibit little caretaking; and leave-taking is frequent.

As suggested earlier, the stages of ego development easily fit these types of families, with the optimal family being headed by parents who are at the autonomous stage of development, the midrange families headed by parent figures who are at the conformist stage, and the disturbed families headed by parent figures who are at stages of development simpler than the conformist stage. This framework suggests that to function at a minimum level of adequacy, a family must be headed by parent figures who have achieved at least the conformist stage of development. But how does Bales's system fit in? Beavers' centripetal-centrifugal dimensions appear to be a consequence of where the parental figures fall on Bales's positive-negative dimension. If they fall on the negative side, they will be unable to integrate the family members effectively, thus producing a centrifugal family. If they fall on the positive side, they will produce a centripetal family; but because they tend to be rigid and authoritarian, they will produce a somewhat stifling family atmosphere that will fail to meet the members' needs fully and thus generate covert conflict. Rigid authoritarianism suggests not dominance but insecurity in the ability to control.

Beavers observed, in studying healthy and distressed families, that the members of optimally functioning families had about twice as many positive as negative interactions. Healthy families had less conflict than did either adequate or distressed families and were able to solve their conflicts. Adequate and distressed families had more negative than positive interactions.

To sum up simply, the type of family one grows up in reflects the parents' levels of ego development. More love is expressed in healthy or optimal families than in other families. And, finally, the total structure of the family members may be diagrammed by locating the members individually in particular parts of the space described by Bales.

There are, of course, many other descriptions of family structure than those outlined here (e.g., Olson, Russell, & Sprenkle, 1983), but the purpose here is to sketch a framework of family structure as a background for personality development in the family, with broader descriptions of the dimensions that underlie both interpersonal relationships and groups.

Relationships among family systems

The structure outlined in the preceding section applies primarily to a household, a group of persons living together under the same roof at the same time—a nuclear family. Nuclear families do not, however, live in isolation from other households. Especially do they maintain contact with the parents of the parents, the children's grandparents. They also maintain contact with the families of the parents' brothers and sisters. Whatever the interaction with the members of these other households, it affects the specific family being studied. Particularly do the families of origin of the parents (the parents of the father and the mother) continue to exert an influence upon the family (Boszormenyi-Nagy & Spark, 1973; Leader, 1975). The family is not a closed system, but a partly permeable system that is influenced by impinging social forces, the strongest of which come from the other families in the larger unit. Further, as mentioned earlier, the unsettled accounts of past generations persist, so that patterns of behavior are repeated from one generation to another. The likelihood is that the parents in a particular family will behave toward their children as their own parents behaved toward them (Bales, 1970) and that the parents will tend to recreate approximately the same family structure as that of the family in which they were reared.

Not only do the nuclear families overlap and interact with one another, but significant one-to-one relationships cross household boundaries. Perhaps the most important of these relationships is the grandparent-grandchild relationship, which may have a significant impact upon the family itself (Robertson, 1976; R. H. Turner, 1970). The relationship with the grandparents is an important one to the child, and it may either support or undercut the parent-child relationship. In healthy families, the outside relationships tend to support and confirm parent-child and child-child relationships; in dysfunctional families, the grandparent-grandchild relationship adds to the conflict and chaos. Other outside relationships, such as that between a special aunt or uncle and a niece or nephew, may also be significant. The relationship that the parents maintain with their own parents may be a source of satisfaction and support or a source of added conflict and tension (Cicirelli, 1981; Johnson & Bursk, 1977).

CHANGE AND THE FAMILY

The family does not exist in a vacuum. Not only does it overlap with other relatives, but it also exists within a society and a culture whose trends affect family functioning and relationships (Levinger, 1977a, 1977b).

The more complex the society, the more differentiated are the stages of adult development and the more abstract are the developmental goals toward which life is directed (Giele, 1980). The greater the complexity that a person must cope with in the workplace, the more complex is the person's cognitive development (Kohn, 1969, 1980). The complexity of work is greater when it involves data and people, and this is precisely the direction in which work in the United States is developing (Naisbitt, 1982). This increased complexity appears to be reflected in family relationships: Those whose work is more complex are more likely to use internal and verbal means to control and discipline their children; those whose work is less complex use physical methods of discipline (Gecas & Nye, 1974; Kohn, 1969).

Personality changes in the U.S. population have been observed for the past 25 years. We might speculate that changes in society have been a major factor in the development of these personality changes. As the number of autonomous, self-generating people declines (Fiske, 1980), the gap widens between the commitments of academics and artists and the remainder of the population. Fiske has speculated that more complex, autonomous people can live satisfying lives in our time only if they belong to a more privileged class for whom lifestyle options remain open. This observation, if correct, suggests that we will have a sizable and growing population pushing for increased choice, thus pushing for social change that will provide more options.

Demography is also a factor in social change, a factor whose effect upon intimate relationships we may have overlooked. Glick (1975) suggested that the excess of marriageable women in recent years has influenced the development of the women's movement. The women's movement has, of course, had a major impact upon the relationships between the sexes, an impact not yet fully studied or understood. The growing number of the elderly will certainly increase the number of grandparents and great-grandparents who will be around to influence the families of their children, grandchildren, and great-grandchildren (Swensen, 1983a, 1983b).

Role relationships within the family appear to be changing (Csik-szentmihalyi, 1980), and three new roles for males appear to be emerging: the therapeutic, the recreational, and the sexual. For females, three traditional roles—child care, child socialization, and provider—appear to be stable; but two traditional roles—kinship (obligations to kin) and housekeeper—appear to be weakening.

Husbands and wives are indeed two different persons. Their personal growth does not occur at the same rate (Gould, 1980) or in the same direction (Fiske, 1980). This lack of coordination in the direction and the rate of growth is a basic source of conflict. When the husband wants autonomy, his wife is seeking intimacy, and vice versa. Early in marriage, men are typically most concerned with autonomy; their wives are more concerned with intimacy. Later in the marriage, husbands begin to seek intimacy while their wives are seeking autonomy. Early in marriage, the husband is seeking to advance his career while his wife is concerned with love, family, and children. Later, the husband, weary of his battle with the world, seeks the solace and warmth of home, family, and grandchildren. His wife, meanwhile, has finally reached a stage in life at which she has both the desire and the opportunity to develop and try her skills in the outside world. These differences between husband and wife may produce a growing estrangement, or they may challenge a couple's growth as persons and in their relationship.

Conflicts and conflict resolution

These problems may reveal themselves in specific conflicts about the roles that husbands and wives play and about the way they play them (Pearlin, 1980). Role conflict, basically a dispute about which rules to apply to a situation, is a typical conflict in the marriages of persons at the conformist stage of ego development. Persons at the postconformist stage of ego development can separate the person playing the role from the role itself (Cushman & Craig, 1976, pp. 33–57)—they are not "embedded" (Kegan, 1982) in the role—and can thus isolate the conflict and make the necessary adaptation: revising the rules, applying different rules, or otherwise coping constructively with the conflict. If most adults in our society (i.e., most married persons) are at the conformist stage of ego development, problem solution demands useful rules for solving conflicts.

The universal solvent for marriage problems is commitment, which has been defined as the "avowed or inferred intent of a person to maintain a relationship" (Rosenblatt, 1977, p. 73). A commitment will be greater when it is voluntary, public, and requires some effort. In any long-term relationship come times when the commitment is tested.

A commitment that has passed a test is a stronger commitment. When the partners are strongly committed to each other and are assured of each other's commitment, that commitment provides the foundation for a secure relationship, giving the couple the security to face and cope with their problems. Because their relationship is secure, they need not fear that any particular issue will seriously disturb or destroy their relationship. Marriages in which the husband and the wife are committed to each other as individuals have significantly fewer problems than do marriages in which the commitment is less (Swensen & Moore, 1979; Swensen & Trahaug, 1979).

Commitment as the basis for facing and solving a conflict involves certain steps (Raush et al., 1974): *(a)* introduction of the issue, *(b)* exploration of alternative solutions, *(c)* resolution, *(d)* practical planning about the resolution, *(e)* emotional reconciliation, *(f)* consolidation and reaffirmation of the relationship, and *(g)* return to the conflict to work out future methods for coping with interpersonal issues. A conflict is more likely to be resolved when the discussion remains intellectual and focuses upon a concrete issue (not expanding into a discussion of the partners' personality flaws). Conflict is also more likely to be resolved when communications are clear and unambiguous. (Raush et al., 1974, noted that in a fight the conciliatory initiatives seem to come from the husband.)

Marriage relationship and family structure

Parents found the family and build the family structure, passing on to their children (for good or ill) a certain amount of what was handed to them from their own families of origin (Boszormenyi-Nagy & Spark, 1973; Leader, 1975). They develop the kinds of relationships they learned from their parents (Bales, 1970) and teach their children to relate to others as they themselves relate to each other and to the children.

The three basic kinds of families—chaotic, midrange (adequate), and optimal (Beavers, 1977; Beavers & Voeller, 1983; Lewis et al., 1976)—correspond well to the stages of ego development, as does the hypothesis that family systems grow from chaos to rigidity to flexibility.

Persons who are at the preconformist, the self-protective, or the impulsive stages of development, form and maintain relationships because of the relatively immediate rewards in the relationship. They are not able to form a structure for a family or for any other group, but are dependent upon structures created by others. A family formed by two persons at the self-protective or the impulsive stages of development will thus have a chaotic structure unless the family exists within a larger unit that imposes structure. Further, persons who found chaotic families were themselves reared in chaotic families, which did not provide at each stage of development the necessary experiences that would have allowed them to continue to grow as persons.

Persons who have achieved the conformist stage of ego development will found families that are adequate or midrange. They establish rules for the functioning of the family, rules that the parents learned in their own families. Because these parents are not able to resolve conflicts in the rules, revise or bend the rules when conflicts arise, or revise or bend the rules when they do not seem applicable, they will develop a rather rigid family structure. Husband and wife are not able to resolve the conflicts between them; if they maintain their relationship, they handle the conflicts by avoiding and denying them. A couple may be skilled at avoiding their own unresolved conflicts, but children are not so perceptive or so adept. Children do and say things that bring the conflicts into the open. If the parents of such a family can successfully sweep the problems under the rug, the consequences of those problems work themselves out covertly and are expressed indirectly. If such problems cannot be successfully swept under the rug, open rebellion erupts. Thus, such families are characterized by passive resistance and withdrawal or by open rebellion and conflict or some combination of the two. Such families tend to avoid conflict when possible, put it down with parental force when they cannot avoid it, suffer a certain amount of "closedness" and a degree of alienation among members, and have a collection of topics that are avoided in family discussions. These families have love, but it is an attenuated love. Howard (1978) was referring to them when she wrote that dread, not love, holds families together. Such families are most cohesive when they are threatened by an external problem.

Optimal families have a flexible structure. The hierarchy within the family is clear, but individual members have a high degree of personal autonomy. They communicate clearly with one another. These families are highly permeable to external influences, which are perceived as sources of growth and stimulation rather than as threats. Most of the interactions within such families are positive rather than negative. Such families adapt to changing circumstances and give their children increasing power and autonomy as they get older. Such families have fewer problems and are able to solve the ones that arise. As these families age, they become a loose collection of lovingly respectful adults. We expect this kind of family to be headed by adults who are growing from the conformist to the conscientious and the autonomous stages of ego development. If such parents continue their personal development, they may reach the integrated stage by the time they become grandparents. Such parents create a family environment that provides the love necessary for the personal growth of their children.

CONCLUSION

A relationship is a function of the persons involved in the relationship and of the situation within which the relationship exists, or

Relationship $= f$(Person 1, Person 2, . . . Person n) Environment

This paradigm gives us four kinds of variables: relationship variables, person (or personality) variables, variables of the structure of the relationship among the persons, and environmental or situational variables.

The structure of the relationships of members of a family may be plotted on space defined by the dimensions of dominance versus submission, positive versus negative orientation toward other people, and promoting versus objecting to the goals toward which the family seeks to move. Within this structure, families may be classified as chaotic, adequate (midrange), and optimal. The kind of family structure that develops in a given family depends upon the stage of ego development achieved by the parents. An optimal family, with postconformist parents, provides the love necessary for the children's continued growth through adolescence and into adulthood. Conformist parents in an adequate, or midrange, family promote the growth of children to adolescence, but the rigidity of the structure creates a growing estrangement as the children grow older and produces adults who recreate the same limited family structure. The chaotic family produced by preconformist parents fails to provide the children with the love or the family structure necessary for personal growth.

The main environmental factors that impinge on the family are the extended family of which the particular family is a part, the wider social group, and the culture within which the family lives. Changes in the wider family, the social group, and the culture compel changes in the relationships within the family. The changes now occurring in our culture are in the direction of greater choice and complexity. These changes are both a strain on family relationships and a challenge to growth.

REFERENCES

Anderson, R. I never sang for my father. In R. G. Lyell (Ed.), *Middle age, old age.* New York: Harcourt Brace Jovanovich, 1980.

Bales, R. F. *Personality and interpersonal behavior.* New York: Holt, Rinehart & Winston, 1970.

Bales, R. F., & Cohen, S. P. *SYMLOG: A system for the multiple level observation of groups.* New York: Free Press, 1979.

Beavers, W. R. *Psychotherapy and growth: A family systems perspective.* New York: Brunner/Mazel, 1977.

Beavers, W. R., & Voeller, M. N. Family models: Comparing and contrasting the Olson circumplex model with the Beavers systems model. *Family Process,* 1983, *22,* 85–98.

Boszormenyi-Nagy, I., & Spark, C. M. *Invisible loyalties.* New York: Harper & Row, 1973.

Cicirelli, V. G. *Helping elderly parents: The role of adult children.* Boston: Auburn House, 1981.

Clayton, R. R. *The family, marriage, and social change.* Lexington, Mass.: D. C. Heath, 1975.

Cohler, B. J. Autonomy and interdependence in the family of adulthood: A psychological perspective. *The Gerontologist,* 1983, *23,* 33–39.

Csikszentmihalyi, M. Love and the dynamics of personal growth. In K. S. Pope (Ed.), *On love and loving.* San Francisco: Jossey-Bass, 1980. Pp. 206–326.

Cushman, D. P., & Craig, R. R. *Explorations in interpersonal communication.* Beverly Hills, Calif.: Sage Publications, 1976.

Erikson, E. H. *Childhood and society.* New York: W. W. Norton, 1950.

Fiske, M. Changing hierarchies of commitment in adulthood. In N. J. Smelser & E. H. Erikson (Eds.), *Themes of work and love in adulthood.* Cambridge, Mass.: Harvard University Press, 1980. Pp. 238–264.

Friedlander, S., & Morrison, D. C. Childhood. In K. S. Pope (Ed.), *On love and loving.* San Francisco: Jossey-Bass, 1980. Pp. 27–43.

Gecas, V., & Nye, F. I. Sex and class differences in parent-child interaction: A test of Kohn's hypothesis. *Journal of Marriage and the Family,* 1974, *36,* 742–749.

Geller, J. D., & Howenstine, R. A. Adulthood: Men. In K. S. Pope (Ed.), *On love and loving.* San Francisco: Jossey-Bass, 1980. Pp. 61–88.

Giele, J. Z. Adulthood as transcendence of age and sex. In N. J. Smelser & E. H. Erikson (Eds.), *Themes of work and love in adulthood.* Cambridge, Mass.: Harvard University Press, 1980.

Glick, P. C. A demographer looks at American families. *Journal of Marriage and the Family,* 1975, *37,* 15–26.

Gould, R. L. Adult life stages: Growth toward self-tolerance. *Psychology Today,* February 1975, pp. 74–78.

Gould, R. L. *Transformations: Growth and change in adult life.* New York: Simon & Schuster, 1978.

Gould, R. L. Transformations during early and middle adult years. In N. J. Smelser & E. H. Erikson (Eds.), *Themes of work and love in adulthood.* Cambridge, Mass.: Harvard University Press, 1980. Pp. 213–237.

Hogan, R. Dialectical aspects of moral development. *Contributions to Human Development,* 1976, *2,* 53–59.

Howard, J. *Families.* New York: Simon & Schuster, 1978.

Johnson, E. S., & Bursk, B. J. Relationships between the elderly and their adult children. *The Gerontologist,* 1977, *17,* 90–96.

Jourard, S. M. Marriage is for life. *Journal of Marriage and Family Counseling,* 1975, *1,* 199–208.

Kantor, D., & Lehr, W. *Inside the family.* San Francisco: Jossey-Bass, 1975.

Kegan, R. *The evolving self.* Cambridge, Mass.: Harvard University Press, 1982.

Kohn, M. L. *Class and conformity.* Homewood, Ill.: Dorsey Press, 1969.

Kohn, M. L. Job complexity and adult personality. In N. J. Smelser & E. H. Erikson (Eds.), *Themes of work and love in adulthood.* Cambridge, Mass.: Harvard University Press, 1980. Pp. 193–210.

Leader, A. I. The place of in-laws in marital relationships. *Social Casework,* 1975, *56,* 486–491.

Levinger, G. The embrace of lives: Changing and unchanging. In G. Levinger & H. L. Raush (Eds.), *Close relationships: Perspectives on the meaning of intimacy.* Amherst: University of Massachusetts Press, 1977. Pp. 1–16. (a)

Levinger, G. Re-viewing the close relationship. In G. Levinger & H. L. Raush (Eds.), *Close relationships: Perspectives on the meaning of intimacy.* Amherst: University of Massachusetts Press, 1977. Pp. 137–162. (b)

Levinson, D. J. Toward a conception of the adult life course. In N. J. Smelser & E. H. Erikson (Eds.), *Themes of work and love in adulthood.* Cambridge, Mass.: Harvard University Press, 1980. Pp. 265–290.

Levinson, D. J., Darrow, C., Klein, E., Levinson, M., & McKee, B. *The seasons of a man's life.* New York: Alfred A. Knopf, 1978.

Lewin, D. *Field theory in social science.* New York: Harper & Row, 1951.

Lewis, J. M., Beavers, W. R., Gossett, J. T., & Phillips, V. A. *No single thread: Psychological health in family systems.* New York: Brunner/Mazel, 1976.

Loevinger, J. *Ego development.* San Francisco: Jossey-Bass, 1976.

Naisbitt, J. *Megatrends: Ten new directions transforming our lives.* New York: Warner Books, 1982.

Nettles, E. J. *Ego development and sex role expectations in marriage.* Unpublished doctoral dissertation, Washington University, 1978.

Olson, D. H., Russell, C. S., & Sprenkle, D. H. Circumplex model of marital and family systems: VI. Theoretical update. *Family Process,* 1983, *22,* 69–83.

Pearlin, L. E. Life strains and psychological distress among adults. In N. J. Smelser & E. H. Erikson (Eds.), *Themes of work and love in adulthood.* Cambridge, Mass.: Harvard University Press, 1980.

Raush, H. L., Barry, W. A., Hertel, R. K., & Swain, M. A. *Communication, conflict and marriage.* San Francisco: Jossey-Bass, 1974.

Riegel, K. Adult life crises: A dialectic interpretation of development. In N. Datan & L. Ginsberg (Eds.), *Life-span developmental psychology: Normative life crises.* New York: Academic Press, 1975.

Riegel, K. Dialectical operations of cognitive development. *Contributions to Human Development,* 1976, *2,* 60–71.

Robertson, J. F. Significance of grandparents: Perceptions of young adult grandchildren. *The Gerontologist,* 1976, *16,* 137–140.

Rosenblatt, P. C. Needed research on commitment in marriage. In G. Levinger & H. L.

Raush (Eds.), *Close relationships: Perspectives on the meaning of intimacy.* Amherst: University of Massachusetts Press, 1977. Pp. 73–85.

Smelser, N. J. Issues in the study of work and love in adulthood. In N. J. Smelser & E. H. Erikson (Eds.), *Themes of work and love in adulthood.* Cambridge, Mass.: Harvard University Press, 1980. Pp. 1–26. (a)

Smelser, N. J. Vicissitudes of work and love in Anglo-American society. In N. J. Smelser & E. H. Erikson (Eds.), *Themes of work and love in adulthood.* Cambridge, Mass.: Harvard University Press, 1980. Pp. 105–119. (b)

Swensen, C. H. *Introduction to interpersonal relations.* Glenview, Ill.: Scott, Foresman, 1973.

Swensen, C. H. Ego development and interpersonal relationships. In D. Nevill (Ed.), *New frontiers in humanistic psychology.* New York: Gardner Press, 1977. Pp. 35–66.

Swensen, C. H. Assessment of ego development. In R. H. Woody (Ed.), *Encyclopedia of clinical assessment.* San Francisco: Jossey-Bass, 1980. Pp. 331–340. (a)

Swensen, C. H. Ego development and a general model for counseling and psychotherapy. *Personnel and Guidance Journal,* 1980, *58,* 382–388. (b)

Swensen, C. H. Post-parental marriages. *Medical Aspects of Human Sexuality,* 1983, *17*(4), 171–194. (a)

Swensen, C. H. A respectable old age. *American Psychologist,* 1983, *38,* 327–334. (b)

Swensen, C. H., Eskew, R. W. & Kohlhepp, K. A. Factors in the marriages of older couples. Report of NIMH Grant No. RO1–MH–26933. W. Lafayette, Ind.: Purdue University, 1977.

Swensen, C. H., Eskew, R. W., & Kohlhepp, K. A. Stage of family life cycle, ego development, and the marriage relationship. *Journal of Marriage and the Family,* 1981, *43,* 841–853.

Swensen, C. H., & Moore, C. Marriages that endure. In E. Corfman (Ed.), *Families today: Strengthening the family* (NIMH Science Monographs, DHEW Publication No. ADM 79–896). Rockville, Md.: National Institutes of Mental Health, 1979. Pp. 249–288.

Swensen, C. H., & Trahaug, G. *Mental problems of older people* (Report of Norwegian Research Council Grant No. B.61.01.088). Bergen, Norway: University of Bergen, 1979.

Turner, J. G. Patterns of intergenerational exchange in developmental approaches. *The International Journal of Aging and Human Development,* 1975, *6,* 111–115.

Turner, R. H. *Family interaction.* New York: John Wiley & Sons, 1970.

Vaillant, G. E. *Adaptation to life.* Boston: Little, Brown, 1977.

Chapter 4

Social and Family Psychology

LYNDA D. TALMADGE
R. BARRY RUBACK

Social psychologists have traditionally studied the effect of situational factors—including the presence, statements, and behavior of others—on the thoughts, feelings, and actions of an individual (Allport, 1968). Although this definition includes virtually all of normal adult human behavior, much of social psychological research has been conducted with only one population, college students. Moreover, social psychologists have tended to focus on individual rather than group processes (Pepitone, 1981; Sampson, 1977). Surprisingly, social psychologists have generally ignored the one pervasive, naturally occurring group of interacting persons, the family, within which it is possible to study the effect of the group on any one individual as well as the effect of the individual on the rest of the group (Hill & Hansen, 1960). In recent years there have been numerous calls for social psychologists to study the family (e.g., Framo, 1982; L'Abate & Thaxton, 1983; Walbridge, 1976, pp. 14–17).

Although social psychologists may be criticized for their failure to study the family, family researchers and therapists may be equally criticized for their failure to test and apply social psychological theory and research to the family. Part of the reason for their failure to utilize this theory and research may simply be that they are not aware of the work that is either directly or indirectly relevant to understanding family interaction.

This chapter strives to bridge the gap between social and family psychology. To do that, we present theory and research from social psychology that we believe is relevant to the study of families. The chapter is divided into three parts. The first part discusses two theoretical frameworks in social psychology that can be usefully applied to understanding family interactions: attribution theory and social exchange theory. The second part of the chapter is a review of research by social psychologists relevant to studying the family. These areas include marriage and divorce, parent-child relations, adolescence, and family structure. The third part of the chapter describes how social psychological research can be applied to family therapy and suggests several research questions that could profitably benefit from the combined research and practical expertise of social and family psychologists.

Before describing social psychological theory and research, we want to indicate that there may be limitations in applying research findings directly to families, primarily because until recently there was very little research that involved families. For example, in his review of the small-group literature, Framo (1965) found almost no studies that used the family as the group of interest. Subsequent reviews (e.g., Waxler & Mischler, 1978) have found more studies, although the most-recent textbooks summarizing the social psychological research on small groups (Forsyth, 1983; Shaw, 1981) do not even list families in their subject index. Though much of the research is experimental, the relevance of studies on small groups of interacting strangers is an open question (Harre & Secord, 1976), since there are several dimensions along which ad hoc groups and families may differ from one another (Weick, 1971).

Even though not all social psychological theory and research may be generalizable to families, we believe that much of it is relevant and can be useful to family researchers and therapists.

THEORETICAL PERSPECTIVES

As in many areas of psychology, there are a number of important theories in social psychology. In this section, we examine two general perspectives on human behavior: attribution theory and social exchange theory. These frameworks have generated a great deal of research and have been employed to help understand the behavior of actors in a number of contexts outside the laboratory (e.g., Greenberg & Ruback, 1982).

Attribution theory

Attribution theory is concerned with how people determine the causes of their own and others' behaviors. There really is no one theory of attribution; rather, several theorists use similar concepts to understand the attribution process. There are several books that are good introductions to attribution theory, including books by Shaver (1975) and Harvey and Weary (1981). Chapters on more specific topics in attribution are in edited books by Jones, Kanouse, Kelley, Nisbett, Valins, and Weiner (1972) and by Harvey, Ickes, and Kidd (1976, 1978, 1981). This section will very briefly introduce some of the ideas of the social psychologists who developed the theories and some of the research that has been used to test the theories. Following this general introduction, the more recent work relating attributional questions to marital interaction will be discussed.

Early theoretical work. The person who is usually considered to be the seminal figure in the area is Heider (1958). He argued that people divide causality into that which can be attributed to the person and that which can be attributed to the environment. The person can be further divided into three parts: intention, motivation, and ability. If a person's ability is sufficient to overcome the task difficulty of the environment, a state of "can" is said to exist. When a person completes an act, therefore, an observer can say with confidence that the person intended to complete the act, that the person was motivated to perform the act, and that the state of "can" existed.

Theorists subsequent to Heider have made more specific predictions about when observers attribute causality to the person as opposed to the environment. Jones and Davis (1965) suggested that observers try to make correspondent inferences—that is, inferences that explain both the observed action of the person and the disposition that is presumed to underly the reason for the person having performed the action. Jones and Davis argued that confidence in a correspondent inference is likely to be highest when there are few reasons that could explain why the person chose one action over another and when the action that the person performed is one that is low in social desirability (i.e., low in the frequency with which it is performed).

Kelley (1967) has argued that causality is attributed to a stimulus, to a situation, or to the perceiver based on a series of comparisons. Thus, for example, if a husband and wife always get into a fight when they talk about money, the wife would want to know if it was something about her husband (the stimulus), the subject of money (the situation), or her (the perceiver). Kelley argued that the wife would make comparisons along three dimensions: *(a)* compare her husband to other people along an entities dimension; *(b)* compare the subject of money to other situational factors along a time/modalities dimension; and *(c)* compare herself to others along a perceivers dimension. According to Kelley, the wife would be most confident of an attribution to her husband if she got into arguments with her husband and no one else (high distinctiveness), if she and her husband argued over things besides money (high consistency), and if her husband got into arguments with everyone else (high consensus). The wife would be most confident of an attribution to the topic of money if she got into arguments with everyone else (low distinctiveness) only about the subject of money (high consistency) and if everyone else got into fights over money (high consensus). Finally, the wife would be most confident of an attribution to herself if she got into arguments with her husband and everyone else (low distinctiveness), about the subject of money and all other topics (high consistency), and if no one else got into fights with her husband (low consensus).

In a later paper, Kelley (1972) suggested that the attribution process can be summarized in terms of three principles: covariation, discounting, and augmentation. The covariation principle suggests that we attribute causation to the cause that is present when the effect is present and is absent when the effect is absent. Thus, if a husband and wife get into a fight only when the husband's mother is visiting them, then causation can be attributed to the mother-in-law. The second principle, discounting, suggests that when two or more possible causes of an event are present, we are less confident that any one of them is the true cause. For example, if a husband buys a gift for his wife because he wants to show his love for her and because he forgot their anniversary, then the wife is less confident that he bought the gift because he loves her. The third principle, augmentation, suggests that when an event occurs in the presence of reasons that should reduce the likelihood of its occurring, then we tend to believe that the reasons that produced the event must be especially strong. Thus, for example, if a wife stays married to her husband even though he is very sick and out of work, then we are fairly confident of attributing her staying with her husband to her love for him.

Another major theorist in the attribution area is Weiner (Weiner, Frieze, Kukla, Reed, Rest, & Rosenbaum, 1972), who was concerned with the common attributions people make for achievement-related behavior. These common attributions for success and failure on different kinds of tasks are ability, effort, task difficulty/ease, and luck. These four attributions can be considered in terms of two dimensions: locus of control (internal or external to the person) and stability over time (stable or unstable). Thus, ability is internal to the person and stable over time; effort is internal to the person and unstable over time; task difficulty/ease is external to the person and stable over time; and luck is external to the person and unstable over time. Weiner et al. suggest that attributions to internal causes are more likely to produce praise or blame than are attributions to external causes. In addition, Weiner et al. suggest that attributions to stable causes carry with them the prediction of similar behavior in the future, whereas attributions to unstable causes carry no such prediction.

Although the preceding summary of the major attribution theories might imply that the theorists assume that people are rational and logical, there is a fairly substantial body of work that suggests that the average person's perceptions of causation are subject to a number of biases. One such bias has been termed the *fundamental attribution error* (L. D. Ross, 1977), the tendency to overattribute responsibility to a person and to underattribute responsibility to the environment. A second attributional bias, related to the fundamental attribution error, is the divergent-perspectives hypothesis or the actor-observer difference (Jones & Nisbett, 1972). This difference is the tendency for actors to attribute their own behavior to situational causes, whereas observers have a tendency to attribute an actor's behavior to dispositional causes (i.e., factors internal to the person).

Much of the research on attributions in couples has been concerned with the attributions couples make for marital conflict and negative interpersonal behavior. For example, Orvis, Kelley, and Butler (1976) asked each partner in 41 couples (who were married, living together, or dating) to give examples of important behaviors for which the two partners had different explanations. Analyses of the attributions provided support for Weiner's internal-external and stable-unstable dimensions. In addition, Orvis et al.'s results were consistent with Jones and Nisbett's actor-observer difference; they found that actors tended to attribute their behavior to situational factors, whereas partners tended to attribute the same behavior to dispositional factors. Orvis et al. hypothesized that the mediating factors for actors and partners in a dating relationship may be characterized by more justification and defensiveness than those made when the actors and observers are strangers, as in the typical study of college students. Harvey, Wells, and Alvarez (1978) found sex differences in attributions for conflict; men placed more importance on sexual incompatibility and disloyalty, whereas females place more importance on financial problems and the stress associated with one or both partners' work or educational activities.

Although not described in any of the formal attribution theories, research suggests that positive-negative attitude toward spouse is an important dimension underlying attributions for negative behavior (Passer, Kelley, & Michela, 1978). Doherty (1982) found that wives' tendency to attribute negative traits or intentions to a character in a vignette was related to their verbal criticism of their husbands but that husbands showed no such tendency toward their wives.

There is some evidence that blaming one's spouse is negatively related to happiness. Marital satisfaction was inversely related to wives' blaming their husbands for negative situations (Madden & Janoff-Bulman, 1981). Divorced women who attributed their divorce to aspects of their interaction with their spouse rather than to traits and behaviors of their spouse were happier, more socially active, and more optimistic one to three years after the divorce (Newman & Langer, 1981).

In the context of the family, research is needed on the attributions family members (parents and children) make not only for each other's behavior but also for the behavior of the family as a whole. Moreover, although the research on attribution theory is fairly extensive, more work is needed on the degree to which attributions affect behavior. The assumption is that attributions are important but not exclusive factors affecting individuals' behavior. Among other factors are the rewards and costs involved in the relationship with others. These rewards and costs relate to a second general theory in social psychology, social exchange theory.

Social exchange theory

Social exchange theorists assume that social interest is anchored in self-interest, that people join together only insofar as they believe it in their best interest to do so. Within the exchange context, the bartering of rewards and costs between partners determines the flow of the relationship, its development or dissolution (Huston & Burgess, 1979).

Thibaut and Kelley (1959) are usually considered the originators of social exchange theory in social psychology. The focus of their book was the dyad. They suggested that the outcomes of two individuals (A and B) could be considered in terms of a matrix of possible interactions and outcomes. One axis of the matrix represents A's possible behaviors, while the other axis represents B's possible behaviors. In each cell of the matrix are the outcomes for both A and B for that particular combination of behaviors. Thibaut and Kelley argued that A and B will continue their interaction only if both consider their outcomes to be adequate. Adequacy, Thibaut and Kelley suggested, is determined using two standards: (a) whether or not the outcome is above what the person feels he or she deserves (comparison level), and (b) whether or not the person's available alternative opportunities would produce greater outcomes (comparison level for alternatives).

Blau (1964) and Homans (1961) are usually considered the originators of the exchange tradition in sociology. Homans derived his theory of social exchange from behavioral psychology (largely animal studies) and elementary economics. He defined social behavior as "exchange of activity, tangible or intangible and more or less rewarding or costly, between at least two persons" (p. 13). Blau basically concurred with Homan's definition and suggested two fundamental principles of exchange: (1) An individual who supplies rewarding services to another obligates the other person. The second must, thus, furnish benefits to the first. (2) Profits from exchange decrease with the number of exchanges simply because having more of whatever is exchanged lowers its value. The focus here is on extrinsic benefits, not those intrinsic to the association itself. This is perhaps one of the weaknesses of the theory in its early development by the sociologists. Kelley and Thibaut (1978) and Kelley (1979) built on their earlier work to incorporate the intrinsic rewards of relationship exchanges in personal relationships. Both Kelley and Thibaut and Levinger and Huesmann (1980) attempt to account for the symbolic or relational level of social exchange in close relationships. These elaborations will be considered in a later section.

Social exchange is best considered as an aggregate of theories rather than as a single, unified theory. According to Hatfield, Utne, and Traupmann (1979), there are three major schools of thought subsumed under social exchange: *(a)* equity theory, *(b)* reciprocity/quid pro quo, and *(c)* the power or economic model.

Equity theory.   Equity theory was developed to explain and predict *(a)* how individuals judge whether or not a relationship is equitable, and *(b)* if the relationship is inequitable, how individuals deal with the inequity. Equity theory has four major assumptions:

1.   Persons try to maximize their outcomes.
2.   Groups try to promote equity among their members and will employ rewards and punishments to do so.
3.   Inequitable relationships cause the involved individuals to experience distress.
4.   These distressed persons will attempt to restore equity by either a real behavior change or a change in their perception of the situation (Walster, Walster, & Berscheid, 1978).

The formula that is usually used to define an equitable relationship for two individuals A and B is the ratio of outcomes in a relationship (where outcomes equal rewards minus costs) to investments into the relationship:

$$\frac{\text{A's rewards} - \text{A's costs}}{\text{A's investments}} = \frac{\text{B's rewards} - \text{B's costs}}{\text{B's investments}}$$

Thus, according to equity theorists, equity is not absolute; rather, it is relative to what the other person in the relationship receives.

Equity theory has generated predictions concerning four major areas of interaction: *(a)* philanthropist/recipient, *(b)* business, *(c)* exploiter/victim, and *(d)* intimate. Regarding parent-child relations, equity theorists are at the point of speculation, since "no data exist" (Walster et al., 1978, p. 197). Our concern is the intimate relationship, especially as it is found in the family.

Intimate relationships differ from casual ones on several dimensions. Compared to casual relationships (see also Chapter 13), intimate relationships involve (a) more intense liking and loving, (b) more exchange of information, in terms of both depth and breadth, (c) longer time periods, thus making it more difficult to determine if equity exists (since inequity may exist in the short run), (d) the exchange of resources of greater value and greater variety, and (e) greater substitutability of resources (Hatfield, et al., 1979).

Research on equity theory in marriage supports two hypotheses: (a) mismatched relationships are unhappy and (b) the overbenefited partner has to try harder in order to restore an equitable balance. More generally, partners who perceive their relationship as equitable feel content and happy. Those who see themselves as underbenefited feel angry, and those who see themselves as overbenefited feel guilty (Walster et al., 1978). Hatfield, Greenberger, Traupmann, and Lambert (1982) conducted a study that showed greater sexual and personal satisfaction with their relationship if equity existed. There is a tautological aspect to this research which defines contentment, satisfaction, happiness, and equity so similarly that they seem synonymous. That is, these studies correlate two phenomenological, subjective experiences and may tell us only that if one perceives a relationship to be fair and equitable, then one perceives himself or herself to be happy. Equity theory would be better tested if perception were related to behavior.

One such study correlated subjective perception of equity in the relationship with extramarital affairs (Walster, Traupmann, & Walster, 1978). If the partners felt overbenefited or equitably treated, they waited an average of 12 to 15 years before having an extramarital affair. However, if they felt underbenefited, the affair occurred on an average between six and eight years after marriage.

Although equity theory is fairly broadly based, Leventhal (1976, 1980) has argued that it is far too narrow a focus to account for the process of allocating resources within a group. Motivational forces other than concern for fairness or justice could powerfully influence perception and behavior: forces such as roles, cultural context, competing goals, and the ordering of priorities within a group or family.

According to Leventhal, groups are concerned with fairness in allocating resources, as equity theory implies, but multiple norms interact to influence the attainment and perception of fairness. Rewards may be distributed according to rules of "contributions," "equality," or "needs." The contributions rule is essentially the norm of equity, that is, outcomes should be proportional to inputs. It is used in situations such as employer-employee relations where productivity is the goal.

The equality rule states that resources should be divided equally among all members of the group and is used in situations where group harmony and solidarity are desired. The needs rule states that resources should be allocated on the basis of need, irrespective of other factors, and is used in groups such as the family, where members have close personal relationships and feel responsible for others. Leventhal argued that situational factors determine which rule is the dominant one. Thus, the contributions rule is likely to be dominant in the workplace, whereas the needs rule is likely to be dominant in the family. However, even this generalization is not always true. For example, parents are likely to use the contributions rule when giving their children money for doing household chores but to use the needs rule with regard to food.

With respect to need, there are several studies using college students as subjects which demonstrate that an individual works harder to help others as the other's involuntary dependence upon that individual increases (Berkowitz, 1969, 1972; Berkowitz & Daniels, 1963; Leventhal, Weiss, & Buttrick, 1973). Social responsibility and need become more salient in the family group than in any other because of the intensity of the connections in this highly personal, interdependent system.

In addition to the amount each member receives, Leventhal (1976, 1980) asserted that there is considerable concern for a fair procedure in deciding how resources should be distributed. He has postulated that group members use both a content and a process component while judging the acceptability of exchange in social relationships. Although he did not apply these principles to the family group per se, his notions of concern about procedural fairness seem especially appropriate to families because of the long-term, intimate connections among the members. What could be more disturbing than depending on a social system in which the procedures violate the individual? One can envision the "allocator" in Leventhal's groups as the parents in a family, responsible for gathering and distributing resources among the members.

Reciprocity or quid pro quo exchange.   In addition to equity, social exchange theory also encompasses reciprocity or quid pro quo exchange. The concepts of reciprocity and quid pro quo in exchange are based on the notion of tit for tat, a sort of scorekeeping arrangement wherein each person is concerned with the payback for a reward received. Hatfield et al. (1979) refer to the quid pro quo or reciprocity concepts of exchange theory as primarily the clinician's domain. Traditionally, clinical behaviorists have instructed couples in negotiating contracts about what a partner is willing to give in order to get something he or she wants (Paolino & McCrady, 1978).

Morton (1978) examined the relationship between intimacy and reciprocity of exchange, using 24 married couples and 24 opposite-sex unacquainted dyads. Results supported the tenets of social penetration theory, which predicts that overall intimacy increases and overall reciprocity decreases as relationships progress in their development. Following the original quid pro quo concept developed by Lederer and Jackson (1968), this study suggests that although couples in distress may need to be taught reciprocity, they also need to be shown how to go beyond it. In fact, some theorists have asserted that it is only when a relationship is of questionable quality that partners are apt to be concerned with calibrating rewards and costs (Huston & Burgess, 1979). For example, Murstein, Cerreto, and McDonald (1977) have argued that marital partners who apply the reciprocity model to their relationships are less satisfied than those who do not. More strongly, Kelley (1979) has stated that the exclusive use of behavioral contracting in marital therapy decapitates the marriage and deprives the partners of the symbolic level of their relationship.

Power or economic exchange model.   The third aspect of social exchange theory, the power/economic position, assumes that the individual is primarily interested in maximizing his or her own benefits— if need be, at the expense of the partner or the relationship (Kelley, 1979; Kelley & Thibaut, 1978). This model emphasizes the competitive relationship between participants and assumes that each participant tries to get for him or herself whatever the market will bear (Hatfield et al., 1979). There are two main groups who view intimate relationships in terms of the power/economic model: sociologists (Blau, 1964; Homans, 1961; Nye, 1978, 1980) and some marriage and family therapists (Bagarozzi & Wodarski, 1977; Brown, 1975; Edwards, 1969).

The work of marriage and family therapists who use this model is particularly relevant to this review. Brown (1975) has used social exchange at the behavioral level to describe how family crises are precipitated. Essentially, Bagarozzi and Wodarski (1977) have operationalized concepts of exchange as explicated by Levinger (1976), not only attending to the attractions of the relationship but also considering the barriers to exiting. Edwards (1969), focusing on exchange among all family members, has stated that different resources and rewards are needed at different stages of relationships and has illustrated this principle in discussing mate selection and family problem solving. Nelson and Nelson (1982) have focused on exchange in reconstituted or blended families. They have examined the roles of stepmother and stepfather, using the frameworks of Kelley and Thibaut's (1978) interdependence outcome matrix and equity theory. Willis and Frieze (1980) have used exchange theory and role theory as an explanation for formation, compatibility, and stability of couple relationships. Underlying all of these works is the assumption that each individual in the family is seeking to maximize his or her own gains in the exchange processes.

On a more general level, Nye's (1978, 1980) rendition of social exchange theory falls prey to a common criticism of the theory, which is that seminal social exchange theory contains few particulars, making it so abstract that it cannot be disproven (Berkowitz, 1972; Gergen, 1980). Nye has assumed the maximize-for-self position; but beyond that, he fails to deal with exchange as meaningful on different levels of interpersonal experience. Nor does he examine what is rewarding, how, why, when, and for whom. In short, he does not address the rules governing exchange in various contexts, especially that of the family.

The work of U. G. Foa (1971), Foa and Foa (1974), (1980) can also be characterized within the power/economic version of social exchange. To test their classification of resources into six classes (love, money, information, status, goods, and services), they have investigated the homogeneity of classes, similarity and substitution of resources, and appropriate exchange responses (Foa, 1971). Their most recent summary of their ongoing research seems sketchy, with little attention to clarification, methodology, and operationalization of variables. Thus, it is difficult to know how important the findings are. The only research they did with the family indicated that married couples reported less need for love than did unmarried couples. Another finding pertinent to the family is that the probability of love exchanges is higher in small rather than large groups (Foa & Foa, 1980).

An alternative. The foregoing models of social exchange have many detractors (Ahrens, 1981; Berkowitz, 1972; Clark & Mills, 1979; Gergen, 1980; Huston & Burgess, 1979; Leventhal, 1976; Scanzoni, 1979). These critics have suggested that, at least in part, intimate relationships are characterized by a different type of exchange interaction. The main objection to the power/economic and reciprocity models is that they emphasize the individual's gain over the well-being of the community or relationship. Raush (1977), Sampson (1977), and Scanzoni (1979) have argued that it is a mistake to assume that individual needs are always at odds with group needs. In fact, as interdependence progresses, so does communal concern, even to the extent that partners may become so perfectly meshed that what is rewarding to one is rewarding to the other (Raush; Scanzoni). At this stage of relating, the participants are apt to think of their relationship more as communion than exchange (Huston & Burgess, 1979). The commitment is not to exchange resources as individuals but to the larger unit that constitutes their mutual relation (Raush).

It has been argued that the focus on reciprocity has caused researchers to ignore selfless action on behalf of others (Berkowitz, 1972). Research indicates that the perception that others are dependent arouses feelings of responsibility toward these others (Berkowitz, 1972; Bowlby, 1969; Leventhal, 1976). Factors affecting helpful exchanges are awareness of the dependence, recall of pertinent social ideals, judgment of the dependence as appropriate or not, and willingness to accept the psychological costs of being helpful (Berkowitz, 1972).

Consistent with the notion of selfless action, Clark and Mills (1979) and Clark (1981) have distinguished "communal" relationships from exchange relationships. The distinguishing factor is the rules governing the exchanges, not the content of the exchanges. The exchange relationship, as they define it, assumes a reciprocity/quid pro quo character wherein obligations are incurred and discharged fairly proximal to one another. In contrast, a communal relationship assumes each person is concerned about the welfare of the other and has a positive attitude about benefiting the other. The communal relationship involves an expectation of a long-term relationship not necessarily present in exchange relationships. Clark and Mills (1979) do not assume that persons are necessarily conscious of the distinctions between the two types of relationships.

Clark (1981) conducted three studies which demonstrated that different rules apply to communal and exchange relationships. Concluding that persons in intimate relationships may become upset if they see tit-for-tat exchanges developing in a relationship (because reciprocity implies a formal, less-valued association), she also argued against equity theory as an explanation of her findings that noncomparable benefits are exchanged among intimates, because keeping track of equitable balance in an ongoing intimate relationship would be a formidable task. It seems more likely, according to Clark, that the partners have an implicit agreement to be responsive to one another's needs. Carrying these ideas one step further, some theorists believe that the reciprocity or economic/power model actually harms intimate relationships and may only appear as the communal relationship deteriorates (Clark & Mills, 1979; Greenberg, 1980; Huston & Burgess, 1979; Murstein et al., 1977).

Similar to the notion of communal relationship is the concept of "bonds of indebtedness" (Ahrens, 1981). According to Ahrens, there is a "conferred exchange" process wherein the human infant/child receives benefits long before he or she can reciprocate. This process predisposes that child to respond to these bonds of indebtedness in future adult intimacy. She asserts that the prime movers in forming and adjusting human relationships are not just pleasure or profit seeking, but also the creation of a secure setting as a basis for social predictability and the building of a consistent basis for self expression (Ahrens, 1981).

In his review of the research and his development of a theory of indebtedness, Greenberg (1980) suggested that *(a)* indebtedness increases when the donor is perceived as altruistic; *(b)* its magnitude is a result of the recipient's perception of net benefits received, perception of cost to donor, and perception of his or her own needs; *(c)* indebtedness increases when the recipient has requested or pleaded; and *(d)* when objective reality is ambiguous, the recipient relies on social reality to determine indebtedness.

Two aspects of indebtedness theory are particularly relevant to families. First, indebtedness is usually accompanied by negative affect. Second, across cultures, debts to parents and family are among those that cannot be repaid; such debts are simply too great. These two aspects of indebtedness may partially explain the intense love/hate relationships found in some conflict-ridden families.

An integration. How can these competing models of social exchange be integrated? Huesmann and Levinger (1976), Kelley (1979), Kelley and Thibaut (1978), and Levinger and Huesmann (1980) have made admirable attempts in that direction. Kelley and Thibaut's theory focuses on interdependence, mutual responsiveness to one another's outcomes, and attribution. The mechanism for viewing interaction between partners is the matrix. Kelley and Thibaut readily admit that a matrix concept is limiting in that it offers the objective rather than subjective view of the interaction and is a static concept. However, what has been needed is a strong objective predictor which is quantifiable in couples' research. Kelley and Thibaut maintain that persons in relationships take a given situation and evaluate its outcome for themselves as individuals. Then they transform the given situation and consider the outcome for the partner and for the relationship. This concept of outcomes reflects the social exchange notions of costs, rewards, and comparison levels. Having established that both prosocial and egoistic transformations occur in personal relationships, Kelley (1979) then posited that they occur on two levels: behavioral and cognitive. He specifies the processes of the symbolic level of functioning as providing a fulfillment in relationships, whereas at the behavioral level, the partners are more concerned with the practicality of their functioning together.

Kelley and Thibaut (1978) and Kelley (1979) have thus effectively integrated exchange and attribution theory; in addition, they have brought together the disparate views of types of exchange. They have enumerated many types of exchange interactions and have noted when and how each might develop in an intimate relationship. They have suggested that it is no more desirable to make prosocial transformations (equity theory, communal exchange) than to make egoistic ones (quid pro quo, power) in response to every situation in an intimate relationship. The point is that it is adaptive for persons to be able to do both, depending upon the situation. In other words, they have argued that it is not either/or but both types of exchange that are required in a personal relationship. Kelley and Thibaut (1978) and Kelley (1979) imply that, though egoistic transformations are a necessary aspect of such relationships, they occur in an overall context of regard for the partner *and* the relationship.

Levinger and Huesmann (1980) described exchange as occurring developmentally and at both the behavioral and the relational levels, which approximate Kelley's (1979) behavioral and symbolic levels. Though theorists have focused primarily on the behavioral level, "higher social rewards frequently result from a state of being, rather than from behaving; one feels rewarded merely from being competent, being accepted, worthwhile, or secure" (Levinger, 1977, p. 174). Relational rewards are pegged to the actor's level of relational involvement. Unlike behavioral rewards, which are received in discrete quanta, relational rewards are received continuously as long as the level of the relationship remains unchanged.

Some relational rewards are direct, such as immediate pleasure, and others are attributional. Attributional rewards arise from one's own or others' interpretation of what has happened. They are difficult to measure, as they may require a lengthy sequence of behaviors and outcomes. Using Kelley and Thibaut's (1978) outcome model, Levinger and Huesmann (1980) suggested that partners who discover a high payoff correspondence are likely to move forward to deeper involvement.

The various aspects of social exchange theory can serve explanatory, sensitizing, organizing, and integrating functions for studying interpersonal relationships (Gergen, 1980). Its critics have accused social exchange proponents of being individualistic, treating people as commodities, and being too abstract. Especially in the family, nonrational factors may tend to overwhelm exchange tendencies (Holman & Burr, 1980). However, social exchange theory sensitizes us to the issues of interdependency of all people and makes explicit that "self-interest is best served by an interest in the collectivity. . . . Only at the most superficial level does exchange theory favor social alienation" (Gergen, 1980, p. 279). Perhaps, then, we need for others to follow the leads of Kelley, Thibaut, and Levinger in probing the various levels of interdependent exchanges if we are to use the theory in family psychology.

SOCIAL PSYCHOLOGICAL RESEARCH ON THE FAMILY

In an effort to either substantiate or refute the charges leveled against social psychologists regarding their neglect of the family, we conducted a review of five major journals in which social psychologists publish, from 1968 to the present. They are: *Journal of Personality and Social Psychology, Journal of Social Psychology, Social Psychology Quarterly, Journal of Social Issues,* and *Personality and Social Psychology Bulletin.* Since the *Journal of Social Issues* is a multidisciplinary publication, we selected only those articles authored by social psychologists. The areas of content which emerged are *(a)* marriage and divorce, *(b)* parent-child relations, *(c)* adolescence, and *(d)* family structure. We omitted cross-cultural studies, since those are more anthropological in nature. The studies are described by methodology as well as content. Before any of the specific content areas are described, we briefly review the types of methodology used in social psychology.

Methodology

Although there is an increasing emphasis on studies of family interaction in their homes (e.g., McHale & Huston, in press), most social psychological research relevant to the family has involved undergraduate students who participate to fulfill a requirement of an introductory psychology course. Probably the most common methodology is the attitudinal questionnaire. With this type of procedure, subjects are called on to give their attitudes about another person they have just met or whom they know only through an indication of the other person's attitudes on some other issues (e.g., Byrne, 1971). In addition to attitudinal questionnaires, social psychologists have also created situations in which they can observe subjects' behavior toward others. In these types of experiments, there is usually some sort of deception involved so that subjects do not try to perform socially desirable behaviors.

Marriage and divorce

Method. In this review, we found 13 studies using observational methods with couples (Birchler, Weiss, & Vincent, 1975; Birsky & Dion, 1978; Doherty & Ryder, 1979; Douglas, 1980; Gottman, Notarius, Markman, Banks, Yoppi, & Rubin, 1976; Knudson, Sommers, & Golding, 1980; Levenson & Gottman, 1983; Levinger, 1964; McCarrick, Manderscheid, & Silbergeld, 1981; Noller, 1980, 1981, 1982; Sabatelli, Buck, & Dreyer, 1982). In addition, six studies used some version of the traditional social psychological experimental laboratory method (Davis

& Martin, 1978; Hill, Blackham, & Crane, 1982; Murstein & Christy, 1976; Price & Vandenberg, 1979; J. A. Ross, 1973; Stone, 1973). Three studies used interview techniques (Bahr & Harvey, 1980; Levinger, 1966b; Levinger & Breedlove, 1966). Thirteen studies used questionnaire measures (Antill, 1983; Barton & Cattell, 1972; Burke, Firth, & McGratta, 1974; Driscoll, Davis, & Lipetz, 1972; Eidelson, 1980; S. S. Hendrick, 1981; Johnson & Leslie, 1982; Levinger & Senn, 1967; Levinger, Senn, & Jorgensen, 1970; Meyer & Pepper, 1977; Rosenblatt & Budd, 1975; Scherf & Kawash, 1976; Winter, Stewart, & McClelland, 1977). Two studies were devoted to developing questionnaire measures (Rubin, 1970; Schumm, Benigas, McCutchen, Griffin, Anderson, Morris, & Race, 1983). Thus, the total number of empirical studies regarding marriage in the five major social psychological journals is 37, a relatively small percentage of the total number of studies reported in these journals.

Empirical studies on divorce or dissolution of unmarried romantic relationships totaled four. One was an archival study (Levinger, 1966a) and three were questionnaire studies (Hill, Rubin, & Peplau, 1976; Kulka & Weingarten, 1979; Rockwell, Elder, & Ross, 1979). There were also three reviews (Levinger, 1965; Moles & Levinger, 1976; Levitin, 1979) and one theoretical article (Levinger & Moles, 1976).

Content.   Levinger has proposed a three-level model of involvement in relationships (Levinger, 1974; Levinger & Snoek, 1972). Level 1 is a unilateral awareness of another; level 2 is surface contact; and level 3 is mutuality, wherein two persons respond to each other as unique individuals. Levinger (1974) has argued that there are few studies at level 3 for two reasons: (a) it is not possible to create this level artificially, and (b) deep relationships are complex, making it more difficult to disentangle the causal variables. Consequently, most social psychological studies are conducted at levels 1 and 2.

Levinger (1977) discussed four different perspectives on the close relationship: the individual, the dyad, the group, and the society. This seems a coherent framework within which to organize the empirical studies in this review. If we believe the criticisms of social psychology by Sampson (1977), Pepitone (1981), and L'Abate and Thaxton (1983), then we would predict that most of the social psychological studies on marriage and divorce would focus primarily on the individual in the relationship rather than on the relationship itself. In fact, this is the case. Studies are included in this category because they take some measurement on the individuals in the relationship, usually separately, and do not treat the relationship as the unit of measurement and analysis. These individual measures may be opinions about the relationship. Thus, studies that involve each person's perception of the relationship are included here, but not those wherein the relationship itself is observed and measured. Three studies focused on only one individual in the relationship and did not include the partner in any way. One study, using interview techniques, focused on adjustment of young widows several months after the deaths of the husbands. Results indicated education and income predicted good morale (Bahr & Harvey, 1980). Eidelson (1980) focused on individuals as they evaluated five different friendships. Results showed that interpersonal satisfaction increases initially in relationships, declines at intermediate levels of involvement, and rises again at higher levels of involvement. Rockwell et al. (1979) conducted a longitudinal study of 83 women who had married in the 1940s or early 1950s at either a young age or at the norm for that time, age 20–22. They measured six personality dimensions at adolescence and at age 40. Results showed that personal growth from adolescence to midlife characterized the psychological functioning of both young brides and the women who subsequently divorced.

The remaining 18 studies focusing on the individual took measures from each partner and then evaluated the discrepancies and/or correlated them with other measures (Antill, 1983; Barton & Cattell, 1972; Burke et al., 1974; S. S. Hendrick, 1981; C. T. Hill et al., 1976; Johnson & Leslie, 1982; Levinger, 1966a, 1966b; Levinger & Breedlove, 1966; Levinger & Senn, 1967; Levinger, Senn, & Jorgensen, 1970; Meyer & Pepper, 1977; Murstein & Christy, 1976; Noller, 1981; Price & Vandenberg, 1979; Rosenblatt & Budd, 1975; Scherf & Kawash, 1976; Winter et al., 1977).

Variables of interest included personality dimensions, stress, relationship satisfaction and involvement, complaints of couples applying for divorce, distortion in spouses' reports of preferred and actual sexual behavior, interpersonal attraction and agreement, disclosure of feelings in marriage, value consensus and need complementarity, need compatibility, communication, territoriality, androgyny, couple withdrawal, and husband's power motives as per wife's career level.

Those studies dealing with the dyad as the unit of study were largely observational in method. Birchler et al. (1975), Douglas (1980), and Gottman et al. (1976) investigated marital interaction from the social learning/behavioral viewpoint. Nonverbal as well as verbal communication were studied (Birsky & Dion, 1978; Levenson & Gottman, 1983; Noller, 1980, 1982; Sabatelli et al., 1982). Knudson et al. (1980) investigated interpersonal perception between spouses and their mode of approaching conflict as a couple. Assertiveness and locus of control within the dyad were examined by Doherty and Ryder (1979). Levinger (1964) tested the Bales proposition that task and social roles were divided between husband and wife respectively. He found that task performance is specialized, while social behavior in marriage is a mutual matter.

Three other studies of the dyadic relationship come under the rubric of traditional social psychological laboratory experimentation (Davis & Martin, 1978; R. D. Hill et al., 1982; Stone, 1973). With the exception of Hill et al.'s on personal space, these laboratory manipulations did not yield as rich or as useful data as the observational methodology used in the other studies.

Focusing on the group context in which the couple is embedded, we found only four studies. Johnson and Leslie (1982) investigated the dyadic withdrawal hypothesis, finding that couples selectively withdrew from portions of their social network. Friendships decreased in number and level of involvement at marriage. Some couples increased involvement with kin, others decreased it. Disclosure to kin did not decrease dramatically, but importance of kin opinions did decrease sharply after marriage. Driscoll, Davis, and Lipetz (1972) investigated parental interference and romantic love, finding that they were highly correlated. However, such interference by parents also fostered increased criticalness, bothersome behaviors, and decreased trust within the couple. In a third one, long-term effects of parental divorce on adult adjustment were less than would be expected (Kulka & Weingarten, 1979). The fourth study observed gender differences in competition and dominance during married couples' group therapy. Findings indicate more indiscriminate competition between males than females. Although females compete with males under certain conditions, males do not compete with females. Instead, they dominate, i.e., interrupt. Females were also found to be somewhat more submissive with their husbands than with the other males (McCarrick et al., 1981). Though these studies of couples' group context are by far the fewest in number, they are among the most interesting and creative in the review.

Parent-child relations

Method. We found 27 studies which were classified as dealing with how parents and children might be affecting each other. Six of the studies used observation as part of the methodology (Kraut & Price, 1976; Lott, 1978; Lytton, Conway, & Sauve, 1977; Randall, 1981; Seashore, Leifer, Barnett, & Leiderma, 1973; Tower, 1980). Kraut and Price, Lott, and Seashore et al. also used questionnaire measures. Lytton et al. used interviews and a lab experiment as well as the observational methodology, while Tower supplemented observations with ratings and psychological tests.

Three of the studies employed interviewing as a primary means of data collection, supplementing with a questionnaire (Hoffman, 1975; McClelland & Pilon, 1983; Ra, 1977). Nine others used the questionnaire as the main method of gathering data (Becker & Cross, 1977;

Busse, Busse, & Busse, 1979; Dielman, Barton, & Cattell, 1973; Kraut & Lewis, 1975; Li, 1974; Miller, 1972; Nijhawan & Verma, 1975; Prasad, Sinha, & Prasad, 1979; Sivern & Nakamura, 1973). The total number of studies using questionnaires in this topic area is 14, about half of the studies.

Only four studies employed experimental laboratory methods in data collection. Three involved compliance of the mother to advice regarding her child. Crisci and Kassinove (1973) manipulated level of expertise of the professional helper, strength of advice given, and setting to test their effects on mothers' posttesting compliance to their suggestions about the child. J. A. Ross (1973) used expert status versus peer status as the independent variable in a similar study on compliance of mothers. Expert status prevailed over race as well as referent group. However, the variable of gender confounds the results. Wasserman and Kassinove (1976) used type of recommendation, attire of psychologist, and perceived expertise of the psychologist as the independent variables. The fourth experimental study involved teaching mothers how to teach cognitive and perceptual skills to their preschool children. A control group did not receive the treatment. Both groups of children were given pretests and posttests for cognitive and perceptual skills. Results showed that mothers could be taught to increase these skills in their children (Coleman, Ganong, & Brown, 1981).

One longitudinal study used IQ and personality tests with all available adopted and biological children in 300 families which had adopted children, as well as scores on the same tests which had previously been collected during pregnancy on the unwed mothers of the adopted-out children (Loehlin, Willerman, & Horn, 1982). Another study was a validation of a scale, the Family Attitude Measure (Barton, Dielman, & Cattell, 1973).

Content. Of the 27 studies dealing with parent-child relations, 11 dealt only with the mother and one child, adhering to the tradition of much developmental research. Content of these studies included mother's compliance to expert advice (Crisci & Kassinove, 1973; J. A. Ross, 1973; Wasserman & Kassinove, 1976), effects of observers on mother's behavior in the laboratory (Randall, 1981), effects of teaching mothers to teach their preschool children cognitive and perceptual skills (Coleman et al., 1981), mother's response and child's self-concept (Miller, 1972), mother's attitudes and child's achievement motivation (Li, 1974), and television viewing patterns of mothers of small infants (Hollenbeck, 1978).

Three longitudinal studies were particularly noteworthy. Seashore et al. (1973) studied the effects of early mother-infant separation on the mother's self-confidence as a caretaker. Questionnaire and observational data were obtained on four occasions for mothers of premature infants ranging from the neonate stage to one month postdischarge. A control group was also used. The early separation affected primiparous mothers negatively, but not multiparous mothers. McClelland and Pilon (1983) conducted an interesting follow-up to the original Sears, Maccoby, and Levin (1957) interviews of mothers. They collected questionnaire, test, and interview data on 118 of the children (at ages 31–32) whose mothers had participated in the 1951 study. McClelland and Pilon were looking for what specific parent practices contribute to which social motives in the grown child, e.g., achievement, affiliation, intimacy, and power. The questions were only partly answered. Scheduled feeding and severe toilet training predicted high achievement motives in the children. Children permitted some freedom in expressing sexual and agressive urges had higher power motives. Permissiveness in other areas had no such effect. However, the authors caution against overinterpretation of these results because only 10–30 percent of the variance in adult motives could be accounted for by these childhood variables. A third longitudinal study compared personality test scores of unwed mothers during pregnancy with scores of their adopted-away offspring when the children were at least three years old (Loehlin et al., 1982). There was a tendency for the adopted children to be more extroverted and emotionally stable than their biological siblings in the adoptive families. Extroversion of unwed mother and adopted-away child was similar. On the variable of emotional stability, however, there was a negative correlation between unwed mother and adopted-away child. The authors make a case for a genetic influence on personality which seems unwarranted from their results.

At the individual level, staying with Levinger's levels of analysis, seven of the studies involving parent-child relations took measures on either the child(ren) or both parents, but not both. Barton et al. (1973) validated the Family Attitude Measure, using only parents. Dielman et al. (1973) factor analyzed a questionnaire on parenting completed by parents of junior high school students. The remaining studies at the individual level collected data only from the child. Topics included college men's perceptions of women via memories of parents (Becker & Cross, 1977), students' and parents' political views (Kraut & Lewis, 1975; Silvern & Nakamura, 1973), parental attitudes and need achievement (Prasad et al., 1979), and naming of children (Busse et al., 1979). All were questionnaire studies except Becker and Cross, which included a laboratory stimulus as well as a questionnaire.

The remaining studies on parent-child relations took measures from both the parents and one child in the family. Because the unit of study was not the group—i.e., the family—we classify these studies at the dyadic level: parents and child. The real unit of interest in these studies was the child, not the family system. In one study, the parents provided ratings on the child as additional data on child attachment to the television (Ra, 1977). Other studies with similar emphasis on the child sought factors in the parents' behavior or attitude to correlate with or explain the child's behavior. Topics included parental sex typing as per child's creativity (Lott, 1978), parental attitude toward altruism as per child's observed behavior (Hoffman, 1975), parental authoritarian attitudes as per child's conservative or democratic attitudes (Nijhawan & Verma, 1975), parental Machiavellianism scores as per child's Machiavellian behavior on an observed task (Kraut & Price, 1976), and parental self-concepts as per child's behavior (Tower, 1980). The most impressive study of this group actually investigated parent-child interaction, using observation (Lytton et al., 1977). Twin boys at 2½ years had fewer verbal exchanges with parents than singleton 2½ year olds and fewer demonstrations of affection. The authors explained the twins' lower verbal facility by the parents' reduced speech.

Two articles were theoretical. Bardwick (1974) proposed an ethological analysis of parenting behavior, and Russo (1976) examined a proposed cultural mandate to have two children.

Adolescence

Method.   Of the six studies in this category, two used some laboratory experimental design (Fodor, 1972; Klos & Singer, 1981; see also Jurkovic and Ulrici, Chapter 7 of this *Handbook*). One used interviews (Fox & Inazu, 1980). Three used questionnaires (Jackson, 1980; Miller, 1976; Scarr, Webber, Weinberg, & Wittig, 1981).

Content.   Two of the six studies gathered data only from the adolescent. Fodor (1972) used a laboratory situation and a questionnaire to examine cheating and perceived style of parental discipline. Klos and Singer (1981) used college students in a laboratory situation of improvised conflict with parents. The remaining four studies used measures from the adolescent and one or both parents. Miller (1976) examined adolescent self-esteem as per facilitative skills of the mother. Jackson (1980) studied female undergraduates' valuation of marriage and career as per parental ideology. Scarr et al. (1981) examined personality similarity between adolescents and their parents in a study on biological versus adoptive families. This study concluded that most of the variance in personality is not accounted for by either genetic or environmental factors, but by individual differences within the same family. Thus, the experience of siblings within the same family must be sufficiently different so that personality development proceeds quite differently. This finding is of import to those who contemplate the relationship between the individual and the family system. Another study of great relevance is one in which both mother and adolescent daughter were interviewed separately regarding attitudinal and behavioral aspects of sexuality and their communication regarding sexuality (Fox & Inazu, 1980). Higher frequencies of current communication were associated with more responsible patterns of daughters' sexual behavior.

Family structure

Method. Eight studies in the review examined some aspect of family structure. Of these, two used laboratory manipulation of variables (Fink, Rey, Johnson, Spenner, Morton, & Flores, 1975; Maceachron & Gruenfeld, 1978). Three used observational methods (Clingempeel, 1981; Deutsch, 1983; Hadley & Jacob, 1973). Two used questionnaires to collect data (Grotevant, Scarr, & Weinberg, 1977; Miller & Rose, 1982). One was an archival study which reanalyzed questionnaire, self-report, and test data collected in 1968 (Tesser, 1980).

Content. The individual level of analysis was employed in four of the studies. Deutsch (1983) observed 35 first-born preschoolers in a study of single-parent families. Fink et al. (1975) and Maceachron and Gruenfeld (1978) used family occupational type, family authority structure, and socioeconomic status as independent variables in a laboratory experiment using individual subjects. Tesser (1980) reanalyzed test data from undergraduates to test a self-esteem maintenance model.

The dyad (i.e., marital quality) was the unit of analysis in a study of blended families (Clingempeel, 1981). Partial families were the subjects in the remaining three studies. Miller and Rose (1982) used twins and their parents in a study of familial resemblance of internal-external locus of control. Pair-wise resemblance was assessed for twins, spouses, and single-parent offspring, making this actually a dyadic unit of analysis. Adolescent children and their parents were the unit of analysis in a study of interest similarity in adoptive and biological families (Grotevant et al., 1977). Another study using adolescent males and their parents examined family power (Hadley & Jacob, 1973).

Summary

It is clear from the review that, though their major emphasis during the last 15 years has not been the family, neither have social psychologists ignored it as they have been charged with doing. Certainly, family therapists would prefer to see more interactional research which focuses on the characteristics of the family system, not on those of individuals. Perhaps they would also implore social psychologists to investigate the processes and outcomes of family therapy.

Riskin and Faunce (1972), in a review of family interaction research, indicated several characteristics which might well be applied to the social psychological family research we have reviewed:

1.   Striking interdisciplinary isolation in family interaction research, with investigators seemingly unaware of others' work and continuing to use outdated, inadequate techniques. The charge of isolationism, which has earlier been leveled against social psychology vis à vis the family, takes on a new perspective as we see that this lack of continuity and cooperation is a problem for the family field in general.

2.   Lack of replication. This is also the case with the social psychologists' work, probably because they are so recently into the family field that they have not yet replicated studies.

3.   A lack of comparable sample populations. This was less the case with social psychologists, since (more often than not) their entry into the family has been through a college student.

4.   A family-based nosology was beginning. This is not the case for social psychologists, who largely focus on the individual vis à vis the family group.

5.   Sloppiness in methodology. This was not the case overall in the social psychological studies. A complaint which might be lodged instead is that of relevance of the research question.

6.   Much of the research involved parents only or parents and one child, rather than complete families. The social psychologists fall prey to the same shortcoming for the same reasons: inaccessibility of families and difficulty in measuring them.

OTHER RESEARCH

In addition to the theories and empirical work described above, there are other topics of research in social psychology that are relevant to the family. Three such topics that are worthy of mention are interpersonal attraction, the confluence model of children's intellectual development, and self-esteem maintenance in the family.

Interpersonal attraction

The social psychological literature on liking and loving is extensive and can only briefly be summarized here. One of the most dominant factors affecting two individuals' liking for one another is their proximity to one another (Festinger, Schachter, & Back, 1950). Individuals who come into contact with one another more often are more likely to discover that they have similar attitudes and beliefs (Newcomb, 1961). In addition, merely seeing others more frequently may lead to increased liking because of the "mere exposure effect" (Zajonc, 1968). Based on both experimental and correlational evidence, it appears that with novel stimuli of all sorts (faces, Turkish words, Chinese ideographs) the more often they are shown the more they are liked.

A second group of factors relevant to liking relates to characteristics of the stimulus person. One of these characteristics is physical attractiveness (Berscheid & Walster, 1974). Across a number of studies, results have shown that physically attractive people are preferred as dates, are judged more likely to possess desirable traits (e.g., intelligence, sociability, success, competence), and appear to bring increased ratings on these and similar variables to those with whom they are connected in a romantic relationship (Sigall & Landy, 1973).

In addition to physical attractiveness, work by Byrne (1971) and his colleagues indicates that people are attracted to individuals who hold similar attitudes, beliefs, and values. Work by Byrne suggests that the proportion of similar attitudes may be more important than the absolute number. Most of Byrne's work has been conducted with college students who are given attitude questionnaires ostensibly filled out by another student and who are then asked to rate how much they like the person who allegedly completed the attitude questionnaire. Nevertheless, the finding that similarity leads to attraction has been replicated in experimental studies with children, with elderly individuals, and in other countries.

A third factor about the stimulus person concerns how much that person likes us. Not surprisingly, subjects in experiments who were evaluated highly by the stimulus person rated that person higher than did subjects who were evaluated less highly (Byrne & Rhamey, 1965). This finding also seems to be true when the stimulus person shows a gradual change in evaluation from disapproval to approval (Aronson & Linder, 1965).

The confluence model

One of the most interesting areas of work by social psychologists concerns the relationship between family size, spacing between children, and the intellectual development of the children. According to the confluence model of Zajonc (1976, 1983; Zajonc & Markus, 1976; Zajonc, Markus, & Markus, 1979), a child's intellectual development is a result of the changing "average intellectual environment" of the family. The model predicts that a child will have lower intellectual attainment if his or her family is larger, if the gap between siblings is smaller, and if he or she does not have the opportunity to teach a younger sibling. The model has received support (e.g., Berbaum & Moreland, 1980) but is not without its critics (e.g., Ernst & Angst, 1983; Galbraith, 1982; Grotevant et al., 1977). Recent research has focused on sex differences in how family size affects intellectual growth (e.g., Paulhus & Shaffer, 1981; Steelman & Mercy, 1983).

Self-esteem maintenance

Tesser (1980) has argued that a family member's self-esteem is an interactive function of three factors: *(a)* how psychologically close the other member is to the family member (i.e., the extent to which the two belong together), *(b)* how well the other member performs on some dimension, and *(c)* how relevant the dimension is (i.e., the extent to which the family member defines himself or herself based on this ability). According to Tesser, if the "other" does very well and the relationship is close, the family member will have higher self-esteem through basking in reflected glory. On the other hand, if the other does very well and the relationship is close, the family member may have lower self-esteem because he or she looks worse by comparison. Whether reflection or comparison processes are invoked depends on how relevant the dimension is. Tesser argued that comparison processes are likely to be important when relevance is high. Thus, a good performance by other threatens self-esteem, particularly when the relationship is close. In contrast, reflection processes are likely to be important when relevance is low. Thus, a good performance by other should bolster the family member's self-esteem, particularly when the relationship is close.

According to Tesser, individuals act so as to maintain their self-esteem. Thus, if their self-esteem is threatened, they can reduce the relevance of an ability, decrease their closeness to other, interfere with other's performance, or do some combination of these three. Tesser has tested his model, using both experimental and correlational methods. One of the more interesting tests was an analysis of biographical data from 25 famous male scientists and their fathers. The model would predict that, if the father and the son were in similar occupations (high relevance), their relationship should be distant, whereas if they were in dissimilar occupations (low relevance), their relationship should be close. The data were consistent with this prediction.

IMPLICATIONS FOR THERAPY AND RESEARCH

In this final section, we suggest how social and family psychology both can benefit from the application of social psychological knowledge to the family. Implications for therapy are discussed first, followed by a discussion of implications for research.

Implications for therapy

Social psychology is relevant to family therapists because *(a)* mental and emotional problems are often problems in interpersonal behavior and *(b)* therapy is a social interaction between the therapist and the client(s) (Gurman & Kniskern, 1981; C. Hendrick, 1983). Because it is the discipline centrally concerned with human interaction, social psychology provides the basis for constructs in psychotherapy. Family therapists have increasingly employed social psychological theory as they have developed relationship-oriented methods of psychotherapy (C. Hendrick). Though most of the theory in family therapy is derived from general systems theory, the underpinnings are clearly related to social psychological principles, even if not expressed in those terms. Moreover, novel ways of conceptualizing the family therapy process can be expected from social psychologists who are interested in the family because they are "behind the mirror," looking in, whereas the therapist is inside the room, involved in the emotional, phenomenological field.

One of the most important ways that family therapists can use social psychological knowledge is in terms of attributional questions: *(a)* to divert attention from influence processes so the client believes he or she is changing spontaneously because of some inner desire and thereby can save face (Strong & Claiborn, 1982), *(b)* to help the family understand the attribution process (Kelley, 1979), and *(c)* to cause the family to reattribute causes for behavior in the family (Barton & Alexander, 1981). Therapists have coined their own terms for these procedures: *paradoxical intention* and *reframing.* Barton and Alexander consider reattribution to be the central theme of family therapy: "Family members cannot change their behavior until they change their view of themselves and other family members" (p. 421). The change they strive for is relabeling person attributions as interpersonal or situational, thus reversing the emotional valence of the attributions in the process.

Implications for research

In addition to its theoretical contribution to family therapy, social psychology can also offer much in terms of research on both the outcome and the process of family therapy. Gurman and Kniskern (1981) have suggested several areas that need attention in terms of comparative-outcome research (the effectiveness of individual versus cotherapists, the effectiveness of individual versus family therapy). In his review of family therapy process research, Pinsof (1981) suggested the use of sequential interaction analysis. Social psychologists have the methodological tools to answer these questions raised by family therapists. In addition to studying the process of family interaction, it may also be useful to study the process of attributional negotiation—how, for instance, a couple's conversation proceeds regarding their different attributions for one or both members' behaviors.

Most studies of attributions in families have involved attributions for negative behavior. More research needs to be conducted on the process of how these negative attributions are made, the role that affect plays (Fincham & O'Leary, 1983), and the implications they have for separation (Harvey, et al., 1978). In addition, more work is needed on how a couple's production of positive versus negative attributions relate to effective decision making and other aspects of well-functioning families. It has also been suggested that social psychologists should study the everyday speech and behavior of individuals to understand folk attributions and social rules (e.g., Kroger, 1982). "Ethogeny," as this approach is known, is currently a popular technique in Europe and may be particularly applicable to the study of the family.

Another implication of social psychology for family therapy is the extent to which research on families affects relationships in the family. It may be that simply completing questionnaires and being asked to think about the structure and dynamics of the family affects the family. Rubin and Mitchell (1976) reported that almost 90 percent of the couples in their research discussed their answers to the questions they completed, although almost 80 percent of the couples stated that the study did not affect the degree of cohesiveness in their relationship. Although there are ethical questions raised by conducting research with families, it is possible that such research may be useful for therapists.

A recent book has remedied many of the past criticisms that social psychologists have not seriously examined the family. In their book, Kelley, Berscheid, Christensen, Harvey, Huston, Levinger, McClintock, Peplau, & Peterson (1983) proposed a framework for analyzing close relationships that can serve to integrate the seemingly disparate research that has been conducted. The framework provides for examining events in interaction (affect, cognition, and behavior), descriptive properties of the interaction, internal causal dynamics (both intra- and interpersonal), external causal conditions, and causal links among the conditions, as well as between them and events. This framework is one within which investigators can locate their particular problems, highlighting conceptual and methodological issues that are common in research on interpersonal relationships: *(a)* causal loops, *(b)* causal processes within dyadic interaction, *(c)* distal versus proximal analysis of causation, and *(d)* downward versus upward causal links.

Implications for social psychology

Although the benefits of a partnership between social and family psychology might seem to be greater for family researchers and therapists, social psychologists will also gain from such research. Families are not only different from college student populations, they are also likely to be more diverse. Thus, research with families is likely to promote the development of theory that has both greater breadth and depth than is now possible. Moreover, since social psychology as a discipline is becoming more of an applied science (C. Hendrick, 1983), research on the family and interactions with family therapists could help maintain its viability and expand its realm of influence. Both social psychology and family psychology share a number of common interests. Joint ventures could benefit both areas if we can overcome artificial divisions between clinical and social psychology (Harari, 1983).

REFERENCES

Ahrens, A. "Conferred exchange" and the intrinsic rewards of family life—A functional expansion of social exchange theory. In *Theory and Methods Preconference Workshop.* Workshop conducted at the annual conference of the National Council on Family Relations, October 1981.

Allport, G. W. The historical background of modern social psychology. In G. Lindzey & E. Aronson (Eds.), *The handbook of social psychology* (Vol. 1). Reading, Mass.: Addison-Wesley Publishing, 1968.

Antill, J. K. Sex role complementarity vs. similarity in married couples. *Journal of Personality and Social Psychology,* 1983, *45,* 145–155.

Aronson, E., & Linder, D. Gain and loss of esteem as determinants of interpersonal attractiveness. *Journal of Experimental Psychology,* 1965, *1,* 156–171.

Bagarozzi, D. A., & Wodarski, J. S. A social exchange typology of conjugal relationships and conflict development. *Journal of Marriage and Family Counseling,* 1977, *3,* 53–60.

Bahr, H. M., & Harvey, C. D. Correlates of morale among the newly widowed. *Journal of Social Psychology,* 1980, *110,* 219–233.

Bardwick, J. M. Evolution and parenting. *Journal of Social Issues,* 1974, *30* (4), 39–62.

Barton, C., & Alexander, J. F. Functional family therapy. In A. S. Gurman & D. P. Kniskern (Eds.), *Handbook of family therapy.* New York: Brunner/Mazel, 1981.

Barton, K., & Cattell, R. B. Marriage dimensions and personality. *Journal of Personality and Social Psychology,* 1972, *21,* 369.

Barton, K., Dielman, T. E., & Cattell, R. B. Item factor analysis of intrafamilial attitudes of parents. *Journal of Social Psychology*, 1973, *90*, 67–72.

Becker, M. R., & Cross, H. J. College men's perception of women and memories of their parents. *Personality and Social Psychology Bulletin*, 1977, *3*, 450–453.

Berbaum, M. L., & Moreland, R. L. Intellectual development within the family: A new application of the confluence model. *Developmental Psychology*, 1980, *16*, 506–515.

Berkowitz, L. Resistance to improper dependency relationships. *Journal of Experimental Social Psychology*, 1969, *5*, 283–294.

Berkowitz, L. Social norms, feelings and other factors affecting helping behavior and altruism. In L. Berkowitz (Ed.), *Advances in experimental social psychology* (Vol. 6). New York: Academic Press, 1972.

Berkowitz, L., & Daniels, L. R. Responsibility and dependency. *Journal of Abnormal and Social Psychology*, 1963, *66*, 429–436.

Berscheid, E., & Walster, E. Physical attractiveness. In L. Berkowitz (Ed.), *Advances in experimental social psychology* (Vol. 7). New York: Academic Press, 1974.

Birchler, G. R., Weiss, R. L., & Vincent, J. P. Multimethod analysis of social reinforcement exchange between maritally distressed and nondistressed spouse and stranger dyads. *Journal of Personality and Social Psychology and Supplement*, 1975, *31*, 349–360.

Birsky, J. E., & Dion, K. K. Affect and nonverbal behavior in couples—power of liking. *Personality and Social Psychology Bulletin*, 1978, *4*, 349.

Blau, P. M. *Exchange and power in social life*. New York: John Wiley & Sons, 1964.

Bowlby, J. *Attachment and loss* (Vol. I). New York: Basic Books, 1969.

Brown, A. H. A use of social exchange theory in family crisis intervention. *Journal of Marriage and Family Counseling*, 1975, *1*, 259–267.

Burke, R. J., Firth, J., & McGratta, C. Husband-wife compatibility and management of stress. *Journal of Social Psychology*, 1974, *94*, 243–252.

Busse, T. V., Busse, K., & Busse, M. Identical first names for parent and child. *Journal of Social Psychology*, 1979, *107*, 293–294.

Byrne, D. *The attraction paradigm*. New York: Academic Press, 1971.

Byrne, D., & Rhamey, R. Magnitude of positive and negative reinforcements as a determinant of attraction. *Journal of Personality and Social Psychology*, 1965, *2*, 884–889.

Clark, M. S. Noncomparability of benefits given and received: A cue to the existence of friendship. *Social Psychology Quarterly*, 1981, *44*, 375–381.

Clark, M. S., & Mills, J. Interpersonal attraction in exchange and communal relationships. *Journal of Personality and Social Psychology*, 1979, *37*, 12–24.

Clingempeel, W. G. Quasi-kin relationships and marital quality in stepfather families. *Journal of Personality and Social Psychology*, 1981, *41*, 890–901.

Coleman, M., Ganong, L., & Brown, G. E. Effects of multi-media instruction on mother's ability to teach cognitive skills to pre-school children. *Journal of Social Psychology*, 1981, *115*, 89–94.

Crisci, R., & Kassinov, H. Effect of perceived expertise, strength of advice, and environmental setting on parental compliance. *Journal of Social Psychology*, 1973, *89*, 245–250.

Davis, D., & Martin, H. J. When pleasure begets pleasure—recipient responsiveness as a determinant of physical pleasuring between heterosexual dating couples and strangers. *Journal of Personality and Social Psychology,* 1978, *36,* 767–777.

Deutsch, F. Classroom social participation of preschoolers in single-parent families. *Journal of Social Psychology,* 1983, *119,* 77–84.

Dielman, T. E., Barton, K., & Cattell, R. B. Cross-validational evidence on structure of parental reports of child rearing practices. *Journal of Social Psychology,* 1973, *90,* 243–250.

Doherty, W. J. Attribution style and negative problem solving in marriage. *Family Relations,* 1982, *31,* 23–27.

Doherty, W. J., & Ryder, R. G. Locus of control, interpersonal trust, and assertive behavior among newlyweds. *Journal of Personality and Social Psychology,* 1979, *12,* 2212–2220.

Douglas, M. A. Behavior control by happily-married couples in conflict situations. *Personality and Social Psychology Bulletin,* 1980, *6,* 177.

Driscoll, R., Davis, K. E., & Lipetz, M. E. Parental interference and romantic love—Romeo and Juliet effect. *Journal of Personality and Social Psychology,* 1972, *24,* 1.

Edwards, J. N. Familial behavior as social exchange. *Journal of Marriage and the Family,* 1969, *31,* 518–526.

Eidelson, R. J. Interpersonal satisfaction and level of involvement—curvilinear. *Journal of Personality and Social Psychology,* 1980, *39,* 460–470.

Ernst, C., & Angst, J. *Birth order: Its influence on personalities.* New York: Springer-Verlag, 1983.

Festinger, L., Schachter, S., & Back, K. *Social pressures in informal groups: A study of a housing community.* New York: Harper & Row, 1950.

Fincham, F., & O'Leary, K. D. Causal inferences for spouse behavior in maritally distressed and nondistressed couples. *Journal of Social and Clinical Psychology,* 1983, *1,* 42–57.

Fink, E. L., Rey, L. D., Johnson, K. W., Spenner, K. I., Morton, D. R., & Flores, E. T. Effects of family occupational type, sex, and appeal style on helping behavior. *Journal of Experimental Social Psychology,* 1975, *11,* 43–52.

Foa, E. B., & Foa, U. G. Resource theory: Interpersonal behavior as exchange. In K. J. Gergen, M. S. Greenberg, & R. H. Willis (Eds.), *Social exchange: Advances in theory and research.* New York: Plenum Press, 1980.

Foa, U. G. Interpersonal and economic resources. *Science,* 1971, *171,* 345–351.

Foa, U. G., & Foa, E. B. *Societal structures of the mind.* Springfield, Ill.: Charles C. Thomas, 1974.

Fodor, E. M. Resistance to temptation, moral development, and perceptions of parental behavior among adolescent boys. *Journal of Social Psychology,* 1972, *88,* 155–156.

Forsyth, D. R. *An introduction to group dynamics.* Monterey, Calif.: Brooks/Cole Publishing, 1983.

Fox, G. L., & Inazu, J. K. Patterns and outcomes of mother-daughter communication about sexuality. *Journal of Social Issues,* 1980, *36,* 1, 7–29.

Framo, J. L. Family psychology and intimate contexts: Neglected areas in social psychology. *Society for the Advancement of Social Psychology Newsletter,* April 1982.

Framo, J. L. Systematic research on family dynamics. In I. Boszormenyi-Nagy & J. L. Framo (Eds.), *Intensive family therapy*. New York: Harper & Row, 1965.

Galbraith, R. C. Sibling spacing and intellectual development: A closer look at the confluence models. *Developmental Psychology*, 1982, *18*, 181–191.

Gergen, K. J. Exchange theory: The transient and the enduring. In K. J. Gergen, M. S. Greenberg, & R. H. Willis (Eds.), *Social exchange: Advances in theory and research*. New York: Plenum Press, 1980.

Gottman, J., Notarius, C., Markman, H., Banks, S., Yoppi, B., & Rubin, M. E. Behavior exchange theory and marital decision making. *Journal of Personality and Social Psychology*, 1976, *34*, 14–23.

Greenberg, M. S. A theory of indebtedness. In K. J. Gergen, M. S. Greenberg, & R. H. Willis (Eds.), *Social exchange: Advances in theory and research*. New York: Plenum Press, 1980.

Greenberg, M. S., & Ruback, R. B. *Social psychology of the criminal justice system*. Monterey, Calif.: Brooks/Cole Publishing, 1982.

Grotevant, H. D., Scarr, S., & Weinberg, R. A. Intellectual development in family constellations with adopted and natural children: A test of the Zajonc and Markus model. *Child Development*, 1977, *48*, 1699–1703.

Gurman, A. S., & Kniskern, D. P. Family therapy outcome research: Knowns and unknowns. In A. S. Gurman & D. P. Kniskern (Eds.), *Handbook of Family Therapy*, New York: Brunner/Mazel, 1981. Pp. 742–775.

Hadley, T. R., & Jacob, T. Relationship among measures of family power. *Journal of Personality and Social Psychology*, 1973, *27*, 6–12.

Harari, H. Social psychology *of* clinical practice and *in* clinical practice. *Journal of Social and Clinical Psychology*, 1983, *1*, 173–192.

Harre, R. Ethogeny: Theory and practice. In L. Berkowitz (Ed.), *Advances in experimental social psychology* (Vol. 11). New York: Academic Press, 1977.

Harre, R., & Secord, P. F. Experimentation in psychology. In L. Strickland, F. Aboud, & K. Gergen (Eds.), *Social Psychology in transition*. New York: Plenum Press, 1976.

Harvey, J. H., Ickes, W. J., & Kidd, R. F. (Eds.). *New directions in attribution research* (Vol. 1). Hillsdale, N.J.: Lawrence Erlbaum Associates, 1976.

Harvey, J. H., Ickes, W. J., & Kidd, R. F. (Eds.). *New directions in attribution research* (Vol. 2). Hillsdale, N.J.: Lawrence Erlbaum Associates, 1978.

Harvey, J. H., Ickes, W. J., & Kidd, R. F. (Eds.). *New directions in attribution research* (Vol. 3). Hillsdale, N.J.: Lawrence Erlbaum Associates, 1981.

Harvey, J. H., & Weary, G. *Perspectives on attributional processes*. Dubuque, Iowa: Brown, 1981.

Harvey, J. H., Wells, G. L., & Alvarez, M. D. (Eds.). Attribution in the context of conflict and separation in close relationships. In J. H. Harvey, W. Ickes, & R. F. Kidd (Eds.), *New directions in attribution research* (Vol. 2). Hillsdale, N.J.: Lawrence Erlbaum Associates, 1978.

Hatfield, E., Greenberger, D., Traupmann, J., & Lambert, P. Equity and sexual satisfaction in recently married couples. *Journal of Sex Research*, 1982, *18*, 18–32.

Hatfield, E., Utne, M. K., & Traupmann, J. Equity theory in intimate relationships. In *Social exchange in developing relationships*. New York: Academic Press, 1979.

Heider, F. *The psychology of interpersonal relations.* New York: John Wiley & Sons, 1958.

Hendrick, C. Clinical social psychology: A birthright reclaimed. *Journal of Social and Clinical Psychology,* 1983, *1,* 66–78.

Hendrick, S. S. Self-disclosure and marital satisfaction. *Journal of Personality and Social Psychology,* 1981, *40,* 1150–1159.

Hill, C. T., Rubin, Z., & Peplau, L. A. Breakups before marriage—end of 103 affairs. *Journal of Social Issues,* 1976, *32,* 147–168.

Hill, R., & Hansen, D. A. The identification of conceptual frameworks utilized in family study. *Marriage and Family Living,* November 1960, pp. 299–311.

Hill, R. D., Blackham, R. E., & Crane, D. R. The effect of the marital relationship on personal-space orientation in married couples. *Journal of Social Psychology,* 1982, *118,* 23–28.

Hoffman, M. L. Altruistic behavior and parent-child relationship. *Journal of Personality and Social Psychology,* 1975, *31,* 937–943.

Hollenbeck, A. R. Television viewing patterns of families with young infants. *Journal of Social Psychology,* 1978, *105,* 259–264.

Holman, T. B., & Burr, W. R. Beyond the beyond: The growth of family theories in the 1970s. *Journal of Marriage and the Family,* 1980, *42,* 7–19.

Homans, G. C. *Social behavior: Its elementary forms.* New York: Harcourt Brace Jovanovich, 1961.

Huesmann, L. R., & Levinger, G. Incremental exchange theory: A formal model for progression in dyadic interaction. In L. Berkowitz & E. Walster (Eds.), *Advances in experimental social psychology* (Vol. 9). New York: Academic Press, 1976.

Huston, T. L. An analytical tour de force (review of *personal relationships*). *Contemporary Psychology,* 1981, *26,* 325–326.

Huston, T. L., & Burgess, R. L. Social exchange in developing relationships: An overview. In R. Burgess and T. Huston (Eds.), *Social exchange in developing relationships.* New York: Academic Press, 1979.

Jackson, J. A. Parental ideology and adolescent conventional behavior. *Personality and Social Psychology Bulletin,* 1980, *6,* 184–185.

Johnson, M. P., & Leslie, L. Couple involvement and network structure: A test of the dyadic withdrawal hypothesis. *Social Psychology Quarterly,* 1982, *45,* 34–43.

Jones, E. E., & Davis, K. E. From acts to dispositions: The attribution process in person perception. In L. Berkowitz (Ed.), *Advances in experimental social psychology* (Vol. 2). New York: Academic Press, 1965.

Jones, E. E., Kanouse, D. E., Kelley, H. H., Nisbett, R. E., Valins, S., & Weiner, B. (Eds.). *Attribution: Perceiving the causes of behavior.* Morristown, N.J.: General Learning Press, 1972.

Jones, E. E., & Nisbett, R. E. The actor and the observer: Divergent perceptions of the causes of behavior. In E. E. Jones, D. E. Kanouse, H. H. Kelley, R. E. Nisbett, S. Valins, & B. Welner (Eds.), *Attribution: Perceiving the causes of behavior.* Morristown, N.J.: General Learning Press, 1972.

Kelley, H. H. Attribution theory in social psychology. In D. Levine (Ed.), *Nebraska Symposium on Motivation* (Vol. 15). Lincoln: University of Nebraska Press, 1967.

Kelley, H. H. Attribution in social interaction. In E. E. Jones, D. E. Kanouse, H. H. Kelley,

R. E. Nisbett, S. Valins, & B. Weiner (Eds.), *Attribution: Perceiving the causes of behavior.* Morristown, N.J.: General Learning Press, 1972.

Kelley, H. H. *Personal relationships: Their structure and processes.* Hillsdale, N.J.: Lawrence Erlbaum Associates, 1979.

Kelley, H. H., Berscheid, E., Christensen, A., Harvey, J. H., Huston, T. L., Levinger, G., McClintock, E., Peplau, L. A., & Peterson, D. R. *Close Relationships.* San Francisco: Freeman, 1983.

Kelley, H. H., & Thibaut, J. W. *Interpersonal relations: A theory of interdependence.* New York: John Wiley & Sons, 1978.

Klos, D. S., & Singer, J. L. Determinants of the adolescent's ongoing thought following simulated parental confrontations. *Journal of Personality and Social Psychology,* 1981, *41,* 975–987.

Knudson, R. M., Sommers, A. A., & Golding, S. L. Interpersonal perception and mode of resolution in marital conflict. *Journal of Personality and Social Psychology,* 1980, *38,* 751–763.

Kraut, R. E., & Lewis, S. H. Alternate models of family influence on student political ideology. *Journal of Personality and Social Psychology,* 1975, *31,* 791–800.

Kraut, R. E., & Price, J. D. Machiavellianism in parents and their children. *Journal of Personality and Social Psychology,* 1976, *33,* 782–786.

Kroger, R. O. Explorations in ethogeny: With special reference to the rules of address. *American Psychologist,* 1982, *37,* 810–820.

Kulka, R. A., & Weingarten, H. Long-term effects of parental divorce in childhood on adult adjustment. *Journal of Social Issues,* 1979, *35*(4), 50–78.

L'Abate, L., & Thaxton, L. The family as a unit of psychological study and practice. *Academic Psychology Bulletin,* 1983, *5,* 71–83.

Lederer, W. J., & Jackson, D. D. *The mirages of marriage.* New York: W. W. Norton, 1968.

Levenson, R. W., & Gottman, J. M. Mental interaction: Physiological linkage and affective exchange. *Journal of Personality and Social Psychology,* 1983, *45,* 587–597.

Leventhal, G. S. The distribution of rewards and resources in groups and organizations. In L. Berkowitz & E. Walster (Eds.), Equity theory: Toward a general theory of social interaction. *Advances in experimental social psychology* (Vol. 9) New York: Academic Press, 1976.

Leventhal, G. S. What should be done with equity theory? New approaches to the study of fairness in social relationships. In K. Gergen, M. S. Greenberg, & R. H. Willis (Eds.), *Social exchange: Advances in theory and research.* New York: Plenum Press, 1980.

Leventhal, G. S., Weiss, T., & Buttrick, R. Attribution of value, equity, and the prevention of waste in reward allocation. *Journal of Personality and Social Psychology,* 1973, *27,* 276–286.

Levinger, G. Task and social behavior in marriage. *Sociometry,* 1964, *27,* 433–448.

Levinger, G. Marital cohesiveness and dissolution: An integrative review. *Journal of Marriage and the Family,* 1965, *27,* 19–28.

Levinger, G. Marital dissatisfaction among divorce applicants. *American Journal of Orthopsychiatry,* 1966, *36,* 803–807. (a)

Levinger, G. Systematic distortion in spouses' reports of preferred and actual sexual behavior. *Sociometry,* 1966, *29,* 291–299. (b)

Levinger, G. A three-level approach to attraction: Toward an understanding of pair related-ness. In T. L. Huston (Ed.), *Foundations of interpersonal attraction*. New York: Academic Press, 1974.

Levinger, G. A social psychological perspective on marital dissolution. *Journal of Social Issues*, 1976, *32*(1), 21–47.

Levinger, G. Reviewing the close relationship. In G. Levinger and H. Raush (Eds.), *Close relationships*. Amherst: University of Massachusetts Press, 1977.

Levinger, G., & Breedlove, J. Interpersonal attraction and agreement: A study of marriage partners. *Journal of Personality and Social Psychology*, 1966, *3*, 367–372.

Levinger, G., & Huesmann, L. R. An "incremental exchange" perspective on the pair relation-ship: Interpersonal reward and level of involvement. In K. J. Gergen, M. S. Greenberg, & R. H. Willis (Eds.), *Social exchange: Advances in theory and research*. New York: Plenum Press, 1980.

Levinger, G., & Moles, O. C. In conclusion: Threads in the fabric. *Journal of Social Issues*, 1976, *32*(1), 193–207.

Levinger, G., & Senn, D. J. Disclosure of feelings in marriage. *Merrill-Palmer Quarterly of Behavior and Development*, 1967, *13*, 237–249.

Levinger, G., & Snoek, J. D. *Attraction in relationships: A new look at interpersonal attraction*. Morristown, N.J.: General Learning Press, 1972.

Levinger, G., Senn, D. J., & Jorgensen, B. W. Progress toward permanence in courtship: A test of the Kerckhoff-Davis hypotheses. *Sociometry*, 1970, *33*, 427–443.

Levitin, T. E. Children of divorce—introduction. *Journal of Social Issues*, 1979, *35*(4), 1–25.

Li, A. K. F. Parental attitudes, text anxiety, and achievement motivation. *Journal of Social Psychology*, 1974, *93*, 3–11.

Loehlin, J. C., Willerman, L., & Horn, J. M. Personality resemblances between unwed mothers and their adopted-away offspring. *Journal of Personality and Social Psychology*, 1982, *42*, 1089–1099.

Lott, B. Behavioral concordance with sex-role ideology related to play areas, creativity, and parental sex typing of children. *Journal of Personality and Social Psychology*, 1978, *36*, 1087–1100.

Lytton, H., Conway, D., & Sauve, R. Impact of twinship on parent-child interaction. *Journal of Personality and Social Psychology*, 1977, *35*, 97–107.

Maceachron, A. E., & Gruenfeld, L. W. Effects of family authority structure and socioeco-nomic status on field independence. *Journal of Social Psychology*, 1978, *104*, 49–56.

Madden, M. E., & Janoff-Bulman, R. Blame, control, and marital satisfaction: Wives' attribu-tions for conflict in marriage. *Journal of Marriage and the Family*, 1981, *44*, 663–674.

McCarrick, A. K., Manderscheid, R. W., & Silbergeld, S. Gender differences in competition and dominance during married couples' group therapy. *Social Psychology Quarterly*, 1981, *44*, 164–177.

McClelland, D. C., & Pilon, D. A. Sources of adult motives in patterns of parent behavior in early childhood. *Journal of Personality and Social Psychology*, 1983, *44*, 564–574.

McHale, S. M., & Huston, T. L. Men and women as parents: Sex role orientations, employ-ment, and parental roles with infants. *Child Development*, in press.

Meyer, J. P., & Pepper, S. Need compatibility and marital adjustment in young married couples. *Journal of Personality and Social Psychology*, 1977, *35*, 331–342.

Miller, J. Z., & Rose, R. J. Familial resemblance in locus of control—a twin-family study of the internal-external scale. *Journal of Personality and Social Psychology*, 1982, *42*, 535–540.

Miller, T. W. Cultural dimensions related to parental verbalization and self-concept in child. *Journal of Social Psychology*, 1972, *87*, 153.

Miller, T. W. Effects of core facilitative conditions in mother on adolescent self-esteem. *Journal of Social Psychology*, 1976, *100*, 147–148.

Moles, O. C., & Levinger, G. Divorce and separation—introduction. *Journal of Social Issues*, 1976, *32*(1), 1–4.

Morton, T. L. Intimacy and reciprocity of exchange: A comparison of spouses and strangers. *Journal of Personality and Social Psychology*, 1978, *36*, 72–81.

Murstein, B. I., & Christy, P. Physical attractiveness and marriage adjustment in middle-aged couples. *Journal of Personality and Social Psychology*, 1976, *34*, 537–542.

Murstein, B. I., Cerreto, M., & McDonald, M. G. A theory and investigation of the effect of exchange orientation on marriage and friendship. *Journal of Marriage and the Family*, 1977, *39*, 543–548.

Nelson, M., & Nelson, G. M. Problems of equity in the reconstituted family: A social exchange analysis. *Family Relations*, 1982, *31*, 223–231.

Newcomb, T. M. *The acquaintance process*. New York: Holt, Rinehart & Winston, 1961.

Newman, H. M., & Langer, E. J. Post-divorce adaptation and the attribution of responsibility. *Sex Roles*, 1981, *7*, 223–232.

Nijhawan, H. K., & Verma, P. Children's attitudes towards social change in relation to parental attitudes towards child rearing. *Journal of Social Psychology*, 1975, *96*, 293–294.

Noller, P. Misunderstandings in marital communication—a study of couples' nonverbal communication. *Journal of Personality and Social Psychology*, 1980, *39*, 1135–1148.

Noller, P. Gender and marital adjustment level differences in decoding messages from spouses and strangers. *Journal of Personality and Social Psychology*, 1981, *41*, 272–278.

Noller, P. Channel consistency and inconsistency in the communications of married couples. *Journal of Personality and Social Psychology*, 1982, *43*, 732–741.

Nye, F. I. Is choice and exchange theory the key? *Journal of Marriage and Family*, 1978, *40*, 219–233.

Nye, F. I. Family mini theories as special instances of choice and exchange theory. *Journal of Marriage and Family*, 1980, *42*, 479–489.

Orvis, B. R., Kelley, H. H., & Butler, D. Attributional conflict in young couples. In J. H. Harvey, W. Ickes, & R. Kidd (Eds.), *New directions in attribution research* (Vol. 2). Hillsdale, N.J.: Lawrence Erlbaum Associates, 1976.

Paolino, T. J., & McCrady, B. S. (Eds.). *Marriage and marital therapy: Psychoanalytic, behavioral and systems theory perspectives*. New York: Brunner/Mazel, 1978.

Passer, M. W., Kelley, H. H., & Michela, J. L. Multidimensional scaling of the causes for negative interpersonal behavior. *Journal of Personality and Social Psychology*, 1978, *36*, 951–962.

Paulhus, D., & Shaffer, D. R. Sex differences in the impact number of older and number of younger siblings on scholastic aptitude. *Social Psychology Quarterly,* 1981, *44,* 363–368.

Pepitone, A. Lessons from the history of social psychology. *American Psychologist,* 1981, *36,* 972–985.

Pinsof, W. M. Family therapy process research. In A. S. Gurman & D. P. Kniskern (Eds.), *Handbook of family therapy.* New York: Brunner/Mazel, 1981.

Prasad, M. B., Sinha, B. P., & Prasad, A. Perception of parental expectations and need achievement. *Journal of Social Psychology,* 1979, *103,* 301–302.

Price, R. A., & Vandenberg, S. G. Matching for physical attractiveness in married couples. *Personality and Social Psychology Bulletin,* 1979, *5,* 398–400.

Ra, J. B. Comparison of preschool children's preferences for television and their parents. *Journal of Social Psychology,* 1977, *102,* 163–164.

Randall, T. M. Effect of an observer's presence on the behavior of middle-class and working-class mothers. *Journal of Social Psychology,* 1981, *113,* 193–199.

Raush, H. L. Orientation to the close relationship. In G. Levinger & H. Raush (Eds.), *Close relationships: Perspectives on the meaning of intimacy.* Amherst: University of Massachusetts Press, 1977.

Riskin, J., & Faunce, E. E. An evaluative review of family interaction research. *Family Process,* 1972, *11,* 365–456.

Rockwell, R. C., Elder, G. H., & Ross, D. J. Psychological patterns in marital timing and divorce. *Social Psychology,* 1979, *103,* 399–404.

Rosenblatt, P. C., & Budd, L. G. Territoriality and privacy in married and unmarried cohabiting couples. *Journal of Social Psychology,* 1975, *97,* 67–76.

Ross, J. A. Influence of expert and peer upon Negro mothers of low socioeconomic status. *Journal of Social Psychology,* 1973, *89,* 79–84.

Ross, L. D. The intuitive psychologist and his shortcomings: Distortions in the attribution process. In L. Berkowitz (Ed.), *Advances in experimental social psychology* (Vol. 10). New York: Academic Press, 1977.

Rubin, Z. The measurement of romantic love. *Journal of Personality and Social Psychology,* 1970, *16,* 265–273.

Rubin, Z., & Mitchell, C. Couples research as couples counseling: Some unintended effects of studying close relationships. *American Psychologists* 1976, *31,* 17–25.

Russo, N. F. Motherhood mandate. *Journal of Social Issues,* 1976, *32*(3), 143–153.

Sabatelli, R. M., Buck, R., & Dreyer, A. Nonverbal communication accuracy in married couples-relationships with marital complaints. *Journal of Personality and Social Psychology,* 1982, *43,* 1088–1097.

Sampson, E. E. Psychology and the American ideal. *Journal of Personality and Social Psychology,* 1977, *35,* 767–782.

Scanzoni, J. Social exchange and behavioral interdependence. In R. L. Burgess and T. L. Huston (Eds.), *Social exchange in developing relationships.* New York: Academic Press, 1979.

Scarr, S., Webber, P. L., Weinberg, R. A., & Wittig, M. A. Personality resemblance among adolescents and their parents in biologically related and adoptive families. *Journal of Personality and Social Psychology,* 1981, *40,* 885–898.

Scherf, G. W. H., & Kawash, G. F. Husband-wife comparisons of price-quality relationships in post-purchase situation. *Journal of Social Psychology,* 1976, *100,* 99–106.

Schumm, W. R., Benigas, J. E., McCutchen, M. B., Griffin, C. L., Anderson, S. A., Morris, J. E., & Race, G. S. Measuring empathy, regard, and congruence in the marital relationship. *Journal of Social Psychology,* 1983, *119,* 141–142.

Sears, R. R., Maccoby, E. E., & Levin, H. *Patterns of child rearing.* Evanston, Ill.: Row & Peterson, 1957.

Seashore, M. J., Leifer, A. D., Barnett, C. R., & Leiderma, P. H. Effects of denial of early mother-infant interaction on maternal self-confidence. *Journal of Personality and Social Psychology,* 1973, *26,* 369–378.

Shaver, K. G. *An introduction to attribution processes.* Cambridge, Mass.: Winthrop, 1975.

Shaw, M. E. *Group dynamics: The psychology of small group behavior* (3d. ed.). New York: McGraw-Hill, 1981.

Sigall, H., & Landy, D. Radiating beauty: The effects of having a physically attractive partner on person perception. *Journal of Personality and Social Psychology,* 1973, *28,* 218–224.

Silvern, L. E., & Nakamura, C. Y. Analysis of relationship between students' political position and extent to which they deviate from parents' position. *Journal of Social Issues,* 1973, *29,* 111–132.

Steelman, L. C., & Mercy, J. A. Sex differences in the impact of the number of older and younger siblings on IQ performance. *Social Psychology Quarterly,* 1983, *46(2),* 157–162.

Stone, W. F. Patterns of comformity in couples varying in intimacy. *Journal of Personality and Social Psychology,* 1973, *27,* 413–418.

Strong, S. R., & Claiborn, C. D. *Change through interaction: Social psychological processes of counseling and psychotherapy.* New York: John Wiley & Sons, 1982.

Tesser, A. Self-esteem maintenance in family dynamics. *Journal of Personality and Social Psychology,* 1980, *39,* 77–91.

Thibaut, J. W., & Kelley, H. H. *The social psychology of groups.* New York: John Wiley & Sons, 1959.

Tower, R. B. Parents' self-concepts and pre-school children's behaviors. *Journal of Personality and Social Psychology,* 1980, *39,* 710–718.

Walbridge, R. H. Social psychology joins the family. In R. Manderscheid & F. Manderscheid (Eds.), *Systems science and the future of health.* Washington, D.C.: Society for General Systems Research, 1976.

Walster, E., Traupmann, J., & Walster, G. W. Equity and extramarital sexuality. *Archives of Sexual Behavior,* 1978, *7,* 127–142.

Walster, E., Walster, W., & Berscheid, E. *Equity: Theory and research.* Boston: Allyn & Bacon, 1978.

Wasserman, T., & Kassinove, H. Effects of type of recommendation, attire, and perceived expertise in parental compliance. *Journal of Social Psychology,* 1976, *99,* 43–50.

Waxler, N. E., & Mischler, E. G. Experimental studies of families. In L. Berkowitz (Ed.), *Group processes.* New York: Academic Press, 1978.

Weick, K. E. Group processes, family processes, and problem solving. In J. Aldous, T. Condon, R. Hill, M. Strauss, & I. Tallman (Eds.), *Family problem solving: A symposium on theoretical, methodological, and substantive concerns.* Hinsdale, Ill.: Dryden Press, 1971.

Weiner, B., Frieze, I., Kukla, A., Reed, L., Rest, S., & Rosenbaum, R. M. Perceiving the causes of success and failure. In E. E. Jones, D. E. Kanouse, H. H. Kelley, R. E. Nisbett, S. Valins, & B. Weiner (Eds.), *Attribution: Perceiving the causes of behavior.* Morristown, N.J.: General Learning Press, 1972.

Willis, R. H., & Frieze, I. H. Sex roles, social exchange, and couples. In K. J. Gergen, M. S. Greenberg, and R. H. Willis (Eds.), *Social exchange: Advances in theory and research.* New York: Plenum Press, 1980.

Winter, D. G., Stewart, A. J., & McClelland, D. C. Husband's motives and wife's career level. *Journal of Personality and Social Psychology,* 1977, *35,* 159–166.

Zajonc, R. B. Attitudinal effects of mere exposure. *Journal of Personality and Social Psychology Monograph Supplement,* 1968, *9,* 1–27.

Zajonc, R. B. Family configuration and intelligence. *Science,* 1976, *192,* 227–236.

Zajonc, R. B. Validating the confluence model. *Psychological Bulletin,* 1983, *93,* 457–480.

Zajonc, R. B., & Markus, G. B. Birth order and intellectual development. *Psychological Review,* 1975, *82,* 74–88.

Zajonc, R. B., Markus, H., & Markus, G. B. The birth order puzzle. *Journal of Personality and Social Psychology,* 1979, *37,* 1325–1341.

Section Two

Individual and Family Life Cycles

Chapter 5

Individual and Family Life-Span Development: A Critique and Assessment of Current Trends*

MICHAEL BERGER
STEPHEN D. BERGER

INTRODUCTION

This chapter is not organized like a conventional literature review. Such a review typically summarizes the major conceptual and research traditions within an area of study, reviews the empirical and theoretical work within the different conceptual traditions, noting their findings and commenting on their limitations, and concludes with suggestions for future work. The very structure of such a review takes for granted that a reasonably meaningful and coherent literature exists to be summarized. Such a structure will not be employed, because the literatures of concern to this chapter are in a preparadigm stage and should not be codified in their present form. More importantly, a conventional literature review would reify the present segregation between the literatures on individual and family development; as others have indicated (e.g., Dollard, 1935; Mills, 1959; Spiegel, 1971), only a unified and humane social science can properly deal with the question of human development over the life span.

This chapter, therefore, will proceed differently, beginning with an examination of classic views of individual and family development.

* Michael Berger wishes to thank Martha Foster, Ph.D., and Marjorie Blum, Ph.D., for their comments on earlier drafts of the chapter. Stephen Berger wishes to thank the library staff of New Hampshire College—in particular, Carol West, the interlibrary loan librarian—for their assistance. As a scholar working in a small city, his work would not have been possible without the help of the interlibrary loan system. Both authors wish to acknowledge the good-natured and competent secretarial contributions of Majella Hardie and Donna Floyd.

Next, with the help of criteria developed by Dollard (1935) for the study of life-history materials and by Spiegel (1971) for the study of transactional processes in living systems, the issues, foci, and processes which a life-cycle literature should consider shall be set forth. Then, the current individual and family life-cycle literatures will be reviewed. Following this review, we will consider the influence that the idea of the family life-cycle has had on the field of family therapy; while the literature on individual lifespan development has had little effect on individual psychotherapy, the notion of the family life cycle has become quite important in family therapy. Finally, this chapter will conclude with some speculations as to the reasons behind the recent boom in life-cycle studies.

The aim of this chapter is to think about the major conceptual traditions within the individual and family life-cycle literatures rather than to detail the findings of these literatures. For this reason, also, this chapter will not present an exhaustive review of these literatures. Furthermore, since the focus (when examining particular materials) is on their utility for the study of lifespan development, virtues in the materials may well be overlooked—for example, their utility as studies of some aspect of individual or family development or behavior, that are irrelevant to our concerns.

CLASSIC VIEWS OF THE HUMAN LIFE CYCLE

In this section, three classic literary statements about the human life cycle—two of them western, one eastern—shall be examined: *(a)* the riddle of the Sphinx from the Sophocles play *Oedipus Rex; (b)* the "Seven Ages of Man" speech from Shakespeare's *As You Like It;* and *(c)* the Hindu view of the four stages of life. Considering these statements, one will find that they differ in their view of development for men and women; in whether development is viewed primarily in terms of biological metaphors (that is, as the unfolding of something inherently present from the organism's beginning) or in terms of social relationships; and in whether development is viewed as inevitable or as capable of being altered.

The two most famous literary expressions of change over the course of the life cycle are the riddle of the Sphinx in *Oedipus Rex* and the "Seven Ages of Man" speech in *As You Like It.*

As everybody knows,[1] the Sphinx posed a riddle to all people entering or leaving Thebes and tore them to pieces if they could not answer it. The kingship of Thebes (and marriage to the queen, Iocasta) was offered to anyone who could solve the riddle, which was: "What crea-

---

[1] To show that "everyone knows this," this quote is from a children's version (D'Aulaine & D'Aulaine, 1962, pp. 150–160).

ture is it that walks on four feet in the morning, on two at noon, and three in the evening?" Oedipus solves the riddle and becomes King of Thebes (as the Sphinx dashes herself to pieces on the rocks) by answering "It is man. As a child he crawls on four. When grown he walks upright on his two feet, and in old age he leans on his staff."

This story leaves us with the bare picture that the stages of a man's life are three: infancy, adulthood, and old age. Of this picture, there are three things to be noted:

1. It is a metaphor of growth and decline.
2. It is a metaphor of man's growth and decline—as Muriel Rukeyer's (1973) recent poem shows wonderfully:

> Long afterward, Oedipus, old and blinded, walked the roads. He smelled a familiar smell. It was the Sphinx. Oedipus said, "I want to ask one question. Why didn't I recognize my mother?" "You gave the wrong answer," said the Sphinx. "But that was what made everything possible," said Oedipus. "No," she said. "When I asked, 'What walks on four legs in the morning, two at noon, and three in the evening,' you answered Man. You didn't say anything about women." "When you say Man," said Oedipus, "you include women too. Everyone knows that." She said, "That's what you think." (p. 20)

3. The metaphor which identifies aging with the diurnal cycle of day and night implies that the growth and decline is natural, a movement from within that is biological. Hence it is neither subject to alteration nor does it depend on interrelationships with others.

We are left, then, with a simple metaphor of natural growth and decline, and the unstated assumption that men develop (but women do not?). This is our legacy from Oedipus and the riddle of the Sphinx.

Consider now Jaques' famous "Seven Ages of Man" speech from *As You Like It*:

> All the world's a stage
> And all the men and women merely players:
> They have their exits and their entrances;
> And one man in his time plays many parts,
> His acts being seven ages. At first the infant,
> Mewling and puking in the nurse's arms.
> Then the whining school-boy, with his satchel
> And shining morning face, creeping like snail
> Unwillingly to school. And then the lover,
> Sighing like furnace, with a woeful ballad
> Made to his mistress' eyebrow. Then a soldier,
> Full of strange oaths, and bearded like the pard,
> Jealous in honor, sudden and quick in quarrel,
> Seeking the bubble reputation
> Even in the cannon's mouth. And then the justice,

In fair round belly with good capon lined,
With eyes severe and beard of formal cut,
Full of wise saws and modern instances;
And so he plays his part. The sixth age shifts
Into the lean and slipper'd pantaloon,
With spectacles on nose and pouch on side,
His youthful hose well-saved, a world too wide
For his shrunk shank; and his big manly voice
Turning again toward childish treble, pipes
And whistles in his sound. Last scene of all,
That ends this strange eventful history,
Is second childishness and mere oblivion,
Sans teeth, sans eyes, sans taste, sans every thing. (*AYLI*, 2, vii.)

It is a common rhetorical ploy for modern social science lifespan discussions to begin by quoting this speech (in part, at least) as if it reflected some sort of basic and hard-to-disown insight, though those who cite it rarely state clearly just what that insight is. If fundamental insight is what we are searching for in the speech, there would seem to be three candidates:

1. Lifestages are like parts, or roles. We have not seen this notion put forward by students of development, though noting that Shakespeare said that "All the world's a stage" is a common way of starting a discussion of role theory. We suspect that there is something to be gained by exploring the metaphor of lifestages as prescribed roles. We will return to this point later.

2. Life falls into a fixed number of distinctive periods. The assumption that life does fall into some number of distinctive periods seems to be commonplace in most cultures (Turnbull, 1983), though how many periods are to be defined and what they are is far from obvious (see, for example, the discussions in Cuisenier, 1977).

3. That life is an up and then a down. This is the way literary critics tend to see the speech. Thus, Professor Barber (1959) tells us that Jaques is simplifying. "For it is only *one* aspect of the truth that the roles we play in life are settled by the cycle of growth and decline" (p. 226). Critics focus on the last stage of the speech, the supposedly inevitable decline, and tell us that the action of the play at the time—the strong activity of the servant Adam—contradicts Jaques' cynicism, and so we should *not* take the speech as a reflection of Shakespearian wisdom but rather of Jaques' fake wisdom (Goddard, 1951; Wain, 1964).

We have not, in our survey of the literature, found any discussion of the specific stages described in the speech or of their meaning. Even the obvious fact that Jacques' speech at best only describes male development is hardly noticed or discussed. There does seem to be some difficulty in seeing women as capable of developing.

We are left here, then, only slightly beyond the riddle of the Sphinx:

1. It (the life cycle), is portrayed in this speech, as in the riddle, as a metaphor of growth *and* decline.
2. Like the riddle, it is a metaphor of *men's* growth and decline.
3. The metaphor of seven ages implies that the cycle of growth and decline is natural.
4. *But,* the metaphor of parts to play and the social scripting of the parts (infant and nurse, schoolboy, lover and mistress, soldier in war, justice in his court—the last two stages lacking clear social definition) suggest the possibility of social aspects to the development of the individual. And it is social in two senses: scripted by society (let us call this cultural) and played out in interaction with others (let us call this social in a narrower sense).

This appears to be the (relatively undeveloped) legacy from Shakespeare and the "Seven Ages of Man."

There is a third classic statement on lifespan development which may be worth looking at, since it takes us out of the Western set of cultural traditions. That is the Hindu view of four stages of life. Embree (1966) has provided a convenient summary of this view:

> The second great ideal (after that of the four classes of people) that undergirded the social and religious structure was the conception of four stages *(ashrams)* of life. Just as society as a whole was understood to be divided into classes performing mutually exclusive functions that came together under the general working of *dharma,* each individual life was divided into stages that were distinct but in the end produced a harmonious totality. These stages, it should be noted, were taken to be applicable mainly to members of the three "twice-born" classes and only to men and boys. After initiation, the boy became a celibate student, living in the house of his teacher or *guru.* Then he married and observed the obligations and enjoyed the pleasures of the life of a householder. . . .
>
> Following the fulfillment of his duties as a householder and having assured the continuance of his family, a man next becomes a hermit in the forest, meditating and studying the scriptures. Then finally comes the fourth stage when, abandoning all earthly ties, he wanders about unhindered by family, home, or possessions. Here as everywhere, the assumption is that *dharma* is not the same at every stage of life, just as it is not the same for all men. . . .
>
> The third ideal construction, the four ends of life, related the religious understanding of the nature of existence to the conduct of everyday life. The four legitimate ends to be pursued were *dharma,* or duty; material gain *(artha);* the pleasures of physical sense *(kama);* and salvation *(moksha).* Since it was assumed that not only did men differ in

their needs and capabilities according to their class but also according
to their stage of life, these legitimate ends were defined in terms appropriate for one's particular station. (pp. 76–78)

This view obviously has some differences from, as well as some similarities to, the riddle of the Sphinx and Jaques' speech:

1. It is not a metaphor of growth and decline, but is more akin
to a metaphor of continuous growth, a shedding of the previous stage
(see 5 below).

2. It is a metaphor that ascribes development only to men. Women
are seen as follows, in the *Manu Smriti:*

> Day and night must women be kept in dependence by the males of
> their families, and if they attach themselves to sensual enjoyments, they
> must be kept under one's control. . . . in youth, and her sons protect
> her in old age; a woman is never fit for independence.
>
> Reprehensible is the father who gives not his daughter in marriage
> at the proper time; reprehensible is the husband who approaches not
> his wife in due season; and reprehensible is the son who does not protect
> his mother after her husband has died.
>
> The production of children, the nurture of those born, and the daily
> life of men, of these matters woman is visibly the cause. (Embree, 1966,
> pp. 88–89)

We may glimpse here a three-stage view of the circumstances (though
not development) of women: prior to childbearing and rearing; childbearing and rearing; post childbearing and rearing. Growth and decline
of a sort.

3. The metaphor is not natural, but religious. Further, development beyond the householder stage is seen as permissible, not prescribed: "When a householder sees his skin wrinkle, and his hair white,
the sons of his sons, then he may resort to the forest" (Embree, 1966,
p. 90). "But having thus passed the third part of a man's natural term
of life in the forest, he may live as an ascetic during the fourth part
of his existence, after abandoning all attachment to worldly objects"
(pp. 71–72). Thus the statement to the individual is not, "This is the
next stage you will go through," but something like "This is the next
stage and its characteristics. You may choose to enter if you would
go further towards salvation."

4. There is a clear social element to each stage: the first stage as
a student in the house of the *guru;* the second stage as a married
householder and parent; the third stage as a (not necessarily isolated)
"hermit," or "guestdweller" (in this stage, the hermit could even be
living with his wife); the fourth stage as an isolated, possessionless wan-
derer. In each case, the social element includes other people (or their
absence) in specific roles, a social location, and socially appropriate
possessions (or their lack).

5.   There are specific virtues associated with each stage, which are *not* appropriate for other stages. This is an extraordinarily interesting way of dealing with human conflicts over the plurality of values—by assigning each to stages, choices are made nonexclusively but dialectically. Over a time, a number of virtues are both accepted and rejected.

6.   There is some suggestion that the first two stages involve doing one's duty for the society, the second two allow individual (if impersonal) development. This, at least, is the view of the German Indologist Heinrich Zimmer (1951):

> Everyone tends to become petrified, dehumanized, stabilized, and purged of spontaneous individuality—in proportion to the degree of perfection he achieves in the intensely stylized enactment of his timeless role. In the second half of the individual's life cycle, therefore, these brittle roles are to be put aside. Having identified himself wholly with the functions of his social personality (his social actor's mask or *persona*), he must now as radically step away from that—throw off possessions and all the concerns of wealth *(artha)*, break from the desires and anxieties of his now flowered and variously fruitful life-in-marriage *(kama)*, turn even from the duties of society *(dharma)* which have linked him to the universal manifestation of Imperishable Being through the stable archetypes of the human tragicomedy. His sons are now bearing the joys and burdens of the world; himself, in late middle life, may step away. (p. 157)

This view closely resembles Jung's. Since we know that Jung and Zimmer worked together, it is difficult to know who influenced whom.

7.   There is also a suggestion that cultural definitions mediated through ritual and magic may help the individual make the transition from one stage to the next. This was Zimmer's (1957) view:

> In some cultures there are sacramental formulas for putting off the old Adam—initiatives, demanding and causing a complete breakup of the existing mold that has bewitched and bound its wearer. He is invested with an entirely new costume, which brings him under the spell of a new magic and opens to him new paths. . . . Civilizations like that of India, founded on a cornerstone of magic, help their children through these necessary transformations that men find it so hard to accomplish from within. This they do by means of undisputed sacraments. The bestowal of the special vestments, implements, signet rings, and crowns, actually re-create the individuals. Changes of food and the reorganization of the outer ceremonial of life make possible certain things, certain actions and feelings, and prohibit others. (pp. 18–19)[2]

This view brings us close to the anthropology of the rituals of transition initiated by the Belgian anthropologist Van Gennep in his classic *The Rites of Passage* (1908/1960). It also suggests the importance of the

---

[2] Other discussions of the Hindu four stages may be found in Erikson (1969, especially pp. 34–39), Kakar (1968), and in Smith (1958).

role of helpers and society in easing transitions. This is a point that has been made repeatedly in the therapy literature, in the description of the therapist as (to use Zuk's, 1978, term) a *celebrant* who aids individuals and families in making life-cycle transitions (see also Friedman, 1980; Haley, 1973).

The classical picture of *family* development in the West (though it is less frequently referred to as paradigmatic than are the riddle of the Sphinx and the "Seven Ages of Man" speech) is the biblical story of Adam and Eve in Genesis. In it, the following are emphasized:

1. The wife becomes (is created out of) part of the husband, and this justifies/requires that the man leave behind his family of origin: "Therefore shall a man leave his father and his mother and shall cleave unto his wife: and they shall be one flesh" (Gen. 2:24). That is, it is taken for granted that a woman leaves behind her family of origin. What is seen as problematic and needing to be stressed is the man leaving *his* family.
2. By implication, both are young; but the woman is still younger than the man, since she is created out of him.
3. There is a movement from innocence to shame, mediated by knowledge/sin in opposition to the dictates of authority.
4. The act of opposition to authority, the act of sin, is punished as follows:
    (a) Women shall have children "in sorrow,"
    (b) Women's desire shall be limited to their husbands (Gen. 3:16),
    (c) Men shall sweat and eat of the products of the ground (rather than the tree) and shall die (return to the ground) (Gen. 3:17–19).
5. They make love and have children.
6. After having children, Adam dies. (Eve's death is not mentioned.) In fact, as generation succeeds generation, sons and daughters are conceived and born, but only the sons are named in the chapter which details the succession of generations (Gen. 5).

The simplest summary, then, is that in the post-Edenic world, in shame and sorrow, men and women form families to raise (especially male) children and for the men to work. The slightly more complicated version is that family formation requires sin in the form of a desire for knowledge which constitutes disobedience to (male) authority and that family life ends in the death of the parents.

SCIENTIFIC VIEWS OF THE HUMAN LIFE CYCLE

One of the things that "everybody" knows about a science (as compared, say, to an art) is that it progresses. Over time, scientists within a given field or discipline obtain more and more precise information about the issues they study. While the limitations of this assumption have been stressed by Kuhn (1970), he himself reiterates this very point in a later collection of essays (Kuhn, 1977).

How have the two fields under study in this chapter—the fields of individual and family life-cycle development—progressed beyond the historically classic views described above? To answer this question, some standards need to be made clear: This will be done by delineating a series of criteria devised almost 40 years ago by Dollard (1935) for the analysis of life-history material. Sarason (1974) has correctly noted that the title of Dollard's book *Criteria for the Life History* radically understates what Dollard is undertaking: Dollard is doing nothing less than setting forth criteria for the meaningful scientific study of human personality. Such study, Dollard repeatedly points out, must be the study of human development in a particular culture, because personality and human beings do not exist outside of culture. Such studies, Dollard passionately argues, cry out for a unified discipline that would study the interrelationships between culture and human beings in all their complexity, rather than chopping up this ecosystem (to use Bateson's phrase) into parts that neatly fit into disciplinary boundaries. Indeed, almost leaping off the page is Dollard's hope that an intelligent understanding of the kinds of knowledge that would be needed to understand the life history, would lead to a unified field of social science. This hope has not, of course, been realized. Dollard's seven criteria are:

1. *The subject must be viewed as a specimen in a cultural series.* By this, Dollard means that all human beings are born into a particular culture with a specific social life that is organized and systematized and which will impose itself upon the new member added to the already existing cultural group. "To state the point in an extreme manner, we can think of the organic man as the mere toy of culture, providing it with a standardized base, investing its forms with affect but creating very little that is new alone or at any time" (1935, p. 16). If the social scientist does not take this view into account, Dollard argues, he or she will fall into error by mistaking for accidental or individual much that is culturally patterned.

2. *The organic means of action ascribed must be socially relevant.* This, Dollard says, "means merely that in order to have a theory of motivation we must make some statements about the body and what it can and will do; the organic properties which we assume as the basis of the life of the individual in the group must be of a kind that they will submit to social elaboration. The organic activities of the body must come to meet the social influences we have just described" (1935, pp. 17–18).

3.   *The particular role of the family group in transmitting the culture must be recognized.* "Why," Dollard asks, "should we jump from
the organic nature of man to the family? The answer is not difficult.
The 'group' into which the child comes has a cultural lineage; it is
not formed just previously to the birth of the child for the purpose
of taking care of him" (1935, p. 21). Thus, Dollard stresses the special
importance of the family (which for the young child *is* the culture),
both for the early transmission of opportunities and limitations characteristic of the wider culture and as a target for the emotional life of
the child; and he notes the fact that family values and interaction
patterns are themselves culturally patterned.

4.   *The specific method of elaboration of organic materials into
social behavior must be shown.*

> The useful life history of the future will begin (theoretically) at the
> bottom; that is, with the organism and it will show in detail how this
> organism slowly becomes capable of social life in its particular group.
> We have noticed already that this group is represented at the outset
> by the parents who exercise its molding pressures and permissive tenden-
> cies on the growing person. This translation from the sheer "socially
> relevant biological" to socialized motivational forces must be carefully
> delineated and formulated theoretically because it is of the utmost impor-
> tance that we get this straight. Otherwise, we will have our person fitted
> out as a mature individual with a set of attitudes corresponding to a
> culture but we will have no idea how he got this way and we are likely
> to miss altogether the initial and continuing importance of the biological
> substratum of the social life of the person. (1935, p. 24)

5.   *The continuous related character of experience from childhood
through adulthood must be stressed.* By this, Dollard means in part
that any significant aspect of an individual's life must be considered
in the light of the rest of the individual's life.

> Some writers treat life history material as if it were a series of uncoordi-
> nated, unrelated events without any sequence or necessary relationship.
> If they wish to study the religious behavior of adolescents, for instance,
> they simply drop a statistical bucket into the well of adolescent experi-
> ence and draw it out; they will view their bucketful of data as self-explana-
> tory and not as a part of an individual unified life. If our criterion is
> accepted this procedure would be found invalid. The religious behavior
> of adolescents could not be seen except as part of the continuous experi-
> ence of the individual adolescent and the "religious events" would have
> to be set in series with the rest of the life of the person. It might well
> be that we would miss the whole sense of adolescent religious experience
> unless we understand the organic problems of adolescents and the partic-
> ular character form which adolescents *in our culture* bring forward at
> this age level. (1935, p. 26)

Dollard intends that this criterion means that the theorist must consider his or her subject's life as beginning at birth rather than at a later age chosen at the theorist's convenience.[3] Dollard does not mean, however, to assert that all events in an individual's life have equal importance.

> Some experiences will be more important for the determination of character than others, and some few will be of central crucial character. Such events will leave the individual with a formed character and a central feeling core which will be of highest relevance for any later behavior which we attempt to explain. . . . This is not a cultural view; it is, however, set off against the cross-cultural institutional view of behavior. It shows . . . the culture as coagulated around a center of feeling. From this point of view the life history record shows a center of feeling and positive motivation moving through a culture, over time. The culture offers to this moving center of feeling its preferred barriers and permitted exits, much as in the psychologist's maze. An important difference is that the culture "maze" is not experimentally thought out in advance; nor is the moving organism a rat. (1935, p. 29)

6. *The "social situation" must be carefully and continuously specified as a factor.* Individuals live, Dollard notes, by encountering a large number of socially defined situations; out of these encounters they acquire their present culture, including their sense of themselves within that culture. These socially defined situations through which people develop can themselves be defined in at least two ways: there is an objective or sort of average view of the situation, and there is also an extremely personal view of the situation to which the individual actually reacts.

> In the adequate life history we must constantly keep in mind both the situation as defined by others and by the subject; such a history . . . will let us see clearly the pressure of the formal situation and the force of the inner private definition of the situation. One of the acutest needs in cultural theory is to specify the series of situations through which the average organism in the culture must come; this specification will probably turn out to be a more specific view of the culture patterns, a view of the culture as it is actually experienced by emerging members of the group. (1935, p. 32)

Dollard continues by noting that the usual error with regard to this criterion is to overvalue the current and formally defined situation.

---

[3] In fact, there is good reason to start before the individual's birth. Fried and Fried (1980) discuss the cultural patterning of birth, and Galinsky (1981) analyses some possible patterns in the parents' preparation for the birth.

It is, however, equally erroneous to overlook this aspect of the situation and to deal "only with the former experience of the individual as though the current situation were a mere recapitulation of past experience. With such a view one might well overlook, for example, the whole existence of the economic order and its pressure on an individual while reveling in his recollections of a childhood experience" (1935, p. 33).

7. *The life-history material itself must be organized and conceptualized.* The subject, whose material "is already conditioned and limited in a great number of ways, not least by the taboos which every culture has on communicating certain kinds of material" (1935, p. 33) cannot provide a coherent theoretical organization of his own life, at least not one that is "meta" to the organizing concepts of his or her culture. Thus, the social scientist must filter the life-history material through his or her own set of conceptual nets in order to organize it: it will not organize itself. Indeed, as Whitehead has been credited with noting, many of the most taken-for-granted assumptions of any culture at a given time will not be mentioned by subjects because they seem so obvious as not to be noticed by the subject.

Dollard's criteria demand that the individual and the family group and the culture within which individual and family life occurs be seen as patterned wholes, and as patterned wholes which can change.[4] (Given this focus, it is curious that Dollard neglects that cultures themselves, often dramatically, undergo historical change. Elder, 1975, provides a fine discussion of the relevance of historical change to the study of individual and family development.) In terms of the individual, this means that his or her development must continually be seen as a transaction between organic motives and possibilities and culturally presented and defined situations; as the individual matures, it is a set of transactions between motivations which have themselves come into being as a result of culture-organic motive transactions but which, once in existence, as an active force are themselves affecting present and future individual-cultural situation transactions.

Two points deserve to be stressed here, for they seem crucial for any reasonable life-cycle literature. The first is the necessity for viewing both people and the cultures in which they live as patterned, coherent, and active forces; the second is the necessity of noting that both people and cultures can change. As Dollard's own analysis of the six documents he reviews in his book—case histories by Freud, Adler, and Jessie Taft;

---

[4] This is actually an unacceptable reification. In any specific case, the degree to which a culture is consistently patterned and encompasses the whole of an individual or group's experience needs to be investigated, not assumed. Most current cultures in the West are not consistently patterned in Dollard's sense.

two sets of life-history materials gathered by members of the Chicago school of sociology; and H. G. Wells' autobiography—shows, these criteria are rarely met. Rather, we have materials in which the individual is portrayed as dynamic and his or her developing motivations, cognitions, and behaviors may even be appropriately linked to organic underpinnings and to his or her family transactions, but the culture in which he or she lives is depicted as static or is not even portrayed, but rather taken for granted—dismissed, in Hartman's phrase, as "the average expectable environment." Such materials are characteristically produced by psychologists and therapists. Or, we have sociological materials in which the culture is described in great detail and with great care to portray significant patterns and interrelationships within it, but the individual is then described as something close to a mere passive responder to the culture. The first view denies both the importance of cultural patterns and the possibility of cultural change; the second denies the possibility that individuals can change and, in so doing, can also change the culture.

The demands that Dollard's criteria set for the researcher studying life-history materials are stringent. It is possible that some of his criteria become less relevant if, instead of studying life-history materials, one is interested in development over shorter periods of time than the full life cycle. For example, Dollard's concern for demonstrating the continuous character of development would be less stringent if one were studying development over, say, adolescence (e.g., Lerner & Spanier, 1980). Still, if one takes, for example, the literature in developmental psychology—a literature which characteristically focuses on development over short periods of time—it is clear that many of Dollard's criteria have not been met and that the failure to meet these criteria diminishes the value of the literature. For example, except in explicitly cross-cultural studies, it is rare in the developmental literature to have a sense, much less a precisely defined portrayal, of the culture in which the persons being studied live.[5] It is even rare in developmental studies of children to note that children both influence and are influenced by other family members, although in the past 35 years, developmentalists have moved from noting that children have mothers to seeing that children have mothers and fathers to noting that children are influenced not only by direct contact with their mother and father

---

[5] An exception here is the work in ecological psychology of Barker and his collegues (Barker, 1963, 1968, 1978; Barker & Gump, 1964; Barker & Schoggen, 1973; Barker & Wright, 1951, 1955). Even this work, however, does not take into account either the history of the community in which the behavioral settings which they study are situated or the relationship between that community and the larger society, a relationship that may well influence the structure and life of that community (see Vidich & Bensman, 1958). Their work also tends to ignore the people who move through the behavioral settings.

but by indirect influences among family members (Bristol & Gallagher, 1983; Lerner & Spanier, 1978).

Let us not be cavalier. Noticing the obvious, in this case that children have two parents and are also affected by both indirect and direct family influences, creates huge methodological and conceptual problems. In a superb essay on research methods suitable for the study of developmental reciprocity in families, Klein, Jorgensen, and Miller (1978, pp. 110–111) remark that, for example, in a family with two parents and three children, the following 12 questions are reasonable and worthy of study:

1. How do spouses affect each other?
2. How do parents affect their children, and vice versa?
3. How do siblings affect each other?
4. How does the relationship between spouses affect their children, and vice versa?
5. How does the relationship between parent and child affect the other parent, and vice versa?
6. How does the relationship between parent and child affect the other children, and vice versa?
7. How do the relationships between siblings affect the parent, and vice versa?
8. How do the relationships between siblings affect the other children, and vice versa?
9. How does the relationship between spouses affect the relationship between siblings, and vice versa?
10. How does the relationship between spouses affect the relationship between parent and child, and vice versa?
11. How does the relationship between parent and child affect the relationship between siblings, and vice versa?
12. How does the relationship between one parent and the children affect the relationship between the other parent and the children?

To make matters more complicated, Klein et al. correctly note that the preceding questions are not sufficient to capture the richness of family interaction. All of the following facts, they continue, are ignored by this scheme:

1. Due to cultural, social structural, and situational factors, some families have either more or fewer than two functioning parents.
2. A family member may affect and be affected by his or her relationship with other family members (for example, a couple's spousal relationship may affect their parental relationship, and vice versa).
3. Family members also have relationships with individuals,

groups, and other social systems that lie outside the members' nuclear family. We may ask, for example, how a boy's relationship with his peers at school affects his relationship with his parents, and vice versa?

4. The effects between relational networks may be indirect, suggesting that several of the networks could be linked together (e.g., the husband may affect the wife in either her parental or spousal role in such a way that she treats one of her children differently, and that will influence how that child treats another of his or her siblings.)

5. Family members may act "in concert" with one another or be jointly affected by the actions of other family members. Thus, at least some of the important reciprocal relationships in families may involve coalitions and other collective units (1978, p. 112).

That these criteria place huge demands on researchers and theorists should be obvious. That they are, however, reasonable—that is, appropriate to the complexity of issues involved in development—is a view increasingly articulated by psychologists, sociologists, anthropologists, and systems therapists (Auerswald, 1983; Baltes, Reese, & Lipsitt, 1980; Berger & Jurkovic, 1984; Bronfenbrenner, 1979; Clausen, 1972; Elder, 1975; Erikson, 1950; Gerth & Mills, 1953; Hoffman & Long, 1969; Lowenthal, Thurnher, & Chirigboga, 1975; Scheflen, 1980; Spiegel, 1971). Yet, if one looks at the two literatures under review in this chapter for studies which do justice to this complexity, one looks almost in vain. Rather, one encounters a series of repeated conceptual errors which have been well classified by Spiegel (1971): (1) the overestimation of one focus; (2) the skipping of foci; (3) the fading of foci; and (4) the collapsing of foci.

Spiegel notes that the first error is the most common. "Typically, proponents of the focus in question push it forward as the most valuable area of knowledge and rate other areas as secondary or of no importance. The terms of devaluation of the other foci may vary. They may be called unscientific; or if allowed to be known as scientific, their yield of knowledge will still be judged trivial" (1971, pp. 58–59). With regard to our two areas of study, the form that this error takes is that researchers and theorists characteristically focus on only one unit of analysis or focus such as the individual (e.g., Baltes et al., 1980; Erikson, 1950; Levinson, Darrow, Klein, Levinson, & McKee, 1978) or the family (e.g., Aldous, 1979; Reiss, 1980) or the culture (e.g., Friedenberg, 1965) and ignore other relevant foci. Thus, studies in these two literatures tend to portray the individual as dynamic and complex while the family and the cultural contexts in which he or she lives are relatively ignored; or the family system is described in great detail but without reference to the lives of individuals within the family or to the larger cultural context (Rosman, 1979); or cultural contexts are described with great complexity while individuals and families are viewed as mere passive responders to these contexts. While it is theoretically possible that a useful synthesis might emerge out of a series of such one-sided studies, this synthesis has not occurred. It is interesting that such syntheses have not occurred in a number of other fields such as physics (Kuhn, 1977), molecular biology (Judson, 1979), and biology (Allen, 1975) in which researchers and theorists, while recognizing the inextricably transactional character of the phenomena they are studying, focus on only one aspect of the transaction.

The second type of error—skipping of foci—occurs when the investigator acknowledges the interdependence of systems but then adopts the attitude that any system within any of the foci may be observed at any time and correlated with any other, rather than respecting the order of interrelations of foci in their field. Spiegel (1971) argues that the nature of the transactional field (see pp. 41–55 for his description of the transactional field) "requires that the foci to be included in an investigation be taken up in their order of succession and that no focus be passed. In other words, if an investigator wishes to relate somatic phenomena (any genetic factors) to social phenomena (any social-class variables) then he must take into account, in *some systematic fashion,* of the intervening psychological and group factors" (pp. 61–62).

The third type of error—fading of foci—is, Spiegel cautions, a bit difficult to describe, because it is unplanned and not under full conscious control. It is "a little noted and somewhat mysterious event which occurs when three adjacent foci (or systems of any kind) are lined up for simultaneous investigation. The system in the middle tends to fade from awareness, to be difficult to keep in focus" (1971, p. 66). This phenomenon may be a concrete example of the recency and primacy effects typically found in learning curves.

The final type of error—collapsing of foci—occurs when:

> foci which should be maintained in careful differentiation from each other are fused, usually under some conceptual tag which obliterates the boundaries between them. A typical example is the use of the word 'milieu' in studies of mental hospitals. This word has achieved a certain popularity in the literature of social psychiatry. Its use frequently makes it unnecessary for the investigator to specify what aspect of the hospital is under observation. It may refer to the physical aspects—color scheme of rooms, layout of buildings, presence of locked or open doors. . . . It may refer to the value orientations and belief systems of hospital personnel and of the community in which the hospital exists. Or it may mean the decision as to what therapeutic technique will be practiced in the hospital. . . . It may refer to the parts of the wider social system with which the hospital is in contact, such as the upper or middle class which

a private mental hospital serves versus the working class served by public facilities; or it may refer to the internal organization of the hospital. . . . Or it may refer to the interpersonal relations which obtain in various wards of the hospitals. . . . Often it refers simultaneously to a bit of all of these operating together. (1971, pp. 68–69)

Spiegel's description of the interrelationships between adjacent foci in the transactional field calls attention to another problem in the two literatures under review. When we are dealing with more than one focus, he notes, we must specify how processes from one focus are transformed into processes within the other—for example, how somatic processes become psychological processes, and vice versa. To do this, we must either possess a theory that can convincingly explain processes at the many different foci or levels of analysis (in our case, at least the individual, the family, the social network, the community, and the culture) or possess at least a set of conceptually coherent notions which collectively can account for these processes and their transformations (Keeney, 1983). Not only do we currently lack such theories, but there seems to be little interest in creating them and little sense of what we are missing by not having them (Bowen, 1978; Spiegel, 1971; Scheflen, 1980).

INDIVIDUAL LIFE-SPAN DEVELOPMENT

We shall divide this literature into two branches. In the first, which contains theories and descriptions of life-cycle stages, the metaphor of development as a planned unfolding is taken from biology and botany and applied to human beings.[6] In this branch of the literature, it is asserted that there are predictable stages through which all human beings (at least those living in our culture) must pass (Erikson, 1950; Gould, 1978; Levinson et al., 1978; Valliant, 1977; White, 1966). This is a literature whose metaphors are growth (development) and change, and it is implied that both of these processes are natural rather than cultural.

In the second branch of the literature, in which the largest area is lifespan developmental psychology (see the review of this literature by Baltes et al., 1980), the term *development* is used broadly to mean any kind of change, and we are told that human beings continue to change. It is not, however, argued that these changes are totally predictable or that they proceed in typical stages. It is implied that change is inevitable, although cultural and historical factors can influence the

---

[6] The metaphor of development has a variety of quite different meanings within developmental psychology, ranging from the unfolding of genetically programmed processes to change in general. For a good discussion, see Harris (1957).

timing and degree of change (Baltes & Brim, 1979; Baltes et al., 1980; Bronfenbrenner, 1979; Datan & Ginsberg, 1975; Lowenthal et al., 1975; Turner & Reese, 1980).

The two branches of the life-span development literature will be reviewed in turn, beginning with the work of the doyan of the first literature, Erik Erikson, then moving on to consider the recent and celebrated study of men's midlife transitions by Levinson and his colleagues (Levinson et al., 1978), and then concluding with an examination of the literature in life-span developmental psychology, the second main branch of the individual lifespan literature.

Although preceded by other European (e.g., Buhler, 1928) and American work (e.g., the culture and personality tradition embodied in Dollard, 1935), Erikson's (1950) book *Childhood and Society* can fairly be said to have brought into American social science the notion of adult development, of life-cycle stages after adolescence. Erikson's eight-stage theory delineated particular developmental tasks for each stage, the adequate resolution of which, he argued, was necessary for the successful resolution of subsequent lifestyle tasks. Erikson's early work in this area focused mainly on the traditional developmental stages (that is, on lifestyle stages through adolescence), but in his later work (e.g., Erikson, 1968, 1969), he has paid increasing attention to later life-cycle stages. While Erikson's is a stage theory, it is a dialectical one, since he argues that different issues and different virtues are preeminent at different life-cycle stages. This argument is similar to the traditional Hindu view discussed earlier; indeed, Erikson (1969, 1976) has noted that his thinking in the last 15 years has been influenced by his encounters with the Hindu tradition.

While Erikson's work has been widely cited as having great theoretical influence (Clausen, 1972; Elder, 1975; Lerner & Busch-Rossnagel, 1981), few elements of his argument have received empirical support. There is little evidence to support his argument for the utility of his eight stages, for his contention that it is necessary to successfully resolve the tasks of one stage in order to move on adequately to the next, or for the idea that specific developmental tasks are centered in a given life-cycle stage (Clausen, 1972; Douvan & Adelson, 1966; Jurkovic & Ulrici, Chapter 7 of this volume).

Also fascinating is what is taken for granted or omitted in Erikson's description of life-cycle stages and tasks. To give one example, while Erikson treats parents as significant actors in the lives of children until the children are about five, they then almost cease to figure in Erikson's work and certainly (at least as parents) cease to develop. For another, the successful realization of many of Erikson's stage goals requires particular cultural arrangements which Erikson seems to view as *natural* phenomena. Erikson's famous description of identity formation in adolescence as occurring through intimate relationships and mean-ingful work, for example, assumes that most adolescents and young adults live in a cultural milieu in which access to meaningful work is possible. This is clearly not so (Friedenberg, 1965; Goodman, 1960; Haan, 1981).

Nor does Erikson pay much attention to the kinds of occupational settings in which individuals work or to the effects of occupational arrangements on the individual's ability to care for children, one major way in which individuals manifest generativity. (For the necessity for such attention, see Aronowitz, 1973; Berger, 1979; Miller, 1976; Mills, 1959; Rapoport & Rapoport, 1978; Walker & Wallston, Chap. 23 of this *Handbook*.) Reading Erikson's (1950) book, it would be difficult to learn, for example, that many American women work and that most American men work in settings that are organized in such a fashion that it is difficult for them to spend much time caring for children.

Analogous lacunae can be seen in the work of Levinson et al. (1978). It is true that they articulately note that "a man's life has many compo-nents: his occupation, his love relationships, his marriage and family, his use of solitude, his roles in various social contexts—all the relation-ships with individuals, groups, and institutions that have significance for him" (p. 41). Yet, reading the book closely, we find an emphasis on occupational career as viewed by the individual subjects (but little sense of the institutional structures which govern the occupational settings), on the subject's view of his love and family relationships (but no information on the point of view of the lover or spouse or children, and no observation or discussion of family interaction), and on the subject's view of himself (but little information about the ongo-ing relationships and societal contexts which provide the situations through which the men construct their view of themselves). To put it sharply, while Levinson and his colleagues take theoretical note of the importance of cultural context and of cultural and institutional forces, their book is primarily psychological in nature, focusing on indi-vidual, intrapsychic behavior.

The book's best-known finding, that there is a definite progression of stages from young adulthood to midlife, is in line with this orienta-tion, since the data underlying that assertion come from the inferences about the subjects' "life structure"—that is, the basic pattern or design of a person's life at a given time (Levinson et al., p. 41)—made by the research staff. This is a construct which puts primacy on intra-psychic experience. Levinson and his colleagues argue that "the life structure evolves through a relatively orderly sequence during the adult years" (p. 49). This argument is not convincing. Rather, seeing the change in perspective on one's life that comes from reaching (or seeing that one is about to reach) the plateau of one's current career, which came to subjects in their late 30s or early 40s, Levinson and his colleagues mistake the change for an almost biological, implacable, natural stage of life. Note some counterexamples. Studying blue-collar couples, Rubin (1976) described the men in her sample as reporting the same kinds of concerns in their early or late 20s (when their careers had already reached their limits) that Levinson's subjects reported in their late 30s and early 40s. Second, examining the marriages of influential politicians in Washington, Cuber & Haroff (1965) note that their subjects either do not share the experiences of Levinson's subjects or have them either much later in life when they lose an election. Finally, the lives of numerous people about whom we have biographical information (for example, Mozart, Churchill, Robert Moses, Schubert, Lyndon Johnson, and Douglas MacArthur) cannot gracefully be fitted into Levinson's schema.

The most important contribution of this literature is that it has taught us that adult life is not a mere repetition of early childhood experience. Hence, there is merit in studying adults and the contexts in which they live and change. This literature has also increased our sensitivity to issues and choices experienced by adults in our society and to the diverse ways adults face these issues and make these choices. In short, this literature has increased our understanding of how problematic and complicated it is to be an adult in our society.

However, as previous comments have suggested, this is a literature which overly focuses on individual experience and process, almost wholly ignores the family, and tends to reduce institutional and societal-level phenomena to vague generalities. Moreover, the assumptions of this literature not only lack empirical support but can be conceptually challenged. Writing of Erikson's work, Clausen (1972) makes a number of points that are relevant to this entire literature:

> Individual and group departures from Erikson's postulated sequence are frequent, and there is little evidence to support the thesis that autonomy, initiative, and intimacy—or even identity—tend to be definitively achieved *at* any given stage or *by* any given time. Each of these attributes has different meanings at different age levels, as Erikson himself notes, and some degree of each may be demanded at more or less specified times in any given social milieu, but phase movements differ sharply. (pp. 460–461)

Finally, it is curious that, for all the complexity of description of tasks to be mastered in a given life-cycle stage, the general assumptions of this literature are not dissimilar from the riddle of the Sphinx: development is natural, and there is a growth and decline, of sorts. The decline needs qualification because the writers in this literature find more virtue, or at least more interest, in the later stages of men's lives. It is curious also that, while this literature describes stages apparently applicable to both genders, the subjects characteristically studied or cited as examples are almost invariably men. It is apparently still hard to think of women as developing.

In the second branch of the individual life-span literature fall theorists and researchers interested in adult behavior who believe that human beings change throughout their entire life span but who do not believe that the form, the timing, or the content of these changes are predictable. Writers in this literature share not only the above assumptions but also some beliefs about the kinds of influences which produce lifespan development (Baltes et al., 1980; Bronfenbrenner, 1979; Riegel, 1975, 1976). The three major influences focused upon in this literature are:

1.   Age-graded or epigenetic influences, that is, biological or environmental determinants which have (in terms of onset and duration) a fairly strong relationship with chronological age. These events are normative if they tend to occur in highly similar ways for all individuals in a given culture or subculture.

2.   Normative history-graded influences which are events which occur to most members of a given age cohort in similar ways, though they may differ for different cohorts living at the same time in the same culture. Examples of such influences are economic depressions and wars.

3.   Nonnormative life events, that is, determinants that do not occur in any normative age or history-graded manner for most individuals (Baltes et al., pp. 75–76).

Following these assumptions, studies in this literature attempt to trace the relative importance and interaction among these influences either on a given cohort, on a given aspect of personality such as memory, intelligence, or cognitive development, or on adaptation to particular life-cycle stages or transitions (Baltes, 1979; Binstock & Shanas, 1976; Bronfenbrenner, 1979; Buss, 1979; Chandler, 1976; Datan, 1977; Datan & Ginsberg, 1975; Dragastin & Elder, 1976; Eisenstadt, 1956; Lerner & Busch-Rossnagel, 1981; Lerner & Spanier, 1978, 1980; Lowenthal et al., 1975; Porges, 1976; Schaie, 1979; Turner & Reese, 1980; Wohlwill, 1973).

These studies are often fascinating and add to our understanding of personality and development. They also have the virtue of stressing the importance of both age-graded and historical factors, and of calling attention to areas both of stability and of change in the development of persons living in a given culture at a given time.

Yet, this literature shows little sign at present of coalescing into a framework or theory that would be capable of understanding development throughout the life span. A glance at what Baltes and his colleagues (Baltes et al., 1980) term the *methodological assumptions* about the major influences on development should indicate why this is so. First, while these assumptions call our attention to three kinds of influences (age-graded, history-graded, and nonnormative), the third category is not defined but is rather a basket category for all possibly important factors that do not fit into categories one and two. So we are left with two categories of influences, and terra incognita beyond. These two categories have clearly been the province of different branches of the sciences, with the work of scientists concerned with intraindividual or individual-level phenomena represented in the age-graded category (e.g., biologists and psychologists) and scientists concerned with institutional or societal phenomena (e.g., historians, sociologists, anthropologists) represented in the history-graded category. However, as Spiegel (1971) has noted, if these different level of phenomena are to be combined, there must be a clear picture of the processes which transform phenomena at one level into phenomena at another level. Such description is lacking in this literature. Lacking also is attention to the foci which Spiegel views as intermediate between the individual and society: the family. Lacking, in fact, is attention to any group larger than the individual but smaller than the society. It is interesting that in a literature which talks frequently of dialectics (see, for example, Riegel, 1975, 1976) and of individuals as "producers of their development" (to give the title of Lerner and Busch-Rossnagel's, 1981, book), no attention is paid to the fact that individuals combine with one another to form political groups which act in concert to change things. The existence of power and social structure, of interests which act to preserve social arrangements, and of other interests which act to change these arrangements is ignored in this literature which is finally, therefore, ahistorical and politically conservative (M. Harris, 1979; Mills, 1959).

Lastly, it is clear that the lifespan developmental literature is too parochial, too much a literature of psychologists (see, for example, the final section in Baltes et al., 1980) because the conception in this literature of societal factors (i.e., history-graded influences) is so vague as to confound historians, sociologists, or historically minded men and women of letters. To talk of events such as depressions or wars as "occurring to most members of a given age-cohort in similar ways" is extremely simplistic and false, as historians (Keegan, 1976), sociologists (Elder, 1974), and novelists (e.g., Tolstoi) should have taught us by now.

Thus far, the assumptions of this literature are not that different from Jaques' "Seven Ages of Man" speech. People change (interpreted as growth), and this change is influenced both by biological (age-graded) and societal (history-graded) factors. This literature is more optimistic than Jaques in that it speaks of change rather than decline, and it does view women as developing, though little attention has been paid either to the differences and similarities in how men and women change or to the factors which influence how men and women change.[7]

THE FAMILY LIFE CYCLE

Current notions of the family life cycle entered the literature through the work of family sociologists Hill and Duvall (Duvall, 1971; Hill & Rodgers, 1964; Rodgers, 1977) in the late 40s and 50s. In the past two decades, the family life-cycle schema has increased in influence and is currently a major organizing framework in family sociology (Aldous, 1979; Rodgers, 1977). The family life-cycle schema centers around the idea that there are predictable times of transition for families, times when tasks, membership, roles, statuses, and family structure are likely to change.[8] While there is no agreement among researchers and theorists as to the number and timing of these stages—estimates range from 5 to 24—there are several life-cycle stages cited by almost everyone in this literature. These include: moving from being a couple to being married; the birth of the first child; children entering school; children entering adolescence; children leaving home (the empty nest); and retirement from work (Aldous, 1979; Carter & McGoldrick, 1980; Duvall, 1971; Rodgers, 1973, 1977).

Writings on the family life cycle have focused on the tasks involved in a particular life-cycle stage such as marriage (Rapoport, 1972) or parenting a first child (e.g., La Rossa, 1977; LeMasters, 1957), or on the issues involved in making the transition from one stage to another, or on difficulties involved in juggling the various roles played by different family members (e.g., Aldous, 1979; Hill, 1970; Rapoport & Rapoport, 1976, 1978; Rubin, 1976), or on the difficulties adult family mem-

---

[7] The work of Gilligan (1980) and Lowenthal (Lowenthal et al., 1975) and recent work influenced by the feminist movement are notable exceptions to this statement.

[8] Modern theories of stages of family life agree with the classical (Genesis) paradigm in seeing the basic function of the family as raising children and in defining the family as the separation by movement of the married couple from their families of origin into a separate household. Modern stage theories of the family go beyond the Genesis paradigm in being explicitly interested in family stages after the children have all left the parental home and after retirement from the work world.

Modern family theorists, however, show little understanding of the historical and cultural relativity of such stages: that they do not everywhere and always occur. In 18th-century American families, for example, one parent had been dead, on the average, for nine years when the last child left the house: there was no empty nest at all (Wells, 1973). This lack of understanding is only one example of the relative lack of sensitivity to demographic considerations among our theorists despite the fact that the demographer Glick (1947, 1955; Glick & Parke, 1965) is one of the creators of the family life-cycle notion.

bers have in juggling the various roles each of them plays (Gluck, Dannefer, & Milea, 1980).

This literature is important because it calls attention to the fact that, at different points in time, family members face different sets of tasks both within the family and outside of it and have differential resources to draw upon to meet these tasks (Hill, 1977; Kearns & Berger, 1980; Lerner & Spanier, 1978; Rodgers, 1977). This literature is also helpful in that it makes us notice that families commonly try to juggle sets of tasks and resources and often find it hard to meet the needs of all members of the family. Further, this literature forces us to see that any pattern of family interaction and resource allocation is likely to have to change due either to alterations in the extrafamilial involvements of family members (e.g., when an adult loses a job or a grandparent dies who was involved in child care) or through changes in the developmental needs of family members (for example, when a wife rejoins the work force or a young child grows into adolescence). In short, as Hill (1977) notes, this literature makes us consider the question of how human systems deal with time—how family members synchronize activities, keep on schedule, and maintain a sense of both individual and family identity over time (Bott, 1971; Hill, 1970; Reiss, 1980).

However, as with the individual lifespan literature, there are empirical and conceptual problems with the family life-cycle schema. Empirically, it has not been possible to establish agreement as to when certain stages are reached (how, for example, one knows that a child has definitely left home) or to show that most families with children in the appropriate age range fit comfortably into the schema (Elder, 1975; Eriksen & Tiller, 1977; Kamiko, 1977; Spanier & Sauer, 1979; Trost, 1977).

Conceptually, the very name of the schema is misleading. Rather than being a *family* life cycle, this is more precisely a description of changes over time in the relationship of children and their primary caretakers (Goode, 1977; Kamiko, 1977; Rodgers, 1977). Further, the schema equates family with two-generational constellations consisting of two parents and children of their issue, thus excluding couples, multigenerational families, single-parent families, and blended families.[9] It is also unclear how to categorize families with more than one child or families with children who are not developing normally

_____

[9] While there have been recent attempts to extend the family life-cycle framework to encompass single-parent and blended families (e.g., Aldous, 1979), the family life-cycle schema still takes for granted the "traditional" two-parent family with children (see Trost, 1977). It is fascinating also to see how little attention has been paid to the adult lives of childless couples.

(Rodgers, 1977). The schema also fails to take into account that parents work and have interests beyond their children (Elder, 1975; Foster, Berger, & McLean, 1981; Goode, 1977; Rapoport & Rapoport, 1976, 1978). Lastly, the schema underestimates how hard individuals strive, both conceptually and emotionally, to integrate their different interests and concerns. Too often, this literature reduces family members to family role-holders and misses the complexity of their inner experience.

The family life cycle and family therapy

The family life-cycle schema was brought to the attention of family therapists by Haley (1973) in his book on the work of Milton Erickson. For Haley, psychiatric symptoms are signals that a family is having difficulty in getting past a stage in the life cycle. For example, Haley would read an anxiety attack in a mother when she gives birth to a child as an expression of that family's difficulty in achieving the child-rearing stage of development.

In terms of a concern with developmental stages per se, Haley is not so much concerned with what goes on within a given life-cycle stage as he is with the problems of making the transition from one stage to the next. Stages exist as a frame through which to describe problems of transition. Or, to put it slightly differently, an individual has problems in dealing with the stage of life s/he is in, because the family matrix in which the individual is embedded is not making the transition from one stage to another which it needs to make in order to free the individual to directly face and negotiate the issues of the individual's developmental stage. Haley's framework, although explicitly couched in terms of the family life cycle, is in fact a complex interweaving of family and individual developmental cycles. For example, while the particular schema of family development that Haley uses (courtship, mating, nest building, childrearing, the dislodging of offspring into a life of their own, and retirement) is a simple one, Haley's particular flair is apparent when he starts with courtship in its social context—namely, the individuals' families of origin which must successfully launch their offspring into autonomous lives of their own in order for courtship to proceed and succeed.

In the main, family therapists' use of the family life-cycle schema has been similar to that of family sociologists, focusing therapists either on the tasks of a given life-cycle stage, or on conflicts between the life-cycle tasks or needs of different family members, or on the difficulties of negotiating transitions between stages (Carter & McGoldrick, 1980; Combrink-Graham, 1983; Haley, 1980; Hoffman, 1980; Liddle, 1983; Rosman, 1979).

The life-cycle heuristic has had many uses for therapists. It has called their attention to the fact that families change over time and cannot be regarded as stable systems[10] (Hoffman, 1980; Hughes, Berger, & Wright, 1978; Liddle & Saba, 1983). The schema has helped therapists notice that there is no one correct family style and that the most appropriate style for carrying out the tasks of one particular life-cycle stage may not be the best style in which to carry out the tasks of another stage (Combrink-Graham, 1983; Minuchin & Fishman, 1981). This idea, as Liddle and Saba (1983) have recently stressed, suggests the utility of devising specific interventions to solve particular life-cycle dilemmas, such as the work of Haley (1980) in dealing with families where children have not left home successfully. Lastly, as our discussion of Haley's work earlier noted, the life-cycle concept has focused therapists on the difficulties many families have in negotiating life-cycle transitions, transitions which require family reorganization.

However, the utility of the schema has sharp limits. In the first place, as we noted earlier, it just does not fit the experience of many families. Secondly, the concept is now being used so diffusely as to make it unclear, if not meaningless. For example, in a recent collection of essays on the clinical utility of the family life-cycle concept (Liddle, 1983), the various authors use the concept to mean family tasks within a given life-cycle stage, difficulties in negotiating transactions between stages, or difficulties in negotiating tasks thought to be present throughout the life cycle. Unless the concept is to dwindle into a mere shibboleth reminding us that families change over time, it now requires much greater specification (Liddle & Saba, 1983). Or it may be that the schema has limited conceptual utility for therapists, and it is enough that it reminds us (as Haley has noted) to look for the life-cycle transition that is not being made successfully when a family presents for therapy without a clear presenting problem.

CONCLUSIONS

It is sociological commonplace to notice that the models of human behavior and human potential held by scientists reflect the cultural and social structure of the society within which the scientist lives and works, the particular position which the scientist occupies in that culture and that social structure with its interests and commitments, and

---

[10] There has been a major controversy in the family therapy literature about whether it is meaningful to say that family systems display homeostasis or whether it is more accurate to say they are always changing (Dell, 1982; Hoffman, 1981). A more accurate position is that some parts of the system are generally changing at a faster rate than others and that families are capable of choosing to act as if parts of their system are stable if they wish to do so.

the particular "angle of vision" available from that position (Mills, 1959).

It should therefore not be surprising that developmental notions, though theoretically applicable to the entire life span, developed first with reference to infants and children (Oerter, 1972). Not surprising because that development—the equation of "developmental psychology" with child psychology—coincided with the development of institutions, and hence positions, from which social scientists would either deal directly with children (e.g. schools, institutions for the feeble-minded) or would advise those such as pediatricians, teachers, or child development specialists who were themselves dealing directly with children (Ehrenrich & English, 1978).

As more people live longer, it is not surprising that aging becomes a theme of investigation and advice. And as people live longer and space their children more closely, many more married adults spend more of their life in units without children. Thus, the empty-nest and retirement stages become foci for study. More recently, the popular literature on midlife crises has focused awareness on stages of adultness between adolescence and the empty nest.

The emergence of popular literatures on these subjects suggests that adult life, at least from middle age onward, has become more problematic—or at least that there are few clear and universally accepted guidelines in the culture as to what to expect in these periods, how to make them meaningful and important, and how to make sense of them. In this circumstance, the major function of the new lifespan development literature and the family life-cycle literatures is essentially the same as the function of the popular literature: namely, to help people prepare for these stages by telling them what to expect and what the stages mean.

This function can be seen clearly in the way the notion of predictable stages in adult life is introduced in the book which popularized the idea of adult life stages, Sheehy's *Passages* (1976).[11] She begins with an incident which occurs while she is reporting in Northern Ireland and its effect on her: a young boy she is talking to has his face blown off as she is speaking with him. She calls her man, who neither understands nor comforts her. Nor does he bring her to safety. She survives but finds that she cannot work, loses her temper, gets rid of her man, fires her secretary, loses her housekeeper (and apparently sends her daughter to her ex-husband).

She has a series of frightening experiences in which she is afraid she is going crazy or that she will commit suicide. She is concerned

---

[11] Lest it be thought that Sheehy's account of her work is due in some fashion to her lacking credentials as a professional social scientist, note that a very similar, though less dramatic, incident and conclusion is to be found at the beginning of Gould's (1978) book *Transformations*.

that she is all alone (having made herself all alone). She says several times that she is trying to find the right person to help her.

Somehow, she survives. Having done so, she immediately describes what has happened to her as a midlife crisis which had coincided with a terrible accident (she does not notice that it is no accident that people are killed in wars): "An awesome life accident had coincided with a critical turning point in my own life cycle. It was this experience that made me eager to find out everything I could about this thing called midlife crisis" (1976, pp. 13–14).

Describing what has happened to her as a midlife crisis appears to give Sheehy great solace, even as she suggests that there is no way of really facing death. And what does she then want to do with the description? She seeks to discover whether "there were, in fact, turning points in the lives of adults that were *predictable*" (1976, p. 14). As if predicting and naming what will happen to one gives one control over it: the magic paradigm.

In short, by describing adult life in terms that make it seem orderly and predictable, the life-cycle literature serves an essentially religious, meaning-creating, and stability-asserting function: it gives meaning and placement to an otherwise literally upsetting time. Indeed, the structure of the life-cycle literature (with its emphasis on the tasks, issues, and solutions of a given stage of life), draws our attention away from the fact that, as we grow older, we are moving closer to death.[12]

There can be no argument with such a religious view when it is presented as such. We do have problems with it being presented as science and with the systematic confusion of description with prescription. By using metaphors of *natural* development, this view radically underestimates the degree to which the social world is, or can be, a human creation and thus can be further changed by human action. The life-cycle literature is, therefore, politically conservative: It easily leads to the identification of the status quo with nature; and the world with which one should be concerned is identified with the world of essentially private experience, with life as an individual and as a family member. It is a cramped world which omits any possibility of public action. In such a world, human suffering is portrayed as natural.

In the *Poetics,* Aristotle had argued that man is a political animal: that human beings only achieve their full humanity in the public world of the *polis* as opposed to the private worlds of household, family, and work (Arendt, 1958; Habermas, 1969). Only a social psychology which places individuals and families in their wider social, economic,

---

[12] Notice how easily culturally accepted metaphors make us forget that we know. "Moving closer to "death" . . . That death occurs at the aged end of life is only roughly true now and was largely not true in the past: the metaphor reflects the drastic decline in infant mortality in the 20th century Western world.

and political settings and allows them to act there, as well as being acted upon, will be an acceptable and effective social psychology which is both scientifically accurate and meaningfully enlightening.[13]

To rephrase Galileo's comment upon emerging from his recantation before the Inquisition: But the wider world still moves. In a sense, we may see social scientists as being tested for their worthiness for full citizenship in that wider world. This is appropriate, since the social sciences came into being as one outgrowth of that very Enlightenment faith that human beings could and would choose to know; and knowing, would act. As Mozart's holiest character, Sarastro pronounces (in music that George Bernard Shaw termed "the only music fit to issue from the mouth of God"): "Wen solche Lehren nicht erfreun/Verdienet nicht ein Mensch zu sein." [Whom such teaching does not delight, does not deserve to be a human being, to be part of humanity.]

REFERENCES

Aldous, J. *Family careers.* New York: John Wiley & Sons, 1979.

Allen, G. *Life science in the twentieth century.* New York: John Wiley & Sons, 1975.

Arendt, H. *The human condition.* Chicago: University of Chicago Press, 1958.

Aronowitz, S. *False promises.* New York: McGraw-Hill, 1973.

Auerswald, E. The Gouveneur health services program: An experiment in ecosystemic community health care delivery. *Family Systems Medicine,* 1983, *i,* 5-24.

Baltes, P. Life-span developmental psychology: Some converging observations on history and theory. In P. Baltes & O. Brim (Eds.), *Life-span development and behavior.* New York: Academic Press, 1979.

Baltes, P., & Brim, O. (Eds.). *Life-span development and behavior.* New York: Academic Press, 1979.

Baltes, P., Reese, H., & Lipsitt, L. *Life-span developmental psychology.* Palo Alto, Calif.: Annual Reviews, 1980.

Barber, C. *Shakespeare's festive comedy.* Princeton: Princeton University Press, 1959.

Barker, R. (Ed.). *The stream of behavior.* New York: Appleton-Century-Crofts, 1963.

Barker, R. *Ecological psychology.* Stanford, Calif.: Stanford University Press, 1968.

Barker, R. (Ed.). *Habitats, environments, and human behavior.* San Francisco: Jossey-Bass, 1978.

Barker, R., & Gump, P. *Big school, small school.* Stanford, Calif.: Stanford University Press, 1964.

Barker, R., & Schoggen, D. *Qualities of community life.* San Francisco: Jossey-Bass, 1973.

Barker, R. & Wright, H. *One boy's day.* New York: Harper & Row, 1951.

---

[13] This is why the paradigmatic analysis of family in Genesis is limited and hence inaccurate: It neglects or downplays the larger political context of God's domination (see Burke, 1961).

Barker, R., & Wright, H. *Midwest and its children.* New York: Harper & Row, 1955.

Berger, M. Therapeutic consequences of men's new family roles. *The Family Coordinator,* 1979, *28,* 638–646.

Berger, M., & Jurkovic, G. (Eds.). *Family therapy in context: Practicing systemic therapy in community settings.* San Francisco: Jossey-Bass, 1984.

Binstock, R., & Shanas, E. (Eds.). *Handbook of aging and the social sciences.* New York: Van Nostrand Reinhold, 1976.

Bott, E. *Family and social network.* New York: Macmillan, 1971.

Bowen, M. *Family theory and clinical practice.* New York: Jason Aronson, 1978.

Bristol, M., & Gallagher, J. *Psychological research on fathers of young handicapped children: Evolution, review, and some future directions.* Paper presented at NICHD Conference on "Research on families with retarded persons," Rougemont, N.C., September 1983.

Bronfenbrenner, U. *The ecology of human development.* Cambridge, Mass.: Harvard University Press, 1979.

Buhler, C. *Kindheit und Jugend.* Leipsig: S. Herzel, 1928.

Burke, Kenneth. "The first three chapters of Genesis." In *The Rhetoric of Religion.* Boston: Beacon Press, 1961.

Buss, A. Dialectics, history, and development. In P. Baltes & O. Brim (Eds.), *Life-span development and behavior.* New York: Academic Press, 1979.

Carter, E., & McGoldrick, M. (Eds.). *The family life cycle.* New York: Gardner Press, 1980.

Chandler, M. Social cognition and life-span approaches to the study of child development. *Advances in Child Development and Behavior,* 1976, *11,* 225–239.

Clausen, J. The individual life course. In M. Riley, M. Johnson, & A. Foner (Eds.), *Aging and society,* (Vol. 3). New York: Russell Sage Foundation, 1972.

Combrink-Graham, L. The family life cycle and families with young children. In H. Liddle (Ed.), *Clinical implications of the family life cycle.* Rockville, Md.: Aspen, 1983.

Cuber, J., & Haroff, P. *Sex and the significant Americans.* New York: Penguin Books, 1965.

Cuisinier, J. (Ed.). *The family life cycle in European societies.* The Hague: Mouton, 1977.

Datan, N. The narcissism of the life cycle. *Human Development,* 1977, *20,* 191–195.

Datan, N., & Ginsberg, L. (Eds.) *Lifespan developmental psychology: Normative life crises.* New York: Academic, 1975.

D'Aulaine, I., & D'Aulaine, E. *The book of Greek myths.* Garden City, N.Y.: Doubleday Publishing, 1962.

Dell, P. Beyond homeostasis: Toward a concept of coherence. *Family Process,* 1982, *21,* 21–42.

Dollard, J. *Criteria for the life history.* New Haven, Conn.: Yale University Press, 1935.

Douvan, E., & Adelson, J. *The adolescent experience.* New York: John Wiley & Sons, 1966.

Dragastin, S., & Elder, G. (Eds.). *Adolescence in the life cycle.* Washington, D.C.: Hemisphere, 1976.

Duvall, E. *Family development.* Philadelphia: J. B. Lippincott, 1971.

Ehrenreich, B., & English, D. *For her own good.* Garden City, N.Y.: Doubleday Publishing, 1978.

Eisenstadt, S. *From generation to generation.* New York: Free Press, 1956.

Elder, G. *Children of the great depression.* Chicago: University of Chicago Press, 1974.

Elder, G. Age differentiation and the life course. In A. Inkeles, J. Coleman, & N. Smelser (Eds.), *Annual review of sociology.* Palo Alto, Calif.: Annual Reviews, 1975.

Embree, A. *The Hindu tradition.* New York: Random House, 1966.

Eriksen, J., & Tiller, P. Social change and the child-rearing phase: Resources and network of the modern urban family in Norway. In J. Cuisenier (Ed.), *The family life cycle in European societies.* The Hague: Mouton, 1977.

Erikson, E. *Childhood and society.* New York: W. W. Norton, 1950.

Erikson, E. *Identity, youth, and crisis.* New York: W. W. Norton, 1968.

Erikson, E. *Gandhi's truth.* New York: W. W. Norton, 1969.

Erikson, E. Reflections on Dr. Borg's life cycle. In E. Erikson (Ed.), *Adulthood.* New York: W. W. Norton, 1976.

Foster, M., Berger, M., & McLean, M. Rethinking a good idea: A reassessment of parent involvement. *Topics in Early Childhood Special Education,* 1981, *1,* 55–65.

Fried, M. N., & Fried, M. H. *Transitions: Four rituals in eight cultures.* New York: W. W. Norton, 1980.

Friedenberg, E. *Coming of age in America.* New York: Random House, 1965.

Friedman, E. Systems and ceremonies. In E. Carter & M. McGoldrick (Eds.), *The family life cycle.* New York: Gardner Press, 1980.

Galinsky, E. *Between generations: The six stages of parenthood.* Alexandria, Va.: Time-Life Books, 1981.

Gerth, H., & Mills, C. W. *Character and social structure.* New York: Harcourt Brace Jovanovich, 1953.

Gilligan, C. *In a different voice.* Cambridge, Mass.: Harvard University Press, 1980.

Glick, P. C. The family cycle. *American Sociological Review,* 1947, *120,* 164–178.

Glick, P. C. The life cycle of the family. *Marriage and Family Living,* 1955, *17,* 3–9.

Glick, P. C., & Parke, R. New approaches in studying the life cycle of the family. *Demography,* 1965, *2,* 187–202.

Gluck, N., Dannefer, E., & Milea, K. Women in families. In E. Carter & M. McGoldrick (Eds.), *The family life cycle.* New York: Gardner Press, 1980.

Goddard, Harold C. *The meaning of Shakespeare.* Chicago: University of Chicago Press, 1951.

Goode, W. Family cycle and theory construction. In J. Cuisenier (Ed.), *The family life cycle in European societies.* The Hague: Mouton, 1977.

Goodman, P. *Growing up absurd.* New York: Random House, 1960.

Gould, R. *Transformations.* New York: Simon & Schuster, 1978.

Graves, R. *The Greek myths.* New York: Penguin Books, 1960.

Haan, N. Adolescents and young adults as producers of their own development. In R. Lerner & N. Busch-Rossnagel (Eds.), *Individuals as producers of their own development.* New York: Academic Press, 1981.

Habermas, Juergen. *Strukturwandel der Oeffentlichkeit.* Neuwied, West Germany: Luchterhand Verlag, 1969.

Haley, J. *Uncommon therapy.* New York: W. W. Norton, 1973.

Haley, J. *Leaving home.* New York: McGraw-Hill, 1980.

Harris, D. (Ed.). *The concept of development.* Minneapolis: University of Minnesota Press, 1957.

Harris, M. *Cultural materialism.* New York: Random House, 1979.

Hill, R. *Family development in three generations.* Cambridge, Mass.: Schenkman, 1970.

Hill, R. Social theory and family development. In J. Cuisenier (Ed.), *The family life cycle in European societies.* The Hague: Mouton, 1977.

Hill, R. & Rodgers, R. The developmental approach. In H. Christensen (Ed.) *Handbook of marriage and the family.* Chicago: Aldine, 1964.

Hoffman, L. *Foundations of family therapy.* New York: Basic Books, 1981.

Hoffman, L., & Long, L. A systems dilemma. *Family Process,* 1969, *8,* 211–234.

Hoffman, L. Discontinuous change. In E. Carter & M. McGoldrick (Eds.), *The family life cycle.* New York: Gardner Press, 1980.

Hughes, S., Berger, M., & Wright, L. The family life cycle and clinical intervention. *Journal of Marriage and Family Counseling,* 1978, *44,* 33–40.

Judson, H. *The eighth day of creation.* New York: Simon & Schuster, 1979.

Kakar, S. The human life cycle: The traditional Hindu view and the psychology of Erik Erikson. *Philosophy East and West,* 1968, *18,* 127–136.

Kamiko, T. The internal structure of the three-generation household. In J. Cuisenier (Ed.), *The family life cycle in European societies.* The Hague: Mouton, 1977.

Kearns, D., & Berger, M. Family response to change. *Dimensions,* 1980, *9,* 20–23.

Keegan, J. *The face of battle.* New York: Viking Press, 1968.

Keeney, B. Ecological assessment. In B. Keeney (Ed.), *Diagnosis and assessment in family therapy.* Rockville, Md.: Aspen, 1983.

Klein, D., Jorgenson, S., & Miller, B. Research methods and developmental reciprocity in families. In R. Lerner & G. Spanier (Eds.), *Child influences on marital and family interaction: A life-span perspective.* New York: Academic Press, 1978.

Kuhn, T. *The structure of scientific revolutions.* Chicago: University of Chicago Press, 1970.

Kuhn, T. *The essential tension.* Chicago: University of Chicago Press, 1977.

La Rossa, R. *Conflict and power in marriage: Expecting the first child.* Beverly Hills, Calif.: Sage Publications, 1977.

LeMasters, E. Parenthood as crisis. *Marriage and Family Living,* 1957, *19,* 352–355.

Lerner, R., & Busch-Rossnagel, N. (Eds.). *Individuals as producers of their own development.* New York: Academic Press, 1981.

Lerner, R., & Spanier, G. (Eds.). *Child influences on marital and family interaction: A life-span perspective.* New York: Academic Press, 1978.

Lerner, R., & Spanier, G. *Adolescence in the life span.* New York: McGraw-Hill, 1980.

Levinson, D., Darrow, C., Klein, E., Levinson, M., & McKee, B. *The seasons of a man's life.* New York: Alfred A. Knopf, 1978.

Liddle, H. (Ed.). *Clinical implications of the family life cycle.* Rockville, Md.: Aspen, 1983.

Liddle, H., & Saba, G. Clinical use of the family life cycle: Some cautionary guidelines. In

H. Liddle (Ed.), *Clinical implications of the family life cycle.* Rockville, Md.: Aspen, 1983.

Lowenthal, M., Thurnher, M., & Chiraboga, D. *Four stages of life.* San Francisco: Jossey-Bass, 1975.

Miller, J. *Toward a new psychology of women.* Boston: Beacon Press, 1976.

Mills, C. W. *The sociological imagination.* New York: Oxford, 1959.

Minuchin, S., & Fishman, H. C. *Family therapy techniques.* Cambridge, Mass.: Harvard University Press, 1981.

Oerter, R. Development. In H. J. Eysenck, et al. (Eds.), *Encyclopedia of psychology,* London: Herder & Herder, 1972.

Porges, S. Cohort effects and apparent secular trends in infant research. In K. Riegel & J. Meacham (Eds.), *The developing infant in a changing world.* Hawthorne, N.Y.: Aldine Publishing, 1976.

Rapoport, R. The study of marriage as a critical transition for personality and family development. In P. Lomas (Ed.), *The predicament of the family.* London: Hogarth, 1972.

Rapoport, R., & Rapoport, R. *Dual-career couples reexamined.* New York: Harper & Row, 1976.

Rapoport, R., & Rapoport, R. (Eds.). *Working couples.* New York: Harper & Row, 1978.

Reiss, D. *The family construction of reality.* Cambridge, Mass.: Harvard University Press, 1980.

Riegel, K. Toward a dialectical theory of development. *Human Development,* 1975, *18,* 50–65.

Riegel, K. The dialectics of human development. *American Psychologist,* 1976, *31,* 689–700.

Rodgers, R. *Family interaction and transaction: The developmental approach.* Englewood Cliffs, N.J.: Prentice-Hall, 1973.

Rodgers, R. The family life cycle concept: Past, present, and future. In J. Cuisenier (Ed.), *The family life cycle in European societies.* The Hague: Mouton, 1977.

Rosman, B. *Developmental perspectives in family therapy with children.* Paper presented at the American Psychological Association Annual Meeting, New York, September 1979.

Rubin, L. *Worlds of pain.* New York: Basic Books, 1976.

Rukeyser, Muriel. *Breaking open,* New York: Random House, 1973.

Sarason, S. *The psychological sense of community.* San Francisco: Jossey-Bass, 1974.

Schaie, K. The primary mental abilities in adulthood: An exploration in the development of psychometric intelligence. In P. Baltes & O. Brim (Eds.), *Life-span development and behavior.* New York: Academic Press, 1979.

Scheflen, A. *Levels of schizophrenia.* New York: Brunner/Mazel, 1980.

Sennett, R., & Cobb, J. *The hidden injuries of class.* New York: Random House, 1972.

Seyffert, O. *Dictionary of classical antiquities.* 3d ed. 1894. Reprinted, Cleveland: World Publishing Company, 1956.

Sheehy, G. *Passages.* New York: E. P. Dutton, 1976.

Smith, H. *The religions of man.* New York: Harper & Row, 1958.

Spanier, G., & Sauer, W. An empirical evaluation of the family life cycle. *Journal of Marriage and the Family,* 1979, *41,* 27–40.

Spiegel, J. *Transactions.* New York: Science House, 1971.

Trost, J. The family life cycle: a problematic concept. In J. Cuisenier (Ed.), *The family life cycle in European societies.* The Hague: Mouton, 1977.

Turnbull, C. *The human cycle.* New York: Simon & Schuster, 1983.

Turner, R., & Reese, H. *Life-span developmental psychology: Intervention.* New York: Academic Press, 1980.

Vaillant, G. *Adaptation to life.* Boston: Little, Brown, 1977.

Van Gennep, A. *The rites of passage.* Reprinted, Chicago: University of Chicago Press, 1960.

Vidich, A., & Bensman, J. *Small town in mass society.* Princeton, N.J.: Princeton University Press, 1958.

Wain, John. *The living world of Shakespeare.* London: Pelican, 1966.

Wells, R. Demographic changes and the life cycle of American families. In Theodore K. Robb and Robert J. Rotberg (Eds.), *The family in history.* New York: Harper & Row, 1973.

White, R. *Lives in progress.* New York: Holt, Rinehart & Winston, 1966.

Wohlwill, J. *The study of behavioral development.* New York: Academic Press, 1973.

Zimmer, H. *Philosophies of India.* New York: Pantheon Books, 1951.

Zimmer, H. *The king and the corpse.* New York: Pantheon Books, 1957.

Zuk, G. *Family therapy: A triadic-based approach.* New York: Human Sciences Press, 1978.

Chapter 6

Sibling Relationships throughout the Life Cycle*

VICTOR G. CICIRELLI

Although scientific interest in the study of siblings has been strong since the 19th century, most early interest in the subject was focused on the effects of birth order on the characteristics of the individual. The voluminous literature devoted to this topic has been attested to by bibliographies devoted solely to birth order studies (Miley, 1969, Vockell, Felker, & Miley, 1973). Most such studies have been severely attacked on methodological grounds, however (Schooler, 1972).

WHAT CONSTITUTES A SIBLING RELATIONSHIP?

A second major line of inquiry has been concerned with effects of sibling structure on the characteristics of the individual. Sibling structure variables which have been investigated include family size, sex of the individual and of sibling, age, age spacing between the siblings, and numerous variables derived from the more basic variables characterizing the sibling constellations. Although such studies have been considered to be outdated (Lamb, 1982), replaced by more recent interests in the processes of family relationship which lead to such structural effects, the effect of sibling structure on the characteristics of the individual remains an important area. Sibling structure studies continue to be of value in the prediction of individual characteristics and in the study of individual differences (Cicirelli, 1978b; Clausen,

---

* Certain of the author's research on sibling relationships in adulthood and old age reported in this chapter was supported by grants from the American Association of Retired Persons Andrus Foundation.

1966; Sutton-Smith & Rosenberg, 1970; and Wagner, Schubert, & Schubert, 1979). Such studies, however, do not in themselves provide evidence as to how or why sibling structure came to be associated with individual characteristics.

Sibling structure and birth order studies have provided a basis for much theorizing about the causes of their effects on individual characteristics. The earliest of such theories was Adler's (1959) notion that a causal factor in sibling rivalry is the trauma associated with the child's dethronement by the arrival of a sibling. A more recent example is Walberg's conception of parental attention varying inversely as the number of children in the family increased, resulting in lower intelligence and achievement among children from larger families (Walbert & Marjoribanks, 1976). Among the most mathematically elaborate of such theories is the confluence model (Zajonc & Markus, 1975), which applied a modified growth function to explain intellectual development in terms of both the average intellectual ability of parents and siblings and the child's opportunity to teach a younger sibling. What such theories have in common is their use of family process concepts to explain individual characteristics. Each makes use of at least one sibling structure variable, but none takes all sibling structure variables into account. Each rests on assumptions about processes that go on between siblings within the family, but does not seek to explain or predict such processes themselves.

More recent work in sibling research has focused on the relationship between siblings (or between siblings and other family members) in itself. Studies have been concerned with describing and explaining the interaction between siblings, with relating the interaction between siblings to other dimensions of the sibling relationship (e.g., feelings and attitudes, knowledge about the sibling) and to sibling characteristics, and with the relationships between siblings and other family members. This inquiry into the sibling relationship will be the major concern of the present chapter. In it, we will attempt to bring together existing findings pertaining to sibling relationships over the life span and to examine the theoretical formulations which have been applied to explain sibling relationships.

Meaning of relationship

Before proceeding further, it is important to clarify what we mean by a sibling relationship. A relationship is the state of being connected by consanguinity, or the state of being mutually or reciprocally interested. The sibling relationship is an example of both definitions. Biological siblings are connected by consanguinity since they have both parents in common. Also, most siblings are mutually or reciprocally interested in one another. However, the formal definition of siblings is of little value in understanding the relationship from a psychological perspective, while the concept of mutual or reciprocal interest in one another is not sufficiently precise to be useful from a scientific standpoint.

Other attempts at definition seem to be equally unsatisfactory for a psychology of sibling relationships. Bossard and Boll (1960) define the sibling relationship in terms of the range of contacts between siblings and the ways in which they influence one another. Another definition is the classical sociological one (Becker & Useem, 1942) of a dyadic relationship, where "intimate face-to-face relations have persisted over a length of time sufficient for the establishment of a discernible pattern of interacting personalities" (p. 13). The Bossard and Boll definition is rather ambiguous as to what is meant by contacts, while in the Becker and Useem definition, it is unclear just how intimate the relationship must be, how long it must persist, or how a discernible pattern of interacting personalities is identified in order to be able to say that a relationship exists. Still another definition (Lee, 1975) regards the relationship as "social exchange involving processes of continual reaction, mutual exchanges in which each partner continually affects the other" (p. 214). Further, Schvaneveldt and Ihinger (1979) define a sibling relationship as "the nature of the interaction between brothers and sisters," where interaction refers to "the social behaviors involved when two or more persons interstimulate each other by any means of communication and hence modify each other's behavior" (p. 457). All of these definitions have in common the notion of mutual interaction and interdependence, while some contain the idea of mutual influence and others the concept of temporal duration.

Hartup (1975), Hinde (1981), and Huston and Robins (1982) introduced two important aspects to the concept of a relationship: cognitive and affective. By these we mean the knowledge, perceptions, attitudes, beliefs, and feelings of each individual about the other. Two siblings do not simply interact, with one person's behavior serving as the stimulus for the response of the other. Rather, the behavior of the first is perceived from the perspective of the second's beliefs, knowledge, attitudes, and feelings, all of which dispose the second individual to respond in a certain way or to intitiate some other behavior. These cognitive and affective aspects of the relationship are long-lasting and relatively stable, although they are affected by the interaction between the two. Huston and Robins term this *psychological interdependence.* The cognitive and affective dispositions account for the influence of the sibling in his/her absence, for continuation of the relationship over periods when there is no behavioral interaction, and for the motivation to make contact after a separation.

Drawing from such antecedents, we regard sibling relationships as the total of the interactions (actions, verbal and nonverbal communication) of two (or more) individuals who share common parents, as well as their knowledge, perceptions, attitudes, beliefs, and feelings regarding each other from the time when one sibling first became aware of the other. Thus, we regard the sibling relationship as having behavioral, cognitive, and affective components and as existing over an extended time period. (For purposes of this chapter, the term *siblings* will be used to refer to individuals who share common biological parents. Stepsiblings, half-siblings, and adoptive siblings will be referred to specifically where appropriate.)

Although the relationship between siblings has been described as a quasi-small group, there are a number of important differences between sibling relationships and those among members of other small groups. Siblings share a biological heritage from their parents, with more than 99 percent of sib pairs having from 33 to 66 percent of their genes in common (Scarr & Grajek, 1982). Siblings also have a commitment to maintain the relationship, usually over their entire life span (Walters, 1982); indeed, it is rare for siblings to break off their relationship or to lose touch completely with one another (Cicirelli, 1980b). The relationship has a longer course than most other human relationships, beginning at the birth of the younger child and continuing, for most, throughout the life span. If, as Graziano and Musser (1982) contend, a relationship begins when one person becomes aware of another, then the sibling relationship may well begin within the younger child's first year of life. Dunn and Kendrick (1982a) have evidence of sibling interaction by nine months of age. Indeed, for the older child, the cognitive and emotional aspects of the relationship may begin in the months before the younger child's birth (Nadelman & Begun, 1982), when the older child learns of the impending arrival of a sibling. Finally, the sibling relationship has a long shared history of intimate experiences which distinguish it from nonfamily small groups. Sibling relationships differ from other family relationships as well, by the fact that they typically endure over a longer portion of life and are more egalitarian in nature (Sutton-Smith & Rosenberg, 1970).

All relationships can be viewed as having a unique developmental/aging history (Graziano & Musser, 1982; Kimmel, 1979), with an initiation phase, a maintenance phase, and a dissolution phase. Sibling relationships, too, must be viewed within such a developmental perspective, although the time frame of the relationship typically extends over the entire life span. The relationship's initiation phase occurs in early childhood as basic attachments develop. Then the relationship undergoes a long maintenance phase, during which the intensity of the relationship fluctuates as one sibling or the other encounters various life events such as entry into school, puberty, departing the parental home, getting a job, getting married, having children, loss of parents, and so on. Siblings may interact with greater frequency at one time period then another, and there may be periods when they do not meet or communicate directly for rather extended intervals. Yet, the relationship does go on (Hinde, 1981), with parents, other siblings, or other kin providing the linkage of communication or simply through the persistence of the image of the sibling maintained in the cognitive and affectional system of the individual. Finally, although intentional dissolution of the sibling relationship is rare, the relationship may end abruptly with the death of a sibling or gradually dissolve with other declining functions in very advanced old age. In studying sibling relationships, then, one cannot speak of a relationship which remains invariant over all stages of life, but must rather consider the relationship at various points over its entire course. We will attempt to do this within the present chapter.

THE SIBLING RELATIONSHIP WITHIN THE FAMILY AND SOCIAL CONTEXT

The sibling relationship does not take place in isolation, but typically takes place within the confines of the family and within the broader social context. Further, the nature of the relationship appears to be dependent, at least to some degree, on the type of family and culture within which it is found.

When viewing the sibling relationship within the family context, perhaps the most productive conceptual scheme is that of the family as a system. The family system involves three major subsystems: the parent-parent (or spousal) subsystem, the parent-child subsystem, and the child-child (or sibling) subsystem. With such a frame of reference, sibling relationships must be understood in terms of the effects of relationships with other subsystems rather than as an effect of an external stimulus alone. Siblings' perceptions, feelings, and behaviors are considered within the context of their relationships with others. What happens within the parent-child or parent-parent subsystem has an effect upon (and is affected by) what happens within the sibling subsystem. Thus, siblings socialize each other indirectly through parental mediation (Schvanefeldt & Ihinger, 1979).

Family systems theory has had its greatest use as a guide to family therapy. Among such theories are those of Minuchin (1974), Bank and Kahn (1975, 1982), and Kantor and Lehr (1975). While detailed consideration of these theories is not relevant to present concerns, all consider relationships with siblings to be an important factor in child therapy.

The sibling relationship, like other family relationships, is also influenced by its cultural context. Weisner (1982) has described cross-cultural differences in child caretaking of younger siblings in various cultures, as well as in regard to marriage and property customs. Within the United States, sibling relationships may vary depending on socioeconomic status level (Adams, 1968) or ethnicity (Johnson, 1982). While there is relatively little research on this topic, we must be careful in considering sibling relationships to examine the broader cultural context within which they are found, before attempting to generalize from existing findings.

The sibling subsystem

Although we will attempt to keep the larger family system in mind and to present findings which are pertinent, relationships between siblings will be the main focus of attention.

In studying sibships consisting of more than two siblings, we must also consider the existence of minisubsystems of siblings. These are often found within the larger sibling subsystem and consist of coalitions of two or more siblings for the purpose of exercising power (Bank & Kahn, 1975, 1982; Schvanefeldt & Ihinger, 1979) or as alliances based on mutual interests (Minuchin, 1974). Such minisubsystems may consist of dyads, triads, or larger groups, depending on such sibling structure variables as age, sex, and age differences as well as on special interests, geographic proximity (in adulthood), and the like. The minisubsystems may be relatively permanent, or they may be quite fleeting in nature.

The researcher of siblings is thus confronted with the question of identifying the appropriate unit for study. Should it be the entire family, the sibling subsystem, a minisubsystem, or simply a sibling dyad? Obviously, the unit of study should be selected with regard to the purpose of the inquiry. Another consideration is the existence of methods for the study of larger units. Sutton-Smith and Rosenberg (1970) have demonstrated the rapidly increasing complexity of studying siblings as the number of siblings in the family increases. The number of unique sibling status positions based on sex and birth order alone rises from 8 in the two-child family to 24 in the three-child family to 160 in the five-child family; if age and age spacing are also considered, the number of identifiable sibling status positions rises even more sharply. For this reason, these authors recommended studying the two-child family. A further reason for concentrating on the sibling dyad in the two-child family is the diminishing size of the American family, with two-child families becoming much more prevalent. If this is the family of the future, then it is important to accumulate knowledge about sibling relationships in the two-child family, and the study of sibling dyads takes on added significance. Finally, the body of accumulated knowledge in regard to siblings is largest in regard to two-child families, making study of the dyad more relevant. One should not pursue a given topic simply because it has been more widely studied in the past. However, for all the reasons stated above, we have selected the sibling dyad as the basic unit of study for the chapter. Larger sibling groups will be discussed where possible, as will the interactions between the sibling subsystem and the larger family.

Nearly all of the research into sibling relationships which has been carried on thus far has dealt with true biological siblings who share the same mother and father. Yet, the number of children who are reared in intact nuclear families has been declining as the divorce rate increases. It has been estimated that half of all current marriages will end in divorce, with about three fourths of the former partners remarrying. Often, the new marital partners each bring children from a former marriage, and there may be additional children from the new union. Thus, the family in which a child is reared may contain half- or stepsiblings, while true siblings may or may not reside in the same home. Although it is difficult to estimate the number of children with half- and stepsiblings, it may be as great as 1 in 7 or even larger (Furstenberg, Spanier, & Rothschild, 1982). Indeed, by 1990, as many as a third of all children will have experienced the dissolution of their parents' marriage by the time they reach age 18. When adopted children, children with a deceased parent, children with single parents, and the like are also taken into account, it is clear that those who work with siblings cannot assume the existence of a traditional nuclear family system. Studies of the blended or reconstituted families which result following remarriage are beginning to appear (e.g., Duberman, 1975). Based on interviews with parents, Duberman found that 38 percent of children in such families had poor relationships with stepsiblings, but that relationships tended to be better when there was a good relationship with the stepparent and between the new spouses themselves. We need to focus attention on the sibling subsystem in these exceedingly complex families to understand how children interact with half- and stepsiblings as well as with their true biological siblings. This should be an important area for future investigations.

Changes in the sibling subsystem over the life cycle

According to Schvaneveldt and Ihinger (1979), sibling interaction is a "continuous developmental process not limited to the early critical years" (p. 456). Of the three major family subsystems, the sibling subsystem is potentially the most enduring, with many sibling dyads in exis-tence for 80 or 90 years. Over the long span of this dyadic relationship, there are many changes. The individual enters the family system as an infant and either enters into an existing sibling subsystem at birth or does so with the birth of a younger child. As the individual grows older, the family system and the individual's roles within that system change. Beginning in the role of child in the family of origin, the individual "rises" in the system to assume the roles of spouse and then parent in the family of procreation and finally the roles of grand-parent and possibly great-grandparent. At the same time, certain roles (e.g., dependent child) are relinquished with the passage of time. The family system in adulthood and later life may be looked upon as com-posed of overlapping nuclear family systems, with the middle-aged adult child taking the role of parent in the nuclear family which he or she heads and taking the role of child in the nuclear family of origin. When grandparents die, the role of grandchild is no longer available, and when elderly parents die, the role of adult child is given up.

Thus, over the life span of the individual, the sibling subsystem retains its identity while there are changes in the kinship structure which affect the system of which the sibling subsystem is a part. Over the years, the individual's family of procreation expands while the family of origin gradually disintegrates as its members die. Only frag-ments of the original nuclear family system remain, in the form of sibling dyadic relationships. The subsystem continues to endure after the whole is gone, with the whole continuing to exist only as memories within the remaining individuals (Cicirelli, 1982b).

The sibling subsystem is most interdependent with the other subsys-tems of the family early in life. As the family ages, the sibling subsystem becomes more autonomous. The subsystems become a loose federation in adulthood, but the system moves toward greater integration when a family crisis occurs. Eventually, the sibling subsystem becomes more important than the whole family as the family of origin gradually disin-tegrates with the death of its members. The implication of this concep-tion of the sibling subsystem as moving toward greater autonomy is that the sibling relationship can be studied somewhat independently of the other family subsystems, particularly in later life.

On this basis, we will focus attention on the sibling subsystem (espe-cially the sibling dyad) in this chapter, describing the sibling relation-ship as it exists, the maintenance of the relationship, changes over time, and the antecedents of such relationships. We will begin by con-sidering the three main aspects of the sibling relationship: emotions and feelings, cognitive aspects (knowledge, perceptions, and judg-ments), and interactions between siblings.

ASPECTS OF THE SIBLING RELATIONSHIP: EMOTIONS AND FEELINGS

Among the emotions and feelings which siblings have for one another, first to come to mind are love and affectional closeness on the one hand and the opposing feelings of jealousy and rivalry on the other. They will be considered in this portion of the chapter, as well as feelings of involvement and indifference, and so on.

Attachment and closeness of feeling

Considerable evidence exists that most siblings feel some degree of affectional closeness for one another throughout their lives. We may then ask: How and when do such feelings develop? How are they maintained over the life span? Do they decline in later years?

Siblings respond to each other from infancy onward, but can they be said to have feelings toward the other at an early age? This is an issue which has not been settled as yet, with some arguing that the child does not have sufficient cognitive development for such feelings to have relevance and others arguing that such feelings do develop quite early in life and may be clearly inferred from children's behavior (Borke, 1972; Bretherton & Beeghly, 1982; Burlingham & Freud, 1944; Dunn & Kendrick, 1982b). Dunn and Kendrick observed siblings from before the birth of the younger sibling, when the older child was between 1½ and 2 years of age, until the younger child was 14 months old; over this time period, they observed both behavior of the older sibling which was warm and affectionate toward the younger child and friendly behavior on the part of the infant. At the same time, the older child interpreted the younger child's actions in terms of feelings. On this basis, we would agree with Dunn and Kendrick that children's recognition of their own and their siblings' feelings comes well before age three. Obviously, a more sophisticated understanding and greater differentiation of emotions and feelings develops more gradually.

While relationships between infants and their preschool older siblings are quite variable, in most cases there is evidence of some behavior that indicates warmth and affection toward the sibling (Dunn & Kendrick, 1982a, 1982b), such as smiling, touching affectionately, giving, comforting, and so on. Median values of 70 percent of the infant's and 55 percent of the older child's approaches to each other were positive in nature. Older individuals have typically been asked to indicate their feelings for siblings on self-report instruments. Bowerman and Dobash (1974) found that 65 percent of a large sample of junior and senior high school students reported feeling close or extremely close to their siblings; only 13 percent said that they did not feel close. Greater closeness was reported by girls and by same-sex siblings. In larger families, a child frequently feels particularly close to one or two siblings. When college women were asked to indicate how close they felt to this closest sibling, mean closeness was 6.10 (SD = 1.14) on a seven-point scale; this was significantly closer than they felt to their fathers and only slightly less close than they felt to their mothers (Cicirelli, 1980a). Closeness to other siblings in the family was not as great and did not depend on sibling structure variables. It was expected that sibling relationships would be unusually close during the college years, with siblings being particularly supportive of efforts to establish independence from parents and to take on new roles and values.

When siblings leave the parental home in young adulthood to establish careers and new homes of their own, feelings of closeness seem to persist in spite of geographic separation. In Adams' (1968) survey of young to middle-aged adults (median age 33 years), 48 percent of those interviewed reported a high degree of closeness. Pairs of sisters were closest of all, 60 percent reporting a high degree of closeness, with cross-sex pairs intermediate and pairs of brothers lowest in closeness. More than half reported feeling closer in adulthood than they did while growing up. Cicirelli (1982a) asked both middle-aged and elderly adults how close they felt to the sibling with whom they had the most contact, with responses on a four-point scale. In middle age, 68 percent reported feeling close or very close to their siblings, and only 5 percent did not feel close at all. In the elderly group, 83 percent reported feeling close or very close to their sibling. Although these studies suggest that feelings of closeness to siblings increase with increasing age (and there was a significant linear trend in the data), this must be considered only a tentative conclusion since there are no longitudinal data on sibling relationships in later life. Different cohorts may vary in their willingness to express their feelings about their siblings. Sisters were named most frequently as the sibling to whom these adults felt closest.

Existing evidence (Cicirelli, 1980b) indicates a decline of contact with siblings in the latter portion of the life span. However, it appears that there is not only no decline in feelings of closeness to siblings in adulthood and later life but very possibly an increase. Since the usual truism is that we feel closest to those we see most often, how can such a situation be explained? What explains the persistence of sibling relationships over time and distance, when most peer relationships tend to fade away in such circumstances?

Attachment theory (Ainsworth, 1972; Bowlby, 1979, 1980) can aid in understanding the sibling relationship as well as the bond between mother and child (see Section 5 of this *Handbook*). According to the theory, the child's attachment can be inferred from its attempt to maintain proximity, contact, or communication with the parent and thus represents an internal state within the individual. Attachment refers to an emotional or affectional bond between two people and is essentially being identified with, in love with, and having the desire to be with another person. The attachment bond continues, even though proximity-seeking behaviors may appear only occasionally. The young child leaves the parent for varying distances and times, returning to renew contact with the parent. Somewhat later in time, a protective aspect of attachment develops in which the child desires to protect the attached figure; this is distinct from attachment behavior and complementary to it in that it is concerned with preserving or restoring the threatened existence of the attached figure rather than merely maintaining or restoring proximity. According to Bowlby, attachment does not end in childhood or early adolescence, but endures throughout life. However, the attachment, exploratory, and protective behaviors are modified as appropriate to the stage in life. In adulthood, feelings of attachment are manifested in periodic communication, visiting, and responses to reunions, while protective behavior is shown in helping and care-giving behavior that attempts to maintain the survival of the attached figure and preserve the emotional bond. The reader should be aware that there is currently a great deal of conceptual and theoretical diversity in the literature on attachment (see Lerner & Ryff, 1978, for a discussion of the various approaches). We will not attempt to debate the various approaches in this chapter, but will remain generally in the Ainsworth-Bowlby tradition.

Attachment is not restricted to the mother; multiple attachments to other objects (father, other family members, friends) can develop (Hartup & Lempers, 1973; Troll & Smith, 1976) through such mechanisms as conditioning (Gewirtz, 1976) or self-promoted feedback (Kalish & Knudtson, 1976; Knudtson, 1976). Recent studies (Dunn & Kendrick, 1982; Stewart, 1983) have concluded that young children display toward their older siblings behaviors which imply an attachment to the sibling. Although Lamb (1978) observed that both infants and their older siblings interacted more with their mother than with each other in a triadic situation and concluded that the siblings were not attached, Stewart (1983) observed young siblings when the mother was absent and found that the older siblings served as subsidiary attachment figures. They comforted and reassured their younger siblings, and the younger child used the older as a secure base of exploration in the presence of a stranger.

Bank and Kahn (1982), based on clinical study of siblings, also noted the strong affectional bond that can exist between siblings. They use the terms *sibling attachment* and *sibling loyalty*, but regard this sort of bond as having an incomplete, unsatisfactory, and anxious nature. According to Bank and Kahn, the bond of deep sibling loyalty develops when there is weakness, failure, or absence of parents (either physically or emotionally) to provide for the children and there is a relative unavailability of parent surrogates. Even in situations where a competent mother is available, a sibling may be used as a secondary attachment figure in making a transition away from the mother toward greater autonomy. Bank and Kahn seem to regard the sibling bond as a rather perilous tie which can easily lead to emotional problems. It remains to be seen, however, just how applicable this view of the sibling relationship is to children in the average family.

Troll and Smith (1976) devised a measure of attachment to study the dyadic bonds among family members and friends. The measure included such things as knowledge of the individual, amount of present influence, strength of relationship, quality of relationship, obligation, and responsibility. In a small study of university graduate students, the affectional bond was found to be independent of proximity. Attachment scores were higher for parents and intimate friends than for siblings, but were higher for siblings than for other kin. Sisters were rated more positively than were brothers. We can conclude from this evidence that there is a relatively close attachment to siblings which overrides separation and distance. Indeed, according to Troll and Smith, the bond can persist after the death of the attached figure.

To explain the maintenance of the attachment bond over space and time, we can argue that the propensity for closeness and contact with the attached figure continues through the life span (although it may vary in intensity at different stages of life), but is satisfied on a symbolic level (Cicirelli, 1983). Identification is the mechanism by which symbols are used to establish closeness and contact on a psychological level. Love is the essential ingredient of the affective bond, and identification is the essence of love (Fromm, 1956); it is a process whereby the individual takes over the features of another person to make them a part of his own personality. Through identification, the person can feel close to the attached figure by calling forth the symbolic representation of the person and experiencing a sense of closeness on this level through the similarity of certain personality characteristics. The individual can thus continue to feel a bond to the absent sibling, use the sibling as a model for certain actions, and so on, by using the psychological representation. This symbolic contact can be supplemented by periodic visits, telephone communication, letter writing, and messages or information conveyed through another family member or third party.

The importance of identification processes in the sibling relationship has also been stressed by Bank and Kahn (1982). They distinguish three main levels of identification: close identification, in which the person feels great similarity with a sibling (and may have difficulty in establishing a separate identity); partial identification, in which the person feels some identification with a sibling (experiencing closeness, comfort, and guidance, but also freedom to determine his/her own destiny); and distant identification, in which the person feels little similarity and great difference with a sibling (often leading to rejection or disowning of that sibling).

Further support for the role of symbolic processes in maintaining the attachment bond to siblings comes from a series of detailed discussions with adults about sibling relationships (Ross, Dalton, & Milgram, 1980; Ross & Milgram, 1982). Feelings of closeness to siblings were seen as originating in childhood; memories of early closeness and internalized shared values, goals, and interests maintained the sense of continuity of this closeness in spite of separation in adulthood. Contact with the sibling in periodic reunions tended to be highly valued, as did other forms of communication.

In sum, the available evidence on feelings of closeness between siblings leads to the conclusion that a majority of siblings (although not all) have close feelings of affection for each other, that feelings of closeness increase in later adulthood and old age, and that there is an attachment bond between siblings which accounts for the persistence of sibling relationships over separations of time and distance. Closeness to various siblings in the same family varies, but there tends to be greater closeness to sisters than to brothers. It should be remembered, however, that except for some of the data in early childhood, most of the findings were based on the reports of one sibling about the relationship. Further study of both siblings involved in a sibling relationship is needed to determine whether there is mutuality of these feelings.

Rivalry, jealousy, competition, and conflict

Rivalry between siblings has been written about from the earliest recorded history and, with the advent of psychoanalysis, has been regarded by many as a major force in child development. Adler (1959) considered the dethronement of the older child from a position of being the focus of attention in the family by the birth of a younger sibling, as a trauma responsible for feelings of sibling rivalry. The younger child is, at the same time, in a weaker position in comparison to the older child and must constantly strive to overcome this inferiority.

Sibling rivalry involves competition of the siblings for rewards such as love, approval, recognition, and so on. It has as its basis comparisons and evaluations of the siblings—either by one or both of the siblings or by someone else—on traits, achievements, appearance, or other dimensions of concern. Most often, sibling rivalry involves a sibling's weakness on some dimension and the rival sibling's strength on the same dimension (Ross & Milgram, 1982), along with an evaluative comparison of the two. The feeling of rivalry is usually accompanied by the emotion of jealousy of the sibling. Rivalry can exist in all degrees from very slight to very intense, depending on characteristics of the children themselves, relationships with parents, family values, and so on. At its mildest, it may be an amicable competition on some dimension. At greater intensity, there may be feelings of hatred and a desire to do harm. In many cases, such feelings erupt in aggressive behaviors directed against the sibling.

We have already seen that there is considerable variability in siblings' positive feelings toward one another in early childhood, as indicated by their behaviors and the older child's statements. What evidence is there of feelings of rivalry in early childhood? According to Nadelman and Begun (1982), as many as 40 percent of the mothers they interviewed regarding their older child's adjustment to the impending birth of a sibling reported that the older sibling had ambivalent reactions to the new sibling, while 64 percent had negative reactions in the few weeks following birth. Dunn and Kendrick (1982a, 1982b) found wide variation in the extent to which firstborns exhibited hostility toward their infant siblings, ranging from none for some of the children they studied to 100 percent of all interactions with the baby for others, with a median of about 45 percent of hostile reactions. By contrast, only about 30 percent of the infants showed hostility to their older siblings. These findings are in rough agreement with early studies (Levy, 1937; Smalley, 1930) which found that about half of all firstborn children showed jealousy of their younger siblings, with more jealousy of a same-sex than of an opposite-sex sibling. Among older preschool sibling pairs (Abramovitch, Pepler, & Corter, 1982), there was also a great deal of hostile behavior. The various studies make clear that these young children exhibit behaviors which may readily be termed hostile or agonistic. The real question is whether one can infer the existence of feelings of rivalry and jealousy from such behaviors. As we have argued in the case of positive feelings, quite young children are able to recognize their own feelings and to interpret the actions of others in terms of feelings; there is no reason to believe that this does not occur with negative feelings as well, particularly when hostile and aggressive behaviors are as prevalent as they are. Certainly, there are anecdotal reports of young children with strong feelings of jealousy toward a sibling (e.g., Bank & Kahn, 1982).

Studies of siblings in middle adulthood provide more definite evidence of feelings of sibling rivalry. When brothers differed in certain dimensions of personality or traits, the one who suffered in the comparison experienced feelings of rivalry toward the brother who excelled, while the older brother also experienced some negative feelings in the relationship (Pfouts, 1976, 1980). Similarly, when one sibling is perceived as receiving preferential treatment from the parent, both siblings experience ill will toward each other, not just the less-favored child (Bryant, 1982; Bryant & Crockenberg, 1980). Both studies demonstrate the importance of comparison processes in sibling rivalry.

Ihinger (1975) has theorized about the importance of the parent's role in sibling rivalry. In her view, the parent has control over the distribution of rewards in the family. When there is conflict between the siblings over a certain reward, the parent acts in the role of referee to allocate the reward. When the parent is consistent and behaves according to clearly stated moral principles, there is less rivalry than there is in families where the parent is inconsistent or fails to state moral rules. Feelings of rivalry and hostility occur when the child's sense of justice is violated.

Whether or not Ihinger is correct about the importance of parental consistency and rule setting in relation to sibling rivalry, others (Dunn & Kendrick, 1982b; Nadelman & Begun, 1982) have found parental behavior to be important in preschool children. Rivalry was less when mothers discussed the motives, intentions, and feelings of the younger child with the older child, as well as when fathers helped to ensure that both children received adequate parental attention following the birth of the younger child.

To what extent does rivalry between siblings persist into adult years? Once children grow up and leave the parental home, do feelings of rivalry continue or do they gradually dissipate once siblings are no longer competing for limited rewards at home? Certainly, sibling rivalry can last until the end of life. One 80-year-old man whom we interviewed felt such hostility toward his brother that he refused to even speak of him in the interview. But, to what extent is this typical?

In younger adulthood, there is evidence of sibling rivalry. Adams (1968) found that there was more competitiveness, ambivalence, and jealousy between pairs of brothers than between any other sibling combination, although some rivalry was reported within every sibling group. Troll (1975) concluded that adults use their siblings as "measuring sticks" by which to evaluate their own success or lack of it and that ill feelings tend to result when a sibling is perceived as getting too far ahead. Adams (1968) found the relationship between brothers to be the poorest when they were at different occupational levels. Further, the most-satisfied workers were those who felt that they were doing better occupationally than their brothers, while the least-satisfied workers were those who felt that their brothers were doing better than they (Form & Geschwender, 1962). The centrality of rivalry to many adults was borne out by findings (Noberini, Brady, & Mosatche, unpublished) that those with hostile feelings toward siblings in adulthood tend to be cautious, rigid, anxious, stereotyped, and conventional, while those who perceive their siblings as being jealous of them tended to be more self-assured, outgoing, sincere, stable individuals. Thus, well into adulthood it appears that the feeling that one is the least-favored sibling can damage not only the sibling relationship but the individual's outlook on life.

Rivalry continues into later life as well, although for most it appears to be abated somewhat. In a study of middle-aged adults, Cicirelli (1981b) found that only 2 percent felt frequent feelings of competition with the sibling, and only 3 percent reported frequent arguments with the sibling. Even this weak evidence of sibling rivalry was found to decline with age. Allan (1977) has argued that sibling rivalry dissipates as individuals get older, largely because interaction between siblings in later life is limited in frequency in comparison to earlier years and the nature of the interaction is such that siblings can avoid rivalrous conflicts. When siblings are brought together by family concerns, such as the care of aged parents or the settling of an estate, there may be a regression to earlier rivalry and hostility (Berezin, 1977). Thus, it may be that sibling rivalry does not truly disappear in adulthood, but exists in a latent state.

Many people may find it difficult to admit to feelings of sibling rivalry in adulthood (Ross & Milgram, 1980, 1982). Such feelings are usually actively discouraged by parents, and children are led to feel that it is shameful, immature, or immoral to feel jealousy or hostility toward siblings. Thus, sibling rivalry, as a socially undesirable feeling, is likely to be underestimated by self-report measures. Ross and Milgram conducted small-group interviews with adults ranging from 25 to 93 years of age, feeling that self-disclosure about rivalrous feelings would be stimulated in a clinical setting. They found that 71 percent of the adults reported rivalrous feelings with a sibling at some point in their lives, with these feelings arising early in childhood or in adolescence. Some 26 percent reported that they were able to overcome earlier sibling rivalry, but 45 percent still experienced rivalry in their adult years. Many of those who still felt rivalry attributed it to a continuation of patterns from childhood into sibling interactions in adulthood, while others felt that the rivalry developed in adulthood.

Ross and Milgram (1982) found that the maintenance of sibling rivalry in adulthood depends on continued parental favoritism, competitive behaviors between siblings, feeling excluded from interactions of other family members (e.g., coalitions), family-assigned roles and labels, and never mentioning the rivalrous feelings to the siblings involved. However, in spite of these factors contributing to maintenance of rivalry, even Ross and Milgram's data indicate that earlier feelings of rivalry had diminished for many in the adult years. By late adulthood and old age, the repair and renewal of sibling relationships takes on importance to many people; when reasons for feelings of rivalry are reevaluated from the more mature perspective of later adulthood and changes in both siblings are taken into account, the intensity of the rivalry may well diminish.

Ambivalent and mismatch relationships

Is it inconsistent for feelings of closeness and rivalry toward a sibling to exist at the same time? Researchers who see love-hate or friendliness-hostility existing as a bipolar scale (e.g., Wish, Deutsch, & Kaplan, 1976) would seem to characterize an interpersonal relationship in terms of some point on the continuum, so that one would expect a rivalrous relationship to have little closeness. However, Troll, Miller, and Atchley (1978) theorize that there is a basic love-hate ambivalence in human relationships and that strong positive feelings cannot arise where there are not strong negative feelings at the same time. People who are not closely enough involved with each other do not feel either love or hate. Further, relationships are not constant, with positive and negative feelings varying in the ebb and flow of the relationship. The heights of love in a marriage can be followed by a violent quarrel and by a subsequent making up, as is well known. Similarly, the stereotype of siblings as fighting between themselves yet basically close is equally well known.

Ambivalence of feelings toward a sibling apparently exists from the beginning of the relationship. Mothers reported prebirth ambivalence toward a sibling in 40 percent of the children and ambivalent initial reactions to the baby in 26 percent (Nadelman & Begun, 1982). Dunn and Kendrick (1982a, 1982b) have also noted ambivalence toward the sibling as evident in the children's behavior patterns. The same children were often observed to behave in both a friendly and a hostile manner toward their sibling; relatively few sibling relationships were uniformly warm or uniformly hostile. In middle childhood too, ambivalence appears characteristic of the sibling relationship (Bryant, 1982), with greater ambivalence between closely spaced siblings than between those with wider age spacings (Bigner, 1974a). Ambivalence toward siblings continues in adulthood as well and may be an inevitable factor in sibling relationships, given the nature of sibling comparison processes.

We have speculated elsewhere (Cicirelli, 1982a) on the existence of a closeness-rivalry dialectic between siblings which leads to individual growth and growth in the relationship. Excessive closeness can interfere with the development of an individual identity, while excessive rivalry can be totally destructive (Bank & Kahn, 1982). However, a certain degree of rivalry can be an incentive to personality growth and individual achievement, while feelings of closeness can provide the warmth and support within which such growth can more easily take place. Thus, the successful resolution of rivalry may lead to growth and new dimensions of closeness in the relationship. Further comparison processes could induce rivalrous feelings in some new dimension, conflicting with feelings of closeness and leading to yet another resolution. Such a process would explain the value that many older people place on the renewal or repair of sibling relationships in later years. On the other hand, one can conceive of both closeness and rivalry as situation-specific emotions, with rivalry appearing strongly in certain circumstances and closeness appearing in others. However, the fact that many siblings do experience conflict between feelings of closeness and feelings of rivalry argues against such a situation-specific view.

Are feelings between siblings reciprocated, or are "mismatch" relationships common? Other than some observational studies in childhood, there are few studies involving both members of a sibling dyad. Among preschool children, Dunn and Kendrick (1982a) remarked on the incidence of such mismatch relationships, with younger siblings' positive approaches often meeting with older siblings' negative responses. Bank and Kahn (1982) provide anecdotal evidence of a much-younger sibling who idolizes a much-older sibling, but who is actively rejected by the older. In our own studies of adult sibling relationships, we have found that later-born siblings feel closer to firstborns than firstborns feel to later-borns. One member of a sibling dyad feels stronger rivalry as a result of being the inferior one in a comparison; however, the other member of the dyad also experiences some degree of negative feelings (Pfouts, 1980). In view of the fact that siblings rarely discuss rivalrous feelings with each other in adulthood (Ross & Milgram, 1982), it is certainly possible that one sibling's feelings of rivalry are neither perceived nor returned by the other. However, although few relationships may be completely reciprocated, most sibling pairs know when they have a mutually close relationship or one in which there is bad feeling and estrangement. This area is one where careful study of both members of the sibling dyad is needed before reaching any final conclusion in the matter.

Involvement and indifference

Sibling relationships also vary according to the degree of the siblings' emotional involvement in the relationship. Siblings who are close confidants are more emotionally involved than are siblings who are widely separated by age and interests. Johnson (1982) has found, for example, more emotional involvement in the sibling relationship among Italian-American adults than among those of European Protestant backgrounds. Wish et al. (1976), using techniques of multidimensional scaling, were able to isolate four bipolar dimensions of human relationships. One of these was a superficial-intense dimension; this would seem to be an indicator of the degree of emotional involvement. A number of young adults' relationships were rated on the dimension. Sibling relationships were rated as less intense than relationships with parents or spouse, but more intense than relationships with classmates, co-workers, or casual acquaintances. Also they tend to regard current relationships with siblings as slightly less intense than sibling relationships in childhood.

A recently completed study explored the question of indifference to siblings by asking middle-aged and elderly adults to indicate the extent to which they felt indifferent toward their closest sibling. Some degree of indifference was reported by 26 percent of the elderly group and by 39 percent of the middle-aged group; only 7 percent of each group reported quite a bit or more-extreme levels of indifference. Clinical data (e.g., Bank & Kahn, 1982), indicate very high levels of emotional involvement in the relationship among some sibling pairs. While very high involvement in a sibling relationship in adulthood can be indicative of adjustment problems, those with very low involvement miss the emotional support which siblings can give in dealing with major life events.

Other feelings

Although feelings of closeness and feelings of rivalry come most readily to mind when one thinks of the emotional aspect of a sibling relationship, there are other feelings which also bear examination. However, there is little or no research evidence which pertains to these topics.

In childhood, some relationships are characterized by much physical and verbal aggression, particularly by an older, larger sibling against a younger. In such a situation, the weaker sibling can experience fear and anxiety in the presence of the older. Bank and Kahn (1982) cite some case histories in which such fear and anxiety played a part. In our own interviews of elderly siblings (unpublished), interviewees were asked to use a five-point scale to indicate the degree to which they felt "nervous and tense" when the sibling was around. The mean rating was 1.60, which indicated that such feelings were low for most adults, but did exist in some degree for a minority of the elderly siblings.

Not known is whether such feelings are aroused as a by-product of sibling rivalry or come about as a result of differences in temperament or lifestyles.

Death of a sibling can have a profound effect on the surviving children in a family. Loss of a sibling in childhood is not as common in our society as it is in underdeveloped nations, but nevertheless it occurs in many families. A child who has seen a sibling die may be haunted by feelings of horror, fear, and anxiety long after the event. If there has been rivalry between the siblings, feelings of guilt often predominate. On the other hand, if the siblings were extremely close, the surviving sibling often feels a loss of identity. Parent grief can force the surviving child into the role of substituting for the deceased sibling, with resulting identity confusion (Bank & Kahn, 1982). When sibling death occurs in later adulthood, it is more readily accepted as part of the life course, but surviving siblings can still feel intense grief. In our own interviews of elderly people regarding the effects of a sibling's death (unpublished), most mentioned the loss of the feeling of family togetherness and the sense of sadness and loneliness at being the last or nearly the last member of the sibling group. In this sense, feelings of grief for a sibling are different than feelings engendered by the loss of a parent, child, spouse, or other loved one.

ASPECTS OF THE SIBLING RELATIONSHIP: KNOWLEDGE, PERCEPTIONS, JUDGMENTS

The cognitive aspect of the sibling relationship consists of the individual's knowledge, perceptions, and judgments about the sibling and about the relationship.

Shared family history

Siblings who grow up together in the parental home share many years of experiences which are on a highly intimate level. In early years, they work and play together, eat together, and often bathe and sleep together. The relationship is one of great frankness and, according to Bossard and Boll (1960), is like "living in the nude, psychologically speaking." As a result, siblings come to feel that they know and understand each other very well. In addition, they share knowledge of many family and personal events from a perspective which is unique to the sibling subsystem.

This richness of early knowledge about siblings raises a number of questions. How well do siblings agree on knowledge and perceptions of each other? Do perceptions and judgments of siblings change in adulthood, or are they based largely on childhood impressions? How are perceptions and judgments of siblings related to feelings of closeness and rivalry?

Perceptions and judgments of the sibling

Bigner (1974b) studied the change in children's perceptions of their older siblings over the elementary school years, with the child asked to describe the older sibling in terms of what the sibling did, as well as what the child liked about the sibling. From kindergarten through the eighth grade, the number of constructs used to describe siblings increased, while their quality also changed from concrete, egocentric descriptors to more abstract nonegocentric descriptors. Further, the children described the liked characteristics of their siblings in more concrete terms, while disliked characteristics were described in a more general way, especially when siblings were close in age. That negative characteristics tend to be described in terms of pervasive qualities may help in understanding the persistence of sibling rivalry. Bigner concluded that as children grow older, their perceptions of siblings become both more elaborated and more cognitively complex.

From grade school through college, firstborn children tend to be perceived by their younger siblings as more bossy and powerful. These siblings are able to recount in exquisite detail the tactics which each member of the sibling pair used to maintain power or as a defense against it (Sutton-Smith & Rosenberg, 1970).

A recent series of studies (Schachter, 1982; Schachter, Gilutz, Shore, & Adler, 1978; Schachter, Shore, Feldman-Rotman, Marquis, & Campbell, 1976) is of great interest in that they illustrate how processes in the relationship between siblings shape their perceptions of their own and siblings' characteristics. College students from two- and three-child families were asked to judge whether they were alike or different in personality from each of their siblings in regard to 13 bipolar personality traits (which included a set of semantic differential scales). Judgments of being different from the sibling were regarded as deidentification judgments. In three-child families, percentages of deidentification were greatest in the case of "first pairs" (firstborn and second-born), intermediate for "second pairs" (second-born and third-born), and lowest for "jump pairs" (firstborn and third-born). Percentage of deidentification in two-child families (first pairs) was higher than for second pairs and jump pairs in three-child families, but was not as high as for first pairs in three-child families. Schachter argues that these results are explained by a rivalry-defense hypothesis. In this view, the variations in sibling deidentification correspond to expected variations in sibling rivalry, with first pairs likely to be the most rivalrous (since they had undiluted competition before the third sibling arrived), and jump pairs likely to be the least rivalrous (with competition likely to be diluted by the presence of the intervening sibling). Same-sex siblings, who are more rivalrous than opposite-sex siblings, also deidentify more. Schachter theorizes that deidentification is a defensive, socially acceptable form of expressing rivalrous feelings between siblings. By so doing, the individual can feel superior to the sibling in certain areas, while the sibling can feel superior in other areas which are not central to the individual's view of self. Since these siblings each see their strong points in different areas, they do not feel the need to compete in these areas, and negative feelings abate. While the rivalry-defense hypothesis bears some similarity to Bossard and Boll's (1960) notion of sibling role differentiation or to social comparison theory, these other positions fail to predict the differences between the first, second, and jump pairs. Schachter was able to cross-validate findings with mothers' judgments of similarities and differences between their six-year-old children and their siblings. Further support was provided by the later work of Tesser (1980), who found that the relative importance of comparison with a sibling is determined by the relevance of the sibling's performance to the individual's self-definition.

We looked at judgments of sibling traits in a study of adults ranging in age from 30 to 90 (Cicirelli, 1981a). The traits which were studied were surface traits of the individual (fair, selfish, kind, etc.) which are important for interpersonal relationships; since the trait judgments were highly intercorrelated, an overall trait score was obtained. As age increased, siblings' traits were judged more positively; males' judgments of sisters were most positive of all. Closeness of feeling was associated with more positive trait judgments, while rivalry was associated with more negative trait judgments.

Although the existing evidence on knowledge, perceptions, and judgments of the siblings is meager at the present time, results clearly point to the interrelationship between the emotional and cognitive aspects of the sibling relationship. How both of these bear on the actual interactions between siblings will be considered next.

ASPECTS OF THE SIBLING RELATIONSHIP: INTERACTIONS

Sibling interaction is the exchange of verbal and nonverbal communications and actions between siblings. Because of the long history of the relationship, there are stable and enduring patterns in the interactions between a sibling pair which tend to characterize their relationship. These patterns may be relatively unique to a given sibling dyad, or there may be commonalities which characterize certain stages of life or certain sibling status positions (e.g., sisters may interact differently in some ways than do brothers or sister-brother pairs). In this portion of the chapter, we will try to answer some of the following questions: What kinds of interactions do siblings have? Do these interactions depend on sibling status? How do sibling interactions change over the life span of the sibling concerned?

The literature dealing with sibling interactions consists in large part of reports by only one member of the sibling dyad about the interaction or reports by a parent, teacher, or other observer about the siblings' interaction. While these studies are not without some value in that they provide knowledge about certain areas of sibling interaction that would be difficult or impossible to obtain in other ways, they are subject to bias and inaccuracy on the part of the individual providing the information and need independent verification; reports have typically not been obtained from both members of the sibling pair. Observational studies of the interaction between siblings, particularly in early childhood, are becoming more frequent. However, these studies at best have sampled only a small portion of sibling behavior. When they are carried out in the laboratory using a standardized situation, they suffer from problems of ecological validity, since one does not know whether siblings would behave in the same way in their usual environment. Home observations are an improvement in this respect, but here as in the laboratory the presence of the observer may alter the siblings' behavior so that normal patterns of interaction are not observed. Most observational studies to date have dealt with interactional data by summarizing frequencies of certain types of behavior and employing category systems of various degrees of complexity and richness of detail. Relatively few studies attempt to determine how one sibling responds to the previous behavior of the other or to use recent techniques of sequential analysis (e.g., Gottman, 1983) in the data analysis. Detailed observational studies require a great deal of time in observations, coding, and data analysis (Gottman spent six years on coding and data analysis alone), and it remains to be seen whether the insights and understanding of sibling interactional processes which can be gained by such methods will justify the high research costs.

Sibling interactions are varied in nature, involving affectionate exchanges, conflict and aggressive interactions, exchange of confidences and emotional support, helping interactions, teaching and learning interactions, sexual interactions, shared reminiscences, and formation of coalitions and alliances. Each of these types of sibling interaction will be considered in turn.

Exchanging confidences, affection, and emotional support

We have already discussed some of the affectionate interactions between siblings in early childhood in connection with feelings of closeness toward the sibling. According to Dunn and Kendrick (1982a,

1982b), some 70 percent of the infant's and 55 percent of the older child's approaches to each other were positive. Such behaviors as smiling, touching affectionately, giving, and so on are examples of these positive interactions. The two- to three-year-old siblings tended to use shortened and repetitive speech patterns in communicating with the baby, as well as diminutives and endearments. In such ways, the older sibling seeks to make the baby understand and, at the same time, seems able to grasp the baby's feelings, needs, and desires. The frequency of interactions increased as the younger sibling grew older; there were also more positive interactions between same-sex sibling pairs (particularly sisters) than between opposite-sex pairs. Similar findings have been reported (Abramovitch et al., 1982) for slightly older sibling pairs, although they did not find differences which varied according to the sex composition of the dyad. Older siblings initiated the majority of the interactions, but the younger siblings initiated about a third of all prosocial interactions and responded more positively to such behaviors than did their older siblings. Lamb (1978), by contrast, found little interaction between siblings, with younger siblings more likely to simply watch the older; however, Lamb's observations were made in a laboratory situation in the presence of the parents, while those of Dunn and Kendrick and Abramovitch et al. were home observations of the siblings together.

In middle childhood, children typically spend a great deal of time interacting with their siblings. Presumably, they share confidences and offer each other mutual support (Bossard & Boll, 1960). However, most studies of siblings in this stage of life have focused on rivalry and competition, power relationships, and other topics. College women reporting on their relationships with siblings (Cicirelli, 1980a) felt more friendly and relaxed and better understood by their closest sibling than by their parents. There were closer relationships with sisters and with siblings who were close in age. Adams (1968) also found that pairs of sisters were very close in adulthood, sharing common interests in marriage, home, and children; they communicated and visited with each other because they gained enjoyment from each other's company. In interactions with siblings in middle age, it was found that 78 percent felt a high degree of compatibility with their siblings; only 4 percent got along poorly (Cicirelli, 1982a). Yet, substantially fewer (49 percent) felt that they would discuss topics of an intimate nature with their siblings, and only 8 percent frequently talked over important decisions with them. Compatibility with siblings was even higher in old age: 88 percent felt high compatibility, 66 percent could discuss intimate topics with the sibling, and 16 percent talked over important decisions. They communicated most often in regard to family matters, but shared views on many other topics. The studies which are available suggest that sibling interactions become more compatible as the individuals mature into adulthood and old age.

Conflict and aggressive interactions

In infancy and the preschool years, rivalrous conflict between siblings takes the form of hitting, pinching, shoving, taking toys, and the like (Abramovitch et al., 1982; Dunn & Kendrick, 1982b). The older child is more likely than the younger to initiate such behaviors and to counterattack in response when the other starts the hostilities. The younger child tends to submit to the behavior by crying or whining, withdrawing, asking the other child to stop, obeying the sibling, or giving up the toy. Less frequently, the child who was the target of the aggressive behavior simply ignores it and continues with ongoing activity. In middle childhood (Sutton-Smith & Rosenberg, 1970), the overall pattern of such interactions appears to be little changed, although aggressive behaviors are more differentiated. In addition to physical attacks, the aggressive sibling inflicts damage to the other's property, interferes with the other's activities, argues, or attempts to embarrass or otherwise get the other in trouble. As in early childhood, the sibling who is the target counterattacks, submits, ignores, or attempts to explain, apologize, or otherwise resolve the situation. Direct attack behaviors are used most often by older brothers, while sisters make greater use of verbal and other behaviors.

By later adolescence and adulthood, direct physical aggression between siblings becomes relatively rare, with rivalrous conflicts tending to be expressed verbally. By old age (Cicirelli, 1982a), conflict between siblings tends to be quite low. What conflict there is tends to revolve around criticism of the sibling's habits, spouse, children, or friends; intrusiveness into the other's activities; opinions of their parents; and differences in temperament, views, and lifestyle. Although actual conflict is low, most expect that it would escalate if the siblings had to live together again. Thus, by later life, use of distancing appears to be quite effective as a technique for dealing with sibling rivalry.

Companionate and recreational interactions

Siblings, by the very nature of the family situation, are available to each other for play and other recreational activities through the childhood years. Sibling companionship becomes more important when same-age peers do not exist in the child's neighborhood or when contact with peers is limited. Dunn and Kendrick (1982b) note the range of play activities between siblings: verbal games, fantasy games, formal games, and active games. At many times, both children gained great enjoyment from these shared play activities; at others, the activity led to argument and conflict. Similarly, school-age children enjoy many play activities with siblings while, at the same time, engaging in lengthy arguments over rules and proper behavior. Such interactions are of considerable value to the children involved, as they learn sharing, behavioral give and take, rules and norms, and so on. At the same time, more than half of all children reported that they had fun in games with their siblings (Sutton-Smith & Rosenberg, 1970).

In adulthood and old age, most sibling relationships tended to be companionate in nature (Adams, 1968; Cicirelli, 1982a; Johnson, 1982; Troll et al., 1978). Although some sibling contacts involved ritual family occasions, most involved sharing of family news and common interests. Taking part in formal recreational activities with siblings (sports events, movies, etc.) is less common than simply getting together for conversation, but occurs more frequently when siblings live at a distance and pay each other longer visits. As Johnson points out, sibling companionship in adulthood assumes even greater importance among some ethnic groups.

Power and dominance

Closely allied to the topic of sibling rivalry is that of sibling power and dominance. By middle childhood, most children view relationships with their siblings as involving elements of power. Firstborns, particularly boys who tend to use physical force, are viewed as more powerful and bossy than are younger siblings (Bigner, 1974a; Bryant, 1982; Sutton-Smith & Rosenberg, 1970). The firstborns are hypothesized to engage in a hierarchical power relationships with their parents. In relationships with younger siblings, they tend to model the power tactics used by the parents. Younger siblings will react in a counteractive fashion aimed at upsetting the power of the older. Sutton-Smith and Rosenberg found much the same perceptions of family power relationships among college students as among elementary school children. However, somewhat older young adults (Wish et al., 1976) reported that their relationship had moved to one of greater equality in adulthood as compared to childhood years. In our studies of the elderly, only 12 percent reported any degree of bossiness on the part of siblings. Although Minuchin (1974) regards power relationships as a central aspect of family relationships, leading to the formation of coalitions either to maintain power or to avoid domination, we maintain that it is only one of many important facets of the sibling relationship.

Teaching and learning

A major function of the sibling relationship is the teaching/learning process. Siblings can serve as teachers, role models, challengers, and reinforcers. Siblings who serve as teachers profit as much as, if not more than, their younger siblings; according to the Zajonc confluence model of intellectual development (Zajonc & Markus, 1975), the experience of teaching a younger sibling is a factor adding to the intellectual development of all but the youngest child.

In infancy and early childhood, imitation of the older sibling occurs with some frequency. Dunn and Kendrick (1982b) observed imitation of an older sibling's behaviors by a 14-month-old child, with both verbal imitation and imitation of actions occurring. There was about twice the frequency of imitation among same-sex than among opposite-sex pairs. Curiously, the older child imitated the baby to about the same degree as the baby imitated the older sibling. Abramovitch et al. (1982) concurred only in part with the findings of Dunn and Kendrick, reporting much more imitation of the older sibling by the younger than vice versa. Lamb (1978) also found evidence of imitation of the older sibling in infancy.

In laboratory studies of sibling teaching/learning on a concept teaching task in middle childhood (Cicirelli, 1972, 1973, 1975), girls teaching their siblings tended to use a deductive teaching method, while boys used an inductive method; both sexes taught differently with non-siblings. Girls were also more effective as teachers. Younger siblings were more ready to accept direction from an older sister than from an older brother, perhaps attributable to greater rivalry with brothers. Bryant (1982) views sibling teaching and caretaking as another means of asserting power over a younger sibling; thus, resisting sibling teaching may be a way of resisting domination. Yet, older siblings at wide age spacings were found to be more effective teachers than those at close age spacings, although those at wide age spacings should clearly be perceived as more powerful.

Sibling relationships can also be viewed as socializing the sibling pair for adult roles (Essman, 1977). Through play in childhood, siblings practice roles they will later assume. Also, older siblings model school behaviors, dating behaviors, employment behaviors, marriage and parent behaviors, and responses to life crises throughout their lifetime. Siblings directly instruct each other in many skills, as well as give advice on many topics. In addition, there is mutual regulation (Schvaneveldt & Ihinger, 1979) of role behaviors as siblings interact to shape each other's behaviors according to common family or community values.

Helping interactions

One aspect of the sibling relationship is the help and support siblings can provide for each other. Even in early childhood, there is evidence of some altruistic behavior toward siblings (Dunn & Kendrick, 1982b), with siblings responding to the other's distress with attempts at comforting, giving toys, and so on. In middle childhood and adolescence, too, siblings help each other in terms of shared tasks and activities (Weisner, 1982), sharing and lending possessions, and helping each other in avoiding parental displeasure and otherwise dealing with parents. In some cases, an older sibling will function as a substitute parent (Bank & Kahn, 1982).

The use of older siblings as caretakers for younger ones is very widespread, especially in less-advanced cultures (Weisner, 1982; Weisner & Gallimore, 1977). In our own country, it is more prevalent in lower socioeconomic status groups and among children of working mothers. The style and extensiveness of sibling care varies widely across cultural groups. In many cases, there is mimicry of adult care-giving patterns, often resulting in excessive authoritarianism, with older children tending to tyrannize, harass, and threaten younger siblings. In other cases, there is overindulgence, with younger children becoming overdemanding, or older siblings may simply neglect the younger. In most cases, sibling care takes place within an area where the mother or other adults are available, but differs in terms of the responsibility placed upon the siblings. Most sibling caretaking is delegated to older sisters, with boys freed for play or other tasks. Thus, in this area of sibling interaction as in many others, sisters play a special role.

Often sibling help as well as sibling care-giving is strongly resisted by younger siblings, who perceive it as an attempt to assert dominance and control rather than as a well-intentioned desire to help. Thus, it may be only a veiled power maneuver and is responded to as such (Bryant, 1982).

Once siblings leave the family home, helping behaviors continue to some extent. Adams (1968) found mutual aid between young adult siblings to be relatively infrequent, occurring most often between pairs of sisters and pairs of brothers. It is clear that the greater similarity of roles leads to greater help from same-sex siblings. Also, help was more frequent among those siblings who felt affectionally close.

In middle age, siblings are seen as a source of aid in time of crisis (Troll, 1975), caring for children, sharing household responsibilities, and even making funeral arrangements when this becomes necessary. More important, they provide companionship and support to each other in time of crisis or serious family problem.

Among the elderly, siblings sometimes provide a great deal of help. After the death of their mother, older sisters may assume the mother's earlier role in looking after the brothers in the family (Townsend, 1957). Also, a sister may assume many of a deceased wife's duties for her brother, or a brother may take on some of the deceased husband's roles for a widowed sister. Such role substitution helps to explain the growth in closeness to cross-sex siblings that has been observed in later life. In our own studies (Cicirelli, 1979), siblings were seen as a primary source of help in the area of psychological support for some 7 percent of all elderly. Smaller percentages regarded siblings as primary helpers with business dealings, protection, and homemaking and as a source of reading materials and social and recreational activities. Surprisingly, siblings became more important among the oldest age groups. If occasional and supplementary help had been considered in the study, the contribution of siblings would surely have been much greater.

Perhaps the most important feature of sibling help in adulthood and old age is that most siblings are ready to help one another if needed, although such help is called upon only infrequently.

Sexual interactions

Interaction between siblings may take the form of sexual activity, ranging from mutual curiosity about one another's bodies and sex play in early childhood to sexual intercourse and sexual relationships of considerable intensity and duration. As a result of the incest taboo in our society, few individuals ever tell anyone about such sexual experiences, and there is little reliable information about them. Finkelhor (1980) surveyed college undergraduates in New England and found that 15 percent of the females and 10 percent of the males reported some type of sexual experience with a sibling. Younger children engage more often in genital exhibition, while touching and fondling genitals occurred in all age groups, and intercourse tended to occur in the latency period of middle childhood and in adolescence. In about 25 percent of the cases, force was used by an older sibling. In about a third of the cases, a single incident was never repeated; in 27 percent, the sexual relationship continued for periods from a year to 10 years. Experiences where there was force or threat of force or where there was a large age difference between siblings were most likely to be regarded by the participant as having a negative effect, while mere genital exhibition tended to be regarded more positively. About as many regarded the experience positively as regarded it negatively. From a clinical perspective, however (Bank & Kahn, 1982), sibling sexual interaction can be traumatic and confusing, particularly for younger children who have been exploited by older siblings. These authors distinguish power-oriented incest of the exploitive, coercive type from nurturance-oriented incest which occurs by mutual consent and involves elements of love and erotic pleasure. However, even the second type involves considerable anxiety and pathos, if only from the burden of maintaining secrecy.

Shared reminiscing

Because siblings share a long and unique history, reminiscing about earlier times together is an activity in which siblings engage at many points in the life span. Such reminiscing with siblings seems to become more important in the latter portion of life as individuals go through, in the life review process, detailed reconsideration and evaluation of experiences throughout life. At the same time, the nuclear family of origin erodes through the deaths of its members until perhaps only a few sibling dyads remain. In examining topics of communication of elderly people with their siblings and children, we found more discussion of old times together with siblings than with adult children, indicating that siblings do play an important role in reminiscing (Cicirelli, 1982b): the fewer the remaining siblings in the family, the greater the extent of the reminiscing. As the remaining members of their families of origin, siblings can use reminiscences of old times together to validate and clarify events and relationships that took place in earlier years and to place them in mature perspective. Ross and Milgram (1982) observed that sharing recollections of happy childhood experiences appears to be a source of comfort and pride for the elderly, evoking the warmth of early family life and contributing to a sense of integrity that life had been lived in harmony with the family.

Sibling coalitions and alliances

In larger families, siblings seem to organize themselves into relatively stable subgroups, usually dyads. When there are three or five children, the odd man is often left to himself. The sibling coalition or alliance most often involves siblings of the same sex with a small age difference, although other combinations also occur (Bank & Kahn, 1982; Blood, 1972; Schvaneveldt & Ihinger, 1979). Coalitions may form in order to exert power over other siblings, parents, or peers or to resist domination by others. Siblings can also form alliances based on closeness of feeling and common interests, exchanging confidences and sharing activities.

INTERFACE OF SIBLING SUBSYSTEM WITH OTHER FAMILY SUBSYSTEMS

Parents

The relationship of siblings with each other depends also on the kinds of interactions which occur within the family between the parents and between the parents and other siblings. We have already seen how sibling rivalry in early childhood can be augmented or lessened by the kind of relationship between mother and child (Dunn & Kendrick, 1982a, 1982b; Nadelman & Begun, 1982), as well as the father's role. Firstborn children get more attention than later-born children when alone with their mothers, but are relatively neglected when the sibling is present. Also, there may be little evidence of sibling attachment when the parent is present, but rather clear evidence when the siblings are alone together (Lamb, 1978; Stewart, 1983). There is also some evidence of longer-term effects (Kendrick & Dunn, 1983), as the relative friendliness and hostility of a young sibling dyad was found to depend on the degree of maternal involvement in quarrels six months earlier. In middle childhood, too, the behavior of the children toward each other was found to be dependent on the mother's responsiveness to the child's needs (Bryant & Crockenberg, 1980). A mother's helping behavior toward her younger child in a learning task situation (Cicirelli, 1976, 1978a) varied depending on the sex of the older sibling and whether the sibling was present or absent, with the mother implicitly relinquishing some of the caretaking functions when there is an older sister.

Coalition formation is highly affected by the relationships with parents (Bank & Kahn, 1982; Blood, 1972; Schvaneveldt & Ihinger, 1979). When the parent subsystem is strong, there are strong coalitions between siblings. When one parent is dominant, another parent-child coalition may result as well as coalitions between other siblings to resist the parent-child dyad. These situations may become very complex.

One sibling, usually an older one, often performs a pioneering function with the parents for the sibling group by adopting a new or forbidden behavior, thus making it more acceptable for younger siblings (Bank & Kahn, 1982). Siblings often mediate and negotiate with parents for others in the sibling group, explaining feelings and actions that a child might be unwilling or unable to communicate directly (Schvaneveldt & Ihinger, 1979).

Peers

The kind of relationship a child has with siblings also influences the relationship with friends. Children who took high-power roles with siblings were found to take low-power roles with friends, and vice versa (Sutton-Smith & Rosenberg, 1970). Also, close and highly involved relationships with siblings may be associated with lower involvement with peers in childhood (Bank & Kahn, 1982) as well as in adulthood (Johnson, 1982). In old age, the relationship with a sister appears to

stimulate elderly women to maintain social skills and relationships with
people outside the family (Cicirelli, 1982a).

Spouse and children

When there is a close relationship between siblings, the relationship
with a spouse can become less close in certain aspects (Cicirelli, 1982a;
Johnson, 1982); similarly, a very intense relationship with a spouse
can leave little room for a sibling relationship.

Toman's (1976) work has dealt with the theory that the more nearly
a marital partner duplicates the sibling relationships of one's youth,
the more successful and free from conflict the marriage would be.
Thus, for Toman, the best marital partner for the oldest sister of brothers would be the youngest brother of sisters, and so on. The theory
has also been extended in a similar way to include relationships with
one's children.

CONCLUSIONS

The present chapter has attempted to bring to the reader an overview of the present state of the art in the study of sibling relationships.
A wide variety of topics fall within the domain of a psychology of
sibling relationships, but as yet we know really very little about some
of these areas.

What then are the priorities for future research? First of all, we
need to focus on the study of processes in sibling relationships. That
is, we need to understand what goes on in sibling relationships and
why. How do siblings come to socialize each other? How are feelings
and attitudes toward siblings shaped, and how are they changed? We
need to know how well sibling phenomena are explained by existing
developmental and social small-group psychologies, and where new
explanations are needed.

Second, we need to look at the sibling relationship, not in isolation
but in the context of the larger family system and cultural milieu.
There are promising beginnings in this area, but these need to be
expanded. Newer techniques of network analysis may be of value here.

Third, we need more studies in which there is direct participation
and observation of sibling and family relationships in a naturalistic
setting. The work of Dunn and Kendrick (1982a, 1982b) illustrates
the richness of understanding that can be gained from studies of this
type. Where interviewing is used, it should attempt to increase understanding of contemporaneous sibling interactions and not merely seek
information retrospectively. We need to study both members of a
sibling dyad, not just one. Methods of sequential analysis should be

attempted to determine how one sibling's behaviors lead to certain responses on the part of the other, as well as what later effects of such sequences might be.

Fourth, we need a better understanding of effects of genetic similarity on sibling relationships; Scarr and Grajek's (1982) work provides a beginning in this direction. We need to understand how basic differences of temperament or mood between siblings may lead to differences in closeness of the sibling relationship throughout life and to conflict in sibling interactions.

Fifth, we need studies that will link sibling interactional processes with existing findings regarding sibling status variables and individual differences in abilities and traits. If sibling relationships have an influence on these abilities and traits, how does it come about? How do sibling processes shape sex role identification, for example?

Sixth, we need to extend existing studies across the life span of the sibling relationship, particularly naturalistic observation and participation studies. We now know very little of how adult siblings behave when they interact under various circumstances or how sibling interactions, feelings, and attitudes change with age and critical life events. We need to know how sibling relationships are maintained over long separations and how other siblings and family members help to maintain the relationship.

Finally, we need studies to determine how the sibling relationship is affected by changing family patterns. The rapid increase in divorce and alternative lifestyles is resulting in family systems that are quite complex, involving relationships between half- and stepsiblings as well as between biological siblings. The increase in the number and proportion of older people in our society will affect the availability of siblings in old age; we need to understand how sibling relationships may be affected by such changes.

As yet, we have no clear, unified theory of sibling relationships and sibling influence to guide our inquiries, although there are various theoretical ideas which seem to have some application to a psychology of sibling relationships. It is hoped that such a theory will evolve as we come to understand more of what the relationship is about. Central to the theory must be an explanation of the three aspects of the sibling relationship (cognitive, emotional, behavioral) and how each of the aspects affects and is affected by the others, how each of the aspects develops and changes over the duration of the relationship, and how each is affected by the larger family and social system. This is a large order, considering the relatively primitive stage of our knowledge about sibling relationships at the present time. Yet, the importance of sibling relationships to us all indicates that it would be a worthwhile effort.

REFERENCES

Abramovitch, R., Pepler, D., & Corter, C. Patterns of sibling interaction among preschool-age children. In M. E. Lamb & B. Sutton-Smith (Eds.), *Sibling relationships: Their nature and significance across the life span*. Hillsdale, N.J.: Lawrence Erlbaum Associates, 1982. Pp. 61–86.

Adams, B. N. *Kinship in an urban setting*. Chicago: Markham Publishing, 1968.

Adler, A. *Understanding human nature*. New York: Fawcett, 1959.

Ainsworth, M. D. Attachment and dependency: A comparison. In J. L. Gewirtz (Ed.), *Attachment and dependency*. New York: John Wiley & Sons, 1972. Pp. 97–137.

Allan, G. Sibling solidarity. *Journal of Marriage and the Family*, 1977, *39*, 177–184.

Bank, S. P., & Kahn, M. D. Sisterhood-brotherhood is powerful: Sibling subsystems and family therapy. *Family Process*, 1975, *14*(3), 311–337.

Bank, S. P., & Kahn, M. D. *The sibling bond*. New York: Basic Books, 1982.

Becker, H., & Useem, R. Sociological analysis of the dyad. *American Sociological Review*, 1942, *7*, 13–26.

Berezin, M. A. Partial grief for the aged and their families. In E. Pattison (Ed.), *The experience of dying*. Englewood Cliffs, N.J.: Prentice-Hall, 1977.

Bigner, J. J. Second borns' discrimination of sibling role concepts. *Developmental Psychology*, 1974, *10*, 564–573. (a)

Bigner, J. J. A Wernerian developmental analysis of children's descriptions of siblings. *Child Development*, 1974, *45*, 317–323. (b)

Blood, R. O. *The family*. New York: Free Press, 1972.

Borke, H. Interpersonal perception of young children: Egocentrism or empathy? *Developmental Psychology*, 1972, *7*, 107–109.

Bossard, J. H. S., & Boll, E. S. *The sociology of child development* (3d ed.). New York: Harper & Row, 1960.

Bowerman, C. E., & Dobash, R. M. Structural variations in intersibling affect. *Journal of Marriage and the Family*, 1974, *36*, 48–54.

Bowlby, J. *The making and breaking of affectional bonds*. London: Tavistock Publications, 1979.

Bowlby, J. *Attachment and loss* (Vol. III): *Loss, stress, and depression*. New York: Basic Books, 1980.

Bretherton, I., & Beeghly, M. Talking about internal states: The acquisition of an explicit theory of mind. *Developmental Psychology*, 1982, *18*, 906–921.

Bryant, B. K. Sibling relationships in middle childhood. In M. E. Lamb & B. Sutton-Smith (Eds.), *Sibling relationships: Their nature and significance across the lifespan*. Hillsdale, N.J.: Lawrence Erlbaum Associates, 1982. Pp. 87–121.

Bryant, B. K., & Crockenberg, S. Correlates and dimensions of prosocial behavior: A study of female siblings with their mothers. *Child Development*, 1980, *51*, 529–544.

Burlingham, D., & Freud, A. *Infants without families*. Winchester, Mass.: Allen & Unwin, 1944.

Cicirelli, V. G. The effect of sibling relationships on concept learning of young children taught by child teachers. *Child Development*, 1972, *43*, 282–287.

Cicirelli, V. G. Effects of sibling structure and interaction on children's categorization style. *Developmental Psychology*, 1973, *9*, 132–139.

Cicirelli, V. G. Effects of mother and older sibling on the problem solving behavior of the younger child. *Developmental Psychology*, 1975, *11*, 749–756.

Cicirelli, V. G. Mother-child and sibling-sibling interactions on a problem-solving task. *Child Development*, 1976, *47*, 588–596.

Cicirelli, V. G. Effect of sibling presence on mother-child interaction. *Developmental Psychology*, 1978, *14*, 315–316. (a)

Cicirelli, V. G. The relationship of sibling structure to intellectual abilities and achievement. *Review of Educational Research*, 1978, *48*(3), 365–379. (b)

Cicirelli, V. G. *Social services for elderly in relation to the kin network*. Report to the NRTA–AARP Andrus Foundation, May 31, 1979.

Cicirelli, V. G. A comparison of college women's feelings toward their siblings and parents. *Journal of Marriage and the Family*, 1980, *42*, 95–102. (a)

Cicirelli, V. G. Sibling influence in adulthood: A life span perspective. In L. W. Poon (Ed.), *Aging in the 1980s*. Washington, D.C.: American Psychological Association, 1980. (b)

Cicirelli, V. G. *Feelings toward siblings in adulthood and old age*. Paper presented at the 89th Annual Convention of the American Psychological Association, Los Angeles, August 1981. (a)

Cicirelli, V. G. Interpersonal relationships of siblings in the middle part of the life span. Paper presented at the Biennial Meeting of the Society for Research in Child Development, Boston, April 1981. (b)

Cicirelli, V. G. Sibling influence throughout the life span. In M. E. Lamb & B. Sutton-Smith (Eds.), *Sibling relationships: Their nature and significance across the lifespan*. Hillsdale, N.J.: Lawrence Erlbaum Associates, 1982. Pp. 267–284. (a)

Cicirelli, V. G. *Similarities and contrasts in quality of child and sibling relationships with elderly*. Paper presented at the 35th Annual Scientific Meeting of the Gerontological Society, Boston, November 19–23, 1982. (b)

Cicirelli, V. G. Adult children's attachment and helping behavior to elderly parents: A path model. *Journal of Marriage and the Family*, 1983, *45*, 815–825.

Clausen, J. A. Family structure, socialization, and personality. In M. L. Hoffman & L. W. Hoffman (Eds.), *Review of child development research* (Vol. 2). New York: Russell Sage Foundation, 1966. Pp. 1–53.

Duberman, L. *The reconstituted family*. Chicago: Nelson-Hall Publishers, 1975.

Dunn, J., & Kendrick, C. Siblings and their mothers: Developing relationships within the family. In M. E. Lamb & B. Sutton-Smith (Eds.), *Sibling relationships: Their nature and significance across the lifespan*. Hillsdale, N.J.: Lawrence Erlbaum Associates, 1982. Pp. 39–60. (a)

Dunn, J., & Kendrick, C. *Siblings: Love, envy, and understanding*. Cambridge, Mass.: Harvard University Press, 1982. (b)

Essman, C. S. Sibling relations as socialization for parenthood. *Family Coordinator*, 1977, *26*, 259–262.

Finklehor, D. Sex among siblings: A survey on prevalence, variety, and effects. *Archives of Sexual Behavior*, 1980, *9*, 171–194.

Form, W. H., & Geschwender, J. A. Social reference basis of job satisfaction: The case of manual workers. *American Sociological Review*, 1962, *27*, 232–233.

Fromm, E. *The art of loving.* New York: Harper & Row, 1956.

Furstenberg, F. F., Spanier, G., & Rothschild, N. Patterns of parenting in the transition from divorce to remarriage. In P. W. Berman & E. R. Ramey (Eds.), *Women: A developmental perspective.* Washington, D.C.: U.S. Department of Health and Human Services, Public Health Service, National Institute of Health, 1982 (NIH Publication No. 82–2298). Pp. 325–348.

Gewirtz, J. L. The attachment acquisition process as evidenced in the maternal conditioning of cued infant responding (particularly crying). *Human Development,* 1976, *19,* 143–155.

Gottman, J. M. How children become friends. *Monographs of the Society for Research in Child Development,* 1983, *48*(3), Whole No. 201), 1–86.

Graziano, W. G., & Musser, L. M. The joining and the parting of the ways. In S. Duck (Ed.), *Personal relationships* (Vol. 4): *Dissolving personal relationships.* New York: Academic Press, 1982. Pp. 75–106.

Hartup, W. W. The origins of friendships. In M. Lewis & L. A. Rosenblum (Eds.), *The origins of behavior* (Vol. 4): *Friendship and peer relations.* New York: John Wiley & Sons 1975. Pp. 11–26.

Hartup, W. W., & Lempers, J. A problem in life span development: The interactional analysis of family attachments. In P. B. Baltes & P. W. Schaie (Eds.), *Life-span developmental psychology: Personality and socialization.* New York: Academic Press, 1973.

Hinde, R. A. The bases of a science of interpersonal relationships. In S. Duck & R. Gilmour (Eds.), *Personal relationships* (Vol. 1): *Studying personal relationships.* New York: Academic Press, 1981. Pp. 1–22.

Huston, T. L., & Robins, E. Conceptual and methodological issues in studying close relationships. *Journal of Marriage and the Family,* 1982, *44,* 902–925.

Ihinger, M. The referee role and norms of equity: A contribution toward a theory of sibling conflict. *Journal of Marriage and the Family,* 1975, *37,* 515–524.

Johnson, C. L. Sibling solidarity: Its origin and functioning in Italian-American families. *Journal of Marriage and the Family,* 1982, *44,* 155–167.

Kalish, R. A., & Knudtson, F. W. Attachment versus disengagement: A life-span conceptualization. *Human Development,* 1976, *19,* 171–181.

Kantor, D., & Lehr, W. *Inside the family.* San Francisco: Jossey-Bass, 1975.

Kendrick, C., & Dunn, J. Sibling quarrels and maternal responses. *Developmental Psychology,* 1983, *19,* 62–70.

Kimmel, D. C. Relationship development and initiation: A life-span developmental approach. In R. L. Burgess & T. L. Huston (Eds.), *Social exchanges in developing relationships.* New York: Academic Press, 1979. Pp. 351–377.

Knudtson, F. W. Life span attachment: Complexities, questions, considerations. *Human Development,* 1976, *19,* 182–196.

Lamb, M. E. Interactions between 18-month-olds and their preschool-aged siblings. *Child Development,* 1978, *49,* 51–59.

Lamb, M. E. Sibling relationships across the lifespan: An overview and introduction. In M. E. Lamb & B. Sutton-Smith (Eds.), *Sibling relationships: Their nature and significance across the lifespan.* Hillsdale, N.J.: Lawrence Erlbaum Associates, 1982. Pp. 1–11.

Lee, L. C. Toward a cognitive theory of interpersonal development: Importance of peers. In M. Lewis & L. A. Rosenblum (Eds.), *The origins of behavior* (Vol. 4): *Friendship and peer relations.* New York: John Wiley & Sons, 1975. Pp. 207–221.

Lerner, R. M., & Ryff, C. D. Implementation of the life-span view of human development: The sample case of attachment. In P. B. Baltes (Ed.), *Life-span development and behavior* (Vol. 1). New York: Academic Press, 1978. Pp. 1–44.

Levy, D. M. Sibling rivalry. *American Orthopsychiatric Association, Research Monograph No. 2,* 1937.

Miley, C. H. Birth order research 1963–1967: Bibliography and index. *Journal of Individual Psychology,* 1969, *25,* 64–70.

Minuchin, S. *Families and family therapy.* Cambridge, Mass.: Harvard University Press, 1974.

Nadelman, L., & Begun, A. The effect of the newborn on the older sibling: Mothers' question-naires. In M. E. Lamb & B. Sutton-Smith (Eds.), *Sibling relationships: Their nature and significance across the lifespan.* Hillsdale, N.J.: Lawrence Erlbaum Associates, 1982. Pp. 13–37.

Noberini, M. R., Brady, E. M., & Mosatche, H. S. *Personality and adult sibling relationships: A preliminary study.* Unpublished.

Pfouts, J. H. The sibling relationship: A forgotten dimension. *Social Work,* 1976, *21,* 200–204.

Pfouts, J. H. Birth order, age-spacing, IQ differences, and family relations. *Journal of Marriage and the Family,* 1980, *32,* 517–531.

Ross, H. G., Dalton, M. J., & Milgram, J. I. *Older adults' perceptions of closeness in sibling relationships.* Paper presented at the 33rd Annual Scientific Meeting of the Gerontologi-cal Society, San Diego, California, November 1980.

Ross, H. G., & Milgram, J. I. *Rivalry in adult sibling relationships: Its antecedents and dynamics.* Paper presented at the Annual Meeting of the American Psychological Asso-ciation, Montreal, September 1980.

Ross, H. G., & Milgram, J. I. Important variables in adult sibling relationships: A qualitative study. In M. E. Lamb & B. Sutton-Smith (Eds.), *Sibling relationships: Their nature and significance across the lifespan.* Hillsdale, N.J.: Lawrence Erlbaum Associates, 1982. Pp. 225–249.

Scarr, S., & Grajek, S. Similarities and differences among siblings. In M. E. Lamb & B. Sutton-Smith (Eds.), *Sibling relationships: Their nature and significance across the lifespan.* Hillsdale, N.J.: Lawrence Erlbaum Associates, 1982. Pp. 357–381.

Schachter, F. F. Sibling deidentification and split-parent identification: A family tetrad. In M. E. Lamb & B. Sutton-Smith (Eds.), *Sibling relationships: Their nature and significance across the lifespan.* Hillsdale, N.J.: Lawrence Erlbaum Associates, 1982. Pp. 123–151.

Schachter, F. F., Gilutz, G., Shore, E., & Adler, M. Sibling identification judged by mothers: Cross-validation and developmental studies. *Child Development,* 1978, *49,* 543–546.

Schachter, F. F., Shore, E., Feldman-Rotman, S., Marquis, R. E., & Campbell, S. Sibling deidentification. *Developmental Psychology,* 1976, *12,* 418–427.

Schooler, C. Birth order effects: Not here, not now! *Psychological Bulletin,* 1972, *78,* 161–175.

Schvaneveldt, J. D., & Ihinger, M. Sibling relationships in the family. In W. R. Burr, R. Hill, F. I. Nye, & I. L. Reiss (Eds.), *Contemporary theories about the family* (Vol. 1): *Research-based theories.* New York: Free Press, 1979. Pp. 453–467.

Smalley, R. E. Two studies in sibling rivalry: II. The influence of differences in age, sex and intelligence in determining the attitudes of siblings toward each other. *Smith College Studies of Social Work,* 1930, *1,* 23–40.

Stewart, R. B. Sibling attachment relationships: Child-infant interactions in the strange situation. *Developmental Psychology,* 1983, *19,* 192–199.

Sutton-Smith, B., & Rosenberg, B. C. *The Sibling.* New York: Holt, Rinehart & Winston, 1970.

Tesser, A. Self-esteem maintenance in family dynamics. *Journal of Personality and Social Psychology,* 1980, *39,* 77–91.

Toman, W. *Family constellation: Its effects on personality and social behavior* (3d ed.). New York: Springer Publishing, 1976.

Townsend, P. *The family life of old people: An inquiry in East London.* New York: Free Press, 1957.

Troll, L. E. *Early and middle adulthood.* Monterey, Calif.: Brooks/Cole Publishing, 1975.

Troll, L. E., Miller, S., & Atchley, R. *Families of later life.* Belmont, Calif.: Wadsworth, 1978.

Troll, L. E., & Smith, J. Attachment through the life span: Some questions about dyadic bonds among adults. *Human Development,* 1976, *19,* 156–170.

Vockell, E. L., Felker, D. W., & Miley, C. H. Birth order literature 1967–1971: Bibliography and index. *Journal of Individual Psychology,* 1973, *29,* 39–53.

Wagner, M. E., Schubert, H. J. P., & Schubert, D. S. P. Sibship-constellation effects on psychosocial development, creativity, and health. In H. W. Reese & L. P. Lipsitt (Eds.), *Advances in Child Development,* (Vol. 14). New York: Academic Press, 1979, 57–149.

Walberg, H. J., & Marjoribanks, K. Family environment and cognitive development. *Review of Educational Research,* 1976, *46,* 527–552.

Walters, L. H. Are families different from other groups? *Journal of Marriage and the Family,* 1982, *44,* 841–850.

Weisner, T. S. Sibling interdependence and child caretaking: A cross-cultural view. In M. E. Lamb & B. Sutton-Smith (Eds.), *Sibling relationships: Their nature and significance across the lifespan.* Hillsdale, N.J.: Lawrence Erlbaum Associates, 1982. Pp. 305–327.

Weisner, T. S., & Gallimore, R. My brother's keeper: Child and sibling caretaking. *Current Anthropology,* 1977, *18,* 169–190.

Wish, M., Deutsch, M., & Kaplan, S. J. Perceived dimensions of interpersonal relations. *Journal of Personality and Social Psychology,* 1976, *33,* 409–420.

Zajonc, R. B., & Markus, G. B. Birth order and intellectual development. *Psychological Review,* 1975, *82,* 74–88.

Chapter 7

Empirical Perspectives on Adolescents and Their Families

GREGORY J. JURKOVIC
DONNA ULRICI

After decades of scientific neglect, the American adolescent has become an object of increased systematic study (see Hodgman, 1983; L'Abate, 1971). The adolescent's position in the life cycle raises complex and multifaceted questions. Perhaps most basic is how to define this age period. Derived from the Latin verb *adolescere,* the term *adolescence* means "to grow up" or "to grow into maturity" (Harvey, 1984). Maturity, however, can be defined from different vantage points (Lerner & Spanier, 1980). Stone and Church (1984), for example, have distinguished biological adolescence from cultural or psychological adolescence. Whereas the former refers to the span of time between the prepubertal growth spurt and full physical maturity, cultural adolescence is a distinct age period characterized by special psychological attributes—many of which are socially determined.

Indeed, from a sociohistorical perspective, adolescence can be seen as an artifact of contemporary industrialized society. Providing no clear-cut rites of passage (Van Gennep, 1960), our culture requires lengthy preparation for adult roles. Neither adolescents nor parents know exactly when and how this socially defined age period ends (Elder, 1980). "All we have," according to Conger (1979, p. 43), "is a hotch-potch of often inconsistent and loosely-enforced rules . . . about when a young person may drink, drive a car, leave school, marry, or own property." The few specific rituals that exist, such as the first communion, bar mitzvah, and confirmation, may no longer serve a significant boundary-making function (Ford, 1970). However, as Friedman (1980) has observed, concern primarily with the culture that defines these rules or events or with the changing individual, ignores the central role of the family. It can be argued from the point of view of family systems theory that the family rather than the culture sets the emotional tone for different socially determined life-cycle markers and ultimately specifies which events or rules will be used as rites (Friedman; Handel, 1965).

Consideration of these definitional problems points to the ineluctable interplay of personal and sociofamilial processes in the young person's transition from childhood to adulthood. Yet, to date, individual psychological studies have dominated the literature. Their monadic orientation has brought the teenager's inner world into sharp focus; however, the social context of which this world is a part has remained largely in the background. Curiously, even when contextual factors have been examined, the peer group has received as much if not more empirical attention than the family—the adolescent's *primary* group. A chapter on family process, for example, is conspicuously absent from the *Handbook of Adolescent Psychology* (Adelson, 1980), although one on friendship and peer groups is included.

In this chapter, we will consider the growing empirical literature on the family context of adolescent development. Investigators of this problem have concerned themselves mainly with (1) normative trends in the adolescent's family relationships; (2) the role of familial variables, such as control, closeness, and conflict, in his or her negotiation of phase-specific tasks and personal growth; and (3) processes that differentiate functional from dysfunctional families of adolescents. After presenting representative research related to each of these points, we will discuss the implications of the findings for various theories of adolescent development as well as for research and clinical practice.

NORMATIVE TRENDS: DESCRIPTIVE DATA

It is well documented that the family plays a major nurturing and socializing role in the lives of young children. But, as Lerner and Spanier (1980) ask, what about adolescents? How involved are families in the lives of adolescents, and what impact do they have? Is it true, as many lay and professional persons assume, that the family's influence diminishes precipitously as peer influence increases during the teenage years? Descriptive data bearing on these questions will be considered first before presenting research dealing specifically with the nature of the adolescent's family relationships.

Peer and family influences

Surprisingly few investigators have explored how adolescents spend their time. In his self-report survey of males and females in 10th, 11th, and 12th grade attending suburban high schools in the Midwest, New-man (1972) found that on the average the students talked most often during out-of-school hours to close friends and parents, followed by siblings, girlfriends or boyfriends, extrafamilial adults, relatives, and clergy. During school hours, the students reported interacting almost six times as frequently with other students as with teachers.

Using a different methodology, Csikszentmihalyi, Larson, and Prescott (1977) randomly sampled the daily activities and experiences of 25 boys and girls ranging in age from 13 to 18. The youngsters were issued electronic paging devices so that they could be signaled (5–7 times per day between the hours of 8 A.M. and 11 P.M. for one week during the school year) when to complete self-report forms. Of the 753 observations, the most prevalent primary activities were talking with peers, watching TV, and studying. The adolescents interacted verbally with peers most frequently in public or in school and with adults mostly in their homes, suggesting that adult talk occurred typically with parental figures. Television watching took place usually at home and about equally with family or alone. Lower-socioeconomic youngsters tended to talk more to peers, and those ranked lower in sibling birth order conversed more with adults.

In comparison to nonworkers, high school students who work part-time were found by Greenberger, Steinberg, Vaux, and McAuliffe (1980) to spend less time with family but not with peers. Employment had little effect on the students' perceived quality of family and peer relationships although, for females, working related to relatively weak emotional ties to parents. Greenberger et al. also discovered that the students did not form close relationships with others at their workplace.

These studies support earlier findings (e.g., Douvan & Adelson, 1966) indicating that adolescents spend more time with peers than with parents. However, it appears that they interact most with immediate family members (parents and siblings) when not in school and more with parental figures than with any other adult role group. Thus, while peer interaction clearly represents a major context for socialization, the family continues to be significantly involved in the lives of adolescents (Newman & Newman, 1979).

Unfortunately, data are not available to determine whether this pattern of peer-versus-family time commitment is markedly different from that during the middle school-age years. Moreover, it cannot be concluded that because adolescents spend more time with age-mates, they are most influenced by them (Lerner & Spanier, 1980). Indeed, the available evidence indicates that both parents and peers are influential, the relative degree of which varies as a function of age, situation, and family involvement.

In general, there appears to be substantially less discordance between parents and peers than popular and clinical lore suggests. Douvan and Adelson (1966), for example, found in their analysis of interview data from a representative cross section of males in grades 7 through 12 (N = 1,045) and females in grades 6 through 12 (N = 2,005) that peers are chosen whose values and attitudes overlap significantly with those of parents. These results perhaps should come as no surprise inasmuch as the different generational groups (peer and family) to which adolescents belong generally share similar social, economic, religious, educational, and geographic characteristics (Mussen, Conger, & Kagen, 1974).

Floyd and South (1972) have shown that, while orientation to parents declines from grades 6 to 12 for males and females, older adolescents tend to exhibit a mixed orientation. Further evidence for the dual influence of peers and parents and the increasing self-determination of teenagers has been presented by Meisels and Canter (1971) and Munns (1972). Their data reveal that older adolescents perceive their own attitudes and values as falling between the perceived attitudes and values of peers and parents. Specifically, they see themselves as more progressive than their parents but not as liberal as their agemates.

Whether adolescents orient to one reference group or another appears to fluctuate according to the situation or issue at hand. For example, Floyd and South (1972) found that the teenagers in their study were more likely to orient to parents than to peers in areas in which they perceived their parents to have special knowledge. (For further discussion of variables that influence the adolescent's orientation to parents or peers, see Manaster, 1977; Lerner & Spanier, 1980; and Biddle, Bank, & Merlin, 1980.) Biddle et al. have also considered processes by which these two groups affect high school students. Their findings suggest that peers gain influence through modeling of behaviors, in contrast to parents whose impact is mediated by expression of normative standards.

Another important familial variable relates to the nature of the parents' involvement in the life of their teenage son or daughter. Larsen (reported in Mussen et al., 1974) found that "parent-adolescent affect" (amount of shared family activity, parental interest, understanding, and support) interacts with age in determining degree of parent and peer influence. Although this variable did not figure into the orientation of young adolescents, its significance increased in middle and late adolescence such that those who were emotionally estranged from parents oriented more to peers. There is also evidence that favorable family relationships can mitigate or override the effects of potentially problematic peer involvement. For example, Pittel and his colleagues (reported in Conger, 1977b) empirically demonstrated in the late 1960s that the best predictor of subsequent social integration (defined by stable relationships, regular employment, unproblematic drug use) for a group of 154 San Francisco "hippies" was a cohesive and supportive family background. In view of various findings, Bronfenbrenner (1975) cogently argues that the segregation of parents from children (e.g., in the workplace, school) in contemporary society is contributing to the increasing alienation and peer orientation of youth. His observations point to the often-ignored role of larger societal factors in determining sources of influence on the adolescent's behavior.

Summary   That peers and parents are both integral features of the social fabric of adolescence is supported by the empirical findings. While peers may offer greater opportunity than parents for egalitarian relating, it appears that most adolescents comfortably move between these two generational groups and that members of each are probably more similar than different in basic values and attitudes. Thus, the role of the family in adolescent development is not eclipsed by peers. Rather, as Campbell (1969) concludes:

> Any scholarly attempt to describe and dramatize the growth of peer group influences, the power of youth culture, the adolescent's struggle for freedom, etc., must eventually come to terms with the fact that family structures endure through the entire period of adolescence—as residential, affectional, and companionship units. (p. 829)

We agree with Mussen et al. (1974) that the question of peer versus parental influence reflects a false dichotomy. The more interesting question is how the youngster's orientation toward these two groups is affected by the transaction of various individual, familial, and social processes.

Family relationships

Descriptions of the family context of adolescence in the past have been based primarily on clinical work with white, middle-class teenagers (Offer, 1969). Not surprisingly, consistent with the impression that adolescence involves considerable turmoil (A. Freud, 1975), crises (Erikson, 1968), or storm and stress (Hall, 1904), serious intergenerational conflict has been seen as the norm rather than the exception in parent-adolescent interaction. The generalizability of these characterizations to the modal adolescent, however, has been seriously questioned by investigators who have studied teenagers and their families in nonclinical contexts. Unfortunately, most of this research relies on self-report data, thus limiting the validity of the findings for understanding family interaction. Nevertheless, the results are interesting in their own right and provide the only empirically based picture that we have of various normative aspects of the teenager's family life.

Researchers have focused mainly on the following dimensions of parent-adolescent relating: closeness and affect, control and authority, and conflict. In this section, we will examine normative trends in these areas. How the findings relate to different aspects of adolescent development will be considered later.

Closeness and affect. After carefully selecting a normal group of 73 white, middle-class males, Offer and his colleagues (Offer, 1969), beginning in 1962, followed the youngsters through their high school years and beyond. In addition to interviews, psychological testing, and self-report surveys of the boys, data were collected from parents and teachers. Questions about closeness revealed that 59 percent of the boys were identified with their fathers, although most felt that their mothers understood them better emotionally. Nearly all also indicated being closer to one or the other parent; few reported being equally close to both. About 33 percent of the parents, on the other hand, observed that neither parent was close to the youngster, while about 33 percent perceived a closer bond between the boy and his mother. The parents who were interviewed separately showed a high degree of agreement (95 percent). On the average, these findings remained about the same throughout the youngsters' high school years, although different adolescents reversed their position over time.

The boys' descriptions of their home environment during the second wave of testing in their sophomore year also indicated that they were pleased with the emotional atmosphere in the family. The "worst things" mentioned related to their physical surroundings (e.g., sharing rooms with siblings, having only one family car). There were few reports of physical or severe emotional trauma.

Findings by other investigators also suggest that adolescents generally feel close to their parents and satisfied with their home. Niles's (1979) investigation of 262 adolescent girls, for example, revealed highly favorable attitudes toward parents. Even the most peer-oriented participants in this study perceived their parents as being more loving than friends (see also Bengtson, 1970; Campbell, 1969; Offer & Offer, 1975). Interestingly, in their large-scale survey of 13,000 high school students, Moore and Holtzman (1965) discovered that 73 percent of the youths placed high value on their parents and felt a lifelong responsibility to them; about 75 percent reported that they were in no hurry to marry and leave home.

Henggeler and Tavormina (1980) evaluated emotional expressiveness in their study of 64 well-adjusted families (mother, father, and 14- to 16-year-old) who varied as a function of social class, ethnicity, and sex of adolescent. Although the different family members across groups generally rated their relationships to one another as warm on the self-report measures, the lower-class mothers coded their marital relationships as more affectionate than did middle-class mothers. By contrast, qualitative ratings of observed family interaction indicated that each middle-class dyad was warmer than corresponding lower-class dyads. This effect, however, did not obtain significance when verbal IQ and family size were statistically controlled through covariance procedures. Both of these variables correlated highly with social class, pointing to their importance as sources of variance in family interaction.

Henggeler and Tavormina's direct observational data also revealed that father-son relationships were rated as less affectionate than father-daughter relationships. That boys may wish greater closeness to paternal figures can be inferred from Meissner's (1965) investigation of 1,278 high school males. Consistent with stereotypic role patterns, he found that fathers were perceived as being colder, less understanding, more unreasonable, more indifferent, and more old-fashioned than mothers, while mothers were seen as more friendly and nervous than fathers. Nevertheless, 74 percent of the boys reported that they were not only proud of their parents but also liked having them meet their friends. Research by Martin (1979) suggests that adolescent females may desire greater nurturance from their fathers as well. Fathers in this study expressed concern about not having been more emotionally available and giving to their daughters.

Although the findings in this area indicate that patterns of closeness to parents vary as a function of several variables, adolescents on the whole appear favorably disposed toward parental figures. That this attitude is being expressed at a time when they are becoming increasingly independent is noteworthy. Indeed, findings from both Douvan and Adelson's (1966) and Offer's (1969) studies reflected a steady movement toward autonomy from parents. Douvan and Adelson, however, found differences in this area between boys and girls. In most respects the boys appeared behaviorally dependent for a longer period of time than girls, although boys reported sharing fewer leisure activities with their families. Boys, however, achieved emotional autonomy at a significantly faster pace. For example, in comparison to girls, they were less likely to choose intrafamilial models for adult roles, especially same-sex models, and were more likely to break rules. Reflecting differences in sex role socialization, Douvan and Adelson's findings also suggest that independence is a more important concern for boys than for girls. Only 25 percent of the oldest female participants reported that independence was a parental expectation. That these sex differences in autonomy probably still persist today is suggested in several recent research reports (Gilligan, 1982; McDermott, Robillard, Char, Hsu, Tseng, & Ashton, 1983).

Control and authority.   Another important aspect of family life concerns the way power and control are exercised, as reflected in parents' disciplinary patterns, children's freedom to participate in setting rules, and so forth. Based on respondents' answers to the question, "If you do something wrong, how do you get punished?", Douvan and Adelson (1966) distinguished three disciplinary approaches: physical, deprivation, and psychological. Deprivation was most commonly reported (66 percent), followed by psychological (21 percent), and physical (14 percent). With advancing age, the reported use of physical punishment declined (see Newman & Newman, 1979), and participation in rule-making increased for the girls.

Responses in different content domains (punishment, authority, autonomy, and conflict) sampled by Douvan and Adelson (1966) clustered in such a way as to suggest distinct family styles. A significant number of the adolescents (approximately 33 percent) displayed an authoritarian orientation, a pattern associated in part with parents who rely on physical punishment and who do not allow their youngsters to share in behavior regulation. This orientation was overrepresented in the lower socioeconomic strata of the sample (see Elder, 1963). The most prevalent mode of parent-child interaction, however, was basically equalitarian in nature. Between one half and two thirds of the time, parents and adults were characterized as "reasonable, lenient, well intentioned," leading Douvan and Adelson to conclude that for the most part the "American family provides for its adolescents an easygoing, libertarian milieu" (p. 172).

In contrast to Douvan and Adelson's findings, 80 percent of the parents in Offer's (1969) study still physically punished their youngsters; all scolded; only 7 percent of the boys reported that their parent used love withdrawal. Interestingly, mothers were perceived by the boys as more strict than fathers. While some of the adolescents felt their parents were too lenient (20 percent) or too strict (20 percent), the majority (60 percent) suggested that they were disciplined in a variable and unpredictable fashion. Yet despite these concerns, 88 percent reported general satisfaction with their parents' disciplinary measures.

Weller and Luchterhand (1977) found in their study of 1,820 inner-city youths (grades 7 through 12) a negative relationship between parental control and grade in school. The results also indicated that as the youngsters grew older, they turned less to their parents for advice while at the same time becoming closer to them.

It is interesting, however, that even though American teenagers seem generally accepting of their parents' disciplinary style, they may be subject to harsher treatment on the average than their counterparts in other areas of the world. For example, in comparison to family relationships in Denmark, adolescent self-report data collected by Kandel and Lesser (1969) indicate that families in the United States are significantly more autocratic and less democratic. About one half of the American adolescents sampled perceived their parents as autocratic, about one third saw them as democratic, and the remainder felt their parents dealt with them permissively.[1] The adolescents from the United States also perceived their fathers as autocratic in contrast to their mothers, who were seen as democratic (see Elkind & Weiner, 1978, for further descriptive statistics derived from Kandel & Lesser's study).

As research by Jessop (1981) suggests, perhaps contributing to American adolescents' satisfaction with power relationships in the family are biases in how they assay their relative degree of influence. Jessop's examination of the self-reports of high school students and their parents (N = 3,988) on various relational dimensions of family life revealed low levels of agreement. However, further analyses indicated that systematic response biases were evident in response to questions concerning the power dimension. Both parents and adolescents tended to exaggerate the amount of perceived control they had in their relationship.

The few investigators who have studied normal families of adolescents, using direct observational procedures, have provided relevant information on the control dimension as well. Jacob (1974) evaluated the interactions of 44 family triads, comprised of middle- and lower-class families with 11- or 16-year-old boys. The results suggested in part that the older boys were more influential than the younger boys. This shift in power appeared to be at the expense of mothers in middle-class families and at the expense of fathers in lower-class families. A subsequent study by Steinberg and Hill (1978) suggests that these changes are more closely associated with physical maturity than with changes in chronological age or cognitive development (acquisition of formal operational thinking), at least within middle-class families. They found that over the course of the pubertal cycle, boys from middle-class homes became more power-assertive in their verbal interactions with parents. This change was independent of both age and cognitive ability.

Although Henggeler and Tavormina (1980) found little difference in observed control or dominance across the various groups they studied, their self-report findings indicated that in lower-class families, male adolescents influenced their fathers to a greater extent than did female adolescents. In middle-class families, however, males reported less influence with fathers than did females. In addition, daughters in white

---

[1] Recall that only about 33 percent of the subjects sampled by Douvan and Adelson (1966) reported an autocratic or authoritarian pattern. The discrepancy may be due to differences in methodology and/or the historical time period when the data were collected.

families were found on the self-report measures to have greater influence with mother than sons, whereas sons in black families were more influential with mothers than were daughters.

Conflict. Evidence from different time periods, including the turbulent 1960s when parents and adolescents were portrayed in the media as perhaps most polarized, indicates that teenagers are positively oriented toward their parents and gain increasing influence with them as they progress through the adolescent period. It follows that adolescent-parent interaction is probably not marked by excessive conflict or turmoil. Indeed, the literature supports this conclusion.

Douvan and Adelson (1966) found that most female respondents in their survey perceived their parents to be fair. To the extent that they reported disagreements with parents, personal grooming emerged as the area of greatest discord in early adolescence, social activities (e.g., dating, friendship choice, driving in cars) during middle adolescence, and ideology (e.g., politics) during middle and especially late adolescence. Douvan and Adelson view these conflicts as falling on a continuum from an initial concern with narcissistic issues, followed by issues centering on social involvement and sexual conduct, and later the wider world of ideas, values, and opinions. There was also suggestive evidence that while the mother was the antagonist in these conflicts for young adolescents, the father increasingly assumed this role as the girls matured.

Although similar conflict data were not collected for the male sample, the impression from Douvan and Adelson's results is that neither sex generally experiences significant conflict with their parents. Douvan and Adelson conclude:

> The normative adolescent tends to avoid overt conflict with his family. Now this is not to say that conflict is not present; but it is largely unconscious conflict. . . . Even when we do find overt conflict one senses that it has an "as if" quality to it, that it is a kind of war game, with all the sights and sounds of battle but without blood being shed . . . parent and child play out an empty ritual of disaffection, that they agree to disagree only on token issues, or teen issues, and in doing so are able to sidestep any genuine encounter of differences. (p. 352)

Echoing the results of Douvan and Adelson (1966), Offer (1969) found little conflict between parents and adolescents as well. Both reported fewer disagreements once the student started high school. Eighty percent of the youngsters also indicated that their parents approved of their future plans. Relatedly, with the exception of four parents, all expressed approval of their sons and regarded the problems they had as minor. Conger (1977b) has reviewed other attitude surveys of adolescents that provide additional support for these findings.

The research in this area also indicates that parents and adolescents hold similar values (see Coleman, 1978; Offer, 1969). When differences are found, they are often in the areas of musical taste, dress, and other superficial qualities (see Mussen et al., 1974). Even more substantive differences in underlying social and moral attitudes toward contemporary social issues (drug use, sexuality) tend to involve different levels of agreement or disagreement (e.g., parents moderately agree, while the adolescent strongly agrees) rather than directional differences (e.g., parents strongly agree, and the adolescent strongly disagrees) (see Lerner & Spanier, 1980).

Results of studies conducted by Feather (1975, 1978) in this area, however, point to some value discrepancies that appear rooted in differing life tasks of parents and adolescents. For example, on the value survey (Rokeach, 1973), adolescents placed greater weight on such values as close companionship with others and excitement and pleasure, while parents assigned more importance to values concerning family and national security, self-respect and responsibility. Feather's data also indicated that the daughters were closer to their parents in value orientation than were the sons. Douvan and Adelson (1966) also found similar sex differences, which they interpreted as further evidence of the girls' greater emotional dependence on parents.

Neither serious conflict with parents nor turmoil and rebellion appear endemic to adolescence. Offer (1969) found that while rebellious behavior was evident in the early adolescence of his subjects, it usually did not assume the form of a tumultuous crisis. Those in his sample (21 percent) who did exhibit such "tumultuous growth" came from unstable backgrounds marked by marital conflict and emotional distance in the family. They were also members of the lower middle class, the lowest class represented in Offer's study. The other participants were characterized by "continuous growth" (23 percent) and "surgent growth" (35 percent). In contrast to the latter, who experienced various family crises (death, divorce, serious illness in the family), the histories of the continuous-growth youngsters were free of such life-cycle events. They also came into conflict with their parents less often than did the surgent-growth adolescents. To an even greater extent than Offer's study suggests, data from the Berkeley longitudinal studies (Haan & Day, 1974) indicate that the modal adolescent proceeds smoothly toward adulthood, displaying considerable continuity in information processing, interpersonal reactions, responses to socialization influences, and manner of self-presentation.

Results from direct observational studies (Jacob, 1974; Steinberg & Hill, 1978), discussed earlier, are also generally supportive of self-reports indicating that the rise in conflict during early adolescence declines over time. Jacob found as well that middle-class families exhibited less overall discord (as defined by degree of initial agreement among family members using an unrevealed-difference technique) than lower-class families. They also appeared to have a stronger parental alliance, in that disagreement between parents was less than parent-child disagreement to a significantly greater degree in the middle-class than in the lower-class families. Henggeler and Tavormina's (1980) data, however, raise questions about social-class differences in conflict. In addition to finding no differences in self-report ratings as a function of this variable, their direct observational results yielded a mixed picture. For example, while middle-class marital dyads had less initial disagreement on an expressive task than did lower-class dyads, they were rated as more conflictual and demonstrated more simultaneous speech. The differences in qualitative ratings, however, did not remain significant with verbal IQ statistically controlled.

Summary. Despite the impression that "readiness for adulthood comes about two years later than the adolescent claims, and about two years before his parents will admit" (Stone & Church, 1968, p. 447), normative data suggest that the relationship between adolescents and parents becomes increasingly harmonious with age. The initial discord experienced between the generations during early adolescence presages changes in power relationships in the family; the adolescent's influence increases, and the parents' control decreases. Although adolescents appear generally satisfied with their home environments, many report that their fathers are autocratic and emotionally distant. These concerns may not greatly affect their overall ratings of family satisfaction, however, inasmuch as such paternal behavior is role-conforming. Evidence that family conflict is greater in lower-class than in middle-class homes is equivocal.

The results reported in this section shed little direct light on processes that mediate normal adolescent development and adaptive family functioning. For example, information about the absolute degree of conflict experienced by modal adolescents and their parents leaves unanswered how different modes of conflict resolution affect adolescent development. These and related issues are considered in the next two sections.

FAMILY RELATIONSHIPS AND ADOLESCENT DEVELOPMENT

Numerous theorists have described tasks that adolescents in contemporary industrialized societies must master to become mature and well-adjusted young adults. Conger (1973) suggests that the following are particularly important: adjusting to physical changes and new drives accompanying puberty, establishing autonomy from parents, developing affective relationships with same- and opposite-sex peers, preparing for a vocation, constructing a value system, and creating a sense of identity. These tasks are not faced by the adolescent alone; rather, his or her whole family participates in their negotiation and crucially influences and is influenced by the process. Perhaps the most significant challenge for parents is the transition from a parent-child, or complementary, relationship to an increasingly adult-adult, or symmetrical, one (L. Hoffman, 1980). This familial process does not occur in a social vacuum either. Indeed, wider cultural values and socialization patterns, sociopolitical trends, and economic conditions crucially affect the lives of families. The developmental changes and tasks of adolescence, therefore, cannot be sufficiently described by simple lineal models (see Adelson, 1980; Berger & Berger, Chap. 5 of this volume; Feather, 1975; Lerner & Spanier, 1980). Illustrative of the complexities involved is research on the role of family relationships in the adolescent's personality and social growth.

Douvan and Adelson's (1966) analyses, for example, revealed that teenage girls who displayed a pattern of autonomy in self-report and projective test data came from families who allowed participation in setting rules and relied heavily on psychological punishments (verbal, guilt-inducing). Interestingly, those girls below age 14 not permitted to contribute to rule making reported fewer disagreements with parents than girls who did participate. However, no differences between these groups emerged during middle adolescence, and fewer disagreements were reported by the latter above age 16. Physical punishment was related in Douvan and Adelson's data to a submissive orientation to authority and dependent tendencies in both girls and boys, although boys appeared to suffer the most ill effects. They also showed signs of rebellion or covert resentment, poor internalization of control, social isolation, low self-confidence, and restricted time perspective.

Other researchers have also reported that the adolescent's emerging independence covaries with power relationships in the family. In an often-cited study in the literature on adolescence, Elder (1963) investigated the influence of level of perceived parental power and power legitimization. Junior high and high school students' responses to the question, "In general, how are most decisions made between you and your (mother/father)?", were grouped by Elder into three power levels: autocratic (participation in decision making and self-regulation are not allowed), democratic (participation in decision making is encouraged, but parents ultimately decide), and permissive (adolescent's input carries more weight than the parents'). Power legitimization was defined in terms of the frequency of parental explanations of rules and decisions. In part, the youngsters of permissive and democratic parents who legitimized their rules through frequent explanations were self-

confident and autonomous decision makers. By contrast, such legitimization at the autocratic level related to dependency with varying
confidence in the youngsters; infrequent explanation at this level was
associated with a lack of both self-assuredness and independence in
decision making. Elder also generally found that youngsters whose
mothers and fathers often explained rules were most likely to model
their parents and to associate with parent-approved peers. Moreover,
democratic parents were perceived as more attractive models than
the other parental types, regardless of frequency of explanations. As
Newman and Newman (1979, p. 234) note, these and other findings
(e.g., Kandel & Lesser, 1969, who extended Elder's work) point out
an intriguing paradox: "The same conditions that foster a sense of
independence also build a bond of closeness and affection between
parents and children" (p. 230).

Democratic relating with parent-defined limits, frequent explanations, and child involvement also contribute to the development of
moral judgment. In a series of studies in this area, M. L. Hoffman
and his colleagues (see M. L. Hoffman, 1980, for a review) have demonstrated that inductive disciplinary practices (involving reasoning) in
conjunction with expression of affection in nondiscipline contexts correlate significantly with an internalized moral code and high guilt in
youngsters (see also Miller & Swanson, 1966). Power assertion (use of
physical force, deprivation, or threats of deprivation), on the other
hand, relates to a moral orientation rooted in a fear of punishment
and detection. Although the other type of discipline identified by Hoffman, love withdrawal (nonphysical expression of anger or disapproval),
has not been shown to relate consistently to moral orientation, some
data suggest that it may contribute to inhibition of anger (see M. L.
Hoffman, 1980).

Observational research by Jurkovic and Prentice (1974) and Holstein
(1972) of family discussions of moral dilemmas also reveals that youngsters' moral maturity, as determined by Kohlberg's (1976) moral judgment interview, relates positively to parental encouragement and negatively to parental hostility and dominance. The association of
reciprocity in parent-child relationships and moral development has
also been found by Parikh (1980) in 15- to 16-year-old Indian children,
although this finding did not obtain for younger adolescents (12 to
13 years). The intellectual debate and mutual perspective-taking that
encouraging, supportive, and reciprocal family discussions induce can
be seen as contributing to the youngster's development of higher-order
moral cognitions. It is likely that disagreement in these families is not
only better tolerated and negotiated but also relates to different content
issues than in families who do not support active discussion. Indeed,
Douvan and Adelson (1966) found that teenage girls who participated

in making rules relevant to their behavior tended to disagree with their parents about ideas (opinions, values) rather than, like their less-involved counterparts, about dating and riding in cars. Such intellectual disagreement has been found in the family backgrounds of college students who exhibit principled or postconventional moral reasoning *à la* Kohlberg (Haan, Smith, & Block, 1968).

Of course, it could be argued that parental encouragement, reciprocal relating, and intellectual sparring in the family are merely responses to the behavior of a morally and cognitively sophisticated youngster. However, that this is probably not entirely the case was demonstrated recently in an experimental study by Stanley (1978). Her manipulation of family interaction patterns through skills training in the area of democratic conflict resolution produced positive and lasting changes in the moral-developmental level of the adolescent participants.

The importance of affective dimensions (parental warmth, supportiveness) in moral development, as found in several of the investigations already considered, has also emerged in studies of cognitive and affective role taking. Keller (1976) suggests that positive family affect establishes at a young age favorable expectations relating to social interaction and, thus, incentives to take the role of others. (See M. L. Hoffman, 1980, for more elaborate theorizing about the relation of cognition, affect, and various socialization experiences.) Empirical data collected by Keller revealed globally that perceived parental supportiveness and severity related, as expected, to the ability of seventh-grade boys and girls to take the role of others cognitively (as measured by the Feffer (1970) role-taking task). A more recent study by Adams, Jones, Schvaneveldt, and Jensen (1982), however, suggests that these findings may not generalize to the development of affective aspects of role taking—that is, to the adolescent's emotional sensitivity to or empathy with another's feelings. They found that an interpersonally supportive relationship with mothers and fathers is predictive of high scores only for males on the Mehrabian and Epstein (1972) empathy scale. Eisenberg-Berg and Mussen (1978) obtained similar results, leading them to hypothesize that the salience of affective sensitivity in stereotypic female sex role socialization (see Gilligan, 1982) obscures the effects of specific parental socialization practices on girls. It is plausible that Keller did not find sex differences in her study because she used a cognitive rather than an affective measure of perspectivism; cognitive role taking may be less sensitive to wider social influences on sex role development.

Both parental affect and control and such family characteristics as father absence and maternal employment have been shown to relate to other aspects of adolescents' personal and social development as well (see Conger, 1979; Elkind & Weiner, 1978; Goslin, 1969; Lerner

& Spanier, 1980; Newman & Newman, 1979; Walters & Stinnett, 1971). Research in this area has recently taken a refreshingly new twist, however. A few investigators, influenced by family systems theorists such as Minuchin (1974), have not only pointed to the possible importance of several previously unstudied familial variables but also have attempted to take into account the multivariate and interdependent nature of the family system (Forman & Forman, 1981). For example, Bell and Bell (1979) provide suggestive evidence for the problematic effects of triangulation on adolescents. The personal and interpersonal growth of 15- to 17-year-old girls sampled by the Bells related negatively to parental tendencies to focus on their daughter's problems or to invite their daughter's support against the other spouse when experiencing marital stress. In his family interview study of 53 normal 11th and 12th grade males, Kleiman (1981) also discovered that functional parental alliances and generational boundaries are associated with optimal psychosocial adaptation during adolescence (as measured by the Offer self-image questionnaire). Lewis's (1978) research points as well to the significance of these variables in adolescent development, along with many other family dimensions such as closeness and efficiency in negotiation and problem solving.

Another interesting study by Prasinos and Tittler (1981) found that humor-oriented adolescent boys reported lower cohesion scores and higher conflict scores on the Moos family environment scale and greater distance from the father on Kueth's figure placement test than did their less humor-oriented peers. Prasinos and Tittler propose a family distance model of humor in which humor is seen as one way to relate to others from a distance. Forman and Forman (1981) have also reported a number of other significant relationships between adolescent personality development and family systems variables as operationalized by Moos's measure. As would be expected from a family systems perspective, they did not find any single family variable that accounted for major portions of the variance; rather, their multivariate analysis led them to conclude that "child behavior varies with total system functioning, more than with separate system factors" (p. 163). Forman and Forman's findings are also consistent with evidence reported by Olson and his colleagues (Olson, Sprenkle, & Russell, 1979; C. S. Russell, 1979) that optimal functioning is associated with families who score in the moderate range on various family dimensions.

Summary.   Research reviewed in this section indicates that the family continues to play an important role in the socialization and personality development of youngsters during adolescence. Over the years, this research has become more complex. Initial efforts to define relationships between isolated parental and adolescent variables are slowly being supplanted by multivariate and systemic approaches that recognize the many varied and interrelated aspects of family process. Investigators with a Piagetian orientation have also begun to explore the family context of different lines of sociocognitive development. Interestingly, their findings are underscoring the importance of dimensions of family relating, such as democratic conflict resolution, that are increasingly emerging in theory and research (e.g., L'Abate, 1976; Lewis, 1978) as central not only to other aspects of individual adaptation (e.g., autonomous functioning) but also to family adaptation generally. Research comparing functional and dysfunctional families, which we will turn to next, makes this point even clearer.

FAMILY INFLUENCE AND ADOLESCENT PROBLEMS

Although it has been long assumed that adolescent disturbance is related to family functioning (Erikson, 1968; Hall, 1904; Healy & Bronner, 1936; Johnson & Szurek, 1952), the empirical literature in this area has focused mainly on two problem areas: juvenile delinquency and, more recently, teenage drug use. Related to the young person's interactions with society, these issues appear to reflect the prevailing concerns of parents and other members of the social community. Clinical investigators have shown an increasing interest in the family context of other forms of adolescent psychopathology as well (Hetherington & Martin, 1979); but with the exception of schizophrenia (for reviews see Doane, 1978; Goldstein & Rodnick, 1975; Jacob, 1975), the findings are based largely on clinical case studies. In keeping with our empirical focus, we will concentrate on family-oriented research of court- and drug-involved adolescents.

Sheldon and Eleanor Glueck's (1934, 1940, 1950, 1962, 1970) well-known work represents a basic reference point in this area. In 1950, using self-report questionnaires and family interviews, they compared the family characteristics of 500 delinquent boys to those of 500 nondelinquent boys matched for residence in underpriviledged areas, ethnic origin, age, and global intelligence. The delinquents experienced more inconsistent discipline by fathers, more father absence, less supervision and more lax discipline by mother, and more tenuous bonds of affection with both parents; their parents also placed less emphasis on family loyalty and future accomplishments. In addition, the delinquents had a greater incidence than did nondelinquents of criminal and delinquent behavior as well as emotional disturbance in their family backgrounds, along with a less financially stable and routinized home environment. (See also Andry, 1960; Bonney, 1941; McCord, McCord, & Zola, 1959; and Nye, 1958.)

Subsequent research comparing the self-reports of delinquents and nondelinquents also reveals that parent-child relationships are perceived by the delinquent to be more hostile, rejecting, and punitive (Deitz, 1969; McCord & McCord, 1964; Medinnus, 1965); moreover, their overall family concept is more negative (Anolik, 1980). Fathers are viewed as more neglecting and distant (Andry, 1960; Bandura & Walters, 1959; Biller & Meredith, 1975; Lang, Papenfuh, & Walters, 1976; and Robinson, 1978) and are more likely to have a nonfunctioning role in the family (Clausen, 1961). Mothers are seen as less warm and loving (McCord & McCord, 1964; Streit, 1981).

Similar findings have emerged in studies of drug-abusing adolescents. Adolescents who perceive their relationship with parents as positive, involved, and supportive and who express feelings of attachment to their family are less likely to report drug involvement than adolescents who perceive greater friction and distance among family members (Adler & Lotecka, 1973; Jessor & Jessor, 1975, 1977; Lawrence & Vellerman, 1974; McBride, 1978; J. S. Russell, 1972; Shibuya, 1974; Wechsler & Thum, 1973). Generally, it appears that the probability of drug involvement by adolescents increases as their affinity toward the family decreases. (For reviews, see Barnes, 1977; Glynn, 1981; Stanton, 1979.)

Studies of the relation of "broken homes" to delinquency and to drug abuse have been less consistent. Whereas numerous investigators (e.g., Chein, 1964; Monahan, 1960; Nye, 1958; Shore, 1971) have found a higher rate of divorce and separation in delinquent and drug-abusing groups, others (e.g., Wilgosh & Paitich, 1974) report no significant relationship between broken homes and delinquent behavior. It has generally been concluded that the stress associated with marital discord is more significant than whether parents are separated or divorced (Bennett, 1959; Browning, 1960; Dancy & Handal, 1980; Glueck & Glueck, 1970).

The role of parental discipline and decision-making style in the development of delinquent and drug-abusing behaviors has also received considerable attention. Lax and inconsistent discipline has most often been cited as a precursor to delinquency (Jessor & Jessor, 1974; Nye, 1958; Streit, 1981; West, 1967); McCord, McCord, & Howard, (1961) and Duncan (1971) further report that parents of delinquents are more likely to use physical punishment. Jenkins (1968) also found that undersocialized, aggressive youth came from homes where mothers were critical, punitive, and inconsistent, whereas socialized delinquents were more likely to live in large, neglectful families with an absence of parental control, particularly paternal control. Although most of the research in this area has relied solely on the adolescent's perception of parental behavior, Robinson (1978) used mothers' and fathers' reports of their own behavior as well as adolescents' reports of parental behavior. Her results strongly support other findings in the literature. Parents of delinquent adolescents were described by all sources to be more inconsistent in setting and reinforcing rules, less likely to praise, encourage, and show an interest in their child, and higher in hostile detachment. However, it is noteworthy that, in both groups, the adolescents described parents as being significantly less positive and more inconsistent than their parents reported themselves to be.

Relatedly, parents who are perceived as applying a quasi-democratic mode of discipline, where they maintain a basic firmness but also express an openness to communication and reasonable negotiation, are more successful in minimizing drug involvement than parents who are seen as overly rigid and dominating or parents who are permissive or lax in their disciplinary approach (Blum & Associates, 1969, 1972; Braucht, Brakarsh, Follingstad, & Berry, 1973; Hunt, 1974; Jessor & Jessor, 1977). A comprehensive study by Blum et al. (1971) of 211 adolescents who were designated as high, medium, or low risk for drug abuse suggests that parenting styles have an influence on the youth's general social orientation as well as on specific behaviors. For example, children from low-risk families characterized by a benevolent dictatorship with diversity of self-expression and an emphasis on discipline, self-control, and family tradition tend to be reliable, honest, and sensible but conservative, inflexible, and often dogmatic in social beliefs. Children from medium-risk families, who maintain a basic firmness but provide greater allowance for freedom and adherence to the child's perspective, are more self-reliant, flexible, enthusiastic, and curious. The authors observed that even though these children engaged in minor drug experimentation, they showed the best overall adaptation.

There are also indications in line with Glueck and Glueck's earlier findings that parents of delinquents and drug abusers may provide poor role models. For example, in comparison with parents of nondelinquents, parents of delinquents display more antisocial and morally unstable personality traits (Bennett, 1959; Herzog, 1973) and lower levels of maternal moral development (Hudgins & Prentice, 1973). Robins, West, and Herjanic (1975) also found high correlations between parents' and son's involvement in legal transgressions (see Glueck & Glueck, 1950).

Studies that have focused on adolescent use of alcohol have also consistently reported that parental drinking behavior appears to be a strong mediating factor (Annis, 1974; Braucht et al., 1973; George, 1975; Gorsuch & Butler, 1976; Scherer, 1973; Smart & Fejer, 1972). In fact, several investigators (Akers, 1968; Bacon & Jones, 1968; Maddox, 1970) have concluded that parental attitudes toward drinking and their own drinking behaviors are the best predictors of the drinking patterns of their children, consistent with a modeling theory of drug use (Annis, 1974; Bandura & Walters, 1963; Maddox, 1970). Although it has also been noted that children of alcoholics are at high risk for developing drinking problems (Adler & Lotecka, 1973; Kandel, 1974; Lerner, Ronald, & Burke, 1974; Smart & Fejer, 1972), theorists and researchers (e.g., Chafetz Blanc, & Hill, 1971; Sutherland & Cressey, 1966) studying the problem of alcoholism argue that learned drinking patterns may affect one's initiation into the use of alcohol, but alcohol dependency is the result of family instability (see Barnes, 1977; Selden, 1972).

In contrast to the well-documented link between parental and adolescent drinking behavior, research of marijuana use (especially casual use) suggests that peer models and influences may play a more significant role, (Goode, 1969, 1970; Hochman, 1972; Jessor, 1976; Jessor & Jessor, 1975, 1977; Stone, Miranne, & Ellis, 1979). Kandel (1973, 1974, 1975), for example, obtained data from triads of high school students, best friends, and parents. Her major finding was that marijuana use by peers was a better predictor than drug use by parents, and peers were found to exert a greater influence than parents. However, a subsequent analysis of these findings by Stanton (1979) revealed that the highest rates of marijuana use were reported by youngsters whose best friend and parents were both drug users. Smart and Fejer (1972), who discovered significantly higher rates of tranquilizer, barbituate, and stimulant use by parents of marijuana users than parents of nonusers, also point to the importance of parental factors.

For adolescents whose drug use extends beyond marijuana to include other illicit drugs, research has consistently shown that peer influence is relatively minimal. Rather, serious drug abuse appears more highly related to negative parent-adolescent relationships (Cannon, 1976; Sanborn, Daniels, Jones, Salken, & Shonick, 1971; Selden, 1972) and to parents' use of alcohol and other prescription and illicit drugs (Bushing & Bromley, 1975; Fejer, 1972; Goode, 1975; Kandel, 1978a, 1978b; Stenmark, Wackwitz, Pelfrey, & Dougherty, 1974; Tec, 1974a, 1974b). Kandel, Tec, and Goode have observed intergenerational continuities in drug use; differences are more highly related to the type of psychoactive substance used than to use or nonuse.

That ongoing patterns of family interaction are important in the development and perpetuation of delinquency and adolescent drug abuse has been suggested by family systems theorists (see Alexander, 1973; Kaufman, 1980; Stanton, 1980, 1982). To study these processes, Olson et al. (1979) developed an objective self-report measure called the Family Adaptability and Cohesion Evaluation Scales (Faces II). This test was administered before and after family-oriented treatment to 29 families with female juvenile offenders (Olson, McCubbin, Barnes,

Larsen, Muten, & Wilson, 1982). On pretest, families as a whole were found to be disengaged and chaotic, in contrast to their more moderate scores on the posttest. Although the pretest findings are generally consistent with the literature describing delinquent families, Olson et al. (1979) did not include a control group. That Faces II may not differentiate delinquents and nondelinquents emerged in a study by Schratz (1983). In addition to finding no significant differences between these groups, the raw scores of delinquents did not differ from national norms reported by Olson et al. (1982). However, Schratz's study was confounded by the fact that his delinquent and nondelinquent subjects differed in socioeconomic status.

C. S. Russell (1979) evaluated family triads of mother, father, and daughter, which were subdivided into high- and low-functioning units according to whether the daughters had seriously considered running away from home. Based on their participation in a structured family interaction game and their responses to self-report inventories, Russell found that high-functioning triads exhibited moderate levels of adaptability and cohesion. Low-functioning families had extreme scores on both of these dimensions.

Other investigators have also directly observed family interactions of delinquents and drug-abusing adolescents. Their findings have generally been consistent with subjective reports of family life. Jurkovic and Prentice (1974), for example, compared dyadic interactions of mothers and delinquent sons to those in nondelinquent families. They found delinquent interactions were higher on maternal hostility, conflict, and maternal dominance and lower on maternal warmth than were nondelinquent dyads.

Alexander's (1973) evaluation of supportive and defensive communications in parent-adolescent triads revealed greater defensiveness in delinquent than in nondelinquent families. Parents in both groups supported their youngsters, but the delinquent boys were less supportive than nondelinquent boys. Further analyses indicated that in comparison to interactional sequences in delinquent families, supportive rather than defensive communications were reciprocated to a greater extent in nondelinquent triads.

In a subsequent study examining the effects of attributional set on supportive and defensive communications and on talk time, Barton and Alexander (1984) observed delinquent and nondelinquent families interacting under experimentally induced competitive and cooperative conditions. Although families in both groups interacted more adaptively within a cooperative set, the delinquent families did not relate as capably as their nondelinquent counterparts. The findings are suggestive of communication skill deficiencies in delinquent families that cannot be remedied through changes in attributional set alone. Consistent with stereotypic role patterns, fathers in both groups were also more controlling and defensive than other family members. As Barton and Alexander note, that these paternal behaviors were not specific to delinquent families challenges the assumption that stern, harsh fathers cause delinquency. Indeed, evidence of the detrimental effects of paternal neglect suggests that father involvement, even if domineering, is better than no involvement (Jessor, 1976; Lang et al., 1976).

A series of studies initiated by Ferreira (1963) compared interactions of normal family groups to groups with a delinquent, schizophrenic, or maladjusted youngster (Ferreira & Winter, 1965, 1966, 1968; Ferreira, Winter, & Poindexter, 1966; Winter & Ferreira, 1967). In comparison to the controls, the delinquent families displayed less spontaneous agreement on likes and dislikes prior to information exchanges, less individual choice fulfillment in family decisions, and more silence during family discussions. Comparison of delinquent groups to other abnormal groups on these variables revealed that they were less pathological than the schizophrenic families, but generally more pathological than the maladjusted families. In general, they seemed interested mainly in quickly completing the experimental tasks without becoming too involved. These findings appear consistent with self-reports of delinquents that their parents are indifferent and detached.

Using the same decision-making task as Ferreira and Winter (1965), Mead and Campbell (1972) compared families with and without a drug-abusing adolescent. Findings revealed members of drug-abusing families had less overall spontaneous agreement on what they liked and disliked and displayed less individual choice fulfillment in areas of disagreement. In comparison to Ferreira and Winter's (1965) findings, both delinquent and drug-abusing families appear to exhibit a pseudo-mutual orientation. Both resolved disagreements quickly and superficially, shifting the focus to areas of agreement.

Gantman (1978) directly examined the family interaction patterns of families with a normal, drug-abusing, or emotionally disturbed adolescent. Compared to the other groups, normal families displayed less scapegoating of the adolescent; more positive communications; more freedom of expression, cooperation, and sensitivity; clearer communication; and greater equality of participation. However, no significant differences were noted between emotionally disturbed and drug-abusing families. Gantman concluded that adolescent drug abuse is secondary to other family problems.

Stabenau, Tupin, Werner, and Pollin (1965) compared family groups with a schizophrenic, delinquent, and normal adolescent. Family groups consisted of mother, father, index subject, and normal sibling. Family interactions were evaluated by a revealed-difference task. All individuals were given an object-sorting task to assess conceptual abstraction abilities, and parents were given the Thematic Apperception Test (TAT). Findings from the revealed-difference task were as follows: schizophrenic families evidenced overcontrol of emotion, inappropriate affect, imbalanced leadership, fragmented communication, and conformity to external standards. Parents were rigid, and the index child was inactive. In contrast, delinquent families showed uncontrolled emotion, artificial affect, undifferentiated leadership, choatic communication, and self-centered goals. Parents were in conflict, and the index child was active. Modulated emotion, appropriate affect, organized leadership, clear communications, and empathic awareness emerged in the responses of normal families. Congruent trends were found on the TAT. On the object-sorting test, normal index subjects were found to have significantly higher ability in conceptual abstraction than schizophrenic or delinquent youngsters who did not differ from each other. Parents of normal subjects had greater abstraction abilities than parents in the other groups; however, siblings in all groups did not differ.

Finally, a few studies have observed family interactions of delinquents differentiated according to various diagnostic criteria. Duncan (1971) assessed the interactions of mothers and fathers of nondelinquent, individual-delinquent, and social-delinquent girls. Parents of nondelinquents displayed higher levels of verbal activity, less conflict, more egalitarian control, less rejection, and more flexibility. Parents of social delinquents were more verbally active and controlling than the individual-delinquent group.

Hetherington, Stouwie, and Ridberg (1971) investigated family interactions of normals and three subgroups of delinquent boys and girls: neurotic, psychopathic, and social (see Quay & Werry, 1979). They found that family interactions varied according to the sex and diagnostic category of the adolescent. For males, findings indicated in part that (a) neurotic-delinquent families were mother-dominated, (b) social- and psychopathic-delinquent families were father-dominated, and (c) normal families displayed no differential patterns of dominance between parents. For females, findings partly revealed that (a) neurotic-delinquent families were mother-dominated, (b) social- and psychopathic-delinquent families displayed little parental dominance or control, and (c) normal families again exhibited no differential patterns of dominance. Research by Duncan (1971) and Hetherington et al. underscore the importance of not viewing delinquents as a homogeneous group.

Summary. Studies of the family context of court-involved and drug-abusing adolescents point to many of the same variables that have been empirically linked to personal and sociocognitive growth during this age period. For example, whereas lax, neglectful, and inconsistent discipline is related to behavioral dysfunction, a quasi-democratic approach typifies parental control in families of well-adjusted adolescents. However, findings reported in this section more clearly reflect the continuing importance of parental models and family communication and systems processes in the behavioral adjustment and development of adolescents. It is apparent that both drug-abusing and delinquent teenagers reside in families characterized by deviant parental behavior and dysfunctional family interaction patterns. By contrast, common observations of functional families include adult modeling of prosocial behaviors, significant spontaneous agreement among members, genuine expression of affect, efficient and supportive decision making, and clear parental control.

IMPLICATIONS FOR THEORY, RESEARCH, AND PRACTICE

The investigative work reviewed does not represent an exhaustive sampling of research on adolescents and their families; however, it is reflective of the many different kinds of content issues, methodological approaches, and empirical trends that characterize this literature. We intentionally avoided detailed consideration of theory initially to highlight the descriptive value of the studies considered. Although many of them suffer from methodological and conceptual problems, the findings have begun to cohere in ways that promise not only to redress previous theoretical distortions but also to improve further study and clinical practice in this area.

Theory

As Offer, Ostrov, and Howard (1981) noted recently, theoretical speculation and popular commentary have tended to emphasize the *Sturm und Drang* qualities of adolescence and attendant discontinuities between the generations (see Blos, 1961; Deutsch, 1967; Erikson, 1968; A. Freud, 1946, 1975; Hall, 1904). Psychodynamic theorists, for example, have assumed that adolescent identity formation requires emotional separation from, and opposition to, parents. Only by experiencing a psychosocial moratorium, according to Erikson, can the youngster prepare for his or her eventual reentry into the social mainstream as a new and autonomous individual. Of course, it was recognized that not every young person proceeds through his or her adolescent years in this fashion: Some fail to resolve their identity crisis; others do not experience one at all (or at least maintain remarkable intrapersonal and interpersonal equanimity). Both adaptations were seen as problematic, however.

Evidence reviewed here seriously questions the validity of traditional personality theory (see Elkind & Weiner, 1978; Offer, 1969, Offer et al., 1981). From the perspective of normative findings and systematic observation of nonclinical groups, adolescence for most young people and their parents is not significantly destabilizing. In addition to remaining relatively tension free personally, the middle-range teenager spends considerable time with family members, shares many of their values and expectations, interacts with acceptable peers, feels close to at least one parent, avoids ongoing familial conflict, expresses general satisfaction with parental childrearing methods, and becomes increasingly influential in family interactions. Studies of socialization patterns and abnormal groups further suggest that family process plays a crucial mediating role in the adolescent's intrapersonal and interpersonal development. Rather than merely representing obstacles that teenagers resist or maneuver around to define their individuality, parents are active participants in their growing up.

Although empirical studies of adolescents with behavior problems are consistent with previous clinical reports of marked intergenerational conflict, their generalizability to normal groups can now be viewed as limited. The normative data have led some investigators to conclude that adolescent rebellion and the generation gap are mythical constructions (see Elkind & Weiner, 1978) or at least grossly overstated problems (see Conger, 1973; Manaster, 1977). Offer (1969, Offer et al., 1981) and his colleagues, along with others (Elkind & Weiner, 1978; Weiner, 1982), have thus called for new theoretical formulations that accord with normative findings.

While we generally agree that tensions between the generations have clearly been exaggerated, closer inspection of the self-report and observational findings suggests that maturational changes in normal adolescents are coincident with increased familial conflict and rigidity. Difficulties in adaptation, however, are followed by an increasingly pleasant mode of adolescent-parent relating, marked in part by a greater balance of power (see Douvan & Adelson, 1966; Jacob, 1974; Offer, 1969; Steinberg & Hill, 1978). Although further empirical validation of this trend is needed, it is consistent with theoretical accounts of the family life cycle. L. Hoffman (1980), for example, posits that change in a youngster's developmental status ushers in a period of disequilibrium in the family during which members struggle to construct a more adaptive organizational pattern. This new pattern is assumed to be discontinuous with previous relational modes. It is plausible that empirical evidence of phasic conflicts between the generations reflect transformational processes in the adolescent's family system. It is likely that second-order or qualitative shifts in the families of well-adjusted adolescents are part of a long-standing intergenerational process in which parents and youngsters mutually accommodate each other in graduated steps (see Bowen, 1974). Coleman's (1974, 1978) focal theory of adolescence is consistent with this view. Based on a large-scale study of teenagers, he discovered that concern about different relational issues peaked at different times. Rather than facing all of the demands of this age period at once, adolescents appear to deal with them serially.

In an effort to understand the morphology of expectable conflict (however intense) at different points in the family life cycle, L. Hoffman (1980) speculates that paradoxical injunctions or "simple binds" characterize relationships in transition. Family interactions are governed by conflicting sets of rules: the old and the new. The adolescent, for example, is enjoined by parents to be more independent and thus symmetrical to them, but their injunction defines the relationship in familiar complementary (parent-child) terms. These simple binds are typically resolved, according to Hoffman, when parents reinforce adolescents for behaving in a developmentally progressive manner. However, responses that disconfirm mature behavior create a double bind—the message is "change but don't change."[2]

Whereas most adolescents and their families appear to successfully avoid long-standing double binds, simple binds may be the norm. Interestingly, democratic parents may occasion these simple relational contradictions at an earlier point in their teenager's development than autocratic parents. Recall Douvan and Adelson's (1966) finding that conflict in early adolescence is most characteristic of youngsters whose parents encourage their input into childrearing decisions. Parents who disallow such input, thus maintaining a uniformly complementary relationship with their teenage offspring, tend to experience intergenerational conflict later, if at all.

Families distinguished by intra- and interparental inconsistency and conflict are likely to support double binds that prevent or retard movement to new developmental levels in both the adolescent and the family.[3] Although these qualities are typically found in families of iden-

---

[2] Following Hoffman's logic, we would add that adolescents also place their parents in simple binds. For example, consider the peremptory demands of a 15-year-old to be accorded adult privileges—a request for independence (symmetry) framed in a childish (complementary) fashion. Teenagers who behave maturely when given the opportunity to demonstrate age-appropriate independence increase the likelihood that parental expectations will shift to a new relational level. An immature response, however, is nonreinforcing to parents who may then react to the form rather than to the content of their adolescents' pleas for independence by continuing to treat them as children. Predictably, their youngsters' requests become even more strident, completing a circular sequence in which the original simple bind transforms into a double bind.

[3] Dammann (1973) has presented strong evidence for irregular parental reinforcement schedules and communication patterns in the families of disturbed adolescents. Her data lend support to Hoffman's hypothesis that emotional disturbances in family members are related to disconfirmation of desired behavior.

tified problem groups, such as delinquent and drug-abusing adolescents, they may appear in nonclinical families as well. "Normal" adolescents and their families are not a monolithic group (Elkind & Weiner, 1978; Offer, 1969). Differing widely, they respond to numerous factors that can interfere with smooth life-cycle transitions. Our enthusiastic embrace of data exposing biases in prior theoretical formulations ignores evidence of disharmonies in the lives of many families of adolescents in this country. For example, it can be inferred from the research reviewed that traditional role patterns contribute to parental disagreement about childrearing methods and to teenagers' less-favorable evaluation of fathers than of mothers. The disruptive effects of poverty are reflected by findings that low-socioeconomic families, especially the very poor, look worse on various measures of conflict, affect, and control than do their more advantaged counterparts.[4] The adolescent period also appears difficult for families experiencing such life stresses as death, divorce, or physical illness.

We point out these exceptions or extreme positions on the "normative intergenerational curve" to emphasize that new theories adhering solely to a statistical definition of normality may oversimplify the nature of the adolescent's family relationships. Theoretical formulations are needed that address transactions among variables associated with different levels of analysis: individual, family, and sociocultural (Berger & Berger, Chap. 5 of this volume). Recent efforts by Lerner and Spanier (1980) to conceptualize adolescence within a life span, dynamic interactionalist model represent an excellent example of such a multilevel transactional approach. The conceptual frameworks of many others (e.g., Bronfenbrenner, 1979; Carter & McGoldrick, 1980; L. Hoffman, 1980; Holland, 1970; L'Abate, 1976; Minuchin, 1974; Spiegel, 1970; Stierlin, 1967) also offer additional scaffolding for theory construction in this area.

Within these models, it is apparent that intergenerational relationships cannot be understood without consideration of their larger social context. To return to research of low-socioeconomic families, it is likely that many of their relational qualities, such as low cohesion, are adaptive in view of the overcrowding and lack of privacy that characterize impoverished living settings (C. S. Russell, 1979). Yet, in reference to normative trends within the population at large, these characteristics will appear statistically abnormal. Just as psychometric intelligence test results of disadvantaged children are being increasingly compared to norms for their own reference group, family relationships perhaps should be evaluated in the same way. A cohesion score of an impover-

---

[4] See, however, Henggeler and Tavormina (1980), whose research indicates that family size and verbal IQ rather than social class per se may account for the variance in this area.

ished family that is normatively low even for their socioeconomic level may say more about that particular family's adaptation than evidence that such a score is low in the population generally.[5]

On the other hand, even though the modal relational structure of low-socioeconomic families appears to fit their wider social context, it may interfere with the youngster's optimal personal and interpersonal development. Indeed, increasing evidence underscores this point (see Chilman, 1975; Elkind & Weiner, 1978). Thus, what is adaptive at one level (family) can be maladaptive at another (individual) (see L. Hoffman, 1980). These patterns are not self-evident in normative data without consideration of the level at which statistical norms are being interpreted.

Research

Douvan and Adelson (1966) expressed concern some 18 years ago about the schism between theory and research on adolescence. Unfortunately, this schism contributed to a line of theorizing that misled clinicians, educators, parents, and others charged with responsibility for supporting and facilitating the adolescent's development. Without adequate empirical grounding, new theories may be equally misinformed and misinformative.

Although the data base in this area has grown, serious questions can be raised about methodology. For example, the heavy reliance in the past on self-reports of one family member to assess family process variables has doubtful validity. While such reports can provide useful information about individual perceptions of family interaction, they alone are not helpful in constructing an accurate picture of family process. If self-reports are used for this purpose, then observations from at least two or more members are needed to generate data from the divergent perspectives. (For further discussion of this issue, see Cromwell & Peterson, 1983; Keeney, 1983.)

Of course, direct observational procedures offer an even better view of family relationships. However, only a limited number of investigators have used these procedures, and most of what has been done has involved comparative analyses of disturbed and normal groups rather than examination of normative trends or family influences on socialization processes and personality development (see Handel, 1965).

The design of much of the research in this area has been descriptive and cross-sectional in nature, although a few major longitudinal projects

---

[5] Yet, as Berger and Berger (Chapter 5, this volume) point out, it is simplistic to assume that all families react similarly to such broadly defined social conditions as poverty. More information is needed about transactions between particular familial and sociocultural variables.

have been undertaken. More longitudinal research is needed that combines self-report and observational methods. In line with the complexity of current theorizing about adolescent development that transcends simple parent-child, cause-effect models, investigators are also increasingly using multivariate procedures. We further recommend the use of various sequential analyses to trace patterns of family interaction.

Also needed are experimental studies. Stanley's (1978) analysis of the implications of family negotiation training for the moral development of individual family members exemplifies how an experimental approach can illucidate relationships between different levels of functioning (family and individual). Numerous researchers have studied the effects of family therapy and social skills training (see Gurman & Kniskern, 1981; L'Abate, 1981). They, however, have typically not included outcome measures of individual-level personality and developmental variables (e.g., moral development, perspective-taking, etc.). In light of research reviewed earlier, family systems interventions predictably influence these variables as well and thus deserve greater attention in future studies of treatment outcome.

Another major methodological issue is the importance of controlling or systematically evaluating variables that are relevant to family relationships during adolescence. One long-overlooked variable, for example, is how family members interpret the research context. As Barton and Alexander's (1984) study illustrates, attributional set can significantly affect the family's performance on experimental tasks (see also Framo, 1972; Reiss, 1983; Terkelson, 1983; Zuckerman & Jacob, 1979). Other important variables include socioeconomic status, family size, IQ, sex of adolescent, family structure (blended, single-parent, etc.), ethnicity, diagnostic classification (e.g., psychopathic, neurotic, social delinquency), birth order, stage of adolescence (early, middle, late), age of parents, and birth cohort. Concerning the latter, much of the important descriptive work in this area is based on observations made during the 1950s and 1960s. Because family relationships cannot be understood independently of their historical context (Elder, 1980; Lerner & Spanier, 1980), empirical descriptions need to be updated using more advanced methods. (For further consideration of relevant factors, see Handel, 1965; Henggeler & Tavormina, 1980; Hetherington & Martin, 1979; Jacob, 1975; Lerner & Spanier, 1980; Walters & Stinnett, 1974.)

There are also a number of specific content areas warranting additional empirical study. The role of different family subsystems (individual, sibling, marital, grandparental)—in addition to the parental subsystem—has scarcely been addressed. It is also not clear how these different subsystems reciprocally interact. For example, how do particular attributes of the adolescent (sex, age, physical maturity, cognitive development) influence family interaction patterns (see Steinberg & Hill, 1978)? Are there concurrent changes in parents' relationships to each other and to their own parents (see L. Hoffman, 1980)? Does their level of differentiation as marital partners affect their parental behavior (see L'Abate, 1976)? Do adolescent family members potentiate identity conflicts in parents (see Fulmer, Medalie, & Lord, 1982; Levi, Stierlin, & Savard, 1972; Stierlin, 1967, 1974)? Are some adolescents selected by parents to bear their ambivalence about their own midlife development? Labeled by Stierlin (1974) as "delegated" children, do these young persons achieve only a limited degree of self-differentiation, and experience difficulties leaving home? What are the varieties of leaving home in late adolescence and early adulthood, and how do family relationship patterns shift at this point (see Stierlin, 1974)? How do familial and societal processes mutually affect the sex role development of children and adolescents? Do our male-biased theories of adolescent development fit the experiences of female youngsters and their families (see Gilligan, 1982)?

Practice

Just as research is essential to theory construction, so it is important for clinical practice. In the absence of normative data, clinicians have struggled to differentiate the expectable, age-related difficulties of their adolescent clients from serious deviancy (see Everett, 1976). The tendency has been to be overly conservative in identifying problems that warrant intervention. It is now apparent, however, that normalization of personal and familial conflicts of the adolescent (especially if middle class) without serious consideration of their possible clinical significance, represents poor clinical practice (see Offer et al., 1981; Weiner, 1981).

Unfortunately, a recent study by Offer et al. (1981) suggests that mental health professionals continue to operate on misinformation and biased perceptions. When asked to complete the Offer self-image questionnaire as would a "mentally healthy/well-adjusted adolescent" of their same sex, clinical psychologists, psychiatric residents, psychiatric nurses, and psychiatric social workers were unable to predict how normal teenagers would describe themselves. The descriptions by these mental health professionals were not only less positive than those of well-adjusted youngsters but also less positive than self-descriptions of either emotionally disturbed or delinquent adolescents. Graduate psychology students without formal clinical training completed the questionnaire in much the same way as did the normal adolescents. As Offer et al. intimate, in addition to deficiencies and biases in their training, clinicians may cling to the notion that psychopathology is endemic to the adolescent period to help them better tolerate working with disturbances of this age group.

Other therapeutic implications of research in this area have been addressed, in part, by Conger (1973). Noting similarities between the effective parent and the effective therapist, he concludes that both need to develop with the adolescent a mutually respectful relationship that appropriately balances issues of autonomy and control (see also Weiner, 1970). An authoritative rather than an autocratic, permissive, or neglectful approach is recommended for both. Conger's comments are directed mainly to psychotherapists who work with teenagers individually rather than in the context of their family, although his conclusions are applicable to family systems therapists as well.

Many argue, however, that family therapy is contraindicated for adolescents because it threatens their growing autonomy from family members. We find this position perplexing in light of reviewed evidence clearly indicating that members of normal families all participate in this process and, unlike their less-successful counterparts who develop problems, possess such skills as the ability to negotiate conflicts, to regulate emotional distance, and to establish age-appropriate rules. These are skills, as family therapists have demonstrated (see Gurman & Kniskern, 1981), that families of behavior-problem adolescents can be helped to exercise or to develop as an essential step in facilitating both the family's and the adolescent's development. Family systems therapy, of course, rules out neither individual sessions with adolescents nor special sensitivity to the intrapersonal issues of this age group. However, ongoing individual work with an adolescent that is not coordinated with family-level processes may perturb the individual/family system in deleterious and unpredictable ways. The recent movie *Ordinary People,* in which the "successful" individual treatment of a depressed adolescent is accompanied by his parents' separation, graphically illustrates this point. The paradox of family therapy with adolescents, at least when viewed from a traditional individualistic perspective, is that family members are brought together so they can learn to differentiate (Minuchin, 1974). In the process, as a growing number of studies intimate, they become even closer to each other.

Yet family therapists must pay greater attention to the research data. Barton and Alexander's (1984) study, for example, suggests that it may not be sufficient with disturbed families merely to alter their attributional set through reframing or relabeling their problematic behavior or relational patterns. Although reframing may create a more cooperative atmosphere in which to conduct therapy and even an initial reduction in symptomatic behavior, these effects are not likely to endure without increasing the family's repertoire of functional relational skills through direct training or other evocative procedures.

It is also imperative that therapists, regardless of their orientation, develop a better appreciation for larger contextual factors such as socioeconomic status, federal funding patterns, and urbanization that influence the functioning of adolescents and their families. For example, to expect impoverished, inner-city families to establish greater cohesion to enhance the development of their child members may be unrealistic for reasons discussed earlier. Yet, this fact does not excuse therapists in their role as responsible change agents and citizens from attempting to alleviate pressures (e.g., overcrowding, unemployment) contributing to a particular family's disengagement and to work with policymakers in redressing social conditions that are debilitating to the lives of large groups of families (Jurkovic, Berger & Associates, 1984).

CONCLUSIONS

The various lines of empirical investigation considered in this chapter lead to a number of conclusions. Perhaps foremost is that, despite the growing influence of peers, the family is centrally important in the adolescent's development. Normative research of patterns of closeness, control, and conflict during this age period suggests that modal teenagers remain connected to family members, although they often experience a period of familial discord in early adolescence. They also become increasingly influential in family decision making, especially concerning the regulation of their own behavior. Nonclinical groups who deviate from these norms are likely to live in households experiencing various life-cycle stressors such as divorce or illness.

Review of familial variables related to the adolescent's personal and interpersonal development points to the limitations of simple causal models. Studies that consider the multivariate and interrelated aspects of family process appear to account more adequately for the variance in this area. Democratic conflict resolution, along with parental encouragement, support, and legitimization of power, are key correlates of optimal development in adolescence. Problems in these areas are apparent in families of behavior-problem teenagers.

The normative findings challenge previous accounts of adolescents and their families based on clinical analyses. Theoreticians and clinicians alike are well advised to inform themselves of this data base in their future constructions of adolescence. It is important, however, that evidence of intergenerational readjustments and accompanying tension not be ignored in debate about the fact or myth of adolescent turmoil (Coleman, 1978). Although the degree of turmoil is substantially less than suggested in earlier theorizing, disequilibrating shifts in family interaction do appear to take place. It is also critical that caution be exercised in generalizing from data associated with one group of adolescents and their families to other groups and from observations of family interaction to individual-level processes. Further theory building and clinical practice in this area could greatly benefit from research of diverse samples using methods sensitive to multiple levels of analysis (individual, family, and sociocultural).

REFERENCES

Adams, G. R., Jones, R. M., Schvaneveldt, J. D., & Jenson, G. O. Antecedents of affective role-taking behavior: Adolescent perceptions of parental socialization styles. *Journal of Adolescence,* 1982, *5,* 259–265.

Adelson, J. *Handbook of adolescent psychology.* New York: John Wiley & Sons, 1980.

Adler, P. T., & Lotecka, L. Drug use among high school students: Patterns and correlates. *International Journal of Addiction,* 1973, *8,* 537–548.

Akers, R. L. *Teenage drinking, a survey of action programs.* University of Washington, Institute of Sociological Research, 1968.

Alexander, J. F. Defensive and supportive communication in normal and deviant families. *Journal of Consulting and Clinical Psychology,* 1973, *40,* 223–231.

Andry, R. G. *Delinquency and parental pathology.* London: Methuen, 1960.

Annis, H. M. Patterns of intra-familial drug use. *British Journal of Addiction,* 1974, *69,* 361–369.

Anolik, S. A. The family perceptions of delinquents, high school students and freshman college students. *Adolescence,* 1980, *60,* 903–911.

Bacon, M., & Jones, M. B. *Teen-age drinking.* New York: Thomas Y. Cromwell, 1968.

Bandura, A., & Walters, R. H. *Adolescent aggression.* New York: Ronald Press, 1959.

Bandura, A., & Walters, R. H. *Social learning and personality development.* New York: Holt, Rinehart & Winston, 1963.

Barnes, G. M. The development of adolescent drinking behavior: An evaluative review of the impact of the socialization process within the family. *Adolescence,* 1977, *48,* 571–591.

Barton, C., & Alexander, J. F. *The effects of competitive and cooperative set on normal and delinquent families.* Unpublished manuscript, Davidson College, 1981.

Bell, L. G., & Bell, D. C. Triangulation: Pitfall for the developing child. *Group Psychotherapy, Psychodrama, and Sociometry,* 1979, *32,* 150–155.

Bene, F., & Anthony, J. *Manual for the family relations test.* London: National Foundation for Educational Research in England and Wales, 1957.

Bengtson, V. L. The generation gap: A review and typology of social-psychological perspective. *Youth and Society,* 1970, *2,* 7–32.

Bennett, I. *Delinquent and neurotic children: A comparative study.* New York: Basic Books, 1959.

Berger, M., Jurkovic, G. J. & Associates. *Practicing family therapy in diverse settings.* San Francisco: Jossey-Bass, 1984.

Biddle, B. J., Bank, B. J., & Merlin, M. M. Parent and peer influence on adolescents. *Social Forces,* 1980, *58,* 1057–1079.

Biller, H. B., & Meredith, D. *Father power.* New York: Anchor Press/Doubleday, 1975.

Blos, P. *On adolescence.* New York: Free Press, 1961.

Blum, R. H., & Associates. *Students and drugs.* San Francisco: Jossey-Bass, 1969.

Blum, R. H., & Associates. *Horatio Alger's children.* San Francisco: Jossey-Bass, 1971.

Bonney, M. B. Parents as the makers of social deviates. *Social Forces,* 1941, *20,* 77.

Bowen, M. *Family theory in clinical practice.* New York: Jason Aronson, 1978.

Braucht, G. N., Brakarsh, D., Follingstad, D., & Berry, K. L. Deviant drug use in adolescence: A review of psychosocial correlates. *Psychological Bulletin,* 1973, *79,* 92–106.

Bronfenbrenner, U. The split-level American family. In W. C. Sze (Ed.), *Human life cycle.* New York: Jason Aronson, 1975.

Bronfenbrenner, U. *The ecology of human development.* Cambridge, Mass.: Harvard University Press, 1979.

Browning, C. J. Differential impact of family disorganization on male adolescents. *Social Problems,* 1960, *8,* 37–44.

Bushing, B. C., & Bromley, D. G. Sources of nonmedical drug use: A test of the drug-oriented society explanation. *Journal of Health and Social Behavior,* 1975, *16,* 50–62.

Campbell, E. Q. Adolescent socialization. In D. A. Goslin (Ed.), *Handbook of socialization theory and research.* Skokie, Ill.: Rand McNally, 1969.

Cannon, S. R. *Social functioning patterns in families of offspring receiving treatment of drug abuse.* Roslyn Heights, N. Y.: Lybra Publishers, 1976.

Carter, E. A., & McGoldrick, M. The family life cycle and family therapy: An overview. In E. A. Carter & M. McGoldrick (Eds.), *The family life cycle: A framework for family therapy.* New York: Gardner Press, 1980.

Chafetz, M. E., Blanc, H. T., & Hill, M. J. Children of alcoholics: observations in a child guidance clinic. *Quarterly Journal of Studies and Alcohol,* 1971, *32,* 687–698.

Chein, I. Narcotics among juveniles. In R. Cavan (Ed.), *Readings in juvenile delinquency.* Philadelphia: J. B. Lippincott, 1964.

Chilman, C. S. Child-rearing and family relationship patterns of the very poor. In W. C. Sze (Ed.), *Human life cycle.* New York: Jason Aronson, 1975.

Clausen, J. A. Drug addiction. In R. R. Merton & R. A. Nesbit (Eds.), *Contemporary social problems.* New York: Harcourt Brace Jovanovich, 1961.

Coleman, J. *Relationships in adolescence.* London: Routledge & Kegan Paul, 1974.

Coleman, J. Current contradictions in adolescent theory. *Journal of Youth and Adolescence,* 1978, *7,* 1–11.

Conger, J. J. *Adolescence and youth.* New York: Harper & Row, 1973.

Conger, J. J. *Adolescence and youth: Psychological development in a changing world* (2d ed.). New York: Harper & Row, 1977. (a)

Conger, J. J. Parent-child relationships, social change, and adolescent vulnerability. *Journal of Pediatric Psychology,* 1977, *2,* 93–97. (b)

Conger, J. J. *Adolescence: Generation under pressure.* New York: Harper & Row, 1979.

Cromwell, R. E., & Peterson, G. W. Multisystem-multimethod family assessment in clinical contexts. *Family Process,* 1983, *22,* 147–163.

Csikszentmihalyi, M., Larson, R., & Prescott, S. The ecology of adolescent activity and experience. *Journal of Youth and Adolescence,* 1977, *6,* 281–294.

Dammann, C. *Patterns of family interaction and the ability of parents to administer accurate reinforcement.* Paper presented at the Annual Meeting of the Southeastern Psychological Association, New Orleans, 1973.

Dancy, B. L., & Handal, P. J. Perceived family climate of black adolescents: A function of parental marital status or perceived conflict? *Journal of Community Psychology,* 1980, *8,* 208–214.

Davison, P., & Davison, J. Coming of age in America. *New York Times Magazine,* March 9, 1975.

Deitz, G. E. A comparison of delinquents with nondelinquents on self-concept, self-acceptance, and parental identification. *Journal of Genetic Psychology,* 1969, *115,* 285–295.

Deutsch, H. *Selected problems of adolescence.* New York: International Universities Press, 1967.

Doane, J. The role of the family in psychiatric disorders: An interpretative review of family interaction and communication deviance in disturbed and normal families. *Family Process,* 1978, *17,* 357–376.

Douvan, E., & Adelson, J. *The adolescent experience.* New York: John Wiley & Sons, 1966.

Duncan, P. Parental attitudes and interactions in delinquency. *Child Development,* 1971, *42,* 1751–1765.

Eisenberg-Berg, N., & Mussen, P. Empathy and moral development in adolescence. *Developmental Psychology,* 1978, *14,* 185–186.

Elder, G. H. Parental power legitimation and its effects on the adolescent. *Sociometry,* 1963, *26,* 50–65.

Elder, G. H., Jr. Adolescence in historical perspective. In J. Adelson (Ed.), *Handbook of adolescent psychology.* New York: John Wiley & Sons, 1980.

Elkind, D., & Weiner, I. B. *Development of the child.* New York: John Wiley & Sons, 1978.

Erikson, E. H. *Identity, youth, and crisis.* New York: W. W. Norton, 1968.

Everett, C. A. Family assessment and intervention for early adolescent problems. *Journal of Marriage and Family Counseling,* 1976, *2,* 155–165.

Feather, N. T. *Values in education and society.* New York: Free Press, 1975.

Feather, N. T. Family resemblances in conservation: Are daughters more similar to parents than sons are? *Journal of Personality,* 1978, *46,* 260–278.

Feffer, M. Role-taking behavior in the mentally retarded. Washington, D.C.: U.S. Government Printing Office, 1970.

Ferreira, A. Decision making in normal and pathologic families. *Archives of General Psychiatry,* 1963, *8,* 68–73.

Ferreira, A., & Winter, W. Family interaction and decision making. *Archives of General Psychiatry,* 1965, *13,* 214–223.

Ferreira, A., & Winter, W. Stability of interactional variables in family decision-making. *Archives of General Psychiatry,* 1966, *14,* 352–355.

Ferreira, A., & Winter, W. Decision-making in normal and abnormal two-child families. *Family Process,* 1968, *7,* 17–36. (a)

Ferreira, A., & Winter, W. Information exchange and silence in normal and abnormal families. *Family Process,* 1968, *7,* 251–276. (b)

Ferreira, A., Winter, W., & Poindexter, E. Some interactional variables in normal and abnormal families. *Family Process*, 1966, *5*, 60–75.

Floyd, H. H., Jr., & South, D. R. Dilemma of youth: The choice of parents or peers as a frame of reference for behavior. *Journal of Marriage and the Family*, 1972, *34*, 627–634.

Ford, C. S. Some primitive societies. In F. H. Seward & R. C. Williamson (Eds.), *Sex roles in changing society*. New York: Random House, 1970.

Forman, S. G., & Forman, B. D. Family environment and its relation to adolescent personality factors. *Journal of Personality Assessment*, 1981, *45*, 163–167.

Framo, J. L. (Ed.). *Family interaction: A dialogue between family researchers and family therapists*. New York: Springer Publishing, 1972.

Freud, A. *The ego and the mechanisms of defense*. New York: International Universities Press, 1946.

Freud, A. Adolescence as a developmental disturbance. In W. C. Sze (Ed.), *Human life cycle*. New York: Jason Aronson, 1975.

Friedman, E. H. Systems and ceremonies: A family view of rites of passage. In E. A. Carter & M. McGoldrick (Eds.), *The family life cycle: A framework for family therapy*. New York: Gardner Press, 1980.

Fulmer, R. H., Medalie, J., & Lord, D. A. Life cycle in transition: A family systems perspective on counseling the college students. *Journal of Adolescence*, 1982, *5*, 195–217.

Gantman, C. A. Family interaction patterns with normal, disturbed and drug abusing adolescents. *Journal of Youth and Adolescence*, 1978, *7*, 429–440.

Gilligan, C. *In a different voice*. Cambridge, Mass.: Harvard University Press, 1982.

Glueck, S., & Glueck, E. *One thousand juvenile delinquents, their treatment by court and clinic*. Cambridge, Mass.: Harvard University Press, 1934.

Glueck, S., & Glueck, E. *Juvenile delinquents grown up*. New York: Commonwealth Fund, 1940.

Glueck, S., & Glueck, E. *Unraveling juvenile delinquency*. New York: Commonwealth Fund, 1950.

Glueck, S., & Glueck, E. *Family environment and delinquency*. Boston: Houghton Mifflin, 1962.

Glueck, S., & Glueck, E. *Toward a typology of juvenile offenders*. New York: Grune & Stratton, 1970.

Glynn, T. J. From family to peer: A review of transitions of influence among drug-using youth. *Journal of Youth and Adolescence*, 1981, *10*, 363–383.

Goldstein, M., & Rodnick, E. The family's contribution to the etiology of schizophrenia: Current status. *Schizophrenic Bulletin*, 1975, *14*, 48–69.

Goode, E. Multiple drug use among marihuana smokers. *Social Problems*, 1969, *17*, 48–64.

Goode, E. *The marihuana smokers*. New York: Basic Books, 1970.

Goode, E. Sociological aspects of marihuana use. *Contemporary Drug Problems*, 1975, *4*, 390–445.

Gorsuch, R. L., & Butler, M. C. Initial drug abuse: A review of predisposing social psychological factors. *Psychological Bulletin*, 1976, *83*, 120–137.

Goslin, D. *Handbook of socialization theory and research.* Skokie, Ill.: Rand McNally, 1969.

Greenberger, E., Steinberg, C. D., Vaux, A., & McAuliffe, S. Adolescents who work: Effects of part-time employment on family and peer relations. *Journal of Youth and Adolescence,* 1980, *9,* 189–202.

Gurman, A. S., & Kniskern, D. P. Family therapy outcome research: Knowns and unknowns. In A. S. Gurman & D. P. Kniskern (Eds.), *Handbook of family therapy.* New York: Brunner/Mazel, 1981.

Haan, N., & Day, D. A longitudinal study of change and sameness in personality development: Adolescence to later adulthood. *International Journal of Aging and Human Development,* 1974, *5,* 11–39.

Haan, N., Smith, M. B., & Block, J. The moral reasoning of young adults: Political-social behavior, family background, and personality correlates. *Journal of Personality and Social Psychology,* 1968, *10,* 183–201.

Hall, G. S. *Adolescence.* New York: Appleton-Century-Crofts, 1904.

Handel, G. Psychological study of whole families. *Psychological Bulletin,* 1965, *63,* 19–41.

Harvey, G. H. *Initial development of the parent-adolescent expectation scale and a psychoeducational model for its use.* Unpublished doctoral dissertation, Georgia State University, 1984.

Healy, W., & Bronner, A. *New lights on delinquency and its treatment.* New Haven, Conn.: Yale University Press, 1936.

Henggeler, S. W., & Tavormina, J. B. Social class and race differences in family interaction: Pathological, normative, or confounding methodological factors? *Journal of Genetic Psychology,* 1980, *137,* 211–22.

Horzog, E. Social stereotypes and social research. In R. I. Evans & R. M. Rozelle (Eds.), *Social psychology in life.* Boston: Allyn & Bacon, 1973.

Hetherington, F. M., & Martin, B. Family interaction and psychopathology in children. In H. C. Quay & J. S. Worry (Eds.), *Psychopathological disorders of childhood* (2d ed.). New York: John Wiley & Sons, 1979.

Hetherington, E. M., Stouwie, R., & Ridberg, E. Patterns of family interaction and child-rearing attitudes related to three dimensions of juvenile delinquency. *Journal of Abnormal Psychology,* 1971, *78,* 160–176.

Hochman, J. *Marihuana and social evolution.* Englewood Cliffs, N.J.: Prentice-Hall, 1972.

Hodgman, C. H. Current issues in adolescent psychiatry. *Hospital and Community Psychiatry,* 1983, *34,* 514–521.

Hoffman, L. The family life cycle and discontinuous change. In E. A. Carter & M. McGoldrick (Eds.), *The family life cycle: A framework for family therapy.* New York: Gardner Press, 1980.

Hoffman, M. L. Moral development in adolescence. In J. Adelson (Ed.), *Handbook of adolescence.* New York: John Wiley & Sons, 1980.

Holland, D. Familization, socialization, and the university of meaning: An extension of the interactional approach to the study of the family. *Journal of Marriage and the Family,* 1970, 415–427.

Hollstein, C. E. The relation of children's moral judgment level to that of their parents and to communication patterns in the family. In R. C. Smart & M. S. Smart (Eds.),

Readings in child development and relationships. New York: Macmillan, 1972.

Hudgins, W., & Prentice, N. M. Moral judgement in delinquent and nondelinquent adolescents and their mothers. *Journal of Abnormal Psychology,* 1973, *82,* 145–152.

Hunt, D. G. Parental permissiveness as perceived by offspring and degree of marihuana usage by offspring. *Human Relations,* 1974, *27,* 267–285.

Jacob, T. Patterns of family conflict and dominance as a function of child age and social class. *Developmental Psychology,* 1974, *10,* 1–12.

Jacob, T. Family interaction in disturbed and normal families: A methodological and substantive review. *Psychological Bulletin,* 1975, *82,* 33–65.

Jenkins, R. L. The varieties of children's behavioral problems and family dynamics. *American Journal of Psychiatry,* 1968, *124,* 1440–1445.

Jessop, D. J. Family relationships as viewed by parents and adolescents: A specification. *Journal of Marriage and the Family,* 1981, *43,* 95–107.

Jessor, R. Predicting time onset of marihuana use: A developmental study of high school youth. *Journal of Consulting Clinical Psychology,* 1976, *44,* 125–134.

Jessor, R., & Jessor, S. L. Adolescent development versus the onset of drinking: A longitudinal study. *Quarterly Journal on the Study of Alcohol,* 1975, *36,* 27–51.

Jessor, R., & Jessor, S. L. *Problem behavior and psychosocial development: A longitudinal study of youth.* New York: Academic Press, 1977.

Jessor, S. L., & Jessor, R. Maternal ideology and adolescent problem behavior. *Developmental Psychology,* 1974, *10,* 246–254.

Johnson, A. M., & Szurek, S. A. The genesis of antisocial acting out in children and adults. *Psychoanalytic Quarterly,* 1952, *21,* 323–343.

Jurkovic, G. J., & Berger, M. Conclusions: Implications for practice, training, and social policy. In M. Berger, G. Jurkovic & Associates, *Practicing family therapy in diverse settings.* San Francisco: Jossey-Bass, in press.

Jurkovic, G. J., & Prentice, N. M. Dimensions of moral interaction and moral judgment in delinquent and nondelinquent families. *Journal of Consulting and Clinical Psychology,* 1974, *42,* 256–262.

Kandel, D. B. Adolescent marihuana use: Role of parents and peers. *Science,* 1973, *131,* 1067–1070.

Kandel, D. B. Inter and intragenerational influences on adolescent marihuana use. *Journal of Social Issues,* 1974, *30,* 107–135.

Kandel, D. B. Some comments on the relationship of selected criteria variables to adolescent illicit drug use. In D. J. Lettieri (Ed.), *Predicting adolescent drug abuse: A review of issues, methods and correlates* (DHEW Publication No. (ADM) 76–299, National Institute on Drug Abuse). Washington, D.C.: U.S. Government Printing Office, 1975.

Kandel, D. B. Convergencies in prospective longitudinal surveys of drug use in normal populations. In D. B. Kandel (Ed.), *Longitudinal research in drug use: Empirical findings and methodological issues.* Washington, D.C.: Hemisphere, 1978. (a)

Kandel, D. B. Homophily, selection, and socialization of early marihuana use. In G. M. Beschner & A. S. Freedman (Eds.), *Youth drug abuse: Problem issues and treatment.* Lexington, Mass.: Lexington Books, 1978. (b)

Kandel, D. B., & Lesser, G. S. Parent-adolescent relationships and adolescent independence in the United States and Denmark. *Journal of Marriage and the Family*, 1969, *31*, 348–358.

Kaufman, E. Myth and reality in the family patterns and treatment of substance abuse. *American Journal of Alcohol Abuse*, 1980, *7*, 257–279.

Keeney, B. P. Ecological assessment. In J. C. Hansen & B. P. Keeney (Eds.), *Diagnosis and assessment in family therapy*. Rockville, Md.: Aspen, 1983.

Keller, M. Development of role-taking ability: Social antecedents and consequences for school success. *Human Development*, 1976, *19*, 120–132.

Kleiman, J. I. Optimal and normal family functioning. *American Journal of Family Therapy*, 1981, *9*, 37–44.

Kohlberg, L. Moral stages and moralization: The cognitive-developmental approach. In T. Lickona (Ed.), *Moral development and behavior: Theory, research, and social issues*. New York: Holt, Rinehart & Winston, 1976.

L'Abate, L. The status of adolescent psychology. *Developmental Psychology*, 1971, *4*, 201–205.

L'Abate, L. *Understanding and helping the individual in the family*. New York: Grune & Stratton, 1976.

L'Abate, L. Skill training programs for couples and families. In A. S. Gurman & D. P. Kniskern (Eds.), *Handbook of family therapy*. New York: Brunner/Mazel, 1981.

Lang, D. M., Papenfuh, R., & Walters, J. Delinquent females' perceptions of their fathers. *Family Coordinator*, 1976, *25*, 146–153.

Lawrence, T. S., & Vellerman, J. O. Correlates of student drug use in a suburban high school. *Psychiatry*, 1974, *37*, 129–136.

Lerner, R. M., & Spanier, G. B. *Adolescent development: A life-span perspective*. New York: McGraw-Hill, 1980.

Lerner, S., Ronald, L., & Burke, E. Drugs in junior high school—part II. *Journal of Psychedelic Drugs*, 1974, *6*, 51–56.

Levi, L. D., Stierlin, H., & Savard, R. J. Fathers and sons: The interlocking crises of integrity and identity. *Psychiatry*, 1972, *35*, 48–56.

Lewis, J. M. The adolescent and the healthy family. *Adolescent Psychiatry*, 1978, *6*, 156–170.

Maddox, G. L. *The domesticated drug: Drinking among collegians*. New Haven, Conn.: College and University Press, 1970.

Manaster, G. J. *Adolescent development and the life tasks*. Boston: Allyn & Bacon, 1977.

Martin, D. H. The expressive domain of the father–adolescent daughter relationship defined by their perceptions and issues (Doctoral dissertation, University of Northern Colorado, 1978). *Dissertation Abstracts International*, 1979, *39*, 5521B. (University Microfilms International No. 7910308)

McBride, D. *Parental and peer influence on adolescent drug use*. Rockville, Md.: National Institute on Drug Abuse, Division of Research, 1978.

McCord, J., & McCord, W. Effects of parental role model on criminality. In R. Cavan (Ed.), *Readings in juvenile delinquency*. Philadelphia: J. B. Lippincott, 1964.

McCord, W., McCord, J., & Howard, A. Familial correlates of aggression in nondelinquent male children. *Journal of Abnormal and Social Psychology*, 1961, *62*, 79–83.

McCord, W., McCord, J., & Zola, I. K. *Origins of crime*. New York: Columbia University Press, 1959.

McDermott, J. F., Robillard, A. B., Char, W., Hsu, J., Tseng, W. S., & Ashton, G. C. Reexamining the concept of adolescence: Differences between adolescent boys and girls in the context of their families. *American Journal of Psychiatry*, 1983, *140*, 1318–1322.

Mead, D. E., & Campbell, S. S. Decision-making and interactions by families with and without a drug abusing child. *Family Process*, 1972, *11*, 487–498.

Medinnus, G. R. Delinquents' perceptions of their parents. *Journal of Consulting Psychology*, 1965, *29*, 592–593.

Mehrabian, A., & Epstein, N. A measure of emotional empathy. *Journal of Personality*, 1972, *40*, 525–543.

Meisels, M., & Canter, F. M. A note on the generation gap. *Adolescence*, 1971, *6*, 523–530.

Meissner, W. W. Parental interaction of the adolescent boy. *Journal of Genetic Psychology*, 1965, *107*, 225–233.

Miller, D. R., & Swanson, G. E. *Inner conflict and defense*. New York: Schocken, 1966.

Minuchin, S. *Families and family therapy*. Cambridge, Mass.: Harvard University Press, 1974.

Monahan, T. P. Broken homes by age of delinquent children. *The Journal of Social Psychology*, 1960, *51*, 387–397.

Moore, B. M., & Holtzman, W. H. *Tomorrow's parents*. Austin, Tex.: Hogg Foundation for Mental Health, 1965.

Mussen, P. H., Conger, J. J., & Kagan, J. *Child development and personality* (4th ed.). New York: Harper & Row, 1974.

Muuns, M. The values of adolescents compared with parents and peers. *Adolescence*, 1972, *7*, 519–524.

National Institute on Alcohol Abuse and Alcoholism. *A national study of adolescent drinking behavior, attitudes, and correlates*. Report prepared by Research Triangle Park, North Carolina, 1975.

Newman, B. M., & Newman, P. R. *An introduction to the psychology of adolescence*. Homewood, Ill.: Dorsey Press, 1979.

Newman, P. R. Person and setting interactions of the quality and range of social interaction in two suburban high schools. *Dissertation Abstracts International*, 1972, *32*(11–A), 6539–6540.

Niles, F. S. The adolescent girl's perception of parents and peers. *Adolescence*, 1979, *14*, 591–597.

Nye, F. I. *Family relationships and delinquent behavior*. New York: John Wiley & Sons, 1958.

Offer, D. *The psychological world of the teenager*. New York: Basic Books, 1969.

Offer, D., & Offer, J. B. *From teenage to young manhood: A psychological study*. New York: Basic Books, 1975.

Offer, D., Ostrov, E., & Howard, K. I. The mental health professional's concept of the normal adolescent. *General Psychiatry*, 1981, *38*, 149–152.

Olson, D. H., McCubbin, H. I., Barnes, H., Larsen, A., Muxen, M., & Wilson, M. *Family inventories: Inventories used in a national survey of families across the family life cycle.* Unpublished manuscript, University of Minnesota, 1982.

Olson, D. H., Sprenkle, D. H., & Russell, C. S. Circumplex model of marital and family systems: I. Cohesion and adaptability dimensions family types and clinical applications. *Family Process,* 1979, *18,* 3–28.

Parikh, B. Development of moral judgment and its relation to family environmental factors in Indian and American families. *Child Development,* 1980, *51,* 1030–1039.

Prasinos, S., & Tittler, B. I. The family relationships of humor-oriented adolescents. *Journal of Personality,* 1981, *49,* 295–305.

Quay, H. C., & Werry, J. S. *Psychopathological disorders of childhood* (2d ed.). New York: John Wiley & Sons, 1979.

Reiss, D. Critique: Sensory extenders versus meters and predictors: Clarifying strategies for the use of objective tests in family therapy. *Family Process,* 1983, *22,* 165–172.

Robins, L. N., West, P. A., & Herjanic, B. L. Arrests and delinquency in two generations: A study of black urban families and their children. *Journal of Child Psychology and Psychiatry,* 1975, *16,* 125–140.

Robinson, P. A. Parents of "beyond control" adolescents. *Adolescence,* 1978, *49,* 109–119.

Rokeach, M. *The nature of human values.* New York: Free Press, 1973.

Russell, C. S. Circumplex model of marital and family systems: III. Empirical evaluation with families. *Family Process,* 1979, *18,* 29–45.

Russell, J. S. Composite patterns of drug use. In S. Einstein & S. Allen (Eds.), *Student Drug Surveys.* Farmingdale, N.Y.: Baywood, 1972.

Sanborn, B., Daniels, J., Jones, S. G., Salken, B., & Shonick, H. LSD reactions: A family research approach. *International Journal of the Addictions,* 1971, *6,* 497–507.

Scherer, S. Self-reported parent and child drug use. *British Journal of Addiction,* 1973, *68,* 361–363.

Schratz, P. R. *Institutionalized and hidden male delinquents and male nondelinquents. A comparison of their family perceptions.* Unpublished masters thesis, Loyola College, 1983.

Selden, N. E. The family of the addict: A review of the literature. *International Journal of the Addictions,* 1972, *7,* 97–107.

Shibuya, R. R. Categorizing drug users and nonusers on selected personality variables. *School Health,* 1974, *44,* 442–444.

Shore, M. F. Psychological theories of the causes of antisocial behavior. *Crime and Delinquency,* 1971, *17,* 456–468.

Smart, R. G., and Fejer, D. Drug use among adolescents and their parents: Closing the gap in mood modification. *Journal of Abnormal Social Psychology,* 1972, *79,* 153–160.

Spiegel, J. *Transactions.* New York: Science House, 1971.

Stabenau, J. R., Tupin, J., Werner, M., & Pollin, W. A comparative study of families of schizophrenics, delinquents, and normals. *Psychiatry,* 1965, *28,* 45–59.

Stanley, S. F. Family education to enhance the moral atmosphere of the family and the moral development of adolescents. *Journal of Counseling Psychology,* 1978, *25,* 110–118.

Stanton, D. M. Drugs and the family. *Marriage and Family Review,* 1979, *1,* 2–10.

Stanton, D. M. A critique of Kaufman's "myth and reality in the family patterns and treatment of substance abusers." *American Journal of Drug and Alcohol Abuse,* 1980, *7,* 281–289.

Stanton, D. M., Todd, T. C., & Associates. *The family therapy of drug abuse and addiction.* New York: Guilford Press, 1982.

Steinberg, L. D., & Hill, J. P. Patterns of family interaction as a function of age, the onset of puberty, and formal thinking. *Developmental Psychology,* 1978, *14,* 683–684.

Stenmark, D. E., Wackwitz, J. H., Pelfrey, M. C., & Dougherty, F. Substance abuse among juvenile offenders: Relationships to parental use and demographic characteristics. *Addictive Diseases,* 1974, *1,* 43–54.

Stierlin, H. *Separating parents and adolescents: A perspective on running away, schizophrenia, and waywardness.* New York: Basic Books, 1967.

Stierlin, H. *Separating parents and adolescents.* New York: Quadrangel, 1974.

Stone, L. H., Miranne, A. C., & Ellis, G. J. Parent-peer influence as a predictor of marihuana use. *Adolescent,* 1979, *14,* 115–122.

Stone, L. J., & Church, J. *Childhood and adolescence: A psychology of the growing person* (25th ed.). New York: Random House, 1984.

Streit, F. Differences among youthful criminal offenders based on their perceptions of parental behavior. *Adolescence,* 1981, *62,* 409–413.

Sutherland, E., & Cressey, D. *Criminology.* New York: J. B. Lippincott, 1970.

Tec, N. *Grass is green in suburbia.* Roslyn Heights, N.Y.: Lybra Publishers, 1974. (a)

Tec, N. Parent-child drug abuse: Generational continuity or adolescent deviancy? *Adolescence,* 1974, *9,* 351–364. (b)

Terkelson, K. G. Schizophrenia and the family: II. Adverse effects of family therapy. *Family Process,* 1983, *22,* 191–200.

Thomas, A., & Chess, S. Evolution of behavior disorders into adolescence. *American Journal of Psychiatry,* 1976, *133,* 539–542.

Van Gennep, A. *The rites of passage.* Reprinted, Chicago: University of Chicago Press, 1960.

Walters, J., & Stinnett, N. Parent-child relationships: A decade review of research. *Journal of Marriage and the Family,* 1971, *33,* 70–111.

Wechsler, H., & Thum, D. Teenage drinking, drug use, and social correlates. *Quarterly Journal Studying Alcohol,* 1973, *34,* 1220–1227.

Weiner, I. B. *Psychological disturbance in adolescence.* New York: Wiley-Interscience, 1970.

Weiner, I. B. *Child and adolescent psychopathology.* New York: John Wiley & Sons, 1982.

Weller, L., & Luchterhand, E. Adolescents' perceptions of their parents. *Adolescence,* 1977, *12,* 367–372.

West, D. J. *The young offender.* New York: Penguin Books, 1967.

Wilgosh, L., & Paitich, D. Juvenile offenders, grouped according to type of delinquent behavior and their parents: Intelligence, achievement and family interaction. *Canadian Journal of Criminology and Corrections,* 1974, *16,* 68–76.

Winter, W. D., & Ferreira, A. J. Interaction process analysis of family decision-making. *Family Process,* 1967, *6,* 155–172.

Zuckerman, E., & Jacob, T. Task effects in family interaction. *Family Process,* 1979, *18,* 47–53.

Chapter 8

Social Networks, Families, and Mate Selection: A Transactional Analysis

ROBERT M. MILARDO
ROBERT A. LEWIS

A FALLACY

An implied assumption underlies much of the research done on mate selection in particular and dyadic development in general: the fallacy that couples develop in a social vacuum (Lewis, 1973). For example, while most researchers during the last two decades have studied the personal (individual) and interpersonal (pair) factors related to mate selection (Huston, Surra, Fitzgerald, & Cate, 1981), very few researchers have examined the effects of social networks and family members upon the development of couples (Cobb & Jones, 1984; Lewis, 1973; Parks, Stan, & Eggert, 1983; Ridley & Avery, 1979). This apparent neglect of social networks is surprising in view of the fact that heterosexual couples, especially those who marry, are typically embedded in family and other social networks.

Many family therapists and observers of dyadic development and family formation assert that most members of couples do not fully leave their families of orientation when they marry, but instead form even more complex sets of interlocking families and mutual social networks. With tongue in cheek, Whitaker (1982) has defined marriage as the relationship formed by "two scapegoats, trying to recreate their families of origin" (p. 134). In other words, married couples are rarely free of the effects of their families either before or after marriage.

Another part of the fallacy is the assertion found both in popular materials and in some textbooks that mate selection in the United States operates from "complete freedom" by individuals, who have freedom of choice to marry whomsoever they wish to marry. Obviously, this simplistic analysis neglects both the reality that significant others influence one's choice of mate directly and indirectly and the fact that social norms still proscribe large numbers of potential mates as inappropriate and thereby greatly limit freedom of choice.

FAMILIES AND MATE SELECTION: A TRANSACTIONAL ANALYSIS

Although the research is scanty and specific linkages are difficult to trace, several authors have suggested that socialization into mate selection begins very early for children, even in the United States, as parents and other significant persons transmit models of appropriate mates to their offspring. For example, Coombs (1962) found evidence that parents effect indirect reinforcements in their transmission of family values to ensure that the future marital partners of their children will be homogamous. Other researchers and theorists have suggested that parents and other social network members often act as *mediating agents* between sociocultural norms (such as homogamy) and marital choice (Bates, 1942; Coombs, 1962; Kirkpatrick & Caplow, 1945; Lewis, 1975; Ryder, Kafka, & Olson, 1971; Sussman, 1953). Some of the subtle effects of models, symbols, and values with which some parents suffuse their children throughout childhood and preadolescence relate to appropriate marriage partners (Broderick & Rowe, 1968; Hill & Aldous, 1969; Mayer, 1967). Broderick (1966) and Broderick & Rowe (1968) have shown how these values and symbols are constantly reaffirmed in social interaction and are anticipated increasingly by preadolescents and adolescents as a part of socialization into marriage. It is not difficult to assume that many parents, even in an open mate selection society, are effective in delimiting potential mates for their children through early socialization. These influences, however, are more passive and limiting than active and selecting, such as one would find in more closed mate selection societies.

Direct effects of parents

More overt effects of parents in the mate selection process were suggested many years ago by Bates (1942) from interview data with unmarried college students, who reported that their parents had directly influenced their choice of dating partners. Although the percentages were somewhat lower for reports of fathers' influence, 97 percent of the females and 79 percent of the male students reported that their mothers had tried to influence their choice of dates. Sussman (1953) has also reported that parents admit not only to consciously choosing schools and neighborhoods for their children but also to attempting to manipulate directly their children's courtship choices. Waller and Hill (1951) described some such actions of parents and other significant persons in mate selection in terms of a "looking-glass reflection of unity provided by a friendly public" (p. 190). That is, family members may act and react toward a developing couple as a social unit; they may invite them to social and family events as a pair, allow or make arrangements for them to be together, and increasingly think of them as a pair (Lewis, 1973). In spite of these early suggestions, however, few social psychologists have investigated the role that parents in the United States may play in their children's mate selection.

One of a few studies done in this area suggested that parents indeed may play a significant and direct part in affecting pair relationships of their children. Data from a longitudinal study of 316 couple relationships (Lewis, 1973) over a 10-week period suggested that the greater the reactions of significant others (i.e., family members and friends) in reflecting and in labeling the two as a pair at the time of the pretest, the greater the couples' pair commitment, boundary maintenance, dyadic functioning, value consensus, dating-courtship status, and dyadic preference at the time of the posttest. Of course, cause and effect can not be determined from these correlational data. (An analysis of several panels of couples at different points in their courtship progress would help to establish more clearly the time-ordering of effects.) On the one hand, it may be that family support of developing dyads does assist the formation of some couples; on the other hand, family support may come as a "seal of approval" *after* parents consider a future marriage as inevitable (Ryder et al., 1971). It is interesting, however, that the intercorrelations were much stronger for *family* support than for the support of friends at the pretest and the posttest measures of couple quality. Finally, the 96 couples (out of 316) which did not survive over the 10 weeks had significantly lower scores on social support (social reaction) at the pretest time, indicating that the couples which had more positive reflections and labeling at that time were significantly more apt to continue as a couple over the 10-week period.

Two more recent studies in this area (Krain, 1977; Parks et al., 1983) appear to corroborate the findings of Lewis (1973). While Krain found that support from family members and friends was positively linked to courtship progress, Parks et al. found that perceived support from family members was positively and linearly related to romantic involvement (emotional attachment), to the amount of interaction between partners, and to the extent to which individuals expected their relationship to continue. It is interesting also that they found the couples' romantic involvement additionally related to perceived support from the partner's networks and to the number of people in the partner's network. Conversely, these researchers found little support for the Romeo and Juliet effect (Driscoll, Davis, & Lipetz, 1972), which will be discussed in a later section. They found support for the Romeo and Juliet effect in only one sector of the network and only for some levels of some variables.

Explanations of these relationships have varied. Utilizing Heider's (1958) balance theory, one could reason that both couple development and parental support could reflect a partner's need for *structural balance* in both his/her couple relationship and relationships in the family of orientation. Exchange theorists could argue that support for a couple from family members may create greater couple involvement by making it more costly to break up the relationship, since the threatened loss of the couple's relationship might endanger the family relationships as well (Levinger, 1979; Lewis & Spanier, 1979). Finally, Lewis (1973), building on the ideas of Waller & Hill (1951), has also suggested a social-reaction explanation: If family members act and react toward a couple as "a social unit"—e.g., inviting them to social events as a pair, thinking increasingly of them together, and arranging for them to be together—then the partners may increasingly think of themselves as a pair, accept roles prescribed by dyadic norms, and therefore continue and behave as a couple.

A social reaction theory of mate selection

Lewis (1975) offered a set of theoretical assumptions as an initial formulation of a social reaction (SR) theory of mate selection and as an attempt to formally recognize the interaction of pair processes and the pair's social context:

1. Values, role models, and symbols of marital dyadic unity are learned throughout childhood and preadolescence (Broderick & Rowe, 1968; Hill & Aldous, 1969), particularly in the family of orientation (Mayer, 1967).

2. These values and symbols are reaffirmed in social interaction and increasingly anticipated throughout preadolescence and adolescence (Broderick, 1965, Broderick & Rowe, 1968).

3. Loosely joined and low-committed premarital pairs form for indeterminant periods of time as the result of individuals' rewards and pair achievements in the perception of similarity, rapport, self-disclosure, accurate role-taking, and need satisfaction (Lewis, 1972, 1973).

4. Pairs reacted to and labeled as "viable dyads" by significant others are rewarded for their symbiotic interaction and punished for their

individualistic behavior (Bates, 1942; Sussman, 1953; Ryder et al., 1971; Driscoll et al., 1972.)

5. Particularly in times of individual disorientation, pair members are more susceptible to the cues given by the reactions of significant others (Erickson, 1964, p. 88) and at those times are more accepting of dyadic labels and norms (Bolton, 1961).

6. Internalization of dyadic labels and norms enables pairs to play reciprocal roles in conformity to these labels and norms—act and react as comprehensive dyads with increasing interaction and commitment (Waller & Hill, 1951).

In sum, a social reaction theory would suggest that family members and others play key roles in initiating, perpetuating, and crystallizing premarital dyadic commitments. Included in these roles are critical evaluations of a pair by family members and friends, their labeling the two as a viable or nonviable pair, and their reflecting and reacting toward the two actors in terms of their proffered labels. On the other hand, chief roles played by the incipient dyad include their acceptance or rejection of others' reactions and labels which may reinforce conceptualizations of themselves as a viable or nonviable pair. The general assumption is that when positive social reaction and labeling are withheld by significant others, pair relationships are transitory, and few develop into comprehensive dyads; but when such positive reaction and labeling are offered by family members and others and accepted and internalized by the partners, the resulting dyad is more likely to be launched into a more-permanent trajectory, such as a marital career.

Translated into a set of interrelated hypotheses, a testable social reaction theory of dyadic formation would be as follows:

Hypothesis 1: The amount and effectiveness of anticipatory socialization into marital-dyadic values positively influences the degree of initial attraction between pair members of the opposite sex.

Hypothesis 2: The amount and effectiveness of anticipatory socialization into marital-dyadic values positively influences the amount of rewards given by significant others for symbiotic behavior.

Hypothesis 3: The amount and effectiveness of anticipatory socialization into marital-dyadic values positively influences the amount of punishments given by significant others for separatist behaviors.

Hypothesis 4: The amount of visibility of a pair's interaction and dyadic exclusiveness positively influences the

amount of dyadic labeling of heterosexual pair relationships by significant others.

Hypothesis 5: The amount of rewards for symbiotic behavior positively influences the amount of pair members' susceptibility to dyadic labels.

Hypothesis 6: The amount of punishments for separatist behavior
positively influences the amount of pair members'
susceptibility to dyadic labels.

Hypothesis 7: The amount of initial attraction between pair members positively influences the amount of rewards
which accrue to pair members' early interaction.

Hypothesis 8: The amount of rewards within pair members' early
interaction positively influences members' susceptibility to dyadic labels.

Hypothesis 9: The amount of members' susceptibility to dyadic
labels positively influences their internalization of
dyadic labels.

Hypothesis 10: The amount of dyadic labeling by significant others
positively influences the amount of members' internalization of dyadic labels.

Hypothesis 11: The amount of pair members' internalization of
dyadic labels positively influences the amount of the
pair's dyadic interaction and exclusiveness.

Hypothesis 12: The amount of a pair's dyadic interaction and exclusiveness influences the amount of the pair's dyadic
commitment.

Some advantages of a social reaction theory

An SR theory of pair bonding offers several advantages. First, it
offers bridging concepts—such as significant others, definition of the
situation, socialization, role-taking, interaction, reaction, and labeling—
which link the social system and the developing dyad.

This theory secondly places the processes of dyadic formation within
the context of social interrelationships. A critical variable, therefore,
is the social audience, the family members and significant others, which
both acts and reacts to a pair as reflectors and labelers. As Erickson
(1962) has suggested in another context, friends and relatives may act
as a "community screen," thus functioning as filters which select, reinforce, and sustain certain heterosexual pairs in preference to others.
Thus, one value of this theory would be its potential for predicting,
from a direct knowledge of significant others' reactions to the pair,
which heterosexual pairs may survive or be extinguished over time.

Another value of an SR theory of mate selection is its primary focus

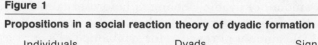

Figure 1

Propositions in a social reaction theory of dyadic formation

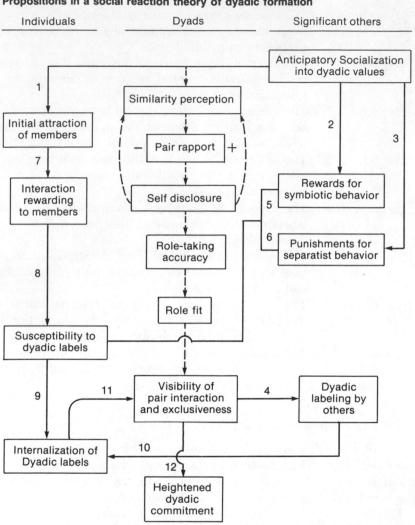

Note: Solid lines and numbers relate to labeling hypotheses. Dotted lines refer to an earlier but related theory of premarital dyadic formation (Lewis, 1972; 1973).
Source: Reprinted from R. A. Lewis, Social influences on marital choice. In *Adolescence in the life cycle,* ed. S. Dragastin & G. H. Elder, Jr. (New York: John Wiley & Sons, 1975), pp. 211–226.

upon transactional analysis. It is therefore a dynamic rather than a static approach and, as such, necessitates sequential (longitudinal) analyses. Dyadic formation can be better understood, therefore, in light of the constant changes which occur for couples as a result of their interaction with significant others, as well as between themselves. In the words of Bolton (1961):

Mate selection must be studied not only in terms of the variables brought into the interaction situation but also as *a process* in which a relationship is built up, a process in which the transactions between individuals *in certain societal contexts* are determinants of turning points and commitments out of which marriage emerges. (p. 235)

SOCIAL NETWORKS AND MATE SELECTION

In the following section, we examine the social environment of courtship processes. The dynamic interplay of couples and their social networks of kith and kin is reflected in the effects each has upon the other. As a pair becomes increasingly involved with one another, they relinquish relationships with their separate friends and initiate mutual friendships with other couples. At the same time, the friends of each member of the romantic pair may seek out alternative friendships, particularly as the romantic pair become more couple-centered in their activities and interests. Kinfolk may demonstrate increased interest in the pair members as they move closer to marriage, at times attempting to directly influence the outcome of the pair relationship. And the romantic partners may themselves attempt to alter the views of kin evaluating the pair's relationship.

Analysis of the interpersonal context of close relationships suggests a variety of questions, including the interconnections of relationship variables with network composition and the degree of social participation; the role of networks in supporting, failing to support, or directly interfering in the continuance or direction of growth of the pair relationship; and the implications of social structures arising during courtship for the later adaptation to changing personal, family, or social conditions. Prior to addressing each of these questions in their substantive form, we briefly consider methods of identifying network memberships.

Identifying network members: Methodological challenges

The membership of an individual's or couple's network may be conceptualized in terms of those people who are considered important to the respondent (i.e., the network of significant others) or the network of individuals with whom the respondent engages in actual face-to-face interaction (i.e., the interactive network). This discrimination is often overlooked, with the two models being fused together conceptually and methodologically. To date, research has focused on identifying those individuals whom the respondent considers important, often including inquiries concerning the respondent's perception of interaction frequency. Survey techniques, reviewed below, have been developed to explore the network of significant others. Curiously, however, studies using behavioral techniques to investigate couples' actual social activity with network members are scant, and a study of the actual social participation of spouses has yet to be published.[1] Nonetheless, methodological strategies are available and may provide some of the most theoretically meaningful and clinically relevant material to date.

Mass survey techniques in network analysis. Fischer and his coworkers have developed a method for investigating the social networks of target individuals that has known psychometric properties, can be employed in survey instruments with minimal time required for completion, and is fully documented to allow application in diverse substantive research areas (see Fischer, 1982, especially chap. 3 and appendix A; Jones & Fischer, 1978). The method avoids several of the theoretical and methodological pitfalls commonplace in less-rigorous approaches.

In a highly structured interview schedule, respondents are first presented with a set of social settings (e.g., personal household, work) and several categories of individuals defined specifically in terms of the probability of rewarding exchanges. Prototypes include a spouse or dating partner if unmarried, people who serve as confidants, or people who provide personal favors including home care, child care, or other symbolic or material resources.

The name-eliciting questions include, for example: "Some people never talk with anyone, either on or off the job, about their work. Other people do discuss things like decisions they have to make, problems they have to solve, and ways to do their work better. Is there anyone you talk with about how to do your work?" (If yes) "Who do you talk with about how you do your work?" and "Which of the following activities have you done in the last three months?" (List activities) "Had someone to your home for lunch or dinner? Went to someone's home for a visit?" and so on. (If any activities participated in) "Who do you usually do these kinds of things with?"

Once a core of network members have been identified, respondents are invited to review the list, adding the names of additional people who are considered important. In general, respondents identify about 13 members of the core network, and they supplement this with another 6 individuals who are thought to be significant (Fischer, 1982). These latter people are usually kin; relationships with them appear to be of an affective or sentimental nature without the inclusion of frequent interaction or the regular exchange of goods or services.

Additional questions concerning the network so identified are de-

---

[1] Huston (1982) and his colleagues have recently collected data on the social activity of newlywed couples. The study, based on daily telephone interviews, is longitudinal in design and includes accounts of the social activity of spouses with network members.

signed to elicit descriptive information on selected members. For instance, "When you are upset about a personal matter—for example, about someone you are concerned about—how often do you talk about it with someone: usually, sometimes, or never? When you do talk with someone about personal matters, which of the people on the list do you talk with? Is there anyone else, either on or off the list, you talk to about personal matters?" Follow-up questions could be inserted as dictated by the particular needs of a research program.

The advantages of the Fischer procedure are several, particularly when compared with less-rigorous survey methods that simply require participants to provide a list of their close friends and kin without specifically defining the criteria to be used for their inclusion. Requiring a respondent to list his/her five closest friends assumes interindividual consistency in the interpretation of closeness, as well as assuming interindividual consistency in the exchange content or function of all close friendships. These assumptions are unsupported by a variety of research. Individuals vary widely in the number of interactants who are considered close; the content of such friendships varies predictably across age and gender; and finally, the attribution of closeness is often unrelated to frequency of face-to-face interaction (Milardo, 1983). By requesting respondents to list their closest associates, without qualifying the criteria to be used for their identification, a demand characteristic is presented that ensures the respondent will identify some close friendships and enough of them to satisfy the needs of a professional social scientist.

The Fischer procedure also implicitly challenges the notion that an individual's degree of social integration or social support can be adequately described by examining network sectors considered close or intimate. Intermediate-level friends and kindred may serve important functions in the conduct of everyday life. For instance, can a researcher safely assume mere acquaintances who are regularly available for child care and to lend household tools are less consequential in determining a family's degree of social integration or social support when compared with close associates who are seen irregularly? Many of these individuals are identified in the core name-eliciting questions employed by Fischer (1982).

Additional network sectors might also be explored where the need arose. In particular, people with whom interaction is typically negative are unidentified as the name-eliciting questions are presently structured. It is important to note, however, that conflict-habituated relationships can serve central functions with both negative and positive consequences. Conflict-habituated relationships with neighbors may have deleterious consequences for a family's level of social integration, for example. On the other hand, conflict may have positive consequences, as in the case of a young mother who finds herself constantly at odds with a neighbor in regard to appropriate childrearing strategies. Under these circumstances, the mother's own attitudes and beliefs may become more concrete as a function of social comparison. In this way, the neighbor, perhaps unwittingly, becomes a source of social support; yet, the relationship between young mother and neighbor is neither close nor of a positive valence.

Possibly more problematic is the procedure's reliance on identifying network constituents with a high probability of rewarding exchange— individuals with whom interaction is regular and involves some transfer of material or symbolic goods and services. Relationships of a purely affective nature with only intermittent contact may be central determinants of the respondent's subjective evaluation of being socially supported, although these relationships would be relatively inconsequential in the provision of direct aid. Moreover, purely affective relationships are apt to characterize the networks of women, whereas exchange-oriented relationships are likely to be characteristic of the networks of men. As a result, a gender bias may be unintentionally introduced when the selection of network members emphasizes one set of criteria or another (Milardo, 1983).

Future research employing questionnaire-based assessments of networks must, without question, be guided by a systematic elicitation of constituents based on comprehensive and distinct criteria that are interpreted in a similar way by a variety of respondents. Further, investigators should not underestimate the importance of intermediate-level friends and distant kin as well as individuals with whom interactions are typically negative. In some ways, contacts with these individuals may be far more consequential than network members considered close, in determining the quality of family relationships, the availability of social supports, and the degree of network interference.

Interactive networks. Perhaps the most common error in network analysis is the assumption that respondents can accurately name those individuals with whom they typically interact or accurately estimate the frequency of social contact with network constituents over time. Neither assumption is supported by data; rather, available evidence demonstrates that individuals do not know with any certainty with whom they typically interact or how often such interactions occur. This does not mean that perceptions of social participation are inconsequential, but simply that perceptions are not a valid proxy for actual behavior. In the following section, we review the factors that attentuate the accuracy of self-report data, and the more promising methods available for gathering accurate indexes of social activity. In particular, we review issues bearing upon immediate versus retrospective accounts of social activity and the seat of responsibility for the aggregation of data.

A respondent may report on a particular social episode immediately following occurrence, or retrospectively for a certain period of time (e.g., over a week, month, or year). Secondly, a respondent may be required to provide aggregate measures of social activity (e.g., the frequency of interaction with a friend over the last week), or the responsibility for aggregation may be assumed by the researcher. With some documentation of separate social interactions, the researcher is able to calculate a summary index of the number of distinct interactants or the frequency of interaction.

Questionnaire items used to generate network data are typically both retrospective and respondent-aggregated. For example: "With whom have you interacted in the last week, month, or year? How often do you interact with kin, friends, or acquaintances? Frequently, seldom, or never?" We would argue that retrospective and respondent-aggregated measures yield less veridical data when compared to accounts of social participation that are based upon "immediate" sources of data later aggregated by the researcher. In fact, there is little reason to believe people are capable of constructing accurate indexes of the people with whom they interact, nor are they capable of accurately computing average measures of the frequency of interaction, particularly when there may be some variability in frequency from week to week or month to month, and no one has yet designed a way to have respondents compute variances.

Bernard and Killworth (1977; Killworth & Bernard, 1979) have addressed these issues by generating unobtrusive measures of social activity among four naturally occurring groups: a deaf community who communicated by teletype and thus produced written records of all communications, a group of amateur radio operators whose communications were electronically monitored, and two separate groups of office personnel whose interactions were recorded by trained observers. Several days following the monitoring of interactions by the experimenters, the participants were required to rank order those individuals with whom they interacted, most to least often. In general, respondents were unable to accurately reconstruct profiles of their social participation.

A more useful and accurate approach to monitoring levels of social participation would require participants to report on their social activity as soon following that activity as possible, and at least daily. Such an "immediate" source of data, by narrowing the gap between the experience of an event and the reporting of that event, minimizes the effects of disturbances in the memory and recall of past events. This contemporary data base could be summarized by the researcher to form aggregate indexes, rather than requiring the respondent to do so, and thus eliminate an additional source of error.

Several procedures for documenting the contemporary social activity of respondents with network members have been developed in order to circumvent the problems noted above. Milardo and his colleagues (Milardo, 1982; Milardo, Johnson, & Huston, 1983) required research participants to report on all their social activity daily for 10 consecutive days. Social-interaction report forms were provided for this purpose and participants were instructed to complete one interaction record for each voluntary social episode over 10 minutes in length. Each record included data on all individuals present during an interaction: their sex, relationship to the participant, relationship to the participant's dating partner, as well as evaluations of the satisfaction and intimacy of each encounter. These records provided a relatively objective definition of the network constituency. All people present during the interactions are de facto members of the respondent's network. Subjective definitions of network membership are avoided, and participants are not burdened with recalling precisely who is significant or with whom interactions have occurred over long periods of time.

Interactive measures of network membership additionally allow the researcher to determine the significance of particular members or groups of members (cliques) based on empirically derived composites of the interaction records. Judgments of significance may be based on measures of the frequency or duration of interactions, contemporary ratings of the intimacy of interactions, or descriptions of exchange content.

Additional technologies have been developed to monitor contemporary interpersonal events. Huston and his co-workers have employed a time-sampling procedure in which newlywed couples were interviewed by phone concerning their social activity with network members during a previous 24-hour period (Huston, 1982; Robins, 1982). Peterson (1979), using an event-sampling technique, had spouses maintain structured diaries of interactions that they judged to be particularly significant. Still others have employed electronic paging devices, and participants reported on their social activity or current emotional state when paged (Larson, Csikszentmihalyi, & Graef, 1980).

At present, strategies for identifying interactive networks (e.g., Milardo et al., 1983) and exchange networks (Fischer, 1982) appear more reliable than traditional measures, but these methods need not produce equivalent results. A number of factors may attenuate correspondence between the divergent methods. Geographic separation or extensive obligations to work and family may preclude interacting with network sectors considered important. Under this condition, time-sampling procedures would be incapable of identifying significant others seen infrequently. There is little reason to presume, however, that the exchange network identified by Fischer accurately or comprehensively represents the actual social activity of respondents.

The overlap between time-sampling and survey methods may be further attenuated by the nature of the information being sought, particularly in regard to its objectivity. For instance, in comparison to the content or intimacy of self-disclosures, the identity of interactants is relatively more objective. Although the constituency of networks defined by well-designed survey instruments and time-sampling procedures may be similar, accurate measures of the frequency of interaction or the content of self-disclosures could be more difficult to obtain because these attributes are more difficult to define objectively. Hence, the correspondence between network methodologies should vary with the character of the traits being investigated. In the future, researchers will need to attend more closely to issues having to do with retrospective versus contemporary sources of data, respondent-aggregated versus researcher-aggregated measures of network attributes, and objective versus diffuse qualities of network variables being sought.

In the following section, we examine the role of social networks in courtship and early marriage. Although research in this area is just beginning to develop, the utility of the network concept is firmly demonstrated, and the issues raised can be shown to generalize to other points in the family life course.

Social withdrawal as an interpersonal process

As partners become increasingly interdependent in a developing couple relationship, their personal or separate social networks shrink in size and their mutual or joint networks expand (Johnson & Leslie, 1982; Milardo, 1982; Milardo et al., 1983). The shrinkage of each pair member's network is thought to result from several factors. Slater (1963) argues that the amount of emotional energy (libido) available to others is limited; thus, once such energy is committed to a dyadic relationship, less is available for investment in other relationships. Marks (1977) as well as Johnson and Leslie (1982), however, suggest that relationships need not consume energy, but rather may in fact increase the individual's social interests and opportunities. Nonetheless, additional constraints of a behavioral or temporal nature are also thought to limit the pair's degree of network participation. Since the absolute time available for social relationships is limited, investments in a close relationship place temporal restrictions on what is potentially available to others (Boissevain, 1974; Shulman, 1975; Slater, 1963). From the perspective of symbolic interactionism, Lewis (1973) has posited that the exclusion of third parties is a necessary component of "dyadic crystallization," in that in order to fully develop a sense of pair identity, couples increasingly view themselves as a unit apart from others, and they may exclude third parties from their interaction (see Krain, 1977).

In an insightful discussion of the social-withdrawal hypothesis, Johnson and Leslie (1982) argue that the withdrawal of a couple from a larger collectivity is not absolutely necessary but is a function of social definition. It is selective rather than universal insofar as pair members need not withdraw from all sectors of the network but only those that are defined as incompatible with developing a highly committed pair relationship. The authors argue that Western conceptions of romantic pairings require the maintenance of monogomous-exclusive relationships. As a consequence, pair members will terminate only those network ties viewed as incompatible with the socially defined ideals of exclusivity and monogamy.

Each of these theoretical bases for the withdrawal of couples from certain network sectors, however, fails to consider the initiation of withdrawal by network members. A friend, for example, may find her tennis partner so embedded in a passionate relationship with another as to be unavailable for weekly matches, and as a result the friend withdraws. The term *dyadic withdrawal* assumes that somehow network members are passive agents in the social activity of pair members, an unlikely occurrence. People are active in maintaining their social worlds, and withdrawal probably occurs as both network and pair members adjust their interconnections to best suit need and circumstance.

Several cross-sectional and retrospective studies have demonstrated that relatively greater pair involvement is associated with a greater probability of exclusive interactions, joint activity, and partner-directed activity (Huston et al., 1981; Lewis, 1973; Mack, cited in Levinger, 1974; Rands & Levinger, 1979). These findings imply a decline in social activity with others as couples become close. In fact, Huston et al. found that the proportion of leisure activity involving the partner increases while similar activities with others decline as pairs move through courtship to marriage.

In a more direct test of the withdrawal hypothesis, Johnson and Leslie (1982) required individuals involved in dating relationships to identify their personal networks of significant others—i.e., "those people whose opinions of your life are important to you." Respondents in the latter stages of courtship reported fewer network members relative to the early stages, and they reported less involvement with those people who remained in the network. These findings, however, were largely restricted to friendships. The number of kin identified as significant others did not vary across stages, although the variance in the number of kin identified increased dramatically across stages of court-ship. The authors interpret these findings as supportive of their position that withdrawal is selective rather than being universal. As couples move from peer-legitimated relationships to the kinship-related stage of engagement and finally marriage, their involvement with friends diminishes. Concurrently, as they become more central in the lives of couples, kin's opinions increase in importance, while kin who disap-prove of the pair's continuing involvement either are dropped from the network or may themselves withdraw. The result of these simulta-neous processes is little change in the average number of kin identified at each stage but an increase in the variance in the latter stages (John-son & Leslie, 1982).

The findings of Johnson and Leslie tend to support a degree of social withdrawal, but they are limited for two reasons. First, the net-work of significant others may not coincide with the interactive net-work of people who are involved in recurrent, sometimes daily contacts with the target person. Perhaps actual interaction patterns remained unchanged while perceptions of who is significant varied. It may be far simpler for a pair member to control perceptions of who is signifi-cant than the people with whom one interacts. Secondly, cross-sectional comparisons of stages of courtship are difficult to interpret. For in-stance, although the engaged partners reported fewer network mem-bers than casually dating partners, it is possible that individuals with large networks are less apt to develop enduring relationships. Thus, people who tend to move to later stages of courtship, as opposed to people who (perhaps perpetually) remain in casual dating situations, may always have had fewer significant others and less involvement with those who remain in the network. Perhaps it is the scarcity of their social network ties that permits or encourages movement toward a deeper pair relationship. A more robust test of the withdrawal hypoth-esis requires the examination of time-ordered variations in social partic-ipation across specific network sectors for dating partners who either move closer together or further apart.

In a combination of cross-sectional and longitudinal designs, Milardo et al. (1983) required research participants to record pertinent network data for all significant social interactions for two 10-day periods sepa-rated by three months. In general, the findings confirmed the hypothe-sized covariations of stage of relationship and network structure and interaction. Network size varied as predicted with people in the early stages interacting with about 31 network members during the first occasion of measurement, while engaged people interacted with about 25 members. The analyses of network size did not yield robust stage differences, however. Far more substantial were the variations in the frequency and duration of interactions. As predicted, casually dating participants interacted more often and for longer periods of time relative to engaged parties.

Longitudinally, there were also significant variations in social participation. The time-ordered changes unexpectedly involved only the frequency and duration of interactions. Network size did not vary with changes in pair involvement over time. In short, advancing relationships demonstrated a reduction in the frequency and duration of contacts with friends, while people in deteriorating relationships increased their social participation with friends.

An overall model of the process of social withdrawal was developed based upon the findings pertaining to network size and the degree of social interaction. The model suggests that the frequency and duration of interaction are sensitive indicators of short-term changes in social activity and that such changes eventually result in changes in the number of social interactants and thus the total size of the network.

When the findings (Milardo et al., 1983) are considered in light of their origin—in the ongoing social activity of participants—several dynamic qualities of interpersonal relations can be addressed, including the initiation and regulation of social relationships. Consider, for example, the duration of interactions between pair members and friends. Unlike network size (i.e., the number of people with whom interactions occur), the duration of interactions is readily manipulated. Friends may initiate interactions and thus become de facto members of the network, but the target person has an even greater capacity to abridge and control the length of such interactions. Reductions in duration are also less costly to pair members than reducing network size by entirely preventing encounters; and pair members may not consider interactions with friends without some reward value. It is perhaps largely a question of relative comparisons of alternatives where interactions with the dating partner become juxtaposed with interactions involving friends. Complete withdrawal from a network member, however desirable, is not simply contingent on the wishes or actions of pair members. Over time, pair members may demonstrate a sufficient lack of availability and interest in the network to result in a decline (in the case of an advancing relationship) in the amount of other-initiated interaction. This process would eventually, but not immediately, result in a reduction in the size of the interactive network.

Yet another hypothesis is tenable: that social withdrawal would be greater from the peripheral sectors of the network than the close sectors. The findings of Milardo et al. (1983) were not in complete agreement with this prediction. Apparently, the degree of social participation is not dependent on the level of friendship under investigation. What does appear to be pivotal is the timing of changes in social activity for close versus peripheral network members. Any change in the degree of affiliation with close friends is gradual and occurs over the long term. Evidence for this prediction is represented in the analyses of frequency and duration of interaction. For close friends, each of these variables declined across stages of courtship; but neither showed any variation over time. One explanation for this finding is that the ties binding close friends are considerable and not easily broken. In general, withdrawal will be gradual when social relationships are based on mutually rewarding exchanges of tangible or intangible resources that are highly valued, considered irreplaceable, with few alternative arrangements available. These interpersonal events and processes are equally applicable to the target person and network member and are suggestive of the manner in which each gradually realigns relations to best reflect current situations.

There seems to be little doubt that as couples become increasingly interdependent, they withdraw from their respective networks. Thus far, withdrawal appears to center on networks of friends and acquaintances; evidence for withdrawal from kin is mixed. Although Johnson and Leslie (1982) found an apparent increase in the variability of the number of kin considered significant based on cross-sectional comparisons of stages of courtship, Milardo et al. (1983) found little change in the means or variances in the size of the kinship network or in the amount of interaction with kin as couples changed their level of involvement with one another. Nonetheless, the importance of kin in the courtship process, particularly during engagement and marriage, should be emphasized. And, while withdrawal from friends is apt to depend more upon social interests and availability, withdrawal from kin may result more from direct interference in the pair relationship. But for many couples and especially women, courtship would increase the number of potential kinship members as the partner's consanguines become known. Engagement and the marriage ceremony itself function to redirect the attention of the couple upon every affectional tie either partner has ever contracted to the extent that an observer might question whether the idea of marriage originated with the couple or the network (Slater, 1963).

We might also expect withdrawal to vary across gender, but current research suggests that both men and women are equally likely to withdraw from their networks of friends. Within marriage, however, a different picture emerges. While husbands tend to increase their social participation with friends, wives continue to withdraw from friends and at the same time become increasingly involved with kin, both consanguines and affines. Marriage and motherhood have deleterious effects on the friendships maintained by women. Working and nonworking wives without children report fewer friends than husbands, and wives with young children report still fewer friends (Davis, 1981; Fischer, 1982; Fischer & Oliker, 1980).

Dobash and Dobash (1979) reported on a sample of Scottish families with a history of spouse abuse. Sixty-one percent of the women and 41 percent of the men in their sample reported *no* separate social life following engagement, having never spent evenings with friends or acquaintances apart from their betrothed. These findings are in accord with those presented earlier, if a bit radical. Following marriage, the curtailment of the social activity of wives continued as the activities of husbands increased. Dobash and Dobash argue that the social withdrawal of wives and mothers is a necessary symbol of commitment to husband and family. In contrast, the social life of newlywed husbands is under few socially sanctioned restrictions. Commitment for men is largely defined in terms of fiscal obligations to provide for their families. The social expectations of husbands and wives in regard to their social participation reflect a patriarchal system with concomitant and differential authority, dependence, responsibilities, and social freedom to initiate and maintain friendships. Thus, although emotional, temporal and behavioral constraints may operate during courtship, the production of gender-based differences in social regression during early marriage suggests a latent ideology of male patriarchy, however unconscious that ideology may be.

Overlapping social networks

Concurrent with social withdrawal, couples are thought to form a joint social network composed of people who are close associates of both members of a pair relationship (Huston & Levinger, 1978; Levinger, 1977). The emergence of a mutual social network occurs for several reasons. Central to Levinger's (1980) model of pair relatedness, as well as Kelley and Thibaut's (1978) social exchange theory, is the concept of behavioral interdependence, reviewed already by Talmadge & Ruback (chap. 4 of this volume). Simply stated, "interdependence refers to the effects interacting persons have on each other" (Kelly, 1979, p. 13). The degree of interdependence of couples is reflected in the thoughts and actions of each person toward the other as well as in the ways pair members separately and jointly view their social environment and interact with that environment. As pairs become interdependent in their personal lives, they will become interdependent in their social lives as well; and the emergence of overlapping networks is largely the result of increasing interdependencies. These intra- and interpersonal events can be usefully summarized in terms of three essential themes with symbolic and behavioral components. Mutually involved pairs develop a jointly held orientation toward themselves, a jointly held orientation toward their social environment, and a jointly held network of relationships that reflect the pair's interdependence with one another and their interdependence with their social environment.

Several investigations of the social networks of spouses suggest both separate and mutual friendships are maintained (Babchuk & Bates, 1963; Bott, 1971; Crawford, 1977; Lowenthal, 1975; Shulman, 1975); however, the size of the joint network and the proportion of mutual to separate associates have remained unspecified, and researchers have not linked the formation of a joint network to the development of a pair relationship.

Direct support for the emergence of a joint network of mutually held network members concurrent with the development of a pair relationship is found in a study of the social activity of dating partners (Milardo, 1982). Measures of network overlap were based on self-reports of social activity completed daily. Both cross-sectional and longitudinal comparisons supported the formation of a joint network. People in the later stages of courtship reported a larger proportion of jointly held friendships (averaging about 77 percent) relative to those in the early stages (averaging about 30 percent). Longitudinally, relationships that advanced over time increased the proportion of mutual friends; relationships that deteriorated reduced this proportion. Equally significant were changes in the absolute number of mutual friends. For example, casually dating individuals reported interacting with about 10 network members who were considered friends of the dating partner. Engaged individuals identified about 19 mutual friends. Finally, variations in network overlap were demonstrated to include cognitive changes in the way friends are viewed (i.e., where pair members redefined their personal or separate friends as mutual friends of both themselves and their partner) as well as behavioral changes in the people with whom interactions occurred (i.e., where entirely new individuals became members of the couple's joint network).

Network interference and support

In addition to examining variations in network structure and in partners' degree of social participation, a few studies have examined the content of interaction between couples and their respective social networks, particularly in terms of network interference in pair relationships. Direct attempts at influencing pair relationships by parents, other relatives, or friends have been reported by several authors (Coombs, 1962; Driscoll et al., 1972; Johnson & Milardo, 1984; Knox & Wilson, 1981; Leslie, 1982; Parks et al., 1983; Ryder et al., 1971; Sussman, 1953). Bates (1942) found a majority of married couples reported that parents attempted directly or indirectly to influence their choice of a spouse, although parents were generally perceived to have played a more significant role in the dating patterns of daughters than of sons. More recent inquiries have failed to support sex differences in the degree of interference by network members in their relationships

(Johnson & Milardo, 1984), while at the same time suggesting that both parents and their offspring attempt to influence each other's evaluation of the current dating partner and the future viability of the dating relationship (Leslie, 1982).

Curiously, rather than center on the supportive function of network members in the development of a pair relationship, as has been the case in marital research, the focus of research has been on network interference (for exceptions, see Lewis, 1973; Parks et al., 1983). The persistence of romantic love in the face of opposition has long attracted the attention of writers. Driscoll et al. (1972), in their now-classic study, hypothesized that parental interference in a pair relationship facilitates the couple's attraction toward one another—the Romeo and Juliet effect. The study is often cited for its support of the positive consequences of interference on pair involvement. Close examination of the findings, however, suggests otherwise. For example, interference was measured by noting the degree to which seriously dating or married respondents complain to their mates that parents interfered in their relationship, express negative sentiments, attempt to place the respondent in a negative light, take advantage of the partner, or refuse to accept the respondent. The measure of interference represents the perceptions of a subjective condition and can not be equated with actual attempts at interference. Although subjective evaluations may be real in their consequences, it is quite a different matter to inquire how perceptions of interference vary with courtship progress, as compared with how actual attempts at interference vary with courtship progress. The perceptions of parental interference may reflect the respondent's attitudes toward parents rather than any particular actions or attitudes of the parents.

The findings of Driscoll et al. demonstrate a moderate degree of association between interference and romantic love. Causal interpretations were tested by correlating change over 6 to 10 months in parental interference and love scores. For the unmarried group this correlation was 0.34, but nonsignificant for the married group. These findings hardly represent strong support for a causal sequencing of interference and courtship progress. The analyses based on changes in the target variables over time merely demonstrate a moderate degree of synchronous covariation between measures of interference and love.

Further attempts to support the Romeo and Juliet effect have failed to demonstrate a significant causal relationship (Leslie, 1982; Parks et al., 1983). Moreover, Driscoll et al. (1972) reported that parental interference was associated with decreased trust, increased criticalness, and an increased frequency of negative behavior within couples. Interference, rather than leading to a closer pair relationship, may lead to its deterioration. In another study, members of dating relationships who reported high levels of interference were also more apt to have terminated their relationships one year following initial assessments of perceptions of network interference (Johnson & Milardo, 1984). And, although different interests of partners or the desire to be independent are the most-often cited problems of couples who break up before marriage, the perception of parental interference is frequently cited as a contributing factor (Hill, Rubin, & Peplau, 1976). Continued and unabated interference is therefore probably deleterious to a relationship's overall quality.

Additional research in the area is necessary to examine the distinct role of actual attempts at interference in pair relationships. We suspect the rate of interference over time is more critical than the absolute magnitude at any one point in time. That is, low levels of interference that continue over long periods of time may have a more negative impact on a relationship's viability, since this would most likely preclude the provision of social support from the interfering party. High levels of interference over short terms may at most mean a temporary lapse in social support, and the overall affect would be rather inconsequential.

Research on the impact of interference should not preclude examining the supportive function of network constituents in the maintenance of pair relationships. To date, the role of social support has been largely restricted to the well-being of individuals (for reviews, see Gottlieb, 1981; Saulnier, 1982), particularly those facing major life transitions such as divorce (e.g., Colletta, 1979; Price-Bonham & Balswick, 1980). Network members may demonstrate support by considering pair members as a unit, by inviting the pair to social events as a couple (Lewis, 1973) or, more directly, by offering material or symbolic aid. The magnitude and diversity of support probably increases as the respective networks of partners merge, with concommitant increases in the contacts with each other's family and friends (Parks et al., 1983).

CONCLUSION

In their pursuit of theories to explain heterosexual, dyadic (pair) formation, social psychologists generally have ignored the social environment in the early development of pair relations and mate selection. This chapter focused attention upon the vital interface between social networks, families, and mate selection—that is, the *transactions* between a developing dyad and significant others such as family members and friends. Assertions explored were: Couples do not develop in a social vacuum but rather within social contexts; some individuals are socialized at an early age to delimit their potential mates in line with their parents' values; some parents exert direct influence in terms of their children's dating partners; and there appears to be a positive relationship between family support for one's pair relationship and courtship process. Finally, a social reaction theory of mate selection was offered as a partial explanation for the relationships between family transactions and dyadic development.

In the second half of the chapter a review of network literature was offered to distinguish various methodologies for studying network effects on dyadic development, and to describe and explain the processes of pair development in relation to social context.

REFERENCES

Babchuk, N., & Bates, A. P. The primary relations of middle-class couples: A study in male dominance. *American Sociological Review*, 1963, *28*, 377–384.

Bates, A. Parental roles in courtship. *Social Forces*, 1942, *43*, 483–486.

Bernard, H. R., & Killworth, P. D. Informant accuracy in social network data II. *Human Communications Research*, 1977, *4*, 3–18.

Boissevain, J. *Friends of friends*. Oxford: Basil Blackwell, 1974.

Bolton, C. D. Mate selection as the development of a relationship. *Marriage and Family Living*, 1961, *23*, 234–240.

Bott, E. *Family and social network*. New York: Free Press, 1971.

Broderick, C. B. Social heterosexual development among urban Negroes and whites. *Journal of Marriage and the Family*, 1966, *27*, 200–203.

Broderick, C. B., & Rowe, G. A scale of preadolescent heterosexual development. *Journal of Marriage and the Family*, 1968, *30*, 97–101.

Cobb, S., & Jones, J. M. Social support, support groups and marital relationships. In S. W. Duck (Ed.), *Personal relationships* (Vol. 5): *Repairing personal relationships*. New York: Academic Press, 1984.

Colletta, N. C. Support systems after divorce. *Journal of Marriage and the Family*, 1979, *41*, 837–846.

Coombs, R. Reinforcement of values in the parental home as a factor in mate selection. *Marriage and Family Living*, 1962, *24*, 155–157.

Crawford, M. What is a friend? *New Society*, 1977, *42*, 116–117.

Davis, K. E. *Friendship through the life-cycle: Age, gender, and race effects on the number and quality of personal relationships*. Paper presented at the Annual Meeting of the American Psychological Association, Los Angeles, 1981.

Dobash, R. E., & Dobash, R. *Violence against wives*. New York: Free Press, 1979.

Driscoll, R., Davis, K. E., & Lipetz, M. E. Parental interference and romantic love; The Romeo and Juliet effect. *Journal of Personality and Social Psychology*, 1972, *24*, 1–10.

Erickson, K. R. Notes on the sociology of deviance. *Social Problems*, 1962, *9*, 307–314.

Erickson, K. R. *Wayward puritans*. New York: John Wiley & Sons, 1964.

Fischer, C. S. *To dwell among friends: Personal networks in town and city*. Chicago: University of Chicago Press, 1982.

Fischer, C. S., & Oliker, S. J. *Friendship, sex, and the life-cycle.* Berkeley: University of California, Institute of Urban and Regional Development, Working Paper No. 318, 1980.

Gottlieb, B. H. (Ed.). *Social networks and social support.* Beverly Hills, Calif.: Sage Publications, 1981.

Heider, F. *The psychology of interpersonal relations.* New York: John Wiley & Sons, 1958.

Hill, C. T., Rubin, Z., & Peplau, L. A. Breakups before marriage: The end of 103 affairs. *Journal of Social Issues,* 1976, *32,* 147–168.

Hill, R., & Aldous, J. Socialization for marriage and parenthood. In D. Goslin (Ed.), *Handbook of Socialization Theory and Research,* Skokie, Ill.: Rand McNally, 1969.

Huston, T. L. *The typography of marriage: A longitudinal study of changes in husband-wife relationships over the first year.* Paper presented at the International Conference on Personal Relationships, Madison, Wisconsin, 1982.

Huston, T. L., & Levinger, G. Interpersonal attraction and relationships. In M. R. Rosenzweig & L. W. Porter (Eds.), *Annual Review of Psychology,* 1978, *29,* 115–156.

Huston, T. L., Surra, C. A., Fitzgerald, N. M., & Cate, R. M. From courtship to marriage: Mate selection as an interpersonal process. In S. Duck & R. Gilmour (Eds.), *Personal Relationships* (Vol. 2). New York: Academic Press, 1981.

Johnson, M. P., & Leslie, L. Couple involvement and network structure: A test of the dyadic withdrawal hypothesis. *Social Psychology Quarterly,* 1982, *45,* 34–43.

Johnson, M. P., & Milardo, R. M. Network interference and pair relationships: A social psychological recasting of Slater's (1963) theory of social regression. *Journal of Marriage and the Family,* 1984, *46.*

Jones, L. M., & Fischer, C. S. *Studying egocentric networks by mass survey.* Berkeley: University of California, Institute of Urban and Regional Planning, Working paper No. 284, 1978.

Kelley, H. H. *Personal relationships: Their structures and processes.* New York: John Wiley & Sons, 1979.

Kelley, H. H., & Thibaut, J. W. *Interpersonal relations: A theory of interdependence.* New York: John Wiley & Sons, 1978.

Killworth, P. D., & Bernard, H. R. Informant accuracy in social network data III. *Social Networks,* 1979, *2,* 19–46.

Kirkpatrick, C., & Caplow, T. Courtship in a group of Minnesota students. *American Journal of Sociology,* 1945, *51,* 114–125.

Knox, D., & Wilson, K. Dating behaviors of university students. *Family Relations,* 1981, *30,* 255–258.

Krain, M. A definition of dyadic boundaries and an empirical study of boundary establishment in courtship. *International Journal of the Family,* 1977, *7,* 107–123.

Larson, R., Csikszentmihalyi, M., & Graef, R. Mood variability and the psycho social adjustment of adolescents. *Journal of Youth and Adolescence,* 1980, *9,* 469–490.

Leslie, L. A. Parental influence and premarital relationship development. Unpublished dissertation, The Pennsylvania State University, 1982.

Levinger, G. A three-level approach to attraction: Toward an understanding of pair relatedness. In T. L. Houston (Ed.), *Foundations of Interpersonal Attraction.* New York: Academic Press, 1974.

Levinger, G. The embrace of lives: Changing and unchanging. In G. Levinger & H. Raush (Eds.), *Close Relationships.* Amherst: University of Massachusetts Press, 1977.

Levinger, G. A social psychological perspective on marital dissolution. In G. Levinger & O. Moles (Eds.), *Divorce and Separation.* New York: Basic Books, 1979.

Levinger, G. Toward the analysis of close relationships. *Journal of Experimental Social Psychology,* 1980, *16,* 510–544.

Lewis, R. A. A developmental framework for the analysis of premarital dyadic formation. *Family Process,* 1972, *11,* 17–48.

Lewis, R. A. Social reaction and the formation of dyads: An interactionist approach to mate selection. *Sociometry,* 1973, *36,* 409–418.

Lewis, R. A. Social influences on marital choice. In S. Dragastin & G. H. Elder, Jr. (Eds.), *Adolescence in the life cycle.* New York: John Wiley & Sons, 1975. Pp. 211–226.

Lewis, R. A., & Spanier, G. B. Theorizing about the quality and stability of marriage. In W. R. Burr, R. Hill, F. I. Yne, & I. L. Reiss (Eds.), *Contemporary theories about the family,* New York: Free Press, 1979. Pp. 482–524.

Lowenthal, M. F. *Four stages of life.* San Francisco: Jossey-Bass, 1975.

Marks, S. R. Multiple roles and role strain: Some notes on human energy, time and commitment. *American Sociological Review,* 1977, *42,* 921–936.

Mayer, J. E. People's imagery of others' families. *Family Process,* 1967, *6,* 27–36.

Milardo, R. M. Friendship networks in developing relationships: Converging and diverging social environments. *Social Psychology Quarterly,* 1982, *45,* 162–172.

Milardo, R. M. Social networks and pair relationships: A review of substantive and measurement issues. *Sociology and Social Research,* 1983, *68,* 1–18.

Milardo, R. M., Johnson, M. P., & Huston, T. L. Developing close relationships: Changing patterns of interaction between pair members and social networks. *Journal of Personality and Social Psychology,* 1983, *44,* 964–976.

Neill, J. R. & Kniskern, D. P. (Eds.). *From psyche to system: The evolving therapy of Carl Whitaker.* New York: Guilford Press, 1982.

Parks, M. E., Stan, C. M., & Eggert, L. Romantic involvement and social network involvement. *Social Psychology Quarterly,* 1983, *46,* 116–131.

Peterson, D. R. Assessing interpersonal relationships by means of interaction records. *Behavioral Assessment,* 1979, *1,* 221–236.

Price-Bonham, S., & Balswick, J. O. The noninstitutions: Divorce, desertion, and remarriage. *Journal of Marriage and the Family,* 1980, *42,* 225–238.

Rands, M., & Levinger, G. Implicit theories of relationships: An intergenerational study. *Journal of Personality and Social Psychology,* 1979, *37,* 645–661.

Ridley, C., & Avery, A. Social network influence on the dyadic relationship. In R. Burgess & T. Huston (Eds.), *Social exchange in developing relationships.* New York: Academic Press, 1979. Pp. 223–246.

Robins, E. *Just the two of us: The distribution of spouses' leisure time in marriage.* Paper presented at the International Conference on Personal Relationships, Madison, Wisconsin, 1982.

Ryder, R. G., Kafka, J. S., & Olson, D. H. Separating and joining influences in courtship and early marriage. *American Journal of Orthopsychiatry,* 1971, *41,* 450–464.

Saulnier, K. Networks, change, and crisis: The web of support. *Canadian Journal of Community Mental Health,* 1982, *1,* 5–23.

Shulman, N. Life-cycle variations in patterns of close relationships. *Journal of Marriage and the Family,* 1975, *37,* 813–821.

Slater, P. On social regression. *American Sociological Review,* 1963, *28,* 339–358.

Sussman, M. Parental participation in mate selection and its effects upon family continuity. *Social Forces,* 1953, *32,* 76–81.

Waller, W., & Hill, R. *The family: A dynamic interpretation.* Hinsdale, Ill.: Dryden Press, 1951.

Chapter 9

The Aged within a Family Context: Relationships, Roles, and Events*

JEFFREY A. GIORDANO

KATHRYN BECKHAM

INTRODUCTION

The importance of the family in modern-day life is paramount, and the family is the primary source of interaction and support for the elderly. As participation in other social institutions declines, the family becomes the primal resource for the social, emotional economic, and health needs of old persons (Seelbach & Hansen, 1980; Troll, 1971). For the most part, family involvement is a positive force in the continued growth and development of the aged. Old people who are isolated from or without families have more problems. They are more likely to be economically disadvantaged, live in substandard housing, and have more serious health and psychological problems (Hendricks & Hendricks, 1977). Indeed, socialization to family life is so pervasive that people isolated from relatives will create substitute families (Troll, Miller, & Atchley, 1979).

A dual perspective that includes the developmental approach and personality development is useful in understanding the aged in a family context. The family life-cycle concept is particularly relevant (Atchley, 1977b; Hill & Rodgers, 1964). Some conceptualizations include three stages (middle years, retirement, and old age), some others designate two stages, while others list five or more stages. There are a variety

* The authors would like to acknowledge the support of the University of Georgia Gerontology Center and the assistance of Dr. James Montgomery, professor of gerontology, for his helpful comments on the manuscript.

of notions as to when aging begins. In this chapter, the latter third of family and individual life cycles are seen as consisting of two stages corresponding roughly to Neugarten's (1975) conceptualization of "young-old" and "old-old." While an individual's life cycle often parallels the family cycle, the two are not one and the same. Retirement is viewed as the transition to the latter third of the family life cycle. Most elderly see old age as being after 65 or when regular work ends (Harris & Associates, 1981).

The aged are not a homogeneous group. People are more similar at earlier stages of life (for example, at two years of age) than in old age. The diversity that exists among the aged increases the difficulty in making generalizations. The notion of continued personality growth has received much less attention than the events and roles of the later years. Research has shown that there is a continuity to the adaptive qualities of personality over the years (Neugarten, 1964; Neugarten, Havighurst, & Tobin, 1968). Further, age seems to increase preoccupation with the inner life and bring a more restricted perceptual system, a reduction in the complexity of personality, and greater personality consistency (Atchley, 1977b, 1983; Neugarten, 1964). Personality variables are intimately related to social networks, especially to those related to the family. Although relatively little attention has been given to the continued development of personality, it remains important to keep in mind that in the later years, personality characteristics do interact with life changes and life tasks.

It was once thought that after retirement, increased dependency and psychological deterioration doomed the family to unresolvable problems. Recently, however, the literature indicates that most older adults experience marital and life satisfactions, increased self-esteem, and the ability to cope with concomitant problems (Atchley, 1983; Cormican, 1980; Steere, 1981). To be sure, the transition to the ranks of the old-old increases the likelihood of dysfunctioning; but family support, coping mechanisms, and social and health services are often applied to restore or stabilize functioning.

Family patterns have traditionally been conceptualized as either nuclear or extended. The pattern of contemporary America is the *modified extended family*—that is, family members living in close proximity and engaged in mutual exchange of goods and support. Most old people prefer to live apart from their children. The most common household arrangements are the married couple or widowed person living alone (Streib, 1977). Further, the family of three and four generations is more common than ever today due to the numerical and proportional increase in the elderly population (Brody, 1979; Sussman, 1968). In turn, the modified extended family often includes two categories of the elderly, the young-old and the old-old.

Information relevant to family psychology and to the aged originated in a number of disciplines and professions. Research in the psychology of aging families is rare (Hoyer, Raskind, & Abrahams, 1984). Research in other fields has been skewed toward the isolated aged and individual adjustment. Nevertheless, within the last 15 years, a considerable body of literature has emerged on family life of the elderly.

This chapter provides a systematic and critical review of roles, relationships, and events characteristic of family life in the later years.[1] Retirement is regarded as the transition to old age. Marital relations, parent–adult child relations, and grandparenting are examined as the primary roles for the older adult. Widowhood is viewed as the major event in the family life cycle. Family dysfunctioning will mainly include late-onset problems. The final section presents information on methods of family intervention.

RETIREMENT TRANSITIONS

For most American families, retirement represents a transition to old age. The majority of adults retire, and the trend in recent years has been toward voluntary, early retirement (Atchley, 1983). While retirement is by definition a sought-after reward for a life of work, it has been characterized as a negative status (Atchley, 1977a; Cohen & Gans, 1978; S. J. Miller, 1965; Rosow, 1974). Research has shown that the loss of the work role and related changes accompanying retirement are not as problematic as once predicted. Further, retirement has been shown not to be responsible for the problems of old age (Palmore, Fillenbaum, & George, 1984; Streib & Schneider, 1971). Generally, after an adjustment period, retirement for most couples is a pleasant and rewarding phase of life.

Couples are retired when neither member holds full-time employment and when the family receives a retirement income (Atchley, 1983). Retirement is typically a family decision and a family event. It usually involves a rite of passage that includes family members. Retirement brings increased opportunities for family interaction within the nuclear and the extended family (Troll, 1971; Troll et al., 1979). Adjustment to retirement and life satisfaction are markedly affected by the family situation, health, income, employment history, and attitudes toward retirement.

A popular notion holds that most retirement results from mandatory retirement policies, but the percentage of mandatory retirements is actually small (Atchley, 1983). Yet, it is common for employers to use subtle and direct pressures to induce retirement, and mandatory retire-

---

[1] Extensive references are provided throughout the chapter for the reader desiring more in-depth information on the areas discussed.

ment policies often have a pervasive, indirect effect on retirement decisions. Retirement is an economic decision even though it is a social event. Atchley (1983) reports that most people "retire as soon as it is financially feasible."

The majority of people retire around the age of 65. It was once thought that poor health was a major reason for retiring, but this has recently been disputed for those over age 65. Palmore, George, and Fillenbaum's (1982) secondary analysis on data from five studies reports that health is a relatively unimportant reason. Early retirement has been shown to be related to poor health (Atchley, 1983; Palmore et al., 1982; Palmore et al., 1984). Perhaps family pressures to retire are often based on concerns about health rather than on health per se.

The retirement transition brings a major change in family life. The husband usually becomes more involved in household activities (Dressler, 1973; Troll, 1971). A blending of male-female roles usually occurs along with an increased egalitarian approach to home-life responsibilities. In general, as the adjustment to the retirement progresses, women become more instrumental and assertive and men more expressive and nurturing (Weishaus, 1979; Williamson, Evans, & Munley, 1980).

Withdrawal from work reduces contact and relationships associated with jobs and careers. Couples usually shift toward one another, and there is greater opportunity for expressive roles for both partners (Troll, 1971). Mutually acceptable and enjoyable friendships and leisurely activities tend to be increased. Greater flexibility to visit and interact with adult children and siblings is afforded. The future-orientation characteristic of early and middle years gives way to more short-term planning of activities.

While most couples feel unprepared for retirement and a difficult adjustment period is frequently reported, there is eventual satisfaction with retirement (Dressler, 1973). However, adjustment problems are reported by researchers who have examined subgroups of the population. Upon retirement, work-oriented men in particular experience low morale (Lowenthal & Robinson, 1976). For men who resist the adoption of expressive roles and greater participation in household tasks, self-esteem may suffer. For example, Kerckhoff (1966) found that positive adjustment to retirement was reported by men who frequently participated in family activities. Women whose sense of importance has rested upon control over the household may be threatened by a spouse's increased involvement in home activities (Williamson et al., 1980). These problems are found mainly in lower socioeconomic classes and for traditional couples. Marital conflict and tension could be expected under these circumstances. Research has not revealed strong evidence of marital discord during the retirement transition, but most research is based on self-report data.

The family's retirement transition usually begins before the retirement event and can last from three months to three years. Once a new lifestyle is established with modified patterns of leisure and social responsibilities, the family has entered another stage of life. The goal for the family is to make changes and adjustments that will facilitate a smooth transition to old age. Continued growth and development with high life satisfaction are realistic expectations for this stage.

MARITAL RELATIONS

In 1981, 77 percent of the men 65 years old and older were married, while only 38 percent of the women 65 and over were married (U.S. Department of HHS, 1981). Increasing proportions of married couples are surviving as two-person families after the last child has left home. More than a third of older people are married and live with their spouses in separate households.

The literature on married life during the later years shows that there is likely to be increased companionship and emotional satisfaction (Steere, 1981), contributing to increased marital satisfaction. Such reports should be studied carefully, however. Data on marital relations of those 65 and over are based on a sample highly biased for survival and also include people who have remarried (Troll, 1971; Troll et al., 1979). Couples who do not grow old together self-eliminate from studies through death, divorce, desertion, or separation. Couples' interpretations of their experiences may also distort information: The longer a couple has remained together, the greater their investment in perceiving their relationship as meaningful and satisfying (Hess & Waring, 1978). Married couples who do survive and enter old age find new situations awaiting them. Most of these situations tend to be normal life events that have an impact on family lifestyles and relations and require readjustment (Bumagin & Hirn, 1982).

Marital satisfaction

Marriage tends to be the focal point in the lives of most older people who have a living spouse (Atchley, 1977b). One factor that researchers have studied in relation to marital satisfaction in later life is sex of spouse. The research results in this area are inconclusive. While most studies have reported differences according to sex (e.g., Lurie, 1974; Stinnett, Collins, & Montgomery, 1970), others have not (e.g., Rollins & Cannon, 1974). Perhaps these differences in marital satisfaction are due to the varied expectations, beliefs, and attitudes individuals have regarding marriage.

Social class and economic status have also been identified as being related to marital satisfaction. Reports of low marital satisfaction tend to be more prevalent among couples of low socioeconomic status (Williamson et al., 1980). Expressed marital satisfaction among old persons tends to rise with socioeconomic status. However, Maas and Kuypers' (1974) data did not support this conclusion. Their longitudinal study included 47 upper middle class couples between 60 and 82 years of age. A rather large percentage of the men in the sample showed low involvement and low satisfaction with the marital relationship.

Another factor affecting marital satisfaction is the past coping ability of each spouse. Those individuals who had the greatest trouble with transitions to adolescence, young adulthood, and middle age tend to have the most trouble with later transitions such as retirement, widowhood, and disabilities (Bumagin & Hirn, 1982; Lowenthal, 1977; Maas & Kuypers, 1974). Conversely, other people experience these same transitions as usual life events and opportunities for growth.

Numerous studies have investigated stages of adult life and marital relations (Blood & Wolfe, 1960; Lopata, 1960; Lowenthal, Thurnher, & Chiriboga, 1975; Taylor, 1964). In a review of these studies, Atchley (1977b) concluded that marriage is a source of great comfort and support for the happily married older couple and that they often express an increasing closeness over the years. As the marriage progresses, there is an increased level of interdependence and relaxation of sex role expectations, particularly in case of illness or feebleness of both partners. The partners will then perform those tasks they can manage best, regardless of sex role (Steere, 1981; Troll, 1971; Troll et al., 1979).

Sexuality of older couples

The pervasive myth that sexual expression, activity, and enjoyment are reserved for the early years of life permeates all age groups (Aiken, 1980; Cleveland, 1976; Friedeman, 1978; Hendricks & Hendricks, 1981; Hyde, 1982). However, sex is an important aspect of older couples' relationships. Kinsey, Pomeroy, and Martin (1948, 1953) documented continued sexual interest and activity past the age of 80. More recent studies have also reported continued sexual interest and activity among older people (Masters & Johnson, 1968; Pfeiffer, Verwoerdt, & Wang, 1969). The loss of interest in sexual activities that does occur with increased age is primarily among widowed, divorced, and single women.

There is a continuity to the pattern of sexual expression from earlier years to old age (Christenson & Gagnon, 1975; Kaplan, 1974; Masters & Johnson, 1966). However, adjustments in these patterns may be required as both partners experience physiological changes. A large number of older people lack understanding of these changes (Friedeman, 1978). The result may be sexual problems that do not confront younger couples (Atchley, 1977b).

In the later years, men are slower to achieve an erection, produce less volume of ejaculate, and have a less-forceful ejaculation (Cleveland, 1976). Their responses are slower, but there is no functional change (Pengelley, 1974). Women who do not understand these physiological changes or the reasons behind them may interpret them as a lack of interest.

The changes in women are not as obvious as those in men. Older women tend to experience a delay in the reaction of the clitoris to direct stimulation, a lower intensity of orgasm, and less lubrication during excitement (Cleveland, 1976). There are no physiological mandates that might place the sexually active female at risk in old age. In fact, hormonal changes may result in an increased sexual interest.

Unless the elderly know about the changes that occur with age, they may hold unrealistic expectations for their sexual performance, misinterpreting the physiological changes. Although physiological disabilities and changes may lessen sexual activities, the prevalence of negative stereotypes are even greater constraints to continued sexual expression. There are a wide variety of erotic activities and alternate forms of sexual expression that can be used to compensate for these normal developments (Cleveland, 1976).

Divorce

Most older marriages are broken by death rather than by divorce (Butler & Lewis, 1982; Williamson et al., 1980). While the divorce rate in the second half of life (as in all age groups) has increased, the divorce rate of the elderly remains far below that of younger cohorts. Therefore, being divorced in old age is still a relatively uncommon experience (U.S. Bureau of the Census, 1979). In 1975, only 1 percent of all divorces were for people aged 65 and over.

The older generations of today grew up in a time when marriage was a lifetime commitment. Once, couples felt obligated to stay together even if they were highly incompatible and unhappy. Now, a reversal in general attitudes may have occurred, resulting in a belief that marriages that are not happy should be terminated (Troll et al., 1979). This increased emphasis on the voluntary nature of marital relationships contributes to an expectation that the divorce rate for those over age 65 will rise substantially. Other factors that may contribute to this phenomenon include: *(a)* an increase in the proportion of the elderly who will be in second or higher-order marriages; *(b)* cohorts entering old age in the future are likely to be much more accepting of divorce; *(c)* increasing economic independence of women; and *(d)* the reduction in mortality rates at earlier ages ("Experience exchange," 1983; Uhlenberg & Myers, 1981).

Chiriboga (1982) found the vulnerability of older persons to the process of divorce to be considerable. Family and kinship relationships are particularly at risk (Uhlenberg & Myers, 1981). Marriage partners lose a spouse who, at some point in time, was a source of emotional and physical support. Adult children, often forced to take sides, may avoid one or both parents (Troll et al., 1979). This may involve a withdrawal of emotional as well as other types of support. Communication may become strained and tense, increasing the stress accompanying divorce. All family members may suffer from the stigma of divorce and a sense of personal failure. On the other hand, divorce may facilitate improved family relationships if viewed as a resolution to overwhelming, lifelong conflicts and may prepare individuals to deal with future losses.

Remarriage

Remarriage of the elderly, after the death or divorce of a spouse, does occur with some frequency (Butler & Lewis, 1982), even though the remarriage rate is reported to have been declining since 1967 (Uhlenberg & Myers, 1981). Older men are more likely to remarry than older women (Glick, 1979; H. Lopata, 1978; Treas, 1975). Not only are older men greatly outnumbered by older women, but they also tend to marry women younger than themselves. This gives men a much larger field from which to choose (Butler & Lewis; Troll et al., 1979). This sex ratio greatly affects marrying in later life (Atchley, 1977b). For example, in 1976, almost twice as many older men married than did older women, yet women outnumbered men by 4.6 million (Butler & Lewis).

Late marriages appear to enjoy substantial success (Williamson et al., 1980). This seems to be especially true in couples where the partners had known each other for a period of years before the marriage. Personal adaptability and financial factors also influence the likelihood of success for late-life marriages (Atchley, 1977b; Troll et al., 1979).

Approval of the marriage by children and friends is important to the success of marriage in later life. Their positive support is needed to offset the apparent social pressure exerted against these marriages (Atchley, 1977b). However, children from an earlier marriage may have negative attitudes, particularly if they believe a parent is being taken advantage of, acting foolishly, or endangering their inheritance (Butler & Lewis, 1982; Treas, 1975). In cases where the parent is widowed, children may feel that remarriage is a betrayal of the deceased parent.

Many children actively encourage parents to find new lives for themselves through remarriage (Butler & Lewis, 1982). These children recognize the parent's need for companionship and independence and recognize their own need for privacy. Furthermore, these "children" may be middle aged (or young-old), dealing with their own life cycle events (Gelfand, Olsen, & Block, 1978). Remarriage of the parent may afford them more time for these events.

ELDERLY PARENTS AND ADULT CHILDREN

An increasing proportion of the population today is likely to have an aging parent (Treas, 1977, 1979). These "children" are the main source of support to the elderly (U.S. Department of HHS, 1981). About 82 percent of all older persons have living children (Brody, 1979; Johnson & Bursk, 1977; Shanas, 1979). Of those over 65 who have children, approximately 10 percent have children who are also over 65 (Atchley, 1977b; Butler & Lewis, 1982; Troll et al., 1979).

Research to date presents a confusing picture with regard to the importance of offspring in elderly persons' psychological adjustment to aging. Results of some studies (e.g., Davidson & Cotter, 1982) suggest offspring play a significant role in their parents' adjustment. Glenn and McLanahan (1981) stated that "one might suspect that the primary rewards derived from having children typically come during and after late middle age. People may tend to enjoy their offspring more when it no longer entails parental responsibilities" (p. 410). Yet, they provisionally concluded that having had children had no important effects on the psychological well-being of older Americans.

Research has typically examined elder parent-adult child relationships in terms of quantitative variables such as frequency of visits. Only in more recent years have researchers (Beckman, 1981; Davidson & Cotter, 1982; Quinn, 1983) incorporated qualitative variables into their research. It is necessary to examine both in attempts to understand variables that affect elder parent–adult child relationships.

Residential proximity

The widely held belief that in contemporary American society old people are alienated from their families, particularly their children, is simply a myth (Shanas, 1979; Streib, 1977). One hypothesis deriving from this myth is that most old people who have children live at great distances from them. It has been proven, however, that in the U.S. most elderly people live close to at least one child and visit often (Shanas).

Almost all of the surveys conducted on residential proximity show that older people prefer to live in their own homes but near their children (Hess & Waring, 1978; Steere, 1981; Streib, 1977). In fact, both younger and older adults express a clear preference for separate households (Shanas, 1979; Sussman, 1968; Troll et al., 1979). Elderly people want to be independent, and their children want to have privacy.

The proportion of old people with children has remained unchanged over the last 20 years. The proportion of old people living in the same household with one of their children has declined, but an increased number live within 10 minutes distance of a child (Shanas, 1979). Of people 65 and older who live with a child, more are likely to live with an unmarried child than with a married one; more with a daughter (54 percent) than with a son (35 percent); and the parent tends to be the head of household (Mindel & Wright, 1982; Troll et al., 1979).

Frequency of parent-child interaction

Among all of the relationships within the family network, contacts with adult offspring appear to be the most frequent (Quinn, 1983). Among older parents not living with a child, Shanas (1979) found that 62 percent had seen a child within the last 24 hours, and 75 percent had seen one within the last week. This frequent contact may be partially explained by evidence that contact with children, especially daughters, is important to satisfy elderly parents' economic, emotional, and service needs (Beckman, 1981; Treas, 1977).

The patterns of frequent interaction among generations of adult family members living independently has been referred to as a modified extended family system (Bromberg, 1983; Litwak, 1965; Troll, 1971). This type of extended kin network in which parents and children are in regular and frequent contact with one another is a fundamental part of intergenerational relations (Streib, 1977; Sussman, 1968). Sustaining meaningful relationships in the absence of frequent interaction (intimacy at a distance) and reestablishing emotional ties when needed or desired (revocable detachment) have also been used to describe other patterns of intergenerational relations (Rosenmayr & Kockeis, 1963).

Contact with children tends to have little effect on an older person's life satisfaction; under some conditions, it may have a negative effect.[2] It has been suggested that since current social policy absolves adult children of caring for their aging parents, ties are now essentially voluntary.

Contact with other people appears to be much more closely associated with psychological well-being of the elderly than does contact with children. Arling (1976) found that contact with family, especially

---

[2] For a summary of studies investigating the effect contact with children has on elderly parents, see Adams (1971) and Larson (1978).

children, showed no correlation with measures of morale for widows aged 65 to 85. Lee (1979) concluded from his data that the morale of aging parents is not consistently or significantly affected by frequency of contact with children. Finally, Beckman's (1981) results supported that the qualitative nature of a relationship is more important than mere frequency of contact. She suggested that quality of contact with nonchildren contributes more substantially to well-being than mere contact with a child. Conversely, Davidson and Cotter (1982) indicated that offspring play a significant role in their parents' adjustment to aging.

Mutual aid and support

With the existence of a modified kin network in American society has emerged a practice which supports older members and binds generations by choice. There are also various patterns of mutual aid (Bromberg, 1983). This mutual aid is a complex pattern of interaction and social exchange (George, 1980). It may be in the form of emotional support, services, money, or goods (Bromberg; Troll et al., 1979). Sex, marital status, social class, and health variables of both generations may affect the type of aid exchanged. For example, adult children with broken marriages provide less help to their elderly parents than do adult children with intact marriages (Cicirelli, 1983). In the middle class, aid continues to flow from old parents to middle-aged children (Shanas, Townsend, Wedderburn, Friis, Milhøj, & Stehouver, 1968). Indeed, the flow of support between generations is bidirectional. Interdependent, rather than dependent, is a more descriptive way of describing mutual-aid patterns in later life (Bromberg).

The stereotype generally envisioned is the elderly parent dependent on young-old or middle-aged children. The term *dependency* is associated with problems and has become a source of shame and guilt (Schwartz, 1979). There has been a tendency socially to induce dependency of the elderly by labeling them as chronically ill, treating them as sick, and expecting behaviors that fit our generalized stereotype of old age (Schwartz).

A portion of the early research on intergenerational family relationships was based on the underlying assumption that the aging parent was competent only to a certain point in the life span, at which time there was a reverting to childlike behaviors. The adult child then assumes the role of parent to his or her own parents—a role reversal (Gelfand et al., 1978; Glasser & Glasser, 1962). However, this phenomenon does not always occur. When role reversal does occur, it is not a reversal of parenting one's children, so the same rules are not applicable (Schwartz, 1979). Further, Blenkner (1965) and Bromberg (1983) hold that role reversal is a pathological rather than a normal development.

Blenkner (1965) views adult children's supportive behavior as a new phase in the developmental sequence which she called "filial maturity." It is a psychological state in which the adult child accepts a personal sense of adult maturity and, at the same time, accepts parents or older relatives as colleagues who may need or give support in a relationship of mutual aid. The development of filial maturity is a reciprocal process in which both the parent and child must cooperate (Brody, 1979; Quinn, 1983; Troll, 1971).

Quality of relationships

Johnson and Bursk (1977) delineated several factors related to the quality of family relationships. Elder parents and adult children rated their relationships as being of high quality when based on similar values, mutual respect, trust, and realistic perceptions. Overall, relationships were perceived as best when they were with parents who were in better health, not restricted in choice of daily activities, and independent.

Quinn (1983) developed a theoretical model of qualitative dimensions for relationships between older parents and adult children. His sample included 143 intergenerational family dyads, and he used expert judges to modify instrument items. Test-retest reliability coefficients showed higher reliability for children than for parents. Quality of relationship had the second strongest direct effect upon psychological well-being of aged parents. Highly correlated with quality of relationship were affection, communication, and consensus. Since the affection variable comprised elements of trust, respect, understanding, and fairness, it may be that the prior state and development of the parent-child relationship is important in determining the present relationship quality. The belief was also confirmed that effective communication enhances the quality of relationships as perceived by parents and children.

Finally, Quinn (1983) observed that filial responsibilities seem to directly influence the quality of the relationship. Thus, adult children who have developed a genuine commitment to their parents' aging experiences may have attitudes conducive to strong family bonds. This, in turn, may enhance the parents' feelings of satisfaction with children.

GRANDPARENTHOOD

Grandparenthood is a common role transition in midlife and later life. Approximately 94 percent of persons over 65 with living children are grandparents, and 46 percent are great-grandparents (Butler & Lewis, 1982). Only about 5 percent of the households headed by older people contain grandchildren (Atchley, 1977b), but nearly half of all American grandparents see a grandchild frequently.

Grandparents are usually free to choose the style of interaction they wish to have with their grandchildren (Troll, 1980a). These interactions seem to be characterized more by ethnic or personality-determined behaviors. In addition, because grandparents have neither formal authority nor responsibility for their grandchildren, they are able to interact more freely with them than are parents (Robertson, 1977).

Robertson (1977) found grandparenting to be enjoyed by grandmothers. Neugarten and Weinstein (1964) concluded that most grandmothers and grandfathers are comfortable in these roles and express pleasure and satisfaction. However, at least one third of their respondents reported the role as being uncomfortable, disappointing, or unrewarding. Reasons for these feelings included the strain associated with recognition of self as a grandparent, conflict with parents over childrearing, and guilt regarding ambivalence over child-care responsibilities. Some older people have reported that being a grandparent had little effect on them or that they felt removed from their grandchildren (Cumming & Henry, 1961; Neugarten & Weinstein). Collectively, these findings indicate that being a grandparent has the potential of either enriching or impoverishing generational relationships (Kivnick, 1982).

Another aspect of grandparenting is the value of the role to the individual. Robertson (1977), in her study on grandmothers, found the most important factor affecting role salience to be lifestyle. Grandparents' own grandchild experiences also contribute to role meaning. Kivnick (1982) conducted one of the few studies that include grandfathers as well as grandmothers in addition to using quantitative and qualitative analysis. Her findings suggested that a meaningful experience as a grandchild and the existence of a favorite grandparent during childhood are associated with a positive grandparenthood experience. These associations are greater for women than for men. Kivnick also suggested that grandparenthood-related experience may be viewed as contributing to psychological well-being.

Some attention has been given to the value that grandchildren have for grandparents and the kinds of gratification grandchildren provide. One study of grandmothers revealed that grandchildren expanded the self beyond one's own lifetime; filled a need for creativity, accomplishment, and competence; reconfirmed their social identities as women; and represented useful work (grandparenting) which provided structure and stability for their lives (Timberlake, 1980). The value of grandchildren to grandmothers differed significantly according to geographical and social proximity. It was suggested that those grandmothers providing child care have a strong personal commitment to their grand-children. The research design and sampling strategy limit generalizability (Timberlake). However, similar kinds of gratification were cited by Neugarten and Weinstein (1964).

Interactions shared by grandparents and grandchildren appear to be greatly influenced by the parents. They serve as mediators in the relationship. They may transfer their attitudes and behaviors toward their parents to their children, thus facilitating or hindering interactions and the bonds between grandparents and grandchildren (Robertson, 1975). Grandparenting activities also seem to be influenced by parental attitudes. Robertson (1977) found that the only behaviors in which grandmothers engaged with high frequency were those initiated by the parent or child. She speculated grandparents may fear that parents view a high frequency of behavior with grandchildren as meddlesome, intrusive, or inappropriate.

A variety of styles of grandparenting have been delineated. Major studies making distinctions in styles include Neugarten and Weinstein (1964), Wood and Robertson (1976), and Robertson (1977). Neugarten and Weinstein identified five styles: *(a)* formal; *(b)* fun-seeker; *(c)* surrogate parent; *(d)* reservoir of family wisdom; and *(e)* distant figure. Few respondents in their study served primarily as reservoirs of family wisdom. Furthermore, few grandparents actually served as surrogate parents, as they did not want to resume parenting activities with their grandchildren (Cumming & Henry, 1961; Lopata, 1973). This style of grandparenting is determined more by necessity than by choice (Neugarten & Weinstein). Researchers also found an age difference in styles. For example, young grandparents had more diverse styles than older ones, the latter usually being formal and distant (Neugarten & Weinstein).

WIDOWHOOD

The death of a spouse presents a major psychological insult. It is highly stressful and disruptive, requiring more readjustment than any other event in life (Barrett, 1979; Cohen & Gans, 1978; George, 1980; Silverstone & Hyman, 1976). Grief and bereavement initially follow a spouse's death and may continue indefinitely. Silverman (1972) suggests that it is more accurate to think of making an adjustment rather than a recovery.

Parkes (1972) has identified four stages of grief that often occur after a death. The first stage, *numbness*, includes shock and denial followed by dread, panic, emotional outbursts, and physical reactions to grief. The second stage is *pining*. At this point, the surviving spouse has a persistent yearning for the loved one, accompanied by anxiety, restlessness, and fear. The third stage, *depression,* brings feelings of defeat and submission, and apathetic withdrawal. This is followed by *recovery,* the fourth and final stage. There are three major tasks to be accomplished at this stage: *(a)* accept the loss intellectually; *(b)* accept the loss emotionally; and *(c)* change one's self-image in relation to the world.

Widowed persons turn to relatives, especially their children (usually daughters), for support and interaction more frequently than they turn to friends (Bumagin & Hirn, 1982; Glick, Weiss, & Parkes, 1974; Lopata, 1973). Adult sons provide the most help in the immediate planning of funerals and other arrangements, while adult daughters provide crucial emotional supports. Daughters tend to provide companionship, emotional outlets, and homemaking services (Treas, 1977).

Family supports may not always be adequate. Bankoff (1983) found that widows received more support from their children than from any other single source, but that support did not appear to make a difference in their psychological well-being. Supports may also be problematic, as children are dealing with their own grief. This may be compounded by an unresolved conflict they had with the deceased or by anger at the loss of the preferred parent, a factor that may intensify the ambivalence toward the surviving parent (Bumagin & Hirn, 1982).

Problems associated with widowhood range from immediate instrumental concerns to emotional, health, and economic problems. Regardless of the types of problems widowed individuals face, most eventually attain acceptable and even satisfying levels of adjustment (George, 1980). Parkes (1972) viewed the multiple factors affecting adjustment and contributing to the outcome of bereavement within a time frame. His three categories were: antecedent factors, such as life crises prior to the death; concurrent factors, including the sex and age of the surviving spouse; and subsequent factors, such as social supports and isolation.[3]

In efforts to adjust to the status of widowhood, a variety of coping methods are employed. When coping with economic problems, a person may reduce spending. The elderly tend to reduce spending for clothing, social and recreational activities, and food (Barrett, 1979; Morgan, 1979). Widows often seek employment to alleviate financial stress, while widowers are more apt to curtail expenditures, particularly for medical care (Balkwell, 1981).

Loneliness is accepted as accompanying the loss of a spouse. Remar-

---

[3] For information on these and other factors, see Balkwell (1981); Barrett (1979); George (1980); Glick, Weiss, and Parkes, (1978); Hiltz (1978); Kivett (1978); Loether (1975); Lopata (1973, 1978); and Morgan (1979).

riage is an option chosen by a minority of the elderly to dispel feelings of loneliness. To enable them to move into new relationships, widows and widowers need to express and cope with loyalties, obligations, and guilts generated from the past marriage (Moss & Moss, 1980). Glick et al. (1974) found that those who chose to remarry had been able to work through grief for the former spouse and establish satisfying marriages. Others organize their lives around an intimate relationship that does not lead to remarriage (George, 1980). Having a confidant, someone to share intimate thoughts and feelings with, also provides a buffer to loneliness (Balkwell, 1981).

Much attention has been focused on widowhood regardless of age, and a variety of formal support systems have been established. These range from the widow-to-widow program to formal therapy programs.[4] These programs are designed to help those who have lost a spouse move through the grief process, identify sources of information or assistance, and share experiences with others who have had similar experiences. While many of the widowed benefit from formal support, not every widowed person needs this type of assistance.

FAMILY DYSFUNCTIONING

As in other stages of life, a large number of old people have serious problems in living which require direct intervention. An important distinction should be made between continuity and stage-specific problems of individuals and families. Many families bring to old age problems, pathologies, and stresses that have existed for some time. Amster and Krauss (1974), using the geriatric social readjustment scale, found that mental deterioration after 65 was related to the frequency and intensity of earlier life crises.

Stage-specific problems which seem to materialize or become problematic for the first time in later life are usually referred to as "late onset" problems (Giordano & Beckham, 1983; Gutmann, Grunes, & Griffin, 1980). These problems may have existed at a manageable level in previous stages but emerged or reemerged under the changes related to later life. In other instances, there may be unique variations of problems common to earlier stages but with different causes, such as in depression (Eisdorfer & Cohen, 1978). This discussion of family dysfunctioning will focus mainly on stage-specific conditions and on extrinsic causal factors.

The dynamics of family ties and bonding provide the context for personal adjustment and maladjustment in later life. Cohler (1983)

---

[4] For a more detailed description of formal support programs, see Balkwell (1981); Hiltz (1978); Silverman (1972); Toth and Toth (1980).

offers three psychological perspectives of the development of social ties that point to a conflict between the needs for autonomy and dependency expectations. Troll (1980b), taking a systems approach to families, suggests that interaction will be determined by the shared family theme and value systems. Scherz (1971) offers a crisis approach to the understanding of family problems and identifies psychological tasks, such as self-autonomy versus responsibilities, that can produce problems unique to later stages of life. Psychiatric research at Northwestern University used naturalistic inquiry to document continued psychological development into old age, and it focused attention on later-life psychoses for childless older women (Gutmann et al., 1980).

Family problems

Family relationships that foster autonomy, minimize the loss of independence, and make adjustments for new roles produce a satisfying later life (Brody, 1979; Steere, 1981). Quinn (1983) found that other than health, the quality of relationships had the strongest effect upon psychological well-being. However, the presence of family conflict and unresolved crises often result in problems for, and victimization of, older individuals (Block & Sinnott, 1979; Busse & Pfeiffer, 1977b; Lau & Kosberg, 1979; Steinmetz, 1983; Viano, 1983). Scherz (1971) holds that caretaking roles of many older children arouse old conflicts about dependency, achievement, and separation. Simos (1973) found that the added stress of old age exacerbated old defensive patterns of parent-child conflicts. It has also been suggested that elderly with unmet expectations of their children will experience more disappointment and lower psychological well-being (Brody, 1970; Quinn, 1983; Seelbach, 1978). For elderly women, midlife family responsibilities extended into later life are a source of stress and decreasing life satisfaction (Cohler, 1983).

Marital discord resulting from changing roles, weak bonding, and unmet needs is a major source of stress for older couples. Often, as the woman shifts to more autonomy and independence, the male experiences emotional problems (Gutmann et al., 1980). Long-term marital discord characterized by hopefulness for resolution during middle years may turn to hopelessness in later years. Marital discord may emerge for the first time as partners realize that the interpersonal patterns and behaviors established in earlier stages are unsatisfying for later life (Bumagin & Hirn, 1982; Troll et al., 1979).

When one spouse becomes a caretaker, the stress of that role has strong implications for both partners. Indeed, a spouse is the most frequent abuser in the most common types (physical and psychological) of elder abuse (N. H. Giordano & Giordano, 1983). Illness can often

reverse long-standing behavior patterns. The dominant spouse may become ill and, for the first time, rely heavily on the more dependent mate (Silverstone & Hyman, 1976).

Family functioning is dramatically affected by losses that characterize the life of aging adults. These losses represent changes that require energy and adjustment. Family responses and support will greatly affect the individual's adjustment. Most families, upon retirement, realize a reduction of income. Often, additional losses (such as loss of friends, status, and community leadership positions) occur during the transition period of retirement. Even more stressful losses occur with the death of friends, relatives, and spouse.

Many adults enter old age with a chronic health problem, and most will develop one or more serious health problems before death. These problems often result in a loss of independence and a feeling of anxiety about becoming a burden on others. Confusion and ambivalent expectations of family members are common, for family members are expected to provide help with personal affairs, financial problems, household activities, transportation, and personal care (Glick et al., 1974; Lau & Kosberg, 1979; Lopata, 1973; Neugarten, 1979). Mindel and Wright (1982), who devised and tested a theoretical causal model of family life satisfaction for the multigenerational household, found that the more dependent elderly had less life satisfaction. The individual's response to declining control over one's life often includes maladaptive behavior such as resignation and alcohol abuse. Further, dependencies induced by losses render the older adult extremely vulnerable to all types of abuse by others (Douglas, Hickey, & Noel, 1980; O'Rourke, 1981).

Some older adults experience multiple losses that occur simultaneously. The feelings of dependency, loss of control, and depression bring about a deep sense of futility. This response, often called "learned helplessness," results in further loss of autonomy and independence (Davidson, Hennessey, & Sedge, 1979; Seligman, 1974). Professional and family attitudes that convey an "irreversible loss" or an "it's just old age" perspective contribute to learned helplessness (Cormican, 1980; Gutman et al., 1980).

Family gerontological research has not satisfactorily identified predictors of maladjustment for individuals without a history of adjustment problems. Part of the difficulty is the confusion regarding cause and effect and the interaction between precipitating events and behavior. For example, is social isolation a result of depression, or is depression the consequence of social isolation and loneliness? One point of view is that serious psychological problems, negative consequences (such as victimization), and increased complications of physical health are manifestations of negative family events characteristic of this stage

(Busse & Pfeiffer, 1977b). With this viewpoint in mind, the literature concerning depression, elder abuse, and alcohol abuse will be reviewed.[5]

Depression

Depression is the most frequent emotional problem experienced by the elderly. The incidence of depression is the highest for those between 55 and 70 years old (Gurland, 1976). Depression is not found only among mental health patients and those who have had a previous episode but also among the elderly who are experiencing life-limiting symptoms of depression for the first time (Botwinick, 1978; Busse & Pfeiffer, 1977b; Lipton, 1976). At the same time, families and friends, while aware of mood changes in an individual, are not likely to be experienced in coping with or counteracting many forms of later-life depression.

Generally, depression is an affective (mood) problem rather than a thought disorder. However, depression as a concept is far too broad to be useful. The confusion, lack of consensus among professionals, and disagreements surrounding the categorization of depression are evident throughout the literature, especially when depression in later life is examined (Botwinick, 1978; Epstein, 1976; Gurland, 1976). Therefore, use of traditional psychiatric nomenclature seems to be of limited value in diagnosing depression in later life.

Where normal depression ends and a psychological illness begins is less important to the understanding of depression than the extent of disruption to everyday life. Classifying depression as endogenous and exogenous has some utility in understanding this phenomenon as it relates to the aged population. Endogenous depression results from internal causes such as guilt, self-hatred, and unresolved conflicts. It is often associated with severe depression, clinically identifiable symptoms, the likelihood of institutionalization, and difficulty of treatment. Severe depression is more likely when a serious physical problem is present (Dovenmuehle & Verwoerdt, 1963). Endogenous depression forms represent a small percentage of depression experienced by the elderly (Gurland, 1976). Since endogenous types often require hospitalization and psychiatric medication, this condition severely limits interaction with family members.

Exogenous depression, on the other hand, is caused by extrinsic life events, such as the unique age-related stresses. The more common

---

[5] Space will not permit discussion of all the mental health and social pathology related to old age in the family. For authoritative texts, see Busse and Pfeiffer (1973, 1977a); Butler and Lewis (1982); and Kosberg (1983).

terms are *reactive depression* or *neurotic depression* (Epstein, 1976; Jarvik, 1976), but they do not correspond precisely. Considerably more knowledge has been amassed about endogenous (severe) depression than exogenous (reactive) depression (Lipton, 1976), since research on the latter requires examination of the general population rather than clinical samples. The elderly person with reactive depression typically will be apathetic, listless, and engage in self-depreciation while less likely to report guilt and anger (Busse & Pfeiffer, 1977b; Epstein, 1976). This form of depression can seriously disrupt individual and family functioning.[6]

Reactive depression may produce emotional symptoms and somatic complaints; but with the elderly, it is often difficult to distinguish between normal grief, temporary adjustment reactions, and more problematic depression (Patterson, 1978). Dunkle (1983) researched a sizable sample of families with an elder in the household. Using multiple regression analysis, she found the contributions to the household resulted in a reduction of depression of older members and that depression diminished as length of time in the residence increased.

Recognition and diagnosis of depression in the elderly is complicated by many factors. Some authorities are concerned about underdiagnosis of depression; however, there is evidence that labeling can be detrimental (Epstein, 1976). Of greater concern has been the extent of inaccurate diagnoses by attributing symptoms of depression to senility, physical illness, or impaired mental functioning (Butler & Lewis, 1982; Epstein, 1976). In addition, the elderly themselves are resistant to revealing symptoms of depression other than somatic complaints.

The influence of environmental stress and the family on later-life depression should not be underestimated (Epstein, 1976; Mendelwicz, 1976). Reactive depression for the aged (as is true of younger counterparts) is episodic, has a tendency to remit, and can be successfully treated with interpersonal techniques, although treatment approaches will differ (Botwinick, 1978; Busse & Pfeiffer, 1977b; Epstein, 1976). Gallagher and Thompson (1983) investigated the effectiveness of brief psychotherapies on elderly depressed outpatients and found that nonendogenous patients responded more favorably than endogenous patients. For the most part, treatment approaches have not included family members as an integral part of the treatment program.

Elder abuse

For elderly who require care and assistance, the primary provider is a family member. Research on family violence and neglect has

---

[6] For instruments used with the elderly to measure depression and stress of life events, see Beck, Ward, Mendelson, Mock, and Erbaugh (1961); Hamilton (1967); Horowitz and Wilner (1980); and Zung (1965).

brought to light the extent of domestic abuse involving the elderly
(Block & Sinnott, 1979; Lau & Kosberg, 1979). Elder abuse in its most
extreme form consists of a dependent old person being "cared for"
and actively abused physically in the home of a relative (O'Rourke,
1981). In its most common and less-dramatic form, abuse includes exploitation, neglect, and psychological mistreatment.

The aging of the population and the trend toward deinstitutionaliza-
tion will increase the number of family members who will care for
their relatives at home. For families where there is conflict, the extra
demands of caring for an elder can lead to abuse and neglect. The
consensus of a number of studies is that older females who are mentally
or physically impaired are the most likely victims and that the abuser
is usually a middle-aged female offspring (Douglas & Hickey, 1983;
N. H. Giordano & Giordano, 1984).

Steinmetz (1983) studied abuse, using a structured interview to obtain information from adult children who were caring for an elderly
relative. She found that about 20 percent of the care givers were 60
years old or older, but that the majority were in midlife and caught
between two or more generations. These middle-aged adult children
are sometimes referred to as the "sandwich generation." According
to Miller (1981), this generation is confronted with loss of youth, recognition of their own aging, the impact of the empty nest, as well as
the stresses of dual responsibilities. The care-giver role can become
overwhelming, especially when crises occur simultaneously for several
members of the family.

Research on elder abuse is in an elementary stage, and most studies
have sought to generate causal hypotheses. Douglas and Hickey (1983)
present a review and summary of research published through 1980.
Close examination of this review reveals that most data have been
obtained by surveying professionals who recall information about elder
abuse. The largest direct case study involved only 39 individuals (Block
& Sinnott, 1979).

Recently, N. H. Giordano and Giordano (1983) presented a rigorous
cross-validated study that obtained data from case files for 600 abused
and 150 nonabused elderly.[7] The study investigated individual and
family circumstances for five specific types of abuse—physical abuse,
neglect, financial exploitation, psychological abuse, and multiple abuse.
The profiles of the abused elderly were different for each type of abuse,
which adds further to the problem of generalizing about elder abuse
unless the specific types of abuse are defined. Several findings contradict those of previous studies. In the discriminate analysis of abuse
and nonabuse, marital problems emerge as an important descriptor.
Further, spouse abuse was found to be a dominant variable in physical,

---

[7] For a presentation of the entire study, see Giordano (1982).

psychological, and multiple abuse. Psychological abuse, the most difficult type to predict, frequently accompanies other forms of abuse.

Alcohol abuse

Many people increase the frequency of their drinking or begin drinking excessively for the first time in later life. Late-onset alcohol abusers are referred to in the literature as Type II alcoholics, while Type I alcoholics have had a history of alcohol-related problems throughout life (Drew, 1968; Rosin & Glatt 1971; Zimberg, 1974).

Alcohol use by old people involves a unique set of problems in addition to those experienced by younger populations. Often, the elderly have less tolerance for alcohol (Barnes, Abel, & Ernst, 1980; Rosin & Glatt, 1971). For example, old people with moderate levels of blood alcohol have more accidents than younger people with the same level of blood alcohol. Old people are also more likely than other age groups to experience alcohol-related complications because of the high incidence of medication use. Alcohol problems are frequently masked by medical problems, rendering them difficult to diagnose (Osborne, 1979).

Alcohol abuse in later life is thought to be more closely associated with external factors of age-related stress (Kola & Kosberg, 1981; Pascarelli & Fischer, 1974; Peck, 1979; Rosin & Glatt, 1971; Schuckit, 1977). Thus, loneliness, loss of spouse, physical or emotional separation from children, ill health, and lack of purposeful employment can precipitate alcohol abuse. Often the elderly person who consumes excess amounts of alcohol is attempting to reduce anxiety, deal with depression, or avoid further family interaction. The situational explanation for excess use of alcohol in later life is based mostly on self-report and retrospective information and should be viewed with caution. Giordano and Beckham's (1983) review of literature related to causes of later-life drinking suggests that situational stress may provide only a partial explanation. They offer alternative causal theories for excessive drinking in later life.

It has been established that most late-onset excessive drinkers have no evidence of severe antisocial behavior or psychiatric problems and have a low incidence of disruptive lifestyles (Royce, 1981). Late-onset alcohol abusers have fewer deep-seated psychological problems and fewer social problems than Type I alcoholics (Rosin & Glatt, 1971; Schuckit, Atkinson, Miller, & Berman, 1980). Carruth (1980) conducted one of the few empirical studies of Type I and Type II abuse involving a sizable sample. He observed that Type I alcoholics reported more alcohol-related problems and heavier and more frequent drinking than the Type II groups.

Hubbard, Santos, and Santos (1979) characterized the late-onset alcohol abusers as individuals who express guilt, drink mostly at home, and lack meaningful role involvement and positive self-concepts. Family contact for this group was moderate, and often their family members expressed denial of alcohol problems. Both the family and the elderly subjects were likely to describe their drinking as medicinal. An alcohol-related medical problem is common for individuals in this group (Schuckit et al., 1980).

The different conditions and motivations for drinking behavior in later life necessitate different treatment approaches. The elderly's life-styles are different from their younger counterparts; their outlook is often focused on past achievements rather than on future goals (Johnson, 1982). Evidence suggests that late-onset problem drinkers actually respond better to treatment than younger alcoholics and that their chances for successful rehabilitation are greater (Snyder & Way, 1979; Williams, 1982). Schuckit (1977) claims that the older alcoholic is more likely than the younger alcoholic to enter treatment voluntarily and to remain in treatment. However, to date, few communities have developed specialized programs to meet the unique needs and different motivations of the late-onset alcohol abuser (Dupree, Broskowski, & Schonfeld, in press).

FAMILY INTERVENTIONS

The need for systematic, professional intervention with the elderly and their families is well established. With the evidence that supports the continuing critical role of the family in the well-being of the individual, family intervention should receive emphasis by practitioners and researchers. However, even though the family context represents a closer approximation of reality, family interventions have received little attention and are underutilized with the aged. Therapeutic intervention with the aged and their families received its greatest impetus with the establishment of life review therapy (Butler & Lewis, 1982; Lewis & Butler, 1978).[8]

For the most part, therapeutic and educational interventions used with the aged and their families are adaptations of intervention techniques that have been used with younger groups. Such modifications may be appropriate, but it should be recalled that the kinds of problems experienced by the aged may be unique in terms of their cause, time of onset, and interpersonal and material resources available. Also, the unique problems experienced by the aging may exacerbate the emotional and family problems of other family members.

---

[8] Life review is a structured and purposeful process that involves the taking of autobiographical information from both the older person and relatives.

The distinction between psychotherapy and educational intervention is difficult to establish. For the purposes of this discussion, family therapy is seen as an intervention that requires an evaluation, is usually problem-focused, and more often than not deals with problems that have an established pattern in the family history. Educational interventions usually have multiple goals, do not require an identified problem, and may be preventive in nature, seeking enhancement of functioning. Application of family therapy to dysfunctioning in later life is rare, and reports of evaluative research are not readily available, but the use of educational techniques is somewhat more prevalent.

Family therapy

Family therapy is used sparingly by practitioners even though it is frequently the treatment method of choice. Individual counseling and psychotherapy are more commonly used with the aged.[9] Most family therapy will include the husband and wife, with the occasional presence of offspring or other relatives. It is important to understand that not all members of a family need to be present at family therapy sessions. Family therapy is also indicated when the children are in individual therapy and the aging parents can be provided supportive treatment.

Family therapy needs to focus on the family group and on the interpersonal relations and communications systems of the family (J. Haley, 1975; Satir, 1967). If family therapy is to be successful, therapists will need to set goals jointly with the family members. The more specific the goal and the greater the degree of commitment by family members, the more likely the therapy will be successful. Further, successful outcome of family therapy may be facilitated by structural modifications. To reduce threat and stigmatization, sessions could be held in the home of one of the family.

Several practitioner-scientists have offered suggestions and models for family therapy based on their clinical practice and observations. Burnside (1978), drawing upon the writings of major family therapists, presents a collection of practical suggestions for family counseling with the elderly. These include suggestions concerning unique age-related circumstances such as the reactions of the family to a younger counselor and dealing with hopelessness. Rathbone-McCuan, Travis, and Voyles (1983) review three models of family intervention appropriate for use with the elderly. The contextual family therapy model is seen as a

---

[9] Much of the literature providing information on individual therapy methods deals with late-onset problems related to life cycle. See, for example, Keller and Hughston (1981); Steury and Blank (1978); and Storandt (1983).

long-term approach to treatment that is grounded in psychoanalytic and existential psychology (Boszormenyi-Nagy & Ulrich, 1980). Problem-centered systems family therapy and task-centered models are viewed as appropriate for short-term age-related issues. The problem-centered systems approach is highly focused with four distinct stages and with the length of therapy usually limited to 12 sessions (Epstein & Bishop, 1980). The task-centered model (Reid, 1977, 1978) has many of the characteristics of crisis counseling. It focuses on defining problems as viewed by the client and setting specific goals with high client involvement.

The use of behavioral techniques within a humanistic context, such as the task-centered approach, holds great promise for working with the elderly and their families. Evaluative research has documented the effectiveness of structured approaches with specific, limited goals (Reid & Hanrahan, 1982). The teaching of behavioral management techniques to family members has been used by W. E. Haley (1983). His approach is designed to assist family members in dealing with the cognitively impaired elderly person. These techniques are considered to be applicable to a number of problems encountered by families.

The Gerontology Alcohol Project (GAP), developed at the Florida Mental Health Institute in Tampa, provides one of the most innovative approaches to dealing with later-life problems of the elderly (Dupree et al., in press). The GAP program was developed as a short-term outpatient intervention model for late-onset alcohol abusers. Each client is initially assessed, and an individualized treatment plan is developed. This program, with its unique blend of psychotherapeutic techniques and educational methodology, offers a model that has great potential for broad application and success.

Educational interventions

Educational interventions are particularly appropriate for the elderly because there has been prior socialization, and they offer an approach to life's problems that is free from labeling or stigmatization. Educational interventions are found in universities or colleges, community agencies, churches, and (more recently) hospitals and mental health centers. These programs, usually referred to as "classes" by the elderly, are structured, have identifiable goals for each session, and have a limited overall time frame. A wide variety of formats and approaches is described in the literature. The effectiveness of programs and the attainment of their goals are highly dependent upon the design and upon the educational technology (Ammons & Giordano, 1982; J. A. Giordano & Giordano, 1983).

Family life education is perhaps the broadest category of educational intervention and has traditionally been associated with cooperative extension services and continuing education departments of colleges and universities. For the most part, family life education provides information and addresses the cognitive domain of participants (L'Abate, 1978). Recently, there has been an expansion of family life education to include the latter part of the life cycle. Family life education has focused directly on the elderly, providing them with such courses as myths and realities of aging, death and dying, managing financial resources, and home health and nutrition courses. Courses to assist adult children in dealing with their aging parents have been among the most popular. While these workshops may be a step in the right direction, Johnson and Spence (1982) have found that they do not necessarily enhance relationships between adult children and older parents.

Marital and family enrichment, which has its roots in the human potential movement, is particularly appropriate for the aged (L'Abate, 1978; Mace, 1979). Enrichment programs are for couples who have a satisfactory relationship and wish to make improvements.[10] Enrichment is particularly appropriate for companionship-oriented marriages typical of later life (Hopkins, Hopkins, Mace, & Mace, 1978). Enrichment programs are experientially oriented, assist people in improving their relationships, and focus on communication skills, with very little time spent on dydactic material (Ball & Ball, 1979; L'Abate, 1978).

Preretirement programs throughout the country are sometimes offered by employers and, equally as often, by community agencies and colleges (Hunter, 1973; Palmore, 1977; Thorson, 1976). These group programs range from small groups of 10 or 12 to large audiences; sometimes they include the spouse. There is a variety of formats and approaches to preretirement programs, some of which have proven to be more effective than others (J. A. Giordano & Giordano, 1983). The effectiveness of many of these efforts has come into question, for it has been suggested that some programs heighten fears and increase anxiety in regards to later life (Lumsden, 1978; Tiberi, Boyack, & Kerschner, 1978). Preretirement programs need to be conducted by professionally trained individuals with a background in both educational technology and gerontology.

CONCLUSION

The growth, potential, and strengths associated with later life have only recently been recognized (Bengston, 1976; Busse & Pfeiffer,

---

[10] There are two well-known package programs. For the Minnesota Couples Communication Program, see Nunnally, Miller, and Wackman (1976); for Marriage Encounters, see Bosco (1976).

1977a; Schiff, 1984). Continued growth and well-being are greatly determined by family experiences. Positive, balanced family interactions are possible and probable where the elder can continue to realize independence, where intimacy at a distance with children is accomplished, and where the quality of marital relations is improved. In turn, this formula will contribute to stable mental health and successful adjustment to health problems. Moreover, once the myths and beliefs held by younger family members about the extent of problems of old age (Harris & Associates, 1981) are dispelled, continued growth and development in later life will be become a reality.

For the field of family psychology of aging, researchers need to redouble their efforts. Some particularly critical areas for research have been gleaned from this review. Paramount is the need for further investigation into the quality of marital relationships in later life. The present state of the art reveals considerable confusion and contradictory evidence surrounding the marital relationships of the elderly (N. H. Giordano & Giordano, 1983; Maas & Kuypers, 1974). Investigation into family strengths and weaknesses on retirement adjustment is needed, since family variables must have at least as much influence on retirement as on earlier-life transitions. Many aspects of retirement have been researched for men; but for women, we are still guided largely by myths and half truths. While the changing roles for middle-aged women have received some attention (e.g., Brody, 1981; Brody, Johnson, Fulcomer, & Lang, 1983; Lang & Brody, 1983; Neysmith, 1981; and Treas, 1977), the implications for the "modern woman" for later life require longitudinal research that should begin immediately. Widowhood as a female experience has received considerable attention, but widowers remain a group about which we have little empirical knowledge.

The generational extended family of the future can be predicted, in part, by some of the current trends. The four-generation extended family will present new challenges for adjustment by individuals. Indeed, the number of young-old caring for old-old is increasing dramatically. The increased capacity of young people to determine the course of their own lives has reduced the obligatory nature of relationships with the aged. More and more, family relationships of all types are becoming voluntary. Sibling relationships for the elderly are of great importance, but such sources of support have seldom been the concern of researchers. The future is likely to bring dramatic changes in later-life sibling relationships (Hess & Waring, 1978). Family life in later life is dynamic and ever changing, with unique features for each generation.

REFERENCES

Adams, D. L. Correlates of satisfaction among the elderly. *The Gerontologist,* 1971, *11*(4, Part 2), 64–68.

Aiken, L. R. Problems in testing the elderly. *Educational Gerontology,* 1980, *5,* 119–124.

Ammons, P., & Giordano, J. A. Designing effective curriculum for family life education. *Social Casework,* 1982, *63*(2), 67–72.

Amster, L. E., & Krauss, H. H. The relationship between life crises and mental deterioration in old age. *International Journal of Aging and Human Development,* 1974, *5,* 51–55.

Arling, G. The elderly widow and her family, neighbors, and friends. *Journal of Marriage and the Family,* 1976, *38*(3), 757–768.

Atchley, R. C. Retirement: Continuity or crisis? In R. A. Kalish (Ed.), *The later years: Social applications of gerontology.* Monterey, Calif.: Brooks/Cole Publishing, 1977. (a)

Atchley, R. C. *The social forces in later life* (2d ed.). Belmont, Calif.: Wadsworth, 1977. (b)

Atchley, R. C. *Aging: Continuity and change.* Belmont, Calif.: Wadsworth, 1983.

Balkwell, C. Transition to widowhood: A review of the literature. *Family Relations,* 1981, *30,* 117–127.

Ball, J., & Ball, O. Strengthening families through marriage enrichment. In N. Stinnett, B. Chesser, & J. DeFrain (Eds.), *Building family strengths: Blueprints for action.* Lincoln: University of Nebraska Press, 1979.

Bankoff, E. A. Social support and adaptation to widowhood. *Journal of Marriage and the Family,* 1983, *45*(4), 827–839.

Barnes, G., Abel, E. L., & Ernst, C. A. S. *Alcohol and the elderly: A comprehensive bibliography.* Westport, Conn.: Greenwood Press, 1980.

Barrett, C. J. Women in widowhood. In J. H. Williams (Ed.), *Psychology of women: Selected readings.* New York: W. W. Norton, 1979.

Beck, A. T., Ward, C., Mendelson, M., Mock, J. E., & Erbaugh, J. An inventory for measuring depression. *Archives of General Psychiatry,* 1961, *4,* 561–571.

Beckman, L. J. Effects of social interaction and children's relative inputs on older women's psychological well-being. *Journal of Personality and Social Psychology,* 1981, *41*(6), 1075–1086.

Bengston, V. L. *The social psychology of aging.* Indianapolis, Ind.: Bobbs-Merrill, 1976.

Blenkner, M. Social work and family relationships in late life, with some thoughts on filial maturity. In E. Shanas & G. Streib (Eds.), *Social structure and the family: Gerontological relations.* Englewood Cliffs, N.J.: Prentice-Hall, 1965.

Block, M. R., & Sinnott, J. D. (Eds.). *The battered elder syndrome.* College Park: University of Maryland, Center on Aging, 1979.

Blood, R. O., & Wolfe, D. M. *Husbands and wives.* New York: Free Press, 1960.

Bosco, A. Marriage encounter: An ecumenical enrichment program. In H. A. Otto (Ed.), *Marriage and family enrichment: New perspectives and programs.* Nashville, Tenn.: Abingdon Press, 1976.

Boszormenyi-Nagy, I., & Ulrich, D. N. Contextual family therapy. In A. S. Gurman & D. P. Kniskern (Eds.), *Handbook of family therapy.* New York: Brunner/Mazel, 1980.

Botwinick, J. *Aging and behavior.* New York: Springer Publishing, 1978.

Brody, E. M. The etiquette of filial behavior. *Aging and human development,* 1970, *1,* 87–94.

Brody, E. M. Aged parents and aging children. In P. K. Ragan (Ed.), *Aging parents.* Los Angeles: Ethel Percy Andrus Gerontology Center, University of Southern California Press, 1979.

Brody, E. M. Women in the middle and family help to older people. *The Gerontologist,* 1981, *21*(5), 471–480.

Brody, E. M., Johnson, P. T., Fulcomer, M. C., & Lang, A. M. Women's changing roles and help to elderly parents: Attitudes of three generations of women. *Journal of Gerontology,* 1983, *38*(5), 595–607.

Bromberg, E. M. Mother-daughter relationships in later life: Negating the myths. *Aging,* fall, 1983, 15–20.

Bumagin, V. E., & Hirn, K. F. Observations on changing relationships for older married women. *The American Journal of Psychoanalysis,* 1982, *42*(2), 133–142.

Burnside, I. M. (Ed.). *Working with the elderly: Group processes and techniques.* North Scituate, Mass.: Duxbury, 1978.

Busse, E. W., & Pfeiffer, E. (Eds.). *Mental illness in later life.* Washington, D.C.: American Psychiatric Association, 1973.

Busse, E. W., & Pfeiffer, E. (Eds.). *Behavior and adaptation in late life* (2d ed.). Boston: Little, Brown, 1977. (a)

Busse, E. W., & Pfeiffer, E. Functional psychiatric disorders in old age. In E. W. Busse & E. Pfeiffer (Eds.), *Behavior and adaptation in old age.* Boston: Little, Brown, 1977. (b)

Butler, R. N., & Lewis, M. I. *Aging and mental health: Positive psychosocial and biomedical approaches* (3d ed.). St. Louis: C. V. Mosby, 1982.

Carruth, F. B. An exploration of some subgroup differences among older alcoholics (Doctoral dissertation, State University of New York, 1979). *Dissertation Abstracts International,* 1980, *40,* 5594A. (University Microfilms No. 80–08864)

Chiriboga, D. A. Adaptation to marital separation in later and earlier life. *Journal of Gerontology,* 1982, *37*(1), 109–114.

Christenson, C. V., & Gagnon, J. H. Sexual behavior in a group of older women. *Journal of Gerontology,* 1975, *30*(4), 469–472.

Cicirelli, V. G. A comparison of helping behavior to elderly parents of adult children with intact and disrupted marriages. *The Gerontologist,* 1983, *23*(6), 619–625.

Cleveland, M. Sex in marriage: At 40 and beyond. *The Family Coordinator,* 1976, *25,* 233–240.

Cohen, S. Z., & Gans, B. M. *The other generation gap: The middle-aged and their aging parents.* Chicago: Follett Publishing, 1978.

Cohler, B. J. Autonomy and interdependence in the family of adulthood: A psychological perspective. *The Gerontologist,* 1983, *23*(10), 33–39.

Cormican, E. J. Social work and aging: A review of the literature and how it is changing. *International Journal of Aging and Human Development,* 1980, *11*(4), 251–267.

Cumming, E., & Henry, W. *Growing old.* New York: Basic Books, 1961.

Davidson, J. L., Hennessey, S., & Sedge, S. Additional factors related to elder abuse. In

M. Block & J. Sinnott (Eds.), *The battered elder syndrome: An exploratory study.* Unpublished manuscript, University of Maryland, 1979.

Davidson, W. B., & Cotter, P. R. Adjustment to aging and relationships with offspring. *Psychological Reports,* 1982, *50,* 731–738.

Douglas, R. L., & Hickey, T. Domestic neglect and abuse of the elderly: Research findings and a systems perspective for service delivery planning. In J. I. Kosberg (Ed.), *Abuse and maltreatment of the elderly: Causes and interventions.* Boston: John Wright, 1983.

Douglas, R. L., Hickey, T., & Noel, C. *A study of the maltreatment of the elderly and other vulnerable adults.* Ann Arbor: University of Michigan, Institute of Gerontology, 1980.

Dovenmuehle, R. H., & Verwoerdt, A. Physical illness and depressive symptomatology. *Journal of American Geriatrics Society,* 1962, *10,* 932–947.

Dressler, D. M. Life adjustment of retired couples. *International Journal of Aging and Human Development,* 1962, *4,* 335–349.

Drew, L. R. H. Alcoholism as a self-limiting disease. *Quarterly Journal of Studies on Alcohol,* 1968, *29*(4), 956–967.

Dunkle, R. E. The effect of elders' household contributions on their depression. *Journal of Gerontology,* 1983, *38*(6), 732–737.

Dupree, L. W., Broskowski, H., & Schonfeld, L. Gerontology alcohol project: A behavioral treatment program for the elderly abuser. *The Gerontologist,* in press.

Eisdorfer, C., & Cohen, D. The cognitively impaired elderly: Different diagnosis. In M. Storandt, J. C. Scigler, & M. F. Elias (Eds.), *The clinical psychology of aging.* New York: Plenum Press, 1978.

Epstein, L. J. Symposium on age differentiation in depressive illness. *Journal of Gerontology,* 1976, *31*(3), 278–282.

Epstein, N. B., & Bishop, D. S. Problem-centered systems therapy of the family. In A. S. Gurman & D. P. Kniskern (Eds.), *Handbook of family therapy.* New York: Brunner/Mazel, 1980.

Experience exchange: "Late life divorce." Aging, 1983, (340), 27–28.

Friedeman, J. S. Factors influencing sexual expression in aging persons: A review of the literature. *Journal of Psychiatric Nursing and Mental Health Services,* 1978, *38,* 34–47.

Gallagher, D. E., & Thompson, L. W. Effectiveness of psychotherapy for both endogenous and nonendogenous depression in older adult outpatients. *Journal of Gerontology,* 1983, *38*(6), 707–712.

Gelfand, D. E., Olsen, J. J., & Block, M. R. Two generations of elderly in the changing American family: Implications for family services. *The Family Coordinator,* 1978, *27*(4), 395–403.

George, L. K. *Role transitions in later life.* Monterey, Calif.: Brooks/Cole Publishing, 1980.

Giordano, J. A., & Beckham, K. *Having a few too many in the later years: An examination of the characteristics of the late-onset alcoholic.* Paper presented at the Southern Gerontological Society Fourth Annual Meeting, Atlanta, Georgia, April 1983.

Giordano, J. A., & Giordano, N. H. A classification of preretirement programs: In search of a new model. *Educational Gerontology,* 1983, *9,* 123–137.

Giordano, N. H. *Individual and family correlates of elder abuse.* Unpublished doctoral dissertation, University of Georgia, 1982.

Giordano, N. H., & Giordano, J. A. Individual and family correlates of elder abuse. Paper presented at the 36th Annual Scientific Meeting of the Gerontological Society of America, San Francisco, California, November 1983.

Giordano, N. H., & Giordano, J. A. Elder abuse: A review of the literature. *Social Work,* 1984, *29*(3), 232–236.

Glasser, P. H., & Glasser, L. N. Role reversal and conflict between aged parents and their children. *Marriage and Family Living,* 1962, *24,* 46–51.

Glenn, N. D., & McLanahan, S. The effects of offspring on the psychological well-being of older adults. *Journal of Marriage and the Family,* 1981, *43*(2), 409–421.

Glick, I. O., Weiss, R. S., & Parkes, C. M. *The first year of bereavement.* New York: John Wiley & Sons, 1974.

Glick, I. O., Weiss, R. S., & Parkes, C. M. The impact of death. In M. M. Seltzer, S. L. Corbett, & R. C. Atchley (Eds.), *Social problems of the aging: Readings.* Belmont, Calif.: Wadsworth, 1978.

Glick, P. C. The future marital status and living arrangements of the elderly. *The Gerontologist,* 1978, *19,* 301–309.

Gurland, B. J. The comparative frequency of depression in various adult age groups. *Journal of Gerontology,* 1976, *31*(3), 283–292.

Gutmann, D., Grunes, J., & Griffin, B. The clinical psychology of later life: Developmental paradigms. In N. Datan & N. Lohmann (Eds.), *Transitions of aging.* New York: Academic Press, 1980.

Haley, J. *Family therapy.* New York: Jason Aronson, 1975.

Haley, W. E. A family behavioral approach to the treatment of the cognitively impaired elderly. *The Gerontologist,* 1983, *23*(1), 18–20.

Hamilton, M. Development of a rating scale for primary depressive illness. *British Journal of Social and Clinical Psychology,* 1967, *6,* 278–296.

Harris, L., & Associates. *Aging in the eighties: America in transition.* Washington, D.C.: National Council on the Aging, 1981.

Hendricks, J., & Hendricks, C. D. *Aging in mass society.* Cambridge, Mass.: Winthrop, 1977.

Hendricks, J., & Hendricks, C. D. *Aging in mass society* (2d ed.). Cambridge, Mass.: Winthrop, 1981.

Hess, B. B., & Waring, J. M. Changing patterns of aging and family bonds in later life. *The Family Coordinator,* October 1978, pp. 303–314.

Hill, R., & Rodgers, R. H. The developmental approach. In H. T. Christenson (Ed.), *Handbook of marriage and the family.* Skokie, Ill.: Rand McNally, 1964.

Hiltz, S. R. Widowhood: A roleless role. *Marriage and Family Review,* 1978, *1,* 1; 3–10.

Hopkins, L., Hopkins, P., Mace, D., & Mace, V. *Toward better marriages.* New York: Acme, 1978.

Horowitz, M. J., & Wilner, N. Life events, stress and coping. In L. W. Poon (Ed.), *Aging in the 1980s: Psychological issues.* Washington, D.C.: American Psychological Association, 1980.

Hoyer, W. J., Raskind, C. L., & Abrahams, J. P. Research practices in the psychology of aging: A survey of research published in the *Journal of Gerontology,* 1975–1982. *Journal of Gerontology,* 1984, *39*(1), 44–48.

Hubbard, R. W., Santos, J. F., & Santos, M. A. Alcohol and older adults: Overt and covert influences. *Social Casework,* 1979, *60*(3), 166–170.

Hunter, W. W. Preretirement educational programs. In R. R. Boyd & C. Oakes (Eds.), *Foundations of practical gerontology* (2d ed.). Columbia: University of South Carolina Press, 1973.

Hyde, J. S. *Understanding human sexuality.* New York: McGraw-Hill, 1982.

Jarvik, L. F. Aging and depression: Some unanswered questions. *Journal of Gerontology,* 1976, *31*(3), 324–326.

Johnson, E. S., & Bursk, B. J. Relationships between the elderly and their adult children. *The Gerontologist,* 1977, *17*(1), 90–96.

Johnson, E. S., & Spence, D. L. Adult children and their aging parents: An intervention program. *Family Relations,* 1982, *31,* 115–122.

Johnson, N. Research centers conduct studies on alcoholism. *National Institute of Alcohol Abuse and Alcoholism Information and Feature Service* (No. 103), December 21, 1982, p. 6.

Kaplan, H. S. *The new sex therapy.* New York: Brunner/Mazel, 1974.

Keller, J. F., & Hughston, G. A. *Counseling the elderly: A systems approach.* New York: Harper & Row, 1981.

Kerckhoff, A. C. Family patterns and morale in retirement. In I. H. Simpson & J. C. McKinney (Eds.), *Social aspects of aging.* Durham, N.C.: Duke University Press, 1966.

Kinsey, A. C., Pomeroy, W. B., & Martin, C. E. *Sexual behavior in the human male.* Philadelphia: W. B. Saunders, 1948.

Kinsey, A. C., Pomeroy, W. B., Martin, C. E., & Gebhard, P. H. *Sexual behavior in the human female.* Philadelphia: W. B. Saunders, 1953.

Kivett, V. R. Loneliness and the rural widow. *The Family Coordinator,* 1978, *27,* 389–394.

Kivnick, H. Q. Grandparenthood: An overview of meaning and mental health. *The Gerontologist,* 1982, *22*(1), 59–66.

Kola, L. A., & Kosberg, J. I. Model to assess community services for the elderly alcoholic. *Public Health Reports,* 1981, *96*(5), 458–463.

Kosberg, J. I. (Ed.). *Abuse and maltreatment of the elderly: Causes and interventions.* Boston: John Wright, 1983.

Kukich, D. Abuse of the elderly. *Enquiry,* 1982, *2*(3), 2–6.

L'Abate, L. *Enrichment: Structured interventions with couples, families, and groups.* Washington, D.C.: University Press of America, 1978.

Lang, A. M., & Brody, E. M. Characteristics of middle-aged daughters and help to their elderly mothers. *Journal of Marriage and the Family,* 1983. *45*(1), 193–202.

Larson, R. Thirty years of research on the subjective well-being of older Americans. *Journal of Gerontology,* 1978, *33,* 109–125.

Lau, E. E., & Kosberg, J. I. Abuse of the elderly by informal care providers. *Aging,* September–October 1979, pp. 10–15.

Lee, G. R. Children and the elderly: Interaction and morale. *Research on Aging,* 1979, *1*(3), 335–360.

Lewis, M. I., & Butler, R. N. Life-review therapy: Putting memories to work in individual and group psychotherapy. In S. Steury & M. L. Blank (Eds.), *Readings in psychotherapy with older people*. Rockville, Md.: National Institute of Mental Health, 1978.

Lipton, M. A. Age differentiation in depression: Biochemical aspects. *Journal of Gerontology*, 1976, *31*(3), 293–299.

Litwak, E. Extended kin relationships in an industrial democratic society. In E. Shanas & G. Streib (Eds.), *Social structure and the family: Generational relations*. Englewood Cliffs, N.J.: Prentice-Hall, 1965.

Loether, H. J. *Problems of aging* (2d ed.). Encino, Calif.: Dickenson, 1975.

Lopata, H. Z. The life-cycle of the social role of housewife. *Sociology and Social Research*, 1960, *51*, 5–22.

Lopata, H. Z. *Widowhood in an American city*. Cambridge, Mass.: Schenkman, 1973.

Lopata, H. Z. Widowhood in America: An overview. In M. M. Seltzer, S. L. Corbett, & R. C. Atchley (Eds.), *Social problems of the aging: Readings*. Belmont, Calif.: Wadsworth, 1978.

Lowenthal, M. F. Toward a socio-psychological theory of change in adulthood and old age. In J. Birren & K. W. Schaie (Eds.), *Handbook of the psychology of aging*. New York: Van Nostrand Reinhold, 1977.

Lowenthal, M. F., & Robinson, B. Social networks and isolation. In R. H. Binstock & E. Shanas (Eds.), *Handbook of aging and the social sciences*. New York: Van Nostrand Reinhold, 1976.

Lowenthal, M. F., Thurnher, M., & Chiriboga, D. *Four stages of life*. San Francisco: Jossey-Bass, 1975.

Lurie, E. E. Sex and stage differences in perceptions of marital and family relationships. *Journal of Marriage and the Family*, 1974, *36*, 260–269.

Lumsden, B. D. Educational implications of research on retirement. *Educational Gerontology*, 1978, *3*, 375–386.

Maas, H. S., & Kuypers, J. A. *From thirty to seventy*. San Francisco: Jossey-Bass, 1974.

Mace, D. Marriage and family enrichment—A new field? *The Family Coordinator*, 1979, *28*(3), 409–419.

Masters, W. H., & Johnson, V. *Human sexual response*. Boston: Little, Brown, 1966.

Masters, W. H., & Johnson, V. Human sexual response: The aging female and the aging male. In B. Neugarten (Ed.), *Middle age and aging*. Chicago: University of Chicago Press, 1968.

Mendelwicz, J. The age factor in depressive illness: Some genetic considerations. *Journal of Gerontology*, 1976, *31*(3), 300–303.

Miller, D. A. The "sandwich" generation: Adult children of the aging. *Social Work*, 1981, *26*, 419–423.

Miller, S. J. The social dilemma of the aging leisure participant. In A. M. Rose & W. A. Peterson (Eds.), *Older people and their world*. Philadelphia: F. A. Davis, 1965.

Mindel, C. H., & Wright, R., Jr. Satisfaction in multigenerational households. *Journal of Gerontology*, 1982, *37*(4), 483–489.

Morgan, L. A. Problems of widowhood. In P. K. Ragan (Ed.), *Aging parents*. Los Angeles: Ethel Percy Andrus Gerontology Center, University of Southern California Press, 1979.

Moss, M. S., & Moss, S. Z. The image of the deceased spouse in remarriage of elderly widow(er)s. *Journal of Gerontological Social Work*, 1980, *3*(2), 59–70.

Neugarten, B. L. *Personality in middle and late life*. New York: Atherton, 1964.

Neugarten, B. L. The future and the young-old. *The Gerontologist,* 1975, *15*(1), 4–9.

Neugarten, B. L. The middle generations. In P. K. Ragan (Ed.), *Aging parents.* Los Angeles: Ethel Percy Andrus Gerontology Center, University of Southern California Press, 1979.

Neugarten, B. L., Havighurst, R. J., & Tobin, S. S. Personality and patterns of aging. In B. L. Neugarten (Ed.), *Middle age and aging.* Chicago: University of Chicago Press, 1968.

Neugarten, B., & Weinstein, K. The changing American grandparent. *Journal of Marriage and the Family,* 1964, *26,* 199–204.

Neysmith, S. M. Parental care: Another female family function. *Canadian Journal of Social Work Education,* 1981, *7*(2), 55–63.

Nunnally, E. W., Miller, S., & Wackman, D. B. The Minnesota couples communication program. In H. A. Otto (Ed.), *Marriage and family enrichment: New perspectives and programs.* Nashville, Tenn.: Abingdon Press, 1976.

O'Rourke, M. *Elder abuse: The state of the art.* Paper prepared for the National Conference on the Abuse of Older Persons, Boston, Massachusetts, March 23–25, 1981.

Osborne, E. The elderly alcoholic. *Journal of Practical Nursing,* 1979, *29*(9), 25–26; 34.

Palmore, E. Preretirement planning model developed: A practical experiment in preretirement planning. Duke University Center for the Study of Aging and Human Development, *Advance in Research,* 1977, *1.*

Palmore, E., Fillenbaum, G. G., & George, L. K. Consequences of retirement. *Journal of Gerontology,* 1984, *39*(1), 109–116.

Palmore, E., George, L. K., & Fillenbaum, G. G. Predictors of retirement. *Journal of Gerontology,* 1982, *37*(6), 733–742.

Parkes, C. M. *Bereavement: Studies of grief in adult life.* New York: International Universities Press, 1972.

Pascarelli, E. F., & Fischer, W. Drug dependence in the elderly. *International Journal of Aging and Human Development,* 1974, *5*(4), 347–356.

Patterson, R. D. Grief and depression in old people. In S. Steury & M. L. Blank (Eds.), *Readings in psychotherapy with older people.* Rockville, Md.: National Institute of Mental Health, 1978.

Peck, D. G. Alcohol abuse and the elderly: Social control and conformity. *Journal of Drug Issues,* 1979, *9*(1), 63–71.

Pengelley, E. J. *Sex and human life.* Reading, Mass.: Addison-Wesley Publishing, 1974.

Pfeiffer, E., Verwoerdt, A., & Wang, H. S. The natural history of sexual behavior in a biologically advanced group of aged individuals. *Journal of Gerontology,* 1969, *24,* 193–198.

Quinn, W. H. Personal and family adjustment in later life. *Journal of Marriage and the Family,* 1983, *45*(1), 57–73.

Rathbone-McCuan, E., Travis, A., & Voyles, B. Family intervention: The task-centered approach. In J. I. Kosberg (Ed.), *Abuse and maltreatment of the elderly: Causes and interventions.* Boston: John Wright, 1983.

Reid, W. J. Process and outcome in the treatment of family problems. In W. J. Reid & L. Epstein (Eds.), *Task-centered practice.* New York: Columbia University Press, 1977.

Reid, W. J. *The task-centered system.* New York: Columbia University Press, 1978.

Reid, W. J., & Hanrahan, P. Recent evaluations of social work: Grounds for optimism. *Social Work,* 1982, *27*(4), 328–340.

Robertson, J. F. Interaction in three generation families, parents as mediators: Toward a theoretical perspective. *International Journal of Aging and Human Development,* 1975, *6*(2), 103–110.

Robertson, J. F. Grandmotherhood: A study of role conceptions. *Journal of Marriage and the Family,* 1977, *39*(1), 165–174.

Rollins, B. C., & Cannon, K. L. Marital satisfaction over the family life-cycle: A re-evaluation. *Journal of Marriage and the Family,* 1978, *35,* 271–282.

Rosenmayr, L., & Kockeis, E. Propositions for a sociological theory of aging and the family. *International Social Science Journal,* 1963, *15,* 410–426.

Rosin, A. J., & Glatt, M. M. Alcohol excess in the elderly. *Quarterly Journal of Studies on Alcohol,* 1971, *32,* 53–59.

Rosow, I. *Socialization to old age.* Berkeley: University of California, 1974.

Royce, J. E. *Alcohol problems and alcoholism: A comprehensive survey.* New York: Free Press, 1981.

Satir, V. *Conjoint family therapy.* Palo Alto, Calif.: Science and Behavior Books, 1967.

Scherz, F. H. Maturational crises and parent-child interaction. *Social Casework,* 1971, *52*(6), 362–269.

Schiff, N. R. The art of aging. *Psychology Today,* 1984, *18*(1), 32–41.

Schuckit, M. A. Geriatric alcoholism and drug abuse. *The Gerontologist,* 1977, *17*(2), 168–174.

Schuckit, M. A., Atkinson, J. H., Miller, P. L., & Berman, J. A three year follow-up of elderly alcoholics. *Journal of Clinical Psychiatry,* 1980, *41*(12), 412–416.

Schwartz, A. N. Psychological dependency: An emphasis on the later years. In P. K. Ragan (Ed.), *Aging parents.* Los Angeles: Ethel Percy Andrus Gerontology Center, University of Southern California Press, 1979.

Seelbach, W. C. Correlates of aged parents' filial responsibility expectations and realizations. *The Family Coordinator,* 1978, *27*(4), 341–350.

Seelbach, W. C., & Hansen, C. J. Satisfaction with family relations among the elderly. *Family Relations,* 1980, *29,* 91–96.

Seligman, M. E. Depression and learned helplessness. In R. J. Friedman & M. M. Katz (Eds.), *The psychology of depression: Contemporary theory and research.* Washington, D.C.: V. H. Winston (John Winston), 1974.

Shanas, E. Social myth as hypothesis: The case of the family relations of old people. *The Gerontologist,* 1979, *19*(1), 3–9.

Shanas, E., Townsend, P., Wedderburn, D., Friis, H., Milhøj, P., & Stehouver, J. *Older people in three industrial societies.* New York: Atherton, 1968.

Silverman, P. R. Widowhood and preventive intervention. *The Family Coordinator,* 1972, *21,* 95–102.

Silverstone, B., & Hyman, H. K. *You and your aging parent: The modern family's guide to emotional, physical, and financial problems.* New York: Pantheon Books, 1976.

Simos, B. G. Adult children and their aging parents. *Social Work,* 1973, *18*(3), 78–85.

Snyder, P. K., & Way, A. Alcoholism and the elderly. *Aging,* January–February 1979, 8–11.

Steere, G. H. The family and the elderly. In F. J. Berghorn & D. E. Schafer (Eds.), *The dynamics of aging: Original essays on the processes and experiences of growing old.* Boulder, Colo.: Westview, 1981.

Steinmetz, S. K. Dependency, stress, and violence between middle-aged caregivers and their elderly parents. In J. I. Kosberg (Ed.), *Abuse and maltreatment of the elderly: Causes and interventions.* New York: John Wiley & Sons, 1983.

Steury, S., & Blank, M. L. (Eds.). *Readings in psychotherapy with older people.* Rockville, Md.: National Institute of Mental Health, 1978.

Stinnett, N., Collins, J., & Montgomery, J. Marital need satisfaction of older husbands and wives. *Journal of Marriage and the Family,* 1970, *32,* 428–434.

Storandt, M. *Counseling and therapy with older adults.* Boston: Little, Brown, 1983.

Streib, G. F. Older people in a family context. In R. A. Kalish (Ed.), *The later years: Social applications of gerontology.* Monterey, Calif.: Brooks/Cole Publishing, 1977.

Streib, G. F., & Schneider, S. J. *Retirement in America.* Ithaca, N.Y.: Cornell University, 1971.

Sussman, M. B. Relationships of adult children with their aging parents in the United States. In M. B. Sussman (Ed.), *Sourcebook in marriage and the family* (3d ed.). Boston: Houghton Mifflin, 1968.

Taylor, P. H. Role and role conflicts in a group of middle class wives and mothers. *Sociological Review,* 1964, *21,* 317–327.

Thorson, J. A. A media approach to preretirement education. *Adult Leadership,* 1976, *24,* 344–346.

Tiberi, D. M., Boyack, V. L., & Kerschner, P. A. A comparative analysis of four preretirement educational models. *Educational Gerontology,* 1978, *3,* 355–374.

Timberlake, E. M. The value of grandchildren to grandmothers. *Journal of Gerontological Social Work,* 1980, *3*(1), 63–76.

Toth, A., & Toth, S. Group work with widows. *Social Work,* 1980, *25*(1), 63–65.

Treas, J. Aging and the family. In D. S. Woodruff & J. E. Birren (Eds.), *Aging: Scientific perspectives and social issues.* New York: Van Nostrand Reinhold, 1975.

Treas, J. Family support systems for the aged: Some social and demographic considerations. *The Gerontologist,* 1977, *17,* 486–491.

Treas, J. Intergenerational families and social change. In P. K. Ragan (Ed.), *Aging parents.* Los Angeles: Ethel Percy Andrus Gerontology Center, University of Southern California Press, 1979.

Troll, L. E. The family of later life: A decade review. *Journal of Marriage and the Family,* 1971, *33*(2), 263–290.

Troll, L. E. Grandparenting. In L. W. Poon (Ed.), *Aging in the 1980s: Psychological issues.* Washington, D.C.: American Psychological Association, 1980. (a)

Troll, L. E. Intergenerational relations in later life: A family system approach. In N. Datan & N. Lohmann (Eds.), *Transitions of aging.* New York: Academic Press, 1980. (b)

Troll, L. E., Miller, S. J., & Atchley, R. C. *Families in later life.* Belmont, Calif.: Wadsworth, 1979.

Uhlenberg, P., & Myers, M. A. P. Divorce and the elderly. *The Gerontologist,* 1981, *21*(3), 276–282.

U.S. Bureau of the Census. *Current population reports.* Series P-23. No. 84. Divorce, child custody, and child support. Washington, D.C.: U.S. Government Printing Office, 1979.

U.S. Department of Health and Human Services. *The need for long-term care: Information and issues. A chartbook of the Federal Council on the Aging* (DHHS Pub. No. OHDS 81–20704). Washington, D.C.: U.S. Government Printing Office, 1981.

Viano, E. C. Victimology: An overview. In J. I. Kosberg (Ed.), *Abuse and maltreatment of the elderly: Causes and interventions.* Boston: John Wright 1983.

Weishaus, S. Aging is a family affair. In P. K. Ragan (Ed.), *Aging parents.* Los Angeles: Ethel Percy Andrus Gerontology Center, University of Southern California Press, 1979.

Williams, M. Alcohol problems in elderly compounded by many factors. *National Institute on Alcohol Abuse and Alcoholism Information and Feature Service* (No. 103), December 31, 1982, p. 1.

Williamson, J. B., Evans, L., & Munley, A. *Aging and society: An introduction to social gerontology.* New York: Holt, Rinehart & Winston, 1980.

Wood, V., & Robertson, J. F. The significance of grandparenthood. In J. F. Gubrium (Ed.), *Time, roles, and self in old age.* New York: Human Sciences Press, 1976.

Zimberg, S. The elderly alcoholic. *The Gerontologist,* 1974, *14*(3), 221–224.

Zung, W. W. A self-rating depression scale. *Archives of General Psychiatry,* 1965, *12*, 63–70.

Section Three

Affect and the Family

Chapter 10

The Family as a Social Network and Support System

BEVERLEY FEHR
DANIEL PERLMAN

The story is told of a couple who lived in a third-story apartment. Bad luck hit them: The husband was laid off from work for several months, so they couldn't pay the rent. Their landlord evicted them. On the way down the stairs, he carried a television in one hand and a vacuum cleaner in the other. She had a lamp and the baby. At the bottom of the stairs, she burst into laughter. The husband, who was not at all amused, said "Dear, this is no laughing matter." She replied, "Yes, it is. This is the first time in five years we've gone out together."

Stories like this abound in our culture. They are told by after-dinner speakers and printed in popular magazines such as *Reader's Digest*. The pun in this particular story revolves around the wife's unfulfilled desire for recreational companionship. A less-salient but equally important component of the couple's leaving their apartment is the image of the spouses working together, helping one another through a crisis.

For some time, social scientists have been very concerned with the companionship and aid family members provide one another. In the early 1950s, Parsons (1951) asserted that the American nuclear family had become isolated. He depicted a breakdown of ties between extended kin. For two decades (Adams, 1970), research on this issue flourished. In the 1970s, the notion of social networks came into vogue. Cassel (1974) and others popularized the idea that one's personal relationships might influence one's physical well-being. Shortly thereafter, the family was discussed as a major source of social support (Caplan, 1976).

In this chapter, we will examine the family as a social network and support system. We will address such questions as "How important are kin in people's social lives?" and "What do family members do for one another?" In answering these questions, we will rely heavily on existing empirical evidence. We will also look at family relations across the adult life cycle. Finally, we want to focus attention on an obvious but often ignored source of social support, one's spouse.

The chapter is divided into four main sections. Section 1 examines the relationship between marital status and well-being. Section 2 considers the family as a network of social relationships. Section 3 looks at helping patterns among family members. Section 4 deals with kin and nonkin social support during selected life transitions.

Since this chapter is based largely on the existing literature about family relations, a few characteristics of this work should be noted. First, the majority of family research is done by sociologists (see Bayer, 1982). Second, most of the research on social support is designed to show the benefits of social ties. Third, much of the literature focuses solely on the family.

Not surprisingly, as psychologists we believe that personality factors, cognitive processes, learning histories, attitudes, and the like, play a crucial role in the family's functioning as a social network and support system. We hope this chapter will stimulate further psychological research and more use of psychological theorizing.

To decide whether kin are an important part of one's social life, a comparative frame of reference must be used. One must also know the importance of nonkin ties. Thus, we have made an effort to go beyond data on the family per se to include evidence showing the relative importance of family and nonfamily members in social networks.

While this chapter will identify several benefits of interpersonal ties, the tensions and disadvantages of social contacts must be kept clearly in mind. For now, three examples of the negative aspects of social relations will suffice as illustrations. First, stereotypes and jokes such as the following are common: "My mother-in-law has a heart as big as a mountain and a mouth twice that size." Ambivalence toward, and outright dislike of, in-laws is believed to be widespread (see Duvall, 1954). Second, Norton and Glick (1979) project that 4 out of every 10 marriages contracted by women born in the late 1940s will end in divorce. Surely, this involves pain and costs for those involved. Third, while estimates of domestic violence do vary, probably some form of physical abuse between spouses occurs in over one quarter of all marriages (see Gelles, 1980). With phenomena such as these, it is not surprising that some authors (Croog, 1970) mention the family as a source of, rather than a solution to, stress.

Basic concepts

The concepts of networks and social support are central to this chapter. A social network consists of a set of people with links between them. When a particular individual's interpersonal ties are studied, they form a personal network. Several characteristics of networks have been identified. These include size, strength of ties, density (the connectedness between members), homogeneity among members, and multistrandedness (the number of different ways an individual is involved with someone else).

It has been customary to think of kin relations as different than friendships (see Hagestad, 1981). For the most part, fellow family members are given, not chosen. Claims have often been made that family interaction patterns are shaped by social norms and prescribed roles. Service to family members is sometimes seen as obligatory. Friendships, on the other hand, have typically been depicted as voluntary bonds formed and regulated by personal preferences. Probably the distinction between family and nonkin relations is not as clear in American society as it once was. In any case, both kin and nonkin—along with neighbors, co-workers, and professionals—are important members of our personal networks.

After commenting on earlier statements, Thoits (1982, p. 147) defines social support "as the degree to which a person's basic social needs are gratified through interaction with others." House (1981) considers several schemes for categorizing supportive behavior. He then synthesizes his views by stating that support is an interpersonal flow of (a) emotional concern (liking, love, empathy); (b) instrumental aid (goods, money, services); (c) information (advice, knowledge useful in problem solving); and (d) appraisal (information specifically relevant to self-evaluation). House notes that support can be conceptualized at either an objective or a subjective level. At the latter level, the emphasis is on the recipient's satisfaction with, and assessment of, what others provide.

We see a common theme in these and most other analyses. Namely, social support involves interpersonal transactions beneficial to the recipient. While the concept of social support has been most frequently used in the literature on stress and well-being, the essential ingredient of support—helpful exchanges—has been a frequent topic of research on the family. This chapter will consider both empirical traditions.

Conceptual and methodological problems in measuring social support have been discussed by Thoits (1982). She notes that a variety of different measures have been used, and most of these have been introduced with little attention to their reliability or validity. We see this diversity as having mixed consequences. On the one hand, it undoubtedly results in some nonsignificant and inconsistent findings. On the other hand, when multiple measures are used and the same results emerge, this increases one's confidence in the findings.

In operationalizing concepts, some researchers have blurred the meaning of social support and networks. They measure social support as the presence of significant others in one's life or in terms of the properties of one's network. We prefer to keep the concepts separate, thinking of networks as a set of people and of support as the provisions they supply.

MARITAL STATUS AND WELL-BEING

Among the simplest questions that can be asked about family networks is: "Who is in your family?" We can have sibs or be an only child, we can grow up having two parents or only one, we can marry or remain single, we have children or have none. Presumably the composition of our family network can have a substantial impact upon us. Falbo (1984) has reviewed the literature on being an only child, and Blechman (1982) has appraised the issue of whether children with one parent are at psychological risk. Given our focus on family relations in adulthood, we will not attempt to summarize these areas of research.

As far as we know, relatively little research has been done comparing older adults with and without grown children. The evidence collected to date shows that the presence of children has surprisingly little impact on the well-being of seniors. Glenn and McLanahan (1981) found that the effects of children on the global happiness of people age 50+ to be negligible or negative. Other studies (e.g., Arling, 1976) on frequency of interaction show that contacts with peers contribute more to the morale of seniors than do contacts with children.

A great deal of research has been done examining the relationship between marital status and personal well-being. This work has focused on three main areas of well-being: physical health and mortality, mental health, and life satisfaction. Collectively, these studies support the conclusion that being married is associated with well-being. Besides reviewing the evidence supporting this conclusion, we will address two ancillary questions: Do men benefit from marriage more than women? Why is marriage beneficial?

Health, mortality, and marital status

Verbrugge (1979) has reported an important analysis of health as a function of marital status. Her data sources were U.S. Census information and self-report health surveys conducted by the National Center for Health Statistics. Since she used several data sets, her operational definitions varied somewhat across analyses. Basically, however, she classified illnesses as acute if they began in the two weeks prior to the interview. Conditions that had persisted for more than three months were considered chronic. "Disabled" persons were those who were partially or completely hindered in their major life activity (work, housework, school) by a health or physical condition. All statistics were age-standardized to control for the effects of age on health. Verbrugge concluded that:

> Divorced and separated people have the worst health status, with highest rates of acute conditions, of chronic conditions which limit social activity, and of disability for health problems. Widowed people rank second for health status, followed by single people. Married people appear healthiest, having low rates of chronic limitation and disability. Their rates of restricted activity are . . . intermediate, but hospital stays tend to be short. (p. 267)

The superiority of the married group was clearest with regard to chronic conditions that limited the individual's major life activity. Among married respondents, under 16 percent had limiting conditions. Among other segments of the population, the proportion with chronic limiting conditions ranged from 21 to 25 percent.

With regard to acute, short-term problems, the married enjoyed better health than the divorced and separated respondents. No consistent, clear conclusion could be reached when comparing married people with the widowed and the never-married segments of society. Married people have average rates of hospitalization, but they are discharged sooner than other groups.

Given their better health status, one might also expect married people to have lower age-adjusted death rates. This appears to be the case. For instance, Berkman and Syme (1979) did a longitudinal study of 6,928 adults in Alameda County, California. The marital status of each member in the sample was determined in 1968, and then mortality rates were determined nine years later. Married people were less likely to die during the period of the study. While both men and women benefited from being married, the benefit was especially strong for men.

Given differences in age-adjusted death rates, one would expect married people to live longer than their never-married counterparts. This is born out by Statistics Canada data (received in a personal communication in 1983). Among males, the average life expectancies for married and never-married individuals are, respectively, 72.1 and 64.5 years. The figures for married and never-married women, respectively, are 78.8 and 75.9 years.

Death can result from many causes. Given that age-adjusted death rates are lower for married individuals, one would naturally expect deaths due to most specific causes to be lower for the married segment of society. This is true (see Bloom, White, & Asher, 1979; Gove, 1973). For instance, the death rates for suicide, accidents and homicide, cirrhosis of the liver and lung cancer, and tuberculosis and diabetes are all lower for married people. Deaths due to leukemia and aleukemia, however, are only mildly, if at all, reduced by being married. Obviously, different causes of death can, as Gove (1973) has noted, be associated with various behavioral antecedents. Suicide appears related to psychopathology, accidents to carelessness, cirrhosis and lung cancer to poor health habits (drinking and smoking), and tuberculosis and diabetes to the effectiveness of disease management (treatment) after onset. With leukemia, which is not affected by marital status, death is presumably due to physical factors. Thus, it appears that marital status primarily affects mortality rates in situations where the onset and course of the disease might be affected by the person's psychological adjustment, lifestyle, or handling of the malady.

Marital status and mental health

In general, married individuals appear to enjoy more positive mental health than other groups. On the basis of 11 studies, Bloom et al. (1975, p. 185) concluded that "admission rates into psychiatric facilities are lowest among the married, intermediate among widowed and never-married adults, and highest among the divorced and separated." Verbrugge (1979) and Gove (1972) have reported complementary evidence. Verbrugge showed fewer married individuals (circa 1970) living in mental hospitals. Gove also showed that the rate of mental illness is lower among the married. He extended his review, however, beyond studies of institutionalized rates to include research on the mental health of community residents.

Marital status and life satisfaction

A commonly used survey research question is: "Taken all together, how would you say things are these days—would you say you are very happy, pretty happy, or not too happy?" Married respondents are the most likely to report that they are very happy (see Bernard, 1972; Glenn, 1975; Veroff, Douvan, & Kulka, 1981). For instance, in Glenn's analysis of NORC (National Opinion Research Center) data, 36 percent of married women said they were very happy, compared to less than 20 percent of the widowed, divorced, or never-married.

Is marriage more beneficial for men than for women?

In her provocative book *The Future of Marriage*, Jessie Bernard (1972) argued that marriage has a differential impact on men and women. She claimed that being married is good for husbands but "only half as good for wives" (p. 25). Elsewhere in the volume, she alludes to the sinister influences that marriage may have on women. She talks of the "grim mental-health picture of wives," "the destructive aspects of marriage," and the "wife's marriage [as] . . . pathogenic" (pp. 36, 37, 49).

Bernard bases her case on a variety of evidence. She starts with data showing that wives report more frustrations and dissatisfactions with their marriages than do husbands. Using the same comparison groups, she next reports that married women have more mental health symptoms than married men. She then compares the mental health of married versus single women, concluding that "the mental-health picture of wives shows up . . . unfavorably when compared with unmarried women" (p. 29). Finally, she acknowledges the large proportion of married women who report high life satisfaction, but discusses this as an anomaly. She offers several reasons why truly depressed, married women would nonetheless verbally report their lives as happy.

Bernard's case warrants careful scrutiny. As she herself acknowledges, the husband-wife differences in reporting mental health symptoms may reflect a sex difference rather than the negative impact of marriage on women. Certainly, sex differences in reporting such problems as depression are well documented.

One key element in Bernard's case is the evidence on the mental health of married and single women. On this matter, her conclusion is at odds with the previously mentioned analysis by Gove (1972) and others showing higher rates of mental illness among the nonmarried. In part, the two camps reached opposite conclusions because they reviewed different data. Of the 17 studies used, only one was used by both Bernard and Gove. In terms of numbers of studies, Gove marshals more evidence than does Bernard (14 versus 4). One difference can be detected in the type of studies they cite. Gove primarily reviews studies of people who have sought some form of treatment for their problems. Bernard concentrates more on symptoms reported by community members.

One might infer that married women are more at risk than single women for such problems of daily living as nervousness, insomnia, and depression, even though they are less likely to receive psychiatric treatment. However, even the idea that marriage produces modest disturbances among married women can be questioned. Not all the evidence is consistent with this view. For instance, in a recent study (Cargan & Melko, 1982), single women were more apt than married women to report anxiety, crying spells, nightmares, guilt, and feelings of worthlessness. Overall, we are not convinced of Bernard's contention that married (as opposed to single) women have poor mental health.

Another way of looking at Bernard's thesis is to ask: Is the advantage of being married rather than single greater for men than women? One can calculate ratios by dividing the incident rate for single people by the incident rate for married people. The higher the number, the greater the disadvantage of being single. If such ratios are higher for males than for females, one can infer men suffer more than women from being single (or conversely, benefit more from being married).

Analyzed in this way, two previously reviewed bodies of evidence, Berkman and Syme's (1979) mortality rates and Gove's (1972) mental illness rates, support Bernard's thesis of marriage being more beneficial to men than to women. Verbrugge's (1979) health data also show some support for Bernard's thesis, but only when comparing chronic disability rates for married versus single people.

Glenn (1975) has suggested correlational analysis of the life satisfaction data to test Bernard's comparative-advantage thesis. He argues that if marriage is more important to the life satisfaction of men, then the correlation between marital status and life satisfaction should be higher among men than among women. This, however, is not the case.

A final indirect way of examining the importance of marriage to the well-being of males and females is to look at the consequences of marital termination. Presumably, the sex that suffers the most is the one that was previously benefiting more. Here the evidence is nonconclusive. With the death of a spouse, it appears that men suffer more (Stroebe & Stroebe, 1983). Divorce and separation have a stronger impact on women (Verbrugge, 1979).

Explanations for the beneficial effects of marriage

Bloom et al. (1979) offer selection and stress as two major explanations for the benefits of marriage. (Role explanations are considered within the stress category.) The selectivity viewpoint assumes that there are underlying differences between the people who do and don't get married. Thus, quite independent of marriage, one might find differences in the health, adjustment, and happiness of these two groups. Stress theorists assert that stressful events can lead to detrimental consequences. They assume the incidence of stressful events is associated with marital status. Indeed, marital disruption itself is a stressful event.

In discussing the effects of marital status on health and mortality, lifestyle and the use of health care services have been considered as explanatory concepts (Berkman & Syme, 1979; Verbrugge, 1979). There is evidence, for instance, that the prevalence of smoking and drinking is high among the divorced population.

To sum up, we believe marriage benefits people in terms of their physical health, their mental health, and their life satisfaction. In some domains, men may benefit more from marriage than do women. However, insinuations that marriage has an overall negative impact on women seem ill-founded.

THE FAMILY AS A NETWORK OF SOCIAL RELATIONS

One can ask several questions when trying to assess the importance of kin as members of our networks. Perhaps the simplest is: What proportion of the people in our networks are relatives, and how often do we interact with them? Given that leisure activities are among our most enjoyable pursuits and are voluntarily chosen, we wondered: Whom do we select as companions during our recreational hours? Finally, we wanted to know: Are there qualitative differences in the time we spend with family and friends?

A note of caution should be mentioned here that applies to the family, both as a network of social relations and as a helping system. Many studies only include married adults and/or overrepresent women. Institutionalized and derelict members of society rarely find their way into surveys. Often, statistics on family interaction are based on subsamples (e.g., adults with living parents). Collectively, these sampling and reporting procedures probably result in a mildly inflated picture of the quantity and quality of family ties.

Kin as a part of our personal networks

Two studies are particularly helpful in shedding light on the composition of personal networks. C. S. Fischer (1982) conducted an extensive survey of 1,050 people living in 50 localities of varying urbanism in northern California. Respondents' personal networks were elicited by asking them to name the people who did, would, or could provide them with various kinds of social support. On the average, 18.5 names were given. Of these, 7.8 (42 percent) were kin.

A second relevant study was conducted in Toronto, Canada (Shulman, 1975), where the sample included 347 adults (146 males, 201 females) aged 18–65. Respondents were asked to name their closest relationships outside their own household to a maximum of six persons. Of the people named, 41 percent were kin, and a slight majority (51 percent) of relationships ranked first in closeness were kin.

Table 1

Kin in social networks by age and life-cycle stage

Life-cycle stage	Percentage reporting one or more kin	Percentage reporting over 50 percent kin
Age		
18–30	60%	32%
31–44	66	29
45–65	77	36
Marital life cycle		
Single	41	16
Married, childless	70	42
Married, children	83	32
Other	81	51

Source: Adapted from N. Shulman, Life-cycle variations in patterns of close relationships, *Journal of Marriage and the Family* 37 (1975), pp. 813–821.

The proportion of kin bonds varies over the life cycle. Table 1 shows data from Shulman's study indicating two points: close kin relations are more common for married adults than for the never married, and such relationships are more common in older adults aged 45–65. Fischer and Phillips' (1982) data on isolation from kin demonstrate roughly equivalent patterns for people aged 22–64, although for their women the effect of age on isolation from kin held for only one of two dependent measures.

A few speculations are in order on why the proportion of kin members in our networks fluctuates over the life cycle. In late adolescence and young adulthood, people may be trying to establish their autonomy and independence; so they are more involved with peers who have similar interests and life styles than with kin. At this point in life, older relatives (especially parents) may not be very important to respondents, even though these same relationships may be reported as important by the older adults. Marriage and children make family life salient since the cultural norms surrounding these events undoubtedly promote extended family relations. With the arrival of children and again with old age, we have additional needs that we turn to kin for help in satisfying.

Instead of looking at the composition of people's networks, other researchers have examined patterns of interaction among family members. For example, in Gibson's (1972) survey of Ohio disability benefit applicants (N = 486), the mean number of nonhousehold kin seen at least monthly was 2.9. Contact between parents and adult children is the most common form of kin contact. Given that they live in the same community, two thirds or more of adults get together with their elderly parents at least weekly (Irving, 1972, p. 49). In Shanas' (1973) multinational study of senior citizens, of the 82 percent of American respondents who had offspring, 78 percent had seen one of their children within the previous week. Table 2 presents data on the frequency of contact a representative sample of married American males have with each of six different relatives.

In an article reviewing the results of 37 studies and including secondary analysis of two additional data sets, Leigh (1982) identified six key correlates of kin interaction.

Close relatives (e.g., parents and children) interact more often than distant relatives (e.g., second cousins).

Females interact more with kin than do males.

Geographical distance decreases the frequency of interaction.

Affectional closeness increases the frequency of interaction between relatives. In Leigh's data sets, closeness was one of the best predictors of interaction, although in another recent investigation, the correlation between these variables was only significant for younger mother-daughter pairs living moderate distances from one another (Walker & Thompson, 1983).

Kin interaction is inversely related to social class: it is more frequent in the lower than the middle class.

Kin contact is enhanced by strong norms endorsing such interaction.

Table 2

Percentage distributions of contacts between 1,061 married American males and their relatives

		Frequency of contact				
Relative	N	Weekly or more	2 to 3 times per month	Every 2 to 3 months	2 to 3 times per year	Once a year or less
Father	237	52.7%	6.8%	13.1%	5.5%	21.9%
Oldest brother	347	31.1	6.6	15.0	10.7	36.6
Grandfather	59*	15.2	20.3	22.0	10.2	32.2
Brother-in-law	314†	19.4	9.6	20.1	13.1	37.9
Male cousin	499	12.8	5.6	18.4	12.8	50.3
Uncle	372‡	10.2	4.8	16.9	10.2	57.8

* Percentages are based on the respondents' interaction with 59 maternal and paternal grandparents, but since some respondents may have had both grandfathers, the number of respondents with grandparents could have been less than 59.
† The question was asked with reference to the husband of the respondent's oldest married sister.
‡ Percentages are based on the respondents' interaction with 372 uncles (the oldest brother of either the respondent's mother or father) but the number of respondents with an uncle may be less than 372.
Source: S. R. Klatzky, *Patterns of contact with relatives* (Washington, D.C.: American Sociological Association, 1971).

Leigh did not find a relationship between frequency of kin contact and stage in the life cycle. These results seem inconsistent with the data on the increasing proportion of kin in people's networks as they get older. The key to this paradox may be a differential rate of decline in social interaction with kin and nonkin. Perhaps interaction with kin remains fairly constant in frequency, while interaction with friends drops off. Then, the relative importance of kin as network members would increase.

Family and leisure

Somewhat surprisingly, the empirical literature on associational patterns during leisure appears limited. Nonetheless, in reviewing the evidence that does exist, Holman and Epperson (in press) conclude that "the family today is clearly the center of most people's leisure activities." Americans want to spend their leisure time with their families. And most of them succeed. For example, Kelly (1978) did a study of residents (N = 374) of three medium-sized communities (a university town, a small industrial city, and a new planned suburb). He asked them what activities they had done in the past year and with whom they usually did each. The results showed over half the activities studied were usually done with family members. Activities not done alone were about three times more likely to be done with family companions than with friends.

Some information is known on how family life-cycle and other factors influence family leisure patterns. Family-centered leisure is undoubtedly less important for adolescents and single young adults than it is for other age groups. Both the presence of preschool children and dual employment limit the amount of leisure activity. Unhappily married couples (Birchler, Weiss, & Vincent, 1975) engage in fewer joint leisure activities than do happily married couples. Family social activities increase on weekends and during the vacation season (Davey & Paolucci, 1980, p. 43). Finally (at least in "Middletown," first studied by the Lynds in the 1920s), families today spend a lot more leisure time together than their counterparts did 60 years ago.

The quality of family relations

In opinion polls and quality-of-life studies, most people evaluate their marriages, their family relations, and their friendships quite positively. Other studies have gone beyond global ratings to sample specific events. Wills, Weiss, and Patterson (1974) had couples (N = 7) keep detailed daily records of their instrumental and affective behaviors for two weeks. Pleasurable behaviors outnumbered displeasurable behaviors by a ratio of approximately 3 to 1.

In another study done at the University of Oregon, Birchler et al. (1975) had couples discuss human relations problems in a laboratory setting. Half the couples selected were happily married, half had low scores on the Locke-Wallace marital adjustment inventory. Besides interacting with their spouses, each participant engaged in a discussion with an opposite-sex stranger (i.e., another subject's spouse). The contents of the conversations were coded as positive or negative. Even for the distressed couples, positive interactions were more common than negative interactions. Of the three types of dyads, strangers interacted more positively when problem solving than did either happily married or distressed couples.

Larson (1983) compared the quality of family and peer relations experienced by 75 high school students. He had these students carry electronic pagers. Paging students at randomly selected times during the day, Larson found that these adolescents spent 18 percent of their time with family and 30 percent with friends. The adolescents' moods were more positive when they were with friends than when they were with family.

EXCHANGE AND HELPING AMONG KIN

The "isolated nuclear family" debate, mentioned at the beginning of this chapter, has subsided (Lee, 1980). In part, this is because both sides have realized the futility of trying to decide if the family is isolated. No mutually acceptable criterion exists; isolation is a relative matter. Nonetheless, this controversy stimulated investigation of the help patterns among family members. Thus, the debate has left a rich legacy.

This section of the chapter will review the research on how family members help each other and on what they exchange. First, findings will be presented on helping in general. Then, the kinds of help that are exchanged will be examined along with a consideration of who gives what kind of support. To assess the importance of kin as helpers, it is necessary to compare the amounts and kinds of help provided by kin with help received from other sources of social support such as friends, neighbors, and co-workers. Attention will be focused on whom people rely on both during normal times and during crises. Thus, the later parts of this section will focus on family supports within the context of other social supports.

General help patterns within the extended family

A first generation of studies (Hill, 1970; Shanas, 1967; Sharp & Axelrod, 1956; Sussman, 1959, 1965) examined help patterns among kin.

Data were collected from urban Americans adults (Sharp & Axelrod; Sussman), members of three generations of the same families (Hill), and senior citizens in the United States, Denmark, and Britain (Shanas). Sample sizes ranged from small (N = 80 in Sussman's study) to substantial (N = 723 in Sharp and Axelrod's survey) to very large (N ≃ 7,500 in Shanas' project). Respondents were asked questions regarding the aid and services they exchanged with relatives.

A major conclusion from these studies was that assistance between kin is almost universal. In Sussman's study, for instance, 93 percent of respondents reported some form of exchange of aid between their own nuclear family and related kin. In Sharp and Axelrod's survey, over 98 percent of those questioned said they were tied to relatives through mutual aid. About 7 out of every 10 couples reported both giving and receiving some kind of help from relatives outside their immediate household.

These studies also provided information about the patterns and correlates of mutual help. Some conclusions from the data are:

Exchanges tend to occur among close relatives—parents, children, siblings as opposed to aunts, uncles, cousins (Sharp & Axelrod).

Exchanges are fostered by geographical proximity (Sharp & Axelrod).

During adulthood, as people get older, they report giving more than they get (Sharp & Axelrod). In intergenerational exchanges, parents typically give more to their children than children give to their parents.

In his three-generational study, Hill found evidence of the middle-generational squeeze: members of this group had the highest level of help giving.

Intergenerational help between parents and children is more common than intragenerational help between adult siblings.

Older adults tend to rely on their daughters for help (Shanas).

More recently, Cicirelli (1983) as well as Walker and Thompson (1983) have shed light on how relationship factors influence the exchange of aid between adult children and their parents. Although done from different theoretical frameworks, these studies both measured a common set of variables at the operational level. Cicirelli's study will be of particular interest to psychologists, since it was cast in terms of Bowlby's attachment theory.

In both studies, more frequent intergenerational contact was associated with more exchange of aid. This was especially true among older mother-daughter pairs where the daughter was middle-aged rather than a young adult.

In computing bivariate correlations, Cicirelli obtained a small but positive association between emotional attachment and helping. Attachment was not retained, however, as an immediate antecedent in a path analysis of helping. In Walker and Thompson's (1983) study, emotional intimacy correlated with how much noneconomic help daughters gave their mothers, but it did not predict how much help mothers gave their daughters. Thus, these investigations provide only qualified support for the importance of affective factors in understanding intergenerational exchanges. Nonetheless, we believe such dyadic variables are a worthwhile avenue for future research.

Types of social support

In demonstrating the existence of extensive, general patterns of mutual help, these early studies also asked: What, in particular, is being exchanged? Who provides which type of service? Does help flow in two directions or just one? To answer these questions, early investigators (e.g., Sussman, 1959; Sharp & Axelrod, 1956) presented respondents with a list of about a half-dozen types of exchange that might occur.

From these lists, baby-sitting, help during illness, and financial aid were common types of aid. Help with housework and advice were less common. For most of these forms of aid, exchanges occurred between parents and their adult children and between siblings. Financial aid, however, was rarely exchanged between siblings; it was usually an exchange between parents and their grown offspring.

In intergenerational exchanges, child-care services and financial aid tend to flow unilaterally downward from parents to their adult children. Household assistance and help during illness follow bilateral patterns. Adult children are as apt to help their parents as vice versa.

Examination of who gives what to whom may help resolve one paradoxical aspect of these early studies. They found evidence of both linear and curvilinear helping patterns over the life cycle. According to the linear view, parents continue to help their children even in advanced old age. According to the curvilinear view, middle-age adults are net providers for both their own children and their very elderly parents. Perhaps both views are partially true. We suspect that when investigators (e.g., Hill, 1970) concentrate on the exchange of services, they obtain a curvilinear pattern. However, when they focus on financial and economic resources (Cheal, 1983), they obtain a linear pattern, with very elderly individuals giving more than they get.

In summarizing the early studies, it is fair to say that family members often help one another, and they help one another in a variety of ways. Yet, to put the importance of familial helping in perspective, one must examine it within the larger context of who else provides us with social support.

Kin compared with nonkin as sources of support during normal times

One of the most important sources of comparative data on kin and nonkin support is C. S. Fischer's (1982) aforementioned study of personal networks. By having respondents list the names of people with whom they engaged in various forms of exchange, he could calculate the proportion of kin for each type of supportive interaction. His results (see Table 3) demonstrate that in most domains, people have more nonkin than kin support-group members. For example, 74 percent of the people respondents would ask to check on their house were friends rather than kin. The clearest exception to this pattern occurred in the financial area: 65 percent of the people from whom respondents would borrow money were kin. In this area, however, banks are probably a more-important source of financial aid than are kin (Gibson, 1972, p. 15).

Naturally, the balance of kin versus nonkin support varies across communities and over time. For example, in C. S. Fischer's (1982) study, residents of urban communities identified fewer kin (especially extended kin) as network members than did residents of small towns. Fischer argues that urban life provides people with alternatives to

Table 3

Kin and nonkin as sources of support

Type of exchange	Source of support		
	Spouse	Kin	Nonkin
Counseling			
Discuss personal matters	17%	32%	51%
Seek advice	24	32	42
Companionship			
Socializing	1	25	75
Discuss hobby	2	14	83
Practical assistance			
Check on house	0	26	74
Household assistance	2	47	50
Discuss work problems	5	7	89
Borrow money	1	64	35

Source: C. S. Fischer, *To dwell among friends: Personal networks in town and city* (Chicago: University of Chicago Press, 1982), p. 386.

relatives. These alternatives include both nonkin friends and institutional, organized forms of support. In urban environments, then, kinship involvement becomes more selective. It does not, however, lose all its importance. Fischer found the qualitative aspects of kin relationships were equally positive in small and large communities. Furthermore, Fischer maintains that urbanites continue to call on close kin in times of need.

Evidence of historical changes can be found in Veroff et al.'s (1981) work. In 1957 and 1976, Veroff and his associates asked representative samples of Americans how they dealt with worries. At both points in time, about 60 percent of married respondents mentioned their spouse as their primary resource for handling worries. However, the exclusive dependence on the spouse and family as a resource decreased from 1957 to 1976, and the reliance on friends increased. Echoing Fischer's viewpoint, Veroff et al. suggest that the importance of the family still persists, yet the use of family support has become more selective.

Kin and nonkin as sources of social support in disasters and ill health

Up to this point, we have been considering the importance of kin and nonkin during normal times. To whom do we turn in times of crises?

A consistent finding in the disaster literature is that kin are a major source of help reported by disaster victims. In reviewing 50 studies, Quarantelli (1960) concluded that in the majority of disasters, anywhere from two thirds to three quarters of the victims received a substantial portion of their rehabilitation aid from relatives. He reports a discernible hierarchy of help-seeking: Victims seek aid first from family members and close friends and second from other friends and neighbors. Next, they turn to anonymous local community residents and to various organizations such as public agencies set up specifically for the aid of disaster victims.

Thus, kin and public agencies differ greatly in their positions in the help-seeking hierarchy. This contrast is made even more salient by Drabek, Key, Erickson, and Crowe (1975), who report that 95 percent of the tornado victims they interviewed indicated that the assistance received from relatives had been voluntarily offered to them. However, nearly half of the families who received aid from the Red Cross had requested it, and nearly a quarter initiated a request for aid from the Salvation Army.

Quarantelli maintains that this hierarchy of help-seeking is consistent across many countries. Moreover, the smaller the disaster, the greater the reliance on kin. With more extensive disasters, there is a greater probability that one's relatives will also be victims, thus diminishing their capacity to provide assistance. Even in these situations, however, aid is most often received from kin—frequently from those relatives living far away.

Kin are an important source of help both in the pre- and postdisaster stages. For example, in a study by Drabek and Boggs (1968), almost one third of the families were warned by relatives of an impending flood. (This is a substantial proportion, given the specially broadcast media announcements of police warnings to evacuate). Relatives also played a key role in the evacuation process, as families most often stayed with kin. The provision of temporary shelter is a type of aid frequently given during disasters. Drabek et al. (1975) report that relatives also supply many other forms of aid such as baby-sitting, food or clothing, and small money loans following the disaster.

Not only in disasters but also in illness, families appear to be an especially important source of support. Rosow (1970) reports that older people look first to their adult children for care during illness, especially for longer illnesses. Neighbors were the second most frequently chosen, particularly for widows and for those living alone. In fact, Rosow found that neighbors may become the primary source of support for those people whose children live far away.

Croog, Lipson, and Levine (1972) studied male (N = 293) myocardial infarction (heart attack) victims aged 30–59. One year after their attacks, patients were asked to note the degree of help they had received from various people. Siblings and parents received the highest ratings as helpers, followed by friends and neighbors. Thus, one can conclude that kin both frequently serve and are especially appreciated as helpers during illness.

SOCIAL SUPPORT ACROSS THE FAMILY LIFE CYCLE

Life is often viewed as a developmental progression. We go from infancy to old age. Along the way, there are various stages and transitions between stages. We have periods of "being married" or "being a grandparent" and passages via which we "become a parent." Besides becoming a parent, three other important family life transitions are getting married, getting divorced, and becoming a widow. People's networks are intertwined with their life changes.

This section of the chapter focuses on networks and family life transitions. More attention will be focused on becoming than on being. We will assume that there is a bidirectional flow of influence between networks and transitions. The major questions to be addressed are as follows:

1. What are the effects of family transitions on the size and composition of networks?
2. Who helps during various transitions and what resources do they provide?
3. What are the effects of the social support on how well people progress through the transition?

The effects of transitions on personal network

Not surprisingly, life transitions often affect the size and composition of people's networks. Overall, there appears to be a trend toward networks declining in size in the transition to marriage, parenthood, becoming divorced, and during bereavement. In the case of the transition to marriage, couples' networks diminish because of increasing overlapping of their networks as they progress toward marriage (Milardo, 1982). Married couples tend to include both the same kin (Turner, 1970) and friends (Lee, 1979) in their respective networks. Concerning network composition, peripheral friends are excluded from the network, and close friends become peripheral as couples progress from occasional dating through to marriage, while kin relationships remain intact (Johnson & Leslie, 1982).

In the transition to parenthood, even though the number of kin mentioned as network members may decline (Saulnier, 1983), it appears that kin relationships become more important or central in the couples' social network. Specifically, Deutscher (1970) reported that couples move in the direction of greater family affiliation as they approach parenthood. Richardson and Kagan (1979) found arrival of a first child resulted in closer ties to the couples' parents, and L. R. Fischer (1981, 1983) reported heightened contact between mothers and daughters when children arrived (although interaction between the daughters and mothers-in-law did not necessarily increase). Ties with friends, particularly friends without children, diminish in the transition to parenthood (Richardson & Kagan).

Social networks also decrease in size during the divorce process. This is especially true for women whose previous networks overlapped considerably with their husbands' (Wilcox, 1981). One reason for the general decline in network size is that former in-laws become less central in the divorced person's network, as is evidenced by an overall reduction in frequency of interaction (Spicer & Hampe, 1975). Regarding the composition of networks, it appears that for some divorced women, family becomes very important (Hagestad, Smyer, & Stierman, 1983; Spicer & Hampe, 1975), while others make friends, especially divorced friends, the hub of their social network (e.g., Chiriboga, Coho, Stein, & Roberts, 1979).

The word *widowed* could be substituted for *divorced* in the preceding paragraph. Family members figure prominently in the social networks of some widows (e.g., Abrahams, 1972; Bankoff, 1983a), while nonkin ties become salient to others (e.g., Arling, 1976). Again, it may be the case that those who turn to family formerly relied on their spouse as the bridge to peer relationships. As Maddison and Raphael (1975) comment, "Obviously, the major social relationships for many of the (widowed) women have previously involved married couples, and the more multidimensional the involvement of a woman in her husband's life, the more disorganized will be her social relationships after his death" (p. 27).

Networks as resources during life transitions

Life changes can alter the bases and alliances underlying family relationships. They can modify our attitudes, our circumstances, our needs, and how others perceive us. Each major transition, as has been documented, changes our network in distinctive ways. In a similar vein, it is reasonable to expect that the type and amount of help received from different network members varies with the life crisis being faced. Families are an important source of social support in the transition to parenthood. Support includes visits, advice, presents, encouragement, respect for the new parents' need to be alone (Fein, 1976), and an increase in financial aid (Sussman & Burchinal, 1962, p. 321). L. R. Fischer's (1983) study of mothers and mothers-in-law revealed that both were equally likely to baby-sit, provide loans, and give gifts, although there was a tendency for mothers-in-law to *give* things and for mothers to *do* things following the birth of the child. Carveth and Gottlieb (1979) found both mothers and mothers-in-law to be important confidantes, while in Fischer's sample, the daughters were four to five times more likely to ask their mothers than their mothers-in-law for child-rearing advice.

One's spouse is an important source of emotional support (Carveth & Gottlieb, 1979; Fein, 1976; Grossman, Eichler, & Winickoff, 1980). The new fathers in Fein's study, however, received little material or emotional support from their co-workers.

Chiriboga et al. (1979) found friends to be the most common source of support for men and women going through a divorce. Next, surprisingly, came spouses, followed by mental health professionals, relatives, and parents. Self-help groups and children were least sought out. Women were more likely to seek out children for support than were men.

The greater tendency of women than men to seek support from their children was also obtained in a study on the impact of divorce in middle age by Hagestad et al. (1983). They, however, found children to be an important source of support both before and after the divorce of their parents. Many of the women received indirect financial support from their children—for example, one third of the sample reported children who paid rent living with them.

Probably age is a key to understanding why children emerged as a more-important source of support in Hagestad et al.'s (1983) study than in Chiriboga et al.'s (1979). In Hagestad et al.'s study, the average respondent was approximately 50 years old, and all respondents had at least one child age 16 or older. In Chiriboga's study, the average respondent was in their mid-30s, and those who had children would typically have had younger children. Presumably, their child's maturity is a crucial factor in whether parents will turn to their offspring for help.

Nearly half the males and three quarters of the females in Hagestad et al.'s (1983) study also discussed their marital problems with their parents. In fact, about one third of the males moved home at some point in the divorce process. However, overall, children were perceived as a more important source of support than were parents in this study.

In bereavement, Abrahams (1972) found that kin were rated as most helpful in dealing with grief and adjustment problems, followed by friends, clergy, other professionals, and club groups. Thus, it appears that in the transition to parenthood, in bereavement, and under some circumstances in divorce, kin are significant suppliers of support. This leaves unanswered, however, what impact this support has on how successfully people navigate through these life transitions.

Effects of social support

One of the cornerstones in the literature on social support is the assumption that support helps people deal with transitions and stressful life events. The model that has most frequently been advanced contains three postulates: First, stress (conceptualized as an external event) has deleterious consequences; it causes "strain" (an internal form of distress). Second, social support can reduce the level of external stress that people experience. Third, social support can mitigate, or buffer, the impact of stress so that people with social support experience less strain than those without social support.

Numerous studies have been done testing this model. Although there have been exceptions and critiques of this literature (Thoits, 1982), the accumulated evidence reviewed in 39 articles and books (see Cobb

& Jones, 1984) is sufficient to conclude that social support sometimes reduces stress, and it sometimes buffers the impact that stress can have. In essence, for some stressors some of the time, social support protects people from experiencing strain.

From studies of stress and social support, it appears that the family can both provide social support and benefit from it. For example, Thoits (1982) demonstrated how undesirable life events have less impact on married than on unmarried people. Other investigations focused on a specific type of event (see House, 1981, chap. 4) show that the family plays a modest role in reducing and protecting employees from job stress. In terms of how the family benefits, the role of support from all sources has been examined vis-à-vis family life transitions. A favorite arena for demonstrating the positive effects of social support has been the transition to parenthood.

A study by Crnic, Greenberg, Ragozin, Robinson, and Basham (1983) is noteworthy because it examined several aspects of the social-support model and used both self-report and observational outcome measures. New mothers ($N = 105$) were asked about the social support and stressful life events they had experienced during pregnancy. Their life satisfaction and satisfaction with parenting was assessed one month after their baby's arrival. Observations of parent-child interaction provided an index of maternal sensitivity.

As predicted by a social-support model, both stress and support significantly predicted the outcome measures. Mothers with greater stress were less positive in their attitudes and less sensitive in their behavior. Mothers with more support were more positive in their attitudes. Intimate support—that is, support from their husbands—proved to have the most general positive effects. Finally, social support moderated the adverse effects of stress on the mother's life satisfaction.

Other studies show similar effects. Carveth and Gottlieb (1979) report a consistent set of inverse relationships between their measures of social support and both objective and subjective measures of strain in new mothers. In a study by Nuckolls, Cassel, and Kaplan (1972) women with high levels of social support (psychosocial assets) had only one third the complication rate during their pregnancy compared to women with low social support. They argue that the complications in pregnancy were not a result of stress, but of stress coupled with low support.

The relationship between stress and social support was further explored in a study by Paykel, Emms, Fletcher, and Rassaby (1980). Their results showed that women who experienced stressful life events and who did not receive emotional support or assistance from their husband were depressed both during pregnancy and postpartum. Lack of a confidant, other than husband, also correlated with depression.

Cutrona (1983) suggests that different kinds of social support are important at different times in ameliorating depressive symptoms in the postpartum period. At two weeks postpartum, knowing that family members could be relied upon for assistance was the only social support variable that predicted depressive symptoms. By eight weeks, women's social needs had broadened; at that time, assistance and guidance from family members were effective deterrents of depression. In addition, reassurance of worth and social integration into friendship and co-worker networks became significant predictors of depression. Cutrona found that women with both high and low levels of stress appeared to benefit from positive social support.

Crockenberg (1981) hypothesized that social support would facilitate responsive mothering under stressful conditions (an irritable baby) and hence made for strong infant-mother attachment. Her results showed that social support enhanced mother-child attachment and had its greatest effect under stressful conditions.

Besides the transition to parenthood, the role of social support has been examined in other family life changes. Concerning adjustment to divorce, Wilcox (1981) reported a tendency for successful adjusters to have larger social networks. He also found that women in high-density networks adjust more poorly than women in larger, low-density groups. A large proportion of social support in the high-density group was provided by kin. On the other hand, women in the low-density group tended to turn to friends for support. They were also more likely to seek help from outside sources. One possible explanation for the detrimental effects of high-density, kin-oriented networks is that kin may express disapproval of the separation and criticize the person getting divorced. Friends, presumably, are less judgmental.

It has been argued that the kind of support most helpful in adjusting to divorce (Leslie, Grady, & Kirby, 1982) and widowhood (Walker, MacBride, & Vachon, 1977) varies as a function of the stage of the transition. Leslie et al. hypothesized that in the early stages of divorce, individuals may have a need for a network which provides emotional and material support to cope with the initial impact of the loss and the resultant changes in daily life. They suggest that this support is provided most effectively by a network which is dense, homogenous, and characterized by strong ties. The prototype of this kind of network is, of course, the family. In the later adjustment period, although the needs for emotional support and material aid continue, individuals can be expected to experience an increased need for information and new social contacts which would foster the development of a new social identity. Thus, at this stage, they propose that a network which is less dense and homogenous would be most conducive to good adjustment. Here the friendship network would seem to meet these criteria.

The Leslie et al. (1982) study offers a direct but preliminary test of this viewpoint. Their results did not support the prediction that family is most important in early stages of divorce, while involvement with friends is important at later stages. However, as the authors point out, their results must be interpreted cautiously, "as our current sample size of 25 does not justify regression analyses with four predictors" (p. 7).

Results of widowhood studies are more encouraging. Interestingly, Abrahams (1972), in her study of widowed men and women who called a widowhead serviceline, comments that "for most people relatives are helpful in the early stages of bereavement, but the callers forming satisfactory relationships later on had found them among friends or at clubs" (p. 60). Bankoff (1983b) found that social support from parents was the best predictor of psychological well-being among middle-aged widows immediately after their spouse's death. Widowed or otherwise single friends were initially important only to those women who had no living parents. While most of the women received help from their children, this support was not significantly related to the widow's well-being.

As time went on, however, the picture changed. For women widowed 19–36 months, support from single friends was the strongest correlate of psychological well-being. The role of parents diminished considerably.

CONCLUSION

Recap

The premise of this chapter has been that the family serves as a social network and support system. We have examined the quantity and quality of family interaction as well as the ratio of kin to nonkin in personal networks. We have looked at recreational and helping patterns among kin. The underlying assumption of the chapter was that such contact with kin can have beneficial effects. To determine this, we reviewed how people evaluate the help they receive from kin, the role of kin (and others) in dealing with life crises, and the effects of marital status on well-being.

Relationships with kin do, in fact, figure prominently in people's lives, as approximately two fifths of their social networks are comprised of kin. This proportion increases with age. Americans tend to participate in recreational activities with their families and to evaluate the quality of their family relations positively.

Kin contact, at least between parents and their adult children, leads to the exchange of aid. Family members exchange many kinds of help.

In most areas of helping, this exchange is mutual, except in the provision of financial aid and child-care services, where help tends to flow from parents to their adult offspring. People most often turn to their families in crises such as disasters and illness and often turn to their families during life transitions. The help offered by kin during illness or bereavement is evaluated especially positively.

Social support, as illustrated by studies of parenthood, helps people deal with life transitions and crises. Sometimes, the support comes from family members. Other times, the well-being of family members benefits from the support nonkin provide. One's spouse, an often-overlooked source of support, plays an important function. Married people generally enjoy better physical and psychological health, longer life expectancy, and greater overall satisfaction with life than do their single counterparts.

The significance of the family must be kept in proper perspective. For example, friends are considered important for socializing and may play a more crucial role than kin in facilitating adjustment during the later stages of coping with divorce and bereavement. Limited evidence also suggests a trend toward more selective use of kin in urban areas. Nonetheless, overall, the family network is alive and well!

Toward a psychological perspective on family support

As we noted at the beginning of this chapter, a large proportion of the research on the family has been done by sociologists. In studies of the family as a social and exchange network, there has been a greater emphasis on description than on the development of theory. We believe future research in this area can be enhanced by greater use of psychological concepts and theories. We also believe the research on social support has importance to society as a whole. In the hope of encouraging more systematic elaboration and application, we will conclude with a few theoretical and practical speculations.

Attitudes, equity, altruism, and attributions are all psychological constructs with potential relevance for understanding the supportive exchanges between family members. An attitude is an evaluative (good/bad) feeling toward a particular object or person. It is generally believed that attitudes predispose people to specific actions, but attitudes and behavior are not perfectly correlated.

In developing an attitudinal approach, one of the first tasks would be to identify attitudes relevant to family interaction and support. Thus, one might assess attitudes toward the importance of the family, toward specific family members, or toward assisting one's relatives. Another task would be to use attitudes to predict behavior. Fishbein and Ajzen (1975) have developed a very helpful model for doing this.

They claim that the person's attitudes plus their belief about how significant others would behave lead to the individual's intentions. These
intentions, in turn, lead to the person's actions. Thus, for example,
people with positive attitudes toward helping kin who believe their
friends would also provide such help, should be especially likely to
offer help.

Another challenge for the attitudinal approach would be to identify
the conditions that enhance or diminish the correspondence between
attitudes and behavior. Several clues are available from past research.
For instance, it has shown that attitude-behavior consistency is increased when the behavioral implications of the attitudes are clear
for the person. Fishbein and Ajzen have pointed out that if you want
attitudes to predict behavior, you should measure them at the same
level of specificity. That is, attitudes toward specific acts (such as having
Sunday dinner with your in-laws) will predict specific behaviors (such
as the number of Sunday dinners eaten together). Global attitudes
will predict multiple-act, composite measures of behavior. Other investigators have demonstrated the importance of personality traits—for
instance, "low self-monitors" behave more consistently with their attitudes than do "high self-monitors."

Equity theory is another approach with high apparent relevance
to kin relations. Equity theorists view relationships in quasi-economic
terms. They think of each party's investments and benefits. Relationships in which one person benefits more than the other are presumed
to be aversive. According to equity theorists, such relationships should
be avoided and/or disliked. Naturally, both actual and psychological
mechanisms can be used to restore equity.

Walster, Walster, and Berscheid (1978) have demonstrated how
equity principles operate in the selection of dating partners and in
determining people's feelings toward their marriage. There have, however, been implications in the literature that an exchange orientation
may be detrimental to marriages (Murstein, Cerreto, & MacDonald,
1977) or less important in close relationships. Mills and Clark (1982)
consider parent-child and marital relations "communal." They argue
that in such relations participants have less concern with giving and
receiving as an exchange. Instead, members are concerned about the
welfare of the other and want to benefit the other person when that
person needs help.

Rook (1983) used equity theory as a framework for examining the
relationships of elderly widows. She asked respondents about what
they received from, and gave to, family and friends. Under-benefited
individuals give more than they get; over-benefited individuals get
more than they give. In relations with friends, Rook found that imbalances in either direction were associated with higher loneliness and

less satisfaction. Imbalances in familial exchanges, however, were not associated with how satisfied the widows were in their relationships with their children.

We suspect the key to applying equity principles to family relations may involve discriminating different classes of family relations and different ways equity operates. For instance, it may be that equity is more simple and salient in the relationships of more distant relatives. Intimate relations may not follow a tit-for-tat, immediate pattern of exchange, although participants may hope to achieve parity over time. Rook assessed equity in the present relations between parents and their children. As she acknowledges, however, in these relationships, equity may be calculated over a longer time span. Being over-benefited today may be seen as a just reward for having been under-benefited at an earlier time.

When we give gifts or provide services to kin without expectation of repayment or reward, our behavior may simply be altruistic. Psychologists have extensively studied such prosocial behavior in recent years (Perlman & Cozby, 1982, chap. 12). Altruism is influenced by such factors as: social rewards and costs, modeling processes, moods, recognition of the other person's plight, empathetic concern for the other person's needs, assuming responsibility for providing help, and recipient characteristics.

It seems highly plausible that these same factors may be useful in predicting family helping behavior. For instance, consistent with the bystander apathy studies showing the importance of recognizing the victim's plight, Cicirelli (1983) recently demonstrated that helping was more common in cases where the children felt their elderly mothers needed help. One wonders if other hypotheses could be successfully transferred from one area to the other. For instance, does the existence of several siblings reduce each child's sense of responsibility to help their parents? Do moods influence when help is given to kin?

In most attitude and altruism research, behavior is the outcome variable; it is an endpoint. In attributional studies, however, actions are more likely to be a starting point. Attribution theorists (see Perlman & Cozby, 1982, chap. 6) are concerned with how lay people explain the causes of behavior. Behavior can be attributed internally to the actor him- or herself or externally to forces in the environment. When external pressures are present, internal causes are discounted. Thus, to the extent that the helping of kin is dictated by social norms and pressures, this should reduce our tendency to attribute the helpful actions to causes within the helper. This perspective applies to a more-limited range of phenomena. Yet it should be helpful in understanding how people interpret their relatives' actions and what dispositions (or personality traits) they assign to their kin.

The enhancement of social support

Given its beneficial effects, researchers and practitioners have—not surprisingly—turned their attention to how social support can be enhanced (see Cobb & Jones, 1984; Pilisuk & Parks, 1983; Rook & Peplau, 1982; Unger & Powell, 1980). One goal of these efforts should be to find ways of fully realizing the potential of the family as a social-support system. But, if the family is already serving many members of society rather well, then it is equally important to find ways of enhancing the support of those people deficient in family ties. Among groups at risk are the unhappily married, the divorced, the widowed (especially widowed men), seniors without children, and individuals living a long distance from their kin. Typically, strategies for enhancing social support include promoting new relationships, enhancing the quality of existing relationships, or replacing informal support via more organized programs.

In terms of promoting new relationships (see Rook & Peplau, 1982), psychologists have developed social skill training programs for both children and adults. Programs have been especially designed to help people overcome specific problems such as shyness and anxiety about dating. Besides professionally developed strategies, a number of businesses and organizations in society exist explicitly or implicitly to help people become acquainted. These include dating services, singles bars, ski clubs, and the like.

While simply expanding one's network may indirectly support the family or the individual, a more direct form of support during crises and transitions comes from contact with similar others. Thus, there are groups for engaged couples, new parents, the recently separated, and the widowed. There are organizations like Parents without Partners. In hospitals, people about to undergo an operation are often given an opportunity to discuss the experience with someone who has already successfully gone through it. Beyond the educational function these contacts provide, the people involved are apt to become integrated within one another's networks. Thus, the ties germinated within more structured settings are often transferred to natural social environments.

While considerable energy has been spent on expanding people's relationships, an even more important task in our view is improving the supportiveness of existing relationships. As Unger and Powell (1980) note, existing networks can be mobilized in times of need. Family, friends, and neighbors can be contacted to provide assistance, become allies in the administration of treatment programs, and the like. Marital enrichment programs are another important vehicle for the enhancement of existing relationships.

When informal ties are stretched to their limits or are not available, a supportive community is important as a supplement and a replacement for them. Naturally, many social agencies and programs exist to assist citizens. The effectiveness of these bureaucratic agencies can undoubtedly be improved by approaches that develop linkages between the organization and the recipient's personal network. For instance, many elderly or handicapped individuals can benefit from having network members contact agencies in their behalf. Reciprocally, many formal agencies can improve their effectiveness by utilizing informal social-support systems.

Beyond social service agencies, community support comes in many forms. Four of these (see Pilisuk & Parks, 1983) include:

1. Institutionalized support for dependent populations (e.g., day hospitals, day-care centers for children, meals on wheels).
2. Organized channels for natural helping (e.g., Big Brother organizations).
3. Self-help groups (e.g., Alcoholics Anonymous).
4. Crises facilities (e.g., crisis hotlines, shelters for abused women).

With further development of programs to provide support and further development of our knowledge about support, momentum toward specificity will undoubtedly grow. We will be asking what kind of support from whom for which crises at what stage? We support this line of questioning, as we believe it may lead to optimal use of our social resources. Yet, we are reminded of the current view of the effectiveness of psychotherapy: It works, but the differential effectiveness of various types of therapy has been difficult to establish. With regard to social support, it may not be so crucial that the optimal match of type, source, problem, and stage occur. Simply enhancing support may have beneficial consequences. As one bumper sticker campaign asked, "Have you hugged your kid today?" Our bottom line, which has undoubtedly long been endorsed by grandmothers around the world, is that such hugs are generally a good idea.

REFERENCES

Abrahams R. B. Mutual help for the widowed. *Social Work,* 1972, *17,* 54–61.

Adams, B. N. Isolation, function, and beyond: American kinship in the 1960s. *Journal of Marriage and the Family,* 1970, *32,* 575–597.

Arling, G. The elderly widow and her family, neighbors and friends. *Journal of Marriage and the Family,* 1976, *38,* 757–768.

Bankoff, E. A. Aged parents and their widowed daughters. A support relationship. *Journal of Gerontology,* 1983, *38,* 226–230. (a)

Bankoff, E. A. Social support and adaptation to widowhood. *Journal of Marriage and the Family,* 1983, *45,* 827–839. (b)

Bayer, A. E. A bibliometric analysis of marriage and family literature. *Journal of Marriage and the Family,* 1982, *44,* 527–538.

Berkman, L. F., & Syme, S. L. Social networks, host resistance, and mortality: A 9-year follow up study of Alameda County residents. *American Journal of Epidemiology,* 1979, *109*(2), 186–204.

Bernard, J. *The future of marriage.* New York: World, 1972.

Birchler, G. R., Weiss, R. L., & Vincent, J. P. Multimethod analyses of social reinforcement exchange between maritally distressed and nondistressed spouse and stranger dyads. *Journal of Personality and Social Psychology,* 1975, *31,* 349–360.

Blechman, E. A. Are children with one parent at psychological risk? A methodological review. *Journal of Marriage and the Family,* 1982, *44,* 179–196.

Bloom, B. L., White, S. W., & Asher, S. J. Marital disruption as a stressful life event. In G. Levinger & O. C. Moles (Eds.), *Divorce and separation: Context, causes, and consequences.* New York: Basic Books, 1979. Pp. 184–200.

Caplan, G. The family as a support system. In G. Caplan & M. Killilea (Eds.), *Support systems and mutual help.* New York: Grune & Stratton, 1976. Pp. 19–36.

Cargan, L., & Melko, M. *Singles: Myths and realities.* Beverly Hills, Calif.: Sage Publications, 1982.

Carveth, W. B., & Gottlieb, B. H. The measurement of social support and its relationship to stress. *Canadian Journal of Behavioural Science,* 1979, *11,* 179–188.

Cassel, J. C. Psychosocial processes and "stress": Theoretical formulations. *International Journal of Health Services,* 1974, *4,* 471–482.

Cheal, D. J. Intergenerational family transfers. *Journal of Marriage and the Family,* 1983, *45,* 827–839.

Chiriboga, D. A., Coho, A., Stein, J. A., & Roberts, J. Divorce, stress, and social supports: A study in help-seeking behavior. *Journal of Divorce,* 1979, *3,* 121–135.

Cicirelli, V. G. Adult children's attachment and helping behavior to elderly parents: A path model. *Journal of Marriage and the Family,* 1983, *45,* 815–825.

Cobb, S., & Jones, J. M. Social support, support groups and marital relationships. In S. Duck (Ed.), *Personal relationships* (Vol. 5): *Repairing personal relationships.* New York: Academic Press, 1984.

Crnic, R. A., Greenberg, M. T., Ragozin, A. S., Robinson, N. M., & Basham, R. B. Effects of stress and social support on mothers and premature and full-term infants. *Child Development,* 1983, *54,* 209–217.

Crockenberg, S. B. Infant irritability, mother responsiveness, and social support influences on the security of the infant-mother attachment. *Child Development,* 1981, *52,* 857–865.

Croog, S. H. The family as a source of stress. In S. Levine & N. A. Scotch (Eds.), *Social stress.* Hawthorne, N.Y.: Aldine Publishing, 1970. Pp. 19–53.

Croog, S. H., Lipson, A., & Levine, S. Help patterns in severe illness: The roles of kin network, non-family resources, and institutions. *Journal of Marriage and the Family,* 1972, *34,* 32–41.

Cutrona, C. E. *Social support and stress in the transition to parenthood.* Unpublished manuscript, University of Iowa, 1983.

Davey, A. J., & Paolucci, B. Family interaction: A study of shared time and activity. *Family Relations,* 1980, *29,* 43–49.

Deutscher, M. Brief family therapy in the course of a first pregnancy: A clinical note. *Contemporary Psychoanalysis,* 1970, *7,* 21–35.

Drabek, T. E., & Boggs, K. S. Families in disaster: Reactions and relatives. *Journal of Marriage and the Family,* 1968, *30,* 443–451.

Drabek, T. E., Key, W. H., Erickson, P. E., & Crowe, J. C. The impact of disaster on kin relationships. *Journal of Marriage and the Family,* 1975, *37,* 443–451.

Duvall, E. *In-laws: Pro and con.* New York: Association Press, 1954.

Falbo, T. *The single-child family.* New York: Guilford Press, 1984.

Fein, R. A. The first weeks of fathering: The importance of choices and support for new parents. *Birth and the Family Journal,* 1976, *3,* 53–58.

Fischer, C. S. *To dwell among friends: Personal networks in town and city.* Chicago: University of Chicago Press, 1982.

Fischer, C. S., & Phillips, S. L. Who is alone? Social characteristics of people with small networks. In L. A. Peplau & D. Perlman (Eds.), *Loneliness: A sourcebook of current theory, research, and therapy.* New York: Wiley-Interscience, 1982. Pp. 21–39.

Fischer, L. R. Transitions in the mother-daughter relationship. *Journal of Marriage and the Family,* 1981, *43,* 613–622.

Fischer, L. R. Mothers and mothers-in-law. *Journal of Marriage and the Family,* 1983, *45,* 187–202.

Fishbein, M., & Ajzen, I. *Belief, attitude, intention and behavior: An introduction to theory and research.* Reading, Mass.: Addison-Wesley Publishing, 1975.

Gelles, R. J. Violence in the family: A review of research in the seventies. *Journal of Marriage and the Family,* 1980, *43,* 873–885.

Gibson, G. Kin family network: Overheralded structure in past conceptualizations of family functioning. *Journal of Marriage and the Family,* 1972, *34,* 13–23.

Glenn, N. D. The contribution of marriage to the psychological well-being of males and females. *Journal of Marriage and the Family,* 1975, *37,* 594–600.

Glenn, N. D., & McLanahan, S. The effects of offspring on the psychological well-being of older adults. *Journal of Marriage and the Family,* 1981, *43,* 409–421.

Gove, W. R. The relationship between sex roles, marital status, and mental illness. *Social Forces,* 1972, *51,* 34–44.

Gove, W. R. Sex, marital status, and mortality. *American Journal of Sociology,* 1973, *79,* 45–67.

Grossman, F. K., Eichler, L., & Winickoff, S. *Pregnancy, birth and parenthood.* San Francisco: Jossey-Bass,1980.

Hagestad, G. O. Problems and promise in the social psychology of intergenerational relations. In R. Fogel, E. Hatfield, S. Kiesler, & J. March (Eds.), *Stability and change in the family. New York: Academic Press, 1981. Pp. 11–46.*

Hagestad, G. O., Smyer, M. A., & Steirman, K. L. Parent-child relations in adulthood: The impact of divorce in middle age. In R. Cohen, S. Weissman, & B. Cohler (Eds.), *Parenthood: Psychodynamic perspectives.* New York: Guilford Press, 1982.

Hill, R. *Family development in three generations.* Cambridge, Mass.: Schenkman, 1970.

Holman, T. B., & Epperson, A. Family and leisure: A review of the literature with research recommendations. *Journal of Leisure Research,* in press.

House, J. S. *Work stress and social support.* Reading, Mass.: Addison-Wesley Publishing, 1981.

Irving, H. H. *The family myth: A study of the relationships between married couples and their parents.* Toronto: Copp Clark, 1972.

Johnson, M. P., & Leslie, L. Couple involvement and network structure: A test of the dyadic withdrawal hypothesis. *Social Psychology Quarterly,* 1982, *45,* 34–43.

Kelly, J. R. Family leisure in three communities. *Journal of Leisure Research,* 1978, *10,* 47–60.

Klatzky, S. R. *Patterns of contact with relatives.* Washington, D.C.: American Sociological Association, 1971.

Larson, R. W. Adolescents' daily experience with family and friends: Contrasting opportunity systems. *Journal of Marriage and the Family,* 1983, *45,* 739–750.

Lee, G. R. Effects of social networks on the family. In W. R. Burr, R. Hill, F. I. Nye, & I. L. Reiss (Eds.), *Contemporary theories about the family* (Vol. 1). New York: Free Press, 1979. Pp. 27–56.

Lee, G. R. Kinship in the seventies: A decade review of research and theory. *Journal of Marriage and the Family,* 1980, *43,* 923–934.

Leigh, G. K. Kinship interaction over the family life span. *Journal of Marriage and the Family,* 1982, *44,* 197–208.

Leslie, L. A., Grady, K., & Kirby, W. A. *Coping with divorce: The relationship between network characteristics and attitude change.* Paper presented at the meeting of the National Council of Family Relations, Washington, D.C., October 1982.

Maddison, D., & Raphael, B. Conjugal bereavement and the social network. In B. Schoenberg, I. Gerber, A. Weiner, A. H. Kutscher, D. Peretz, & A. C. Carr (Eds.), *Bereavement: Its psychological aspects.* New York: Columbia University Press, 1975. Pp. 26–40.

Milardo, R. M. Friendship networks in developing relationships: Converging and diverging social environments. *Social Psychology Quarterly,* 1982, *45,* 162–172.

Mills, J., & Clark, M. S. Exchange and communal relationships. In L. Wheeler (Ed.), *Review of personality and social psychology* (Vol. 3). Beverly Hills, Calif.: Sage Publications, 1982. Pp. 121–144.

Murstein, B. I., Cerreto, M., & MacDonald, M. G. A theory and investigation of exchange-orientation on marriage and friendship. *Journal of Marriage and the Family,* 1977, *39,* 543–548.

Norton, A. J., & Glick, P. C. Marital instability in America: Past, present, and future. In G. Levinger & O. C. Moles (Eds.), *Divorce and separation: Context, causes, and consequences.* New York: Basic Books, 1979. Pp. 6–19.

Nuckalls, K. B., Cassel, J., & Kaplan, B. H. Psychosocial assets, life crisis, and the prognosis of pregnancy. *American Journal of Epidemiology,* 1972, *95*(5), 431–441.

Parsons, T. *The social system.* New York: Free Press, 1951.

Parsons, T. The normal American family. In S. Farber, P. Mustacchi, & R. H. Wilson (Eds.), *Man and civilization: The family's search for survival.* New York: McGraw-Hill, 1965. Pp. 31–50.

Paykel, E. S., Emms, E. M., Fletcher, J., & Rassaby, E. S. Life events and social support in puerperal depression. *British Journal of Psychiatry,* 1980, *136,* 339–346.

Perlman, D., & Cozby, P. C. (Eds.). *Social psychology.* New York: Holt, Rinehart & Winston, 1982.

Pilisuk, M., & Parks, S. H. *Social support and family stress.* Unpublished manuscript, University of California, Davis, 1983.

Quarantelli, E. L. A note on the protective function of the family in disasters. *Marriage and Family Living,* 1960, *22,* 263–264.

Richardson, M. S., & Kagan, L. Social support and the transition to parenthood. Paper presented at the meeting of the American Psychological Association, New York, September 1979.

Rook, K. S. *Reciprocity of social exchange and social satisfaction among elderly widows.* Unpublished manuscript, University of California, Irvine, Program in Social Ecology, 1983.

Rook, K. S., & Peplau, L. A. Perspectives on helping the lonely. In L. A. Peplau & D. Perlman (Eds.), *Loneliness: A sourcebook of current theory, research and therapy.* New York: Wiley-Interscience, 1982. Pp. 351–378.

Rosow, I. Old people: Their friends and neighbors. In E. Shanas (Ed.), *Aging and contemporary society.* Beverly Hills, Calif.: Sage Publications, 1970. Pp. 57–67.

Saulnier, K. M. *Social networks and the transition to motherhood: A longitudinal analysis.* Unpublished doctoral dissertation, University of Manitoba, Winnipeg, Canada, 1983.

Shanas, E. Family help patterns and social class in three countries. *Journal of Marriage and the Family,* 1967, *23,* 257–266.

Shanas, E. Family-kin networks and aging in cross-cultural perspective. *Journal of Marriage and the Family,* 1973, *35,* 505–511.

Sharp, H. K., & Axelrod, M. Mutual aid among relatives in an urban population. In R. Freedman, A. H. Hawley, W. S. Landecker, G. E. Lenski, & H. M. Miner (Eds.), *Principles of sociology* (Rev. ed.). New York: Holt, Rinehart & Winston, 1956. Pp. 433–439.

Shulman, N. Life-cycle variations in patterns of close relationships. *Journal of Marriage and the Family,* 1975, *37,* 813–821.

Spicer, J. W., & Hampe, G. D. Kinship interaction after divorce. *Journal of Marriage and the Family,* 1975, *37,* 113–119.

Stroebe, M. S., & Stroebe, W. Who suffers more? Sex differences in health risks of the widowed. *Psychological Bulletin,* 1983, *93,* 279–301.

Sussman, M. B. The isolated nuclear family: Fact or fiction. *Social Problems,* 1959, *6,* 333–340.

Sussman, M. B. Relationships of adult children with their parents in the United States. In E. Shanas & G. F. Streib (Eds.), *Social structure and the family: Generational relations.* Englewood Cliffs, N.J.: Prentice-Hall, 1965. Pp. 62–92.

Sussman, M. B., & Burchinal, L. Parental aid to married children: Implications for family functioning. *Marriage and Family Living,* 1962, *24,* 320–332.

Thoits, P. A. Conceptual, methodological and theoretical problems in studying social support as a buffer against life stress. *Journal of Health and Social Behavior,* 1982, *23,* 145–159.

Turner, C. Conjugal roles and social networks: A re-examination of an hypothesis. In C. C. Harris (Ed.), *Readings in kinship in urban society.* Elmsford, N.Y.: Pergamon Press, 1970. Pp. 245–260.

Unger, D. G., & Powell, D. R. Supporting families under stress: The role of social networks. *Family Relations,* 1980, *29,* 566–574.

Verbrugge, L. M. Marital status and health. *Journal of Marriage and the Family,* 1979, *41,* 267–285.

Veroff, J., Douvan, E., & Kulka, R. A. *The inner American: A self portrait from 1957 to 1976.* New York: Basic Books, 1981.

Walker, A. J., & Thompson, L. Intimacy and intergenerational aid and contact among mothers and daughters. *Journal of Marriage and the Family,* 1983, *45,* 841–849.

Walker, K. N., MacBride, A., & Vachon, M. L. Social support and networks and the crisis of bereavement. *Social Science and Medicine,* 1977, *11,* 35–41.

Walster, E., Walster, G. W., & Berscheid, E. *Equity: Theory and research.* Boston: Allyn & Bacon, 1978.

Wilcox, B. Social support in adjusting to marital disruption. In B. Gottlieb (Ed.), *Social networks and social support* Beverly Hills, Calif.: Sage Publications, 1981. Pp. 97–115.

Wills, T. A., Weiss, R. L., & Patterson, G. R. A behavioral analysis of the determinants of marital satisfaction. *Journal of Consulting and Clinical Psychology,* 1974, *42,* 802–811.

Chapter 11

Love in the Family

CLIFFORD H. SWENSEN, JR.

"Families as an institution, in one guise or another, will survive, because our need for them is so intense that it approaches the genetic" (Howard, 1978, p. 34).

Most theories of love describe it as a force for unification and growth (Schneider, 1964, p. 97). Love in the family, then, is the force for unification and growth that exists within a group of persons who live together. Our topic, a complex phenomenon, is the force that promotes unification and growth in a group of persons who are formally connected with each other, who maintain contact with each other over long periods of time, and who have some common identity.

How we love reflects our attempts to grapple with personal development (Swidler, 1980). The great repetitive themes in the intimate relationship are autonomy versus intimacy, individuation versus integration. In the classical love situation portrayed in the past, the adult separated from the family of origin, met the dreamed-of mate, fell in love, married, and lived happily ever after. The love themes of the past dealt with the problems of becoming an adult; the themes of more recent popular culture have been reflecting a cultural attempt to deal with adulthood. In the past, the themes dealt with resolving the separation from family of origin and establishing the family of generation. When that resolution was accomplished, the story was over, and presumably the newly, happily married adult "settled down" and lived a stable, unchanging life from that point until death. In more recent years, however, the themes of love have centered on the process of continued growth throughout adulthood and the consequence of this growth on relationships with intimate others.

In the past, the family existed primarily for survival, but in recent decades, the family has existed primarily to meet emotional needs, to meet the need for love. Love, in this context, has increasingly been interpreted as promoting the growth of the other person (Csikszentmihalyi, 1980; Raush, 1977). "To keep love fresh, each partner must grow, that is, provide new challenges to the lover; and the lovers must learn new skills to appreciate and respond appropriately to the changing ways of the beloved" (Csikszentmihalyi, p. 323). This change has been reflected in literature (Swidler, 1980): Novels of the past were about solving the conflicts of life by falling in love and marrying or by avoiding the trap of marriage and remaining autonomous and independent. More recently, however, the themes have centered on the conflict between self-development and the demands of intimacy (see Chapter 3 of this *Handbook*). That is, the love themes in the literature of the past dealt with the problems of becoming an adult; to repeat, now they deal with the problems of being an adult. Changes in society, particularly in the complexity of society and the necessity to make choices throughout life, are reflected in increased literary concern with the effect that these changes have upon intimate relationships.

Continued growth throughout adulthood has consequences for love relationships. Maslow (1970), perhaps the first to describe these consequences, outlined a process of development based upon needs—physiological, safety, love, belongingness, and self-actualization needs. The needs are ordered in a hierarchy so that when one need is met, the next need emerges to demand satisfaction. Physiological needs must be met to maintain life. To survive, a person must have air, water, food, and so on. When these basic needs are met, the need for physical safety emerges. When the person is safe, the need for love (i.e., the need for attention, encouragement, care, support, and physical cuddling) emerges. When this need is met, the need emerges for a group to which one belongs and within which one is accepted. When these needs are met, the need for self-actualization emerges. The need for self-actualization is the need to become the person one has it within the self to become. At the levels of need that are below self-actualization, love relationships are formed to have one's needs met—"need" love. When a person has reached the stage of self-actualization, the love expressed is "being" love. "Being" love flows out of the person as a consequence of being the kind of person one is rather than flowing into the person to meet that person's needs. "Being" love is a selfless, undemanding, unpossessive love, one that allows the other person to be who she or he is. The self-actualized person does not need to "have" love; love is an expression of who that person is. Before a person can be a nonpossessive, self-actualized lover, he or she must first have received love from others. "Need" love must have been received before a person can give "being" love. That is, love is a necessary ingredient for personality development.

Orlinsky (1972) outlined the love relationships needed throughout the life cycle as a function of Erikson's stages of development (1950). Each stage of development is characterized by a love that is appropriate to that stage, a love that must be received if the person is to solve the problems of that stage of development and grow to the next stage. Some of these love relationships are complementary relationships between nonequals (e.g., between parent and child); other relationships are symmetrical relationships between equals (e.g., between husband and wife). The first kind of love relationship is the symbiotic acceptance of the infant. The second is the affectionate responsiveness of the small child. Then come the seductive possessiveness of the oedipal child, the idealization of the juvenile, and the intimate friendship of the adolescent. As one grows to adulthood, there comes the romantic passion of youth, followed by the conjugal mutuality of the mature adult. Finally, somatic, personal, erotic, and cultural nurturances appear in the parent as the children grow from infancy to adulthood.

Each love relationship is a medium for personal growth, and it is through the emotional nurturance of each love relationship that a person progresses to the next stage of development in the life cycle. Each stage involves, first, a process of differentiation and, then, integration of the person's self-images into the images of those with whom he or she is intimately related.

Analyzing the expression of love among family members will describe the intimate interaction among a group of people. Usually, when we say that a group forms a family, we imply a group composed of persons who are related by marriage or by blood, but the described interactions are probably just as applicable to a group of persons who maintain an intimate interaction over long periods of time, whether or not they are formally related.

The two main foci of life are love and work. Love is satisfied primarily in the family; work is satisfied in the person's occupation. It has been observed that work and family are not well integrated in modern life (Levinson, 1980) and that in our culture the split between these two areas of our lives has been widening (Smelser, 1980a, 1980b). As more and more mothers enter the work force, the split becomes more of a problem. Work strains spill over into family life (Pearlin, 1980). Observers of the social scene have noted that as the world outside the family becomes more bureaucratic and highly technological (Howard, 1978; Naisbitt, 1982), intimate relationships become increasingly important. The conclusion appears to be that as life in our society becomes more complex and depersonalized outside the family, the importance of the expression of love within the family increases. Thus, the social trend appears to be toward requiring more satisfying expression of love within the family.

New forms of intimate group life (e.g., Constantine & Constantine,

1973; Murstein, 1978) appear to be an attempt to meet the need for more satisfying love relationships. The increase in the divorce rate also reflects the attempt to meet this need. Such attempts, however, create their own problems. Communal arrangements create more-complex relationships (Kanter, Jaffe, & Weisberg, 1975), making more difficult the achievement of satisfying love relationships; divorce deprives both partners of emotional support and places greater burdens upon the single parent who must also care for the children, adversely affecting the family's ability to perform tasks (Glasser & Navarre, 1965). The modal family form that we now have—the modified extended family—will probably continue to be the dominant family form in the United States (Reiss, 1971); but family members will increasingly demand a family structure that provides emotional support for personal growth, and families will pressure society to make changes to allow the family to meet the emotional needs of its members.

So far, this discussion is essentially a preamble to the main theme of the chapter—the expression of love in the family—but it is a necessary preamble. The expression of love is a function of the people who are involved in the love relationship and of the situation within which their relationship exists. People and situations change; therefore, the expression of love will change. If we are to understand the expression of love among members of a group that endures over a long period of time, we must have some understanding of the dimensions along which varying factors affect love relationships and how this variability relates to the expression of love among family members.

THE BEGINNING OF LOVE RELATIONSHIPS

The love relationship that begins the family is the love relationship between the husband and the wife. This love relationship has its beginning, not at the beginning of life, but after life has already progressed through several stages. This kind of love typically comes somewhere in a person's mid-20s, in the stage that Erikson (1950) described as including the developmental task of intimacy versus isolation, or the stage described as the period of entering the adult world (Levinson, 1980). Each stage of life has its appropriate and needed love (Orlinsky, 1972). The appropriate love for this period is romantic love; and in our society, of course, love is usually the basis for marriage (Reiss, 1971).

People are most likely to fall in love when they are in a transition stage in life, leaving the security of the previous stage of life and facing the developmental challenges of a new stage (Friedlander & Morrison, 1980; Geller & Howenstine, 1980; Walster & Walster, 1978). The developmental task at this stage is to establish oneself as an independent adult in society. For the man, this may consist of finding a woman who will support him in his special dream for his life (Geller & Howenstine). Both a need state and its frustration are central to falling in love. Women whose self-confidence has been shattered are prone to respond to an attractive, accepting man (Berscheid & Walster, 1978). In any case, the stage for falling in love is set when a person is frustrated and uncertain, facing the necessity of moving on to the next stage of life but uncertain about how to do this or even of the ability to do it. A person then meets another who seems to promise help and support to meet the task, to make up for one's own deficiencies, and to share the struggle.

Romantic love has certain characteristics that distinguish it from other kinds of love. Although different characteristics have been listed in various sources, agreement is general that romantic love is characterized by (a) a preoccupation with the loved one (lovers gaze more at each other than do other couples, Rubin, 1973), an intense longing to be with the loved one, and a feeling of incompleteness when separated from the loved one (Friedlander & Morrison, 1980; Pope, 1980; Walster & Walster, 1978; Weiner, 1980); (b) an idealization and overvaluation of the beloved (Berscheid & Walster, 1978; Friedlander & Morrison; Weiner); (c) fantasies about the beloved in which the beloved satisfies frustrated needs and brings about an ideal existence (Berscheid & Walster; Friedlander & Morrison); and (d) a narcissistic vulnerability to the beloved and a vigilance to prevent loss of the beloved. At times there may be a loss of ego boundaries between the lovers (Weiner).

The characteristics of romantic love that may also be shared with other kinds of love, particularly the love relationship between small children and their parents, are a high degree of emotional dependency and physiological arousal (Berscheid & Walster, 1978; Walster & Walster, 1978). Of course, the physiological arousal between romantic lovers has a strong erotic component, but this is precisely the component that Freud argued is present in the relationship between small children and their parents. Characteristics that romantic love shares with other kinds of love between adults are caring and concern for the needs of the beloved (Rubin, 1973; Weiner, 1980) and intimate and open communications between the lovers (Rubin).

Sex differences have been observed between men and women in love. Women do not seem prone to fall in love during transition periods, as is true of men (Uchalik & Livingston, 1980). Women fall in love more often than do men, but women are more controlled, skeptical, and cautious than men are. Men are more likely than women to fall in love more quickly, to cling to a dying affair longer, and to suffer more when the affair ends (Walster & Walster, 1978). In spite of their caution, women get a higher high from love than men do. Apparently, women enjoy love more; men suffer more.

Why does a person fall in love with one particular person? The first reason is physical proximity (Berscheid & Walster, 1978). The closer two persons are in space, the more likely they are to be attracted to each other. Even more fundamental is the fact that the closer they are in space, the more likely they are to meet; and one usually falls in love with a person whom one has met.

Two persons having met, the most-frequently cited reason for attraction between them is reward—that is, the more they reward each other, the more they are attracted to each other (e.g., Altman & Taylor, 1973; Clore & Byrne, 1974). As two persons mutually reward each other, they selectively reveal themselves to each other and become more knowledgeable about each other. This self-disclosure begins with the public areas of their personal life: their work, where they grew up and went to school, and so on. As the self-disclosure proceeds, it first broadens into wider areas of the public aspects of their personal lives but then begins to penetrate the deeper areas of their personalities, leading to a disclosure of wishes, needs, personal feelings, conflicts and personal problems, and personal vulnerabilities (Altman & Taylor).

As the intimacy develops, the rate of progress slows down as deeper areas of personality and personal life are touched. Because deeper personal revelations carry substantially greater risk, the potential reward and punishment are significantly greater. Research has suggested (Huesmann, 1980) that deeper involvement brings greater rewards, but to reach a deeper involvement with another person, one must overcome certain obstacles. If the perceived reward is great enough, the lovers will overcome the obstacles, which are most likely to involve conflict between autonomy and intimacy—that is, attaining greater intimacy carries the potential loss of personal autonomy, which a person will not give up unless the perceived rewards of greater intimacy are large enough to justify the perceived risk and the potential cost. In the early stages of love, the obstacle of family opposition heightens love (Rubin, 1973).

Reward appears, in particular, to be the primary basis of attraction for persons at the self-protective stage of ego development (cf. Chapter 3) but not between persons at more-complex stages of ego development. The accuracy of that statement depends, however, on how reward is defined. Kelley (1979) demonstrated how a reward matrix may be transformed so that the greatest reward is obtained by rewarding the other person in the relationship. Homans (1961) noted that altruism is not necessarily excluded from a reinforcement view of relationships, observing that "some of the greatest profiteers we know are altruists" (p. 79).

Walster and Walster (1978) were not convinced that reinforcement comes fully into play when a person falls in love, pointing out that persons often fall in love with those from whom they receive punishment rather than reward. They suggested that fantasy and idealization are the essential elements that lead to falling in love. How do fantasy and idealization function in the process of falling in love? Basically, the idealization is of the other person, who will meet one's needs; and the fantasy is of the heaven that life will be with the other person, if. . . . There is great reward in the fantasy. I suggest that the great distress at a broken love affair comes about because one is forced to give up the fantasy. The grief is for the loss of fantasy, not the loss of the very real, less-than-ideal person with whom one has fallen in love. Falling in love is partly a matter of immediate reward but also a matter of much greater rewards that are anticipated in the future. Clinical observation also leads to the conclusion that people repeat the patterns of past relationships: A person who falls in love with someone who is punishing gains the rewards that have been received in the past from similar relationships. Such a person gains the reward that comes from familiarity and the confirmation of expectations.

People are also inclined to fall in love with those who are selectively hard-to-get (Berscheid & Walster, 1978). That is, one falls in love with another person who is hard-to-get for other people but who is uniquely attracted to him or her. We all find it hard to resist persons who find us irresistible. We are also more likely to be attracted to, and to marry, another who is at the same level of ego development as we are (Lickona & Thomas, 1974; Nettles, 1978).

Finally, after reviewing the research on love, Walster and Walster (1978) concluded that the best way to inspire love in another is to take it for granted that you are loved and act that way. Conversely, the way to end love is to question it constantly.

To get one person to fall in love with another requires a couple of additional elements in the prescription. The first step is to assume that you will be successful in getting the other person to fall in love with you. Working on the hypothesis that physiological or emotional arousal is necessary to falling in love and on the observations that any reward is greater when one has received little of it (Swensen, 1973a, chap. 8) and that the impact of a reward is greater after a series of punishments (Swensen, 1973a, chap. 11), I recommend the following course of action. First, choose the person whom you wish to have fall in love with you and punish that person regularly and systematically. Criticize the person's dress, manners, taste and dog. The criticism should be subtle and realistic, especially applied to areas in which the person is likely to give credence to the criticism. Criticize and punish so consistently that the person's blood pressure rises every time you appear. Then shift to reward, complimenting sensitivity, perceptiveness, eyes and hair, anything that makes your compliments sincere and credible. The strong negative emotion that you stirred up at the beginning of the relationship has now shifted to a strong positive emotion. This formula, of course, is that of the romantic movies of the 1930s and 1940s: At the beginning of the picture, the man and the woman met and immediately hated each other, a sure tip-off that they would fall in love by the end of the picture.

The love relationship goes through certain stages; the following list integrates two different descriptions of these stages (Altman & Taylor, 1973; Weiner, 1980).

1. Orientation: The two persons are just beginning to get to know each other and interact with each other only at a superficial level.
2. Exploratory: A superficial affective exchange begins, the couple gets to know more of the surface characteristics of each other, and their interest in each other begins to rise.
3. Beginning to fall in love: The affectionate interchange rises rapidly, and the two persons begin a deeper and more thorough disclosure and exploration of the deeper aspects of their personalities until the idealization of each other is at its peak.
4. Unmasking: Extended intimacy and mutual self-disclosure and exploration begin to reveal the flaws in both persons.
5. Mutual manipulation: Each attempts to get the other to become the person that he or she wants the other to be.
6. Resolution: Each adapts to the reality of the other; they strike some kind of conscious or unconscious "deal" with each other. Thus begins the development of what becomes a permanent relationship. As we shall see later, the deal that the partners work out with each other comes apart later in the relationship.

The preceding description of falling in love and the characteristics of being in love are not universally applicable. Different ways of being in love have been noted (e.g., Walster & Walster, 1978; Weiner, 1980). We expect the process of establishing love relationships to be different at different stages of ego development (Chapter 3 of this *Handbook;* Lickona & Thomas, 1974; Swensen, 1977). Persons at the impulsive and the self-protective stages of ego development establish relationships that are chaotic and full of conflict; unless the social environment provides a structure that keeps them in the relationship, they are likely to terminate the relationship as soon as the rewards become less than the costs of the relationship or less than the rewards in an alternative relationship. Pathological love is the norm for the love relationships of those who are at the stages of ego development below the conformist level.

The earlier description of the development of the love relationship is most applicable to persons at the conformist stage of ego development. The conformist stage is the one that most adults have attained or, more specifically, the stage that most adults have attained by the period when they are more likely to fall in love. The "typical" process of falling in love and the characteristics of the "typical" case of being in love refer to the "average," or persons at the conformist stage. When the typical person at the conformist stage is asked why he or she married, the standard response is that the person was "in love." Persons at the conscientious level of ego development, however, are more aware of their internal needs and wishes and the needs and wishes of the beloved. We thus expect their course of falling in love and being in love to be more perceptive and more accurate; we expect them to be more realistic in idealizing the beloved and to have more realistic fantasies about the beloved. They would then be less likely to go through a stage of disillusioning unmasking and less likely to attempt to manipulate their loved ones into becoming the persons they want them to be, but would be more successful at resolving conflicts in the love relationship.

Types of love that appear to fit the different levels of ego development have been described as follows:

1. Mania (Lasswell & Lasswell, 1976; Lee, 1977): The person is obsessed with the loved one, possessive, intensely dependent, irrationally jealous, and unable to tolerate the thought of loss of the loved one. This kind of love, associated with low self-esteem and a poor self-concept, is probably typical of persons at the impulsive/self-protective level of ego development.

2. Ludus (Lasswell & Lasswell, 1976; Lee, 1977): The lover is a self-centered game player who plays to get the greatest reward for the least cost and who hates dependency in self or others. This description appears to fit the kind of love relationship that a person at the self-protective stage would develop.

3. Pragma (Lasswell & Lasswell, 1976; Lee, 1977): The lover is practical, sensible, keenly aware of, and realistic about, what can be expected from the relationship and what it is likely to cost, and forms or breaks up a relationship for practical reasons. This kind of relationship also has characteristics of the self-protective stage, but the capacity to assess realistically the pluses and minuses from the mate's point of view indicates some progression beyond the self-protective stage. Because this description contains elements of the conformist stage, perhaps we should place the person who develops this kind of love at the self-protective/conformist level.

4. Eros (Lasswell & Lasswell, 1976; Lee, 1977): In eros, or romantic love, the lover is idealized, the relationship is idealized, and the person is preoccupied with pleasing the beloved. The idealization

of, and concern about, the other is typical of the conformist stage.

5. Storge: Rapport, interdependency, self-disclosure, mutual need fulfillment, and a long-term commitment to the relationship are characteristic. Not the kind of love that one expects to find early in a love relationship, storge is more typical of longtime, intimate friends or the kind of love that one expects to find in an old, happily married couple who have achieved the conscientious stage or the autonomous stage of ego development.

6. Agape: The lover is caring, promotes the best for the beloved, and gives without expectation of, or necessity for, return from the other. One would expect agape from a person at the autonomous or the integrated stages of ego development. Agape is not the kind of love that is likely in two young lovers who have recently fallen in love but might be found in an occasional older couple who have grown to the more complex levels of ego development.

The main content of a love relationship between two adults is communication, and the main method for mutual reward is verbal. For a couple who are in love and who plan to marry (Swensen, 1972), the love (assessed by a scale that measures the various factors in a love relationship, Swensen, 1973b) is expressed through mutual statements of love and affection, self-disclosure, interest in each other's activities, encouragement and moral support, and toleration of the less-desirable characteristics of each other. The amount of self-disclosure that furthers the relationship depends upon the degree to which the couple accept themselves and each other. If they are highly accepting of themselves and each other, high levels of self-disclosure increase their satisfaction with the relationship; if they are less accepting of themselves and each other, greater amounts of self-disclosure (especially negative facts about themselves) decrease their satisfaction with the relationship (Gilbert, 1976). Self-disclosure is higher in persons with higher self-concepts (Shapiro & Swensen, 1977) and is higher in marriage for persons at the postconformist stages of ego development (Swensen, Eskew, & Kohlhepp, 1981). For the average young couple in love, then, a moderate amount of self-disclosure would be expected and would be optimal for the development of their relationship.

Self-disclosure provides information that reduces the uncertainty in the relationship (Livingston, 1980). Uncertainty is an element in the romantic love relationship; ironically, however, that which furthers the development of the relationship also tends to reduce the uncertainty and thus tends to reduce the romance in the relationship.

Communication is the means by which people define their relationships (Morton, Alexander, & Altman, 1976). Crises, which occur in a relationship when the couple disagree about their definitions of the relationship, are most likely to concern autonomy versus intimacy and are resolved through communication (Raush, Barry, Hertel, & Swain, 1974).

Love relationships are characterized by reciprocity. What one reveals, the other reveals. Affection expressed by one is reciprocated by the other. Tolerance expressed by one is reflected in the tolerance of the other. Romantic love relationships typically exhibit stereotypic sex role behavior (Rubin, 1973), an expected characteristic because most couples in love are at the conformist stage of ego development, a stage in which stereotypical views of other persons are typical.

Falling in love is not confined to the young, although it is most frequent in the young. Older persons fall in love also, and the recommendations for a successful marriage in old age are very much like those for the young (Paterson & Payne, 1975).

Finally, we come to the question that concerns most young persons: Is this "real" love or mere infatuation? Walster and Walster (1978) suggested, perhaps a bit sarcastically, that if it lasts, it is "real" love; if it ends, it is mere infatuation. Actually, the more accurate answer is that love is a relationship, and all relationships change with time. If the partners are capable of making and maintaining a relationship (i.e., if they are at the more complex levels of ego development), they know themselves and each other fairly accurately and have the ability to make the adjustments that are necessary to maintain a relationship through the vicissitudes of life. Persons in the middle, at the conformist stage of ego development, are those most likely to ask the question and are those for whom the answer has the most significance.

LOVE THROUGHOUT THE COURSE OF MARRIAGE

Love changes during the course of marriage. The emotional intensity of romantic love gives way to the calm warmth of what has been called "companionate love" (Berscheid & Walster, 1978; Walster & Walster, 1978). The average love of the average married couple consists of all of the factors in a love relationship: verbal expression of affection, physical expression of affection and sex, mutual self-disclosure, moral support and encouragement, material support, and tolerance (Swensen, 1972). These expressions are reciprocal, or equal, for husbands and wives (Shapiro & Swensen, 1969; Swensen et al., 1981).

In the average love relationship of the average couple (i.e., most, but not all couples), the couple tend to disengage, the bonds between them weaken, and the relationship tends to become more conventional, passive, and congenial (Altman & Taylor, 1973; Levinger, 1977a, 1977b; Reedy, 1977). The amount of love that is expressed in the relationship declines (Cimbalo, Faling, & Mousaw, 1976; Swensen et al.,

1981; Swensen & Moore, 1979; Swensen & Trahaug, 1979; Walster & Walster, 1978). Although "love" declines, liking does not. What seems to decline most is verbal expression of affection, self-disclosure, and moral support and encouragement: The partners talk less but continue to have affectionate feelings for one another that are not verbally expressed, and they continue to tolerate each other and to provide mutual support.

Along with this decline in talking and the mutual expression of affection, change occurs in the couple's problems. Problems increase with the arrival of children and decline as the children leave home (Swensen et al., 1981; Swensen & Moore, 1979; Swensen & Trahaug, 1979). Problems decline primarily in relationships with other persons; parents and in-laws die, children grow up and leave home, and relationships with troublesome relatives and friends are discontinued. Problems in the expression of affection, making decisions, and determining the goals of the marriage continue, however, throughout the marriage, although they lose some of their intensity as the couple becomes accustomed to them.

The decline in the expression of love is a consequence of the growth of a certain disengagement between the husband and the wife, but the disengagement serves a protective function. As a couple becomes more intimate, areas of conflict emerge. Conflict may basically be dealt with in two ways: One way is to face the conflicts and try to resolve them; the other is to avoid them, withdraw from them, and repress them (Altman & Taylor, 1973; Raush et al., 1974). The longer two persons maintain a relationship, the more areas of potential conflict there are to avoid. As the areas of undiscussed potential conflict accumulate, disengagement increases, and the total amount of intimate interaction thus decreases. If the partners and the relationship are to grow, the partners must be open to each other, to new experiences, to the exploration of new areas, and to solving the conflicts that prevent personal and interpersonal growth (Altman, Vinsel, & Brown, 1981; Csikszentmihalyi, 1980). The consequence of avoiding conflict is that the relationship stagnates and becomes devitalized.

Raush et al. (1974), in their research on marriage, concluded that married couples who avoid conflict are about as happy and satisfied with their lives as are those who face and grapple with their difficulties; however, they studied couples in the beginning years of their married lives. Had they followed these couples throughout their entire married lives, I think they would have found that those couples who used avoidance, denial, withdrawal, and repression to cope with conflict had marriages that steadily became devitalized.

Couples who use denial do so because they believe that their relationships are too fragile to endure change. For such couples, conflict and change threaten the relationship. When a couple decides to make their relationship permanent, they reach a certain arrangement, or deal, with each other. Conflict indicates problems with the original deal, but facing that conflict and bringing about the changes that the conflict demands threaten the whole relationship. Rather than face that threat, the partners avoid conflict and change. The relationship is thus preserved, but at the cost of stagnation. The irony of the situation is that a relationship, if it is to remain vital, must adapt to changing life circumstances and to the personal growth of the partners. By using avoidance to protect the relationship, the couple condemns their relationship to a slow, steady devitalization. Because vital relationships are necessary for personal growth (Orlinsky, 1972), not only does the relationship stagnate but the partners as individuals also stagnate.

The described devitalization in marriage applies to the "average" married couple, or, more accurately, is the average of all married couples. "Average," of course, obscures the fact that different couples take different courses. Most married couples—perhaps 50 to 60 percent—are persons at the conformist stage of ego development. They tend to form relationships that are based upon rules. When the rules do not seem to apply or when the husband and wife disagree about which rules should be accepted and applied, the couple faces a problem. Because they are not so sensitive to, aware of, or knowledgeable about the internal needs, wishes, and conflicts that motivate personal behavior, they have difficulty coping with problems. They lack the resources to revise the rules, develop compromise rules, or, better yet, transcend the rules and make their own rules which are unique to themselves, their spouses, and their relationship. Some married couples, however, have not yet achieved the conformist stage of development and tend to be self-centered: If their spouses do not provide the rewards that they consider necessary, they terminate the relationship and look for another that will be more satisfying. If they stay in the relationship, it is because external social forces keep them in it rather than because of their own actions. Their relationships are likely to be characterized by continuous, overt conflict rather than avoidance, denial, or repression.

Couples who have achieved levels of development beyond the conformist stage are perceptive about, and sensitive to, their own and their spouses' internal psychological processes. They are able to perceive conflict, to perceive the sources of conflict, and have the resources to cope with conflict. They are the persons most likely to create a relationship that has the flexibility to cope constructively with conflict and resolve it, thus promoting growth both in their relationship and in each other as individuals.

Jourard (1975) suggested that problems in a marriage are a sign of growth and a challenge to growth. Perhaps a new "rule" might be introduced into the rule book for marriage: A problem in a marriage is a sign either that one of the partners is growing, which is a challenge to growth in the relationship, or that the situation within which the marriage exists has changed, thus challenging both partners to grow. The rule has a corollary: Growth means that the rules must be revised.

Growth follows the process of differentiation and integration. When differentiation occurs in one partner, that partner moves away from the other. That is, when individuation occurs, that partner becomes more concerned with personal autonomy. The basic issue (or source of problems) in marriage is the dialectic of, and conflict between, autonomy and intimacy. For example, if a couple has conflict about whether or not to visit the wife's parents on vacation, the issue basically is which rules to follow in deciding the vacation, which in turn becomes an issue of the wife's autonomy versus the husband's autonomy. If the wife gives in to the husband, she has given up some of her autonomy to maintain intimacy. If the husband agrees to visit her parents, he gives up some of his autonomy. If the relationship is to continue, some sort of equity (Berscheid & Walster, 1978), or reciprocity (Pearlin, 1980), must be maintained in the sacrifice of autonomy for the sake of intimacy.

Finally, although total love as well as total problems decrease throughout marriage, what has been termed companionate marriage does not decline (Walster & Walster, 1978). For those who have achieved the postconformist stages of ego development, the amount of love expressed increases (Swensen et al., 1981), and many couples in the postparental years of marriage find the flame of love still burning brightly (Traupman, Eckels, & Hatfield, 1982). These husbands and wives, who are able to help each other grow, thus keep their relationship alive and growing.

LOVE AMONG PARENTS AND CHILDREN

As observed in subhuman mammals (Harlow, 1971) as well as humans, love is necessary to normal growth. Orlinsky (1972) described the kinds of love in childhood as the symbiotic acceptance of the infant, the affectionate responsiveness of the small child, the seductive possessiveness of the oedipal child, and the idealization of the juvenile. The parent-child relationship is a complementary relationship in which the parent is dominant, meeting the material and emotional needs of the child. The infant is totally dependent upon the parent, but as the infant grows older and more competent, the parent places more demands upon the child and meets fewer of the child's needs. The child development literature about the parent-child relationship is voluminous and need not be recapitulated here. Nevertheless, the loss of love during childhood not only interferes with the child's normal development but has negative consequences for the individual's health and successful life throughout the life span (Glasser & Navarre, 1965; Lynch, 1977).

Love from parents to children is characterized particularly by material support, moral support, encouragement and advice, and (decreasingly as the child ages) self-disclosure and verbal and physical expressions of affection (Swensen, 1972). Reciprocity in love relationships is important not only between adults but in all relationships. Initially, the infant cannot perceive the parents as other persons. As the infant and the growing child learn to perceive the parents as other persons, they try to repay in kind. With the small child, this may be only by providing entertainment for the parents, but the growing child tries to perform chores and behave in ways that the child perceives (or misperceives) are valued by the parents.

Grandparents are also a significant source of love for children (Robertson, 1976; R. H. Turner, 1970). For the small child, the grandparent-grandchild relationship is a special and privileged one in which the grandparent is a kind of fairy godparent who gives the child undemanding affection—verbally, materially, and physically—without the drawback of a compensating insistence that the child meet certain standards of performance.

The relationship between brothers and sisters is, on the average, the weakest relationship within the family (Swensen, 1972). It is marked by tangibles such as performing chores and giving gifts, but it does not have the drive of material necessity that exists in the parent-child relationship. The sibling relationship is also expressed in moral support, encouragement, and advice, but these kinds of support do not have the strength or the significance that they have when they come from the older, wiser, and more-experienced parents. Love is also expressed through tolerance for the sibling. Siblings, as they grow older, increase meaningful communication in which they consensually validate one another's experience, but this level of communication is beyond the capacity of the young child. The sibling relationship may have a complementary quality (the older sibling holding more power in the relationship), but the complementary quality is likely to be a source of strain in the relationship because it is typically resented by younger siblings (Sutton-Smith & Rosenberg, 1968).

The kind of love Orlinsky (1972) described as necessary for growth at this stage of life is intimate friendship in the early years and romantic love in the later years. The intimate friendships of adolescence may be considered almost a part of love in the family. If the family is flexible and relatively open to the close friends of the family members, the intimate chums of the teenage members of the family become almost additional, or "unofficial," family members. Although perhaps more the rule than the exception in the optimal family, this acceptance is less likely in the more rigid structure of the midrange family (see Chapter 3).

The love relationships of intimate friends at this stage are expressed mostly through communication; self-disclosure, moral support and encouragement, and advice giving are the modes of expressing this kind of love (Swensen, 1972). Love relationships with the parents, on the other hand, are expressed chiefly through material goods, encouragement, and moral support. Parents express love materially by providing material support for the child; the child's material expression of love is primarily through performing chores. At this stage, the love relationship of parent and child goes through its most difficult phase. The parent-child relationship is less reciprocal than at any other stage of life other than infancy: Parents give more materially and receive less. Such unbalanced relationships produce guilt in the one who is receiving the most and resentment in the one who is giving the most (Walster & Walster, 1978). The estrangement between adolescent and parent is reflected in the disagreement between parents and children in the late stages of adolescence about what they have discussed with each other about each other (DeLeon, 1969). The strain between adolescents and their parents affects the relationship between the parents, who have the greatest number of marital problems when their children are teenagers (Swensen et al., 1981). The strain is hard on the children also, but is more difficult for boys, who receive less praise and support from their parents than do girls (Stinnett, Farris, & Walters, 1974). Although the relationship with grandparents declines in significance as the child gets older, grandparents are still an important source of emotional support to teenage children and have an important influence upon them (Robertson, 1976).

As both the parents and the children age and as the children leave home, the structure and the power balance in the family change (J. G. Turner, 1975; R. H. Turner, 1970). The relationship between husband and wife improves, at least in the sense that their marriage problems decrease (Swensen et al., 1981). For couples at the postconformist stages of ego development, the amount of expressed love increases, as do the verbal expressions of affection, self-disclosure, encouragement, and moral support. Life satisfaction increases when the last child is married (Pearlin, 1980).

The relationship between the parents and the children becomes a looser and more-distant relationship among adults, with the children gaining more power and the parents losing power. Older adults want and seem to need more autonomy (Cohler, 1983). They prefer to live separately from their children (Nydegger, 1983), although they still need and want the support of a social network and frequent communication with their children and are more satisfied if at least some of the children live within easy commuting distance (Swensen & Trahaug, 1979). Older adults seek intimacy at a distance. Part of the motivation for this distance is that they have grown tired of meeting the dependency needs of other people.

CONCLUSION

Love is a relationship that promotes intimacy and growth in the persons involved. Love is not an object but a relationship; as such, it changes over time. The paradigm indicates that love changes because of changes in the persons involved in the relationship and because of changes in the environment within which the relationship exists: When the situation or the people change, the love relationship will change.

The personality variable of primary significance to love relationships is ego development. People develop throughout their lives. Their love relationships promote their continued growth and development, and the relationships change as a consequence of their growth and development. The individual grows from an undifferentiated, unintegrated personality structure to an increasingly differentiated, integrated personality structure. In this growth, individuals change from being self-centered in their relationships to being aware and considerate of the needs of others. They grow from being unable to form relationships on their own to being able to relate deeply and harmoniously to other people.

How much love of which kind is necessary for optimal growth and satisfaction at each stage of human development? What are the typical sources of this love? If the typical sources are not available, what substitute sources are available? In the past, we have been concerned with determining and meeting minimum nutritional requirements for optimal physical growth. We now need to devote effort to determining the minimal requirements of the right kind of love for optimal personal growth. If love is the fundamental power and creative substance in the universe and the fundamental force for growth in individuals, we have clearly only begun to study the nature and the effect of this most-fundamental force.

REFERENCES

Altman, I., & Taylor, D. A. *Social penetration: The development of interpersonal relationships.* New York: Holt, Rinehart & Winston, 1973.

Altman, I., Vinsel, A., & Brown, B. B. Dialectic conceptions in social psychology: An application to social penetration and privacy regulation. *Advances in Experimental Social Psychology,* 1981, *14,* 107–160.

Berscheid, E., & Walster, E. H. *Interpersonal attraction* (2d ed.). Reading, Mass.: Addison-Wesley Publishing, 1978.

Cimbalo, R. C., Faling, V., & Mousaw, P. The course of love: A cross-sectional design. *Psychological Reports,* 1976, *38,* 1292–1294.

Clore, G. L., & Byrne, D. A reinforcement-affect model of attraction. In T. L. Huston (Ed.), *Foundations of interpersonal attraction.* New York: Academic Press, 1974. Pp. 143–170.

Cohler, B. J. Autonomy and interdependence in the family of adulthood: A psychological perspective. *The Gerontologist,* 1983, *23,* 33–39.

Constantine, L., & Constantine, J. *Group marriage: A study of contemporary multilateral marriage.* New York: Macmillan, 1973.

Csikszentmihalyi, M. Love and the dynamics of personal growth. In K. S. Pope (Ed.), *On love and loving.* San Francisco: Jossey-Bass, 1980. Pp. 306–326.

DeLeon, P. H. *Concomitants of self-disclosing behavior.* Unpublished doctoral dissertation, Purdue University, 1969.

Erikson, E. H. *Childhood and society.* New York: W. W. Norton, 1950.

Friedlander, S., & Morrison, D. C. Childhood. In K. S. Pope (Ed.), *On love and loving.* San Francisco: Jossey-Bass, 1980. Pp. 27–43.

Geller, J. D., & Howenstine, R. A. Adulthood: Men. In K. S. Pope (Ed.), *On love and loving.* San Francisco: Jossey-Bass, 1980. Pp. 61–88.

Gilbert, S. J. Empirical and theoretical extensions of self-disclosure. In G. R. Miller (Ed.), *Explorations in interpersonal communication.* Beverly Hills, Calif.: Sage Publications, 1976. Pp. 197–215.

Glasser, P., & Navarre, E. Structural problems of the one-parent family. *Journal of Social Issues,* 1965, *21,* 98–109.

Harlow, H. F. *Learning to love.* San Francisco: Albion Publishing, 1971.

Homans, G. C. *Social behavior in its elementary form.* New York: Harcourt Brace Jovanovich, 1961.

Howard, J. *Families.* New York: Simon & Schuster, 1978.

Huesmann, L. R. Toward a predictive model of romantic behavior. In K. S. Pope (Ed.), *On love and loving.* San Francisco: Jossey-Bass, 1980. Pp. 152–171.

Jourard, S. M. Marriage is for life. *Journal of Marriage and Family Counseling,* 1975, *1,* 199–208.

Kanter, R. M., Jaffe, D., & Weisberg, D. K. Coupling, parenting, and the presence of others: Intimate relationships in communal households. *Family Coordinator,* 1975, *24,* 433–452.

Kelley, H. H. *Personal relationships: Their structures and processes.* Hillsdale, N.J.: Lawrence Erlbaum Associates, 1979.

Lasswell, T. E., & Lasswell, M. E. I love you but I'm not in love with you. *Journal of Marriage and Family Counseling,* 1976, *2,* 211–224.

Lee, J. A. A typology of styles of loving. *Personality and Social Psychology Bulletin,* 1977, *3,* 173–182.

Levinger, G. The embrace of lives: Changing and unchanging. In G. Levinger & H. L. Raush (Eds.), *Close relationships: Perspectives on the meaning of intimacy.* Amherst: University of Massachusetts Press, 1977. Pp. 1–16. (a)

Levinger, G. Re-viewing the close relationship. In G. Levinger & H. L. Raush (Eds.), *Close relationships: Perspectives on the meaning of intimacy.* Amherst: University of Massachusetts Press, 1977, Pp. 137–162. (b)

Levinson, D. J. Toward a conception of the adult life course. In N. J. Smelser & E. H. Erikson (Eds.), *Themes of work and love in adulthood.* Cambridge, Mass.: Harvard University Press, 1980. Pp. 265–290.

Lickona, K., & Thomas, A. A cognitive-developmental approach to interpersonal attraction. In T. L. Huston (Ed.), *Foundations of interpersonal attraction.* New York: Academic Press, 1974. Pp. 31–59.

Livingston, K. R. Love as a process of reducing uncertainty—cognitive theory. In K. S. Pope (Ed.), *On love and loving.* San Francisco: Jossey-Bass, 1980. Pp. 133–151.

Lynch, J. J. *The broken heart.* New York: Basic Books, 1977.

Maslow, A. H. *Motivation and personality* (2d ed.). New York: Harper & Row, 1970.

Morton, T. L., Alexander, J. F., & Altman, I. Communication and relationship definition. In G. R. Miller (Ed.), *Explorations in interpersonal communication.* Beverly Hills, Calif.: Sage Publications, 1976. Pp. 105–125.

Murstein, B. I. (Ed.). *Exploring intimate life styles.* New York: Springer Publishing, 1978.

Naisbitt, J. *Megatrends: Ten new directions transforming our lives.* New York: Warner Books, 1982.

Nettles, E. J. *Ego development and sex role expectations in marriage.* Unpublished doctoral dissertation, Washington University, 1978.

Nydegger, C. N. Family tioc of the aged in cross-cultural perspective. *The Gerontologist,* 1983, *23,* 26–32.

Orlinsky, D. E. Love relationships in the life cycle: A developmental interpersonal perspective. In H. Otto (Ed.), *Love today: A new perspective.* New York: Association Press, 1972. Pp. 135–150.

Paterson, J. A., & Payne, B. *Love in the later years.* New York: Association Press, 1975.

Pearlin, L. E. Life strains and psychological distress among adults. In N. J. Smelser & E. H. Erikson (Eds.), *Themes of work and love in adulthood.* Cambridge, Mass.: Harvard University Press, 1980.

Pope, K. S. Defining and studying romantic love. In K. S. Pope (Ed.), *On love and loving.* San Francisco: Jossey-Bass, 1980. Pp. 1–26.

Raush, H. L. Orientations to the close relationship. In G. Levinger & H. L. Raush (Eds.), *Close relationships: Perspectives on the meaning of intimacy.* Amherst: University of Massachusetts Press, 1977. Pp. 163–188.

Raush, H. L., Barry, W. A., Hertel, R. K., & Swain, M. A. *Communication, conflict, and marriage.* San Francisco: Jossey-Bass, 1974.

Reedy, M. N. *Age and sex differences in personal needs and the nature of love: A study of happily married young, middle-aged and older adult couples.* Unpublished doctoral dissertation, University of Southern California, 1977.

Reiss, I. L. *The family system in America.* New York: Holt, Rinehart & Winston, 1971.

Robertson, J. F. Significance of grandparents: Perceptions of young adult grandchildren. *Gerontologist,* 1976, *16,* 137–140.

Rubin, Z. *Liking and loving.* New York: Holt, Rinehart & Winston, 1973.

Schneider, I. *The world of love.* New York: Braziller, 1964.

Shapiro, A., & Swensen, C. H. Patterns of self-disclosure among married couples. *Journal of Counseling Psychology,* 1969, *16,* 179–180.

Shapiro, A., & Swensen, C. H. Self-disclosure as a function of self-concept and sex. *Journal of Personality Assessment,* 1977, *41,* 144–149.

Smelser, N. J. Issues in the study of work and love in adulthood. In N. J. Smelser & E. H. Erikson (Eds.), *Themes of work and love in adulthood.* Cambridge, Mass.: Harvard University Press, 1980. Pp. 1–26. (a)

Smelser, N. J. Vicissitudes of work and love in Anglo-American society. In N. J. Smelser & E. H. Erikson (Eds.), *Themes of work and love in adulthood.* Cambridge, Mass.: Harvard University Press, 1980. Pp. 105–119. (b)

Stinnett, N., Farris, J. A., & Walters, J. Parent-child relationships of male and female high school students. *Journal of Genetic Psychology,* 1974, *125,* 99–106.

Sutton-Smith, B., & Rosenberg, B. C. Sibling consensus on power tactics. *Journal of Genetic Psychology,* 1968, *112,* 63–72.

Swensen, C. H. The behavior of love. In H. A. Otto (Ed.), *Love today: A new perspective.* New York: Association Press, 1972. Pp. 86–101.

Swensen, C. H. *Introduction to interpersonal relations.* Glenview, Ill.: Scott, Foresman, 1973. (a)

Swensen, C. H. Scale of feelings and behavior of love. In J. W. Pfeiffer & J. E. Jones (Eds.), *The 1973 handbook for group facilitators.* La Jolla, Calif.: University Associates, 1973. Pp. 71–85. (b)

Swensen, C. H. Ego development and interpersonal relationships. In D. Nevill (Ed.), *New frontiers in humanistic psychology.* New York: Gardner Press, 1977. Pp. 35–66.

Swensen, C. H., Eskew, R., & Kohlhepp, K. A. Stage of family life cycle, ego development, and the marriage relationship. *Journal of Marriage and the Family,* 1981, *43,* 841–853.

Swensen, C. H., & Moore, C. Marriages that endure. In E. Corfman (Ed.), *Families today: Strengthening the family* (NIMH Science Monographs, DHEW Publication No. ADM 79–896). Rockville, Md.: National Institutes of Mental Health, 1979. Pp. 249–288.

Swensen, C. H., & Trahaug, G. *Mental problems of older people* (Report of Norwegian Research Council Grant No. B.61.01.088). Bergen, Norway: University of Bergen, 1979.

Swidler, A. Love and adulthood in American culture. In N. J. Smelser & E. H. Erikson (Eds.), *Themes of work and love in adulthood.* Cambridge, Mass.: Harvard University Press, 1980.

Traupman, J., Eckels, E., & Hatfield, E. Intimacy in older women's lives. *The Gerontologist,* 1982, *22,* 493–498.

Turner, J. G. Patterns of intergenerational exchange in developmental approaches. *International Journal of Aging and Human Development,* 1975, *6,* 111–115.

Turner, R. H. *Family interaction.* New York: John Wiley & Sons, 1970.

Turner, W. J. *Mozart: The man and his works.* Garden City, N.Y.: Anchor Press/Doubleday, 1955.

Uchalik, D. C., & Livingston, D. D. Adulthood: Women. In K. S. Pope (Ed.), *On love and loving.* San Francisco: Jossey-Bass, 1980. Pp. 89–103.

Walster, E., & Walster, G. W. *A new look at love.* Reading, Mass.: Addison-Wesley Publishing, 1978.

Weiner, M. F. Healthy and pathological love—psychodynamic views. In K. S. Pope (Ed.), *On love and loving.* San Francisco: Jossey-Bass, 1980. Pp. 114–132.

Chapter 12

Emotional Expression in Marital and Family Relationships*

JENNIFER E. SADE
CLIFFORD I. NOTARIUS

INTRODUCTION

The study of emotionality within marital and family relationships provides unique information about family functioning. When we consider intimate relationships, affective expression is often a central component. Though emotional expression has been studied less than the behavioral and cognitive components of relationships, it is certainly no less important. Emotional expression could be expected to operate much differently within the context of intimate relationships than it does out of a relational context. The study of emotional expression in individuals or in groups of strangers may have little bearing on the process of emotional expression among intimates in enduring long-term relationships. Thus, studying emotional expression within the family also can provide unique information about emotionality.

In this chapter, we will focus on the state of knowledge concerning emotional expression in married couples and in families. The chapter is divided into four sections. The first section is concerned with emotional expression as a discriminator of distressed and nondistressed marriages. Emotional expression has often been defined in terms of nonverbal communication skills, and these skills appear to be related to marital satisfaction. Deficits in nonverbal communication skills have

---

* Paul Benson, Margaret Cunningham, and Nelly Vanzetti provided valuable commentary on an earlier draft of this chapter. We would like to extend a special thanks to David Pellegrini; his insightful critique has made a strong contribution to our final product.

been assessed in senders and receivers, since communication problems could be due to errors in sending, receiving, or both. Frequency of affective expression and reciprocity of affect have also been shown to discriminate distressed from nondistressed couples.

The second section focuses on differences in emotional expressiveness between males and females. On a variety of different measures, females have been found to be more expressive than males. This gender difference may cause stress in the marital relationship, due partly to differences in communication style as well as to differences in expectations for the marital relationship.

The third section focuses on emotional expressiveness in families in which a child has a psychosomatic disorder. We live in a society which encourages the suppression of emotion. Support for the hypothesis that inhibition of emotion is related to the development of psychosomatic disorders is reviewed, and issues are discussed which are related to judging the effects of the inhibition or expression of emotion.

In the final section, we look at the role of emotional expressiveness in schizophrenic disorders. Nonexpressiveness has been hypothesized to play in schizophrenic disorders a role similar to that postulated for psychosomatic disorders. Expressiveness in relatives of hospitalized schizophrenics has also been related to the prediction of symptomatic relapse. Models have been proposed which relate emotional expressiveness with psychosomatic and schizophrenic disorders, and studies have analyzed some aspects of these relationships. However, the processes which mediate the relationships, such as between emotional expressiveness and physiological reactivity, remain unclear.

EMOTIONAL EXPRESSIVENESS IN MARRIAGE

Social-learning conceptualizations of marriage have focused our attention on the behavior exchange process characterizing a marriage (Weiss, 1978). Observational studies of communication processes in distressed and nondistressed couples have shown that these groups can be discriminated on the basis of both verbal and nonverbal behaviors (Gottman, Markman, & Notarius, 1977; Margolin & Wampold, 1981); however, nonverbal behaviors have provided the most potent discriminators (Gottman, et al.). The potency of nonverbal cues was also illustrated by the inability of distressed couples to mask nonverbal signs of distress when asked to present a socially desirable interaction; these distressed couples were able to control their verbal behavior to appear nondistressed (Vincent, Friedman, Nugent, & Messerly, 1979).

The study of nonverbal communication has its roots in the study of feelings or emotions (Friedman, 1979). From a communications theory viewpoint, emotions are seen as "sent" (or encoded) by the person sending the message and "received" (or decoded) by the person receiving the message. The information is transmitted through various channels, which include voice tone, facial expressions, and body gestures or posture. The emotional expression is then analyzed in terms of the emotional information available from the sender and the ability of the viewer to detect various aspects of this information.

The importance of clear and accurate nonverbal communication to successful marital interaction was first studied by Kahn (1970), who developed the Marital Communication Scale (MCS) to measure the accuracy of nonverbal communication by controlling the verbal component of messages. Spouses were asked to communicate a specific attitude or feeling to their partners through a verbal message designated by the experimenter. Since the content of the message was fixed, it was through the use of nonverbal cues that the different attitudes could be conveyed. After each communication was completed, the receiver chose from the three alternative attitudes for that item the one he or she believed the partner had attempted to convey. For half of the items, the husband was the sender and the wife the receiver, while the roles were reversed for the other half. The couple received one combined score since each item required the contributions of both spouses.

Kahn found that dissatisfied couples obtained significantly lower accuracy scores on the MCS than did satisfied couples. However, Kahn did not attempt to separate out the different contributions of the husbands and wives as senders and receivers.

Using a modified version of Kahn's Marital Communication Scale, Noller (1980) studied the relationship between skills in encoding and decoding nonverbal communication and levels of marital adjustment. In order to determine whether an incorrect response on the MCS was an encoding or a decoding error, independent observers rated the messages from videotapes of all the senders. If two thirds of the judges were able to decode an item correctly, then that item was classified as successfully encoded, or a good communication. If a spouse gave an incorrect response to an item which qualified as good communication, then the response was scored as a decoding error. Noller's results replicated Kahn's findings that couples with high marital adjustment obtained higher scores on the MCS than did couples with low marital adjustment.

Looking first at encoding skills, Noller found that those in the low marital adjustment group had significantly fewer of their communications rated as good communication than did those in the high marital adjustment group. Encoding was a greater source of error than decoding for all groups, although neither husbands nor wives had difficulty getting across their negative messages. More of the negative messages were rated by the judges as good communications than were the positive or neutral messages.

In addition to differences between the high and low marital adjustment groups in the percentages of communications rated as "good," sex differences were also found. Males in the low marital adjustment group were the poorest encoders. Their poor performance was primarily responsible for the marital adjustment main effect since the two groups of wives did not display large differences in encoding ability. Overall, wives had significantly more of their communications rated as good communication than did husbands. Though females were only slightly better at sending negative messages than males, they were substantially better at sending positive messages. The encoding superiority of females has also been found in other studies using married or dating couples as subjects (Noller, 1981; Sabatelli, Buck, & Dreyer, 1980; Sabatelli, Buck, & Dreyer, 1982).

Sabatelli et al. (1982) found some support for the prediction that spouses who have partners who are good encoders will report greater marital satisfaction. Subjects watched emotionally loaded slides concerning topics such as "sexual," "children," and "human injuries" and described their feelings. Unknown to the subjects, they were videotaped through a one-way mirror so that their spontaneous facial expressions and gestures were recorded. Independent judges rated the tapes to obtain a general sending-accuracy score. The results showed a relationship between nonverbal sending accuracy and marital satisfaction as measured by a modified Locke-Wallace Short Marital Adjustment Test (Locke & Wallace, 1959) and the Ryder Lovesickness Scale (Ryder, 1973). The relationship between encoding accuracy and marital satisfaction was in the opposite direction for males and females. The most consistent relationship found was that when wives were good nonverbal senders, husbands were more satisfied with the marriage. However, when husbands were good nonverbal senders, their wives reported lower marital satisfaction on the Locke-Wallace. If these findings were replicated, it would seem that facial expressivity has a different role or function for males than for females. One difficulty in interpreting the results of this study is that there was no report of the degree of marital distress of the couples in the sample.

While Sabatelli et al. (1982) suggested that husbands who were satisfied with their marriage had partners who provided clear nonverbal information via facial cues, one also needs to look at the spouses' decoding skills. From the communication deficit hypothesis, skill deficits in decoding of nonverbal communication would be predicted in dissatisfied married couples. Gottman and Porterfield (1981) found support for the communication deficit hypothesis for husbands as receivers but not for wives. Using a modified version of Kahn's Marital Communication Scale, they found that the lower the husband's communicative accuracy, the lower the reported marital satisfaction of the husband and wife. When the data were analyzed to determine the location of the deficit, it appeared that there was a receiver deficit in husbands of dissatisfied marriages. No evidence was found for a significant sender deficit in dissatisfied wives. To answer the question of whether the receiver deficit was specific to the husbands' own marital relationship, an additional group of married couples was used as receiver of each message. This group, called the stranger group, viewed the videotapes of opposite-sexed partners from the spouse group. Thus each message was received both by the sender's spouse and an opposite-sexed, married stranger. The dissatisfied husbands' deficits as receivers were found to be specific to their interactions with their wives. The results of this study suggested a relationship between the marital satisfaction of husbands and wives and the husband's ability to accurately read his wife's nonverbal messages.

Noller's (1980; 1981) studies supported the decoding findings of the Gottman and Porterfield study. When looking at the decoding skills, Noller (1980) found that the low marital adjustment group had a significantly greater percentage of decoding errors than the high marital adjustment group. This difference was largely due to the differences between the males in the two groups. Since the husbands in the high marital adjustment group sent more good communications and made fewer decoding errors than husbands in the low-adjustment group and no similar relationship was found for wives, Noller concluded that husbands' communication skills were an important determinant of marital adjustment.

In a follow-up study, Noller (1981) found that the spouses in the low marital adjustment group decoded as well as the spouses in the high-adjustment group when decoding messages from strangers. This supports Gottman and Porterfield's conclusion that decoding deficits apply specifically to interactions with spouses and do not apply in non-spouse decoding situations. Noller stated that the lower spouse-decoding scores of the low marital adjustment husbands were not due to a lack of decoding skills, since their skills were shown in the nonspouse decoding situation. Since distressed spouses appeared to have the ability to accurately decode messages from a person outside of the marriage, it may be that decoding performance declines as distress increases. Thus, longitudinal study of nonverbal decoding ability within relationships is needed to understand the direction of influence between marital distress and decoding ability.

The results of Sabatelli et al. (1982) seem inconsistent with the results of the other studies which found that the decoding skills of the husbands showed the strongest difference between the nondistressed and the distressed groups. Their results suggested that for decoding as well as encoding skills, the wives' abilities were related to marital happiness. Overall, the receiving abilities of husbands and wives were found to be unrelated to the two measures of marital satisfaction, a modified Locke-Wallace Short Marital Adjustment Test and the Ryder Lovesickness Scale. In order to look more closely at the relationship of communication skills to marital satisfaction, the accuracy of the encoded messages was considered. Each slide sequence was classified as encoded poorly, moderately well, or well, based on the percentage of judges able to correctly categorize that item. They found that both husbands' and wives' marital satisfaction were positively related to the wives' ability to decode the poorly encoded affective facial expressions of the husbands. Thus, when the wives were good at decoding even the poorly encoded messages of their husbands, the spouses reported higher marital satisfaction.

A comparison of the Sabatelli et al. (1982) study with the Gottman and Porterfield (1981) and Noller (1980, 1981) studies reveals some important differences which make a direct comparison of the results difficult. The Sabatelli et al. study did not report the level of marital satisfaction for the couples in the sample. The other studies included a distressed-couple group in their subject population, while it is unknown whether the subjects in the Sabatelli et al. study included distressed couples. In addition, Sabatelli et al. had spouses respond to emotionally laden slides whereas Noller and Gottman and Porterfield had couples act out emotional messages to each other. Spouses in the latter two studies also had access to the full range of nonverbal channels, whereas Sabatelli et al. restricted nonverbal communication to the face and body. Therefore, voice tone was not available to spouses for decoding.

An analysis of the contribution of the visual and auditory channels of nonverbal communication was undertaken by Noller (1980). In the case of husband-to-wife communications, there was no difference in accuracy due to which channel was employed. For wife-to-husband communications, there was greater accuracy when the auditory channel was used. Studies using a combination of channels will thus likely get different results than studies using one channel of communication.

Another dimension of nonverbal behavior which has been used to describe marital functioning is a positive/negative affect dimension. When nonverbal communication is divided into positive and negative nonverbal behavior, the data are often presented as frequencies or base rates.

The use of base rates to discriminate between distressed and nondistressed couples has received mixed support. Looking at positive behaviors, Margolin and Wampold (1981) found that nondistressed couples emitted significantly more positive nonverbal behaviors than did the distressed couples. However, Gottman (1979) found that positive nonverbal codes did not discriminate between the distressed and nondistressed couples. Similarly, while Gottman et al. (1977) found that negative nonverbal behaviors discriminated between groups, Margolin and Wampold failed to find significant differences.

Reciprocity of affect has also been analyzed for its potential for discriminating between distressed and nondistressed couples. Reciprocity of negative affect has received consistent support in discriminating between distressed and nondistressed couples and has been found to be a better discriminator between groups than reciprocity of positive affect.

Margolin and Wampold (1981) found reciprocity of positive affect to be evidenced by both distressed and nondistressed couples. Negative reciprocity, however, was exhibited only by the distressed couples. While the nondistressed group emitted negative behaviors at a rate similar to that of the distressed group, the negative behaviors were not emitted in a contingent fashion. Gottman et al. (1977) also found that clinic spouses (i.e., those who were referred by counseling agencies or who responded to ads recruiting couples who felt their marriages to be unsatisfactory) displayed a stronger tendency to follow negative affect with negative affect than did nonclinic spouses.

Gottman (1980) examined the consistency of nonverbal affect and affect reciprocity across high- and low-conflict tasks. For distressed and nondistressed couples, the dimension with the greatest cross-situational consistency was negative affect reciprocity. Though the nonsequential analyses showed less cross-situational consistency than the sequential analyses, negative affect frequency showed greater consistency than positive affect frequency. Gottman concluded that the greater consistency of the negative affect frequency and negative affect reciprocity variables corresponds well with the greater power of negative affect and negative affect reciprocity to discriminate between distressed and nondistressed couples than the positive affect and positive affect reciprocity variables.

To summarize this section on emotional expression in marriage, a number of measures have demonstrated a strong ability to discriminate between nondistressed and distressed couples. The results of the encoding and decoding studies supported the hypothesis that distressed spouses would display deficits in their nonverbal communication skills. The encoding skills of distressed spouses have been found to be lower than those of nondistressed spouses, with this significant difference being primarily due to the large differences between males in the distressed and nondistressed groups. Deficits in husbands' decoding abilities are associated with low husband and wife marital satisfaction. No such relationship has been found for wives' decoding abilities. Due to the poor nonverbal skills of distressed males, it has been suggested that husbands' communication skills appear to be an important determinant of marital adjustment. To test the hypothesis that skill deficits are a precursor of marital distress would require a longitudinal study; such a study has not been done. However, the finding that the deficits are specific to the marital relationship (distressed spouses are able to communicate to strangers) seems to contradict this hypothesis. Thus, although the direction of cause and effect is not known, it is clear that there is a strong relationship between marital satisfaction and nonverbal communication skills.

Why a distressed spouse might be worse at decoding the messages of his spouse than those of a stranger is open to speculation. One possibility is that a spouse may feel overwhelmed by the emotional displays of his partner. When there is dissatisfaction with the marital relationship, the intensity of the emotional displays may be heightened. The spouse may react by tuning out the emotional displays of the partner. Over time, such a tuning-out process may carry over into less emotionally charged situations, such as the laboratory setting. An alternative possibility is that when a person experiences high arousal, he or she may find it difficult to be sensitive to the feelings of his or her partner.

A similar process may also be implicated in the consistent pattern of negative reciprocity characterizing distressed relationships. Across several studies, distressed spouses displayed a greater tendency to reciprocate their partners' negative messages than did nondistressed couples. In states of arousal, it may be difficult to break the pattern of negative affect exchange. In addition, the relatively poor decoding and encoding of nonverbal cues may set off a series of miscommunications that primes the pump for negative exchanges.

GENDER DIFFERENCES AND THE EFFECTS ON MARITAL FUNCTIONING

As discussed in the studies cited above (Noller, 1980, 1981; Sabatelli et al., 1980), females displayed superior skills in the encoding of nonverbal communication. Hall (1979) has reviewed a large number of studies concerned with nonverbal communication skills, including many in which the skills were not measured in a marital or intimate relational context. Hall found that females were better at encoding than males in 71 percent of 26 studies; this difference was greater for visual than for vocal encoding. Buck (1979) also found that females were better senders than males. Being a better encoder of nonverbal communication is one aspect of a person being overtly more expressive. Buck reported that persons who were more expressive often had smaller electrodermal responses to emotional stimuli than did less expressive persons. Adult females had smaller and less frequent electrodermal responses than males in many affective situations. This parallels females being superior encoders in most situations. One exception which has been found is that in aggressive situations, this sex difference reverses and women are less overtly expressive and more expressive physiologically than men (Buck).

Warren and Gilner (1978) designed a role-play test, the Behavioral Test of Tenderness Expression (BTTE), to measure expression of positive assertive behaviors elicited in intimate relationships. Positive assertive behaviors refer to the expression of feelings such as praise, appreciation, liking, empathy, and self-disclosure. Subjects' responses to the short vignettes were recorded on audiotape and rated by judges on a scale of 1 to 4. The criteria for the least expressive response was a punishing response or no response to the partner, and the criteria for the most expressive was a full expression of feelings and response to the partner's needs. From a sample of 41 couples who had been dating at least nine months, females were significantly more expressive than males on the BTTE.

Dosser, Balswick, and Halverson (1983) hypothesized and found females to be more expressive than males on four measures of emotional expressiveness. They also found that males and females were more expressive in situations requiring positive emotions than in those requiring negative emotions. In this study, subjects responded for both same-sex and opposite-sex best friends on behavioral and self-report tests. Dosser et al. analyzed the data on expressivity levels, taking into account situational variables such as type of feeling and sex of the target person. Looking at specific feelings rather than categorizing them as positive or negative, they found the females to be more expressive of love, happiness, and sadness. They predicted that males would be higher in the expression of anger, but this sex difference was not supported.

Females have also been found to be more expressive of negative emotions than males. In an interactional study, Notarius and Johnson (1982) observed wives to be more negative speakers, based on verbal and nonverbal codes, than their husbands. As listeners, wives also displayed more negative nonverbal behavior than their husbands.

Hinchliffe, Vaughan, Hooper, and Roberts (1977) studied couples of which one spouse was a patient diagnosed as depressed and admitted to a short-term psychiatric unit. In this sample of couples (called the depressed couples), some of the identified patients were male and some female. The control sample of couples was drawn from patients on a surgical unit in the hospital and their spouses. Females in general displayed greater expressiveness than males on a variety of behavioral indexes derived from samples of interactions. In the depressed couples, both the husbands and wives were high in expressiveness at the beginning of hospitalization. The husbands' level of expressivity decreased at follow-up after discharge, while the level displayed by the wives did not change dramatically. The change in expressiveness for the husbands was due largely to a significant reduction in negative expressiveness. The pattern of results for the depressed patients was similar to those just reported for couples in which one spouse was depressed. Depressed males showed a dramatic change in level of expressiveness with recovery; depressed females did not change significantly and remained at a high level of expressiveness. Hinchliffe et al. speculated that the nonacceptance of emotionally charged behaviors in males therapeutically motivated the depressed males more than the depressed females to more rapidly change their behavior.

Hinchliffe et al. found a close parallel in the level of expressivity across sessions for male depressed patients and their wives. A similar parallel for female depressed patients and their husbands was not found. One interpretation of these results is that wives may be more sensitive and reactive to the expressed emotions of their husbands than husbands are to their wives. Data from the Notarius and Johnson (1982) study support the hypothesis of greater reciprocity of affect for females than for males. Wives reciprocated their husbands' positive and negative speaker turns. Husbands tended to follow positive speaking turns of their wives with a neutral speaking turn, and they showed no consistent response pattern to their wives' negative expressions.

The finding that females are more emotionally expressive than males is consistent with the general stereotype of females being more expressive. In Western culture, we often think of thoughts and feelings as unrelated, and we associate the feelings component with irrationality (L'Abate & Frey, 1981; Rubin, 1976). To be rational is considered good and to be irrational is bad. To be emotional is the less desired state; according to Rubin, it is bad, weak, and childlike. Therefore, emotionality becomes something to avoid or suppress.

Rubin (1976) attributed difficulties in marital relationships to the lack of a shared language by which husbands and wives could communicate with one another. Each is trained to relate only to one side of self. Females are trained toward the passive, intuitive, and emotional side, while males are trained toward the active, logical, and unemotional one. When they talk, they each rely on the mode they are most familiar with. When stressed or in a high-conflict situation, they are each likely to stick steadfastly to their usual styles. Thus, the wife becomes progressively more emotional and expressive, and the husband becomes more determinedly rational. Since the rational mode is considered the adult-like and preferred state, the husband's rationality in effect invalidates her feelings.

The male and female sex roles concerning expressivity are postulated by Feldman (1982) to negatively influence intimacy and problem solving in marriage, as each sex is inhibited in the expression of certain kinds of behavior. Feldman's conceptualization of the marital interaction, particularly during conflict, is similar to Rubin's notion of the husband and wife each being stuck in their preferred modes. In addition, Feldman postulated that this interaction forms a mutually reinforcing system. A vicious circle is created in which the husband's lack of expressiveness triggers the wife's overexpressiveness, which in turn further inhibits the husband.

Another effect of gender differences on marital functioning is the conflicting needs of the husband and wife. At the time of marriage, people assume that the behaviors of their partners will serve to fulfill their needs (Chafetz, 1974). However, this assumption is largely false, given that the needs of one are in contrast with the sex role stereotypes of the other. While the wives' needs often involve receiving affection, the masculine sex role discourages the open expression of emotion.

In a study looking at spouse preferences for styles of communicating in their marital relationships, Hawkins, Weisberg and Ray (1980) found that wives tended to see their husbands as falling far short of their preferred communication patterns. The discrepancy between the wife's preferences and the behavior she imputed to him was significantly greater than the husband's discrepancy scores between his preferences and the behavior he imputed to his wife. This gap appeared to be due to differences in perceived behavior more than differences in preferences. The findings of Hawkins et al. are consistent with wives generally being less satisfied in the marital relationship (Kamarovsky, 1964). It may be that females expect more personal gratification from their marital relationship and that males have traditionally turned to their work outside of the home for satisfaction of their needs (Chafetz, 1974).

The higher level of expressiveness shown by females was suggested by Feldman (1982) to be due in part to frustration with the limitations of the female role. The wives' overexpressivity and especially critical comments were believed to be a response to the husbands' sense of superiority and control and the lack of assertiveness in the female role.

Theories on the development and maintenance of sex differences have included the power differential between the sexes as a variable which can explain gender differences in emotional expressivity. Frieze, Parsons, Johnson, Ruble, and Zellman (1978) concluded that women, as the less powerful sex, learn to be more accommodating and thus need to be in tune to the needs of superiors. As the lower-status group, females may have a greater need to attend to the affiliative factors. Sensitivity to the feelings of others may also be related to status, due to the fact that the underdog needs to be able to read the signals or nonverbal behaviors of those with greater power.

Rosenthal and DePaulo (1979) found that though women were better at decoding nonverbal communication, they were more polite than men in their decoding. In decoding deception, women were more likely to read what they were supposed to read, rather than what was true. Also, women's advantage in accuracy of decoding was smaller for brief nonverbal cues which were often less intended and under less control of the sender. This finding was interpreted as women refraining from decoding too efficiently those nonverbal cues which reflected ambivalence and deception of others. They also found that more personally and socially vulnerable women showed the greatest operation of the politeness mechanism. These females were more interpersonally accommodating, as they were more guarded in reading cues that senders may have been trying to hide.

Gender differences in expressivity may be learned through socialization to the male and female sex roles. Balswick and Peek (1971) discussed two masculine stereotypes which epitomize the inexpressive man in American society. Boys are believed to be taught from an early age to value expressions of masculinity, one of which is emotional inexpressiveness.

There is evidence of gender-specific socialization of emotional expressivity at early ages. Phinney and Feshbach (1983) studied the crying behavior of three-and four-year-olds in preschool classes. No sex differences were found in the amount of crying behavior or in the causes of crying. However, the teachers' reactions to the crying behavior varied depending on the sex of the child. Consoling of the crying child occurred 16 times, and in 15 of the 16 examples, the consoling by the teacher was directed towards girls.

Balswick and Peek (1971) reported that inexpressive males need to learn to be situationally expressive. In order for the male to be able to fulfill his role expectations in marriage, he needs to learn to be more emotionally expressive with his wife. Thus, it is necessary for him to change his interpersonal style or choose to be expressive in this situation. Sattel (1976) proposed that males choose to be inexpressive, as it is instrumental for securing and maintaining power. Males are taught to be inexpressive because society expects boys to grow up to become decision makers and the wielders of power. When males are expressive in our society, the expressiveness can be viewed as an effort to control a situation on their terms and to maintain their position.

The labeling of emotions and what composes the concept of emotional expressivity is also subject to a sex bias. Aggressiveness, which is more characteristic of males, is not likely to be labeled as an emotional display (Frieze et al., 1978). In a study by Narus and Fischer (1982), masculinity on the Bem Sex Role Inventory was found to be related to expressivity, and femininity appeared to diminish expressivity. Items such as "defends own beliefs," "willing to take a stand," and "assertive" were related to expressivity in this sample of men. Therefore, the notion of the male sex role not encompassing emotional expressivity seems to depend on how the expressivity variable is defined.

Our review of expressivity and decoding differences in husbands and wives confirms the cultural stereotype for gender effects in emotional behavior. Females appear to be better encoders and decoders of nonverbal information, and they are more expressive and responsive to their husbands. Family therapists and social scientists often take these results as evidence that emotional deficits in the husband are a causal factor in marital distress.

We believe this conclusion oversimplifies the situation. Understanding the role of emotional behavior in marriage demands assessment of the interactive effects between spouses. We cannot examine husbands' and wives' emotional behavior without considering the effects each has upon the other. For example, are wives "provoked" to a higher level of emotional responsiveness by their husbands' lack of emotional behavior? Are husbands more physiologically reactive to intimate emotional situations which leads them to be more controlled than their partners? Paradoxically, the latter alternative would argue against husbands being unfeeling; there may be quite a bit of emotional experience behind males' nonexpressive exteriors.

In any event, current relationships seem to be at risk for difficulties stemming from differences in emotionality between husbands and wives. Enhanced communication between partners may be useful to help each recognize expressive differences and to minimize cognitive elaboration of expressive style differences. For example, it may serve relationships to avoid interpreting nonexpressiveness as "he doesn't care about me" and overt expressiveness as "she is out of control." Helping spouses to help each other may also be a useful strategy, as it can foster the goals of both parties; husbands can learn from their wives how to express themselves more freely, and wives can learn from their husbands how best to get their emotional messages heard. We assume both patterns would be rewarding for all involved.

In the next section, we expand the couples focus to consider family interaction. Specifically, we will explore the relationship between family interaction and physical disturbance. The role of emotional expression in health and disease is becoming clearer, and it is an important area of study.

EMOTIONAL RESPONSIVENESS AND
PHYSIOLOGICAL REACTIVITY

The study of families in which a child has a psychosomatic disorder has resulted in a number of provocative hypotheses relating emotional responsiveness among family members to the physical health of the family and especially the children. Underlying this hypothesis is the researchable proposition that communicative interaction, particularly affective communication, can influence bodily function (Weakland, 1977). Among the interactional patterns that have been said to affect bodily processes, a constrained level of emotional responsiveness has been the most frequently reported correlate of psychosomatic disturbance. For example, Rimon, Belmaker, and Ebstein's (1976) study of juvenile rheumatoid arthritics found the group to be characterized by "shyness, unresponsiveness, passivity, submissiveness, aloofness, feelings of inferiority, and inability to express emotions or to establish contact with fellow patients" (pp. 181–182). Rimon et al. also found the patients' mothers to have "tremendous difficulty in expressing their feelings" (p. 182). These findings are representative of many studies suggesting a link between emotional responsiveness in the family and family health. In this section of the chapter, we will briefly review the research on the relationship between emotional responsivity in the family and somatic functioning and then offer a commentary on the state of knowledge, with suggestions for continued study.

Though few if any well-controlled studies exist, there is an impressive clinical literature describing families with psychosomatic children as affectively constrained. Goldberg (1958) found that the mothers of sons with duodenal ulcers acted to rein in the expression of feeling, especially when the sentiment was negative. Looff (1970) reported that psychosomatic families had greater difficulty verbally expressing their feelings than did families with children diagnosed with other forms of psychopathology. Stewart (1962) found that delinquent youths were relatively free of psychosomatic disturbances and argued this was due to freedom of emotional expression.

Concerning the relationship between emotional responsiveness and physiological reactivity associated with psychophysiological disorders, another source of evidence comes from therapy reports. Waring (1977) reported that an intervention which helped chronic pain patients openly express anger and sadness within the family frequently relieved the chronic pain in very few sessions. Extending these results, Waring (1980) has developed a therapy program for couples in which one partner has a psychosomatic illness. The intervention is structured to help couples verbally express their thoughts and feelings about their relationship, which Waring hypothesized was the specific deficit of these couples.

While these clinical reports illustrate an association between emotional expression and psychosomatic symptom patterns, there has been little direct evidence that family interaction patterns are associated with psychophysiological disorders. Although methodologically weak, the work of Minuchin and his colleagues is often cited as confirming a direct link between family interaction and the pathophysiological reactions of the children. Minuchin, Rosman, and Baker (1978) compared families with a psychosomatic diabetic child to two family control groups containing a nonpsychosomatic diabetic child with or without behavioral problems. Families were monitored throughout a four-part diagnostic interview consisting of (1) 30 minutes during which the child observed parents discuss a family problem from behind a one-way mirror, (2) 30 minutes of the child continuing to observe his or her parents while an interviewer attempted to escalate the family conflict, (3) 30 minutes during which the child joined the parents to help each other decide how they should change, and (4) a final cool-down period during which the family was taken to a comfortable office. Throughout the entire procedure, continuous intravenous blood samples were drawn to measure free-fatty acids (FAA), used as an index of emotional arousal.

As Minuchin et al. (1978) had hypothesized, the psychosomatic diabetic children appeared to differ from the two diabetic comparison groups. The FAA levels of the psychosomatic diabetic children rose continually from the start of the interview to the end of the cool-down period. In both nonpsychosomatic groups, FAA levels of the children did not radically depart from baseline. FAA levels of the psychosomatic child were also plotted against the FAA levels of the parent who was most emotionally aroused during the interview. These plots revealed that the more-aroused parent's FAA levels dropped in the third segment of the interview when the child entered the discussion and that the child's FAA levels continued to rise even through the cool-down period. It seemed that the interactional presence of the psychosomatic child helped reduce the most aroused parent's emotional arousal, thus suggesting a relationship between family interaction patterns and emotional responsivity during conflict.

It is important to recognize that Minuchin et al. (1978) did not provide statistical confirmation of the observed relationship between family interaction and emotional arousal, nor is it possible to evaluate the role of selection in the sample studied. Furthermore, the specific nature of family interaction associated with increased physiological arousal is unknown. Minuchin, Baker, Rosman, Liebman, Milman, and Todd (1975) have hypothesized that the family system of a child with a severe psychosomatic disorder is characterized by enmeshment, over-protectiveness, rigidity, and lack of conflict resolution. Burbeck (1979) attempted to independently evaluate that family interaction model through development and evaluation of a questionnaire designed to assess the four family characteristics (enmeshment, overprotectiveness, rigidity, and lack of conflict resolution) hypothesized to characterize the psychosomatic family. The families of 42 asthmatic children completed the study. Burbeck's data failed to confirm a positive relationship between any of the four family characteristics and the severity of the psychosomatic disorder. Unfortunately, the reliability of Burbeck's scales were sufficiently low to challenge the validity of his findings. Thus, the identification of specific patterns of family interaction and emotional arousal related to psychosomatic symptoms remains an important research agenda.

In a nonclinical couples population, Notarius and Johnson (1982) have reported an inverse relationship between emotional responsivity during a conflict resolution discussion and physiological reactivity, operationalized as skin potential reactivity. In this small sample study, husbands were less overtly responsive to their wives than were wives to their husbands. As nonreactive listeners to their partners' negative messages, husbands tended to display more skin potential responses than did wives. Thus, husbands were less overtly responsive and more physiologically reactive in comparison to their wives. These interactional results provide support for a link between emotional responsivity and physiological reactivity during marital interaction. ·

The influence of interaction among intimates upon autonomic reactivity associated with emotional experience was also demonstrated in a study by Levenson and Gottman (1983). Husbands and wives were observed interacting on both a low-conflict and a high-conflict task while heart rate, skin conductance, pulse transmission time, and somatic activity were monitored. A measure of the degree of interrelatedness among the spouse's physiological responses was found to account for up to 60 percent of the variance in marital satisfaction. Distressed spouses were much more likely than were nondistressed spouses to display similar physiological reactivity patterns. Levenson and Gottman hypothesized that the physiological linkage they observed may be related to feeling "locked into" interactional processes and to a sense of being "trapped" in an intimate relationship. While this study also did not specifically address psychophysiological disorders, it represents a well-controlled study demonstrating the association between marital interaction and physiological reactivity. As this research line continues, we may move closer toward understanding the mechanisms by which emotional interaction affects physiological reactivity patterns among family members.

We would like to pull the investigative lens back to allow a broad perspective on the role of emotional responsiveness in health and dis-

ease in order to examine Western socialization processes that have
been portrayed as contributing to psychophysiological disorders. Groen
and Bastiaans (1982) have argued that Western culture fosters impaired
emotional development owing to conditioned suppression of emotional
communication:

> In general, children in our society have more rights and less duties;
> they are "emancipated." On the other hand, the price they pay for
> their emancipation is a less warm, less supporting family situation. . . .
> The deprivation of mutual bodily touching as a form of human communi-
> cation seems to be a part of a growing tendency in Western cultures
> to suppress emotional expression. . . . More and more, Western people
> learn to speak and act in a "detached" way. In situations they formerly
> reacted to by intense motor, mimic, and vocal discharges to express
> their feelings, they now behave as if they were not experiencing any
> emotion. . . . But too much detachment is potentially harmful because
> speech alone is an insufficient vehicle for the transfer of all the feelings
> that human beings need to convey to each other. Only an adequate
> abreaction of the emotions brings understanding and sympathy from
> others and gives the support that is needed in situations of frustration.
> (pp. 16–17)

Groen and Bastiaans concluded that the socially acquired inhibition
of emotion is related to the development of psychosomatic disorder:

> Psychosomatic diseases are substitute forms of behavior, becoming mani-
> fest when the expression in speech and musculoskeletal action that would
> be appropriate in response to psychosocial stress is inhibited. This inhib-
> ited energy may ultimately find an outlet in increased autonomic, vis-
> ceral, or endocrine activity. . . . The cultural tendency toward greater
> self-control in the Western world is, according to psychosomatic theory,
> one of the main reasons for the increasing frequency of certain psychoso-
> matic disorders in Western culture. (p. 26)

Groen and Bastiaans' (1982) analysis thus focuses squarely on the
role of family communication as a determinant of the family's current
well-being as well as the children's future adjustment. Taken together
with the empirical literature, there appears sufficient mandate for further exploration of the role of emotional responsiveness in the family
system. However, if we are to move beyond the notion that emotional
expression is good and emotional inhibition is bad, we must begin to
consider several important issues.

First, there has been a lack of attention to specific affective states.
Many clinicians have focused attention on the inhibition of anger. We
lack knowledge of the effects of emotional expression or inhibition
upon physiological reactivity of specific affective states including anger,
sadness, fear, happiness, interest, and surprise, as well as blends of
these emotional experiences. What affective expressions are most asso-

ciated with physiological reactivity in what specific contexts remains to be explained.

Second, the underlying processes responsible for a lack of overt emotional responsiveness and concomitant physiological reactivity are largely unknown at this time. Among the rival hypotheses currently being considered are: *(a)* competing incompatible affective experiences (e.g., fear and anger) are vying for an output channel, with each inhibiting the other, *(b)* nonexpressive persons are attempting to control their emotional experience perhaps due to socialization pressures, resulting in increased physiological reactivity patterns, and *(c)* nonexpressive persons have an inability to express their feelings in words and thus experience a dissociation between emotional experience and expression (alexithymia).

Third, it is essential to recognize that cause-effect relationships between emotional expression, phenomenological experience, and physiological reactivity have not been established, despite the tendency to reason that suppression of emotional expression "causes" heightened physiological reactivity. The complex interrelationship between cognitive processes, the social environment, physiological reactions, and behavior displays must be acknowledged and assessed. It will not suffice to make conclusions about the overall interrelationships from the study of isolated components.

Fourth, and perhaps most importantly, there are research findings which argue against the suppression model. A number of investigators have reported either a direct relationship between emotional expression and physiological reactivity (e.g., Lanzetta, Cartwright-Smith, & Kleck, 1976; Zuckerman, Klorman, Larrance, & Spiegel, 1981) or a failure of emotional expression to attenuate physiological reactivity (Keane, Martin, Berler, Wooten, Fleece, & Williams, 1982). Keane et al. reported that both hypertensive and normotensive patients displayed similar nonexpressive characteristics, experienced similar subjective distress, and showed similar cardiovascular reactivity patterns to a social stressor. Such data argue against the psychosomatic hypothesis relating inhibited emotional expression (in Keane et al.'s experiment, it was positive and negative assertion) and distinct psychophysiological disturbances (hypertension). In keeping with the theme of this *Handbook,* however, it is essential to note these research reports were *not* based on the interaction of intimates or family members. We would predict that the nature of the relationship among social interactants affects the observed relationships among emotional expression and physiological reactivity patterns. Hence, future studies must acknowledge the influence of the social setting and account for how this may mediate the relationship between emotional expression and physiological reactivity. What is observed in the laboratory among strangers may not be observed among family members who experience personal conflicts within an ongoing interactional system.

Finally, we must be cautious applying our findings to clinical practice. Already, many therapists have argued for the effectiveness of therapeutic interventions which promote emotional expression (Pierce, Nichols, & DuBrin, 1983). Not only is there insufficient evidence to argue for this procedure with individuals, but also it will often be essential to consider the larger family system if an intervention is to be successful. For example, if father is recognized to have a psychophysiological disorder, it may be a misguided effort to plan an intervention to increase father's level of emotional responsiveness without first understanding what mother's reaction to his emotional expression is and has been. Simply stated, the family is an interactional system which affects and is affected by each family member; system processes must be assessed to understand each family member and to effectively intervene on behalf of the family or any of its members.

EXPRESSIVENESS AND SCHIZOPHRENIA

Not only has the role of emotional expressiveness been implicated in psychosomatic disorders, it has also been hypothesized to play a role in schizophrenia. Specifically, the level and form of emotional expression in the family has been investigated in a number of studies comparing schizophrenic families to various control groups, as discussed by Doane (Chapter 30 of this *Handbook*). Similar to the reasoning applied to psychosomatic families, nonexpressiveness is often viewed as a defense against the expression of felt feelings. The "schizophrenogenic mother" who is construed as cold, distant, impersonal, and nonresponsive exemplifies a model which emphasizes the role of nonexpressiveness in the genesis of psychiatric illness. Mishler and Waxler (1968) summarized these models by noting that the families operated as if there were a "mutual protection pact in which feelings are collectively denied" (p. 81).

In an elaborate observational study which compared families classified as normal with families classified as having a schizophrenic child with a good or poor premorbid adjustment, Mishler and Waxler (1968) attempted to test the hypothesized role of emotional nonexpression in schizophrenic family process. Emotional expression was operationalized with indirect measures based on the literal content of exchanged messages as well as with direct measures based on Bales's Interaction Process Analysis codings made from audiotapes and a typed transcript. Although Mishler and Waxler studied families with both females and males, the number of families with schizophrenic females was very small; thus, we will limit our discussion to their findings pertaining to families with males.

Mishler and Waxler (1968) found that parents of normal sons displayed more directly expressive behaviors than did parents of good premorbid schizophrenic sons. Included in the category of directly expressive behaviors were: (1) shows solidarity, (2) tension release, (3) agreement, (4) disagreement, (5) shows tension, and (6) antagonism. Since parents of schizophrenic males were not differentially expressive when interacting with the patient's well brother, some stability in the family system was demonstrated. The investigators also found no evidence of differences in expressivity between mothers and fathers in either the normal or the schizophrenic families as might have been predicted by role theory (Lidz & Fleck, 1965). Mishler and Waxler offered the following interpretation for their results:

> The . . . findings reflect the operation of a general family norm regarding appropriate levels of expressive behavior. Members of normal families . . . are expected to be more expressive when interacting with each other than are the members of patient families; members of good premorbid families, including the schizophrenic son and his well sibling, are expected to be low in expressive behavior. The rates in good premorbid families are sufficiently low to suggest the possibility that this is defensive; that is, their high levels of instrumental and affectively neutral activity are consistent with an interpretation that they are defending themselves against expressions of affect and feeling. (p. 92)

The results reviewed thus far did not distinguish among the qualities of the emotional expression (for example, whether it was positive or negative). After completing a series of analyses that separately examined positive and negative expressiveness, Mishler and Waxler (1968) reported that normal families were characterized by significantly more positive expressive behavior while parents with a good premorbid schizophrenic son were characterized by a disproportionate amount of negative expression. The experimental results matched the investigators' observation that normal families appeared to enjoy themselves during interactional tasks, while good premorbid families appeared emotionally flat with "occasional expressions of irritation, annoyance, and criticism of each other" (p. 93). The poor premorbid families showed a pattern of expressive quality falling between the patterns exhibited by the normal and the good premorbid families.

Although cautious in interpreting the overall pattern of results, Mishler and Waxler (1968) noted that their findings supported the view of the schizophrenic family as a rigid system organized to defend against direct expression of feeling. While the data confirmed differences between normal and schizophrenic families, they cannot be taken as support for an etiological model. In fact, Mishler and Waxler's failure to find a marked difference between the parents' affective interaction with a well sibling and their affective interaction with the patient suggests emotional expression is not in and of itself a causal determinant of schizophrenia. What other variables it operates with or modifies is presently unknown. Nevertheless, the findings suggest the merit of continued study of emotional expressiveness in normal and schizophrenic families.

Emotional expression in the family has also been studied as a predictor of symptomatic relapse in a group of hospitalized schizophrenics (Brown, Birley, & Wing, 1972). Brown and his associates coined their construct "expressed emotion" and operationalized it as a composite of: (1) the number of critical comments made by a key relative when discussing the patient and the patient's illness, (2) the amount of hostility and criticism contained in the comments, and (3) indications of significant emotional overinvolvement in the interviews. In the Brown et al. study, an individual interview was held with a key relative, and on the basis of expressed emotion (as defined above), families were divided into high or low expressed emotion (EE) homes. The results revealed a relapse rate of 58 percent for schizophrenic patients from high EE homes compared to a relapse rate of 16 percent from low EE homes.

It is worth noting that only the interview held with the relative alone produced the significant effect; expressed emotion based on interviews with the patient alone or with both the patient and the relative were not predictive of relapse.[1] While the measurement of expressed emotion in the Brown et al. (1972) study cannot be taken as behavioral evidence (as the construct name might imply) of differential rates of emotional expression during family interaction with the patient, the differential relapse rates are suggestive that there are behavioral correlates of expressed emotion.

Vaughn and Leff (1976) have provided evidence that a one-hour interview with a key relative yields sufficient data to compute an expressed emotion index to predict relapse in schizophrenics. Reviewing the original results reported by Brown et al. (1972) as well as an additional sample, Vaughn and Leff also demonstrated that the occurrence of critical comments appeared to be the essential component of the expressed emotion score. The authors noted that hostility was associated with criticism and that emotional overinvolvement was not a potent marker for identifying high and low expressed emotion families.

Additional evidence for the significance of expressed emotion was provided in a study by Leff and Vaughn (1980) who investigated the

---

[1] One explanation for this finding may be that family members are sensitive to implicit demands of medical personnel to inhibit overt critical comments in front of the patient. When the doctor is present with the patient, relatives may not express the criticism. When relatives are alone or feel that they are not being observed, then they may freely show their expressed emotion. David Pellegrini suggested this hypothesis and noted a similar process with mothers and children in treatment at child guidance clinics.

interactive effects of life events and relatives' expressed emotion upon a group of schizophrenics and a group of depressive neurotic inpatients. The results confirmed an interaction between life events and expressed emotion in the period before the onset of schizophrenia as well as depression. However, the pattern of results differed between the depressed patients and the schizophrenic patients. The onset of a schizophrenic episode among patients living with high EE relatives was not associated with an excess of life events, whereas there was an association between schizophrenic onset and life events among patients living with low EE relatives. Leff and Vaughn concluded: "The onset or relapse of schizophrenia is associated *either* with high EE *or* with an independent life event" (p. 150). The pattern observed with the neurotic depressives was the reverse. The onset or relapse of a depressive episode was associated with the "*conjunction* of a critical relative and an independent life event" (p. 150). Since the key relative is often a spouse, Leff and Vaughn have speculated that depressive episodes are associated with "nonconfiding" marriages (high expressed emotion) and exposure to life events. It would be interesting to explore *directly* the interaction patterns of couples who differ along the expressed emotion dimension. Such a study could isolate the interactional variables that seem to potentiate life events in the onset of depressive episodes.

Recently Doane and her associates have used a variant of the expressed emotion measure to study families with an adolescent at risk for psychopathology (Doane, Goldstein, & Rodnick, 1981; Doane, Chapter 30 of this *Handbook*). The primary dependent variable used by Doane et al. was labeled "affective style" (AS) and was composed of criticism (personal or benign), guilt induction, and intrusiveness (critical or neutral). The experimental design called for each adolescent subject to interact separately with mother, father, and then as a family triad. The interaction tasks were developed from a revealed-differences procedure (Strodbeck, 1954). Various comparison groups, based on mother's or father's AS score were formed to assess the power of affective style to predict adolescent psychological status. The most potent prediction emerged when Doane et al. simultaneously accounted for *(a)* mother's AS score, *(b)* father's AS score, and *(c)* the consistency among parent's scores when interacting alone with the child and when interacting in a family triad.

Specifically, five comparison groups were constructed: (1) bilateral benign, in which both parents had consistently benign AS scores across all settings (n = 19); (2) unilateral benign, in which one parent was consistently benign while the other parent was not consistent across settings (n = 13); (3) bilateral inconsistent, in which both parents were inconsistent across settings (n = 19); (4) unilateral negative, in which one parent was consistently negative and the other parent was inconsistent across settings (n = 8); and (5) bilateral negative, in which both parents were consistently negative (n = 3). Adolescents showed the least disorder at five-year follow-up when both parents displayed consistently benign affective style toward them. The prognosis was nearly as good for the adolescents of parents who displayed a unilateral benign AS. The adolescents of families with even one parent showing a consistently negative AS had a much poorer prognosis. For example, all three cases of bilateral negative parents and 75 percent of the unilateral negative cases displayed schizophrenic-spectrum disorders at the five-year follow-up. Among the adolescents living in a home with bilaterally inconsistent parents, six of the nine cases showed deterioration in psychiatric status over the five-year period.

To summarize, the expressed emotion construct has been remarkably robust. It has shown utility in predicting *relapse* among schizophrenic patients recently hospitalized (e.g., Vaughn & Leff, 1976) as well as *onset* of schizophrenia-spectrum disorder among a high-risk sample of adolescents (Doane et al., 1981). Taken together, these findings lend support to the hypothesis that expressed emotion is a salient family risk factor in the pathogenesis of serious psychological disorder within families. The very consistency of findings across research settings, patient status, and developmental periods strongly supports the validity of the expressed emotion construct.

Of the completed studies, Doane et al.'s (1981) work appears to be a step ahead of the other expressed emotion work in that the dependent variable is based on a family interaction sample. We say 'step ahead' in the context of a desire to learn more about the nature and function of emotional expression in marriage and the family. This objective has been secondary for researchers studying expressed emotion; their primary objective has been the prediction of relapse or onset of psychiatric disorder in prospective designs. Hopefully, the two different objectives bear some commonalities, for it is usually assumed that the expressed emotion is somehow transmitted through family interaction to affect the offspring. Yet, the network of validating data necessary to demonstrate the proximal effects of expressed emotion or affective style has thus far not been established.

One hypothesis for pinpointing the interactional process associated with expressed emotion is suggested by the interactional studies of distressed and nondistressed marriages. Researchers have consistently found distressed couples to engage in reciprocal negative affect exchanges that nondistressed couples appear able to terminate. Perhaps families who are characterized by high expressed emotion are similarly locked into negative affect exchanges. The report that phenothiazines seem to attenuate the risk associated with high expressed emotion

(Leff, Hirsch, Gaind, Rohde, & Stevens, 1973) may locate an interactional effect of the drug. Perhaps the drug disrupts the negative affect cycles and the accompanying arousal characteristic of distressed communication. If this effect were confirmed, then we would be in a better position to understand *how* drug maintenance affects the risk associated with expressed emotion.

In conclusion, our goal in this chapter has been to review four diverse literatures on emotionality in marriage and the family. We have pointed out areas of consistent findings and targeted several agenda for continued research. The evidence supporting an association among emotional processes and family health and disorder provides a strong mandate for expanding our limited knowledge base of the functional role of emotionality in family process.

REFERENCES

Balswick, J. O., & Peek, C. W. The inexpressive male: A tragedy of American society. *Family Coordinator*, 1971, *20*, 363–368.

Brown, G. W., Birley, J. L. T., & Wing, J. K. Influence of family life on the course of schizophrenic disorders: A replication. *British Journal of Psychiatry*, 1972, *121*, 241–258.

Buck, R. Individual differences in nonverbal sending accuracy and electrodermal responding: The externalizing-internalizing dimension. In R. Rosenthal (Ed.), *Skill in nonverbal communication: Individual differences*. Cambridge, Mass.: Oelgeschlager, Gunn, & Hain, 1979. Pp. 32–67.

Burbeck, T. W. An empirical investigation of the psychosomatogenic family model. *Journal of Psychosomatic Research*, 1979, *23*, 327–337.

Chafetz, J. S. *Masculine/feminine or human?* Itasca, Ill.: F. E. Peacock Publishers, 1979.

Doane, J. A., Goldstein, M. J., & Rodnick, E. H. Parental patterns of affective style and the development of schizophrenia spectrum disorders. *Family Process*, 1981, *20*, 337–349.

Dosser, D. A., Jr., Balswick, J. O., & Halverson, C. F., Jr. Situational context of emotional expressiveness. *Journal of Counseling Psychology*, 1983, *30*, 375–387.

Feldman, L. B. Sex roles and family dynamics. In F. Walsh (Ed.), *Normal family processes*. New York: Guilford Press, 1982. Pp. 354–379.

Friedman, H. The concept of skill in nonverbal communication: Implications for understanding social interaction. In R. Rosenthal (Ed.), *Skill in nonverbal communication: Individual differences*. Cambridge, Mass.: Oelgeschlager, Gunn, & Hain, 1979. Pp. 2–27.

Frieze, I. H., Parsons, J. E., Johnson, P. B., Ruble, D. N., & Zellman, G. L. *Women and sex roles: A social psychological perspective*. New York: W. W. Norton, 1978.

Goldberg, E. M. *Family influences and psychosomatic illness*. London: Tavistock Publications, 1958.

Gottman, J. M. *Marital interaction: Experimental investigations*. New York: Academic Press, 1979.

Gottman, J. M. Consistency of nonverbal affect and affect reciprocity in marital interaction. *Journal of Consulting and Clinical Psychology*, 1980, *48*, 711–717.

Gottman, J. M., Markman, H., & Notarius, C. The topography of marital conflict: A sequential analysis of verbal and nonverbal behavior. *Journal of Marriage and the Family*, 1977, *39*, 461–477.

Gottman, J. M., & Porterfield, A. L. Communicative competence in the nonverbal behavior of married couples. *Journal of Marriage and the Family*, 1981, *43*, 817–824.

Groen, J. J., & Bastiaans, J. Psychosocial stress, interhuman communication, and psychosomatic disease. In J. J. Groen & J. Groen (Eds.), *Clinical research in psychosomatic medicine.* Assen, Netherlands: Van Gorcum, 1982. Pp. 9–28.

Hall, J. Gender, gender roles, and nonverbal communication skills. In R. Rosenthal (Ed.), *Skill in nonverbal communication: Individual differences.* Cambridge, Mass.: Oelgeschlager, Gunn, & Hain, 1979. Pp. 32–67.

Hawkins, J. L., Weisberg, C., & Ray, D. W. Spouse differences in communication style: Preference, perception, behavior. *Journal of Marriage and the Family*, 1980, *42*, 585–593.

Hinchliffe, M. K., Vaughan, P. W., Hooper, D., & Roberts, F. J. The melancholy marriage: An inquiry into the interaction of depression—II. Expressiveness. *British Journal of Medical Psychology*, 1977, *50*, 125–142.

Kahn, M. Nonverbal communication and marital satisfaction. *Family Process*, 1970, *9*, 449–457.

Kamarovsky, M. *Blue-collar marriage.* New York: Random House, 1964.

Keane, T. M., Martin, J. E., Berler, E. S., Wooten, L. S., Fleece, E. L., & Williams, J. G. Are hypertensives less assertive? A controlled evaluation. *Journal of Consulting and Clinical Psychology*, 1982, *50*, 499–508.

L'Abate, L., & Frey, J. The E–R–A model: The role of feelings in family therapy reconsidered: Implications for a classification of theories of family therapy. *Journal of Marital and Family Therapy*, 1981, *7*, 143–150.

Lanzetta, J. T., Cartwright-Smith, J., & Kleck, R. E. Effects of nonverbal dissimulation on emotional experience and autonomic arousal. *Journal of Personality and Social Psychology*, 1976, *33*, 354–370.

Leff, J. P., Hirsch, S. R., Gaind, R., Rohde, P. D., & Stevens, B. C. Life events and maintenance therapy in schizophrenic relapse. *British Journal of Psychiatry*, 1973, *123*, 659–660.

Leff, J. P., & Vaughn, C. The interaction of life events and relatives' expressed emotion in schizophrenia and depressive neurosis. *British Journal of Psychiatry*, 1980, *136*, 146–153.

Levenson, R. W., & Gottman, J. M. Marital interaction: Physiological linkage and affective exchange. *Journal of Personality and Social Psychology*, 1983, *45*, 587–597.

Lidz, T., & Fleck, S. Family studies and a theory of schizophrenia. In T. Lidz, S. Fleck, & A. Cornelison (Eds.), *Schizophrenia and the family.* New York: International Universities Press, 1965. Pp. 362–376.

Locke, H., & Wallace, K. Short marital adjustment and prediction tests: Their reliability and validity. *Marriage and Family Living*, 1959, *21*, 251–255.

Looff, D. Psychophysiologic and conversion reactions in children—selective incidence in verbal and nonverbal families. *Journal of the American Academy of Child Psychiatry,* 1970, *9,* 318–331.

Margolin, G., & Wampold, B. E. Sequential analysis of conflict and accord in distressed and nondistressed marital partners. *Journal of Consulting and Clinical Psychology,* 1981, *49,* 554–567.

Minuchin, S., Baker, L., Rosman, B. L., Liebman, R., Milman, L., & Todd, T. C. A conceptual model of psychosomatic illness in children. *Archives of General Psychiatry,* 1975, *32,* 1031–1038.

Minuchin, S., Rosman, B. L., & Baker, L. *Psychosomatic families.* Cambridge, Mass.: Harvard University Press, 1978.

Mischler, E. G., & Waxler, N. E. *Interaction in families.* New York: John Wiley & Sons, 1968.

Narus, L. R., Jr., & Fischer, J. L. Strong but not silent: A reexamination of expressivity in the relationships of men. *Sex Roles,* 1982, *8,* 159–168.

Noller, P. Misunderstanding in marital communication: A study of couples' nonverbal communication. *Journal of Personality and Social Psychology,* 1980, *39,* 1135–1148.

Noller, P. Gender and marital adjustment level differences in decoding messages from spouses and strangers. *Journal of Personality and Social Psychology,* 1981, *41,* 272–278.

Notarius, C. I., & Johnson, J. S. Emotional expression in husbands and wives. *Journal of Marriage and the Family,* 1982, *44,* 483–489.

Phinney, J. S., & Feshbach, N. D. *Crying behaviors in three- and four- year olds.* Paper presented at the meeting of the Society for Research in Child Development, Detroit, April 1983.

Pierce, R. A., Nichols, M. P., & DuBrin, J. R. *Emotional expression in psychotherapy.* New York: Gardner Press, 1983.

Rimon, R., Belmaker, R., & Ebstein, R. Psychosomatic aspects of juvenile rheumatoid arthritis. *Psychiatria Fennica,* 1976, 177–188.

Rosenthal, R., & DePaulo, B. Sex differences in accommodation in nonverbal communication. In R. Rosenthal (Ed.), *Skill in nonverbal communication: Individual differences.* Cambridge, Mass.: Oelgeschlager, Gunn, & Hain, 1979. Pp. 68–103.

Rubin, L. B. *Worlds of pain: Life in the working-class family.* New York: Basic Books, 1976.

Ryder, R. G. Longitudinal data relating marriage satisfaction to having a child. *Journal of Marriage and the Family,* 1973, *35,* 604–606.

Sabatelli, R. M., Buck, R., & Dreyer, A. Communication via facial cues in intimate dyads. *Personality and Social Psychology Bulletin,* 1980, *6,* 242–247.

Sabatelli, R. M., Buck, R., & Dreyer, A. Nonverbal communication accuracy in married couples: Relationship with marital complaints. *Journal of Personality and Social Psychology,* 1982, *43,* 1088–1097.

Sattel, J. W. The inexpressive male: Tragedy or sexual politics? *Social Problems,* 1976, *23,* 469–477.

Stewart, L. Social and emotional adjustment during adolescence as related to development of psychosomatic illness in adulthood. *Psychological Monographs,* 1962, *65,* 175–215.

Strodbeck, F. L. The family as a three person group. *American Sociological Review*, 1954, *19*, 23–29.

Vaughn, C., & Leff, J. The measurement of expressed emotion in the families of psychiatric patients. *British Journal of Social and Clinical Psychology*, 1976, *15*, 157–165.

Vincent, J. P., Friedman, L. C., Nugent, J., & Messerly, L. Demand characteristics in observations of marital interaction. *Journal of Consulting and Clinical Psychology*, 1979, *47*, 557–566.

Waring, E. M. The role of the family in symptom selection and perpetuation in psychosomatic illness. *Psychotherapy and Psychosomatics*, 1977, *28*, 253–259.

Waring, E. M. Marital intimacy, psychosomatic symptoms, and cognitive therapy. *Psychosomatics*, 1980, *21*, 595–601.

Warren, N. J., & Gilner, F. H. Measurement of positive assertive behaviors: The behavioral test of tenderness expression. *Behavior Therapy*, 1978, *9*, 178–184.

Weakland, J. H. "Family somatics": A neglected edge. *Family Process*, 1977, *16*, 263–272.

Weiss, R. L. The conceptualization of marriage from a behavioral perspective. In T. J. Paolino & B. S. McCrady (Eds.), *Marriage and marital therapy: Psychoanalytic, behavioral and systems theory perspective*. New York: Brunner/Mazel, 1978. Pp. 165–239.

Zuckerman, M., Klorman, R., Larrance, D. T., & Spiegel, N. H. Facial, autonomic, and subjective components of emotion: The facial feedback hypothesis versus the externalizer-internalizer distinction. *Journal of Personality and Social Psychology*, 1981, *41*, 929–944.

Chapter 13

Intimacy*

SADELL Z. SLOAN
LUCIANO L'ABATE

This chapter reviews the theoretical and empirical literature bearing on the concept of intimacy, stressing its importance in family functioning and malfunctioning.

Historically, as Schaeffer and Olson (1981) noted, intimacy has not appeared frequently in the psychological literature. Similarly, Sexton and Sexton (1982) pointed out that there was no formal entry for intimacy as a separate category in *Psychological Abstracts* until the 1970s; they cited the period from 1972 to 1978 as the one in which the psychological study of intimacy emerged and became prominent. Gadlin (1977) outlined changes in middle-class, heterosexual intimate relationships in the United States over the past 300 years and argued that the study of the individual's feelings and inner world did not really get under way until after 1940. Sexton and Sexton suggested that the complexity of the multidimensional nature of intimacy and the difficulty in operational specification may explain why psychologists have only lately begun to research intimacy. For an idea of the complexity to which Sexton and Sexton referred, consider the plethora of intimacy models that have been developed recently: Clinebell and Clinebell's (1970) 10 varieties of intimacy (including marital intimacy); Dahms's (1974), Coutts's (1973), and Ramey's (1976) discussions of three levels, or types, of intimacy (i.e., intellectual, physical, emotional); and Spooner's (1982) presentation of Rytting's (1980) model, which involves a matrix illustrating both the sphere (sexual or nonsexual) and the modality (physical, mental, emotional/spiritual) of intimacy.

---

* This chapter is part of a dissertation (Sloan, 1983) by the first author, under the direction of the second author.

PSYCHOANALYTIC VIEWPOINTS

Sullivan (1953) made an instructive differentiation between the experience of tenderness and caring during infancy and the intimacy that emerges only in late adolescence. Because an infant has dependency needs that must be met by an adult caretaker, the initial experience of warmth and emotional closeness is not between peers but involves a power differential. During the juvenile period, the child seeks a group of same-sex peers. At this stage, the child is capable of cooperation (i.e., playing by the rules of the game to preserve prestige and feelings of superiority and merit). The passage to the preadolescent phase, characterized by an interest in a particular member of the same sex who becomes a close friend, marks the beginnings of the individual's ability to give and receive mature love. In preadolescence, individuals move toward supplying each other with satisfactions and sharing each other's successes. As adolescence begins, the object of intimacy typically changes from the same-sex friend to a partner of the opposite sex.

Beginning in the preadolescent stage and developing more during adolescence, individuals become better able to put aside concerns for individual self-esteem and become more capable of collaborating (i.e., focusing on "we" and "us"). Sullivan's perspective suggests a developmental relationship between power and intimacy. Early in development, the individual approaches interpersonal relationships as the means through which to exert personal power for individual gain. In contrast, later in development, the individual enters into relationships because of the satisfactions of giving to another. In acquiring the ability to give in and give up, the individual in a collaborative intimate relationship experiences mutuality, which in turn leads to an even deeper sense of self-validation than do the power operations of earlier developmental stages.

A study of university students in a psychodrama setting suggests confirmation of Sullivan's distinction between cooperation and intimate collaboration. McAdams and Powers (1981) found that those students who were high in intimacy motivation tended to surrender manipulative control in relating to others and were perceived by other group members as especially sincere, likable, loving, and natural; rarely were they seen as dominant.

Erickson (1963) also theorized that the ability to be intimate is integral to human development and suggested that the developmental task of late adolescence and early adulthood is to resolve the issues of intimacy versus isolation. Erikson asserted that, developmentally, the individual must consolidate a strong sense of personal identity before he or she can successfully negotiate the task of forming an intimate relationship. With a solid sense of identity comes a readiness for intimacy, "the capacity to commit [oneself] to concrete affiliations and partnerships and to develop the ethical strength to abide by such commitments, even though they may call for significant sacrifices and compromises" (p. 263). Erikson suggested, then, that individual personality development takes place within the context of a committed relationship and requires the ability to communicate and compromise.

Research has generally supported Erikson's theorized relationship between identity and intimacy. Yufit (1956) found that the intimate individual was characterized by stability, sociability, and warmth; the isolate was self-centered, self-doubting, mistrustful, and had relationships that were formal and stereotyped, lacking warmth and spontaneity. Orlofsky, Marcia, and Lesser (1973) studied a sample of male junior and senior college students and, using a combination of semistructured interviews and questionnaires, determined for each subject an identity status (identity achievement, moratorium, foreclosure, identity diffusion, alienated achievement) and an intimacy status (intimate, preintimate, stereotyped relationships, pseudointimate, and isolate).

Results showed significant differences between ego identity and intimacy statuses on such variables as intimacy, autonomy, affiliation, and social desirability. Those who were most intimate were also most autonomous. Identity achievement subjects generally had successful, mature, intimate relationships, thus confirming the relationship between identity and intimacy.

Kacerguis and Adams (1980), who used a methodology similar to that of Orlofsky et al. (1973) in studying a sample of female junior and senior college students, found that advanced ego identity status was associated with higher intimacy formation. Women and men who had explored occupations before making a commitment were significantly more likely to develop mature, deep interpersonal commitments than were those peers who experienced role confusion or who had made commitments without exploration. Matteson pointed out the complex interaction likely to exist between identity and intimacy: "In every real sharing experience, both persons grow; identities are rediscovered and altered. There is no clear pattern to suggest that identity must precede intimacy; intimacy also alters identity" (1975, p. 161). The authors also suggested the need for longitudinal research into the association between identity and intimacy.

Marcia (1976) adopted a longitudinal design and demonstrated a positive association between identity and intimacy among a group of men who were reinterviewed six years after an initial identity status interview that had taken place during their college years. Identity was related to intimacy, both concurrently and predictively. Although the identity categories were generally stable over time, the factors contributing to change in identity status are pertinent to the relationship between intimacy and personality development. For example, a man who had been characterized by diffusion identity status (i.e., uncommitted) as a college student was now in the identity achievement class (period of decision making followed by commitment). He attributed the change in himself to his relationship with his wife, who "opened my eyes about people" (p. 155).

Just as a marital relationship may facilitate personal growth, Marcia's (1976) data also suggested that the marital relationship may enable an individual to adhere rigidly to patterns that result in stagnation and lack of personal growth. Marcia suggested that although men in the foreclosure category (static position involving unsynthesized childhood identifications) had perhaps (in the early college years) gone through some decision making about their occupations, once they had embarked on their career plans they had conceived a rather constricted life plan based on occupational advancement, apparently making work the focus of their own and their families' lives. In addition to their constricted and rigid work focus, the men in the foreclosure group, although married, seemed bound to their parents. Thus, although these men could be viewed as contented and productive, they could also illustrate rigidity in the identity development process.

These findings are corroborated somewhat by the clinical observations of L'Abate and L'Abate (1981), who noted the following characteristics in the marriages of successful executives who were excessively and exclusively absorbed in their occupations: (a) inability to deal with the issues of intimacy in the marriage, so that the partners become isolated from each other in an "arrangement" rather than a marriage; (b) enmeshment with families of origin; (c) delegation from parents and loyalty binding; and (d) inexpressive husband, expressive wife. These dysfunctional marriages thus share all of the marriage characteristics of the foreclosures and support the notion that lack of involvement in a truly intimate relationship may be linked to the inability to continue to develop identity during adulthood.

Just as Marcia (1976) presented evidence to suggest that the marriages of foreclosures maintain identity stagnation, Dicks (1967) and Boszormenyi-Nagy (1965) described what happens when spouses do not successfully attain identity and separation—developmental stages that are necessary for individuation. These couples collude to become a joint personality. They maintain, through projective identification, a relationship in which each provides qualities that necessarily complement the qualities of the spouse. This establishes a "single psychic identity" (Zinner, 1976) or a "merger" (Boszormenyi-Nagy). The selves of the partners are so inexorably intertwined that neither, because of fears of ego loss and object loss (Karpel, 1976), can risk change or growth. Intimacy in these circumstances is therefore impossible.

HUMANISTIC/EXISTENTIAL PERSPECTIVES

In addition to the psychodynamic-developmental theorists, humanistic and existential writers have also addressed the issues of personality development and intimacy. Maslow (1967) theorized that individuals have two kinds of needs—basic needs and metaneeds (i.e., growth needs). Among such basic drives as hunger, thirst, and sex, Maslow included the basic need for affection. In Maslow's (1968) theory, the pursuit of self-interest, or self-actualization, does not preclude acting for the benefit of the partner. Maslow (1970) suggested that self-actualizing individuals tend to have only a small circle of intimates with whom they experience a deeper and more profound bond than that experienced by other adults. Maslow (1968) associated the development of individual autonomy with the ability to love another and the ability to foster the partner's growth.

Fromm (1956) also assumed that the ability to love depends on the individual's level of development. Fromm described several stages of personal growth that preclude the experience of mature erotic loving—including the exploitive, or hoarding, orientation, in which the act of giving is experienced as deprivation and sacrifice. By contrast, a person who has developed to the marketing orientation is willing to give, but only in exchange for receiving; for such a person, giving without receiving is to be cheated. The individual whose development has progressed to the productive orientation, however, experiences giving as the highest expression of potency because, in the act of giving, he or she enriches the other's sense of aliveness. Thus, Fromm distinguished simple reciprocity from intimate mutuality, a shared experience born of a creative use of self in the presence of the other. Fromm further described the individual at the productive stage of development as having overcome dependency, narcissistic omnipotence, and the wish to exploit others. Such a person has acquired faith in self and the courage to rely on his or her own powers to attain goals.

Thus, the productive individual is capable of active loving, which to Fromm (1956) implied the elements of care, responsibility, respect, and knowledge. According to Fromm, a spouse who "knows" his or her partner is able to respond not only to the partner's anger but to the deeper, unexpressed feelings of anxiety and pain. Fromm appreciated the paradox of loving—"that two beings become one and yet remain two" (p. 17)—and held that "love is union under the condition of preserving one's integrity and individuality" (p. 17).

Puckett's (1977) study supported the notion that individuation and intimacy are related and, furthermore, are associated with spouses' abilities to relate satisfactorily. Couples who were high in self-actualization communicated better than did those who were low in self-actualization. Puckett also reported that individuals who were high in self-actualization had more effective interaction styles than did those who were low in self-actualization.

Kirkpatrick (1975), however, criticized the humanistic view of individualism as precluding true intimacy. He defined identity as one's own sense of sameness over time and suggested that identity is fostered by the "presence of others who have shared our past and bear witness to our personal history" (p. 3) and by maintaining a balance between continuity and change. Kirkpatrick argued that because the basis for human relationships is commitment over time, the two promises of the human potentials movement—intimacy and community—have been undermined by emphasis on the present. He criticized Esalen-type experiences for confusing intense, brief emotional experiences with real intimacy and community, which can only be achieved in lasting relationships over time. Such groups may be marked by a high degree of self-disclosure; but self-disclosure, Kirkpatrick asserted, is not the measure of the depth of a relationship—it is quite easy to disclose oneself to strangers or casual acquaintances whom one is not likely to see again or with whom there is no real danger of commitment.

One must distinguish some clinical practices of the human potentials movement from the theoretical underpinnings of humanistic psychology. Kirkpatrick himself recognized this distinction and acknowledged that Maslow (1968) had warned of the dangers inherent in the quest for self-actualization (i.e., refusal to make choices and commitments because, in making a choice, one may have to limit pursuit of other potentials). Maslow admitted that "a problem we psychologists have been ducking is the problem of responsibilities, and necessarily tied in with it, the concept of courage and will in personality" (p. 81).

SOCIAL PSYCHOLOGICAL VIEWPOINTS

The relationship between personality development and intimacy helps us to appreciate that the dimension of time is important not only to individual growth and development but also to development of the relationship itself (Kantor & Lehr, 1975; L'Abate, 1976).

All of the theorists discussed thus far have noted the importance of such concepts as reciprocity and mutuality. How and under what conditions relationships develop so that they facilitate intrapersonal growth and intimate sharing has been the focus of sociological and social psychological studies.

L. Hoffman (1981) suggested that a primary function of the family system is to provide the members with "an orderly access to intimacy [through] an invisible systole and diastole of connecting and withdrawing" (p. 191). She cited the work of Chapple (1970), who hypothesized the necessity for a daily "interaction quota" by which each individual maintains a balance of the various physiological rhythms of the body. Chapple suggested that "any old interaction will not do" (p. 48). Rather, the individual needs to interact and withdraw at a tempo within the natural limits of his or her repertoire and thus "experience a maximum degree of synchronization with the other person" (p. 48).

Support for Chapple's hypothesis comes from Jourard and Lasakow (1958), who found that there were no differences between married and unmarried subjects (college sophomores and juniors) in total amount of disclosure. Married subjects, however, disclosed less to parents and same-sex friends than did unmarried subjects, and married subjects disclosed more to the spouse than to any other target person. Jourard and Lasakow concluded that although marriage did not change the amount of disclosure, it did alter the pattern of self-disclosure so that the spouse became the major recipient of self-disclosure. Similarly, Burke and Weir (1975) found that, of all their possible social contacts, both men and women tended to select their spouses as the persons to whom they would most likely turn for help with problems and anxieties.

Altman and Taylor's (1973) social penetration theory, Walster, Walster, and Berscheid's (1978) equity theory, and M. Davis's (1973) philemics are three models of intimate relationship development that may explain why the spouse is the primary target of self-disclosures that relate to personal problems and needs. Social penetration theory suggests that "the growth of an interpersonal relationship is hypothesized to be a joint result of interpersonal reward/loss factors, personality characteristics, and situational determinants" (Taylor, Altman, & Sorrentino, 1969, p. 325). Equity theory asserts that individuals try to maximize their outcomes, that systems develop rules for equitably apportioning resources among members, and that when individuals perceive that they are participating in inequitable relationships, they become distressed and attempt to end that distress by restoring equity. Restoration may be made through actual material equity or through psychological equity—changing members' perceptions of the situation (i.e., from a systems perspective, positively reframing as equitable a transaction previously labeled inequitable).

Social penetration theory, equity theory (as discussed by Hatfield, Utne, & Traupman, 1979), and philemics (the study of intimate relations) suggest that relationships develop sequentially. Generally, these models suggest that as relationships progress over time, interactions become more flexible on a variety of dimensions, and a systemic character, or identity ("we-ness"), develops, which permits deeper levels of intimate self-disclosure than is possible with strangers or during the early stages of a relationship. Support for these concepts—that relationships pass through stages over time, resulting in greater flexibility and systemic uniqueness—comes from studies that have compared dyads of varying degrees of intimacy.

Morton (1978) found that among college student pairs of either spouses or strangers, spouses communicated with more descriptive intimacy (i.e., private facts) but not more evaluative intimacy (i.e., personal feelings or opinions) than did strangers, and spouses reciprocated intimacy less. Both findings support equity and social penetration theories; both theories hold that strict reciprocity is highest at the beginning of a relationship, then declines in a well-established relationship, and that as a relationship grows, more intimate information is shared. Moreover, Morton reported that although strangers tended to trivialize intimate topics, married partners tended to personalize nonintimate topics. This finding supports the theoretical propositions that communication becomes more unique, efficient, and synchronized as the relationship develops (Altman & Taylor, 1973; M. Davis, 1973) and that in long-term relationships, the unit of analysis shifts from the individual to the system (Hatfield et al., 1979). Morton also found that married couples personalized nonintimate subject matter more during conjoint communications (in which simultaneous talking, interruptions, and rapid turnover dialogue occurred) than during unbroken monologue.

Similarly, Strauss's (1974) study of married couples whom the community had judged especially loving supports the equity theory hypothesis that as a relationship becomes more intimate, the unit of analysis shifts from the individuals to the relationship itself. Strauss found that such couples referred spontaneously to "working at" their relationship and were committed not to exchanging resources as individuals (i.e., norm of reciprocity) but to the larger unit that constituted their mutual relationship.

Evidence for the hypothesis that relationships develop greater flexibility on a variety of dimensions as time passes comes from a study by Heiss (1962). Heiss asked dating couples to discuss an issue on which their disagreement had been established. Interactional analyses indicated that in the majority of couples, structuring activities occurred more frequently in the male, affective responses in the female. Although this pattern was marked for casual daters, sex role differences tended to vanish with increasing intimacy and commitment to the relationship, suggesting that shared control may be a feature of well-developed intimate relationships.

Stone (1973) studied patterns of conformity in an autokinetic task performed by couples whose intimacy varied. Long-term couples conformed significantly less than did stranger dyads or short-term couples, a difference that held for both men and women. One may interpret these results as supporting Altman and Taylor's (1973) proposition that persons in more-intimate relationships increase their ability to evaluate and convey positive and negative judgments about their partners.

Similarly, Birchler (1973) found that people demonstrated more positive affect, or approval, in interactions with strangers than with their own spouses. Therefore, these studies also suggest that although people in longer-term intimate relationships develop a couple identity demonstrated through increased synchrony, efficiency, and substitutability (i.e., flexibility) in their interactions, they also show signs that they are freer to express differing views. In other words, intimate sharing in a relationship that has developed commitment over time is associated with increased individual differentiation.

INTIMACY AND ADJUSTMENT

Studies of individual personality development and relationship development thus suggest an association, on both personal and marital (i.e., systemic) levels, between adjustment and intimacy in a committed relationship. A growing body of data supports the hypothesis that adjustment is linked to the ability to be intimate. Vaillant's (1977) study of Harvard graduates revealed that virtually all subjects judged "best outcomes" (i.e., achieving successful adjustment) had enjoyed at least 10 years of a stable, satisfying marriage. Haas-Hawkins (1978) discussed the importance of a stable, intimate relationship in moderating the stress of widowhood. Lowenthal and Weiss (1976) discussed how the intimacy of friendship (because it embraces mutual trust, support, understanding, and sharing of confidences) serves as a major source of comfort and defense in the presence of major life crises across the life span. Furthermore, Lowenthal and Weiss suggested that the experience of personal and societal crises may facilitate the development of intimate relationships. Cunningham and Strassberg (1981) demonstrated a difference between the abilities of men with normal and with neurotic MMPI profiles to respond appropriately to levels of intimate disclosure: Neurotics spent little time in intimate self-disclosure, regardless of the level of intimacy they received. Dion and Dion (1978) found that highly defensive women were less likely than less-defensive women to report that they had experienced romantic love.

Rosenblatt, Titus, Nevaldine, and Cunningham (1979) discussed the relationship between physical and emotional intimacy and the potential for conflict and physical abuse between spouses. Nichols (1978), discussing cases of chronic pain in one spouse, suggested that the physical symptom reflected interpersonal alienation, with the marital conflict an attempt to calibrate the psychological closeness/distance between the spouses.

Waring, McElrath, Mitchell, and Derry (1981) reported that high levels of intimacy were associated with marital adjustment and that low ratings of marital intimacy were significantly associated with non-psychotic emotional illness and psychiatric help-seeking. Hames and Waring (1980), using a self-report questionnaire in a clinical sample, showed a statistically significant correlation between the level of non-psychotic emotional illness and the lack of intimacy in marriage. Waring, McElrath, Lefcoe, and Weisz (1981) found a relationship among marital adjustment, intimacy, and the absence of conflict.

Waring (1980) discussed difficulties in the marriages of psychosomatic patients. Typically, one spouse does not wish to discuss personal matters. The partners do not share feelings or engage in cognitive self-disclosure, resulting in a profound lack of intimacy (Waring & Russell, 1980). Waring suggested that cognitive self-disclosure, defined as "the sharing of a private cognition about the couple's relationship and that of their parents" (p. 596), serves as the primary determinant of an affective, or emotional, variable—a couple's feeling of closeness, or intimacy. Waring (1980, 1981) reported that cognitive family therapy, based on the work of Zuk (1971), Bowen (1975), and Framo (1976), has been helpful in improving psychosomatic symptoms, mental adjustment, and family relationships.

In contrast to Waring's (1980) emphasis on the relationship between dysfunctions in cognitive self-disclosure and the lack of intimacy in the marriages of psychosomatic patients, Sifneos and his colleagues (Sifneos, 1973; Sifneos, Apfel-Savitz, & Frankel, 1977) have focused on the affective dysfunctions of the psychosomatic patient. Sifneos proposed the term *alexithymic* to describe psychosomatic patients, who exhibited constriction in emotional functioning, tended to act impulsively (as a substitute for emotional expression and as a way of avoiding conflicts) in conflicting or frustrating situations, and—most strikingly—could not find appropriate words to describe their feelings. Unfortunately, Sifneos did not report any data concerning alexithymic psychosomatic patients and the level of their marital adjustment and intimacy. His work suggests, however, that alexithymic patients—who typically engage in endless, boring descriptions of peripheral details and have difficulty in communicating—would have difficulty in a relationship characterized by emotional intimacy.

A number of researchers have associated clinical depression with the inability to be intimate. Bullock, Siegel, Weissman, and Paykel (1972) found striking deficiencies in autonomy and the capacity for intimacy in a sample of depressed wives. Similar findings were reported by Friedman and Zaris (1964) and by Wasli (1977). Brown, Brolchain, and Harris (1975) demonstrated that the absence of a close, confiding relationship was one of four vulnerability factors in women's development of depression under adverse circumstances. Adler (1980) asserted that experiencing intimacy and communication on an equal basis with others is alien to depressed persons because they fear that they will be exposed as inadequate and, thus, powerless. Fast and Broedel (1967) discussed the tendency of persons prone to depression to form relationships that combined fusion with sharp separation, apparently because they struggled to overcome the fear that total separation would result from the slightest lack of unity. Such depressed persons seemed unable to achieve relations in which intimacy and individuation were not mutually exclusive. Jessee and L'Abate (1982, 1983) suggested that marital intimacy may be an antidote for depression.

CLINICAL MODELS AND RESEARCH FINDINGS RELATING INTIMACY, INDIVIDUATION, AND RISK TAKING

The dysfunctions associated with difficulties in being intimate with a significant other in a sustained relationship point to the importance of a couple's ability to negotiate their emotional space successfully. Clinically derived models of intimacy and experimental research appear to confirm the proposition that the toleration of risk is related to adjustive intimacy/individuation patterns.

L'Abate and Frey (1981) suggested that emotionality governs distance in relationships. Pointing out that family/systems theories hypothesize that individuals in relationships experience both a movement toward others to maintain the relationship system and a movement away from the relationship to maintain the self, L'Abate and Frey contended that individuals in systems use emotionality to express both their separateness and their togetherness.

Farley (1979) presented a model of family development that focuses on the system's tolerance for ranging between merging and individuation. According to this model, the family's homeostasis reflects the system's tolerance for states of intimacy and individuation in the family members' relationships with one another. Farley maintained that both states—intimacy and individuation—are essential to growth and that curtailment of one seriously disrupts and limits the other.

Both Farley (1979) and Byng-Hall (1980) acknowledged the anxiety and the potential for symptomatic behavior when family members get too close or too far apart, relative to the family homeostasis. On the other hand, they asserted that these cases of disequilibrium in the intimacy/individuation psychological space patterns can be opportunities for therapeutic change and growth. Such points of disequilibrium are anxiety provoking because they entail risk. One may move "too close," risking the disintegration of the ego, or "too far," risking the loss of a love object. L. Hoffman (1981) has noted that such points of disequilibrium in the psychological space of the family may turn out

not to be calamitous but to be more comfortable and desirable, resulting in a recalibration of the "safe distance." These writers thus suggested relationships among intimacy, individuation (i.e., continued
identity development), and the ability to tolerate situations with inherent ambiguity and risk (i.e., disequilibrium in the system's homeostatic
closeness/distance patterns).

Perlmutter and Hatfield (1980) defined intimacy as encompassing
the qualities of commitment, confirmation of self and other, and willingness to take risks. They discussed clinical examples of enhanced
intimacy in family relationships in which intentional metacommunication (i.e., talking consciously about the relational context of the messages sent) took place. They linked such metacommunication to second-
order change because such communication often involved risk taking,
which led to the use of previously unknown strategies and tactics,
thereby "suspending the rules of interaction which maintain the system
. . . [and causing spouses to] step into an exciting/terrifying unknown"
(p. 20).

The relationship among confirmation of self and other, risk taking,
and enhanced intimacy and marital adjustment was explored by
Betcher (1977). Results suggested that intimate play and regression
in the presence of the spouse may afford immunization against marital
dissatisfaction.

Gilbert (1976), reviewing patterns of self-disclosure, intimacy, and
communication in families, hypothesized that intimacy may be inversely related to needs for safety and positively related to commitment
in the relationship. She asserted that "needs for security may override
needs for depth in the relationship, such that 'rocking the boat' becomes more risky than maintaining the status quo" (p. 228). Gilbert,
like Kirkpatrick (1975), distinguished the disclosure of intimate information in a low-risk context (e.g., the stranger-on-the-train phenomenon) from intimate sharing. Intimate sharing involves a demonstration
of commitment. Gilbert maintained that in an intimate relationship,
something must transcend the needs for safety. That "something" is
the ability to risk and the desire for intimate commitment and acceptance in the deepest form, not only of the disclosure itself but of the
person making it. Gilbert implied that the challenge of optimum, intimate marital relations may be to learn how to deal with the information, disappointments, and conflicts that hold the highest risk for the
spouses. Thus, Gilbert's concept of intimacy suggests a relationship
between good communication and negotiation skills and intimacy.

The relationship between commitment and conflict in an intimate
dyad was also discussed by Feldman (1979). He asserted that, although
the desire for intimacy is a major motivation for forming and maintaining a marital relationship, the wish for intimacy and fears of intimacy

exist side by side. Such fears of intimacy include fear of *(a)* merger, *(b)* exposure, *(c)* attack, *(d)* abandonment, and *(e)* one's own destructive impulses. According to Feldman, conflict is one way to avoid risk and to distance from the partner at the point at which one feels most anxious and unable to deal with one's own fears or inadequacies. By threatening the partner's self-esteem, one avoids one's own fears and anxieties.

Mace (1976) described a "deadly love-anger cycle" and maintained that the greatest obstacle to intimacy is the "incapacity of the couple of cope with their own and each other's anger" (p. 131). Mace described the pattern of the couple who seek intimacy: In the process of moving closer, the partners discover differences that are threatening and that cause disagreement. The closer they move toward one another, the more painful and risk-laden becomes the disagreement, which heats up into conflict. Disillusionment, shock, and hurt attend the anger of conflict, and the couple distances, settling for a relatively superficial relationship. Thus, rather than risk further distance, the couple develops a "safe distance," or homeostasis, which is also devoid of deeper emotional intimacy. Mace advocated anger management (including acknowledging and then renouncing anger, followed by asking the spouse for help) to break the cycle.

The relationship between the tolerance for risk taking and the achievement of emotional intimacy is given prominence in the approach of L'Abate and his colleagues (Frey, Holley, & L'Abate, 1979; L'Abate, 1977; L'Abate & L'Abate, 1979). L'Abate (1977) argued that "anger is the result of hurt feelings and fear. . . . [Furthermore,] underneath anger there is a great deal of unexpressed pain and fear of further hurt" (p. 13). Instead of seeing how a couple handles anger as primary to their ability to maintain meaningful emotional intimacy, as Ellis (1976) and Bach and Wyden (1968) have argued, L'Abate defined intimacy as the ability to risk the sharing of hurt feelings. Discussing the paradoxes of intimacy, L'Abate and L'Abate (1979) noted that "we only hurt the ones we love" (p. 179) and pointed out the importance of recognizing the inevitability of hurt.

L'Abate and L'Abate (1979) asserted that to be with a hurting spouse without feeling compelled to do anything or to get or give material things (as a substitute for feeling), one needs a sufficient feeling that one is a differentiated self (L'Abate, 1976). Such a differentiated person is separate enough to be with the other's hurt without fusion or entanglement. In emphasizing the sharing of hurt rather than anger as the sine qua non of emotional intimacy, L'Abate and L'Abate thus expressed ideas similar to those of Fromm (1956) and Brown (1979), who also suggested that the sharing of humiliations represents the sharing of the deepest aspect of the self. In summary, then, these writers suggested that the risk of sharing our hurt and vulnerability involves a deeper level of intimacy than does the risk of showing anger and power, which we share during conflict.

Frey et al. (1979) conducted two studies designed to check the validity of three models for dealing with anger: (a) calm, rational discussion, (b) fair fighting, and (c) sharing of hurt feelings. In the first study, subjects identified (at a statistically significant level) a videotaped conflict resolution scene featuring the sharing of hurt feelings as more intimate than scenes featuring Bach and Wyden's (1968) fair fighting or Ellis's (1976) calm, rational approach. In the second study, married couples were exposed to enrichment lessons based on the three approaches. The fair fighting method was liked best, the method that subjects preferred to learn, and the one they became most involved in. Calm, rational discussion was chosen as most suited to interpersonal style, and the sharing of hurt feelings was chosen as the most intimate. Neither study found significant differences between males and females.

The authors interpreted the findings as supporting a vertical, hierarchical, developmental model of intimacy, with self-presentational, phenotypic, and genotypic levels (L'Abate, 1976) akin to the levels of Altman and Taylor's (1973) social penetration model. Frey et al. (1979) concluded that their finding—that subjects preferred to learn calm, rational discussion or fair fighting—supported their conceptual model that the genotypic level of intimacy (involving the sharing of hurt feelings), although seen by subjects as producing greatest intimacy, was also seen as the riskiest and the most threatening.

Gender differences in intimacy

A relevant question for research on intimacy is whether there are gender differences that may affect a couple's establishment of an intimate relationship. Cozby (1973) discussed the inconsistent findings on self-disclosure and gender, pointing out that some studies have found that females disclosed more than males but that other studies found no gender differences in self-disclosure. No study, however, reported greater male disclosure, and Cozby suggested that researchers pay closer attention to kinds of self-disclosure items and situations, which may help to explain gender differences.

Morton (1978), who studied stranger dyads and husband/wife pairs, reported that women used more evaluative intimacy (communication of feelings and judgments) than did men. In related work, Balswick has suggested that because of differing societal role expectations for the two sexes, men and women differ in emotional expressiveness (Balswick, 1979; Balswick & Peek, 1970). For example, research has shown that males express less than females the emotions of love, happiness, sadness, fondness, and pleasure (Balswick & Averett, 1977; Balkwell, Balswick, & Balkwell, 1978).

In a study of college dating couples, Rubin, Hill, Peplau, and Schetter (1980) found no significant differences between the sexes in total disclosure scores. The item least shared by men and women was "things about myself I am most ashamed of." However, superimposed on this general tendency (of both men and women) toward open, mutual emotional sharing were significant gender differences on specific topics. The data of Rubin et al. indicate a pattern in which both men and women have difficulty sharing their sense of their own vulnerability on issues that may directly affect the relationship, but in which women show greater ease in sharing vulnerability concerning issues that are probably external to the relationship ("the things in life I am most afraid of").

Although J. Davis (1978), studying intimacy patterns among unmarried college student dyads, found that experimentally constituted, mixed-sex dyads followed stereotypic sex role behaviors, Heiss (1962) and Stone (1973) found no gender differences but did find patterns of shared control between males and females in established dyads (i.e., either engaged or married couples).

M. Hoffman (1977), reviewing studies of gender differences in empathy, concluded that the overall differences between males and females were small. Hoffman suggested that the sexes are equally adept at assessing how a person in an emotional situation feels; however, "in females the awareness of the other's feeling is more apt to be accompanied by a vicarious affective response" (p. 716). Males, more often than females, tended to respond to an interpersonal emotional situation by considering action alternatives rather than by empathizing—preferring to act rather than to feel (Hoffman & Levine, 1976).

The tendency of males to confuse acting with feeling and the tendency of females to emphasize feeling and deemphasize problem solving (i.e., thinking in order to plan action) offers support for L'Abate, Frey, and Wagner's (1982) emotionality-rationality-activity-awareness-context (E–R–A–Aw–C) model. This model suggests the need to differentiate emotionality, rationality, and activity as equally important spheres of experience. It also emphasizes the importance of being aware of each sphere and its context. Because Hoffman and Levine's (1976) findings were based on a sample of children, we must ask how relevant these conclusions are for adults in general and married adults in particular.

Burke, Weir, and Harrison (1976), studying a sample of married couples in which husbands were professionals (accountants or engineers), reported that wives disclosed their problems to their partners significantly more often than husbands did. Wives' most-frequent reasons for not disclosing their tensions to their husbands included not wanting to worry or burden them with their problems and viewing the spouse as not interested, responsive, or receptive to such disclosures. In contrast, husbands' most-frequent reasons for not disclosing to their wives were that they felt the spouse lacked knowledge relevant to the specific problem or they believed that they should not bring work-related problems home.

The results of Burke et al. (1976) offer some suggestions about how the childhood patterns described by M. Hoffman (1977) may be exhibited in the interactions of married adults. Evidently, wives felt that their husbands could not handle the burden of their disclosures of problems and did not think that their husbands would be emotionally responsive, reactions that might be expected from the childhood pattern in which boys react to emotional situations with less vicarious affect than do girls and tend to find solutions rather than to feel in response to emotional situations. If husbands saw their wives as reacting emotionally to problem situations (as M. Hoffman reported as more typical of girls than boys), their decision not to disclose problems to their wives may be related to their expectation that their wives would react with emotions rather than with concrete solutions. The finding that no working wife cited separation of work and home as a reason not to disclose to her husband suggests that when women disclose problems, they wish emotional support rather than practical advice, as apparently favored by men. This interpretation of the results is strengthened by the desired changes in spouse behavior and attitudes reported by wives and husbands. Wives wanted their husbands to be more responsive and receptive (i.e., more tuned in to their emotional needs); husbands wished that their wives would react to problems less emotionally and respond in a manner that would minimize the probability that additional stresses would develop.

Burke et al. (1976) also reported, however, that the greater the tendency for both husband and wife to disclose their problems and tensions to the spouse, the more positive their standing on both marital satisfaction and life satisfaction measures. In general then, the married men and women in the sample appeared to value different sorts of reactions to problem situations, but husbands and wives who tended to value and practice mutual disclosure of problems (i.e., sharing areas of vulnerability with the spouse) showed higher levels of marital satisfaction than did those who tended not to disclose vulnerability to one another.

In related findings, Levinger (1965) reported that maritally more-satisfied spouses were more likely than were less-satisfied spouses to disclose unpleasant feelings when the feelings concerned external events (e.g., a bad day at work). Levinger also found, however, that more-satisfied spouses, compared with less-satisfied spouses, disclosed fewer unpleasant feelings when such feelings pertained to their mates. Happily married couples may be wary of rocking the boat (i.e., less willing to say something that will cause problems when none currently appear to exist). The risk level of sharing a feeling of vulnerability when one perceives the spouse as the source of the feeling is, of course, greater than when the vulnerability concerns events and persons outside the marriage. Unfortunately, Levinger and Senn (1967), who reported the results of the unpublished Levinger (1965) study, did not mention any differences between husbands and wives in the likelihood of sharing vulnerability concerning the spouse versus an external source.

Tognoli (1980) suggested that, from the studies of Fasteau (1975), Goldberg (1976), and Pleck (1976), there is evidence that men overinvest themselves emotionally in a close relationship with one woman, creating a dependency on the woman, especially in facilitating verbal expression of feelings. This argument is bolstered by Parelman's (1983) finding that the husbands in her sample of university couples reported more togetherness (e.g., "need only my spouse to meet all my emotional needs") than did wives. Similarly, Levinger, Rands, and Talaber (1977) found that women emphasized emotional caring and outcome correspondence (i.e., what happens to partner affects oneself) and that men emphasized uniqueness (i.e., how irreplaceable they consider the relationship) and self-disclosure.

Parelman reported that the dimensions of ideal emotional intimacy did not differ significantly for husbands and wives in her sample of university couples. For the entire sample, as for husbands and wives separately, the major dimension of ideal emotional intimacy was caring and emotional support. For the entire sample, this factor included items that express emotional closeness, trust, and commitment to the relationship.

Separate analyses of results for men and for women showed a greater interrelatedness among caring and emotional support, empathic helping, and verbal expressiveness for the women. Because these components of ideal marital closeness empirically separated out for men, the tendency not to do so for women indicates a gender difference. Thus, Parelman's (1983) finding concerning the differences between men's and women's ideal concepts of intimacy parallels the findings of Burke et al. (1976) and suggests that men do not value these aspects equally or that they, unlike women, do not view them as inseparable.

The studies reviewed suggest that wives may be the facilitators of their partners' emotional expression and may view caring and emotional sharing as more inseparable than do their husbands. Although they may view sharing their hurts with as much trepidation as do their husbands (Frey et al., 1979), we might expect that if couples were given conjoint opportunities to share angry and hurt feelings, wives might be more willing and readier than their husbands to take advantage of such opportunities.

Intimacy and being

L'Abate, Sloan, Wagner, and Malone (1980) proposed a model called the triangle of living, which suggests that differentiation through the family life cycle occurs along three resource exchange (Foa & Foa, 1974) dimensions—being (love and status), doing (services and information), and having (money and goods). They further proposed that functional role performance over time would involve comparable attention to being, doing, and having. *Being* involves a creative receptivity to one's (and one's partner's) existential meaning, a nonjudgmental attitude essential to authentic sharing and caring and to the establishment and maintenance of intimacy (L'Abate & L'Abate, 1979). In contrast, *doing* involves activity in discharging role responsibilities, and *having* involves the acquisition of possessions over relationships.

L'Abate and L'Abate (1979) pointed out that a separate, differentiated sense of self (L'Abate, 1976), based mainly on being rather than on having or doing, allows one to be and remain close without any demands for solution, thereby facilitating intimacy.

CONCLUSION

This chapter has attempted to summarize most of the theoretical and empirical literature on intimacy. From the many implications of intimacy, it appears that this construct is important to personality development in the family throughout the life span.

REFERENCES

Adler, K. Depression and suicide as they relate to intimacy and communication. *Modern Psychoanalysis,* 1980, *5,* 167–176.

Altman, I., & Taylor, D. *Social penetration: The development of interpersonal relationships.* New York: Holt, Rinehart & Winston, 1973.

Bach, G., & Wyden, P., *The intimate enemy.* New York: Avon Books, 1968.

Balkwell, C., Balswick, J., & Balkwell, J. On black and white family patterns in America: Their impact on the expressive aspect of sex-role socialization. *Journal of Marriage and the Family,* 1978, *40,* 743–747.

Balswick, J. The inexpressive male: Functional conflict and role theory as contrasting explanations. *Family Coordinator,* 1979, *28,* 330–336.

Balswick, J., & Averett, C. Differences in expressiveness: Gender, interpersonal orientation, and perceived parental expressiveness as contributing factors. *Journal of Marriage and the Family,* 1977, *39,* 121–127.

Balswick, J., & Peek, C. The inexpressive male and family relationships during early childhood. *Sociological Symposium,* 1970, *4,* 1–12.

Betcher, R. *Intimate play and marital adaptation: Regression in the presence of another.* Unpublished doctoral dissertation, Boston University Graduate School, 1977.

Birchler, G. Differential patterns of instrumental affiliative behavior as a function of degree of marital distress and level of intimacy (Doctoral dissertation, University of Oregon, 1972). *Dissertation Abstracts International,* 1973, *33,* 4499B–4500B.

Boszormenyi-Nagy, I. A theory of relationships: Experience and transaction. In I. Boszormenyi-Nagy & J. L. Framo (Eds.), *Intensive family therapy: Theoretical and practical aspects.* New York: Harper & Row, 1965.

Bowen, M. Family therapy after twenty years. In S. Arieti (Ed.), *American Handbook of Psychiatry,* 1975, *5,* 367–392.

Brown, E. Intimacy and anxiety in psychotherapy. *Voices,* 1979, *15,* 21–23.

Brown, G., Brolchain, M., & Harris, T. Social class and psychiatric disturbance among women in an urban population. *Sociology,* 1975, *9,* 225–254.

Bullock, R., Siegel, R., Weissman, M., & Paykel, E. The weeping wife: Marital relations of depressed women. *Journal of Marriage and the Family,* 1972, *34,* 488–495.

Burke, R., & Weir, T. Giving and receiving help with work and non-work-related problems. *Journal of Business Administration,* 1975, *6,* 59–78.

Burke, R., Weir, T., & Harrison, D. Disclosure of problems and tensions experienced by marital partners. *Psychological Reports,* 1976, *38,* 531–542.

Byng-Hall, J. Symptom bearer as marital distance regulator: Clinical implications. *Family Process,* 1980, *19,* 355–365.

Chapple, E. *Culture and biological man.* New York: Holt, Rinehart & Winston, 1970.

Clinebell, H., & Clinebell, C. *The intimate marriage.* New York: Harper & Row, 1970.

Coutts, R. *Love and intimacy: A psychological inquiry.* San Ramon, Calif.: Consensus Publishers, 1973.

Cozby, P. Self-disclosure: A literature review. *Psychological Bulletin,* 1973, *79,* 73–91.

Cunningham, J., & Strassberg, D. Neuroticism and disclosure reciprocity. *Journal of Counseling Psychology,* 1981, *28,* 455–458.

Dahms, A. Intimate hierarchy. In E. A. Powers & M. W. Lees (Eds.), *Process in relationship: Marriage and family.* St. Paul: West Publishing, 1974.

Davis, J. When boy meets girl: Sex roles and the negotiation of intimacy in an acquaintance exercise. *Journal of Personality and Social Psychology,* 1978, *36,* 684–692.

Davis, M. *Intimate relations.* New York: Free Press, 1973.

Dicks, H. *Marital tensions: Clinical studies towards a psychological theory of interaction.* London: Routledge & Kegan Paul, 1967.

Dion, K. K., & Dion, K. C. Defensiveness, intimacy, and heterosexual attraction. *Journal of Research in Personality,* 1978, *12,* 479–487.

Ellis, A. Techniques of handling anger in marriage. *Journal of Marriage and Family Counseling,* 1976, *2,* 305–315.

Erikson, E. *Childhood and society* (2d ed.). New York: W. W. Norton, 1963.

Farley, J. Family separation-individuation tolerance: A development conceptualization of the nuclear family. *Journal of Marital and Family Therapy,* 1979, *5,* 61–67.

Fast, I., & Broedel, J. Intimacy and distance in the interpersonal relationships of persons prone to depression. *Journal of Projective Techniques and Personality Assessment,* 1967, *31,* 7–12.

Fasteau, M. *The male machine.* New York: McGraw-Hill, 1975.

Feldman, L. Marital conflict and marital intimacy: An integrative psychodynamic behavioral systemic model. *Family Process,* 1979, *18,* 69–78.

Foa, U., & Foa, E. *Societal structures of the mind.* Springfield, Ill.: Charles C Thomas, 1974.

Framo, J. L. Family of origin as a therapeutic resource for adults in marital and family therapy: You can and should go home again. *Family Process,* 1976, *15,* 193–210.

Frey, J., Holley, J., & L'Abate, L. Intimacy is sharing hurt feelings: A comparison of three conflict resolution models. *Journal of Marital and Family Therapy,* 1979, *5,* 35–41.

Friedman, J., & Zaris, D. Paradoxical response to death of a spouse—three case reports. *Diseases of the Nervous System,* 1964, *25,* 480–485.

Fromm, E. *The art of loving.* New York: Bantam Books, 1956.

Gadlin, H. Private lives and public order: A critical view of the history of intimate relations in the United States. In G. Levinger & H. Raush (Eds.), *Close relationships: Perspectives on the meaning of intimacy.* Amherst: University of Massachusetts Press, 1977, pp. 33–72.

Gilbert, S. Self-disclosure, intimacy, and communication in families. *Family Coordinator,* 1976, *25,* 221–231.

Goldberg, H. *The hazards of being male: Surviving the myth of masculine privilege.* New York: Nash, 1976.

Haas-Hawkins, G. Intimacy as a moderating influence on the stress of loneliness in widowhood. *Essence,* 1978, *2,* 249–258.

Hames, J., & Waring, E. Marital intimacy and nonpsychotic emotional illness. *Psychiatric Forum,* 1980, *9,* 13–19.

Hatfield, E., Utne, M., & Traupman, J. Equity theory and intimate relationships. In R. Burgess & T. Huston (Eds.), *Social exchange in developing relationships.* New York: Academic Press, 1979. Pp. 99–132.

Heiss, J. Degree of intimacy and male-female interaction. *Sociometry,* 1962, *25,* 197–208.

Hoffman, L. Deviation-amplifying processes in natural groups. In J. Haley (Ed.), *Changing families: A family therapy reader.* New York: Grune & Stratton, 1971.

Hoffman, L. *Foundations of family therapy.* New York: Basic Books, 1981.

Hoffman, M. Sex differences in empathy and related behaviors. *Psychological Bulletin,* 1977, *84,* 712–722.

Hoffman, M., & Levine, L. Early sex differences in empathy. *Developmental Psychology,* 1976, *12,* 557–558.

Jessee, E., & L'Abate, L. Intimacy and marital depression: Interactional partners. *International Journal of Family Therapy,* 1983, *5,* 39–53. (a)

Jessee, E., & L'Abate, L. The paradoxes of marital depression: Theoretical and clinical implications. *International Journal of Family Psychiatry,* 1982, *3,* 175–187. (b)

Jourard, S., & Lasakow, P. Some factors in self-disclosure. *Journal of Abnormal and Social Psychology,* 1958, *56,* 91–99.

Kacerguis, M., & Adams, G. Erikson stage resolution: The relationship between identity and intimacy. *Journal of Youth and Adolescence,* 1980, *9,* 117–126.

Kantor, D., & Lehr, W. *Inside the family: Toward a theory of family process.* New York: Harper Colophon Books, 1975.

Karpel, M. Individuation: From fusion to dialogue. *Family Process,* 1976, *15,* 65–82.

Kirkpatrick, W. *Identity and intimacy.* New York: Dell Publishing, 1975.

L'Abate, L. *Understanding and helping the individual in the family.* New York: Grune & Stratton, 1976.

L'Abate, L. Intimacy is sharing hurt feelings: A reply to David Mace. *Journal of Marriage and Family Counseling,* 1977, *3,* 13–16.

L'Abate, L., & Frey, J. The E–R–A model: The role of feelings in family therapy reconsidered: Implications for a classification of theories of family therapy. *Journal of Marriage and Family Therapy,* 1981, *7,* 143–150.

L'Abate, L., Frey, J., & Wagner, V. Toward a classification of family therapy theories: Further elaborations and implications of the E–R–A–Aw–C model. *Family Therapy,* 1982, *9,* 251–262.

L'Abate, L., & L'Abate, B. The paradoxes of intimacy. *Family Therapy,* 1979, *6,* 175–184.

L'Abate, L., & L'Abate, B. Marriage: The dream and the reality. *Family Relations,* 1981, *30,* 131–136.

L'Abate, L., Sloan, S., Wagner, V., & Malone, K. The differentiation of resources. *Family Therapy,* 1980, *7,* 237–246.

Levinger, G. *A comparative study of marital communication.* Unpublished manuscript, 1965.

Levinger, G., Rands, M., & Talaber, R. *The assessment of involvement and rewardingness in close and casual pair relationships* (Tech. Rep. NSFGS33541 and BNS–02575). Amherst: University of Massachusetts, June 1977.

Levinger, G., & Senn, D. Disclosure of feeling in marriage. *Merrill-Palmer Quarterly,* 1967, *13,* 237–249.

Lowenthal, M., & Weiss, L. Intimacy and crises in adulthood. *Counseling Psychologist,* 1976, *6,* 10–15.

Mace, D. R. Marital intimacy and the deadly love-anger cycle. *Journal of Marriage and Family Counseling,* 1976, *2,* 131–137.

Marcia, J. Identity six years after: A follow-up study. *Journal of Youth and Adolescence,* 1976, *5,* 146–160.

Maslow, A. A theory of metamotivation: The biological rooting of the value life. *Journal of Humanistic Psychology,* 1967, *7,* 93–127.

Maslow, A. *Toward a psychology of being* (2d ed.). New York: Van Nostrand Reinhold, 1968.

Maslow, A. *Motivation and personality* (2d ed.). New York: Harper & Row, 1970.

Matteson, D. *Adolescence today: Sex roles and the search for identity.* Homewood, Ill.: Dorsey Press, 1975.

McAdams, D., & Powers, J. Themes of intimacy in behavior and thought. *Journal of Personality and Social Psychology,* 1981, *40,* 573–587.

Morton, T. Intimacy and reciprocity of exchange: A comparison of spouses and strangers. *Journal of Personality and Social Psychology,* 1978, *36,* 72–81.

Nichols, E. Chronic pain: A review of the intrapersonal and interpersonal factors and a study of marital interaction (Doctoral dissertation, University of Tennessee, 1978). *Dissertation Abstracts International,* 1978, *39,* 2997B–2998B.

Orlofsky, J., Marcia, J., & Lesser, I. Ego identity status and the intimacy versus isolation crises of young adulthood. *Journal of Personality and Social Psychology,* 1973, *27,* 211–219.

Parelman, A. *Emotional intimacy in marriage: A sex roles perspective.* Ann Arbor, Mich.: UMI Research Press, 1983.

Perlmutter, M., & Hatfield, E. Intimacy: Intentional metacommunication and second order change. *American Journal of Family Therapy,* 1980, *8,* 17–23.

Pleck, J. The male sex role: Definitions, problems, and sources of change. *Journal of Social Issues,* 1976, *32,* 155–164.

Puckett, J. The intimacy/individuation conflict: A study of the relationship between level of self-actualization and couple interaction (Doctoral dissertation, California School of Professional Psychology, 1977). *Dissertation Abstracts International,* 1977, *38*(6), 2880B–2881B.

Ramey, J. W. *Intimate friendships.* Englewood Cliffs, N.J.: Prentice-Hall, 1976.

Rosenblatt, P., Titus, S., Nevaldine, A., & Cunningham, M. Marital system differences and summer-long vacations: Togetherness, apartness, tensions. *American Journal of Family Therapy,* 1979, *7,* 77–84.

Rubin, Z., Hill, C., Peplau, L., & Schetter, C. Self-disclosure in dating couples: Sex roles and the ethic of openness. *Journal of Marriage and the Family,* 1980, *42,* 305–319.

Rytting, M. *Creative limits: Exploring the paradoxes of intimacy.* Paper presented at the Midwest Regional Conference of the Association for Humanistic Psychology, Chicago, May 1980.

Schaeffer, M., & Olson, D. Assessing intimacy: The PAIR inventory. *Journal of Marital and Family Therapy,* 1981, *7,* 47–60.

Sexton, R., & Sexton, V. Intimacy: A historical perspective. In M. Fisher & G. Stricker (Eds.), *Intimacy.* New York: Plenum Press, 1982. Pp. 1–20.

Sifneos, P. E. The prevalence of "alexithymic" characteristics in psychosomatic patients. *Psychotherapy and Psychosomatics,* 1973, *22,* 255–262.

Sifneos, P. E., Apfel-Savitz, R., & Frankel, F. The phenomenon of "alexithymia": Observations in neurotic and psychosomatic patients. *Psychotherapy and Psychosomatics,* 1977, *28,* 47–57.

Sloan, S. Z. *Assessing the differential effectiveness of two enrichment formats in facilitating marital intimacy and adjustment.* Unpublished doctoral dissertation, Georgia State University, 1983.

Spooner, S. Intimacy in adults: A developmental model for counselors and helpers. *Personnel and Guidance Journal,* 1982, *61,* 168–171.

Stone, W. Patterns of conformity in couples varying in intimacy. *Journal of Personality and Social Psychology,* 1973, *27,* 413–418.

Strauss, E. *Couples in love.* Unpublished doctoral dissertation, University of Massachusetts, 1974.

Sullivan, H. *The interpersonal theory of psychiatry.* New York: W. W. Norton, 1953.

Taylor, D., Altman, I., & Sorrentino, B. Interpersonal exchange as a function of rewards and costs and situational factors: Expectancy confirmation-disconfirmation. *Journal of Experimental Social Psychology,* 1969, *5,* 324–339.

Tognoli, J. Male friendship and intimacy across the life span. *Family Relations,* 1980, *29,* 273–279.

Vaillant, G. *Adaptation to life.* Boston: Little, Brown, 1977.

Walster, E., Walster, G., & Berscheid, E. *Equity: Theory and research.* Boston: Allyn & Bacon, 1978.

Waring, E. Marital intimacy, psychosomatic symptoms and cognitive therapy. *Psychosomatics,* 1980, *21,* 595–601.

Waring, E. Facilitating marital intimacy through self-disclosure. *American Journal of Family Therapy,* 1981, *9,* 33–42.

Waring, E., McElrath, D., Lefcoe, D., & Weisz, G. Dimensions of intimacy in marriage. *Psychiatry,* 1981, *44,* 169–175.

Waring, E., McElrath, D., Mitchell, P., & Derry, M. Intimacy and emotional illness in the general population. *Canadian Journal of Psychiatry,* 1981, *26,* 167–172.

Waring, E., & Russell, L. Family structure, marital adjustment, and intimacy in patients referred to a consultation-liaison service. *General Hospital Psychiatry,* 1980, *3,* 198–203.

Wash, E. Dysfunctional communication response patterns of depressed wives and their husbands in relation to activities of daily living (Doctoral dissertation, Catholic University of America, 1977). *Dissertation Abstracts International,* 1977, *38,* 142B.

Yufit, R. *Intimacy and isolation: Some behavioral and psychodynamic correlates.* Unpublished doctoral dissertation, University of Chicago, 1956.

Zinner, J. The implications of projective identification for marital interaction. In H. Grunebaum & J. Christ (Eds.), *Contemporary marriage.* Boston: Little, Brown, 1976.

Zuk, G. *Family therapy: A triadic approach.* New York: Behavioral Publications, 1971.

Section Four

Relational Sexuality

Chapter 14

Introduction to Sexuality

WILLIAM C. TALMADGE

INTRODUCTION TO PREMARITAL AND MARITAL SEXUALITY

Sexuality is a pervasive and integral force—a dynamic and physiological one—in the life of every individual. In light of recent research it might be thought of as a mind, body, and spirit interaction. We come into this world as sexual beings, and that continues until death. Sexuality is an active, organic, and evolving force. It is a force not likely to be denied without heavy expense to the individual. This force continues to evolve over the period of our lives. The evolution of the individual's sexuality does not occur in isolation. Sexuality of the person develops in the context of the relationship.

A sexual script emerges from one's development, interaction with others, and the social context. Although new areas of the script are discovered, explored, and renovated during the life process, the foundation of the script is established early in life. One begins to develop his/her sexual script in those early human contacts (Bowlby, 1969). Ethological research has demonstrated the importance of this period of our lives (Harlow, 1958). We are dependent on our care providers for survival in this highly vulnerable period. The quality of affectional contact with significant others in these beginning years colors our relationships of the future, influencing our capability for attachment and intimacy. Over the years of our lives, we continue to change and develop in our sexual scripts as a result of our relationships with others. The interactions of the individual with the social context and others is the key to the ever-emerging sexual script. Sexual attitudes and behavior are dynamic and interrelated phenomena that change over time in response to our relationships, our maturity, and cultural factors (Clayton & Bokemeier, 1980).

The sexual script is based upon five factors: (1) family history, (2) personality dynamics of the individual, (3) cultural context, (4) the interaction of these factors within the individual, and (5) the interaction of all of the above variables between the two persons in the relationship. These factors form a complex network of variables that are interacting within the individual and within the relationship. Although the sexual script has its foundation in early childhood interactions, the script continues to be reshaped, evolved, changed, and developed in our everyday confrontation with others.

The sexual script is confronted in premarital and marital sexuality. These forms of sexual experience allow the individual to continue in the understanding and formation of his/her sexual script. As a result of the relational process involved in these interactions with others, the sexual script may be better understood, changed, or left the same. The collective sexual script of our Western culture has changed radically just in the past 200 years. During the last century, significant changes have taken place. The sexual attitudes and behavior of males and females are becoming more similar. For instance, in premarital sexual expression, fewer differences between the sexes are observed, both in behavior and attitudes. Robison and Jedlicka (1982) examined changes in sexual attitudes and behavior of college students from 1965 to 1980. In their research, they found that males and females no longer held to the old double standard of premarital sex being acceptable for males but not females. They observed fewer differences in sex attitudes and behavior between men and women than in the past. Schulz, Bohrnstedt, Borgatta, and Evans (1977) investigated the sexual behavior and attitudes of college students as freshmen and four years later as seniors. They also found fewer differences between the sexual behavior of males and females. These same types of findings have been made by other researchers (Bauman & Wilson, 1976; Glenn & Weaver, 1979; Athanasiou & Sarkin, 1974; Peplau, Rubin, & Hill, 1977).

Another major change in the collective social script of Western culture can be seen in sex roles. Sex roles no longer dictate or influence career choices for women and men as much as they once did. As a result of increased liberalization and technological and scientific advancement, women and men have broader choices in their sexual attitudes and behavior. Gunter Schmidt (1982), in his presidential address to the Seventh Annual Meeting of the International Academy of Sex Researchers, stated that sexuality has changed in the last 20 years: there is more sexual freedom, increased liberalization, and a less-restrictive sexual code of behavior.

Similar changes have been observed in the sexual script of the individual. Marshall and Neill (1977) have demonstrated how a change in the individual within the context of a relationship affects one's sexual relationship and thereby alters the individual's sexual script. Marshall and Neill investigated the effects on the marriages of 12 patients who underwent intestinal bypass surgery for extreme obesity. They observed major changes in the sexuality of the couple and the dependency/independency of the partners. The surgery patients generally reported a more-positive sexual image and an increase in sexual desire and arousability. Overall, the spouses generally felt threatened by the changes in their partners. This is an example of how a change in the individual not only alters the relationship but also changes the sexual script of the individual.

Eysenck (1971) has emphasized that the quality of sexual behavior is greatly influenced by the personality of the individual. Through his investigations, he has found that extroverts who need stronger stimuli in general likewise need stronger sexual stimulants. They are more likely to have premarital and extramarital sexual intercourse, to have coitus at an earlier age and with more partners. Individuals having high neurotism scores are prone to experience more anxiety and perceive sexuality as a problem. Changes within the personality of the individual, in light of Eysenck's findings, would support a change in the sexual script of the individual. Another example of a change that can be observed in the sexual script of the individual is the marital partner who has an extramarital relationship. This individual, who may have viewed himself/herself as unattractive, may have a new self-perception of being attractive as a result of having sexual interactions with partners outside the marriage. This change in body image alters the sexual script of this individual and changes the relationship of the couple.

The following two chapters discuss the continued development of sexuality of the individual within the context of premarital and marital sexuality. It is the author's contention that the sexual script of the individual is altered through experiences of premarital and marital sexual expression. The primary purpose of these chapters is twofold: (1) to review the major investigations of premarital and marital sexuality in terms of methodology and findings, and (2) to formulate a transactional pattern of factors that are involved in premarital and marital sexuality.

When one elects to engage in sexual activity either premaritally or maritally, a number of forces—social, relational, and individual— are brought to bear. Some of the components of these forces are self-image, guilt, religiosity, attitudes of parents, intimacy of the relationship, and commitment of the relationship. These factors are involved in a complex set of interactions. In fact, when two individuals—a couple—decide to engage in sexual activity or are in the process of making that decision, each of the individuals' sexual scripts and the sexual script of the couple are continually confronted. The interaction of these individual, relational, and social factors will be discussed in the next two chapters as they relate to premarital and marital sexuality.

REFERENCES

Athanasiou, R., & Sarkin, R. Premarital sexual behavior and postmarital adjustment. *Archives of Sexual Behavior,* 1974, *3*(3), 207–225.

Bauman, K. E., & Wilson, R. R. Premarital sexual attitudes of unmarried university students: 1968 versus 1972. *Archives of Sexual Behavior,* 1976, *5*(1), 29–37.

Bowlby, J. *Attachment.* New York: Basic Books, 1969.

Clayton, R. R., & Bokemeier, J. L. Premarital sex in the seventies. *Journal of Marriage and the Family,* 1980, *42*(4), 759–775.

Eysenck, H. J. Personality and sexual adjustment. *British Journal of Psychiatry,* 1971, *118*, 593–608.

Glenn, N. D., & Weaver, C. N. Attitudes toward premarital, extramarital and homosexual relations in the U.S. in the 1970's. *Journal of Sex Research,* 1979, *15*, 108–118.

Harlow, H. F. The nature of love. *American Psychologist,* 1958, *13*, 673–685.

Jessen, C. J. Male responses to direct verbal and sexual initiatives of females. *Journal of Sex Research,* 1978, *14*, 118–128.

Marshall, J. R., & Neill, J. The removal of a psychosomatic symptom: Effects on the marriage. *Family Process,* 1977, *16*(3), 273–280.

Peplau, L. A., Rubin, Z., & Hill, C. T. Sexual intimacy and dating relationships. *Journal of Social Issues,* 1977, *33*(2), 86–109.

Robison, I. E., & Jedlicka, D. Change in sexual attitudes and behavior of college students from 1965 to 1980: A research note. *Journal of Marriage and the Family,* 1982, *44*(1), 237–240.

Schmidt, G. Sex and society in the eighties. *Archives of Sexual Behavior,* 1982, *11*(2), 91–97.

Schulz, B., Bohrnstedt, G. W., Borgatta, E. F., & Evans, R. R. Explaining premarital sexual intercourse among college students: A causal model. *Social Forces,* 1977, *56*(1), 148–165.

Chapter 15

Premarital Sexuality

WILLIAM C. TALMADGE

Traditionally, premarital sexuality has been investigated in three different ways. First, the surveyists have investigated the rates and changes in sexual attitudes and behavior. Generally, they have been concerned with the social context. These investigations have been useful in recording the rates and changes in different types of sexual behavior among various populations, increasing our understanding of attitudes which influence premarital sexual behavior and changes within the social context over time. These surveys have been greatly enhanced by the use of national probability samples, more sophisticated statistical techniques, and the use of longitudinal designs and cross-cultural analysis.

Secondly, family relations investigators and social psychologists have studied the relationship between premarital sexuality and the family, the couple's relationship, and significant reference groups. These studies have focused on the relationships between premarital sexual attitudes and behavior in relation to parental sexual standards, commitment in the couple's relationship, degree of affection, and peer group sexual standards. The design and methodology of this research has been improved by the use of discriminant analysis and path analysis. However, there have been only a small number of these studies.

Thirdly, individual, psychodynamically oriented investigators have studied how individual dynamics have related to premarital sexuality. Although Eysenck (1971) strongly encouraged the investigation of sexuality in relation to personality dynamics, few studies have been conducted in this regard. Overall, there is a great need for more studies to address the latter two types of investigations, and the greatest need is for a transactional approach of the effects of all three types on sexual behavior and attitudes.

TRENDS IN PREMARITAL SEXUAL BEHAVIOR

Many sex researchers have recently found nonmarried young people are having coitus at an earlier age, and the differences between males and females continue to decline. Udry, Bauman, and Morris (1975) studied changes in premarital coital experiences of urban white and black women. Their study was based on a sample of 100 white and 100 black ever-married women aged 15 to 44. They were interviewed through area sample surveys of low-income neighborhoods in 16 selected cities during the period from 1969 to 1970 and again in 1973 to 1974. These investigators, using cohort analysis, were interested in the differences in premarital coitus of these women over the various age groups. The findings showed an increase in premarital coitus over the various cohort periods, with the most-rapid increase appearing for those in the age group 15 to 19 in the late 1960s. Each successive age group had coital experiences before marriage at an earlier age than the previous group.

Robison and Jedlicka (1982) investigated changes in sexual behavior among college students from 1965 to 1980. Measures of sexual behavior were made in 1965, 1970, 1975 and 1980. The surveys were from a sample of college students in a state-supported southern university. The overall findings of this study support a continued but asymptotic increase in reported premarital sexual behavior of both males and females. Schulz, Bohrnstedt, Borgatta, and Evans (1977) investigated the sexual behavior of college students at the University of Wisconsin. Subjects were the 1964 matriculating class. The participants were questioned in 1964 as freshmen and in 1968 as seniors. As freshmen, 94 percent of the class responded, and 77 percent responded as seniors. Questions about sexual behavior were specifically asked only of the seniors who reported a willingness to answer personal questions about their sexual life. Eighty-one percent of this sample chose to respond. The findings were that 65 percent of the males and 56 percent of the females reported having sexual intercourse.

Simon, Berger, and Gagnon (1972), through a 1969 national survey, reported premarital sexual intercourse among 68 percent of the males and 44 percent of the females among college students. An investigation conducted among unmarried college students in 1968 and 1972 by Bauman and Wilson (1976) found an increase in premarital sexual intercourse. The students in 1968 reported 50 percent of themselves to be nonvirginal as compared to 70 percent in 1972.

Lewis and Burr (1975) investigated premarital coitus among college students with a large sample of 2,453 students from seven colleges and universities throughout the United States. Undergraduates from sociology classes at these schools were administered a questionnaire regarding their courtship and sexual behavior. These investigators found that 59.5 percent of the men and 28.7 percent of the women had had at least one experience with coitus prior to marriage. Lewis and Burr state that these overall findings do not appear different from findings of other sex researchers in terms of frequency of sexual coitus before marriage.

Mercer and Cohn (1979) investigated the sexual behavior of 224 college students who attended a large coeducational university. In terms of sexual behavior, 74 percent of the males and 60 percent of the females reported having had coitus. Twenty-seven percent of the males and 32 percent of the females reported that they had had sexual intercourse with one person, while 47 percent of the males and 28 percent of the females reported having had coitus with two or more partners. This data indicates a significant difference in the number of coital partners among males. Mosher (1979) conducted an investigation with 87 male and 88 female students and found no significant differences in the level of sexual experience for the students based on sex. There was a significant difference between men and women in terms of sexual behavior with face-to-face coitus. Fifty-three percent of the males and 38 percent of the females had experienced face-to-face coitus.

MacQuordale and DeLamater (1979) compared the premarital sexual activity among college students with that of nonstudents. These young adults, aged 18 to 23, were interviewed by undergraduates, graduate students, and former graduates of the university. A number of instruments were administered to the subjects along with specific questions about their sexual behavior. Among the college men, 75 percent had had sexual intercourse by the average age of 17.6; by comparison 79 percent of the nonstudent group had had intercourse by the average age of 17.2 years. The only significant difference between male students and nonstudents was in the category of oral genital relations, with the nonstudents having had more experience. In the comparison of female students and nonstudents, 60 percent of the female students by the average age of 17.9 had their first coital experience, whereas 72 percent of the nonstudent females had had intercourse by the average age of 18.3 years. The nonstudents were also more experienced in oral genital sex.

Peplau, Rubin, and Hill (1977) investigated the sexual behavior of steadily dating college students. The participants of this study were from four Boston area colleges. There were 231 college-age couples that were recruited by letters mailed to a random sample of 5,000 sophomores and juniors. This data was based on a research study conducted over a two-year period on the development of dating relationships. These college-age dating couples were divided in their commitment as follows. One third had been dating for five months or less, one third between five and 10 months, and another third for longer than 10 months. Approximately 75 percent of the couples were dating their partner exclusively, although few had concrete plans for marriage. Each couple completed a 40-page questionnaire concerning their background, dating behavior, and sexual attitudes and behavior. Follow-up questionnaires were administered to these college-age dating couples six months, one year, and two years after the initial contact period. It was found that 82 percent of the couples had had coitus in their current relationship. This figure of 82 percent is higher than the percentage of most college-age students having had sexual intercourse. When the current relationship of the dating couples began, 38 percent of the females and 26 percent of the males reported being virginal.

Overall, these studies support a growing trend of increased sexual intercourse among nonmarried college students and nonstudents. However, most of the research on premarital sexual behavior has been conducted with college students. Future research needs to be aimed at a more-general population of young people.

TRENDS IN PREMARITAL SEXUAL ATTITUDES

Many investigators have reported a trend of increased sexual permissiveness toward premarital sexual activity. The following studies support such a trend. The other noticeable difference has been a convergence in sexual attitudes between men and women, with less adhering to the old double standard. Over the period from 1965 to 1980, fewer differences have been observed between males and females in terms of their premarital sexual attitudes and behavior (Robison & Jedlicka, 1982). These investigators report increased levels of premarital sexual behavior for both sexes; at the same time, however, these students see premarital sexual behavior as generally sinful and immoral. This implies a conflict between sex attitudes and behavior. A similar conflict has been noted by Miller and Lief in their examination of masturbatory behavior and attitudes. He has reported high incidences of masturbation; however, people continue to feel very guilty about this behavior. This same type of phenomenon occurs with premarital coitus; although most unmarried college students participate in sexual intercourse, they tend to feel guilty.

Utilizing a U.S. national probability sample from the 1972 and 1975 National Opinion Research Center's general social survey, Mahoney (1978) investigated age differences and attitudes toward premarital intercourse. Respondents were broken down by sex in 10-year age groups (18 to 29, 30 to 39, 40 to 49, 50 to 59, 60 to 69, and 70 years and older). The findings of this investigation showed an increase in permissiveness in every age group between 1972 to 1975. The age group 18 to 29 was the most liberal but did not exhibit the greatest change. The greatest change in attitudes was in the age group 30 to 39. It was found that this age group was rapidly approaching the liberalism of the younger age group. The greatest amount of change among any group in sexual attitudes was the female age group 30 to 39; and this change was so remarkable as to produce an intersex convergence in this age group.

Another study, conducted by Bauman and Wilson (1976), investigating the premarital sexual attitudes of single university students also found a convergence of sexual attitudes among males and females. The only significant difference between males and females in their 1972 sample was that women were less permissive about having intercourse without affection toward their partner. Overall, the students supported a more permissive attitude toward premarital sexual behavior by both males and females, and fewer differences in attitudes between men and women were observed. It was also observed that there was less adherence to the double standard.

Glenn and Weaver (1979) investigated the premarital sexual attitudes of a large national sample during the period 1972 through 1978. Results of this study indicated an increase in permissive attitudes toward premarital sexual intercourse during the six-year period from 1972 to 1978. However, it was found that there were still some restrictive attitudes toward permarital sex among older persons, especially older persons with little formal education. Fifty-nine percent of the 1978 respondents reported permissive attitudes toward premarital sex.

Mercer and Cohn (1979) investigated sexual attitudes and behavior as well as gender differences with a group of 134 male and 90 female undergraduate students. Their findings were that the females were significantly more conservative on the sex attitude scale than the men. The sex attitude items which differentiated males from females were as follows: (1) wanting spouse to be a virgin; (2) guilt, if engaging in sexual relations with a person to whom I was not engaged or married; (3) feeling guilty if I engaged in sexual relations with a person whom I did not love. All of these items are related to the degree of commitment in the relationship.

Mendelsohn and Mosher (1979) investigated the effects of premarital sexual attitudes in relation to sex guilt and sexual myths. Subjects participated in a sex education role play with a 13-year-old girl who had just experienced her first menstrual period. It was found that women who scored higher on sex guilt or who held more conservative premarital sexual attitudes communicated less accurate information and endorsed more sexual myths. This study observes a relationship between sexual knowledge, guilt, and conservative sexual attitudes.

Peplau et al. (1977) studied sexual attitudes and behavior among dating couples. As with other studies, these researchers found that men and women are becoming more similar in their sexual attitudes and behavior. Approximately 95 percent of the men and women believed the same sexual intercourse standards should apply to both men and women in love relationships. As has been shown in previous studies, attitudes toward premarital sex are becoming more permissive. In this study, 80 percent of the couples believed that for couples who love each other, having intercourse was completely acceptable. Sexual intercourse with casual acquaintances was less acceptable, 20 percent of the students indicating casual sex to be completely acceptable.

Overall, these studies support that males and females are becoming less different in their sexual attitudes. The sexual attitudes of students and young people are becoming more permissive, and the degree of commitment in the relationship is a determining factor in the sexual behavior. In addition, the more conservative sexual attitudes appear associated with sexual myths and guilt.

Reiss and Miller (1979) have further worked these propositions into "an autonomy theory of heterosexual permissiveness." Since the original formulation of that theory of premarital sexual behavior, numerous investigations have been conducted in an effort to substantiate these factors (Singh, 1980; Clayton & Bokemeier, 1980; Reiss & Miller). Reiss has offered a broad understanding of the many factors which influence premarital sexual attitudes and behavior. The reformulation of his original propositions offers a broad and complex set of propositions which will encourage a great deal of future research into the area of premarital sexuality. However, many of these new propositions are being tested in the current research. Premarital sexual behavior is becoming an anachronistic misnomer as more and more unmarried and never-married persons participate in sexual intercourse. With a larger divorced and never-married population, new considerations must be given for the sexual behavior of these people. Another major consideration which is influencing the sexual behavior of this group of people is genital herpes and AIDS.

FIVE FACTORS OF SEXUAL SCRIPT FOR PREMARITAL SEXUALITY

Premarital sexual behavior is a private choice of the individual which is based upon the characteristics of the individual and his/her significant relationships. Based on the sexual-script theory previously stated, there are five primary factors involved in premarital sexual behavior: (1) family history; (2) personality structure of the individual; (3) cultural context; (4) the interaction of these factors within the individual; and (5) the interaction of all the above variables between the two persons

Table 1

Five factors of sexual script

Factor 1:   Family
   Parental attitudes
   Parental acceptance
   Family responsibilities
   Sex myths
   Career orientation

Factor 2:   Personality characteristics
   Self-image
   Self-esteem
   Body image
   Guilt
   Religiosity
   Locus of control
   Moral reasoning
   Authoritarianism
   Transitional events

Factor 3:   Social context
   Peers
   Gender identity
   Age
   Race
   Eduction
   Sexual myths

Factor 4:   Interaction of family, personality dynamics,
      and social context of the individual

Factor 5:   Relationship of the couple
   Commitment
   Equity
   Degree of affection
   Consensual agreement
   Dating behavior
   Relationship reasoning
   Developmental process of relationship
   Intimacy

---

in the relationship. These five components account for the who, what, when, where, and how of premarital sexual behavior. In Table 1, these five factors are arranged in a complex set of components, as they have been investigated.

Family

Libby, Gray, and White (1978) investigated the importance of the reference group and role correlates of premarital sexual permissiveness. Their investigation was based upon data gathered from 421 undergraduate students at a northwestern state university in 1973. This study was only a small part of a much-larger, ongoing study of premarital sexual attitudes and behavior. Items from Reiss's perceived reference group closeness were used. Students were asked to compare their own sexual standards with those of their peers, friends, mother, father, and dates. Using path analysis, it was found that closeness to mother's sexual standards was highly predictive of self-permissiveness as was perceived parental liberality. However, closeness to father's sexual standards and family happiness contributed little to the path models. Libby et al. concluded, "When the perceived reference group and role variables are operationalized and tested in path models, the data do not support Reiss's emphasis on the positive influence of courtship (peers and friends as well as dates) as a stronger predictor of self-permissiveness than the negative influence of the family (parents) on premarital permissiveness" (p. 90).

Adamant virgins, potential nonvirgins, and nonvirgins were investigated by Herold and Goodwin (1981a). In a chi-square analysis of data gathered from 514 single high school and college women, it was found that age, religiosity, career aspirations, parental acceptance of premarital intercourse, peer acceptance of premarital intercourse, peer experience with premarital intercourse, dating commitment, and dating frequency were the significant characteristics. However, using discriminate analysis, parental acceptance of premarital intercourse contributed little, while peer experience with premarital intercourse, dating commitment, and religiosity were highly predictive of virginity status. The authors explain that parental permissiveness did not significantly contribute to the prediction of virginity in the discriminate analysis because almost all of the females in each of the various groups indicated that their parents would be highly upset to find out that they were having premarital intercourse.

Parental sexual conservatism and sexual myths contribute to the belief in sexual myths by adolescents and young adults. Mosher (1979) and Mendelsohn and Mosher (1979) have shown that those subjects having more restrictive premarital sexual attitudes tended to believe in more sex myths and that the males tended to believe in more sexual myths than the females. In addition, it was found that those adhering to more sexual myths tended to also feel guilty about their sexual relations.

Overall, there has been little investigation into the effects of parental attitudes and sexual behavior on premarital sexuality of young people. As Clayton and Bokemeier (1980) have noted, this would be a fruitful area for future research. It is believed that parental attitudes toward permarital sexual behavior, family responsibility, sexual myths, and parents' sexual behavior, contribute greatly to premarital sexuality.

Personality characteristics

Personality variables such as self-image, guilt, religiosity, locus of control, moral reasoning, and authoritarianism contribute to the formation of premarital sexual attitudes and behavior. The personality dynamics of the individual are influential in the young person's decision to participate in premarital intercourse. However, little investigation has been conducted into how personality variables relate to sexual attitudes and behavior within the individual. In terms of premarital sexual attitudes and behavior, there have been a few studies which have investigated the relationship between various personality variables and sexuality.

MacQuordale and DeLamater (1979) investigated the relationship between self-image and sexuality. They defined self-image as being composed of self-esteem, the evaluation of self as a social actor, the evaluation of self as a moral actor, and body image. They were interested in sexuality as both a behavioral and attitudinal process. In their study, they compared undergraduates with a noncollege group. The ages of the participants were between 18 and 23. The instruments used in the study were Sherwood's semantic differential, Secord and Jourard's body cathexis scale, and a modified version of Reiss's permissiveness scale. The subjects also responded to questions about their sexual behavior and their parents'. The authors of this study found no consistent relationship between overall self-image and premarital sex; however, there were a number of significant associations between some components of self-image and sexuality across the subsamples. For example, among female students, there was a significant relationship between higher levels of self-esteem and reports of more lifetime intimate behavior. Among the male students, there was a strong significant relationship between high scores on the desirability scale and more permissive premarital sexual attitudes and intimate lifetime behavior.

MacQuordale and DeLamater (1979) found that there was a stronger relationship between components of self-image and sexual behavior than between self-image and sexual attitudes, and it was a consistent relationship. Self-esteem was found to relate less to sexual behavior than did evaluation of self as a social object, which related more consistently to sexual behavior. In both groups of men, there was a significant relationship found between the number of coital partners and their desirability scale. Men with high desirability showed a relationship with a higher number of intercourse partners. These investigators also found a relationship between body image as measured by the Secord-Jourard scale and premarital sexual behavior. The relationship was strongest between the ratings of the face and genitals of the body image scale with sexual behavior. The MacQuordale and DeLamater study demonstrates a relationship which many theorists have thought to exist between self-image and sexual behavior and attitudes. However, the relationship of different components of self-image seems much stronger with sexual behavior than with attitudes. This study represents the only investigation between self-image and sexual behavior that was found. Future investigations should concentrate in this area.

Another personality dynamic which has been investigated more thoroughly is guilt. Herold and Goodwin (1981b) investigated the relationship between guilt and premarital sexual behavior. The study was conducted with 355 single, sexually active females from ages 13 to 20 who attended 10 different birth control centers in Ontario, Canada. The authors found that 41 percent of these young females experienced guilt after their first intercourse. However, as time lapsed and when asked how they felt about their sexual experience later, only 8 percent experienced guilt. It was found that those women who were against premarital sex were the ones more likely to experience guilt as a result of violating their or perhaps their family's standards. These investigators found that 26 percent of the variance in the current sexual guilt of these females was explained by the variables of the number of sexual experiences, personal attitudes toward premarital intercourse, planning for their first intercourse, and self-esteem. With increased sexual experience, the young adolescent female becomes less dependent upon the standards of others and relies more on her own standards in reacting to her sexual behavior. The authors also found that those females having higher self-esteem were less likely to experience guilt at the onset of their first intercourse experience. This study supports the MacQuordale and DeLamater (1979) study which demonstrated that self-image is related to sexual behavior in a positive way. Theoretically, guilt has been thought to have a mediating effect upon sexual behavior.

Mosher and Cross (1971) defined sex guilt as a generalized expectation for self-mediated punishment which results from violating or expecting to violate one's sexual standards. In their study, they found that college students who had high guilt were less sexually experienced than those with less guilt. This would conform to the previous study by Herold and Goodwin (1981b). A study by D'Augelli and Cross (1975) investigated the relationship of sex guilt and moral reasoning to premarital sexual behavior among college women and in couples. Each subject was given Kohlberg's moral dilemmas questionnaire, Mosher's forced-choice guilt inventory, and the sex experience inventory of Brady and Levitt. Each subject was interviewed one week after completing the various questionnaires. In the interview, such things were discussed as their present sexual relationships and types of sexual behavior and personal and parental attitudes toward premarital sex. Based upon the subjects' sex experience inventory, they were divided into two groups. One was the sex experience group, and the other, sexual expression. There were five categories of sex experience: (1) neckers; (2) light petters; (3) heavy petters; (4) technical virgins; and (5) nonvirgins. There were six categories in the sexual expression group: (1) inexperienced virgins; (2) adamant virgins; (3) potential nonvirgins; (4) engaged nonvirgins; (5) liberated nonvirgins; and (6) confused nonvirgins. Interrater reliability for the sexual expression was based on a percentage of agreement in 20 interviews across four judgments. The agreement averaged to be 85 percent. These authors, like other investigators, found that high sex guilt was negatively related to the amount of sexual experience. Those having high sex guilt were less likely to engage in the more extreme forms of sexual behavior. Sex guilt was found to be inversely related to sexual experience. Those less guilty showed higher liberality of sexual philosophy, and those with high levels of guilt were the adamant virgins.

The second part of the D'Augelli and Cross (1975) study dealt with dating couples. The couples came to the interview and were separated. While one was being asked various interview questions, the other one was completing different questionnaires. The questionnaires that were given were the revised sex experience inventory, Mosher's forced-choice guilt inventory, and Kohlberg's moral dilemmas questionnaire. The authors found that men and women who were at the law-and-order stage of moral reasoning had higher sex guilt than those in the other stages of moral development according to Kohlberg's moral dilemmas. The men who showed higher sex guilt were less sexually experienced. It was also found that the couple's sexual experience was best predicted by the sex guilt of the male partner. Thus once again, sex guilt was found to be significantly related with sexual experience and with moral reasoning. Those who were most guilty tended to have rigid moral codes, less sexual experience, and more guilt feelings for the sexual behavior in which they had participated.

In a study conducted by Mendelsohn and Mosher (1979), they investigated the effects of sexual guilt upon premarital sexual attitudes. The scales that were used were Reiss's premarital sexual permissiveness scale, Mosher's sex myth inventory, and the female form of Mosher's forced-choice guilt inventory. The subjects then participated in three role-play situations. The first was a warm-up dialogue in which the subject was giving academic advice to a role played by one of the experimenters. The second role play was a sex education dialogue in which the subject was giving advice to a role-play 13-year-old girl who was having her first menstruation. The third role play was a sexual advice dialogue. In this role play, the subject was approached by a role-play college freshman who comes to seek advice about her first coital experience. As might be expected, the sex guilt of these women greatly influenced the role-play situations in terms of the type of sexual information and advice that was given. It was found that those women who had higher scores in sex guilt tended to be more restrictive in their premarital sexual attitudes and communicated less accurate information in the role-play interaction with the 13-year-old girl. Those who tended to have higher sex guilt and more restrictive sexual attitudes demonstrated more sexual myths and less accurate sexual information. Once again, sex guilt is shown to have an inhibiting effect not only on sexual behavior but upon sexual attitudes and sexual information.

In another study by Mosher (1979), an investigation was conducted into the relationship of sex guilt and sex myths in college men and women. The subjects were given the Mosher's forced-choice guilt inventory, his sex myth inventory, and the sex experience inventory of Brady and Levitt. It was found that the men tended to score lower on sex guilt, but showed significantly more sexual myths than the women. Once again, an inverse relationship was found between sex guilt and sex experience. Mosher sees sex guilt as having an inhibiting effect upon sexual behavior instead of the sexual behavior creating more of the guilt. The investigator also found, as others have, that there was a significant correlation between sex myth and sexual guilt for both women and men. Mosher states:

> This can be interpreted as reflecting the interaction of cognitive and emotive processes in developing the affective-cognitive structure of self sex guilt and in learning sex myths. Through the punitive socialization of emotions related to sexuality by the parents, children begin to experience intense negative emotions including guilt in sexual situations. (p. 232)

Mosher has noted that sexual guilt is a personality dynamic—that is, an affective cognitive process which has cognitions about sexual behavior and attitudes and an affective and behavioral component that inhibits or encourages different types of sexual behavior. Time after time, sexual guilt has been shown in numerous studies (Langston, 1973; Mosher & Abramson, 1977) to be negatively related to sex experience, frequency of sexual intercourse, the number of sexual partners, and sexual myths. Overall, sex guilt tends to have a strong inhibiting effect upon sexual development. This inhibiting effect has significant influence upon premarital sexual attitudes and behavior and how a young person continues to think of himself or herself as a sexual being.

Another personality dynamic which has received just a little attention is locus of control. Research on locus of control has shown that internally oriented individuals tend to be more assertive, powerful, active, and independent than the externally oriented individual (Applebaum, Tuma, & Johnson, 1975; Hersch & Scheibe, 1967). It is believed that internally oriented people tend to be more active and assertive in influencing the sexual situation, while the externally oriented person tends to be more passive in the sexual encounter.

Two studies have looked at how locus of control orientation (Rotter, 1966) affects an individual's sexual behavior in influencing premarital sexuality. In a study by LaPlante, McCormick, and Brannigan (1980), sexual script, gender identity, and locus of control were studied. The authors predicted that the internally oriented subjects would be more active and influential in the premarital sexual behavior of a couple and that the externally oriented individual would be more passive. Subjects completed different questionnaires, the Rotter locus-of-control scale, and a sexual-script questionnaire. The sexual script gave 2 samples each of 10 strategies for having intercourse and 9 strategies for avoiding it. After reading these strategies, the students were to rate the likelihood of the person being male or female, how frequently they had used this approach, and how frequently this approach had been used on them. Unlike what was predicted, these authors found that internally oriented students failed to be the influencing agent in the sexual encounter more often than the external. Also as was not expected, externals were found not to be the ones who were influenced more in the sexual encounter than the internals. This study found that locus-of-control orientation appears not to have much influence upon sexual script. The authors note the power of the overriding cultural sexual script in influencing college students' sexual behavior and attitudes. They suggest that perhaps personality and attitudinal variables really have little impact on a person's actual sexual role decision and behavior.

In a later study on locus-of-control orientation, Lee and Mancini (1981) further investigated the effects of locus-of-control orientation upon sexual behavior. A sexual questionnaire and the seven first-person items from Rotter's locus-of-control scale were administered to 600 female and 482 male undergraduate college students. These authors found that externally oriented men were more likely to have a greater number of sexual partners, while internally oriented men had more-frequent intercourse. It was found that the internally oriented women were more likely to use effective forms of contraception than the externally oriented females. (This author notes that there needs to be much greater investigation into the effects of personality variables and how they may influence premarital sexual behavior.) Lee and Mancini discussed the possibility that the differences in premarital sexual behavior by internally and externally oriented people may relate more to the difference in the types of relationships that these individuals develop. They suggest that future research must look at the interaction effect of personality and social variables such as commitment to the relationship and attitudes toward different sexual activity.

Another personality variable which has received very little attention is authoritarianism. In a classic investigation conducted by Adorno, Frenkel-Brunswick, Levison, and Sanford (1950), they studied the effects of the authoritarian personality style upon orientation to living. They found that those who scored high on authoritarianism were more conventional in their sexual attitudes and values. The individuals high in authoritarianism are thought to be more conservative and rigid in sexual values and behavior, while those less-authoritatively oriented would be more liberal and permissive in their sexual attitudes and behavior.

Mercer and Cohn (1979), in another investigation of authoritarianism, found the males to be slightly less authoritarian than the females. The authors correlated authoritarianism with a number of other variables such as religious attendance, sexual experience, number of partners, a drug-use permissiveness scale, sexual attitudes, and sex urge. The authors found that these variables were interrelated differently for the males and females. To clarify these differences, factor analysis was undertaken for each gender. For the males, they found two factors emerging: The first was sex urge and activities, and the second factor was related to sexual attitudes, drug-use attitudes, authoritarianism, religious attendance, and marijuana use. They found that these two factors were highly correlated, and together they accounted for 57 percent of the total variance. These authors note the complexity of this personality variable interacting with a combination of a number of other variables.

Another personality variable which has received some investigation is moral reasoning. Moral reasoning is a cognitive variable that is characterized by consistency of logic and values in judging moral situations. It is thought that this can have an inhibiting effect upon sexual behavior. However, little investigation has been devoted to its effect upon sexual attitudes and behavior. Jurich and Jurich (1974) found that subjects with lower degrees of moral development tended to be more traditional, hold double standards, and/or be more permissive. They were also less likely to have any particular formation of relationship, such as having high affection within the relationship. Those showing more-moderate styles with cognitive development were permissive, but needed more affection within the relationship in order to express their sexuality. The final group was more permissive and less affectionate in their relationship formation.

In the D'Augelli and Cross (1975) study discussed above, they studied the relationship of sex guilt and moral reasoning to premarital sexuality among college students. One of the instruments administered was Kohlbert's moral dilemmas questionnaire. Similar to the previous study by Jurich and Jurich (1974), these authors found that those who were at a lower level of moral development, such as the law-and-order stage, were significantly less sexually experienced than those who were at the stages of personal concordance or social contract development. It was also found that the virgins were more likely to be at the law-and-order stage than the nonvirgins. Overall it was found that those who were at the law-and-order stage were more likely to be guilty, to be virgins sexually, and to have had less sexual experience. It is strongly hypothesized that cognitive moral styles are highly influential in sexual decision making. It would appear that those who had more rigid moral processes would be less likely to be sexually experienced and would be more prone to guilt, as this research has demonstrated.

Social context

Social context has received more attention in the investigation of premarital sexual attitudes and behavior than other areas. Theories have been formed about the impact of reference groups upon sexual attitudes and behavior. Other variables of social context which have been investigated are gender identity, religiosity, education, race, and age. This section will review the influence that these variables have had upon premarital sexual attitudes and behavior. Reiss, in his propositions about premarital sexual attitudes and behavior, has stated that the individual will perceive permissiveness along a continuum, with the parents perceived as being on the low end of the continuum and the individual's peers being perceived as highly permissive. He states that the individual will see his/her permissiveness as being more closely aligned to that of his or her peers, with the greatest alignment being with those to whom the individual feels closest. The importance of reference groups has received much attention in its impact upon behavior (Kemper, 1968; Mirande, 1968; Newcomb, 1943, 1958).

Teevan (1972) investigated the impact of parents, friends, and other college students upon the individual's premarital sexual attitudes and behavior. Teevan believed that the individual's sexual attitudes and behavior are strongly influenced by his or her relationship with parents. However, he found that this hypothesis was only weakly supported. The greatest impact was made by the peer reference group. This group was most predictive in determining the sexual permissiveness of the student. The overall norms of the college community in general were very important in predicting the sexual attitudes and behavior of the individual. Teevan also found that the individual tended to align more closely with the norms held by the reference group than with those held by his parents. This author notes that future studies should be devoted to investigating how reference groups are chosen and the strength of the relationship between the individual and his peers and friends.

Schulz et al. (1977) developed research trying to explain premarital sexual intercourse among college students. In their study of a group of University of Wisconsin students that were interviewed as freshmen and again as seniors, they found that one of the most powerful variables predicting sexual behavior was the student's friends. These investigators found that the impact of friends upon the students not only influenced their sexual behavior but also influenced their associations with other college students, their frequency of dating, and their fraternity/ sorority membership. In terms of sexual behavior, it was found that each additional friend out of five who had had premarital intercourse increased the likelihood that the student would engage in premarital sex by 12 to 14 percent. This was found to hold true for both male and female students.

Herold and Goodwin (1981a) investigated the impact of various variables upon types of virginity or nonvirginity. The subjects in this study were 408 single college women and 106 single high school women from the Ontario, Canada, area. Fifty-two percent of these females had had premarital intercourse. Using the significant variables from a chi-square analysis, a discriminate analysis was conducted. Two of the five significant variables which contributed to these subjects' premarital sexual behavior were related to their reference group. The most-important variable was the peers' experience with premarital intercourse. Another variable significantly related in predicting the sexual behavior of these women was the peer group's acceptance of premarital intercourse. This study is very supportive of, and concurs with, the previous study by Schulz et al. (1977).

Using path analysis, Libby et al. (1978) conducted a sophisticated investigation on how the reference group and role correlates with premarital sexual permissiveness. This study was only a part of a much-larger, ongoing study on premarital sexual attitudes and behavior. Questionnaires about sexual behavior and attitudes along with many demographic variables were administered to the subjects in small groups. The variables considered in this study were as follows: (1) premarital permissiveness, (2) family relationship, (3) courtship involvement, (4) perceived closeness to peer standards, (5) perceived closeness to friends' standards, (6) perceived closeness to fathers' standards, (7) perceived closeness to mothers' standards, (8) perceived closeness to dates' standards, (9) family happiness, (10) church attendance, and (11) perceived parental sexual liberality. The authors developed a path model for both males and females. With the males, they found that perceived closeness to mothers' standards was significantly related to permissiveness, along with perceived closeness to peers' and friends' standards. However, perceived closeness to fathers' standards and closeness to dates' standards and family happiness were not significantly related. For the females, perceived closeness to mothers' standards is the only significant predictive variable of female permissiveness. Libby et al., based upon their research, reformulated Reiss's sixth proposition which was aimed at the importance of the reference group. They reframed this proposition into three separate propositions:

1. The closer one perceives his/her premarital sexual standards as being to his/her parents' (particularly the mother's) standards, the lower one's self-permissiveness will be.
2. The closer males perceive their premarital sexual standards as being to their peers' and close friends' standards, the higher male permissiveness will be.
3. Female permissiveness will be reduced by perceived closeness to mother's sexual standards and to a lesser extent by perceived closeness to father's standards; male permissiveness will also be negatively influenced by perceptions of mother's standards but positively affected (though slightly less) by closeness to peers' and friends' standards. (p. 88)

This study emphasizes the importance of reference groups, particularly the impact of mothers' sexual standards on premarital sexual permissiveness.

Another social context variable which has been given some consideration is age. It has been noted by numerous researchers that the age at which young people have intercourse has been decreasing through the last decades. However, the decrease in age has not continued with the rapidity that was presumed. Udry et al. (1975) investigated changes by age in premarital coital experience of urban American women. In their analysis, age groups were broken down by decades. Overall, the data show an increase in premarital intercourse for each successive cohort. The most dramatic change occurred for those females who were age 15 to 19 in the late 1960s. This investigation suggests that women are having their first coital experience at an earlier period in their lives.

Glenn and Weaver (1979) investigated attitudes toward premarital sex, extramarital sex, and homosexuality during the period from 1972 through 1978. This investigation demonstrated an increase in sexual conservatism with age. The younger the respondent, the greater the likelihood of more liberal premarital sexual attitudes. It was found that the most restrictive attitudes toward premarital sex existed among older persons, especially older persons with little formal education. The authors note:

> In the total sample in 1978, 41% of the respondents with an opinion reported restrictive attitudes and if the 1972 to 1978 rate of change should continue, more than a fourth of American adults would still have restrictive attitudes in 1990. Premarital sex relations are not yet 'generally accepted' nor are they likely to be in the near future. (p. 112)

Another study by Herold and Goodwin (1981a), which has been previously described, found a significant age difference between the potential nonvirgins and nonvirgins, with more of the younger women being potential nonvirgins. Once again, these authors have shown the relationship between age and virginity or age and onset of first intercourse. A study by Singh (1980) investigated trends in premarital sexual attitudes. Data was based upon five national surveys that were conducted in 1972, 1974, 1975, 1977, and 1978 by the National Opinion Research Center. This research shows an increase of liberalization toward premarital sexuality over the period of time from 1972 to 1978; there is an increase in liberalization of about 2 to 3 percentage points per year.

In general, what is shown in the social context of the age variable is that over time there has been an increase in liberalization toward premarital sexuality. The onset of first coitus is not continuing at as drastic a rate as one might believe. Also, there are many other intervening variables which need to be taken into account, such as religiosity, social class and liberalism, and influence and impact of peer group and friends.

Another social context variable which has received some investigation is education and how it affects sexual attitudes and behavior. Udry et al. (1975) found women with lower educational rates to have consistently higher rates of sexual involvement. The higher the educational attainment, the lower the percentages of coitus in each cohort. Glenn and Weaver (1979), in a previously mentioned study, explored attitudes toward premarital, extramarital, and homosexual relations. Basing their study on the general social surveys conducted by the National Opinion Research Center from the period 1972 through 1978, these investigators made similar findings in relation to premarital sexual attitudes and education: Those persons having more than 12 years of education tended to be more permissive, while those having less than 10 years tended to be more restrictive in their premarital attitudes. Overall, the findings of this research show that there is an increase in liberalization of attitudes toward premarital sex with higher levels of education.

Singh's (1980) previously mentioned study found that sexual attitudes varied in liberalization with education.

In general, the findings from these three studies support more-permissive attitudes toward premarital sexuality as a result of education and an association between levels of education and premarital sexual behavior. It appears that lower levels of education are associated with earlier premarital sexual coitus and more restrictive premarital sexual attitudes, while higher levels of education are associated with later age periods of first premarital coitus and more permissive sexual attitudes.

Another social context variable which has received very little investigation is that of race: the difference between premarital sexual behavior of blacks and whites. Zelnik and Kanter (1977, 1980) investigated premarital coitus among teenagers from the ages 15 to 19 from a national probability sample. These two studies show an increase in prevalence of premarital intercourse from 1972 to 1977 for both blacks and whites. The increase in premarital intercourse for whites was from 21 percent to 31 percent, while for blacks it was from 51 percent to 63 percent. The authors note that at this later period of 1977, the relative racial differences in premarital sexual behavior were considerably smaller than at the earlier periods. Similar findings have been noted by Udry, Bauman, and Morris (1975), who found the percentage of premarital coitus among blacks was significantly higher than for whites. However, over the later time frames, this difference has become substantially smaller. In future investigations of the race variable, intervening variables such as income and educational level of parents and the subject need to be considered.

Another variable which is beginning to receive more attention is that of sex roles or gender identity. In a study on sexual intimacy in dating couples, Peplau et al. (1977) investigated the nature of sex role-playing in couples. Data from this study was from a much broader two-year study on the development of dating relationships. Data was gathered on all subjects concerning their sexual attitudes and experience, background, and dating relationships. These authors were interested in investigating traditional sex roles which prescribe certain roles that males and females should play in their sexual interactions. The role that young men are expected to play is that of initiating sex, while the female's role is to set the limits on the couple's sexual behavior. These authors chose to divide the participants into three groups based upon their sexual behavior. The first group was sexual traditionalists, who abstained from sexual intercourse. The next was the sexual moderates who had intercourse only after emotional intimacy had been established. The third group was the sexual liberals who tended to have intercourse first without any type of emotional intimacy between the couple. Among the 42 couples who abstained from sex (18 percent of the total sample), the females were the ones who restrained the couple from intercourse. It was also found that the men were more interested than the female in having intercourse and that the females were aware of this. As might be expected, the couples in this group were more restrictive in their sexual attitudes than the couples in the other two groups. These couples also had significantly less sexual experience. Overall, it was found that the sexual attitudes of males and females were quite similar. However, when it came to actual sexual behavior, traditional sex roles were found to still play an important part in the determination of when intercourse would occur, and the females controlled this decision.

In another study, LaPlante et al. (1980) investigated the relationship between gender and locus of control on the influence of sexual behavior and attitudes among college students. As hypothesized by the investigators, the students rated 10 strategies for having sex as masculine strategies and all 9 strategies of avoiding sex as being feminine. As might be expected, the men reported that they had used both indirect and direct strategies significantly more than the women to persuade their dates to have intercourse. The females reported that they had used both indirect and direct strategies significantly more than the males to avoid sexual intercourse. The findings of this study support the findings of the study by Peplau et al. (1977). However, they seem to be in conflict with Jesser's (1978) and McCormick's (1979) investigations in which few differences were found between the sexes for influencing sexual behavior. LaPlante et al. state that "unlike the present study the wording of Jesser's and McCormick's questions oblige students to put themselves in the role of an influencing agent in a sexual encounter" (p. 351). In these two studies, subjects were forced to take the assertive role of initiating sex while in LaPlante et al.'s study, subjects were just asked what types of strategies they used to have and avoid coitus. These authors state that "the unique wording of our questions made it possible for students to indicate whether their actual sexual experiences reflected the sexual script" (p. 351). From this and Peplau et al.'s studies, it can be seen that gender identity has played a significant role in influencing sexual behavior among college students. It would be expected that for young people not in college, the traditional sex roles would be even stronger in influencing their sexual behavior. This area of gender identity and its impact upon sexual behavior still appears to be a very fertile area for future investigation.

Another variable which has received wide attention is that of religiosity and its effects upon premarital sexual attitudes and behavior (Christensen & Johnson, 1978; Clayton & Bokemeier, 1980; Glenn &

Weaver, 1979; Harrison, Benett, & Globetti, 1969; Herold & Goodwin, 1981b; Libby et al., 1978; Mercer & Cohn, 1979; Schulz et al., 1977; Singh, 1980). Religiosity has typically been investigated and defined as the frequency of attendance at religious services. Generally, there has been an inverse relationship between religiosity and permissive sexual attitudes and behavior. However, some authors have stated that this variable has been influenced by other, intervening variables such as race and the relationship of the couple.

Schulz et al. (1977) found religiosity exerted a significant inhibiting effect upon premarital sexual behavior. Glenn and Weaver (1979) investigated the attitudes toward premarital, extramarital, and homosexual relations in the United States during the 1970s. They found that the most permissive sexual attitudes toward premarital sex existed among those persons not having a religious preference. Another study, by Mercer and Cohn (1979), found that attendance at religious services (religiosity) had an inhibiting effect upon sexual attitudes and behavior. However, it was found that it was a better predictor of conservative attitudes and behavior for males than for females. The authors stated that perhaps attendance at church services had a different meaning for males than for females.

In their investigation of adamant virgins, potential nonvirgins, and nonvirgins, Herold and Goodwin (1981a) found, using discriminative analysis, that religiosity was their third-best predictor of virginity status. In the sophisticated study by Libby et al. (1978), church attendance was found to have a significant negative effect upon permissive sexual attitudes. These authors state that their data support Reiss's propositions that there is a significant negative relationship between church attendance and permissiveness. They were unable, however, to support his claim that church attendance has a stronger effect upon females than males. These authors found that church attendance had a strong significant relationship to both male and female perceptions of closeness to the mother's standard, which was their strongest predictor of premarital sexual attitudes.

From these investigations, it can be seen that religiosity (church attendance) has been found to have a significant inverse relationship with permissive premarital sexual attitudes and behavior. However, there is conflicting investigation as to the possibility of other, intervening variables playing a significant role in the investigation of religiosity.

Interaction of family, personality dynamics, and social context of the individual

Very few studies have been conducted in which the interaction effects of the family, personality dynamics, and the social context were investigated in association with premarital sexual attitudes and behavior. One can only hypothesize about the possible interaction effect of personality dynamics (self-image, guilt), social context variables (gender identity and education), and family variables (parental attitudes) upon premarital sexual attitudes and behavior. There is a need for sophisticated studies, such as Libby et al. (1978) and Peplau et al. (1977), which investigate the interaction effects of these variables. Premarital sexuality is a private decision which is reached by two individuals in a couple relationship. Their decision to engage in premarital sexual activity is primarily a function of the personality characteristics of the individuals, the social context in which they live, their familys' backgrounds, and the relationship of the couple. Future investigations of premarital sexuality need to take into account the interaction of these highly important factors. Two studies which have investigated the interaction effect among various variables in premarital sexual behavior have been conducted by Herold and Goodwin (1981a, 1981b). In their investigation of premarital sexual guilt (1981b), the authors used discriminate analysis to investigate the effects of various variables as predictors of premarital sexual guilt in both first and current sexual intercourse. The authors found that those women who felt they were violating important family standards were the ones most likely to feel guilty about premarital sex. In addition, it was found that increasing sexual experience had a significant effect upon lowering the guilt that the individual experienced over time. Overall, these authors found that 26 percent of the variance in current sex guilt was accounted for by the number of sexual experiences, personal attitudes toward premarital intercourse, planning for first intercourse, and self-esteem. In these authors' investigation of adamant virgins, potential nonvirgins and nonvirgins (1981a), they once again used discriminate analysis based upon chi-square analyses. The best predictors for virginity status were peer experience with premarital intercourse, intimacy of the couple (the dating commitment), and religiosity (church attendance).

In the study by Libby et al. (1978), path analysis was used in exploring the relationship between a number of independent variables and premarital permissiveness. In this well-developed study, the investigators explored the relationship between different family and social context variables in predicting premarital sexual permissiveness. The variables that were included in this study were: (1) premarital permissiveness, which was the dependent variable, (2) family responsibility, (3) courtship involvement, (4) perceived closeness to peer standards, (5) perceived closeness to friends' standards, (6) perceived closeness to father's standards, (7) perceived closeness to mother's standards, (8) perceived closeness to date's standards, (9) family happiness, (10) church attendance, and (11) perceived parental sexual liberality. The authors developed a path model for male and female premarital sexual permissiveness. The significant variables in the male model were found to be church attendance, parental liberality, closeness to mother's standards, closeness to peers' standards, and perceived closeness to friends' standards. Closeness to mother's standards was the variable which had the most-significant effect. For females in the path model it was found that only three significant variables—church attendance, parental liberality, and closeness to mother's standards—were involved in the female's premarital sexual permissiveness. Once again, the closeness to mother's standards was the most-significant variable involved.

The authors have observed the importance of the interacting variables of family values, peers' values, and social context for premarital sexual behavior. These studies are excellent examples of the type of sophisticated and complex research needed in investigating the interaction effects of the family, social context, personality dynamics, and the relationship of the couple.

Relationship of the couple

The issue of commitment is receiving more investigative attention in relation to premarital sexual behavior. The media's portrayal of the sexual revolution is that men and women are having sex with one another indiscriminately. However, the scientific investigation of premarital sexual behavior presents a totally different picture. As in other times, commitment within the relationship plays a significant role in the sexual behavior of the couple. Lewis and Burr (1975) studied premarital coitus and commitment among college students from four different geographical areas in the United States. Data for this study was obtained during the period of 1967 to 1968. The researchers were interested in premarital intercourse related to varying levels of relationship commitment. Findings indicated a consistently larger portion of students experiencing intercourse at increasing levels of commitment. The levels of commitment were first date, frequent dating, going steady, and engaged. As expected, as the level of commitment increased, the likelihood of the student having intercourse increased. This held for both males and females; however, for the females, the differences in levels of commitment were greater. The authors state that "the data from this survey support the commitment proposition that the stage of commitment in courtship varies with the permissiveness of sexual behavior" (p. 77). The authors further state that "males and females in more equal numbers are limiting coitus to those with whom they have defined the relationship as one of some affection and commitment" (p. 78).

A study by Kirkendall (1967) investigated the degree of affection and commitment in relationship to premarital sexual behavior. The participants for Kirkendall's investigation were 200 college men who had had sexual intercourse with 668 females. Case histories were taken from the 200 men for each of the 668 sexual contacts that they had had. A scale was developed for the type of sexual partner and the degree of attachment with that partner for each sexual contact. The data from this study led Kirkendall to make several conclusions. First, he stated that the longer a couple knew each other prior to having their first intercourse, the greater the likelihood that their attachment to each other was stronger and the emotional involvement was more intense. Second, he noted that the couple's ability to communicate about their sexuality, whether before intercourse or after it, improved with the degree of emotional attachment within the relationship. Third, those couples who had deeper levels of emotional attachment were more likely to contracept or make plans for coping with the possible pregnancy than those at lesser levels of emotional involvement. Kirkendall's study indicates that the degree of emotional attachment between the couple is a significant factor in determining the sexual behavior between the couple.

Ehrmann (1959) noted that intercourse within the relationship proceeded along parallel lines to the development of emotional intensity and attachment within the relationship. Sexual intercourse was just the culminating event of a strong emotional attachment within the couple. Schofield (1965) studied an English population and noted findings similar to Ehrmann's: that sexual behavior proceeds along emotional attachment lines, with the culminating event being sexual intercourse. Both Ehrmann and Schofield have noted that couples move from no physical contact to hand holding, to kissing and hugging and caressing and fondling, to the culminating event of sexual intercourse. The developmental phases of the relationship play an important role in determining the sexual behavior and emotional intensity within the relationship. Clayton and Bokemeier (1980), in their review of premarital sex in the 70s, stated that a top priority for the future investigation of premarital sexuality should be the development of the sexual behavior of the individual and the couple in relationship to other developmental factors. The implication is simply that premarital sexuality must be studied within the context of the development of the relationship.

D'Augelli and Cross (1975) and D'Augelli and D'Augelli (1977) have studied the importance of moral reasoning and sex guilt within the relationship of the couple in association with premarital sexual behavior. The D'Augellis have stated that the proximal environment of sexual behavior is intrinsically interpersonal: "that is, an understanding of the proximal influences upon a person's decision to engage in a certain sexual behavior should begin with scrutinizing the interpersonal relationship that provides the environment for the behavior" (D'Augelli & D'Augelli, p. 47). In their work with moral reasoning and sexual guilt, they have found that moral decisions about sexuality are based upon the degree of affection within the relationship. They have suggested that the quality of the relationship plays a determining role in the degree of sexuality within the couple. They suggest that one can only understand the sexual behavior of the couple by understanding the meaning given to that sexual behavior by the individual and by the couple. They state that "viewing the behavior without considering the reasoning processes of each partner and of the dyad as a unit leads to a portrait of two bodies coupling instead of two people with unique pasts, presents, and futures engaging in personally and interpersonally meaningful behavior" (p. 61).

D'Augelli and Cross (1975), in their study of sex guilt and moral reasoning, found that the courtship or degree of relationship was a significant variable in determining the sexual experience of the couple. They defined courtship in this study as being various categories of the relationship such as casual dating, going steady, pinned, informally engaged, formally engaged, and living together. In their step-wise multiple regression analysis predicting the couple's total sexual experience, they found that sex guilt, moral reasoning, courtship relationship, and concordance of moral reasoning stage to be the predictors of the sexual experience of a couple. Once again, we can see that the degree of attachment of the couple is a determining factor in the sexual behavior within this relationship.

Herold and Goodwin (1981a), in their investigation of 408 college females and 106 high school females, found that dating behavior and degree of commitment played a significant role in determining the virginity or nonvirginity of the female. From the chi-square analysis of these questionnaires, it was found that dating frequency and dating commitment played significant roles in virginity status. From these chi-square analyses of the significant variables, a discriminate analysis was conducted which also indicated that dating commitment and dating frequency were significant variables in determining virginity status.

Peplau et al. (1977) investigated sexual intimacy in dating relationships in a previously mentioned study based upon a two-year study on the development of dating relationships. Three types of couples emerged in their analysis: sexual traditionalists, sexual moderates, and sexual liberals. This study analyzed not only the sexual experience of the couples but also their attitudes and how these affected their sexual behavior within the couple based upon the type of emotional commitment they had made. The sexually traditional couples, for example, felt that love alone was not sufficient for sexual intercourse and that the more permanent commitment of marriage was the necessary ingredient for sexual intercourse. The sexually moderate couples believed that intercourse could take place within the context of a relationship that was emotionally intimate and close. The third group, the sexual liberals, adhered to sexual standards which Reiss has labeled as permissiveness without affection. This group felt that premarital sexual intercourse without emotional intimacy was acceptable between couples that agree. In summary, Peplau et al. stated:

> The central distinction between these three orientations concerns the lengths between sexual intimacy and emotional intimacy. For traditionals, emotional intimacy developed in the context of limited sexual activity, sexual intercourse is tied not only to love but to a permanent commitment as well. A strong element in this orientation is the belief that premarital intercourse is morally wrong. For moderates, emotional intimacy sets the pace for sexual intimacy. As feelings of closeness and love increase, greater sexual exploration is possible. Moderates are oriented towards romanticism. They emphasize emotional closeness and love in their relationship. In contrast, liberals are more oriented toward eroticism. They view sex as a legitimate dating goal. For them, sexual intimacy and emotional intimacy need not be related. Sex can be enjoyed in its own right or sexual intimacy can be seen as a route to developing emotional intimacy. (p. 99)

In a study by Walster, Walster, and Traupmann (1978), the relationship between equity and premarital sexuality was studied. These investigators studied the effects of equity upon the sexual behavior of unmarried couples. The theoretical formulation for this study was based upon the predicted impact which equity is thought to have upon intimate relationships. They predicted:

> When individuals find themselves participating in inequitable relationships, they become distressed. The more inequitable the relationship, the more distress the individuals feel. . . . Individuals who discover they are in an inequitable relationship attempt to eliminate their distress by restoring equity. The greater the inequity that exists, the more distress they feel and the harder they try to restore equity. (p. 6).

In their study, Walster et al. predicted that the underbenefited male would exert more influence to have sex, while the underbenefited female would exert more influence to avoid having sex. Basically, they expected that the sexuality of the couple would be influenced by the equity/inequity within the couple's relationship. Participants completed Walster's global measures of participant's inputs, outputs in equity/inequity, the Austin measure of contentment/distress, a measure of double standard, a measure of the sexuality within the relationship, and a measure of the stability of the relationship. The results of this study indicated that those couples who felt slightly underbenefited or slightly overbenefited were far more content and happy than those who were greatly underbenefited or greatly overbenefited. The study found that those couples having most equity were the ones who tended to have the most satisfying sexual relationships. It was hypothesized that highly overbenefited or underbenefited relationships would have more sexual activity and the over- or underbenefited individual would exert more control. This hypothesis was not supported. It was found that in these relationships, those that were greatly underbenefited or overbenefited tended to be more restrictive in their sexual behavior.

These studies show how important it is that sexual behavior be investigated within the context of the relationship. The relationship plays a determining role in influencing the sexual behavior of the couple. There are many variables involved in the relationship which have impact upon the sexuality of the couple. Some of these variables are the development of the relationship of the couple, the emotional intimacy within the relationship, the degree of commitment within the relationship, the degree of affection within the relationship, and the equity within the relationship. This systemic approach to understanding sexual relationships continues to be a fertile ground for future investigation into premarital sexual behavior. It would appear that sexual behavior can no longer be investigated within the isolation of only the individual. A transactional approach which takes into account the many complex variables of the relationship needs to be used in future investigations of premarital sexuality.

CONCLUSION

More young people today are having sexual intercourse before marriage than at any point in history. The attitudes of these young people are becoming increasingly more permissive. However, the decision to participate in premarital sexual intercourse is based upon the interaction of a composite set of determining variables: the personality characteristics of the individual, the family of origin, the social context, and the relationship of the couple. Some of the primary factors within these variables which determine premarital sexual behavior are guilt, self-esteem, religiosity, sexual myths, sexual standards of peers and parents, and the degree of affection and commitment within the relationship. These appear to be some of the more-important factors which interact in influencing the sexual behavior of young adults who have never been married.

Another population which must be considered in the future investigation of premarital sexual behavior are those persons who are older and single and those persons who are divorced. This is becoming a very large population in the United States, and the sexual behavior of these people who have no primary love relationships must be considered. Premarital sexual behavior is becoming somewhat of a misnomer in that more and more young people are choosing to have sexual intercourse prior to marriage. However, there appear to be certain set criteria which are influential in helping persons make this decision of when, with whom, and where they choose to become sexually active.

REFERENCES

Adorno, T. W., Frenkel-Brunswick, E., Levison, D. J., & Sanford, R. N. *The authoritarian personality.* New York: Harper & Row, 1950.

Applebaum, A. S., Tuma, J. M., & Johnson, J. H. Internal-external control and assertiveness on subjects high and low in social desirability. *Psychological Reports, 37,* 1975, 319–322.

Athanasiou, R., & Sarkin, R. Premarital sexual behavior and postmarital adjustment. *Archives of Sexual Behavior,* 1974, *3*(3), 207–225.

Bauman, K. E., & Wilson, R. R. Premarital sexual attitudes of unmarried university students: 1968 versus 1972. *Archives of Sexual Behavior,* 1976, *5*(1), 29–37.

Christensen, H. T., & Johnson, L. B. Premarital coitus and the southern black: A comparative view. *Journal of Marriage and the Family,* 1978, *40,* 721–732.

Clayton, R. R., & Bokemeier, J. L. Premarital sex in the seventies. *Journal of Marriage and the Family,* 1980, *42*(4), 759–775.

D'Augelli, J. F., & Cross, H. J. Relationship of sex guilt and moral reasoning to premarital sex in college women and in couples. *Journal of Consulting and Clinical Psychology,* 1975, *43*(1), 40–47.

D'Augelli, J. F., & D'Augelli, A. R. Moral reasoning and premarital sexual behavior: Toward reasoning about relationships. *Journal of Social Issues,* 1977, *33*(2), 46–67.

Ehrmann, W. *Premarital dating behavior.* New York: Holt, Rinehart & Winston, 1959.

Eysenck, H. J. Personality and sexual adjustment. *British Journal of Psychiatry,* 1971, *118,* 593–608.

Glenn, N. D., & Weaver, C. N. Attitudes toward premarital, extramarital and homosexual relations in the U.S. in the 1970's. *Journal of Sex Research,* 1979, *15,* 108–118.

Harrison, D. E., Benett, W. H., & Globetti, G. Attitudes of rural youth towards premarital sexual permissiveness. *Journal of Marriage and the Family,* 1969, *31,* 783–787.

Herold, E. S., & Goodwin, M. S. Adamant virgins, potential non-virgins and non-virgins. *Journal of Sex Research,* 1981, *17,* 97–113. (a)

Herold, E. S., & Goodwin, M. S. Premarital sexual guilt. *Canadian Journal of Behavioral Science,* 1981, *13*(1), 65–75. (b)

Hersch, P. D., & Scheibe, K. E. Reliability and validity of internal-external control as a personality dimension. *Journal of Consulting Psychology,* 1967, *31,* 609–613.

Jesser, C. J. Male responses to direct verbal sexual initiatives of females. *Journal of Sex Research*, 1978, pp. 118–128.

Jurich, A. P., & Jurich, J. A. The effect of cognitive moral development upon selection of premarital sexual standards. *Journal of Marriage and the Family*, 1974, *36*, 736–741.

Kemper, T. Reference groups, socialization and achievement. *American Sociological Review*, 1968, *33*, 31–46.

Kirkendall, L. A. *Premarital intercourse and interpersonal relations.* New York: Julian Press, 1961.

Kirkendall, L. A. Characteristics of sexual decision making. *Journal of Sex Research*, 1967, *3*, 201–211.

Langston, R. D. Sex guilt and sex behavior in college students. *Journal of Personality Assessment*, 1973, *37*, 467–472.

LaPlante, M. N., McCormick, N., & Brannigan, G. G. Living the sexual script: College students' views of influence in sexual encounters. *Journal of Sex Research*, 1980, *16*, 338–355.

Lee, T. R., & Mancini, J. A. Locus of control and premarital sexual behaviors. *Psychological Reports*, 1981, *49*, 882.

Lewis, R. A., & Burr, W. R. Premarital coitus and commitment among college students. *Archives of Sexual Behavior*, 1975, *4*, 73–79.

Libby, R. W., Gray, L., & White, M. A test and reformulation of reference group and role correlates of premarital sexual permissiveness theory. *Journal of Marriage and the Family*, 1978, *40*(1), 79–92.

MacQuordale, P., & DeLamater, J. Self image and premarital sexuality. *Journal of Marriage and the Family*, 1979, *41*(2), 327–339.

Mahoney, E. R. Age differences and attitudes change toward premarital coitus. *Archives of Sexual Behavior*, 1978, *7*(5), 493–501.

Mahoney, E. R. Religiosity and sexual behavior among heterosexual college students. *Journal of Sex Research*, 1980, *16*, 97–113.

McCormick, N. Come-ons and put-offs: Unmarried students' strategies for having and avoiding sexual intercourse. *Psychology of Women Quarterly*, 1979, *4*, 194–211.

Mendelsohn, M. J., & Mosher, D. L. Effects of sex guilt and premarital sexual permissiveness on role played sex education and moral attitudes. *Journal of Sex Research*, 1979, *15*, 174–183.

Mercer, G. W., & Cohn, P. M. Gender differences in the integration of conservatism, sex urges and sexual behavior among college students. *Journal of Sex Research*, 1979, *15*, 129–142.

Mirande, A. M. Reference group theory in adolescent sexual behavior. *Journal of Marriage and the Family*, 1968, *30*, 572–578.

Mosher, D. L. Sex guilt and sex myth in college men and women. *Journal of Sex Research*, 1979, *15*, 224–234.

Mosher, D. L., & Abramson, P. R. Subjective sexual arousal to films of masturbation. *Journal of Consulting and Clinical Psychology*, 1977, *45*, 796–807.

Mosher, D. L., & Cross, H. J. Sex guilt and premarital sexual experiences of college students. *The Journal of Consulting and Clinical Psychology*, 1971, *36*, 27–32.

Newcomb, T. *Personality and social change.* Hinsdale, Ill.: Dryden Press, 1943.

Newcomb, T. Attitude development as a function of reference groups: The Bennington study. In E. E. Macabee, T. M. Newcomb, & E. L. Harley (Eds.), *Readings in social psychology.* New York: Holt, Rinehart & Winston, 1958.

Peplau, L. A., Rubin, Z., & Hill, C. T. Sexual intimacy and dating relationships. *Journal of Social Issues,* 1977, *33*(2), 86–109.

Reiss, I. L., & Miller, D. C. Heterosexual permissiveness: A theoretical analysis. In W. R. Burr, R. Hill, F. I. Nye, & I. L. Reiss (Eds.), *Contemporary theories about the family* (Vol. 1). New York: The Free Press, 1979. Pp. 57–100.

Robison, I. E., & Jedlicka, D. Change in sexual attitudes and behavior of college students from 1965 to 1980: A research note. *Journal of Marriage and the Family,* 1982, *44*(1), 237–240.

Rotter, J. B. Generalized expectancies for internal versus external control of reinforcement. *Psychological Monographs,* 1966, *80*(1), 609.

Schofield, M. *The sexual behavior of young people.* London: Longmans, Green, 1965.

Schulz, B., Bohrnstedt, G. W., Borgatta, E. F., & Evans, R. R. Explaining premarital sexual intercourse among college students: A causal model. *Social Forces,* 1977, *56*(1), 148–165.

Simon, W., Berger, A. S., & Gagnon, J. H. Beyond anxiety and fantasy: The coital experiences of college youth. *Journal of Youth and Adolescence,* 1972, *1*(3), 203–222.

Singh, B. K. Trends and attitudes toward premarital sexual relations. *Journal of Marriage and the Family,* 1980, *42*(2), 387–393.

Spanier, G. B. Sources of sex information in premarital sexual behavior. *The Journal of Sex Research,* 1977, *13*(2), 73–88.

Stratton, J. R., & Spitzer, S. P. Sexual permissiveness and self-evaluation: A question of substance and a question of method. *Journal of Marriage and the Family,* 1970, *29*, 434–441.

Teevan, J. Reference groups and premarital sexual behavior. *Journal of Marriage and the Family,* 1972, *34*, 288–292.

Udry, J. R., Bauman, K. E., & Morris, N. M. Changes in premarital coital experience of recent decade-of-birth cohorts of urban American women. *Journal of Marriage and the Family,* 1975, *37*(4), 783–787.

Walster, E., Walster, G. W., & Traupmann, J. Equity and premarital sex. *Journal of Personality and Social Psychology,* 1978, *36*(1), 82–92.

Zelnik, M., & Kanter, J. F. Sexual and contraceptive experience of young unmarried women in the United States. *Family Planning Perspectives,* 1977, *9*, 55–70.

Zelnik, M., & Kanter, J. F. Sexual activity, contraceptive use and pregnancy among metropolitan area teenagers: 1971–1979. *Family Planning Perspectives,* 1980, *12*, 230–237.

Chapter 16

Marital Sexuality

WILLIAM C. TALMADGE

Marital sexuality is a subject which has received little scientific attention. Sexuality in marriage is one of the most popularly discussed topics with counselors, ministers, and psychotherapists. Next to the parent-child relationship, the marital relationship is the most intimate relationship formed between two people. Most couples go into it expecting that sex will be heavenly and that their marriage will be wonderful. However, couples soon learn that their relationship and their sexuality are not an end but an organic process at which they must continue to work. There are few scientific investigations which have focused upon the sexuality of functional and satisfied couples; very little attention has been given to the development of sexuality within the marital context. Primarily, marital sexuality has been discussed in the context of sexual dysfunction, an approach which offers a sharply skewed viewpoint.

The development of sexuality within the context of the marriage is a complex relationship of multiple variables. The area of debate today is the relationship between marital satisfaction and sexual satisfaction. What brings about sexual compatibility or sexual satisfaction within marriage? Masters and Johnson (1970) assert that the happily married couples have happy sex. Many theorists believe today that happily married couples tend to have more satisfactory sexual relationships with their partner.

Spanier and Lewis (1980) reviewed the scientific investigations that had been conducted on marital quality in the 1970s. They found primarily three areas of focus. These areas were sex differences, the effects of children on marital quality, and the relationship between marital quality and the marital career. Only five articles were found which indirectly dealt with marital quality and sexuality. Three of these articles focused upon marital quality and extramarital relationships (Bell, Turner, & Rosen, 1975; Edwards & Booth, 1976; Glass & Wright, 1977). The other two articles dealt with premarital sexuality and postmarital adjustment (Athanasiou & Sarkin, 1974). From Spanier and Lewis's review of the marital quality literature, it can be seen that very little scientific investigation has been conducted during the 1970s on marital happiness, satisfaction, and adjustment in relationship to marital sexuality.

The purpose of this chapter is to discuss the complex set of factors involved in marital sexuality from a transactional viewpoint. This will be accomplished through the following: (1) a discussion of the purpose of marital sexuality, (2) a description of some of the commonly held myths about marital sexuality, and (3) an examination of the interacting factors of personality, social context, physical state, family history, and personality of the relationship which go into the formation of marital sexuality.

Marital sexuality is an ongoing, dynamic process which is in continual change. These changes in marital sexuality are brought about by personality, social context, physical state, family history, and relationship factors which are interacting within the bond of the married couple. These changes within the sexuality of the couple continue to bring about a new formation of the sexuality of the individual.

Next to the parent-child relationship, the marital relationship is the most intense, vulnerable, and dependent relationship. It is in this type of relationship that sexuality occurs. Each individual in the marital pair brings to the relationship certain expectations, personality dynamics, cultural context, respective physical health, and a distinct familial background. From this complex set of factors, two people are joined together in a bond in which they seek to love and gratify each other for the rest of their lives. This type of marital bond is often a source of pleasure, pain, delight, fear, security, insecurity, happiness, and unhappiness. It is the author's primary assumption that the manner in which this configuration of factors is integrated and acted out is the determinant of the relationship's sexual function and satisfaction. The manner in which this dynamic system operates is the determining force in the compatibility, satisfaction, and happiness of the couple with regard to their marital sexuality. Sex in marriage, when deeply enjoyed and freely given and taken, can be a most intimate bonding experience between the couple.

One of the primary products of this intense bond between husband and wife is affection, a characteristic which often plays an important role in the sexuality of the couple. As Bowlby (1969, 1973) and Harlow (1958, 1962) have shown, affection is one of the most basic dimensions in the primary bonding between parent and child, and this later transforms into the marital relationship (Prescott & Wallace, 1978; Wallace, 1981). The quality of affection within the parent-child relationship is a determining factor in the affectional quality within the marital pair and the subsequent marital sexuality of the pair.

Many theorists believe that having an adequately functioning sexual relationship is an important factor in marital happiness and satisfaction. However, there have been a few studies which have investigated the role of sexuality within married couples (Chesney, Blakeney, Cole, & Chan, 1981; Frank, Anderson, & Rubenstein, 1978; Hoch, Safir, Peres, & Shepher, 1981). These findings support one primary concept: *Marital sexual functioning is based upon a complex set of interacting variables within the relationship of the marriage. It is the couple's total relationship which is the determinant in the sexual adequacy and satisfaction of the marital pair.* These studies are in direct contradiction to older studies which stated, "Coitus is the index to marriage. If the data in this study reinforce any one concept it is that satisfactory sexual relations are necessary to fully successful and adjusted union" (Dickinson & Beam, 1931, p. 56). However, as Gorer (1971) has noted, the vast majority of married couples believe that marital sexuality is very important in marriage, but sex is not the determining factor in making a marriage happy and satisfactory.

Neither Freud (1953) nor Ellis (1938) gave primary attention to marital sexuality. Freud was interested in the sexual instinct in relationship to psychosexual development and personality formation. Ellis was more interested in dispelling sexual myths and surveying and observing sexual behavior. He devoted great energy toward distinguishing between pathological sex and normal sex. However, in *The Psychology of Sex,* Ellis gives one chapter to sexuality in marriage. This chapter attempts to dispel the myth of sexual abstinence within marriage which was being perpetuated during this period by people such as Sylvester Graham and John Harvey Kellogg. These men had laid down strict rules about the permissible frequency of intercourse and discussed the need for constraint of sexual intercourse within marriage. Their reasoning for abstinence was based upon factors of physiology, maturity, and productivity. Thus, in his chapter on marriage and sexuality, Ellis was focusing upon dispelling the myth for sexual abstinence by marital partners.

The marital relationship is traditionally the only relationship in which sexual intercourse is sanctioned. However, throughout history, the need for free expression of sexual intercourse has been debated, and even today, specific types of sexual behavior within marriage are outlawed.

PURPOSES OF MARITAL SEXUALITY[1]

There are basically five purposes of marital sexuality. Each of these will be discussed separately. The first purpose of marital sexuality is *procreation*. Sexual desire and expression in marriage is nature's instinctual drive for the survival of the species. Marital sexuality brings about a union for the perpetuation of the species; it also creates a union or a context in which the species may be born, sheltered, protected, and nurtured. In most societies, marital sexuality has been the means through which infants were brought into the world (Marshall & Suggs, 1971). The marital bond arranges a social context in which the infant can be emotionally, socially, and physiologically nurtured. As noted by Ellis (1938):

> Formerly marriage and procreation were one in aim, indivisible. To recommend marriage meant to permit procreation; to advise against procreation meant to prohibit marriage and permanently to impair the happiness of the lives thus condemned to solitude as well as indirectly to encourage prostitution or other undesirable methods of sexual relief. (p. 207)

Procreation within marriage has many strong biosocial and biopsychological reasons. Thus, procreation is one of the primary ways in which couples may become significantly bonded in marital sexuality. Many couples describe the birth of a child as being one of the times in which they have felt closest to each other.

The second purpose of marital sexuality is *relational*. Marital sexuality is a means of expressing one's affection, fondness, and love for the other. It is a means for couples to be intimate. For marital couples to connect sexually requires that they be trusting, cooperative, vulnerable, open, and dependent. Marital sexuality, when expressed openly between two desiring partners, can be a means of primary physical bonding between the couple. As Morris (1971) has noted, the human adult, unlike other primate species, is able to regain within the marital bond that early intimate attachment between infant and mother.

Morris has stated that humans go through a sequential process which he has divided into 12 stages. Humans proceed through these stages in developing this unique attachment which we call a love affair. Within marital sexuality, we have the means for making both physiological and emotional contact with the loved object. The marital sexual rela-

---

[1] See Chapter 36 on sexual dysfunctions for basic assumptions in the marital relationship which strongly affect the sexuality of the couple.

tionship can be a means of expressing the most deep, intimate, hidden feelings for one another. It can be a time when couples lay aside their shields and facades and openly express to one another in a most-vulnerable way who they really are.

The third purpose of marital sexuality is *recreational*. Marital sexuality can be an enjoyable experience. It can be a means for the couple to play with each other and relax with each other. Marital sexuality is a means of pleasuring each other. However, pleasure was frowned upon during early colonialism and the Victorian period. Historically, Western culture has had a stronger ethic for work productivity than it has had for pleasure. Much of the prohibition against pleasure has had to do with its interference with the productivity of society. Sexuality, with its ability to give pleasure, excitement, and relaxation to the individual, has been prohibited because of its association with pleasure. As Ellis (1938) noted, contraception allows people the opportunity to have sexual pleasure without procreation. This whole notion appears to be in conflict with our puritan ethic of productivity.

Another complicating factor which emerged during the Victorian period was the philosophy that established sexuality as a fixed energy system. This philosophy held that adults have only so many orgasms and that after these orgasms have been depleted, the adult is no longer able to procreate. It is very fitting that the Victorian term for orgasm was *to spend* (Murstein, 1974a). Frequent sexual intercourse was unhealthy because it drained the nervous and the biological systems of the adult. Thus, sexuality was strongly suppressed by the Victorians for what they thought were very good reasons. It has been found through various physiological studies of the sexual response cycle that having frequent orgasms does not deplete the ability to be orgasmic at another time, nor does it deplete fertility.

Also, sexual functioning and sexual intercourse are no longer believed to inhibit mental, mechanical, or athletic functioning. Until the 1950s and 1960s, it was believed by some recreational and physical education experts that having sexual intercourse prior to participating in a sporting activity could inhibit one's performance. Although many of these myths about sexuality in relationship to pleasure and recreation have been dispelled, there is still an underlying inhibition against having pleasure. One of the primary tasks of sex therapists is to enhance, encourage, and incorporate sexual pleasuring into the couple's relationship. The guilt that many individuals feel because of their sexual urges and enjoyment, comes directly from our historical antipleasure roots.

The fourth purpose of marital sexuality is that it is *a means for couples to recognize problems within their relationship*. This purpose assumes that psychogenic sexual problems are a symptom of a difficulty within the marital system. When couples notice that their sexual desire begins to decline over a prolonged period of time, this may be a symbol for the expression of difficulty within the relationship, possibly a lack of intimacy. Therefore, viewing marital sexuality in this manner allows the couple to use their satisfaction with marital sexuality as a barometer of relationship satisfaction.

The fifth purpose of marital sexuality is the *celebration and the symbolic locking of the marital bond* (Jourard, 1961). Marital sexuality can be a life-enhancing force. As some researchers have noted, there is a strong relationship between physical health, happiness, and sexual satisfaction. Marital sexuality in terms of this purpose can be a rejoicing of the couple's union.

MARITAL SEXUALITY MYTHS

1. Sex in marriage comes easy. This myth expresses that marital sexuality is basically an end and not a process. Believers of this myth expect that they will have sex whenever they want it and that there will be no problems. Because of the institution of marriage, there is a belief that sexuality or the expression of one's sexuality will be unencumbered with problems. This myth denies the developmental changes of the individuals and of the marital relationship. For example, the developmental changes in the individual (such as changes in career direction) may have a direct effect on the marital sexuality. It is not uncommon to see an individual have a decline in sexual desire because of job performance and pressures. Developmental changes might be seen in the relationship. A most-common one is the birth of a child. This type of decline in marital coitus and satisfaction has been noted by James (1981) and Cuber (1975).

This myth also denies the importance of sexual communication, which is a most-important variable in marital sexual satisfaction. Researchers have found that the greater the degree of marital sexual communication, the greater the degree of marital sexual satisfaction (Chesney et al., 1981; Hoch et al., 1981; Honeycutt, Wilson, & Parker, 1982). There are many other factors which contribute to satisfied marital sexuality, such as sexual knowledge and myths held by the individuals and the couple, familial sexual attitudes, and the degree of affection within the relationship. The degree to which sex is easy and satisfying within the relationship is much more dependent upon the relationship factors than upon the fact that a couple is simply married.

2. Sexual frequency is a prime indicator of sexual compatibility and marital happiness. This myth has been explored by numerous investigators throughout the past 50 years. Terman (1938) investigated numerous psychological factors in relationship to marital happiness. One of the primary sexual factors which he investigated was frequency of sexual intercourse of the couple. Terman stated that the frequency which sexual intercourse occurs between husband and wife must be to a large extent a function of their sexual drive. But it also may be a function of their general compatibility and even an effective influence enhancing or interfering with compatibility. However, after tabulating his data, Terman stated:

> It appears that in a total population of married couples, the frequency of intercourse is determined by the joint influence of biological factors and of habit and bears little relation to the congeniality of the mates. It seems almost incredible that intercourse should be almost as frequent in the most unhappily mated couples as in the most happily mated, but such seems to be the case. (p. 277)

A study by Heath (1978), which was a longitudinal study of married professional men, found that psychological health does not predict the frequency of marital sexual relations nor the degree of sexual frustration in professional men. The frequency of coitus is not an indicator of marital satisfaction. However, sexual satisfaction, not frequency of intercourse, is highly correlated with marital satisfaction. The *mutuality* of enjoyment is the key factor in marital sexual compatibility.

Another popular misconception is that frequency of sexual intercourse is high initially in the relationship and there is a steady decline over the years. As Cuber (1975) and James (1981) have noted, this myth does not seem to hold true. There is a decline in coitus rates during the first year of marriage; however, over the term of the relationship, coitus rates appear to decline and rise in relation to the mood of the relationship. Gorer (1971), in his study of a large English population, made similar findings to those of Cuber and of James with regard to the misconception of a steady decline of sexual activity in married couples. He states, "This research completely fails to bear out the generalization made by Kinsey and his associates that sexual activity declines consistently from adolescence onwards and that the young are inevitably more potent than their elders" (p. 116).

Two classic studies have been conducted on preferred and actual coitus behavior among married couples. The first was by Wallin and Clark (1958), and a replication of the study was conducted by Levinger (1966). In the Wallin and Clark study, two questions were asked of the husbands and wives: (1) About how many times per month would you prefer to have sexual intercourse? (2) About how many times per month do you think your wife or husband would prefer to have sexual intercourse? The purpose in their study was to examine the cultural sexual ideology that men desire and require sexual intercourse more

Table 1

Mean monthly preferred frequencies of coitus reported for self and spouse*

| | Class A (husband and wife same preference) | | Class B (husband's preference more) | | Class C (wife's preference more) | |
	Wallin and Clark	Levinger	Wallin and Clark	Levinger	Wallin and Clark	Levinger
Number of couples	234	28	149	23	76	9
Husband's ratings						
Of self	7.69	6.71	12.57	13.13	6.49	9.28
Of wife	7.23	5.89	8.89	7.86	6.88	6.50
Wife's ratings						
Of self	7.39	10.07	6.24	10.78	11.67	17.11
Of husband	9.00	6.60	10.62	6.52	11.79	14.66

* Data from Wallin, P., and Clark, A. L., "Cultural Norms and Husbands' and Wives' Reports of Their Marital Partners' Preferred Frequency of Coitus Relative to Their Own," *Sociometry* 21 (1958), pp. 247–54; and Levinger, G., "Systematic Distortion in Spouses' Reports of Preferred and Actual Sexual Behavior," *Sociometry* 29 (1966), pp. 291–99.

often than women. After the couples had completed these questions, they were divided into three groups: Class A was couples in which husband and wife had the same preference; Class B was couples in which the husband's preference was higher than the wife's; and Class C was those in which the wife had the higher preference.

Table I gives a comparison of the Wallin and Clark (1958) data and the Levinger (1966) data with this type of classification of couples. Couple members who differed by three or more in their preferred monthly coital rate were placed in either Class B or Class C. In all three groups, the wives reported that their spouses preferred coitus at a higher frequency than they did. Even in the group of women who preferred coitus at a more-frequent rate, they reported that their spouses desired intercourse more than they did. In general, the wives overestimated their spouses' desired frequency, while the husbands underestimated their wives' desire of coital frequency. Thus, this study would support the cultural belief that men, in the eye of both the man and the woman, require more sexual intercourse than females.

Levinger (1966) made another comparison with the Wallin and Clark (1958) study by dividing the couples into two groups: (1) couples in which one partner perceived their desired frequency of coitus as similar to the other partner's were hypothesized to be more satisfied; (2) those where there was a discrepancy between the partners' desired frequency were hypothesized to be more maritally dissatisfied. The significant findings were that both husbands and wives who perceived high similarity had higher sexual satisfaction than did the less-similar groups. However, with regard to marital satisfaction, only the husbands in both the Levinger and the Wallin and Clark studies had greater marital satisfaction when both husbands' and wives' actual frequency of coitus was similar. Thus, a more-accurate statement of how sexual frequency relates to sexual compatibility and marital satisfaction would be that when couples perceive their desired coital rates as being highly similar, then there is a stronger likelihood for marital and sexual satisfaction. It can be noted that absolute coital frequencies have little to do with sexual and marital satisfaction. Coital rates may have much more to do with such factors as the power in the relationship, submission, poor self-image, assertive/passive styles, or anxiety. It is not uncommon to see a couple in which there is a high frequency of coital interaction and a high degree of marital dissatisfaction. The high rate of coital frequency may be more of a sign of an imbalance of power, adherence to old cultural beliefs, or poor self-esteem in one of the marital partners. The better predictor of sexual and marital satisfaction based upon sexual frequency is to relate the similarity of desired and actual coital frequency as reported by the marital partners. The greater the degree of similarity between the ratings of the partners, the greater the likelihood of marital and sexual satisfaction.

3. Poor sex leads to unhappy marriages and extramarital sexual affairs. The basis for this myth (reverting to the second myth) is that if a person only has high rates of sex, uses many varied techniques, and therefore keeps their partner happy with sex, then the marriage will be happy. There is a belief that high sexual frequency makes good marriages. However, as we have shown in the second myth, this is not the case. Neither high nor low rates of sexual frequency lead to marital happiness or unhappiness. Sexual incompatibility is simply a symptom of marital unhappiness or an imbalance within the relationship and is not the causative factor for the difficulty within the relationship. More likely, the difficulties within the relationship—such as poor communication style, an imbalance in power, lack of equity, and imbalance in independence/dependence styles—are the reasons for the difficulty within the sexual relationship as well as the marital unhappiness. Lederer and Jackson (1968) have stated that "unsatisfactory sexual relations are a symptom of marital discord, not a cause of it" (p. 116). Sexual compatibility in couples leads to neither happy nor unhappy marital relationships. A much better indicator of marital happiness from the sexuality realm would be the degree of similar perception about sexuality among the marital partners and the degree of sexual communication.

Cuber (1975) has noted that extramarital sexual affairs are not brought about by poor marital sexuality. He states, "Spouses may deeply disappoint one another in many ways quite apart from sex; these disappointments may merely be voids such as a lack of companionship, inability to communicate, or simple absence" (p. 54). Sprenkle and Weis (1978) have noted that the motivations for extramarital sexual affairs must be closely examined. One cannot automatically assume that extramarital sexuality is brought about by poor sex. In fact, it has been found that sexuality in the marriage often has very little to do with the extramarital affair, and reasons for extramarital sexual affairs must be examined from both an individual and a relational viewpoint. As these authors have noted, the research on the relationship between extramarital sexual affairs and marital sexual satisfaction appears to be contradictory and not definitive. However, it would seem that marital sexuality has very little to do with whether or not one of the marital partners engages in extramarital sex. The quality of the marital relationship is the area of concern.

4. The sexual relationship and marriage relationship are separate entities.   This type of myth is often expressed in couples where you hear one state, "Just because we aren't getting along, doesn't mean we can't have fun with sex." This myth implies that there is no relationship between the marital factors and the factors which contribute to sexual satisfaction within the couple. However, as numerous researchers have observed, sexual and marital satisfaction are highly related variables (Chesney et al., 1981; Ficher, 1976; Heath, 1978, 1979; Hoch et al., 1981; Levinger, 1966; Meissner, 1978; Roffe & Britt, 1981; Schenk, Horst, & Armin, 1983; Terman, 1938; Udry, 1974). These researchers have demonstrated that the marital relationship factors are significantly related to satisfaction with sexuality in the marriage. Factors which seem to be related between the two are the degree of communication, affective tone within the relationship, self-disclosure, prior experiences with premarital sex, and degree of intimacy. However, there appears to be a small group of couples who may have pathological marital relationships but are highly satisfied with one another sexually. With these couples, it appears that acting sexually is their only means of connecting or communicating with one another (Lederer & Jackson, 1968). Their sexuality serves a grounding function.

5. Sex in marriage creates intimacy.   It is implied in this myth that coital contact or sexual expression between the marital pair causes intimacy within the relationship. This type of mythology is especially prevalent among young married couples and couples within the final phase of courtship. Waring (1981), in his investigation of marital intimacy, found that styles of communication and self-disclosure were more likely the means for establishing marital intimacy. He defined intimacy as being a composite of (1) affection; (2) expressiveness; (3) compatibility, which he defines as the ability of the couple to work and play together comfortably; (4) cohesion, which he defines as commitment; (5) sexuality, which he defines as the couple's ability to communicate their needs and have them satisfactorily fulfilled; (6) conflict resolution; (7) autonomy; and (8) identity, which he defines as the couple's level of self-confidence and self-esteem. Waring suggests that the primary means through which couples may become intimate is through disclosing themselves, one to another. Within his definition, sexuality plays a very small role in the total picture of intimacy.

Another significant factor in determining marital intimacy is the affectional climate in the family of origin and how it affects subsequent affective sexual behaviors. Wallace (1981), conducting this type of investigation with 32 males and 25 females, found that familial affectional climate greatly determined affectional and sexual climate in subsequent relationships. He states:

> In summary and recognizing that inferences may be limited by the uniqueness of the sample, it may be stated with considerable degree of assurance that the affectional climate in the family of origin is not only related to subsequent expression of affection and to attitudes toward sexual expression, but that the three variables are interrelated in a complex fashion with each other and with expressions of sexuality during adulthood. It might prove useful to conceive of the affectional climate in the family out of which current affectional behavior, attitudes and sexual expression emerge. (p. 305)

In conclusion, similar findings (Chesney et al., 1981; Hoch et al., 1981) have been noted as to the importance of affectional climate in determining the intimacy within the relationship.

6. Happily married couples do not have sex problems. This myth states simply that couples who are happily married do not encounter sexual difficulties. This is a great misconception on the part of the general population. For one, it simply denies developmental changes in marital relationships. For example, there is a depression in sexual frequency during the first year after a child's birth (Cuber, 1975; James, 1981). Secondly, couples who have not sought sex therapy and who see their marriage as happy or satisfactory as defined on a number of measures, have experienced various types of specific sexual problems. In their study, Chesney et al. (1981) found that 35.4 percent of the males and 41.7 percent of the females were currently experiencing at least one type of specific sexual difficulty. Hoch and his Israeli group (Hoch et al., 1981) found in an Israeli population that 25 percent of the husbands had had some specific type of ejaculatory difficulty and that 60 percent of the wives had had some problem with reaching orgasm. Similar findings have been noted by Frank et al. (1978) in their investigation of "normal couples." These three studies support that happily married couples do, at some point during their marital relationship, experience specific types of sexual difficulties. However, what makes this a problem for which the couple seeks therapeutic intervention or not *is determined by the marital relationship.* For those couples who have sexual difficulties but do not seek therapeutic intervention, these difficulties do not seem to become significant problems within the relationship. Factors such as the ability to communicate (and communicate about sex), problem resolution, and the affectional quality within the relationship play a significant role in resolving the sexual difficulty within the relationship.

7. If I am only pretty or handsome enough and do all of the right things that my partner wishes, then we will have a most satisfying marital sexual relationship.   This myth denies the individual within the relationship. It implies that if one partner only is and does what the other partner wants, then they will find marital sexual bliss with one another. This misconception denies that one partner may possibly have changes occurring that are outside of the relationship but have an impact upon the relationship. These sorts of outside intervening factors may not be subject to change by the partner within the relationship. A typical example of this myth is the marital couple in which the husband has had a hard day at the office, is angry about a number of situations with his employees, and has driven home in the rush hour traffic. Upon reaching his home, he turns into the driveway, walks into the house, and is greeted by his wife, who is wearing an attractive negligee. In the background is candlelight, champagne, and romantic music, at which point, the husband says, "I think I'll go hit golf balls tonight." Both individuals within this marital bond have a specific agenda in this encounter. Just because the wife is trying to provide her husband with what she thinks he would desire does not necessarily mean that they will be able to find happy sexual satisfaction on that evening. Unfortunately, many couples have accepted this misconception which is portrayed in the media. Couples receive a bombardment from TV, popular magazines, and movies which lead them to believe that if only they will act as romantically as possible—i.e., wearing the "right" type of cologne or perfume, drinking the "right" type of beverages, and going to the "right" places—then they will find marital sexual happiness with one another (Lederer & Jackson, 1968; LoPiccolo & Heiman, 1977).

8. Marital sex is always romantic, exciting, and orgasmic.   This is another popular misconception held by a number of couples in the beginning of their marital relationships. There is the expectation that sex between the couple will always be pleasurable, fun, easy, and delightful. These sexual expectations are unrealistic and often lead to harsh disappointment within the marriage. Unless these high expectations can be resolved, the couple soon finds itself in a state of disappointment and resentment. As noted by Segraves (1982), our representational set of how an event or an individual is going to interact with ourselves and the degree to which this representational set is fulfilled or not greatly determines the amount of marital unhappiness and discord. One of the early tasks in couples psychotherapy is to clarify the expectations which each marital partner holds for the other and the expectations of what the relationship holds. As previously stated, the media has played a significant role in reinforcing these romantic and exciting expectations of marital sexuality. Numerous romantic novels have portrayed the wedding night as a night of sexual ecstasy. However, as Masters and Johnson have noted, the wedding night is often the place where sexual dysfunctions originate. In general, the social context plays a significant role in influencing our expectations of marital sexuality. In conclusion, this popular misconception simply denies the developmental stresses and strains which marital relationships experience. It discounts other reality factors such as physical health, personal and career crises, and self-image which disturb the balance of the marriage.

FACTORS OF MARITAL SEXUAL SATISFACTION

In this section, we will look at the various factors which are involved in marital sexuality. A simple model that can be used in discussing these factors divides the marital relationship into the five interacting vectors. These interacting vectors are the personality of the individual, the social context within which the relationship takes place, the physical state of the individual, the family history of the individual, and the personality of the relationship which is formed from the variables within the interaction. Figure 1 gives an illustration of this type of interaction in marital sexuality. Table 2 is a listing of the variables under each factor.

Personality factors

Eysenck (1971) stated there has been very little investigation into the relationship between personality variables and sexuality. At this point in time, only a small number of scientific investigations have been conducted into the relationship between personality and sexuality (Talmadge, 1979). Masters and Johnson (1970) have stated that pleasurable marital sexual relationships are based on numerous variables

Figure 1

Illustration of marital sexuality interaction

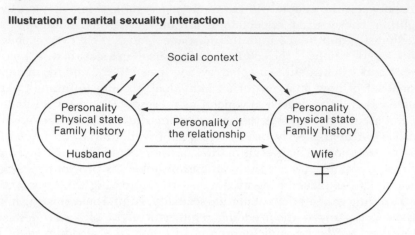

lodged within the personality makeup of the individuals within the relationship. They note that variables such as self-esteem, identity, empathy, and autonomy play significant roles in pleasurable sexual relationships. However, their conclusions were based upon clinical findings and not upon objective measures of personality. One study which would support their clinical findings is that of Heath (1978; 1979). Heath conducted a longitudinal study with professional men which

Table 2

Five vectors of marital sexuality

Personality	Social context	Physical state	Family of origin	Personality of the relationship
Self-image	Development of	Hormones	Sexuality of	Communication
Body image	marriage	Vascular	parents	style
Gender identity	Education	network	Sexual climate	Love
Guilt	Age	General health	of home	Trust
Power	Culture	Obesity	Sex knowledge	Commitment
Defensive	Media	Neurological	and attitudes	Intimacy
styles	Children	network	of parents	Problem resolu-
Autonomy	Transitional	Functioning	Childhood sexual	tion
Dependency	events,	of genital	experiences	Independence/
Intrapsychic	(career,	autonomy	Incest and	dependence
conflicts	deaths, etc.)	Disabilities	sexual trauma	Mutuality
			Affectional	Degree of self-
			climate	disclosure
				Approach/
				avoidance/
				availability

examined the relationship between personality correlates and their marital sexual compatibility. Heath's investigation was based upon 80 men who, as college students, were administered the MMPI, Rorschach, and various questionnaires for self and judged ratings. At age 32, 68 of these men were reinterviewed and tests administered. The question under investigation was how adult psychological health related to marital sexual compatibility. To understand more about the marital relationship, Heath administered a rating questionnaire to the men's wives and to their best friends. He found that adult psychological health did not significantly relate to frequency of marital coital interactions or to the degree of sexual frustration. However, it is significantly related to the degree of sexual pleasure and to marital sexual compatibility. A relationship was found between sexual frustration and psychological immaturity as measured by the ratings of the men's wives, friends, and their colleagues on the self-image questionnaire. Heath summarizes by stating:

> Enjoying sexual relations and being sexually compatible with a spouse are very consistently and strikingly so for sexual compatibility directly related to one's mental health. For the first time, we have convergent evidence from very diverse measures that objectively validate the hypotheses of Masters and Johnson as well as those of many counsellors that sexuality, when integrated with the interpersonal mutuality is like a mirror of one's mental health. The impressive finding that all ten measures of adult mental health were directly related to marital sexual compatibility clearly suggests that sexual mutuality is inextractably integrated with more fundamental personality traits. (p. 114)

This very sophisticated study by Heath indicates the strong relationship between personality characteristics and marital sexual compatibility. However, researchers are challenged to develop future studies which deal with the relationship between personality variables and marital sexual compatibility and satisfaction. Factors which require further investigation are the role of self-image, body image, gender identity, guilt, power, independence/dependence, assertiveness/passivity, and intrapsychic conflicts.

Another study which has dealt somewhat with personality variables and marital sexuality was by Hoch et al. (1981). This research group made a comparison between couples seeking sexual therapy and a control group who were not in sexual therapy. All couples in this group were administered the Israeli Minnesota multiphasic personality inventory (MMPI), Bem sex role inventory, the sim-fan (a game simulation for decision making within the family), anthropomorphical measures of sexual dimorphism, a sociological questionnaire and the Lief and Ebert sexual performance evaluation questionnaire. One problem which exists in the study is the fact that the control group is not a match with the treatment group. The authors found in this study that even though the control group was defined as patients who did not seek sexual therapy, many of these couples had in previous times a specific type of sexual difficulty. Twenty-five percent of the husbands had some ejaculatory problems, and 60 percent of the wives stated that they had had or were having some difficulties with reaching orgasm. Although information is not given in this article which relates to the MMPI and the sexuality of these couples, the data are presented in relationship to the Bem sex role inventory and sexual function within these couples. In relationship to gender identity, the authors found that the couples experiencing the sexual difficulties who were in treatment tended to be less flexible and were more sex stereotyped than those in the control group, while the members within the control group tended to be more flexible and were more likely to be androgynous in their gender identity. The authors relate that the sex-stereotype individuals within the treatment group tended to react in more rigid ways which brought about less flexibility in the relationship and less likelihood of trying new techniques or positions. It would be greatly hoped that in the future, these investigators will present their findings in relationship to the other personality variables which they have studied.

Social context

Social context has played a significant role in relationship to marital sexuality. One only has to view the Victorian era to realize the impact which this period had upon sex roles and sexual outlets and expression. As previously noted, there was rigid adherence to stereotypic sex roles for males and females. Females were viewed as the guardians of moral superiority, and males were viewed as passionate animals who should restrain themselves. The social dynamics of this period greatly influenced the repression of sexuality. This type of severe repression eventually led to the publication of Ellis's studies in the psychology of sex during the period of 1898 through 1910. In his chapter on marital sexuality in *The Psychology of Sex* (1938), the emphasis was on the acceptability for marital couples to partake of sexual intercourse freely within their marital relationship. Sexuality within marriage during the late 1700s through the early 1900s had been viewed as something one does in order to procreate, and couples should therefore restrain themselves from participating in sexual outlets freely. Both Kellogg and Graham gave sound reasons for these beliefs, which were based on physiology and social reasoning. Dr. Sylvester Graham went so far as to prescribe that sexual intercourse between husband and wife should only occur at an interval of once a month. Another important variable which was occurring during this same period in history was the asexuality of women (Haller & Haller, 1974; Murstein, 1974a; Walter, 1974). This type of social impact can be viewed in comparison to the women's movement of today and its impact upon marital sexuality. No longer are women seen as asexual, but are seen as freely expressive sexual beings who have more power and participation in personal, social, political, and economic spheres of living. The changes in these various areas significantly impact upon marital sexuality. Educational and employment opportunities along with changes in birth control and abortion policies have led to the possibility of women having higher self-esteem, more-powerful roles, and lifestyles involving career and parenthood. These types of changes have led to new opportunities in sexual freedom for women within marriage. Masters and Johnson (1970) noted that men stand to gain a great deal from the women's liberation movement. This shift in the relationship between men and women, where women are no longer in a submissive, one-down position but have the opportunity for greater self-esteem and power, is likely to lead to a more balanced relationship with less resentment, anger, and hostility. These changes for females make possible more feeling of mutuality within the relationship. However, equality must not be confused with mutuality. Men have made a number of changes within their perceptions of womanhood and sexuality as a result of the females' new perception of self and sexuality. Numerous clinicians have reported a rise during the 1970s in male sexual dysfunctions, and some clinicians have attributed this to the threat which many males have felt in relationship to their spouses' becoming more powerful within the relationship. These types of changes within the social context are likely to lead to greater responsiveness on the part of both marital partners.

Another type of social context which is more personal and interacts greatly upon marital sexuality is the developmental stages through which the couple grows. A good example of this is during the honeymoon phase of the relationship. James (1981), in his longitudinal study of 21 couples who kept diaries and calendars of coital rates, found that the first year of marriage had the highest rate of sexual frequency during the couple's life span. The frequency of coitus during this initial period of togetherness declines over the first years of marriage. Intercourse frequency is greatly influenced by other variables which occur during the development of the relationship, such as the first pregnancy.

Cuber (1975), in his article on the natural history of sex in marriage, also stated similar findings. During the newlywed period, couples tend to be more sexually active with each other. Further, one of the periods within which marital sexuality demonstrates the greatest change is during the pregnancy and birth of a child. Following the birth of a child, there is deterioration both in the emotional and sexual aspects of the marriage. Dynamically, the couple makes a shift in the relationship from that of a couple to a family. The simple attention and daily rigors of caring for an infant take away from the amount of time that the couple now has to spend with one another. This shift in attention, inavailability of time, and new focus of a love object greatly reduce sexual feeling and opportunity for expression. However, this can be a time of greater bonding in a common union between a couple. Grold (1975), in his commentary on Cuber's natural history of the sexuality of marriage, stated:

> Relationships must be described as dynamic processes in continual change from plateau to crisis to disorganization to attempts at restoration of the homeostatic balance. If learning has taken place, then growth can occur and equilibrium may be established on a more mature level. (p. 73)

Another type of variable in the change in the development of the marital relationship is the 10-year syndrome, more popularly characterized as the 7-year itch. During this developmental change within the relationship, as Whitaker and Warkentin (1966) have described, the couple moves into a period of falling out of love and moves from that more romantic phase of love and fantasy and expectation of one another to a more realistic love and expectation level. During this change within the development of the marital bond, the couple usually goes through an experience of decreased sexual passion and expression. Another, later developmental change within the relationship is the leaving-of-the-nest syndrome, where the final children have left the home and husband and wife are given the time to reunite once again. This can often be a critical period in a marital relationship. For those who make a renewed vow to one another, this may be a period of increased sexual passion and outlet.

Another type of social context factor which is impacting upon marital sexuality today is the influence of the media. Lederer and Jackson (1968) and LoPicollo and Heiman (1977) have discussed the influence of television, movies, and the popular press upon marital sexuality. As LoPiccolo and Heiman have stated, the message of today about sex is that it is okay for both males and females and that you really had better be good at it. Marital sexuality in movies and television has been characterized by high romanticism, easiness, ecstasy, and numerous extramarital sexual affairs. The media has significantly influenced sexual expectation to a high level of passion, arousal, and eroticism only possible in fantasy.

Another important social context variable is that of social background. In this factor, we include the relationship between marital sexuality and such variables as socioeconomic status, educational level, age, and religiosity. Edwards and Booth (1976) investigated the effects on marital intercourse and extramarital involvement of 18 variables related to social background and the marriage. The study was based on a stratified probability sample of Toronto families. The authors found that there is little consistency between variables affecting marital and extramarital sexual patterns. For example, they found that the spouses' ethnicity has a significant effect upon the frequency of marital intercourse, but has no significant effect on extramarital involvement. The authors found that the most consistent variable to influence marital sexual coitus was age. On commenting on the inconsistency of the relationship between social background variables and frequency of marital sexual coitus, the authors stated: "Presumed differences in values and attitudes associated with occupational and educational background and even religious identity simply do not carry over in any significant way to influence our sexual conduct" (p. 81). Edwards and Booth relate the frequency of marital intercourse largely to contextual variables, the nature of marriage, and how the partners perceive their marriage.

Hunt (1974) found that social background variables do not play the extreme role in marital sexual behavior that they once did, as in the era of Kinsey's investigation. As with the Edwards and Booth (1976) study, age seems to be the most consistent social background variable which influences marital sexuality. The questions asked were similar to those in the Kinsey investigation. The author states that the sample closely parallels the American population, with participants from 24 cities throughout the United States.

In comparing the data of Kinsey and Hunt (1974) in relation to marital sexual coitus, there appear to be higher frequencies of coitus for all age groups of the Hunt research. Hunt found, like Kinsey did, that education and occupational status were of little importance in relationship to frequency of marital coitus. However, as Kinsey did, he found that religion did play a significant role in marital coital frequency. According to Hunt, religious devotion has a suppressing effect upon females in relation to frequency of coitus and makes no significant difference among males as measured by regularity of church attendance.

Secondly, the differences in foreplay techniques between college-level subjects and noncollege-level subjects which were vast in Kinsey's study no longer exist in the Hunt study. While the great range of foreplay techniques is broader within the college-educated group than the noncollege-educated group, the differences are much smaller than in the era of Kinsey. However, the greatest difference in terms of a social background variable in relationship to foreplay techniques was age. The younger the age group, the greater the variety in sexual foreplay technique. For example, the age group under 25 spent a significantly longer period of time involved in fellatio and cunnilingus than the age group of 45 and over. Overall, it can be summarized that educational, occupational, and socioeconomic levels and religious devotion play a less-significant role in marital coital interaction than in the era of Kinsey. The greatest differences in social background variables in marital coital interaction appear to be attributed to age. However, in comparing the Kinsey and Hunt studies, it is found that there is an increase in all age groups in relationship to marital coitus interaction and variety of foreplay techniques.

Gorer (1971) investigated sex in marriage in England. The study was conducted by Gorer and the Opinion Research Centre. In this study, 949 men and 1,037 women were interviewed; the age group of the participants ranged from 16 to 45. Many social background variables and sexual information were gathered. Relationships were sought between the frequency of intercourse and educational and income level. It was found that a significant relationship existed between higher educational levels and frequency of intercourse; however, the author states that this correlation may be clouded by the fact that the elder participants tended to have lower educational levels. In terms of income level, there was a significant relationship between higher rates of sexual intercourse and higher levels of income. However, the author notes that this relationship may also be complicated because the low income levels tended to be the people who were under age 20 and the higher-level income among those over 35. Once again, we see the inconsistency of social background variables in relationship to frequency of marital coitus: There are some significant relationships in this study between educational and income level and marital coitus; however, as the author has noted, these significant correlations may be more the product of other intervening variables.

In summary, it can be seen from these three studies that have been presented that age appears to play a significant role in marital coitus, while there is an inconsistency as to the relationship between other social background variables such as educational, occupational, and income levels in relationship to marital sexuality. It appears the more-significant variables are within the context of the relationship. The important area of attention is the overall picture of social background variables in relationship to other variables such as the personality of the individuals and of the relationship.

Physical state

Another influential variable within marital sexuality is the physical health of the marital partners. This type of relationship can be clearly seen in Marshall and Neill's (1977) investigation of 12 marriages in which an obese partner was involved. Their study investigated the effects on the marriage when intestinal bypass surgery for extreme obesity is performed. In general, the surgery patients reported a renewed interest in sexual arousal, self-image, and desire, while the spouses tended to feel threatened by the weight loss and the renewed interest in sexuality. Only 2 spouses reported being pleased with the increased sexual desire of the partners, while the other 10 tended to feel jealous, anxious, and threatened. It was found that some of the nonobese spouses had hidden their homosexuality within their marriage to an obese patient. Others demonstrated a reduction in sexual desire. This study illustrates the profound effects that physical health can have on marital sexuality.

Another example of the effects that physical health has upon marital sexuality can be seen in postmenopausal hormone deprivation of middle- to older-aged women. Typically, with this group there is a tissue inelasticity and a decrease in lubrication, thus making sexual intercourse a physiologically irritating experience. However, as Semmens (1982) has shown, hormone replacement of estrogen can be quite helpful to middle- and older-aged women in increasing their lubricating secretions and improving the physical state of the vagina. In his comparison study of Scandinavian and Charleston, South Carolina, women who were undergoing hormone replacement, he found an increase in lubrication capability and renewed interest in sexuality.

A final factor which has played a significant role in marital sexuality is in the advances made within the contraceptive field in the last 20 years. With the advent and pervasive use of the pill, IUD, and sterilization techniques, couples have greater choices in refraining from procreation. Many advances have been made in oral contraceptives for females; however, this still appears to be a new frontier of investigation for males. The tubal ligation is now an outpatient procedure, and vasectomies are being performed at a much higher rate. These two sterilization procedures have become much more accepted by the public and have allowed couples greater freedom in their sexual expression. Overall, the physiological investigation of human sexuality still appears to be one of the more-important areas of future research.

Family history

The family of origin of the marital partners plays a significant role in the determination of the quality of the marital sexuality. Factors such as the parent-child interaction, the interaction of the parents, values, sexual knowledge, and climate of the parents influences marital sexuality. Most theories of personality attribute much of personality formation to the contributions made by the parents of the individual.

The family of origin contributes to psychosexual development in a similar manner.

In the study by Hoch et al. (1981) which has been previously mentioned, a comparison was made between sexually dysfunctional and functional couples. In determining factors which were likely to lead to the development of sexual dysfunctions, three variables related to family history. These were: (1) early family distress, such as the death or separation of parents; (2) a repressive traditional or religious upbringing in childhood, which had the effect of maintaining similar repressive values in the present relationship; and (3) an adherence to sexual myths regarding sexual performance. These investigators found that these three factors contributed to, and were likely to lead to, potential sexual difficulties within a marital relationship.

Masters and Johnson (1970) have stated that the biosocial factors play a significant role in determining the sexuality of the individual. Masters and Johnson have elaborated upon how negative attitudes within one or both of the marital spouses contribute to a poor quality of marital sexual relatedness. Correlating marital sexual quality to attitudinal and value formation of parents is commonly done. However, the powerful attitudes and values which are portrayed by the parents play a significant role in determining the marital sexuality. A primary example of how this may occur is with the sexual curiosity of the child and the parental response to it. Not only does the content given by the parent play an important role in shaping the attitudes, values, and knowledge of the child, but the metacommunication and the affective tone play a more significant role in shaping the child's sexuality. For example, a mother may give her child very accurate sexual information in regard to menstruation or sexual intercourse; however, while she is imparting this type of information, she may be frowning, speaking in a disgusted tone, and maintaining a physical distance from the child. This type of metacommunication and emotional communication plays a far more significant role than do words in the development of sexual attitudes and behavior of this child. This type of negative sexual information-giving leads to an internalization which becomes a part of the psyche that the individual brings to the marital context. It is from this point that the family of origin acts upon the marital sexuality of the couple.

In a study by Wallace (1981), the affectional climate in the family of origin was investigated to determine what effects it had upon subsequent sexual-affectional behaviors of the individual. As Bowlby (1969, 1973) and Harlow (1958) have stated, the affectional quality of the parent-child interaction plays a determining role in the later adult affectional patterns. Wallace has shown how the affectional climate within the family of origin affects the sexual behavior of the adult. Wallace notes that the uniqueness of this sample group might have an effect on the generalizability of the findings because this group is not likely to be representative of an average adult population. Volunteers for the study were administered the somatosensory index of affection and the affectional history questionnaire.

Factor analysis of the questionnaire items was conducted, which yielded nine factors which accounted for 57 percent of the variance. The first factor, general affectional interaction, was related to such questions as: (1) parents demonstrating affection by hugging, (2) the individual showing affection toward the parents, and (3) mother and father kissing and hugging the child. This factor accounted for 44.7 percent of the variance. The other factors which emerged were parents' interaction, physical closeness with relatives, distancing by the parents, distancing by the relatives, lack of contact with relatives, sexual discussions with parents, physical punishment, and maternal acceptance. These factors played a significant role in determining these subjects' sexual and affectional experiences in adult relationships. Wallace concluded:

> It may be stated with considerable degree of assurance that the affectional climate in the family of origin is not only related to subsequent expression of affection and to attitudes toward sexual expression but that the three variables are interrelated in a complex fashion with each other and with expressions of sexuality during adulthood. It might prove useful to conceive of the affectional climate in the family of origin as the background out of which current affectional behavior, attitudes and sexual expression emerge. (p. 305)

In general, it has been widely accepted that the family of origin of the individual plays an important part in determining sexual attitudes and behavior. This shaping plays an important role in the marital sexuality of the couple. However, our generalizations are largely based upon a small sample number of investigative studies and a large body of clinical intuitions and case studies. Investigators in the future are encouraged to study parental interactions, attitudes, and sexual behavior and their effects upon the subsequent marital sexuality of the child. As of now, little is known as to the effects of the parental sexual climate upon the marital sexuality of the child.

The studies by Chesney et al., (1981) and Edwards and Booth (1976) have shown the importance of the affectional climate within the marriage in determining the quality of sexual satisfaction and in influencing coital frequency.

Personality of the relationship

Through the interaction of the couple, the relationship takes on distinctive factors which form a personality of its own, and a personality of the relationship is born. It is within this area that the most research has been conducted with regard to the various relationship factors which contribute to marital sexuality. Numerous investigators have noted the quality of the marital relationship as being the primary determining factor in marital sexual satisfaction (Chesney et al., 1981; Clark & Wallin, 1965; Lederer & Jackson, 1968; Masters & Johnson, 1970; Talmadge & Talmadge, 1983; Waring, 1981).

The sexuality of the couple depends greatly upon the interaction of the marital partners. If the relationship between sexual satisfaction and various aspects of the relationship remain stable for both partners in the course of the marriage, then the likelihood of healthy sexual satisfaction is more probable. The sexuality of the relationship appears to depend more on the quality of the relationship in the partnership. The more positively the couple perceives of their relationship, the greater the sexual satisfaction within the marriage. Consequently, as one decreases, it is highly likely that the other will decrease also. Sexual satisfaction within the relationship is an ongoing process. It depends greatly upon the couple's commitment to communicate their feelings and desires, to disagree openly, and to express their continuing love and trust for one another. The relationship of the couple as it relates to marital sexuality has focused basically on four variables: communication, affection, intimacy, and problem resolution. In this section, we will also discuss other factors such as respect, the work and play of the couple, commitment, sex drive, and perception of the significant other's satisfaction.

Numerous researchers have discussed the importance of communication in marital sexuality. These investigators have found that the communication of the couple significantly influences their marital sexual satisfaction. Heath (1978), in his study of professional men and marital sexual compatibility, found that the wives' ratings of how well they felt they understood their husbands and the ratings of the husbands as to how well they felt understood were significantly correlated to the sexual compatibility of the couple. The wives of the sexually compatible men believed that they understood their husbands better than did the wives of the less sexually compatible men, and their husbands confirmed this. Waring (1981) has stressed the importance of communication in terms of self-disclosure. Communication is one important variable in his overall-process factors which contribute to marital satisfaction. He discusses the importance of communication between the couple becoming intimate with one another through self-disclosure.

Schenk et al. (1983), in their study of personality traits versus the quality of the marital relationship as the determinant of marital satisfaction, found communication to be a more significant factor in marital sexual satisfaction. These researchers found the correlation between satisfaction in sexual interaction and dimensions of the relationship were significant. The importance of sexuality for the women in the study increased as they felt more appreciative of their partners, were able to express their needs, and if they only experienced little refusal of support. However, the most important variable relating to marital sexual satisfaction was satisfaction within the relationship. There was a significant relationship between couples' perceived overall satisfactory marital relationship and marital sexual satisfaction. This type of finding has also been noted by Hunt (1974): The marital sex life tends to be rated higher in relation to the pleasantness of the overall marital relationship. Ficher (1976) has stated that communication is one of the primary factors which can enhance or detract from the marital sexual relationship. He relates sexual communication to the fear of closeness and intimacy. Those that are more willing to be intimate are likely to have more sexual communication within the relationship.

Chesney et al. (1981), in comparing couples who had sought sex therapy with those who had not, found that "sexual satisfaction depends upon a constant effort by the couples to establish constructive communication patterns, which involves sharing knowledge appropriate to problems at hand in combination with an open, flexible approach to sexual expression" (p. 132). In comparing these two groups of couples, they found that the comparison group had significantly fewer communication problems than those who had sought sex therapy. Although couples in the comparison group experienced some of the same sexual dysfunctions as the treatment group, the major difference appears to be in how the couple perceives its relationship, communication, and sexual communication and how disagreements are resolved. These authors stress the overall importance of how the couple perceives itself and the interaction within the total marital relationship as being the significant variables in determining marital sexual satisfaction.

Honeycutt et al. (1982) studied the degree of happiness related to perceived styles of communicating in and out of the marital relationship. These authors found that a relaxed, friendly, open, dramatic, and attentive communication style was the type which was used most often by the happily married couples. This was a style that was not generally used in relationships outside of marriage. These researchers also found that the levels of marital happiness affected the number of styles predicting a good communicator. Those couples who expressed high degrees of marital happiness tended to have a greater variety of communicator styles, whereas those less happily married tended to have fewer styles of communicating. Hoch et al. (1981), in their study comparing sexually dysfunctional and functional couples, found that sexual communication is one of the most significant variables in influencing the marital sexual functioning. These researchers found that the treatment group (1) was often unable to evaluate their feelings about various forms of sexual activity, (2) did not understand their partner's desire for, or frequency of, certain types of sexual activities, and (3) tended to misperceive in what sexual activity their partners really were interested.

Overall, communication is seen as one of the most significant variables in marital sexual satisfaction. The degree of functional communication within the relationship is significantly related to marital happiness in general. Communication within the relationship relates to the couple's ability to express their needs to one another, have them understood by their partner, and have them addressed. Sexual communication is a significant variable in marital sexual satisfaction. The degree to which a couple may express their sexual likes and dislikes and have these understood is significantly related to the degree of sexual marital satisfaction. The openness a couple has in their sexual communication, meaning the degree to which they can discuss sex openly and honestly, is related to their overall process of becoming a sexually compatible couple. However, for this type of open communication to occur, there must be a marital climate of love, trust, commitment, and respect.

Affection has previously been discussed in relation to marital sexuality and the family of origin. It has been demonstrated that the degree of affection within the family of origin is a determining factor in the subsequent degree of sexual affection within the marital relationship. Masters and Johnson (1970) have discussed affection in terms of touch. They have noted the differences in the gender-identity conceptualizations of touch. Men often make an error in assuming touch to be a means to an end, the end being the culminating sexual act; while females are more accepting of, and desire, touch for touch. The researchers state:

> Touch is an end in itself. It is a primary form of communication, a silent voice that avoids the pitfall of words while expressing the feelings of the moment. It bridges the physical separateness from which no human being is spared, literally establishing a sense of solidarity between two individuals. Touching is sensual pleasure exploring the texture of skin, suppleness of muscle, the contours of the body, with no further goal than enjoyment of tactile perceptions. (p. 253)

Waring (1981) discusses affection in terms of the overall marital intimacy. He discusses affection as communication instead of actual, physical touch. Within his conceptualization, affection is related to being able to express feelings of emotional closeness. Jourard (1961) relates affection more to love and trust. He discusses the importance of love in the Fromm sense. In this way, love is seen more as a caring and a responding to one's needs in a freely acceptable way in which the loved object is given great encouragement and acceptability for autonomy. Jourard believes that this type of love and trust within a marital relationship greatly enhances an exciting and healthy marital sexual relationship. Although important theorists such as Bowlby and Harlow and the work of Wallace and Prescott have demonstrated the importance of affection in relation to sexual satisfaction and bonding between couples, very little research has been conducted as to the relationship between affection and marital sexual satisfaction. It is predicted that the degree of touching and physical affection as an end in itself within a relationship is significantly related to the sexual marital happiness of the couple.

Intimacy is another factor within the personality of the relationship which has been considered to be an important variable in determining marital sexual satisfaction. Waring (1981) and Talmadge and Talmadge (1983) have discussed the importance of marital intimacy within the context of marital sexual satisfaction and the overall satisfaction within the relationship. Waring has noted intimacy to be related to a composite of variables such as expressiveness, compatibility, cohesion, affection, conflict resolution, autonomy, and identity. He discusses these variables as being important to the overall intimacy within the marital relationship and identifies the means through which couples become intimate as self-disclosure.

Talmadge and Talmadge (1983) discuss intimacy as the couple's ability to make known their innermost parts of themselves. They relate variables such as trust, interdependency, vulnerability, power, mutuality, and the knowing and seeking of self as being significant variables in the formation of marital intimacy. They see the degree of intimacy within the marital relationship as a significant factor in determining the sexuality within the marital relationship. In fact, the couple's ability to be intimate with one another determines and colors the sexuality within that relationship.

Several authors have discussed the importance of commitment within the marital relationship as being a determining factor of marital sexual happiness. Masters and Johnson (1970) have discussed the important role that commitment plays in coloring the meaning of the sexual relationship within the marital context. Commitment implies promise. Inherent in this promise is a pledge to continue to work as a couple in establishing the process of marital compatibility and sexual fulfillment. They state, "Becoming committed to someone is, by definition, to entrust one's physical and emotional well-being to that person; it is an act of faith and an acceptance of vulnerability" (p. 274). Chesney et al. (1981) and Heath (1978) found the inverse of commitment, wanting out of the relationship, to be significantly related to marital sexual dissatisfaction and incompatibility. They found a significant relationship between those couples wanting out of the relationship and incompatibility within the sexual relationship of the couple.

A different type of variable which has been studied is the relationship between sex drive and marital sexual compatibility. This type of interaction variable within the relationship has been found by Murstein (1974b) and Ficher, Zuckerman, and Neeb (1981) to be significantly related to marital sexual compatibility. However, this area still is in need of more scientific investigation with regard to marital sexual satisfaction. Murstein found that the perceived influence of personality was significantly related to low sex drive on the part of the male. Generally, he found that those males exhibiting low sex drive made more courtship progress in their relationships than did the males with high sex drive. Another significant finding of his study was that the male sex drive appears to be less dependent upon the interpersonal relationship than does the female's. The sex drive of the female and satisfaction are significantly related to her experience and the quality of the interpersonal relationship which she perceives. Thus, Murstein has found (as have other researchers) that the interpersonal relationship tends to color the sexuality of the couple. This means that the more-positively perceived the interpersonal relationship of the couple, the greater the degree of sexual satisfaction within this pair.

CONCLUSION

The personality factors of the relationship, such as communication, affection, intimacy, problem resolution, commitment, work, play, sex drive, and perception of one's problem, play a significant role in determining the marital sexual compatibility of the couple. It must be remembered that these are all variables which are related to process. None of these variables are ends of themselves. A couple's marital sexual compatibility is greatly determined by their commitment to engage in a long-term process of interacting with one another, expressing their affection, needs, desires, likes, and dislikes in a trusting, caring, vulnerable atmosphere. Thus, marital sexual compatibility is a process which is determined by the personality of the relationship, the social context, the personality of the two individuals within the relationship, and their families of origin.

REFERENCES

Athanasion, R. & Sarkin, R. Premarital sexual behavior and postmarital adjustment. *Archives of Sexual Behavior,* 1974, *3*(3), 207–225.

Bell, R. R., Turner, S., & Rosen, L. A multivariate analysis of female extramarital coitus. *Journal of Marriage and the Family,* 1975, *37,* 375–384.

Berg, P., & Snyder, D. K. Differential diagnosis of marital and sexual distress: A multidimensional approach. *Journal of Sex and Marital Therapy,* 1981, *7*(4), 290–295.

Bowlby, J. *Attachment.* New York: Basic Books, 1969.

Bowlby, J. *Attachment and loss* (Vol. II). New York: Basic Books, 1973.

Chesney, A. T., Blakeney, P. E., Cole, C. M., & Chan, F. A. A comparison of couples who have sought sex therapy with couples who have not. *Journal of Sex and Marital Therapy,* 1981, *7,* 131–140.

Clark, A. L., & Wallin, P. Women's sexual responsiveness and the duration and quality of their marriages. *American Journal of Sociology,* 1965, *71*(2), 187–196.

Cole, C. L., Cole, A. L., & Dean, D. G. Emotional maturity and marital adjustment: A decade replication. *Journal of Marriage and the Family,* 1980, *42*(3), 533–539.

Cuber, J. F. The natural history of sex in marriage. *Medical Aspects of Human Sexuality,* July 1975, pp. 51–73.

Dickinson, R. L., & Beam, L. *A thousand marriages.* Baltimore: Williams & Wilkins Company, 1931.

Edwards, J. N., & Booth, A. Sexual behavior in and out of marriage: An assessment of correlates. *Journal of Marriage and the Family,* 1976, *38*(1), 73–81.

Ellis, H. *Psychology of sex.* New York: Emerson Books, 1938.

Eysenck, H. J. Personality and sexual adjustments. *British Journal of Psychiatry,* 1971, *118,* 593–608.

Farley, F. H., & Davis, S. A. Arousal, personality and assortive mating in marriage. *Journal of Sex and Marital Therapy,* 1977, *3*(2), 122–127.

Farley, F. H., & Mueller, C. B. Arousal, personality, and assortive mating in marriage: Generalizability and cross-cultural factors. *Journal of Sex and Marital Therapy,* 1978, *4*(1), 50–53.

Ficher, I. V. Sex and the marriage relationship. In W. W. Oaks, G. A. Melchiode, & I. Ficher (Eds.), *Sex and the life cycle.* New York: Grune & Statton, 1976.

Ficher, I. V., Zuckerman, M., & Neeb, M. Marital compatibility and sensation seeking trait as a factor in marital adjustment. *Journal of Sex and Marital Therapy,* 1981, *7,* 60–69.

Frank, E., Anderson, C., & Rubenstein, D. Frequency of sexual dysfunction in "normal" couples. *New England Journal of Medicine,* 1978, *299,* 111–115.

Freud, S. *Three essays on sexuality* (Vol. VII, standard ed.). London: Hogarth, 1953.

Glass, S. P., & Wright, T. L. The relationship of extramarital sex, length of marriage and sex differences on marital satisfaction and romanticism: Athanasiou's data reanalyzed. *Journal of Sex and the Family,* 1977, *39*(4), 691–703.

Gorer, G. *Sex and marriage in England today.* London: Thomas Nelson & Sons, 1971.

Grold, L. J. Commentary on Cuber's article. *Medical Aspects of Human Sexuality,* July 1975, pp. 73–75.

Haller, J. S., & Haller, R. M. *The physician and sexuality in Victorian America.* Urbana: University of Illinois Press, 1974.

Harlow, H. F. The nature of love. *American Psychologist,* 1958, *13,* 673–685.

Harlow, H. F. Social deprivation in monkeys. *Scientific America,* 1962, *207,* 136.

Heath, D. H. Personality correlates of the marital sexual compatibility of professional men. *Journal of Sex and Marital Therapy,* 1978, *4*(2), 67–82.

Heath, D. H. Sexual enjoyment and frustration of professional men. *Journal of Sex and Marital Therapy,* 1979, *5*(2), 103–116.

Hoch, Z., Safir, M. P., Peres, Y., & Shepher, J. An evaluation of sexual performance—comparison between sexually dysfunctional and functional couples. *Journal of Sex and Marital Therapy,* 1981, *7,* 195–206.

Honeycutt, J. M., Wilson, C., & Parker, C. Effects of sex and degrees of happiness on perceived styles of communicating in and out of the marital relationship. *Journal of Marriage and the Family,* 1982, *44*(2), 395–406.

Hunt, M. *Sexual Behavior in the 1970s.* Chicago, Playboy Press, 1974.

James, W. H. The honeymoon effect on marital coitus. *Journal of Sex Research,* 1981, *17,* 114–123.

Jourard, S. M. Sex in marriage. *Journal of Humanistic Psychology,* 1961, pp. 23–29.

Lederer, W. J., & Jackson, D. D. *The Mirages of Marriage.* New York: Norton, 1968.

Levinger, G. Systematic distortion in spouses' reports of preferred and actual sexual behavior. *Sociometry,* 1966, *29,* 291–299.

LoPiccolo, J., & Heiman, J. Cultural values and the therapeutic definition of sexual function and dysfunction. *Journal of Social Issues,* 1977, *33*(2), 166–183.

Marshall, D. S., & Suggs, R. C. *Human sexual behavior.* New York: Basic Books, 1971.

Marshall, J. R., & Neill, J. The removal of a psychosomatic symptom: Effects on the marriage. *Family Process,* 1977, *16*(3), 273–280.

Masters, W. H., & Johnson, V. E. *Human sexual inadequacy.* Boston: Little, Brown, 1970.

Meissner, W. W. The conceptualization of marriage and family dynamics from a psychoanalytic perspective. In T. J. Paolino & B. S. McCrady (Eds.), *Marriage and family therapy: Psychoanalytic behavioral and systems theory perspectives* New York: Brunner/Mazel, 1978. Pp. 25–88.

Messersmith, C. E. Sex therapy and the marital system. In D. Olson (Ed.), *Treating relationships.* Lake Mills, Iowa: Graphic Publishing, 1976.

Moore, D. Does good sex bring real intimacy? *Glamour,* October 1980, pp. 232–302.

Morris, D. *Intimate behavior.* New York: Random House, 1971.

Murstein, B. I. *Love, sex and marriage through the ages.* New York: Springer Publishing, 1974. (a)

Murstein, B. I. Sex drive, person perception and marital choice. *Archives of Sexual Behavior,* 1974, *3*(4), 331–348. (b)

Prescott, J., & Wallace, D. Role of pain and pleasure in the development of destructive behaviors: A psychometric study of parenting, sexuality, substance abuse, and criminality. In *Invited Papers: Colloquium on the Correlates of Crime and the Determination of Criminal Behavior.* Washington, D.C.: Mitre Corporation, 1978.

Roffe, M. W., & Britt, B. C. A typology of marital interaction for sexually dysfunctional couples. *Journal of Sex and Marital Therapy,* 1981, *7,* 207–222.

Schenk, J., Horst, P., & Armin, R. Personality traits versus the quality of the marital relationship as the determinant of marital sexuality. *Archives of Sexual Behavior,* 1983, *12*(1), 31–42.

Schmidt, G. Sex and society in the eighties. *Archives of Sexual Behavior,* 1982, *11*(2), 91–97.

Segraves, R. T. *Marital therapy: A combined psychodynamic-behavioral approach.* New York: Plenum Medical Book Company, 1982.

Semmens, J. Hormone replacement of estrogen in older women. 1982 Society for Sex Therapists and Researchers, Charleston, South Carolina.

Spanier, G. B., & Lewis, R. A. Marital quality: A review of the seventies. *Journal of Marriage and the Family,* 1980, *42*(4), 825–839.

Sprenkle, D. H., & Weis, D. L. Extramarital sexuality; Implications for marital therapists. *Journal of Sex and Marital Therapy,* 1978, *4*(4), 279–291.

Talmadge, L. D., & Talmadge, W. C. Relational sexuality: An understanding of sexual desire. Article submitted for publication, 1983.

Talmadge, W. C. *A Sexual Enhancement Workshop for Men.* Unpublished dissertation, Georgia State University, Atlanta, 1979.

Terman, L. M. *Psychological factors in marital happiness.* New York: McGraw-Hill Book Company, 1938.

Wallace, D. H. Affectional climate in the family of origin and the experience of subsequent sexual-affectional behaviors. *Journal of Sex and Marital Therapy,* 1981, *7,* 296–306.

Wallin, P. Religiosity, sexual gratification, and marital satisfaction. *American Sociological Review,* 1957, *22,* 300–305.

Wallin, P., & Clark, A. Cultural norms and husbands' and wives' reports of their marital partners' preferred frequency of coitus relative to their own. *Sociometry,* 1958, *21,* 247–254.

Wallin, P., & Clark, A. L. Religiosity, sexual gratification and marital satisfaction in the middle years of marriage. *Social Forces,* 1964, *42,* 303–309.

Walter, R. G. *Primers for prudery: Sexual advice to Victorian America.* Englewood Cliffs, N.J.: Prentice-Hall.

Waring, E. M. Facilitating marital intimacy through self-disclosure. *American Journal of Family Therapy,* 1981, *9*(4), 33–42.

Wenkart, A. *Healthy and neurotic love.* New York: Auxiliary Council to the Association for the Advancement of Psychoanalysis, 1952.

Whitaker, C. A., & Warkentin, J. Serial impasses in marriage. *(Psychiatric Research Report No. 20).* American Psychiatric Association, 1966.

Section Five

Parenthood and Parenting

Chapter 17

Parental Heritage: Progress and Prospect

NANCY E. MOSS
STEPHEN I. ABRAMOWITZ
GARY R. RACUSIN

The parent-child relationship has long been an object of social and scientific study, with an emphasis on parental socialization practices, parent-child interaction, and parental impact on child development (Anderson, 1981; Becker, 1964; Bell, 1968; Mussen, Conger, & Kagan, 1970; Walters & Walters, 1980). In recent years, increasing interest has been shown in the study of the influence of the child on parental roles and family development (Berardo, Hill, Fox, Wiseman, & Aldous, 1981). Recent investigations of adult development have likewise called attention to parenthood as one among many adult social roles which evolve over the course of the life cycle (Frieze, Parsons, Johnson, Ruble, & Zellman, 1978; Levinson, Darrow, Klein, Levinson, & McKee, 1978; Whitbourne & Weinstock, 1979). An unstated assumption underlying these developments is that parental transmission of a cultural and personal heritage is a central function of the parent-child relationship (Benedek, 1970; Handel, 1970; Hoffman & Hoffman, 1973). Yet, the nature of parental heritage and of its transmission has rarely been investigated directly (Moss & Abramowitz, 1982; Moss, Abramowitz, & Kaschak, 1982). Consequently, knowledge of parental heritage remains largely conjectural.

Psychologists and sociologists have made the major contributions to our implicit understanding of parental heritage, with occasional assistance from historians, anthropologists, and philosophers. Regardless of the writer's discipline, however, content and methodology in this area have tended to be similar. Although psychologists have characteristically examined intrafamilial dynamics and sociologists have tended to focus on intergenerational continuity, there has been considerable overlap. Likewise, the two fields have shared methodological approaches. Both have relied heavily on some theory, large-scale survey data, and a small number of quantitative and qualitative investigations.

Relevant literature from each discipline must be reexamined from the perspective of parental heritage if our knowledge of this phenomenon is to advance from the level of supposition. Inferences from psychological studies of childbearing motivations and sociological studies of the "generation gap," for example, can solidify the framework for the study of parental heritage. The purpose of the present discussion is to facilitate this enterprise.

CONCEPTUAL FRAMEWORK

Parental heritage is first defined as an accumulation of parental assets, either material or psychological, valued sufficiently by the parent to be transmitted intentionally to the child. For instance, the mother who transfers a community leadership position to her grown daughter has passed on a bit of maternal heritage. In contrast, the father who hopes that his son will acquire the professional degree which he himself lacks has communicated a wish for deficit compensation, not a paternal legacy. Likewise, the parent who simply notices replication of the "family temper" in a young son has not conveyed a heritage but rather identified shared family traits. Parental heritage thus connotes an intentional, conscious process of transmission acknowledged and initiated by the parent.

Three conceptual areas of interdisciplinary research provide the framework for the study of parental heritage: (a) sociohistorical context of parent-child relations; (b) social psychological functions of parenthood; and (c) intergenerational dynamics. The relationship between these research areas and parental heritage is illustrated in Figure 1.

Sociohistorical context of parent-child relations

Parent-child relations are embedded in historical time and socioeconomic conditions. Relations are shaped by prevailing definitions of the parent-child tie as well as by social structure and class. As one element of these relations, parental heritage is influenced by the current sociohistorical context. For example, parental heritage would be less relevant in an era which defined the parent-child relationship as a brief, biological connection than in a time when parent-child relations represented cherished, lifelong bonds.

Figure 1

Relationship between areas of interdisciplinary research and parental heritage

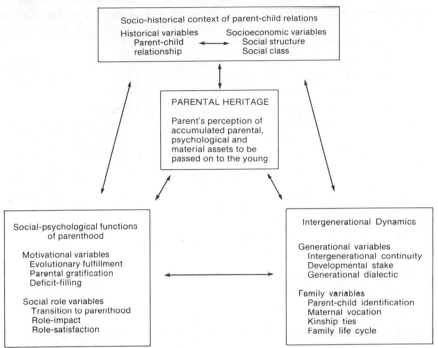

Social psychological functions of parenthood

In all historical periods and socioeconomic positions, parenthood serves a variety of social psychological functions for the parent. Being a parent satisfies a wide array of motives and is a major social role of adult life. Conceptions of parental heritage may vary in relation to different configurations of parenthood motivations and role characteristics. To illustrate, the woman who entered into motherhood to assuage loneliness would be far more restricted in conceptualization of parental legacy than would her counterpart with a valued ethnic tradition to convey.

Intergenerational dynamics

Complex intergenerational dynamics operate at each point within the sociohistorical context introduced above. While the social psychological functions of parenthood pertain to individual psychological motives and role experiences, intergenerational dynamics refer to interactions between entire generations or their representatives within families. Conceptions of parental heritage are influenced by the nature and goals of intergenerational relations. For example, a generation that made great strides in the campaign for women's rights might bequeath a vastly different legacy than its heirs, busy with the private consolidation of those gains.

Each of the three conceptual areas above contribute to conceptions of parental heritage. In addition, the areas themselves are interdependent. For example, historical variables may be linked to motivational variables in their joint influence on parental heritage. The definition of the parent-child relationship as an economic tie may, at a given point in time, motivate adults to become parents to guarantee economic security in old age. Likewise, conceptions of parental heritage may have a reciprocal impact. For instance, prior parental conceptualization of a legacy might itself contribute to parenthood motivations. The man in possession of valued knowledge may become a father to impart that knowledge to his son.

In the interest of advancing our knowledge of parental heritage as the outcome of a complex array of psychological and social forces, this review will emphasize those variables which appear to hold out the most explanatory promise. (The foregoing conceptual scaffold for the study of parental heritage is illustrated in Figure 1.) The review considers theory and research pertinent to each conceptual realm. The material is integrated, current limitations in the study of parental heritage are analyzed, and directions for further work are proposed.

SOCIOHISTORICAL CONTEXT OF PARENT-CHILD RELATIONS

Conceptualization of parental heritage is influenced by both the evolving definition of the parent-child relationship in each era and the socioeconomic structure in which the relationship is embedded during a given time period. Historical variables and socioeconomic variables such as social structure and social class are most salient.

Historical variables

Throughout history, the nature of the parent-child relationship has varied as a function of the interplay between economics and culture (Hareven, 1977). Gilbert (1981) emphasized that parenting research should acknowledge this historical variation. In line with her statement, the historical variation of the parent-child relationship was reviewed by several psychologists to identify critical variables for parent-child interaction.

Lynn (1979) examined the parent-child relationship from ancient to modern times. He noted a steady erosion of the family's identification purely as a self-contained economic unit, complemented by steadily increasing family democratization and affective parent-child attachment. Hagestad (1982) argued that mortality rates play a causal role in this family definitional shift. Lower mortality rates have allowed for more enduring intergenerational attachments, encouraging parents and children to invest themselves more confidently in the family as a sentient rather than corporate group.

Kagan (1977) focused more closely on the increasing salience of parental love. With the movement away from a home-based, subsistence economy around the early 18th century, the child became less an indifferent object of economic utility and more a beloved resource who, with financial and educational preparation, could enhance family status through success in the wider society.

Some researchers focused on culturally sanctioned childrearing goals. Abramovitz (1976) traced four developmental stages in the American parent-child relationship: (a) break the will, 1600–1775; (b) Christian nurture, 1790–1850; (c) individual competition, 1860–1940; and (d) competence and health, 1940–present. During the first three stages, accepted religious and philosophical doctrine authorized parents to prepare their children for roles in an increasingly industrial society. However, "Unlike past generations where survival needs dictated what future plans should be, today the constantly accelerating rate of technological change, multinational corporations, energy crises and nuclear weapons have left mainstream middle-class parents comfortable materially but lacking in confidence to nurture and prepare their children for the future" (p. 46). Likewise, Le Masters (1974) asserted that modern parents face an absence of role clarity regarding parenting goals.

Authorities thus agree that the parent-child relationship has been characterized by decreasing economic and increasing affective ties over the course of history. This development has paradoxical implications for the study of parental heritage. In early times, when parents imparted a legacy of economic skills and social position by necessity, they did not conceptualize the parent-child relationship in socioemotional terms that would make the concept of parental heritage meaningful.

In contrast, the modern, affective parent-child relationship must function within a changing technological and contradictory cultural framework that makes it difficult for parents to amass or identify a heritage relevant to their children's lives. Conceptualization of parental heritage may depend on a balance between societal stability and parent-child affection.

Socioeconomic variables

Interacting with historical factors are socioeconomic conditions that influence childrearing goals and impinge upon the quality of the parent-child relationship (Bernard, 1981). These conditions include social structure and social class.

Social structure. The social structure within which the relationship exists may either facilitate or impede conceptualization and transmission of parental heritage. The social structure in which middle-class women of 19th-century America lived, for example, served a facilitative function (Smith-Rosenberg, 1975). In her historical essay based on primary sources, Smith-Rosenberg chronicled a social order wherein relations between the sexes were strictly formalized, impinging mainly on societal and reproductive conventions. Friendships and family relations between women, however, were a central source of emotional intimacy and practical assistance. A mother brought her growing daughter into a welcoming social network which endured across generations.

In contrast, based upon their anthropological, cross-cultural review of the impact of social structure on mothering patterns, Minturn and Lambert (1968) offered a more sobering view:

> The horde of apparently irrelevant considerations that impinge upon the parents . . . determine the range and content of mother-child "relations" and the context in which the relations must take place. . . . Each [mother] must solve the problems of [her world] and pass on to her children both the problems and their solutions. . . . The message that each [mother] passes to her children is more a function of the problems than of a theory of child-rearing. (p. 557)

Mothers' success in solving the "problems of their worlds" depended largely on the social-support system available to them. Cultures with structural supports for the practice of motherhood, such as child-care help and adult cooperation, were characterized by warmer and more-stable mothering patterns.

Although none of these authors conceived of parental heritage as the focus of their study, it is nevertheless possible to infer that conceptualization and transmission of parental heritage are linked to a social structure which values the parent-child relationship and facilitates parent-child interaction.

Social class. Sociologists refined knowledge of the impact on parent-child relations of historical time and social structure by delineating the role of social class (Duvall, 1946, 1971; Kohn, 1959, 1963). Large-scale survey data reported by both Duvall and Kohn indicated that the nexus of parent-child relations varied according to social position. For example, the lower- and working-class parent-child relationship tended to be oriented toward obedience, in order to assure family respectability. The middle-class parent-child relationship, on the other hand, was more concerned with internalized standards of conduct, leading to independent achievement and self-satisfaction. In all classes, salient life conditions tended to direct parental values and child-rearing behavior. "Parents are most likely to accord high priority to those values that seem both problematic . . . and important" (Kohn, 1959, p. 350). Conceptions of a valuable parental heritage would be dictated, in part, by varying parent-child relations and survival demands in each social class.

In sum, theory and research suggest that conceptualization and transmission of parental heritage are linked to societal definition of the parent-child relationship as a stable, affective tie. This linkage is nourished by a supportive social structure whose orientation varies between social classes.

SOCIAL PSYCHOLOGICAL FUNCTIONS OF PARENTHOOD

Within the sociohistorical context of parent-child relations, the social psychological functions of being a parent are defined by motivational and social role variables. First, parenthood satisfies a variety of motives, such as evolutionary fulfillment, parental gratification, and intergenerational deficit-filling. Second, parenting constitutes an important social role by marking the major transition of adult life, impacting on adult psychological development and having inherent satisfactions and disappointments. Each of these considerations is discussed in turn.

Motivational variables

Idiosyncratic childbearing motives likely contribute to parental concepts of heritage. For example, the middle-aged mother who desires numerous children in order to fulfill religious precepts would tend to transmit a different heritage than a new young mother whose child signified exclusive acceptance and affection. The variety of childbearing motives are discussed below.

Evolutionary fulfillment. Two theoretical statements suggested that childbearing motivation serves an evolutionary purpose. Writing from a psychological perspective, Bardwick (1974) concluded that humankind has a genetically predetermined and hormonally modulated capacity to parent. Particularly powerful in women, "parenthood may be a part of the human need to create and be experienced as the essence of generativity" (p. 59).

Bardwick's (1974) views were echoed several years later in a major sociological essay by Rossi (1977). In her essay, social scientists were asked to deepen their understanding of the family by recognizing "the central biological fact that the core function of any family system is human continuity through reproduction and child rearing" (p. 2). She cited recent discoveries regarding the interaction among neuroendocrine functioning, sex typing, and childbearing as evidence for an important biological substratum in a process many social scientists prefer to construe as purely functional.

These influential assertions of a biological component to parenthood elicited strong reactions from social scientists. Although Bardwick (1974) and Rossi (1977) deplored continued sexual inequality, feminist scholars labeled their work a step backward in the study of both female psychology and women's rights. For example, Gross, Bernard, Dan, Glazer, Lorber, McClintock, Newton, and Rossi (1979) accused Rossi of reviving the dormant nature-nurture controversy and welcoming an era of scientific conservatism rationalized by biological dictum. Rossi's claim of intellectual openness (Gross et al., 1979) evoked apprehension and skepticism.

This area of study has important implications for the investigation of parental heritage. To the extent that Bardwick (1974) and Rossi (1977) are correct in asserting a biological need to reproduce, social scientific research into parental heritage may yield the conscious representation of more basic human capacities.

Parental gratification.   Sociologists (especially demographers) and psychologists have conducted numerous large-scale surveys of childbearing motives. Typically, they utilized questionnaires and structured interview methods. Clinical reflections on childbearing motives have also been contributed. Major childbearing motives mentioned have included instinct, civic responsibility, proof of sexual competence, mental health, parental pride, need for love, marital and family fulfillment, economic security in old age, adherence to religious and cultural norms, and appeasement of the fear of death (Bardwick, 1978; Blauner, 1966; Fawcett, 1970; Hoffman & Hoffman, 1973; Hoffman & Manis, 1979; Kastenbaum, 1974; Lifton, 1973; Rainwater, 1960, 1965; Veevers, 1973; Wheeler & Oles, 1979). Not surprisingly, in discussing the value of children to parents, Walters and Walters (1980) noted that "the precise influence of this variable has not yet been determined" (p. 814).

Often, research in this area has addressed the psychosocial underpinnings of fertility toward the development of benign guidelines for limiting population growth. Two studies helped set the stage for more-direct investigation of parental heritage by mentioning "expansion of self and continuity of the lineage" as a source of parental gratification

(Hoffman & Hoffman, 1973; Hoffman & Manis, 1979). However, this motive was not fully examined. On the contrary, no study has highlighted parental gratification from anticipated transmission of existing attributes, skills, or possessions. Instead, research has focused on parental gratification which derived from interactions within, or benefits of, the parent-child relationship. For instance, fathering a child was more-often intended to cement a marriage than to enable a father to pass on a prized family tradition.

It is currently difficult to discern whether the emphasis on self-directed gratifications in parenting reflects accurate subject report or investigator inattention to parental heritage. Direct study of parental heritage could corroborate the suggestion that parents construe childbearing largely in their own interest. On the other hand, it might suggest in addition or instead the operation of a consciously conveyed parental heritage.

Intergenerational deficit-filling. Theoretical and qualitative empirical contributions from psychologists and sociologists have proposed a childbearing motive often unconsciously fulfilled by parenting. They suggest that the parent vindicates conflicted life choices and remediates personal deficits through childbearing. Moss et al. (1982) termed this parenthood function the *deficit-filling pattern*. On the basis of interview data, they noted that "when asked to name their legacy toward their children, parents instead responded as if they had been asked to describe how their children could fill out the voids in their lives" (p. 6).

Boszormenyi-Nagy and Spark (1973) have proposed that family members retain underlying loyalties to members of their own families of origin. These writers suggest that we look for justice in terms of rewards or compensations for experiences in families of origin and that we allow these "left-over relationships" to exert a corrosive influence on families of procreation. Within the present framework, invisible loyalties and a sense of justice might be seen as helping to shape conceptions of parental heritage. A father who received little help from his own father might resolve to pass on a sizable estate to his son. Or, a mother with covert loyalty to her own mother might not attach sufficiently to her child to want to transmit a legacy. The notions of invisible loyalty and justice as introduced by Boszormenyi-Nagy and Spark thus offer an alternative formulation of the deficit-filling pattern.

Research has indicated that the deficit-filling pattern can be traced across several generations (Harris, 1959; Kagan, 1977; Moss et al.). For example: "Both the mothers and the fathers in our study invariably showed evidence of using their parenthood to continue or to resolve, through their children, some aspects of their own growing up" (Harris,

1959, p. 39); and "Often, the very deficits that the parents assigned to their children . . . were first labeled by current grandparents" (Moss et al., p. 10).

Research has also noted that the quality of parent-child interaction is influenced by parental investment in the deficit-filling pattern (Aberle & Naegele, 1952; Benedek, 1970; Harris, 1959; Levi, Stierlin, & Savard, 1972; Moss et al., 1982). To illustrate this investment, several authors described the impact on father-son compatibility of conflicting paternal ambitions for self and son (Aberle & Naegele; Levi et al.). Another intriguing clinical report described the impact of maternal ambition in a dual-career mother-daughter pair (Smith & Smith-Blackmer, 1981). Additional specific content and correlates of the deficit-filling pattern remain promising areas for further research.

In sum, motivational variables related to parenting include fulfillment of an evolutionary process, personal gratifications, and deficit compensation. Concepts of parental heritage presumably derive in part from the interplay of these psychological functions. The social role variables considered below are likewise reflected in those conceptions.

Social role variables

Personal experience of the parental role no doubt influences behavior in that role. Research has identified three main parental role variables with implications for conceptualization of parental heritage: transition to the parental role, role impact, and role satisfaction.

Transition to the parental role. In a sociological review, Rossi (1968) contended that entrance into the parental role constitutes the major transition of adult life for women. Cultural pressure toward parenthood, incomplete control over when to assume the role, role irrevocability and inadequate role preparation often combine to make the transition stressful and, for many women, ultimately destructive of self-esteem and personal maturation. Rossi (1968) noted a paucity of investigation into parental response to these role characteristics.

Since Rossi (1968) commented upon the sparse study of the transition to parenthood, much research has been done in the area. Steffensmeier (1982) and Alpert (1981) found that the transition to parenthood is not necessarily traumatic. Rather, they held that the nature of the transition is a function of complex interaction between role and event attributes. According to Plemons (1982), the transition to parenthood engenders change in parental personality functioning, most permanently a greater emphasis on security, ease, and contentment. Some authors suggested a differential impact of role transition on mothers and fathers, with a more-negative impact on fathers before birth and the more-negative impact on mothers following the birth (Plemons, 1982; Waldron & Routh, 1981). Michaels, Hoffman, and Goldberg (1982) noted that the transition to parenthood is associated with an increase in family-focused values and decreased interest in societal welfare. These authors underlined the importance of longitudinal research into the transition to parenthood. In particular, they called for researchers to study prebirth and longer postpartum periods to better identify both the inception of the role transition and its lasting effects. Weinberg and Richardson (1981) called for further refinement in this research area and added that "the debate over the degree of crisis inherent in the parenthood transition should be superceded by a concern for identifying the dimensions of stress associated with this life event and their importance to individuals who differ in life circumstances and characteristics" (p. 692).

Role impact.   In a psychoanalytic essay, Benedek (1970) discussed the developmental impact of the parental role on the parent. She underlined an increased sense of responsibility and parental maturation, maintaining a more-positive view of parenthood than Rossi (1968). In particular, Benedek emphasized that "the psychic structure of the parent cannot remain unaffected by the psychological process of child-rearing itself" (p. 133).

Role satisfaction.   Following on Rossi's (1968) comment that parental role satisfaction had been inadequately studied and acknowledging the parental role impact summarized by Benedek (1970), Hoffman & Manis (1978) conducted a large-scale psychological survey of parental role satisfaction. They determined that the birth of the first child has largely positive effects on marital interaction and parental satisfaction. Detrimental effects, such as loss of privacy, were outweighed by rewards associated with rearing offspring. However, the large-scale survey method precluded intensive exploration of the transitional issues raised by Rossi (1968) or the developmental issues noted by Benedek. Later studies suggested that parental role satisfaction may depend on the ease of interaction between the parental role and adult occupational roles (Chilman, 1980; Richardson, 1981).

Scholars agree that the parental role has a profound impact on adult lifestyle and psychological development. Although role characteristics and legacy would appear to be logically connected, studies of the social psychological functions of parenthood have not included conceptualization and transmission of parental heritage. Such concepts have been more-closely approached by the research traditions reviewed below.

INTERGENERATIONAL DYNAMICS

In addition to the social psychological functions of parenthood, complex intergenerational dynamics operate within the sociohistorical context of parent-child relations. These dynamics are defined by generational and intrafamilial variables. On the societal level, generational variables highlight the impact on inter-age-group relations of being in a generation. Included here are continuity across generations, the developmental stake of one generation in another, and the dialectical relationship between successive generations. On the individual level, intrafamilial variables outline the complementary impact of being in a family. These more-idiosyncratic variables include parent-child identification, the influence of maternal vocation on offspring vocational choice, the differential salience of maternal and paternal kinship ties, and the family life cycle. Both sets of variables and their implications for the study of parental heritage are examined below.

Generational variables

Generation membership presumably influences conceptualization of parental heritage. Current historical events, the age and developmental status at which different generations encounter those events, and the differential experience of the historical process by diverse social groups all interact to shape intergenerational relations (Bengston & Troll, 1978; Mannheim, 1923/1952). The middle-class adult generation of the Great Depression, for instance, would likely identify a different parental legacy than would the working-class generation that came of age during the Vietnam War. Features of generation membership relevant to the study of parental heritage are discussed below.

Intergenerational continuity.   Sociologists have made the main theoretical and empirical contributions to the study of "the never ending drama of the succession of generations" (Bengston, 1975; Bengston, Furlong, & Laufer, 1974; Bengston & Troll, 1978). Scholars in this area have typically defined intergenerational continuity as intergenerational similarity. Based on questionnaire and interview data, moderate degrees of similarity have been reported for such variables as value adherence (Bengston), sex role and familial behaviors (Hill & Aldous, 1969), and political party membership, religious affiliation, and intergenerational affection (Bengston & Troll). Some studies have found evidence of a generation gap, primarily in regard to personal and social values (Christenson, 1977; Lichtenstein, 1974) and attributions of power in the intergenerational relationship (Jessop, 1981). In contrast, other studies have found essentially conflict-free intergenerational relations (Coleman, George, & Hall, 1977; Gallagher, 1979; Hamid & Wyllie, 1980).

Equation of intergenerational continuity with intergenerational similarity has provided a descriptive foundation for generational analysis. However, this definition has precluded investigation of the direction of effect in intergenerational continuity. For example, this definition has not addressed the question of whether intergenerational similarity reflects the generations' common exposure to contemporary history, a process of intentional transmission between generations, or an interaction of both possibilities.

Psychologists have demonstrated a related interest in parent-child similarity. Rather than large-scale study of succeeding generations, they have focused on particular attitude correlations among parents and children (Doherty, 1970; Lipman-Blumen, 1972). However, their work has likewise left unresolved the question of direction of effect in parent-child similarity, thereby ignoring parental heritage.

Reconceptualization of intergenerational continuity from the vantage point of parental heritage would suggest new areas of intergenerational study. Knowledge of a mature generation's intentions to transmit a legacy, its conceptions of that legacy, and its acceptance or rejection by a younger generation would greatly enrich our understanding of the degrees of intergenerational similarity already reported. This direct study of parental heritage would benefit, in turn, from incorporation of the following two generational variables.

Developmental stake.   In their survey of intergenerational differences, Bengston and Kuypers (1971) found that college students tended to maximize philosophical and ideological differences between the generations. In contrast, the parent generation tended to minimize such essential differences, concentrating instead on more-trivial issues of personal habits and traits. To account for these opposing views, Bengston and Kuypers introduced the concept of the developmental stake— the investment of one generation in another. The parent generation has a stake in assuring immortality: "Middle generation adults need to orient, socialize, and direct youth . . . to guarantee generational continuity through influence on youth . . . to extend one's personal history into the future" (p. 255). Opposing this stake: "The developmental stake of the young is quite different. They have high investment in establishing their personal lifestyles, in forming their attitudes toward major issues and institutions. . . . They are more concerned with the establishment, as opposed to validation, of values and strategies. Such issues imply freedom to experience and develop" (p. 257). The authors asserted that opposing developmental stakes may thus drastically color the generations' perceptions of one another.

To assess the heuristic value of the developmental stake for the study of parental heritage, it is important to differentiate this concept from both the deficit-filling pattern discussed above (Moss et al., 1982) and the parental heritage itself. The developmental stake is the sociological analogue to the social psychological deficit-filling pattern. Both pertain to vested interests between generations, but the former operates on the generational level and the latter on the individual.

From a sociological perspective, the developmental stake refers to whole generations' reciprocal investments. The older generation seeks an extension into the future via an affinity with the younger generation. For example, a mature generation's assurance that assumption of adult responsibilities inevitably cures the young of disturbing political idealism expresses the generation's developmental stake in the continuity of familiar, comfortably held political beliefs. Conversely, the younger generation pursues the freedom to stake out its social territory. Youth's declaration of enduring political activism represents its developmental stake in laying claim to a new social order, as well as its attempt to establish a generational identity.

From a social psychological perspective, the deficit-filling pattern pertains to the degree to which children's life choices serve to compensate for individual parents' past and current life deficiencies. The mother who pushes her reluctant daughter toward doctoral study to compensate for her own interrupted education offers an illustration of such a pattern.

While the deficit-filling pattern and the developmental stake help to define the parameters of parental heritage, neither notion is equivalent to it. Rather, parental heritage refers to parents' identification of existing parental psychological or material assets that are sufficiently valued to be transmitted to offspring. The father whose lifetime study has yielded a prized political philosophy to be handed down to the young and the professional mother who bestows a carefully collected library on an aspiring daughter both demonstrate conceptualization and transmission of parental heritage.

As suggested above, motivational variables such as the deficit-filling pattern contribute to parental capacity for conceptualizing parental heritage. The parent whose motives for parenthood are limited exclusively to deficit compensation finds it difficult to conceptualize a relevant legacy (Moss et al., 1982). Similarly, generations' developmental stakes may obscure or supplant parental heritage. The parent generation may confuse its legacy with wished-for connectedness to its youth, who in turn may discount the offered heritage in favor of a distinctive world view and social stance.

Studies of parental heritage must thus distinguish among individual parental needs for deficit-filling, generations' developmental stakes in one another, and parental identification of accumulated assets which merit transmission to the young. Likewise, these studies must take into account the oscillating relationship between generations, discussed below.

Generational dialectic. Generations alternate in their political activism and pressure toward social change. Rossi (1973) referred to this alternation as the generational dialectic. To illustrate, Rossi recalled that the adult female generation of the early 20th century agitated for the political reform that culminated in the 19th Amendment to the Constitution. That generation was followed by a quieter, more-private generation which in turn raised the activist generation of 1960s–70s feminists. Rossi asserted that this oscillation represents a continuous process of groundbreaking and consolidation of gains.

Location of a given generation within this generational dialectic may have significant implications for the study of parental heritage. An activist generation may conceptualize a grandiose, impersonal legacy while, in view of changed social rules, a consolidation generation may focus more on validating private life. Direct examination of parental heritage will reveal the accuracy and salience of this generational dialectic concept. The foregoing generational variables are further illuminated by consideration of the following intrafamilial variables.

Intrafamilial variables

Analogous to generation membership, family membership likely exerts an influence over concepts of parental heritage. For example, a wealthy family with a patriarchal tradition of son succeeding father as the local philanthropist would probably conceptualize a different parental heritage than would a matriarchal, working-class family. Patterns of parent-child identification, the impact of maternal vocation, and kinship ties are the aspects of family membership most relevant to the study of parental heritage.

Parent-child identification. Psychologists and sociologists have studied parent-child identification extensively, using a wide range of social science research methods (Maccoby & Jacklin, 1974). Children's identification with parents appears to facilitate their adoption of parental behaviors and personality characteristics (Johnson, 1975; Lynn, 1959, 1969). For example, Chodorow (1978) has suggested that, through identification, individuals tend to reproduce the same-sex parent's child-care role and degree of emotional relatedness.

Much of the literature in this area has focused exclusively on the child's identification with the parent. In order to study parental heritage, however, it is important also to examine the parent's identification with the child. Preliminary examination of such parental identification has been conducted. It appears that when the parent has high self-esteem, identification with the child may promote the child's high achievement and emotional well-being (Baruch, 1976; Harris, 1953). However, in cases of lower parental self-esteem, parental identification approaches symbiosis, and the child's growth and development may be restricted (Johnson, 1975; Lynn, 1959, 1969). Furthermore, such parental overidentification may impede conceptualization of parental heritage (Moss et al., 1982). These authors have suggested that perception of the parent and child as a continuous dyad renders "concepts of a legacy from one individual to the other . . . superfluous" (p. 20). They concluded that "parent-child individuation may be a necessary but not sufficient condition for conceptualization of parental heritage" (p. 23). The relationship between parent-child identification and concepts of parental heritage remains a promising area for further study.

Maternal vocation. Psychological and sociological study of the effects of maternal vocation on children has yielded two main findings. First, maternal employment outside the home tends to facilitate less stereotypic sex role behavior and expectations by family members (Hoffman, 1977), particularly when the mother is engaged in high-status employment (Acock, Barker, & Bengston, 1982). Powell and Steelman (1982) found that maternal employment facilitated more-liberal attitudes only among male offspring, but this finding has not been widely replicated (Acock et al., 1982). Second, the extent to which maternal vocational choice is repeated by daughters appears to be related not to specific choices but to maternal satisfaction with the choices made (Baruch, 1972; Lipman-Blumen, 1972). Lipman-Blumen, for instance, noted that the daughter of a woman forced into a low-status job by economic necessity was less likely to seek a career outside the family than one whose mother was a satisfied professional or businesswoman.

No link has yet been made between the study of maternal vocation and examination of parental heritage. At present, maternal careers have been studied primarily from the standpoint of children's exposure to vocational alternatives but not as possible components of a parental legacy. The extent to which parents may choose specific vocations or other roles in order to amass a heritage for their children remains unexplored territory.

Kinship ties. Salient kinship ties may identify key participants in the conceptualization and transmission of parental heritage. Sociologists and psychologists have investigated the importance and durability of various lineage types. Their work has suggested that, within the middle class, same-sex lineages such as grandfather-father-son are most likely to display regular contact, affection, shared beliefs, and similar familial behaviors (Aldous & Hill, 1965). In addition, research in this area has identified sons as the preferred offspring, through whom lineage values may be best expressed (Dinitz, Dynes, & Clark, 1954; Hoffman, 1977; Norman, 1974; Peterson & Peterson, 1973).

Child-naming patterns in middle-class families have proven to be a useful behavioral index of meaningful kin networks and a child's value as a symbol of clan solidarity. For instance, the mother who gives her daughter the name of a revered paternal grandmother has made an important behavioral statement regarding the older woman's continuing impact as well as the child's capacity to serve as a bridge between the maternal and paternal lines. Rossi (1965) has noted that boys and firstborns are most-often designated as kin name bearers in middle-class families. She has also traced a steady decrease in "naming sons for their paternal kin and daughters for their maternal kin," suggesting a growing "affective social symmetry . . . between the nuclear family's two families of origin" (p. 49).

Information regarding the relative impact of different kinship ties may guide the study of parental heritage. Investigations utilizing behavioral indexes such as child-naming patterns hold promise for illuminating parental legacy within salient kin groups.

Family life cycle. The family moves through a life cycle from formation to reproduction on toward reformation or, in some cases, dissolution. In recent years, authors have suggested that the nature of parent-child interaction at a given point in time depends in part upon the family's place in its life cycle (Duvall, 1971; Hareven, 1977). Hagestad (1982) elaborated on this suggestion, specifying that a parent-child pair's position within a lineage is critical for understanding the pair's interaction. For example, the relationship between the oldest living member of a lineage and her middle-aged daughter would differ greatly from the relationship of a young mother and her school-aged daughter in a lineage that contained a living grandmother and great grandmother.

The concept of a future has also proven to be a critical variable in understanding a family's movement through the life cycle. At early stages of the cycle, there is only a dim conception of the future, while provision for the future becomes more salient later in the cycle (Resnick, 1981).

The study of family life cycle and the concept of the future has striking implications for understanding parental heritage. Likely, conception of parental heritage varies according to stage in the family life cycle. It may well be that a position relatively late in the family life cycle, when belief in the salience of the future is strong, facilitates conception of parental heritage. One study provided tentative support for this formulation. Fischer (1981) noted a rapprochement between mothers and daughters when the daughters, in turn, also became mothers. At that time, both generations expressed increased interest in intergenerational continuity. Such a rapprochement might also entail an increased investment in parental heritage.

Intergenerational dynamics are thus mediated by generational and family variables. Since conceptions of parental heritage may in part reflect complex interactions among them, future investigators would do well to accord high priority to clarifying those interactions.

RESEARCH DIRECTIONS

Development of the infant realm of parental heritage awaits integration and empirical articulation of the diverse conceptual domains discussed above. The psychological functions of parenthood are foremost among the directions that appear to hold out the most promise for advancing such study. Social psychological study of parental gratification and the deficit-filling pattern and intergenerational study of the developmental stake suggest that parenting serves parental self-interest. It is currently unclear, however, whether such self-interest includes transmission of parental heritage. Future work that clarifies whether transmission of a legacy is an additional expression of parental self-interest would help to illuminate the concept of parental heritage.

A second promising area for future study is intergenerational continuity. Research to date has equated intergenerational continuity with intergenerational similarity but has done little to answer questions concerning direction of effect. Thus, previous research has overlooked the possibility that parental conceptions of, and intentions to convey, a heritage may partly account for intergenerational continuity. For example, a high rate of intergenerational continuity in values may reflect deliberate parental transmission of beliefs. On the other hand, it may reflect ongoing cultural influences or inadvertent modeling across generations. More-intensive investigation of the factors that forge similarity across generations would presumably shed light on the content and transmission of parental heritage. Lowenthal (1971) put forth a model for the study of intentionality in adult behavior which might facilitate such investigation.

Finally, reciprocal parent-child identification and its relationship to parent-child individuation have considerable relevance for the study of parental heritage. An intriguing hypothesis can be drawn from preliminary research: Conceptualization of parental heritage appears to depend on an optimal balance between reciprocal parent-child identification and parent-child individuation. Reciprocal parent-child identification must be sufficiently positive and strong to allow for attachment between the parent and child. Yet, at the same time, the two must perceive themselves as distinct personalities between whom meaningful transactions can occur. Confirmation of this hypothesis would represent a major contribution to our understanding of parental heritage.

So as not to relive the history of work on the periphery of this area, we must be mindful to distinguish between the study of parental heritage and more-traditional parent-child study. As noted earlier, previous parent-child researchers have often assumed without evidence that transmission of a cultural and personal heritage is a central function of parenting. This assumption has typically provided the rationale for close examination of various aspects of parent-child relations. Prior assumptions regarding parental heritage must now defer to focused investigation. Before scholars can rely confidently on transmission of parental heritage as a basis for related assertions, they must first clarify its sources, content, and implications.

Research aimed at such clarification must be guided by flexible methodological prescriptions. Controlled social-learning strategies which cast the parent as socializer, linking specific parental inputs with specific child outputs, have articulated one dimension of parent-child interaction. However, to gain answers to new questions regarding parental conceptions and intentions, time-honored methodological techniques must accommodate intensive interviewing and other contextual strategies. To illustrate, an initial study might hypothesize that (a) parents have articulated conceptions of their legacy and that (b) parental self-interest is served by its transmission. Rich information on parental heritage would be yielded by interlacing structured interviews designed to elicit parental conceptions of their heritage with standardized inventories of parental interests and goals.

CONCLUSION

This review has proposed an interdisciplinary conceptual scaffold (Figure 1) on which to base study of parental heritage, an accumulation of psychological and material assets valued sufficiently by the parent to be passed on intentionally to the young. Parental conceptions of a legacy likely assume greatest relevance when the parent-child relationship is defined as a lifelong affective bond, facilitated by a supportive social structure and class. Specific conceptions are shaped by parental motives for evolutionary fulfillment, self-gratification, and deficit-filling as well as the experience of transition into parenthood, the psychological impact of parenting, and parenthood's inherent satisfactions. These conceptions are further influenced by continuity, reciprocal investments, and dialectical relationships between whole generations, and by identification patterns, vocational models, and kinship ties between intrafamilial generations. Future study of parental heritage must clarify the complex interactions among these sociohistorical, social psychological, and intergenerational variables.

Direct study of parental heritage will focus deserved attention on a meaningful and frequently neglected concept in parent-child relations. By illuminating an important intrafamilial transaction, it will further our knowledge of family process. By linking this family interaction to broader social and historical conditions, the study of parental heritage will also contribute to the sociology of the family. Finally, by more-fully articulating a central adult social role, the study of parental heritage will enhance the growing body of knowledge that places parenthood in the broader context of adult development.

REFERENCES

Aberle, D. F., & Naegle, K. D. Middle class fathers' occupational role and attitudes toward children. *American Journal of Orthopsychiatry*, 1952, *22*, 366–378.

Abramovitz, R. Parenthood in America. *Journal of Clinical Child Psychology*, 1976, *5*, 43–46.

Acock, A. C., Barker, D., & Bengston, V. L. Mother's employment and parent-youth similarity. *Journal of Marriage and the Family*, 1982, *44*, 441–455.

Aldous, J., & Hill, R. Social cohesion, lineage type and intergenerational transmission. *Social Forces*, 1965, *43*, 471–482.

Alpert, J. L. Theoretical perspectives on the family life cycle. *Counseling Psychologist*, 1981, *9*, 25–34.

Anderson, C. W. A context for reciprocal developmental influences. *Counseling Psychologist*, 1981, *9*, 35–44.

Bardwick, J. M. Evolution and parenting. *Journal of Social Issues*, 1974, *30*, 39–62.

Bardwick, J. M. Middle age and a sense of future. *Merrill-Palmer Quarterly*, 1978, *24*, 129–138.

Baruch, G. K. Maternal influences upon college women's attitudes toward women and work. *Developmental Psychology*, 1972, *6*, 32–37.

Baruch, G. K. Girls who perceive themselves as competent: Some antecedents and correlates. *Psychology of Women Quarterly*, 1976, *1*, 38–49.

Becker, W. C. Consequences of different kinds of parental discipline. In M. Hoffman & L. W. Hoffman (Eds.), *Review of child development research*. New York: Russell Sage Foundation, 1964.

Bell, R. Q. A reinterpretation of the direction of effects in studies of socialization. *Psychological Review*, 1968, *75*, 81–95.

Benedek, T. The family as a psychologic field. In E. J. Anthony & T. Benedek (Eds.), *Parenthood: Its psychology and psychopathology*. Boston: Little, Brown, 1970.

Bengston, V. L. Generation and family effects on value socialization. *American Sociological Review*, 1975, *40*, 358–371.

Bengston, V. L., Furlong, M. J., & Laufer, R. S. Time, aging and the continuity of social structure: Themes and issues in generational analysis. *Journal of Social Issues*, 1974, *30*, 1–30.

Bengston, V. L., & Kuypers, J. A. Generational difference and the developmental stake. *Aging and Human Development*, 1971, *2*, 249–260.

Bengston, V. L., & Troll, L. Youth and their parents: Feedback and intergenerational influence in socialization. In R. M. Lerner & G. B. Spanier (Eds.), *Child influences on marital and family interaction*. New York: Academic Press, 1978.

Berardo, F. M., Hill, R., Fox, G. L., Wiseman, J. P., & Aldous, J. A prescriptive analysis for the family field in the 1980's. *Journal of Marriage and the Family*, 1981, *43*, 249–270.

Bernard, J. Societal values and parenting. *Counseling Psychologist*, 1981, *9*, 5–11.

Blauner, R. Death and social structure. *Psychiatry*, 1966, *29*, 378–394.

Boszormenyi-Nagy, I., & Spark, G. M. *Invisible loyalties: Reciprocity in intergenerational family therapy*. New York: Harper & Row, 1973.

Chilman, C. S. Parent satisfactions, concerns and goals for their children. *Family Relations*, 1980, *29*, 339–345.

Chodorow, N. *The reproduction of mothering: Psychoanalysis and the sociology of gender*. Berkeley: University of California Press, 1978.

Christenson, J. A. Generational value differences. *Gerontologist*, 1977, *17*, 367–374.

Coleman, J., George, R., & Holt, G. Adolescents and their parents: A study of attitudes. *Journal of Genetic Psychology*, *130*, 1977, 239–245.

Dinitz, S. E., Dynes, R. R., & Clark, A. S. Preferences for male and female children—traditional or affectional? *Marriage and Family Living*, 1954, *16*, 128–130.

Doherty, A. Influence of parental control on the development of feminine sex role and conscience. *Developmental Psychology*, 1970, *2*, 157–158.

Duvall, E. M. Conceptions of parenthood. *American Journal of Sociology*, 1946, *52*, 193–203.

Duvall, E. M. *Family development* (2d ed.). Philadelphia: J. B. Lippincott, 1971.

Fawcett, J. T. *Psychology and population*. New York: Population Council, 1970.

Fischer, L. R. Transitions in the mother-daughter relationship. *Journal of Marriage and the Family*, 1981, *43*, 613–622.

Frieze, I. H., Parsons, J. E., Johnson, P. B., Ruble, D. N., & Zellman, G. L. *Women and sex roles*. New York: W. W. Norton, 1978.

Gallagher, B. J. Attitude differences across three generations: Class and sex components. *Adolescence*, 1979, *14*, 503–516.

Gilbert, L. A. Impediments to research on parenting. *Counseling Psychologist*, 1981, *9*, 63–68.

Gross, H. E., Bernard, J., Dan, A. M., Glazer, N., Lorber, J., McClintock, M., Newton, N., & Rossi, A. Considering a biosocial perspective on parenting. *Signs*, 1979, *4*, 695–717.

Hagestad, G. O. Parent and child: Generations in the family. In T. M. Field, A. Huston, H. C. Quay, L. Troll, & G. E. Finley (Eds.), *Review of human development*. New York: John Wiley & Sons, 1982.

Hamid, P. N., & Wyllie, A. J. What generation gap? *Adolescence*, 1980, *15*, 385–391.

Handel, G. Sociological aspects of parenthood. In E. J. Anthony & T. Benedek (Eds.), *Parenthood: Its psychology and psychopathology.* Boston: Little, Brown, 1970.

Hareven, T. K. Family time and historical time. *Daedalus,* 1977, *106,* 57–70.

Harris, I. D. On recognition of resemblance. *Psychiatry,* 1953, *16,* 355–364.

Harris, I. D. *Normal children and mothers.* New York: Free Press, 1959.

Hill, R., & Aldous, J. Socialization for marriage and parenthood. In D. A. Goslin (Ed.), *Handbook of socialization theory and research.* Skokie, Ill.: Rand McNally, 1969.

Hoffman, L. W. Changes in family roles, socialization and sex differences. *American Psychologist,* 1977, *32,* 644–657.

Hoffman, L. W., & Hoffman, M. L. The value of children to parents. In J. T. Fawcett (Ed.), *Psychological perspectives on population.* New York: Basic Books, 1973.

Hoffman, L. W., & Manis, J. D. Influences of children on marital interaction and parental satisfactions and dissatisfactions. In R. M. Lerner & G. B. Spanier (Eds.), *Child influences on marital and family interaction.* New York: Academic Press, 1978.

Hoffman, L. W., & Manis, J. D. The value of children in the United States: A new approach to the study of fertility. *Journal of Marriage and the Family,* 1979, *4,* 583–596.

Jessop, D. L. Family relationships as viewed by parents and adolescents: A specification. *Journal of Marriage and the Family,* 1981, *43,* 95–107.

Johnson, M. Fathers, mothers and sex-typing. *Social Inquiry,* 1975, *45,* 15–26.

Kagan, J. The child in the family. *Daedalus,* 1977, *106,* 33–56.

Kastenbaum, R. Fertility and the fear of death. *Journal of Social Issues,* 1974, *30,* 63–78.

Kohn, M. L. Social class and parental values. *American Journal of Sociology,* 1959, *64,* 337–351.

Kohn, M. L. Social class and parent-child relations: An interpretation. *American Journal of Sociology,* 1963, *68,* 471–480.

LeMasters, E. E. *Parents in modern America.* Homewood, Ill.: Dorsey Press, 1974.

Levi, L. D., Stierlin, H., & Savard, R. J. Fathers and sons: The interlocking crises of integrity and identity. *Psychiatry,* 1972, *35,* 48–56.

Levinson, D. J., Darrow, C. N., Klein, E. B., Levinson, M. H., & McKee, B. *The seasons of a man's life.* New York: Alfred A. Knopf, 1978.

Lichtenstein, H. The effect of reality perception on psychic structure: A psychoanalytic contribution to the problem of the "generation gap." *Annual of Psychoanalysis,* 1974, *2,* 349–367.

Lifton, R. J. The sense of immortality: On death and the continuity of life. *American Journal of Psychoanalysis,* 1973, *33,* 3–15.

Lipman-Blumen, J. How ideology shapes women's lives. *Scientific American,* 1972, *226,* 34–42.

Lowenthal, M. F. Intentionality: Toward a framework for the study of adaptation in adulthood. *Aging and Human Development,* 1971, *2,* 79–95.

Lynn, D. B. A note on sex differences in the development of masculine and feminine identification. *Psychological Review,* 1959, *66,* 126–135.

Lynn, D. B. *Parental and sex-role identification.* Berkeley, Calif.: McCutchan Publishing, 1969.

Lynn, D. B. *Daughter and parents.* Monterey, Calif.: Brooks/Cole Publishing, 1979.

Maccoby, E. E., & Jacklin, C. M. *The psychology of sex differences.* Stanford, Calif.: Stanford University Press, 1974.

Mannheim, K. The problem of generations. In K. Mannheim, *Essays on the sociology of knowledge.* London: Routledge & Keagen Paul, 1952. (Originally published, 1923.)

Michaels, G. Y., Hoffman, M., & Goldberg, W. *Longitudinal investigation of value system changes at transition to parenthood.* Paper presented at the meetings of the American Psychological Association, Washington, D.C., 1982.

Minturn, L., & Lambert, W. Motherhood and child rearing. In N. W. Bell & E. F. Vogel (Eds.), *A modern introduction to the family.* New York: Free Press, 1968.

Moss, N. E., & Abramowitz, S. I. Beyond deficit-filling and developmental stakes: Cross-disciplinary perspectives on parental heritage. *Journal of Marriage and the Family,* 1982, *44,* 357–366.

Moss, N. E., Abramowitz, S. I., & Kaschak, E. From mother to daughter: Conceptions of parental heritage. *Smith College Journal of Social Work,* 1982, *53,* 1–14.

Mussen, P. H., Conger, J. J., & Kagan, J. *Readings in child development and personality* (2d ed.). New York: Harper & Row, 1970.

Norman, R. D. Sex differences in preferences for sex of children: A replication after 20 years. *Journal of Psychology,* 1974, *88,* 229–239.

Peterson, C. C., & Peterson, J. L. Preference for sex of offspring as a measure of change in sex attitudes. *Psychology Journal of Human Behavior,* 1973, *10,* 3–5.

Plemons, J. K. *The effect of transition to parenthood on adult personality.* Paper presented at the meetings of the American Psychological Association, Washington, D.C., August, 1982.

Powell, B., & Steelman, L. C. Testing an undertested comparison. Maternal effects on sons' and daughters' attitudes toward women in the labor force. *Journal of Marriage and the Family,* 1982, *44,* 349–355.

Rainwater, L. *And the poor get children: Sex, contraception and family planning in the working class.* Chicago: Quadrangle Books, 1960.

Rainwater, L. *Family design: Marital sexuality, family size and contraception.* Chicago: Aldine Publishing, 1965.

Resnick, J. L. Parent education and the female parent. *Counseling Psychologist,* 1981, *9,* 55–62.

Richardson, M. S. Occupational and family roles: A neglected intersection. *Counseling Psychologist* 1981, *9,* 13–23.

Rossi, A. S. Naming children in middle class families. *American Sociological Review,* 1965, *30,* 499–513.

Rossi, A. S. Transition to parenthood. *Journal of Marriage and the Family,* 1968, *30,* 26–39.

Rossi, A. S. Feminism and intellectual complexity. In A. S. Rossi (Ed.), *The feminist papers.* New York: Bantam Books, 1973.

Rossi, A. S. A biosocial perspective on parenting. *Daedalus,* 1977, *106,* 1–31.

Smith, M. O., & Smith-Blackmer, D. The mother-daughter relationship: A dialogue continued.

Some factors effecting professional identity. *Clinical Social Work Journal,* 1981, *9,* 57–68.

Smith-Rosenberg, C. The female world of love and ritual: Relations between women in 19th century America. *Signs,* 1975, *1,* 1–29.

Steffensmeier, R. H. A role model of the transition to parenthood. *Journal of Marriage and the Family,* 1982, *44,* 319–334.

Veevers, J. E. The social meanings of parenthood. *Psychiatry,* 1973, *36,* 291–310.

Waldron, H., & Routh, D. K. The effect of the first child on the marital relationship. *Journal of Marriage and the Family,* 1981, *43,* 785–788.

Walters, J., & Walters, L. H. Parent-child relationships: A review, 1970–1979. *Journal of Marriage and the Family,* 1980, *42,* 807–822.

Weinberg, S. L., & Richardson, M. S. Dimensions of stress in early parenting. *Journal of Consulting and Clinical Psychology,* 1981, *49,* 686–693.

Wheeler, R. W., & Oles, H. Motives for parenthood: A comparison of students and parents values. *Psychological Reports,* 1979, *44,* 1074.

Whitbourne, S. K., & Weinstock, C. S. *Adult development: The differentiation of experience.* New York: Holt, Rinehart & Winston, 1979.

Chapter 18

Characteristics, Consequences, and Determinants of Parenting*

JAY BELSKY

JOAN VONDRA

To even the most casual observer, it is strikingly apparent that families vary immensely in the manner in which they rear their children. A question which confronts every student of parent-child relations involves the origin of these often-dramatic individual differences in parental functioning and the effects of such disparate childrearing practices on child development. Because most empirical and theoretical inquiry has focused on the latter question—that is, the developmental consequences of differing styles and practices of parenting—the first part of the chapter is devoted to this topic, saving for the latter half consideration of the determinants of these individual patterns of parenting.

In seeking to chart parental differences and their comparative effects on children across the entire span of childhood—from infancy to adolescence—it is important to note that parenting itself changes, in a manner which (optimally) corresponds to the developing competencies of the child. There is likely to be both continuity and discontinuity in the progression from infant care giver to adolescent guide. While specific practices obviously metamorphose, the philosophy, the expectations, the foci, and the goals may or may not undergo comparable transitions.

* Work on this paper was supported by grants from the National Science Foundation (No. SES–8108886), the National Institute of Child Health and Human Development (No. R01HD15496–01A1), the Division of Maternal and Child Health of Public Health Service (No. MC–R–424067–02–0), and by the March of Dimes Birth Defects Foundation (Social and Behavior Science Branch, No. 12–64), Jay Belsky, principal investigator.

Thus, the parent who makes few demands on a toddler may have unusually high expectations of a teenager. On the other hand, the parent who places great value on cooperation and social orientation may encourage this from babyhood on. The parenting literature appears primarily to adopt a position stressing continuity: Parenting style (i.e., the more general principles and patterns of parental behavior) is assumed to be fairly consistent over time, allowing extrapolations to both past and future parental and child functioning. In point of fact, however, very little evidence is available on this critical issue.

A second and perhaps more significant characteristic of empirical studies of parenting is their reliance on correlational analysis. Investigations of parenting and child development, as well as those of the determinants of parenting, link proposed cause and consequence concurrently and across time through statistical but not experimental methods. The general tendency, nevertheless, is to interpret empirically established relationships in terms of contextual influences on parenting and of parenting on child development, rather than vice versa. This is in spite of the fact that reported associations, since they are correlational in nature, cannot highlight actual patterns of cause and effect. As some have argued, it may be just as reasonable to interpret such correlational data in terms of child influences on parenting (Bell, 1968) or a third variable of parental personality which governs both parenting and the ecological context in which that parenting is embedded (Belsky, 1984 Burgess & Richardson, 1983).

In light of the current state of the art in the study of parental functioning, we have arranged this chapter to summarize our present understanding of parental influences during infancy, childhood (the preschool and school-age years), and adolescence, before proceeding with a discussion of the probable familial (parental, child, and marital) and extrafamilial (social network and work) determinants of parenting. For the scholar of individual differences in parenting, the task is to assimilate the converging evidence with regard to each domain of inquiry, yet remain alert to the methodological limitations and theoretical presuppositions guiding our efforts to develop a science of parenting.

CHARACTERISTICS AND CONSEQUENCES OF PARENTAL FUNCTIONING

Infancy

The first two years of life have received special attention in the study of parent-child relations for a variety of reasons. Most important is the critical role that traditional psychoanalytic theory (Freud, 1949), more-recent ethological attachment theory (Ainsworth, 1973), and many nonscientists attribute to the initial years of life and to the infant's first interpersonal relationship with mother. It has long been assumed that early development determines or at least places limits upon development in later childhood, adolescence, and even adulthood. In recent years, however, this set of assumptions has been challenged, most forcibly by lifespan theorists who argue, not unreasonably, that the human organism is open to developmental change throughout the life course (Kagan, Kearsley, & Zelazo, 1978). Thus, while parenting practices may certainly influence infants, these early developmental effects need not determine future functioning. Developmental trajectories may be aborted, deflected, or created by influences that arise *throughout* childhood and adulthood. It is in the spirit of this awareness that we review parental influences upon child development during the first two years of life.

Available evidence does suggest connections between early care and development and subsequent functioning. But when linkages are found between parenting during infancy, infant development, and later child behavior, they are likely to be accounted for by complex processes, not simple direct ones. For example, the infant whose parents foster intellectual competence and curiosity may develop into the toddler/preschooler who frequently asks questions of his parents and teachers, receives informative answers, and as a consequence, continues to display intellectual precocity in the preschool and school-age years. Thus, in this instance, it does not appear to be the case that the intellectual brightness fostered by parents during infancy directly determines subsequent intelligence, but rather that a bidirectional and transactional process of parent-to-infant-to-parent-to-toddler-to-parent-to-preschooler effects characterize the connections which link together various developmental periods. We suspect that it will primarily be through such complex reciprocal pathways of influence that parental effects identified during infancy are connected to developmental outcomes and processes beyond the opening years of life.

Intellectual competence. Across an extremely large number of observational studies, several key dimensions of maternal functioning emerge from the vast literature on parental influence during infancy as consistent predictors of individual differences in infant cognitive functioning. These can be ordered along a care-giving continuum ranging from simple, "unembellished" care of infant physical needs to efforts aimed at stimulating development and enriching the bond between mother and child. Toward the end of this continuum, defining the most-limited extent of maternal involvement, are behaviors which require simple maternal *attentiveness* to the infant.

Overall maternal attentiveness repeatedly has been found to relate positively to measures of infant functioning. These measures include performance on standardized infant intelligence tests (e.g., Clarke-Stewart, 1973; Elardo, Bradley, & Caldwell, 1975), assessments of language comprehension (Cohen, Beckwith, & Parmelee, 1978), and measures of exploratory behavior (Rubenstein, 1967). In interpreting these findings, it has been proposed that attentiveness itself may not be the important factor in the relationship between maternal behavior and infant competence. Rather, what occurs as mothers attend to their infants may be more crucial in influencing the infant's development.

In certain respects, this same analysis may explain one reason why *physical contact,* an activity which requires more maternal involvement than merely attending to the baby, has also been linked to intellectual competence in infancy and beyond (e.g., Tulkin & Covitz, 1975). Additionally, the rocking, jiggling, and other active movements of the infant's whole body that frequently accompany physical contact serve to maintain the infant in an optimal state of arousal, which then enables the child to attend to, respond to, and explore people, objects, and events in his/her environment. Such alertness and involvement foster learning and promote cognitive development.

Maternal *verbal or "vocal" stimulation* may be considered the next qualitative level of care-giving, due to its (potentially) reciprocal and cognitive orientation. A number of investigators have noted significant positive relationships between such stimulation (both quantity and quality) and infant competence, particularly in the second year of life (e.g., Clarke-Stewart, 1973; K. Nelson, 1973; Wachs, Uzgiris, & Hunt, 1971). Some investigators have focused on the relationships between maternal language and infant language competence (K. Nelson), whereas others have reported positive correlations between maternal verbal stimulation and more-general measures of infant competence, such as standardized infant test scores (Clarke-Stewart, 1973; Wachs et al.).

Material stimulation is another kind of maternal behavior related to infant cognitive functioning. This kind of growth-promoting mothering consists of deliberate attempts to involve the infant with the environment. Such efforts are typically more overt attempts to facilitate cognitive development than simple attentiveness, physical contact, and even verbal stimulation. Measures of material stimulation ranging from the sheer number of toys provided (Bell, 1971) or provision of age-appropriate toys (Bradley & Caldwell, 1976), to active participation by the mother in material-related activities (Clarke-Stewart, 1973) have each been positively correlated with cognitive functioning, whether in terms of play behavior or performance on standardized tests. Why should such stimulating care-giving facilitate the development of cognitive competence? One suggestion is that stimulating activity furnishes infants with information about the world and teaches them how to focus their attention on objects and events so as to be able to acquire information on their own (Belsky, Goode, & Most, 1980).

In addition to the frequency with which mothers provide cognitively stimulating care, the *responsiveness* of parental behavior also appears to be developmentally important to the infant. It has been found repeatedly that infants whose parents contingently respond to their smiles, vocalizations, and other behaviors display greater intellectual competence both during infancy and at subsequent developmental periods than do age-mates whose parents are less responsive (e.g., Carew, 1980; Clarke-Stewart, 1973; Hardy-Brown, Plomin, & DeFries, 1981; Yarrow, Rubenstein, & Pedersen, 1975). To explain these data it has been proposed that parental behavior that is responsive to infant behavior enables the child to discover that she has control over the world and thereby encourages the child to engage in further activity. Lewis and Goldberg (1969) have spoken in terms of a generalized sense of efficacy the infant develops (even in the first half of the first year) which, through the activity it encourages, generates experiences that are richly informative.

In contrast to the five dimensions of maternal behavior considered up to this point—each associated with positive infant outcomes—the next behavior pattern to be considered, *restriction of exploration,* relates negatively to infant functioning (Clarke-Stewart, 1973; Tulkin & Kagan, 1972). Why should restrictions undermine intellectual growth, as these and other investigations indicate it does? Most likely the answer to this question resides in the effect of such restriction on infant activity and curiosity. By functioning to reduce children's interest in the world, or at least limit the amount of time they have to pursue such interests, long periods of time spent in high chairs and in playpens and frequent noes, don'ts, and stop thats undermine the information gathering upon which intellectual development is based.

On the basis of the preceding discussion, it can be concluded that parents who promote optimal cognitive development during the infancy years function effectively as *sources of stimulation* (by speaking to, and by playing with, the infant) and as *mediators or filters of stimulation* (by directing infant attention to objects and events in the child's world and by restricting the toddler primarily from engaging in dangerous activities). Although we have separately considered several major dimensions of parental care which have been consistently linked with child functioning—both during infancy and beyond—it would be mistaken to assume that these dimensions are unrelated. In fact, in Clarke-Stewart's (1973) investigation linking parenting at 9 months with child functioning at 18 months, mothers found to be attentive to their infants were materially and verbally stimulating, responsive, positively affectionate, and relatively nonrestrictive. Thus, she was led to conclude that, although dimensions of care-giving can be teased apart for purposes of analysis (as we have done here), performance across them tends to be highly related in the real world.

Socioemotional development: Infant-parent attachment. A primary social task for the infant is to establish a close emotional relationship with another human being (Erikson, 1959, Sroufe, 1979). The individual with whom the child develops this first *attachment relationship* is usually the mother, but always an individual who holds a special place in the baby's life. Although all infants develop attachments to some individual, and usually to several persons eventually, individual differences most certainly exist in the quality of the infant-parent attachment relationship. Ainsworth (1973) has characterized this variation along a security-insecurity dimension, on the assumption that infants who by 12 months of life organize their behavior around their care-givers and respond positively to her following brief separations, are developing a sense of trust in the availability and responsiveness of their care-givers. Several longitudinal studies now demonstrate that infants judged secure by 12–18 months look more competent in play, problem solving, and relations to peers during the preschool years (see Sroufe, 1979, for review).

Ainsworth (1979) proposed that the primary determinant of individual differences in quality of attachment is the mother's degree of sensitivity and warmth in responding to infant signals. As a result of their ability to read their infants' often-subtle cues and respond in a manner that addresses the baby's needs in a timely manner, sensitive care-givers are hypothesized to promote in infants a basic trust of the world which is founded upon the experience of being warmly loved and cared for in a manner that is predictable rather than inconsistent. The results of several analyses carried out as part of Ainsworth's longitudinal study of the mother-infant relationship provide support for her thesis (Ainsworth & Bell, 1969; Bell & Ainsworth, 1972). More specifically, mothers of securely attached infants were found in these studies to be, across the infants' first year, more responsive to infant crying (see also Crockenberg, 1981), to hold their infants more tenderly and carefully, to display greater consideration of infant behavior when initiating and terminating breast-feeding, and to be more responsive to infant emotional expressions during face-to-face encounters (Ainsworth, Blehar, Waters, & Wall, 1978). Recently, Belsky, Rovine, and Taylor (1984) reported data consistent with these findings. Indeed, they found that mothers of securely attached infants provided neither too much nor too little interactive stimulation, but rather an intermediate and, presumably, optimal level of not too arousing, yet engaging (i.e., sensitive), social interchange.

Father influence. It must be pointed out that the role of father during infancy has been neglected (Lamb, 1976; Parke, 1978). Consequently, much less is known about the influence fathers exert upon infant development than about that which mothers exert. From a theoretical perspective, there is reason to believe that the same patterns of care identified as being developmentally influential for mother function in a similar way for father. This is because the processes by which stimulating, responsive, and nonrestrictive care are assumed to promote infant competence do not appear dependent upon the gender of the individual providing such care.

It is conceivable, nevertheless, that there are distinct processes of influence for fathers. The only conclusion research currently permits is that quantity of father involvement is related to infant outcome. That is, infants whose fathers are highly involved with them appear to be more intellectually competent and socially oriented toward their fathers (Belsky, 1980b; Wachs et al., 1971). Beyond this general finding, it has been suggested that father's play behavior may be particularly influential (Clarke-Stewart, 1978a), that he may exert greater influence on sons than on daughters (Pedersen, Rubenstein, & Yarrow, 1979), and that he may influence his children by drawing them into the world beyond their intimate relationship with mother (Belsky, 1980b). Since little evidence exists on these points, they must be considered as tentative hypotheses in need of empirical confirmation (Belsky, 1981). Happily, scientific investigation of the father's impact on child development is a field of growing interest, as the knowledge and inferences related here and in later sections indicate it should be.

Childhood

As in infancy, children of preschool (2–5 years) and elementary school age (6–12 years) differ markedly in the manner in which they cope with the various internal and external changes confronting them. The preschool period is a time of moving away from the close attachments of infancy, without breaking the relationships already established, and of venturing forth to explore the material and social worlds beyond the confines of the nuclear family. As Erikson (1950) so succinctly put it, the preschool years are a period of autonomy and initiative. With formal entry into elementary school, the demands upon the developing individual change. The child is expected to master increasingly complex academic subjects as well as be able to get along with age-mates and cooperate with adults in positions of authority.

Again, however, one finds great variability among individual children. Our prime interest in this section is the familial origins of developmental differences in capacities such as intelligence and social competence. Undoubtedly, earlier experiences and congenital factors are responsible for some of the differences that exist between children. But research also indicates that, to a sizable degree, these variations result from the different parental care that children experience in their families during the preschool and childhood years.

Intellectual competence.   The warm, sensitive orientation of mothers that was identified as promoting optimal development during the infant years still functions to promote cognitive competence in the preschool years. During this developmental period, sensitivity continues to denote an acceptance of the child's developmental limits and an understanding of the developmental challenges which the child faces. This challenge translates into providing the child with the freedom to explore the world and to express feelings. In a sense, then, intellectual competence is facilitated by supporting the developmental tendency toward autonomy.

The intellectually stimulating parent of the preschooler does more, however, than merely let children follow their own inclinations. He or she also challenges them and encourages mastery of the developmental tasks which these children confront. Thus, such a parent encourages independence by requiring that they try to solve problems on their own, yet is available to provide supportive assistance as needed. The intellectual abilities of the school-age child have been linked repeatedly to experiences of the child during the preschool period. Mother's earlier involvement in the child's play and her tendency to respond to questions, read to the child, and accompany him on frequent outings beyond the confines of the home have been linked to the older child's general verbal ability (Clarke-Stewart, 1977).

During the school years themselves, the intellectual development of boys and girls appears to relate differentially to the quality of the mother-child relationship. Whereas a continued close relationship with mother seems to facilitate intellectually superior performance in the case of boys, a progressively more distant relationship seems most intellectually stimulating in the case of daughters (Clarke-Stewart, 1977). However, it may not be the case (as a first reading of this finding suggests) that a distant mother-daughter relationship itself facilitates intellectual development; rather, a close relationship between daughter and her nonemployed mother may have discouraged intellectual stimulation in the past through the transmission of traditional female roles. If such intellectual stimulation occurs in mother-daughter relations, it is likely that intellectual development will be facilitated regardless of whether the mother is working.

It appears that sons' and daughters' intellectual competence, as measured by IQ tests, is promoted by high levels of father involvement coupled with an accepting and nurturant orientation and time spent actively involved in teaching. The father's influence on development is especially pronounced in the area of achievement motivation during the school-age years. In the case of boys, father's own success, achievement orientation, and warmth promotes son's orientation to achieve in school. In the case of girls, father's friendliness to his daughter and to his spouse are positively related to achievement motivation (Clarke-Stewart, 1977; Radin, 1981).

Mothers may also play an important role in children's orientation toward achievement; and it is their demand for achievement that seems particularly significant from a developmental standpoint. Achievement standards which are both high and explicit (e.g., "I expect you to do well in science") seem, in particular, to energize a positive orientation toward performance. The parent who encourages achievement during the school-age years is the one who values education and deliberately rewards school success. Showing an interest in the child's daily school work, exam performance, and course grades and encouraging good study habits while praising positive performance facilitates achievement. So too does fostering an intellectual atmosphere in the home, modeling structured work habits, and serving as the child's own teacher where appropriate (e.g., Crandall, Dewey, Kotovsky, & Preston, 1964; Kagan & Moss, 1962).

In summary, for facilitating children's success in school as well as their general intellectual development, the most-effective pattern of parenting seems to involve being nurturant without being restrictive, responsive yet not controlling, and stimulating but not directive. An orientation toward independence and a family structure that expects and rewards such behavior fit the developmental needs of the child—at least as far as intellectual competence is concerned (e.g., Bayley & Shaefer, 1964; Clarke-Stewart, 1977).

Socioemotional competence. A prominent series of reports by Baumrind (1967, 1968, 1972) usefully summarizes much of what is known about parental influence upon social competence during the preschool years. In this research, Baumrind identified three broad types of parents and characteristics of their children that seemed to result from the childrearing and disciplinary practices experienced at home. Importantly, the clusters of parenting behaviors that Baumrind identified as generally co-occurring, and the patterns of child functioning which seemed to result from these styles of care, are relatively consistent with the findings of other studies.

The *authoritarian* parent tries to shape, control, and evaluate the behavior and attitudes of the child in accordance with a preestablished

absolute standard of behavior. Such parents stress the value of obedience to their authority and, as a result, are likely to favor punitive,
forceful disciplinary measures to curb "self-will" whenever the child's
behaviors or beliefs conflict with what the parent thinks is correct.
The children of authoritarian parents tend to be less cheerful and
more moody than others, as well as apprehensive, unhappy, easily
annoyed, passively hostile, and vulnerable to stress. Certainly one
would be hard pressed to describe such children as competent in any
sense of the word.

A second type of parent Baumrind identified is labeled the *permissive* parent. This type of care-giver attempts to behave towards the
child's behaviors, desires, and impulses in a nonpunishing, accepting,
and affirming manner. The parent consults with the child about decisions regarding family "policy" and explains to the child the basis of
family rules. Serving as a resource but not as an active governing agent,
the permissive parent avoids exercising control over the child and,
in fact, often does not encourage the child to obey external (social)
standards. Thus reason, but little overt power, is used by this parent
in his or her attempts to rear the child (Baumrind, 1968, p. 256).

While the experience of permissive rearing (characterized by much
warmth but little overt control) sounds attractive, for the preschooler
trying to master the process of self regulation in a world that she
does not fully understand, this "freedom to be" appears developmentally inappropriate. Evidence to support this claim comes from Baumrind's (1967) observation that permissively reared children tend to
be impulsive-aggressive. More specifically, these children display very
low levels of self-reliance, frequently are out of control, and tend to
have a difficult time inhibiting their impulses. In terms of mood, however, permissively reared children are more cheerful than the con-
flicted-irritable children of authoritarian parents, probably as a result
of the warmth they experience at the hands of their noncontrolling
parents.

The third type of parent which Baumrind identified is labeled the
authoritative parent. Parents who received this label were the most
nurturant in Baumrind's studies, as demonstrated by their high use
of positive reinforcement and infrequent use of punishment; they were
also the most responsive to their children's demands for attention.
By no means was it the case, however, that these loving parents in-
dulged their children. Quite the contrary, in fact; authoritative parents
were very ready to direct and control the child—but in a manner
that displayed awareness of the child's thoughts, feelings, and point
of view as well as his developmental capabilities. It is important to
note that, in addition to being loving and controlling, authoritative
parents were demanding of mature, independent behavior from their

children and frequently explained to them the rationale behind their disciplinary and other controlling actions.

Not surprisingly, it was the children of authoritative parents who looked the most socially competent, so much so in fact that Baumrind characterized them as energetic-friendly. These preschoolers tended to approach novel or even stressful situations with great curiosity and interest and also tended to display high levels of self-reliance, self-control, cheerfulness, and friendly relations with age-mates.

Findings from other studies suggest that the three parenting types identified by Baumrind do indeed exist and that the different parenting styles have contrasting roles in children's development. Coopersmith (1967) found that accepting, supportive, caring, concerned, and loving mothers, who enforced established rules consistently but sought the views of the child in a context of free and open discussion, had sons who were higher in self-esteem than did mothers who treated their sons harshly, gave little guidance, and enforced rules inconsistently. Similarly, Mussen, Harris, Rutherford, and Keasey (1970) found that girls who showed high levels of self-esteem, honesty, and altruism had warm, intimate interactions with their mothers. And as a final example, M. L. Hoffman (1970) reported that the frequent use of power assertion versus induction by a parent is associated with weak moral development in the school-age child. Indeed, children of parents who use power assertion techniques frequently tend to show high levels of aggressive behavior themselves (Feshbach & Feshbach, 1972).

Adolescence

As the child moves into the period of adolescence, a host of new individual and contextual changes occur. For instance, changes associated with puberty alter the adolescent's body, and changes occur socially through entry into new school settings (junior and senior high schools) and new arenas of extracurricular activity (e.g., part-time employment) (Steinberg, Greenberger, Garduque, Ruggiero, & Vaux, 1982). Such changes do not require the adolescent to leave his or her family, but nevertheless broaden the social horizons of earlier childhood, with the result that less time is spent in the family setting. In other words, the family may not so much lose its influence on the adolescent as it must begin to share its influence with other socializing agents. In fact, some theorists (Erikson, 1959) contend that it is the key developmental task of adolescence to establish the separation of self from parents.

Family influences on identity development. Considerable evidence shows that the nature of adolescent interactions with parents,

as well as with other members of the social context, provides a context
for adolescent identity development, perhaps the most-challenging
task for this period. Because, by definition, a sense of identity links
the adolescent to the social world, one likely basis for observed differences in the interpersonal styles of adolescents who have or have not
gained a sense of identity, lies in their individual social-interaction
histories. Certainly such background experiences involve the family,
which acts as society's primary mediator and transmitter of sociocultural rules, roles, and values. Erikson (1959) conceives of identity as
being in part composed of self-esteem. O'Donnel's (1976) finding, that
in 8th- and 11th-grade adolescents the degree of positive feelings toward parents was generally more closely related to self-esteem than
the degree of these feelings to friends, thus may be taken as support
for the saliency of family interaction in identity development. Other
studies show that different family structures—for example, presence
of a working or a nonworking mother (D. D. Nelson, 1971) or father
absence (Santrock, 1970)—are associated with contrasting levels of adjustment in adolescence and with ego development prior to adolescence, respectively. However, none of these investigators suggest what
sort of parental or familial factors may facilitate ego identity development.

Additional studies suggest that, in the context of the family milieu
parents help create, parental personal and interpersonal characteristics
which foster identity development may be transmitted to their offspring. LaVoie (1976) reports that male high school students having
a greater sense of identity reported less regulation and control by
their mothers and fathers and more-frequent praise by their fathers
than did males lower in self-identity. LaVoie found the same pattern
for high school females with respect to maternal restrictiveness and
the freedom to discuss problems with parents. Thus, high-identity adolescents appear to be characterized by a family milieu involving less
parental restrictiveness and better child-parent communication than
do low-identity adolescents. Note how consistent these facilitative styles
of parenting are with those discussed in the preceding two sections
focused on infancy and childhood.

Family influences on school functioning. The fundamental role
which parents continue to play in shaping adolescent development
is apparent even in spheres that are, at times, far removed from home
and family. Indeed, even where the example provided by peers or
other adults outside the family is perhaps most potent—in the school
itself—the influence of parental models is apparent nonetheless. Factors and forces originating from within the family in part determine
both aspirations about, and actual outcomes of, the adolescent's accom-

plishments in school. According to information from the U.S. Bureau of the Census (1978), the college aspirations of high school seniors tend to be correlated with the educational attainment of the head of the household in which they lived.

Over and above parents' own education, there are particular types of parent-adolescent interactions that appear to facilitate successful school functioning. Morrow and Wilson (1961) found that high-achieving adolescents, as compared to a group of low achievers, tended to come from families where they were involved in family decisions, where ideas and activities were shared by family members, and where parents were likely to give approval and praise of the adolescent's performance and show trust in the adolescent's competence. In turn, low-achieving adolescents came from families marked by parental dominance and restrictiveness (Morrow & Wilson). Moreover, both Morrow and Wilson and Shaw and White (1965) found that high-achieving adolescents tend to identify with their parents while low-achieving adolescents do not.

Other researchers have also found that the type of parental behaviors reported by Morrow and Wilson (1961) relate to superior adolescent school achievement. Both Swift (1967) and Rehberg and Westby (1967) report, for example, that parental encouragement and rewards are associated with better adolescent school performance. Similarly, Wolf (1964) found that parent-child interactions that involve both encouragement to achieve and development of language skills are highly correlated with intelligence. Recall that these are many of the same characteristics of parenting found to be related to school achievement and intelligence at younger ages.

Conclusion

It is clear both here and in previous sections that the experience of the child in the family influences cognitive and personality development. In reviewing the data summarized up to this point, it becomes apparent that, across childhood, parenting that is *sensitively* attuned to children's capabilities and to the developmental tasks they face promotes a variety of highly valued developmental outcomes, including emotional security, behavioral independence, social competence, and intellectual achievement (Belsky, Lerner, & Spanier, 1984). In infancy, this sensitivity translates into being able to read babies' often-subtle cues and to respond appropriately to their needs in reasonably brief periods of time. In childhood, sensitivity means continuing the warmth and affection provided in the early years, but increasing the demands for age-appropriate behavior. Parents must be willing and able to direct children's behavior and activities without squelching their developing independence and industry. Ultimately, the sensitive and thus competent parent must be willing to wean the child from this overt control to permit the testing of personal limits through the exercise of internalized rules and regulations. Indeed, by the time the child reaches adolescence, the competent parent has set the stage so that the child has the psychological building blocks to encounter successfully the transition from childhood to adolescence.

DETERMINANTS OF PARENTING

The next questions to pose, then, concern the origins of this parental competence. What factors contribute to sensitive parenting, and what conditions preclude its occurrence? These are the questions which will serve to organize discussion and empirical substantiation throughout the remainder of this chapter. But to better facilitate discussion and understanding, we will present here a conceptual framework on which to hang the often-diverse pieces of evidence which, together, may point out some answers to the questions we ask.

On the basis of both theory and research on the etiology of child abuse and neglect (Belsky, 1980a; Parke & Collmer, 1975), Belsky (1984) proposed a general model of the determinants of parental functioning which details the origins of those patterns of parenting just outlined. This model serves to organize and integrate the many familial and extrafamilial factors hypothesized to influence parenting practices. The model itself, diagrammed in Figure 1, is based upon the assumption that individual differences in parental functioning are shaped by three distinct but interrelated systems of influence. These three systems originate both within and beyond the family, comprising: (1) parental psychological resources, (2) unique characteristics of the child him/herself, and (3) contextual sources of stress and support—specifically the marital relationship, social network, and occupational experiences of parents. As will soon be apparent, each dimension of influence may facilitate competent parenting or, otherwise, interfere with effective parenting.

Additionally, the model posits a series of relationships interconnecting these three sources of influence and uniting them with both parenting and developmental outcomes for children. Thus, one general sequence proposed in the model links parents' developmental histories, marital relations, social networks, and jobs to individual personality and general psychological well-being of parents and, in this manner, to parental functioning and, finally, to child development. By reviewing research pertinent to each level of the relationship just described, support for three general conclusions regarding the determinants of parenting will be provided: (1) parenting is multiply determined; (2) with respect to their influence on parenting, characteristics of the parent,

Figure 1

A process model of the determinants of parenting

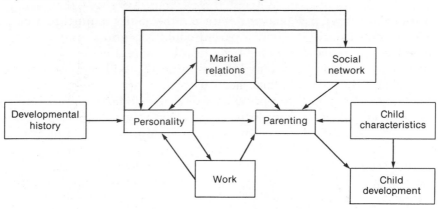

of the child, and of the social context, are *not* equally influential in supporting or undermining growth-promoting parenting; and (3) developmental history and personality may shape parenting indirectly, as well as directly, by first influencing the broader context in which parent-child relations exist (i.e., marital relations, social networks, occupational experience). In marshalling evidence to support the former contention that parenting is multiply determined, discussion will first center around influences on parenting which arise in the immediate context of the family, reserving for a later point analysis of those influences which derive from the broader contexts of neighborhood and workplace.

Within the family

From the outset of this chapter, we are forthright in arguing that consideration of individual differences in parental functioning must reflect the unique but interdependent contributions originating from *both* parent and child. To this end, discussion of influences from within the family comprises an analysis of parental factors, child characteristics, and qualities of the marital relationship.

Parent's contribution. Research on child maltreatment indicates that parenting, like most dimensions of human functioning, may be influenced by enduring characteristics of the individual—characteristics which are, at least in part, a product of one's developmental history (Belsky, 1980a). What kind of person should be able to provide developmentally flexible and growth-promoting care? The sensitive individual, one might argue, is able to decenter and appraise accurately the perspective of others, to empathize with them, and in addition, to adopt a nurturant orientation. Without the capacity to escape the egocentrism of one's own psychological state and the ability to nurture others, it is difficult to imagine how a parent could recognize, much less respond to, immediate and long-term developmental needs of children on a daily basis. Indeed, only by possessing the skills outlined above is it likely that an individual faced with the very real demands and challenges that parenting presents would not abdicate responsibility (as in neglectful and permissive rearing) or rely on absolute power (as in child abuse or authoritarian rearing). Moreover, to function in this way, the individual will likely need to experience a sense of control over his/her own life and destiny, as well as feel that his/her own psychological needs are being met. Since the essence of parenting, especially in the childhood years, involves "giving," it seems reasonable that parents most able to do this in a sensitive, competence-inducing manner will be mature, psychologically healthy adults.

Personality. Direct evidence of a personality-parenting association derives from investigations linking psychological well-being and parental competence. Farber and Egeland (1980) found, for example, that more tense and irritable mothers, who had lower self-esteem, displayed less interest in their newborns, were less effective in soothing their infants, and were less able to maintain synchronous exchanges. Similarly, Heath (1976) observed that men who revealed more personality integration, exhibited less depression and anxiety, and were more independent and stable were more emotionally involved with their children and spent more time playing with them. Consistent with such data is research on psychologically disturbed adults, since it reveals that disturbances like schizophrenia (Baldwin, Cole, & Baldwin, 1982) and depression (Colletta, in press; Weissman & Paykel, 1974) are consistently related to deficits in parenting.

Developmental history. If our principal concern is the determinants of parenting, we need to ask, in the face of findings linking personality and parenting, about the developmental origins of personality—particularly as they pertain to childrearing. Three distinct sets of data illuminate the relationship between developmental history and parenting. Literature on child abuse furnishes the first set by underscoring an association between experience of mistreatment in one's own childhood and mistreatment of one's children. Since this relationship has been discussed elsewhere (Belsky, 1978, 1980a; Parke & Collmer, 1975), little else will be said regarding it. The second set of data linking developmental history and parenting derives from the study of depression (e.g., Heinecke, 1970; Langner & Michael, 1963), and the third from studies of individual differences in father involvement.

Empirical work already cited indicates that depression contributes to difficulties in parenting. Of particular interest here is evidence that early developmental history and susceptibility to depression are correlated, making plausible the postulated process of influence from developmental history to personality and, finally, to parental functioning and, thereby, child development. As part of an investigation specifically concerned with the social origins of depression, Brown and Harris (1978), for example, discovered separation from mother prior to the age of 11 to be one important feature distinguishing female patients (47 percent) from controls (17 percent), though only those individuals who had lost a mother *and* experienced a severely stressful life event or major difficulty actually became depressed. The potential implications of such early experiences for parenting are suggested specifically by several studies revealing a direct association between early separation from parent(s) and subsequent parental dysfunction (Frommer & O'Shea, 1973a, 1973b; Hall, Pawlby, & Wolkind, 1979). When these several studies concerned with the origins of depression and the consequences of separation are jointly considered, there certainly appears to be a basis for concluding that, at least under certain stressful conditions, developmental history influences psychological well-being, which in turn affects parental functioning and, as a result, child development.

The final set of data to be considered regarding the relationship between developmental history and parenting pertains to the functioning of men as parents. Several investigators have found that a father's involvement in parenting is positively related to the involvement exhibited by his own father (Reuter & Biller, 1973). At first glance, these findings suggest that fathers model the behavior of their own fathers. But questions about the accuracy of this simple observational-learning interpretation are raised by other data indicating that unsatisfactory childhood experiences (Gersick, 1979; Mendes, 1976) and insufficient paternal involvement during childhood (DeFrain, 1979; Eiduson & Alexander, 1978) are correlated with *high* levels of parental interest and involvement on the part of fathers. Indeed, such data seem to demand consideration of personality development, especially in regard to processes of identification.

One would expect fathers who are warm, nurturant, and involved to be modeled because their sons are more likely to identify strongly with them. A noninvolved father should generate a weak identification in the son, reducing the likelihood that he will be modeled but perhaps initiating a compensatory process that later prompts the son to parent in a manner expressly opposite that of his own father. Further, weak identification with one's father may generate a more-androgynous, less traditionally masculine sex role orientation, responsible, in part, for high levels of involvement in fathering.

Conclusion: Specification of process. This analysis suggests that mechanisms of influence need to be explicitly investigated when examining the determinants of parenting. The evidence just considered broadly indicates that developmental history influences parenting. If this is indeed the case, it is very possibly because experience shapes personality. At this point progress requires more than demonstrations of relationships between early experience and parental functioning; it requires conceptions of why such relations should obtain. Despite the need for additional work in this area, it seems appropriate to conclude that, in general, supportive developmental experiences give rise to a mature, healthy personality, enabling provision of sensitive parental care which promotes optimal child development.

Child effects on parenting. We have noted already that the parent-child relationship is bidirectional in nature, with parents influencing children and children influencing parents. Before embarking upon an examination of such child effects, two points need to be made. First, the impact of the child upon the parent is very likely to be mediated by the parent's own characteristics of individuality, including his or her own level of psychological development (Sameroff, 1975). Thus, when certain characteristics of the child harmoniously intermesh with the parent's behavioral tendencies, smooth, synchronous, and developmentally facilitative interactions are likely to take place. This "goodness of fit" model will be further elaborated when the effects of temperament are discussed.

A second point that needs to be underscored regarding child effects involves the developmental implications of children's impact upon their parents. Since children, as we will argue, do influence their parents' behavior and since (as we have already seen) parents influence their children's development, the possibility must be entertained that children serve as "producers" of, or at least contributors to, their own development (Lerner & Busch-Rossnagel, 1981). That is, by initiating processes whereby parents are affected by the child and then serve to influence the child, children can have a major impact upon their own developmental trajectories.

It happens to be the case that our capacity to conceptualize the dynamic processes through which children influence the care they receive exceeds our current scientific ability to measure and capture empirically such reciprocal processes of influence (Lerner, Skinner, & Sorell, 1980). As a result, we shall rely in this chapter mostly upon research findings which document unidirectional child-to-adult effects.

Gender. The effect of child gender in shaping parental behavior is evident as early as the opening days of life (Rubin, Provenzano, & Luria, 1974). Although the differential treatment of boys and girls is evident in both parents' behavior during the infancy years, it tends (as is the case throughout childhood) to be more marked for father-son relationships. As early as the first days, weeks, and months of life, fathers apparently look more at sons than daughters and provide sons with more visual and tactile stimulation (Parke, 1978). In the second year of life, fathers verbalize more to boys and engage them in play more regularly.

The quality of mother's behavior during infancy is also susceptible to gender effects, though not as strongly as father's. The one dimension of behavior for which consistent effects of gender have been observed is maternal verbal activity. During the infancy years, mothers are, on the average, more likely to talk to girls and are more verbally responsive to their daughters' vocalizations (Lewis & Ban, 1971). As children grow older, more direct efforts are exerted to have them behave in a manner consistent with traditional sex roles (Fagot, 1978). Girls are encouraged to maintain close family ties and be more dependent, for example. Boys, in contrast, are encouraged to explore more, to achieve more, and to be more independent and competitive. Traditionally, fathers have displayed a special concern for the achievement of their sons and are likely to stress the importance of a career and occupational success (Block, 1976). Daughters, however, are more likely to be encouraged to focus upon interpersonal relationships rather than performance in achievement settings (Block, Block, & Harrington, 1974).

Probably as a result of the strong investment in certain kinds of developmental outcomes for males, boys are also likely to experience more power assertion and less induction in disciplinary encounters with parents than are girls (Zussman, 1978; Block, 1982). Complementing this pattern of parent-son, parent-daughter relations is the finding that higher levels of overall interaction, especially affectionate interchange, seem to transpire between parents and daughters (Noller, 1978).

Developmental status.   Next to gender, the characteristic of children that probably exerts the most-pronounced impact upon the parenting they receive is their age or developmental status. After all, it is babies who are cuddled and smothered with physical affection when they fall down and hurt themselves, not adolescents. While the child's age influences parenting in a variety of ways, it is important to note that it is rarely age per se that is the true source of the influence. Age is simply a "marker" variable for such characteristics as physical size, cognitive ability, and motor coordination. Thus, it is likely that effects which appear to be determined by age are most likely a result of these more-subtle developmental processes.

The effect of the child's behavior upon the care giver becomes most pronounced when various developmental landmarks are attained. The nature of cognitively stimulating parenting styles undergoes modification as the infant and young child develop. Furthermore, as children develop from the preschool years through adolescence, parents' expectations change, in part as a function of children's developing competencies and of the contextual demands that are placed upon them. Several reviews of research suggest, for example, that with development comes increasing emphasis upon independent behavior, responsibility, and achievement (Becker, 1964; Martin, 1975). Thus, as children grow older, parents employ more reasoning, explanations, and giving and withholding of privileges while at the same time displaying less physical affection, becoming less protective, and spending less time with their children (Maccoby, 1980).

Temperament. In their longitudinal study of the course of temperamental differences in children, Thomas and Chess (1977) focused upon nine specific attributes of behavioral style hypothesized to play an important role in development: activity level, rhythmicity (of biological functions), approach-withdrawal, adaptability (to new situations or people), intensity of reaction, threshold of responsiveness, quality of mood, distractibility, and attention span/persistence. In our view, it is just such stylistic characteristics of behavior that give a child's behavioral repertoire its individual distinctiveness, especially at early ages (see Dunn, 1980). Children with contrasting characteristics of individuality elicit different reactions from their parents and siblings, reactions which will likely feed back to these same children, thereby affecting their further development. On the other hand, exactly the same characteristics of individuality may have different consequences in different families. For this reason, the key significance of a definition of temperament as behavioral style, then, is its impact on the social context of the person. But, how may such temperament-context relations be conceptualized, much less empirically investigated?

The approach we favor can be summarized in terms of the goodness of fit between person and context; it emphasizes the significance of a particular characteristic of individuality, like a high activity level, in a particular context, such as a small apartment. As a consequence of characteristics of physical (e.g., sex, body type, or facial attractiveness) and/or psychological individuality (e.g., cognitive style or temperament), people promote differential reactions in their socializing others; these reactions may feed back to people, increase the individuality of their developmental milieu, and provide a basis for their future development. Consider, as one example, the problems of fit which might occur when a child who is highly irregular in his biological functions (e.g., eating, sleep-wake cycles, toileting behaviors) interacts in a family setting composed of highly regular and behaviorally scheduled parents and siblings.

With this conceptualization of goodness of fit in mind, several investigators have attempted to link temperamental difficulty with parental functioning. Difficult infants are characterized as being highly active, moody, distractable, and arrhythmic in nature. Parents who describe their children in such terms, providing some indication of dissonance between characteristics of child and parent, exhibit less than optimal patterns of care-giving and interaction. Campbell (1979) reported, for example, that mothers who rated their infants as having difficult temperaments at three months spent less time in active interchange with them and were less responsive to their cries at three and eight months, relative to control mothers. Similarly, Milliones (1978) discerned a significant negative association between mothers' perceptions of difficultness and outreach workers' ratings of maternal responsiveness when infants averaged 11 months of age. And, as a final illustrative finding, Kelly (1976) reported that mothers of more difficult four-month-olds tended to respond negatively to disagreeable infant emotions.

Conclusion.   Although we have chosen not to pursue the issue of child temperamental contributions in great detail, due to the availability of relatively comprehensive reviews (e.g., Bates, 1980; Plomin, 1982), the limited evidence just reviewed does illustrate the now well accepted point that characteristics of children hypothesized to make them more or less difficult to care for do indeed seem to shape the quantity and quality of parental care they receive. The little work that considers these characteristics in the context of parental factors (e.g., personality, expectations) further suggests that neither temperament nor other adult characteristics per se shape parenting, but rather that it is this goodness of fit between parent and child which shapes the development of parent-child relations (Lerner & Lerner, in press; Thomas & Chess, 1977). In sum, then, there are both empirical and conceptual grounds for concluding that not only do children influence the care they receive, which feeds back to shape their own development, but to understand fully the process by which children contribute to their own development, both characteristics of the child and of the family must be considered.

Marriage and parenting.   To understand how marital relations might affect parenting (and in turn child development) it helps to conceptualize the marriage as a parental support system. Marriages, like other support systems, provide two general types of support: emotional support and instrumental assistance. Emotional support communicates to the parent that he or she is loved, esteemed, and valued and presumably affects the patience that a parent can bring to the care-giving role. Instrumental assistance involves the provision of goods and services and thereby frees up energy that the parent can use in the care-giving role (Belsky, 1984).

It has been suggested that during the infancy years, the influence of fathers on child functioning may be primarily indirect, that is, mediated by the wife in her capacity as mother (Belsky, 1981; Parke, 1978). And indeed, several studies highlight just such indirect effects. One researcher was led to conclude, in fact, on the basis of her investigation of changes in mother-infant reciprocity across the first month of the baby's life, "that the mother's ability to enjoy her infant, and regard it with affection may be in part a function of the quality of her relationship with her husband" (Price, 1977, p. 7). More recently, however, other studies have begun to document a direct marriage → fathering effect. For example, Belsky (1979; Belsky, Gilstrap, & Rovine, 1984) observed that in families in which there was frequent marital communication about the baby, fathers were highly involved with their babies at the ages of 1, 3, 9, and 15 months old.

Evidence relating to the effects of marital support is not confined to the infancy period but, in fact, derives from studies which span all of childhood and adolescence as well (Zur-Spiro & Longfellow, 1981). Working with preschoolers, Sears, Maccoby, and Levin (1957) reported, for example, that mothers' professed esteem for their husbands was systematically related to the praise they directed at their children; and Bandura and Walters (1959) observed that mothers inclined to nag and scold their sons felt less warmth and affection toward their husbands. During the school-age years, Santrock and his colleagues (Santrock, Warshak, Lindbergh, & Meadows, 1982) found that boys 6–11 years old being raised in reconstituted families comprised of a stepfather and biological mother were more socially competent than age-mates reared in families comprised of both biological parents; moreover, such competence was related to the more growth-facilitating care they received which was itself related to more-harmonious marriages. Finally, during adolescence, it has been found that parents who employ disciplinary techniques which we have already seen undermine competent child development (i.e., frequent use of punishment, infrequent use of reasoning) tend to be involved in marriages characterized by hostility and low satisfaction (Dielman, Barton, & Cattell, 1977; Kemper & Reichler, 1976b; Olweus, 1980).

In sum, the data reviewed in this section strongly suggest that to understand parenting and its influence upon child development, attention must be accorded to the marital relationship (Belsky, 1981). At the same time, it is essential to bear in mind the possibility that marital quality is itself a function of the developmental histories and the personalities of the individuals in the relationship. The possibility must also be entertained that marital relations do not affect parenting directly, so much as they do indirectly—by influencing the general psychological well-being of individuals and only thereby the skills they exercise in the parenting role (see Figure 1) (Carveth & Gottlieb, 1979; Johnson & Lobitz, 1974).

Beyond the family

To gain a full understanding of the factors which influence and the processes which underlie parental functioning, it is necessary to look beyond the microsystem of the family to broader arenas of parental activity. Without transcending the same level of day-to-day living, it is easy to identify spheres of daily functioning *outside* the family which are likely to have direct or indirect effects on parental functioning *within* the family. In this final portion of the chapter, two of the more-salient domains of such extrafamilial activity are explored in some detail vis-à-vis their effects on parenting: the parental social network and employment experiences outside the home.

Social network. Having just concluded a discussion of the role of the marital relationship as a system of support for parents, it is most fitting to assess the influence of the social network as an adjunct or extension of this same system. If the marital relationship is the principal support system of parents, as Belsky (1981) suggests, it is likely that the interpersonal relations between parents and their friends, relatives, and neighbors—the significant others in their lives—function as the next most important system of support. In many households, particularly those in which a spouse is not present or the marital relationship is conflicted, the social network may well function as the primary system of support.

A great deal of evidence now exists demonstrating that the availability of significant others and the support received from them exert a beneficial impact upon parent-child relations. For example, during the infancy period, it has been discovered that the qualities of mothering predictive of child competence during the preschool years, namely verbal and emotional responsivity, are more characteristic of mothers who have weekly or more frequent contact with friends (Powell, 1980). Similarly, the presence of a tightly knit social network during the preschool years has been found to be associated positively with parents' sense of competence in the care-giving role—defined as mother's recognition of the malleability of her children, her appreciation of individual differences, and knowledge of how childrearing practices need to be adjusted to match the child's developmental capabilities (Abernethy, 1973)—and with mother's avoidance of punishment and restriction (Pascoe, Loda, Jeffries, & Earp, 1981).

In the case of social network support, just as in the case of the marital relationship, one must speculate on the possible mediating role played by parents' own psychological well-being. That is, social networks may serve to enhance the personal psychological functioning of the parent and, by these means, promote effective parenting behavior and practices. In this regard, Cochran and Brassard (1979) hypothesized that the support which social networks provide can enhance self-esteem and, as a consequence, increase the patience and sensitivity which individuals exercise in the parenting role. Data are available in support of this contention (Aug & Bright, 1970; Belle, 1981).

Work. The final contextual source of stress/support on parenting considered here is suggested by research that links unemployment and labor market shrinkage with child maltreatment (Light, 1973; Steinberg, Catalano, & Dooley, 1981). It is not only investigations of child abuse, however, that highlight the deleterious consequences of unemployment with respect to parent-child relations (Bronfenbrenner & Crouter, 1982). Over four decades ago, Komarovsky's (1940) detailed interview study of intact families with fathers on relief revealed that, especially in households with adolescent children, paternal authority declined with unemployment. Elder's (1974) investigation of children during the Great Depression documented similar consequences and, in doing so, was able to illustrate that when families realigned themselves in order to cope with one pattern of adversity, adolescent offspring (especially sons) could eventually derive benefits from the experience.

Beyond the study of unemployment, the greatest source of information pertinent to the impact of work on parenting is found in the literature on maternal employment. Even though a sizable proportion of studies fail to document any such effects (e.g., see Bronfenbrenner & Crouter, 1982, for a review), several others do suggest that mother's employment status influences both the quantity and quality of her own and her spouse's parenting behavior. Quite a few investigations indicate, for example, that maternal employment creates strain in the father-son relationship in lower-income families (Bronfenbrenner & Crouter, 1982; L. W. Hoffman, 1979). A number of studies also demonstrate that parental expectations of children are greater when both parents are employed outside the home, particularly with respect to those aspects of home and self-maintenance for which children are held responsible. Still other studies record positive developmental outcomes as a consequence of such demands (Bronfenbrenner & Crouter, 1982; L. W. Hoffman, 1979).

A major limitation of many investigations attempting to document the effect of maternal employment on parenting is their undifferentiated classification of employment (Bronfenbrenner & Crouter, 1983; Crouter, Belsky, & Spanier, in press). And research on maternal attitudes toward work clearly establishes the need to consider maternal employment as more than simply a "social address" if an understanding is to be achieved of *how* it impacts parenting and thereby child development. Not only is there evidence that mothers who are dissatisfied with their employment status have offspring whose development is less optimal than those whose mothers are more satisfied with their work situation (Farel, 1980; Hock, 1980; L. W. Hoffman, 1963), but several studies suggest that parenting itself is compromised under such stressful conditions (Stuckey, McGhee, & Bell, 1982; L. W. Hoffman).

The increase in understanding of how work affects parenting which accrues when maternal employment is treated as more than simply a social address is especially evident in research on fathers' work. In his longitudinal study of men in professional jobs, Heath (1976) found the characteristics Kanter (1978) referred to as "work absorption" related to paternal inadequacy. Specifically, the more time and energy fathers devoted to their occupations, the more irritable and impatient they were with their children, as indicated by both husbands' and wives' reports. And in a somewhat different vein, Kemper and Reichler (1976a) and McKinley (1964) found fathers' job satisfaction to be inversely related to the severity of punishment fathers dispensed but directly related to their reliance upon reasoning as a disciplinary strategy.

As was postulated in prior discussions of marital relations and social networks, it is quite conceivable that many of these work-parenting associations are actually mediated by effects that employment and work conditions have upon personality and general psychological well-being. The potential implications for parental functioning of such effects of work on personality are strikingly apparent in Piotrkowski's (1979) small but intensive study of 13 working- and middle-class families. Case analysis indicated that "work experience is brought into the family via the worker-parent's emotional state, which in turn determines in part the person's availability to family members, particularly children" (Bronfenbrenner & Crouter, 1982, p. 28). This perspective is consistent with Heath's (1976) study linking energy invested in the job and irritability and impatience with children.

Taken together, the literature relating social network support and both objective and subjective job conditions to individual differences in parenting illustrates the need for a model of the determinants of parenting that is multiply, reciprocally, and even hierarchically organized. These characteristics form the basis for the model of parenting that has been utilized here. And yet, it is possible to move one step further on a conceptual level by providing some notion of the dynamics which may operate within such a model. We close this chapter with a look at the likely interplay between and within the dimensions of influence that have been outlined in this discussion of the causes and consequences of individual differences in parental functioning.

PARENTING: A BUFFERED SYSTEM

This analysis of the determinants of parental functioning emphasizes that parenting is influenced by a variety of forces, with its three major determinants being the personality/psychological well-being of the parent, the characteristics of the child, and contextual sources of stress and support. Because parental competence is multiply determined, it stands to reason that the parenting system is buffered against threats to its integrity which derive from weaknesses in any single source. When two of three determinants of parenting are at risk, it is proposed that parental functioning is most protected when the personal resource subsystem still functions to promote sensitive involvement and is least protected when only the subsystem of child characteristics fulfills this function. What this implies, of course, is that if something must go wrong in the parenting system, optimal functioning (defined in terms of producing competent offspring) will occur when personal resources of parents are the only determinants that remain intact.

Evidence in support of the claim that risk characteristics in the child are relatively easy to overcome can be found in the literature on high-risk and difficult infants. Premature birth does not compromise subsequent development when rearing takes place in middle-class homes, where both personal resources and support systems are likely to function effectively (Sameroff & Chandler, 1975).

Analogously, disordered infant functioning has been found to predict nonsynchronous patterns of mother-infant and father-infant interaction *only* when marriages were evaluated as low in satisfaction (Vincent, Cook, Brady, Harris, & Messerly, 1979), while a reduced sense of parental competence is reported by mothers primarily in the *absence* of support from people around them, particularly their husbands (Gibaud-Wallston & Wandersman, 1978). Thus, unless the subsystems of support or personal resources are at risk (as they are more likely to be in impoverished homes and in conflicted marriages), we do not find problematic parental functioning in the face of difficult-child characteristics.

No data currently exist to test the hypothesis of the primacy of personal psychological functioning, because students of parent-child relations have not examined, in any single research effort, all three major determinants of parental functioning discussed in this review. The reason for this deficiency may be as much a consequence of the ecology of parent-child relations as it is of the absence of theoretical and conceptual frameworks to stimulate such inquiry. From an ecological perspective, one must bear in mind that in most contexts the influence of the three identified sets of determinants of individual differences in parenting is not independent. Consider, for example, the anecdotal knowledge that individuals with an abundance of personal psychological resources are likely *(a)* to have children who are relatively easy to care for and *(b)* to successfully attract support from their spouse, their friends, their neighbors and relatives, and their jobs. Thus, not only are such individuals likely to be sensitively involved with their offspring because they possess theoretically valuable personal psychological resources, but they are also likely to operate in a parenting system which fosters sensitive involvement as well. In popular phraseology, good things often go together. Unfortunately, the converse is known to be equally true, and the literature on child maltreatment substantiates this claim. Parental dysfunction, numerous studies indicate, is likely to occur *(a)* when parents' own developmental histories have produced individuals with a dearth of personal resources; *(b)* when children are at risk for developmental problems or otherwise are difficult to rear; and *(c)* when social supports are minimal if present at all (Belsky, 1980a; Parke & Collmer, 1975).

REFERENCES

Abernethy, V. Social network and response to the maternal role. *International Journal of Sociology of the Family,* 1973, *3,* 86–92.

Ainsworth, M. D. The development of infant-mother attachment. In B. M. Caldwell & H. N. Ricciuti (Eds.), *Review of child development research* (Vol. 3). Chicago: University of Chicago Press, 1973.

Ainsworth, M. D. *Attachment: Retrospect and prospect.* Presidential address to the biennial meeting of the Society for Research in Child Development, San Francisco, March 1979.

Ainsworth, M. D., & Bell, S. M. Some contemporary patterns of mother-infant interaction in the feeding situation. In A. Ambrose (Ed.), *Stimulation in early infancy.* New York: Academic Press, 1969.

Ainsworth, M., Blehar, M., Waters, E., & Wall, S. *Patterns of attachment.* Hillsdale, N.J.: Lawrence Erlbaum Associates, 1978.

Aug, R. G., & Bright, T. P. A study of wed and unwed motherhood in adolescents and young adults. *Journal of the American Academy of Child Psychiatry,* 1970, *9,* 577–592.

Baldwin, A. L., Cole, R. E., & Baldwin, C. T. Parent pathology, family interaction, and the competence of the child in school. *Monographs of the Society for Research in Child Development,* 1982, *47*(5, Serial No. 197).

Bandura, A., & Walters, R. *Adolescent aggression.* New York: Ronald Press, 1959.

Bates, J. The concept of difficult temperament. *Merrill-Palmer Quarterly,* 1980, *26,* 299–319.

Baumrind, D. Child care practices anteceding three patterns of preschool behavior. *Genetic Psychology Monographs,* 1967, *75,* 43–88.

Baumrind, D. Authoritarian versus authoritative parental control. *Adolescence,* 1968, *3,* 255–272.

Baumrind, D. Socialization and instrumental competence in young children. In W. W. Hartup (Ed.), *The young child: Reviews of research* (Vol. 2). Washington, D.C.: National Association for Education of Young Children, 1972.

Bayley, N., & Shaefer, E. S. Correlations of maternal and child behaviors with the development of mental abilities: Data from the Berkeley growth study. *Monographs of the Society for the Research in Child Development,* 1964, *29*(6, Serial No. 97).

Becker, W. C. Consequences of different kinds of parental discipline. In M. L. Hoffman & L. W. Hoffman (Eds.), *Review of child development research* (Vol. 1). New York: Russell Sage Foundation, 1964.

Bell, R. Q. A reinterpretation of the direction of effects in studies of socialization. *Psychological Review,* 1968, *75,* 81–95.

Bell, R. Q. Stimulus control of parent or caretaker behavior by offspring. *Developmental Psychology,* 1971, *4,* 63–72.

Bell, S. M., & Ainsworth, M. D. S. Infant crying and maternal responsiveness. *Child Development,* 1972, *43,* 1171–1190.

Belle, D. E. *The social network as a source of both stress and support to low-income mothers.* Paper presented at the biennial meeting of the Society for Research in Child Development, Boston, April 1981.

Belsky, J. Three theoretical models of child abuse: A critical review. *International Journal of Child Abuse and Neglect,* 1978, *2,* 37–49.

Belsky, J. The interrelation of parental and spousal behavior during infancy in traditional nuclear families: An exploratory analysis. *Journal of Marriage and the Family,* 1979, *41,* 62–68.

Belsky, J. Child maltreatment: An ecological integration. *American Psychologist,* 1980, *35,* 320–335. (a)

Belsky, J. A family analysis of parental influence on infant exploratory competence. In F. Pedersen (Ed.), *The father-infant relationship: Observational studies in a family context.* New York: Praeger Publishers, 1980. (b)

Belsky, J. Early human experience: A family perspective. *Developmental Psychology,* 1981, *17,* 3–23.

Belsky, J. The determinants of parenting: A process model. *Child Development,* 1984, *55,* 83–96.

Belsky, J., Gilstrap, B., & Rovine, M. Stability and change in mother-infant and father-infant interaction in a family setting: 1-to-3-to-9 months. *Child Development,* 1984, *55,* 692–705.

Belsky, J., Goode, M. K., & Most, R. K. Maternal stimulation and infant exploratory competence: Cross-sectional, correlational, and experimental analyses. *Child Development,* 1980, *51,* 1163–1178.

Belsky, J., Lerner, R., & Spanier, G. *The child in the family.* Reading, Mass.: Addison-Wesley Publishing, 1984.

Belsky, J., Rovine, M., & Taylor, D. Origins of individual differences in infant-mother attachment: Maternal and infant contributions. *Child Development,* 1984, *55,* 706–717.

Block, J., Block, J. H., & Harrington, D. M. Some misgivings about the matching familiar figures test as a measure of reflection-impulsivity. *Developmental Psychology*, 1974, *10*, 611–632.

Block, J. H. Assessing sex differences: Issues, problems, and pitfalls. *Merrill-Palmer Quarterly*, 1976, *22*, 283–308.

Block, J. H. Another look at sex differentiation in the socialization behaviors of mothers and fathers. In J. Sherman & F. Denmark (Eds.), *Psychology of women: Future of research*. New York: Psychological Dimensions, 1982.

Bradley, R., & Caldwell, B. Early home environment and changes in mental test performance in children from six to 36 months. *Developmental Psychology*, 1976, *12*, 93–97.

Bronfenbrenner, U., & Crouter, A. C. Work and family through time and space. In C. Hayes & S. Kamerman (Eds.), *Families that work: Children in a changing world*. Washington, D.C.: National Academy of Sciences, 1982.

Bronfenbrenner, U., & Crouter, A. C. The evolution of environmental models in developmental research. In P. Mussen (Ed.), *The handbook of child psychology*. New York: John Wiley & Sons, 1983.

Brown, G. W., & Harris, T. *Social origins of depression: A study of psychiatric disorder in women*. New York: Free Press, 1978.

Burgess, R. L., & Richardson, R. A. Coercive interpersonal contingencies as a determinant of child abuse: Implications for treatment and intervention. In R. F. Dangel & R. A. Polster (Eds.), *Behavioral parent training: Issues in research and practice*. New York: Guilford Press, 1983.

Campbell, S. Mother-infant interaction as a function of maternal ratings of temperament. *Child Psychiatry and Human Development*, 1979, *10*, 67–76.

Carew, J. V. Experience and the development of intelligence in young children at home and in day care. *Monographs of the Society for Research in Child Development*, 1980, *45*(6–7, Serial No. 87).

Carveth, W. B., & Gottlieb, B. H. The measurement of social support and its relation to stress. *Canadian Journal of Behavioral Science*, 1979, *11*, 179–188.

Clarke-Stewart, K. A. Interactions between mothers and their young children: Characteristics and consequences. *Monographs of the Society for Research in Child Development*, 1973, *38*(6–7, Serial No. 153).

Clarke-Stewart, K. A. *Child care in the family: A review of research and some propositions for policy*. New York: Academic Press, 1977.

Clarke-Stewart, K. A. And daddy makes three: The father's impact on mother and young child. *Child Development*, 1978, *44*, 466–478. (a)

Clarke-Stewart, K. A. Popular primers for parents, *American Psychologist*, 1978, *33*, 359–369. (b)

Cochran, M., & Brassard, J. Child development and personal social networks. *Child Development*, 1979, *50*, 601–616.

Cohen, S. E., Beckwith, L., & Parmelee, A. H. Receptive language development in preterm children as related to caregiver-child interaction. *Pediatrics*, 1978, *61*, 16–20.

Colletta, N. D. At risk for depression: A study of young mothers. *Journal of Genetic Psychology*, in press.

Coopersmith, S. *The antecedents of self-esteem*. San Francisco: W. H. Freeman, 1967.

Crandall, V. J., Dewey, R., Katovsky, W., & Preston, A. Parents' attitudes and behaviors and grade school children's academic achievements. *Journal of Genetic Psychology,* 1964, *104,* 53–66.

Crockenberg, S. Infant irritability, mother responsiveness, and social support influences on the security of infant-mother attachment. *Child Development,* 1981, *52,* 857–865.

Crouter, A., Belsky, J., & Spanier, G. The family context of child development. In G. White-hurst (Ed.), *Annals of Child Development* (Vol. 1). Greenwich, Conn.: JAI Press, in press.

De Frain, J. Androgynous parents tell who they are and what they need. *Family Coordinator,* 1979, *28,* 237–243.

Dielman, T., Barton, K., & Cattell, R. Relationships among family attitudes and child rearing practices. *Journal of Genetic Psychology,* 1977, *130,* 105–112.

Dunn, J. F. Individual differences in temperament. In M. Rutter (Ed.), *The scientific foundations of developmental psychiatry.* London: Heinemann Medical Books, 1980.

Eiduson, B. T., & Alexander, J. W. The role of children in alternative family styles. *Journal of Social Issues,* 1978, *34,* 149–167.

Elardo, R., Bradley, R., & Caldwell, B. The relation of infants' home environments to mental test performance from six to thirty-six months: A longitudinal analysis. *Child Development,* 1975, *46,* 71–76.

Elder, G. H., Jr. *Children of the Great Depression.* Chicago: University of Chicago Press, 1974.

Erikson, E. *Childhood and society.* New York: W. W. Norton, 1950.

Erikson, E. Identity and the life cycle. *Psychological Issues,* 1959, *1,* 18–164.

Fagot, B. I. The influence of sex of child on parental relations to toddler children. *Child Development,* 1978, *49,* 459–465.

Farber, A., & Egeland, B. *Maternal, neonatal and mother-infant antecedents of attachment in urban poor.* Paper presented at the meeting of the American Psychological Association, Montreal, September 1980.

Farel, A. N. Effects of preferred maternal roles, maternal employment, and sociographic status on school adjustment and competence. *Child Development,* 1980, *50,* 1179–1186.

Feshbach, N. D., & Feshbach, S. Children's aggression. In W. W. Hartup (Ed.), *The young child: Review of research* (Vol. 2). Washington, D.C.: National Association for the Education of Young Children, 1972.

Freud, S. A. *An outline of psychoanalysis.* (J. Strachey, trans.). New York: W. W. Norton, 1949.

Frommer, E., & O'Shea, G. Antenatal identification of women liable to have problems in managing their infants. *British Journal of Psychiatry,* 1973, *123,* 149–156. (a)

Frommer, E., & O'Shea, G. The importance of childhood experiences in relation to problems of marriage and family building. *British Journal of Psychiatry,* 1973, *123,* 157–160. (b)

Gersick, K. E. Fathers by choice: Divorced men who receive custody of their children. In A. Levinger & O. C. Moles (Eds.), *Divorce and separation.* New York: Basic Books, 1979.

Gibaud-Wallston, R. B. & Wandersman, L. P. *Development and utility of the parenting sense of competence scale.* Paper presented at the annual meeting of the American Psychological Association, Toronto, August, 1978.

Hall, F., Pawlby, S., & Wolkind, S. Early life experience and later mothering behavior: A study of mothers and their 20 week old babies. In D. Schaffer and J. Dunn (Eds.), *The first year of life*. New York: John Wiley & Sons, 1979.

Hardy-Brown, K., Plomin, R., & DeFries, J. C. Genetic and environmental influences on the rate of communicative development in the first year of life. *Developmental Psychology*, 1981, *17*, 704–717.

Heath, D. H. Competent fathers: Their personality and marriages. *Human Development*, 1976, *19*, 26–39.

Heinecke, C. M. *Parental deprivation in early childhood: A predisposition to later depression?* Paper presented at the Symposium on Separation and Depression: Clinical and Research Reports. Annual meeting of the American Association for the Advancement of Science, Chicago, December 26–30, 1970.

Hock, E. Working and nonworking mothers and their infants: A comparative study of maternal caregiving characteristics and infant social behavior. *Merrill-Palmer Quarterly*, 1980, *26*, 79–101.

Hoffman, L. W. Mother's enjoyment of work and effects on the child. In F. I. Nye & L. W. Hoffman (Eds.), *The employed mother in America*. Skokie, Ill.: Rand McNally, 1963.

Hoffman, L. W. Changes in family roles, socialization, and sex differences. *American Psychologist*, 1979, *32*, 644–657.

Hoffman, M. I. Moral development. In P. H. Mussen (Ed.), *Carmichael's manual of child psychology* (Vol. 2). New York: John Wiley & Sons, 1970.

Johnson, S., & Lobitz, G. The personal and marital adjustment of parents as related to observed child deviance and parenting behaviors. *Journal of Abnormal Child Psychology*, 1974, *2*, 193–207.

Kagan, J., Kearsley, R., & Zelazo, P. *Infancy: Its place in human development*. Cambridge, Mass.: Harvard University Press, 1978.

Kagan, J., & Moss, H. A. *Birth to maturity: A study in psychological development*. New York: John Wiley & Sons, 1962.

Kanter, B. Families, family processes, and economic life: Toward a systematic analysis of social historical research. In J. Demos & S. Boocock (Eds.), *Turning points: Historical and sociological essays on the family*. Chicago: University of Chicago Press, 1978.

Kelly, P. The relation of infant's temperament and mother's psychopathology to interactions in early infancy. In K. F. Riegel & J. A. Meacham (Eds.), *The developing individual in a changing world* (Vol. II). Hawthorne, N.Y.: Aldine Publishing, 1976.

Kemper, T., & Reichler, M. Fathers' work integration and frequencies of rewards and punishments administered by fathers and mothers to adolescent sons and daughters. *Journal of Genetic Psychology*, 1976, *129*, 207–219. (a)

Kemper, T., & Reichler, M. Marital satisfaction and conjugal power as determinants of intensity and frequency of rewards and punishments administered by parents. *Journal of Genetic Psychology*, 1976, *129*, 221–234. (b)

Komarovsky, M. *The unemployed man and his family*. Hinsdale, Ill.: Dryden Press, 1940.

Lamb, M. E. Effects of stress and cohort on mother- and father-infant interaction. *Developmental Psychology*, 1976, *12*, 435–443.

Langner, T. S., & Michael, S. T. *Life stress and mental health*. London: Collier-Macmillan, 1963.

LaVoie, J. C. Ego identity formation in middle adolescence. *Journal of Youth and Adolescence*, 1976, *5*, 371–385.

Lerner, R. M., & Busch-Rossnagel, N. Individuals as producers of their development: Conceptual and empirical bases. In R. M. Lerner & N. Busch-Rossnagel (Eds.), *Individuals as producers of their own development: A life-span perspective.* New York: Academic Press, 1981.

Lerner, R. M., & Lerner, J. Temperament-intelligence reciprocities in early childhood: A contextual model. In M. Lewis (Ed.), *Origins of intelligence* (2d ed). New York: Plenum Press, in press.

Lerner, R. M., Skinner, E. A., & Sorell, G. J. Methodological implications of contextual dialectic theories of development. *Human Development,* 1980, *23,* 225–235.

Lewis, M., & Ban, P. *Stability of attachment behavior: A transformational analysis.* Paper presented at the Symposium on Attachment: Studies in Stability and Change, at the Society for Research in Child Development meeting, Minneapolis, April 1971.

Lewis, M., & Goldberg, S. Perceptual-cognitive development in infancy: A generalized expectancy model as a function of the mother-infant interaction. *Merrill-Palmer Quarterly,* 1969, *15,* 81–100.

Light, R. Abused and neglected children in America: A study of alternative policies. *Harvard Educational Review,* 1973, *43,* 556–598.

Maccoby, E. *Social development: Psychological growth and the parent-child relationship.* New York: Harcourt Brace Jovanovich, 1980.

Martin, B. Parent-child relations. In F. D. Horowitz (Ed.), *Review of child development research* (Vol. 4). Chicago: University of Chicago Press, 1975.

McKinley, D. *Social class and family life.* New York: Free Press, 1964.

Mendes, H. Single fatherhood. *Social Work,* 1976, *21,* 308–312.

Milliones, J. Relationship between perceived child temperament and maternal behavior. *Child Development,* 1978, *49,* 1255–1257.

Morrow, W. R., & Wilson, R. C. Family relations of bright, high achieving and under achieving high school boys. *Child Development,* 1961, *32,* 501–510.

Mussen, P. H., Harris, S., Rutherford, E., & Keasey, C. B. Honesty and altruism among preadolescents. *Developmental Psychology,* 1970, *3,* 169–194.

Nelson, D. D. A study of personality adjustment among adolescent children with working and nonworking mothers. *Journal of Education Research,* 1971, *64,* 1328–1330.

Nelson, K. Structure and strategy in learning to talk. *Monographs of the Society for Research in Child Development,* 1973, *83*(12, Serial No. 149).

Noller, P. Sex difference in the socialization of affectionate expression. *Developmental Psychology,* 1978, *14,* 317–319.

O'Donnel, W. J. Adolescent self-esteem related to feelings toward parents and friends. *Journal of Youth and Adolescence,* 1976, *5,* 179–185.

Olweus, D. Familial and temperamental determinants of aggressive behavior in adolescent boys: A causal analysis. *Developmental Psychology,* 1980, *16,* 644–660.

Parke, R. D. Perspectives in father-infant interaction. In J. Osofsky (Ed.), *Handbook of infancy.* New York: John Wiley & Sons, 1978.

Parke, R. D., & Collmer, C. Child abuse: an interdisciplinary review. In E. M. Hetherington (Ed.), *Review of child development research* (Vol. 5). Chicago: University of Chicago Press, 1975.

Pascoe, J. M., Loda, F. A., Jeffries, V., & Earp, J. A. The association between mothers' social support and provision of stimulation to their children. *Developmental and Behavioral Pediatrics,* 1981, *2,* 15–19.

Pedersen, F., Rubenstein, J., & Yarrow, L. Infant development in father-absent families. *Journal of Genetic Psychology,* 1979, *135,* 51–61.

Piotrkowski, C. S. *Work and the family system: A naturalistic study of working-class and lower-middle class families.* New York: Free Press, 1979.

Plomin, R. Childhood temperament. In B. Lahey & A. Kazdin (Eds.), *Advances in clinical child psychology* (Vol. 6). New York: Plenum Press, 1982.

Powell, D. R. Personal social networks as a focus for primary prevention of child maltreatment. *Infant Mental Health Journal,* 1980, *1,* 232–239.

Price, G. *Factors influencing reciprocity in early mother-infant interaction.* Paper presented at the biennial meeting of the Society for Research in Child Development, New Orleans, March 1977.

Radin, N. Role sharing fathers and preschoolers. In M. Lamb (Ed.), *Nontraditional families: Parenting and child development.* Hillsdale, N.J.: Lawrence Erlbaum Associates, 1981.

Rehberg, R. & Westby, D. Parental encouragement, occupation, education, and family size: Artifactual or independent determinants of adolescent educational expectations. *Journal of Social Forces,* 1967, *45,* 262–274.

Reuter, M. W., & Biller, H. B. Perceived paternal nurturance-availability and personality adjustment among college males. *Journal of Consulting and Clinical Psychology,* 1973, *40,* 339–342.

Rubenstein, J. Maternal attentiveness and subsequent exploratory behavior in the infant. *Child Development,* 1967, *38,* 1089–1100.

Rubin, J. Z., Provenzano, F. J., & Luria, Z. The eye of the beholder: Parents' views on sex of newborns. *American Journal of Orthopsychiatry,* 1974, *44,* 512–519.

Sameroff, A. Transactional models of early social relations. *Human Development,* 1975, *18,* 65–79.

Sameroff, A., & Chandler, M. J. Reproductive risk and the continuum of caretaking casualty. In F. D. Horowitz (Ed.), *Review of Child Development Research* (Vol. 4). Chicago: University of Chicago Press, 1975.

Santrock, J. W. Influence of onset and type of paternal absence on the first four Eriksonian developmental crises. *Developmental Psychology,* 1970, *3,* 273–274.

Santrock, J. W., Warshak, R., Lindbergh, C., & Meadows, L. Children's and parent's observed social behavior in stepfather families. *Child Development, 1982, 53,* 472–480.

Sears, R., Maccoby, E., & Lewin, H. *Patterns of child rearing.* Evanston, Ill.: Row & Peterson, 1957.

Shaw, M. E., & White, D. L. The relationship between child-parent identification and academic under-achievement. *Journal of Clinical Psychology,* 1965, *21,* 10–13.

Sroufe, L. A. The coherence of individual development. *American Psychologist,* 1979, *34,* 834–841.

Steinberg, L., Catalano, R., & Dooley, D. Economic antecedents of child abuse and neglect. *Child Development,* 1981, *52,* 975–986.

Steinberg, L., Greenberger, E., Garduque, L., Ruggiero, M., & Vaux, A. Effects of working on adolescent development. *Developmental Psychology,* 1982, *18,* 385–395.

Stuckey, M., McGhee, P., & Bell, N. Parent-child interaction: The influence of maternal employment. *Developmental Psychology*, 1982, *18*, 635–644.

Swift, D. F. Family environment and 11+ success: Some basic predictions. *British Journal of Educational Psychology*, 1967, *37*, 10–21.

Thomas, A., & Chess, S. *Temperament and development*. New York: Brunner/Mazel, 1977.

Tulkin, S., & Covitz, F. *Mother-infant interactions and intellectual functioning at age six*. Paper presented at the biennial meeting of the Society for Research in Child Development, Denver, April 1975.

Tulkin, S. R., & Kagan, J. Mother-child interaction in the first year of life. *Child Development*, 1972, *43*, 31–41.

U.S. Bureau of the Census. *Statistical abstract of the United States: 1978* (99th ed.). Washington, D.C.: U.S. Government Printing Office, 1978.

Vincent, P., Cook, N., Brady, C., Harris, G., & Messerly, L. *Learning to be a family: Struggle of the emergent triad*. Symposium presented at the biennial meeting of the Society for Research in Child Development, San Francisco, March 1979.

Wachs, T., Uzgiris, I., & Hunt, J. Cognitive development in infants of different age levels and from different environmental backgrounds: An exploratory investigation. *Merrill-Palmer Quarterly*, 1971, *17*, 283–317.

Weissman, M. M., & Paykel, E. S. *The depressed woman: A study of social relations*. Chicago: University of Chicago Press, 1974.

Wolf, R. M. *The identification and measurement of environmental process variables related to intelligence*. Unpublished doctoral dissertation, University of Chicago, 1964.

Yarrow, L., Rubenstein, J., & Pedersen, F. *Infant and environment*. New York: John Wiley & Sons, 1975.

Zur-Spiro, S., & Longfellow, C. *Support from fathers: Implications for the well-being of mothers and their children*. Paper presented at the biennial meeting of the Society for Research in Child Development, Boston, April 1981.

Zussman, J. V. Relationship of demographic factors to parental discipline techniques. *Developmental Psychology*, 1978, *14*, 685–686.

Chapter 19

Becoming a Parent*

DORIS R. ENTWISLE

INTRODUCTION

Earlier writings on the psychosocial consequences of becoming a parent emphasized (1) the family development approach (Duvall & Hill, cited in Hill, 1978), mainly concerned with the developmental tasks set by a family's first pregnancy and birth, or (2) the crisis nature of a couple's first birth, including whether or not a crisis was uniformly perceived (e.g., Blood & Wolfe, 1960). Rapoport (1963) subsequently integrated the family development and crisis themes. In this chapter, we will follow her lead by emphasizing a joint "life course perspective" for individuals and for families. The "life course" of one-parent families, for example, is different from that of two-parent families. The emphasis is timely because the nature of both parents' birth experience and their expectations for family life have changed dramatically in the past decade or two. Pregnancy, birth, and early nurturing of the neonate are increasingly seen as undertakings in which men as well as women take an active role. Additionally, the age and career status of persons becoming parents is more variable than it used to be. There has been an upsurge in adolescent childbearing, a jump in the number of first births to women in their middle or late 30s, and now women often become mothers between episodes of paid employment. In short, there has been a stretching out of the transition to adulthood for both men (Hogan, 1981) and women (C. A. Miller, 1982).

Other recent social changes involve the way the birth event is han-

_____
* Work on this chapter was supported by grants from the National Institute of Child Health and Development (HD13103) and the National Institute of Mental Health (MH15735), Doris Entwisle, principal investigator.

dled. Couples frequently attend childbirth preparation classes together. Births now occur in the home or in birthing centers as well as in hospitals.

A life course perspective stresses the way families and individuals integrate the experience of becoming a parent into a total life pattern. Whether a woman is married and then bears a child, or is single and bears a child without help from a partner, is bound to affect how the transition is negotiated. In 1969, 5.3 percent of all births were to unmarried women; in 1978, the rate was 16.3 percent (U.S. National Center for Health Statistics, 1980). Also, the past affects the future—how people undertake the task of parenting likely affects their parenting or spousal behaviors later on. Do women who experience difficult deliveries have fewer children or space them differently? If a couple copes well with a first birth, is their marital relationship strengthened? Are there any consequences of cesarean deliveries for parent-child relations over the long term? These are only a few of the many questions raised by adopting a life course perspective.

A special merit of this perspective is that it provides a framework for integrating a number of the recent large-scale demographic studies (e.g., the relative timing of marriage and fertility decisions) with the many smaller-scale family and psychological studies of family formation and parenting. For example, to evaluate how having a child affects a woman's labor force participation calls for a large and representative sample, but to understand women's deeper motives for juggling the parent role along with an employee role requires in-depth questioning.

A life course perspective encompasses many ideas, but four will be key in this chapter. (1) A cohort-historical view: Having a first child in the 1980s is different from having a child in earlier decades, in part because the state of the economy, the country's value system, the age distribution of the total population, and other important social contextual factors have changed. (2) Reciprocal causation: Husbands and wives affect each other, and babies are powerful influences on both parents. Focusing exclusively on the baby as recipient of influence is inadequate. A "good" baby can have positive effects on the parents' marriage. Only recently has there been much attention to early parent-infant relationships from the point of view of parental needs and gratifications (Leifer, 1980; Rossi, 1977). (3) Constancy and/or change: becoming a parent adds a new role and perhaps changes performance of spousal roles, but at the same time, it may leave underlying personality traits virtually undisturbed. It is as necessary to establish what does not change as what does. (4) Individuals as producers of their own development: Parenting may be a qualitatively different experience for couples who seek out information about childcare in advance or give careful thought to childbearing-career contingencies, as compared to couples who take no steps to prepare themselves for parenthood. These four themes will organize the extensive research on becoming a parent.

This chapter will concentrate on the *sociopsychological* antecedents and consequences of first-time parenthood, excluding for the most part its biological, medical, political, and economic implications. We will exclude problems of parenthood related to genetic disorders, premature delivery, and handicapped children, but will consider the sociopsychological implications of cesarean delivery since this mode of delivery is becoming so common. Also, we will exclude new parenting of later-born children. There is little research, to our knowledge, on the transition to parenthood for single parents except for the research on adolescents. Also there is little research on becoming a parent as a consequence of marrying a person who already has children. The one study of the transition to parenthood for black couples suggests slightly more difficulty but general similarities to patterns seen for whites (Hobbs & Wimbish, 1977).

In what follows, the transition to parenthood will be discussed under two main rubrics, the birth event itself and the social impact of the event. The birth event occasions physical separation of mother and child, including possible operative delivery and other complications. The social impact of birth includes the social crisis precipitated by the birth and its sociopsychological effects on parents and their spousal relationship.

THE BIRTH EVENT

When this century began, most babies were born at home. Infant mortality rates were high. As a consequence of improved public health and of urbanization, as the century progressed, more and more children were delivered in hospitals. By 1975, 99 percent of all babies in the country were delivered by physicians in hospitals (Querec, 1978).

The nature of the birth event could have profound effects on how the transition to parenthood is negotiated, and the limited research so far available suggests this is true. We will summarize this research in what follows in terms of effects of childbirth preparation classes, personalization of the birth event, effects of father participation in delivery, and the amount of early contact between parents and infants. Delivery mode will be separately considered.

Effects of preparation in pregnancy

Preparation for childbirth now enjoys great popularity. Lamaze preparation, however, is characteristic of better-educated women and of women residing near major population centers (Watson, 1977).

It appears that the major impact of preparation on the woman's birth experience is by way of increasing her level of awareness and by encouraging the husband to participate. Neither preparation nor husband's participation has any substantial effects on pain, and pain is weakly and negatively related to a woman's birth experience (Doering, Entwisle, & Quinlan, 1980).

Personalization

Over the past two decades, young people have begun to see as ends in themselves the quality of mothers' and fathers' birth experience and the gratification parents experience in the very early days of parenting. Young couples increasingly wish to experience a natural (unmedicated) labor and delivery and to have the father and perhaps even close friends present when the birth occurs. They question the quality of parents' emotional experience in old-fashioned hospital obstetric units, with mothers heavily drugged and fathers in waiting rooms. Couples may shop for progressive physicians and hospitals where they can receive the type of care they desire. And some couples are now opting for home births or for delivery at a birth center. The home birth movement began with those living in communes on the West Coast, was picked up on the East Coast, and more and more includes all segments of the population (Mehl, 1978).

A closely related trend is the changing notion of woman's role in childbirth. Feminists insist that women should be allowed to maintain control over the events of labor and birth, and in particular challenge what they see as the devaluation of female patients at the hands of the (usually male) obstetrician. These views are percolating to people at all levels of society (Corea, 1977). For example, the women in the Entwisle and Doering (1981) study, a relatively conservative group, were distinctly unhappy that they received more medication than they wanted during delivery.

Father participation

Many couples now view pregnancy and childbirth as a joint undertaking. Analyses of husband's and wife's birth experiences indicate that each spouse is a strong influence on the other. The man's participation in delivery improves the quality of vaginally delivered women's birth experience (Doering et al., 1980; Norr, Block, Charles, Meyering, & Meyers, 1977), and the quality of a woman's birth experience is a strong predictor of the quality of her husband's birth experience (Entwisle & Doering, 1981). There is even some suggestion that lack of husband support during labor is associated with cesarean delivery

(Klein & Gist, 1982), although these kinds of causal relationships are hard to study.

Active involvement in pregnancy and childbirth apparently has two consequences for the father, one affecting quality of life for the man himself and the other affecting his and his wife's early parenting. The first point requires little elaboration. Some men rate being a participant in the birth of their first child as the most thrilling and profound event in their lives so far (Entwisle & Doering, 1981; Grossman, Eichler, & Winikoff, 1980). The parenting benefits associated with father participation in delivery are largely unresearched, however. Entwisle and Doering tallied the caretaking and emotional reactions of fathers in the first few weeks after delivery according to whether fathers were absent from delivery by choice, absent against their will, or present for delivery. As judged from fathers' reports, in every instance except two (how much the husband held the baby and how soon the man felt like a father), fathers who were present in delivery scored higher on fathering measures than fathers who were absent by choice. But, with minor exceptions, fathers absent against their will scored higher than fathers who were present. Thus the effects of husband participation in delivery on early fathering seem best interpreted as a consequence of both motivation to participate and the effect that actual participation had. Motivation rather than undergoing the actual experience is the key causal element for some fathers.

Early contact between parents and infant

The mechanisms by which very early contact could affect mothers and infants is not clear. Early maternal-infant contact could maintain or enhance hormonal states that heighten maternal feelings (Leifer, Leiderman, Barnett, & Williams, 1972; Seashore, Leifer, Barnett, & Leiderman, 1973). It could also prompt beginnings of synchronous maternal-infant behaviors by way of eye contact (Robson, 1967). Also, there is no need to see attachment as a one-sided process—parents could have strong attachment needs that, if thwarted, have negative consequences. Additionally, attachment of the father, although of little concern in early work on attachment (see especially Bowlby, 1969), is now commanding attention (Greenberg & Morris, 1974; Lamb, 1977). The father, like the mother, may have highly significant attachment experience when the infant is still very young.

The controversy about whether or not early separation of mother and child has negative effects on parents or children is not likely to be settled soon, but empirical evidence continues to appear (McClellan & Cabianca, 1980; Entwisle, 1982; Entwisle, Doering & Reilly, 1983). From a policy perspective, the choice of keeping parents and children together right after the birth is easy because it is hard to see how harm could result even if there are no benefits.

Cesarean delivery

In recent years, the rate of cesarean delivery has gone up sharply, from 5.0 percent in 1968 to 12.8 percent in 1977, while the birth rate has declined 12 percent over the same period (Consensus Development Conference, 1981, p. 6; Marieskind, 1979, p. 1). The cesarean rate in some areas of the country increased more than 300 percent in a dozen years (Consensus, p. 127). The full extent of the increase is not known however because, in contrast with other operative procedures, no central clearinghouse records the number of obstetric operations in the United States.

Numerous reasons are given for the increased number of cesarean births, including the increasing preference to deliver breeches by cesarean section, the increased use of medical technology (especially fetal monitoring), and the increased emphasis on defensive medicine to avoid malpractice suits (Consensus, 1981). The changing demographic characteristics of the parturient population, although substantial, have no apparent effect on the rate (Gibbons, 1976).

If mothers undergo cesarean delivery, the experience ot becoming a parent is different for both spouses compared to becoming a parent when the baby is delivered vaginally. The mother is heavily medicated or unconscious. The father is less likely to participate in the delivery.

Most behavioral studies of cesarean birth enroll families at delivery and then attribute postnatal differences in family functioning to delivery mode. The differences between delivery groups that existed prior to the birth are ignored. Aside from Bradley, Ross, and Warnyea, (1983), only Entwisle (in press) actually uses prepartum data in evaluating the magnitude of cesarean delivery effects.

A cesarean birth and its sequelae likely have different significance for persons in various socioeconomic strata because reactions to stress (Kessler & Cleary, 1980), parent-infant relations (Kilbride, Johnson, & Streissguth, 1977), spousal roles (Bott, 1957), family values (Kohn, 1969), and family functioning (Hess, 1970) all differ along social-class lines. Entwisle (in press) and Reilly (1981) find that effects of cesarean birth are more pronounced for working-class than for middle-class couples. In addition, most sociopsychological effects are *positive*.

Several reports agree that cesarean women have negative birth experiences (Affonso & Stichler, 1980; Entwisle, 1983; Field & Widmayer, 1980; Marut & Mercer, 1979), hardly surprising. There also appears to be increased involvement of cesarean fathers in child care later on in the first year (Pedersen, Zaslow, Cain, & Anderson, 1981; Reilly,

1981; Vietze, MacTurk, McCarthy, Klein, & Yarrow, 1980), but not immediately (Entwisle, in press). The long-term effects for fathers may stem from the more-positive family relations prompted by cesarean delivery. Entwisle (in press) found, for example, that soon after delivery, middle-class cesarean women had more-positive views of husband as father than their vaginally delivered counterparts and that when cesarean couples compare the actual baby to the anticipated baby, it measures up more favorably than is the case for vaginally delivered infants.

Findings for maternal-infant relations are mixed. Pedersen et al. (1981) reported mothers had more problems in the initial adaptation period. Joy (cited in Consensus, 1981, p. 438; see also Williams, Davidson, Joy, & Painter, n.d.), found very few differences in maternal attachment between cesarean and other women, although the cesarean mothers tended to be more depressed than the vaginally delivered. Entwisle (1982) found more depression for working-class mothers and relatively lower ratings of the baby by middle-class mothers. Pedersen et al. (1981) found at five months postpartum that there was less-frequent vigorous stimulation of infants and less reciprocal positive affect between mother and child for the cesarean group. Other workers find positive effects for mothers, especially later in the first year. Field and Widmayer (1980) at four and eight months postpartum found, for low-income black mothers, that 20 cesarean mothers rated their infants' temperament more optimally than did 20 vaginally delivered mothers; and at four months, the cesarean mothers also received more optimal face-to-face and feeding interaction ratings. Likewise, Vietze et al. (1980) report more maternal care-giving and feeding at six months and more stimulation behavior by cesarean mothers at 12 months. Croghan, Connors, & Franz (1980) also reported that cesarean mothers were more responsive to their infants.

Reilly (1981) finds that cesarean women's views of their own maternal competence at one year postpartum are significantly higher than those of their vaginally delivered counterparts. Differential effects of cesarean delivery by class may come about because working-class women make the transition to motherhood faster.

SOCIAL ASPECTS OF BECOMING A PARENT

There is little formal socialization for first-time parents, although becoming a parent is one of the most complex and challenging of life's major transitions. The man must integrate the father role with his prior roles, his husband role, his work role, and others. The woman must integrate the mother role into a role set she possesses, including wife, daughter, and possibly employee. Parenthood has profound social and psychological implications for men *and* women, for their relation to each other, and for their relation to the larger society. Rossi (1968) was among the first to emphasize parenthood as a developmental stage and to delineate the parent role in contrast with the marriage and work role.

Parenthood is also the event that signifies full entrance into adult society (Hill & Aldous, 1969) with all of the responsibilities that such a status carries. In a national sample of married women under 40 years old, Hoffman (1978, p. 344) found that parents of both sexes most often checked "becoming a parent" as the most-important life event in defining adult status. They saw it as "the end of carefree existence" and as a new status characterized by being responsible for others and less egocentric. Before the coming of children, marriage is often more tentative. Afterwards, parents often acquire all those possessions—permanent dwelling, expensive appliances, and the like— that stamp the union as stable. And society is not indifferent to whether persons choose parenthood. In every society, there are strong norms against childlessness, and there is particular pressure on women to produce children.

The birth crisis forces the reorganization of the family as a social system: "Roles have to be reassigned, status positions shifted, values reoriented, and needs met through new channels" (LeMasters, 1957, p. 352). If, as Nye (1976) says, family roles encompass the essential activities of family life and the more competently each spouse enacts these roles, the more satisfactory family life becomes, clearly the first birth can pose a threat to the quality of family life or even to the family's existence. With the advent of a third person, the couples' roles change with respect to each other and to the larger society.

There are two major thrusts to the psychological problems of new parenthood. A first birth challenges the mother and father as individuals. It exposes the husband as well as the wife to high levels of stress. Second, pregnancy challenges "the family"—it tests the bonds between husband and wife. And by producing a third individual who must be socially as well as physically integrated into an already existing group, it tests the viability of the family as a social organization. A three-person group, whatever its nature, is inherently less stable than a two-person group (Simmel, 1950; Stryker, 1964).

Research on the sociopsychological concomitants of pregnancy, birth, and early parenting in the normal, well-balanced adult was rare until about 1970. Since then, however, several detailed reports have appeared of longitudinal research on families over the perinatal period (e.g., Entwisle & Doering, 1981; Grossman, Eichler, & Winikoff, 1980). Even more recently, the journal literature has begun to explode with demographic research on birth and the transition to parenthood. Demographic studies provide a much-needed backdrop against which to evaluate in-depth studies of birth and the family.

Large-scale demographic studies evaluate the impact of a first birth in ways impossible in small-scale studies. A birth to a childless couple, for example, directly reduces income attributable to the husband as well as reducing income via cutting into the wife's hours of employment (Hofferth, 1983). During the first few years after birth of a first child, fathers' earnings do not rise as fast as do those of childless husbands. For this reason, a first birth (in comparison with later births) is the one most affecting family well-being.

In the remainder of this section, we will consider first the extent to which parenthood is voluntary and, second, the motives that impel people to become parents. In later sections, we will discuss the socialization of parents to their new roles and the consequences of parenthood for mothers, fathers, and the marital dyad.

Voluntarism

Becoming a parent now is often, though not always, voluntary. According to Westoff (1978), 5 to 7 percent of couples remain voluntarily childless, and the size of this group may be increasing. Hill (1978), on the other hand, sees childlessness as an epiphenomenon, and on the decrease. Whatever the case, demographic forecasts of fertility have proved exceedingly difficult since the end of World War II, as the pace of social change has quickened.

Intentionality of parenthood is difficult to assess, in part because accidental pregnancy may be quickly rationalized. In a national sample surveyed in 1971–75 of white women married at least 30 months, 5.1 percent experienced a pregnancy when birth was not wanted at all (U.S. Bureau of the Census, 1979). Entwisle and Doering's (1981) small sample revealed 3.3 percent of "completely unplanned" pregnancies acknowledged by the mother and 6.7 percent acknowledged by the father, suggesting that there may be considerable difference between spouses' perceptions of intentionality. There is difficulty also in comparisons across studies because 11 percent of the women in the Entwisle and Doering sample acknowledged an abortion at some time in the past. The rates do suggest, however, that by the mid-70s a very large majority of white women were assuming motherhood voluntarily.

Current rates of conception control contrast sharply with rates reported earlier. The Foundation for Child Development (1977), using data from a national sample of children born between 1964 and 1969, noted that "less than half of the youngsters in the survey were the result of a planned pregnancy, in the sense that the mother 'wanted to become pregnant at that time' " (p. 19). Russo (1979) estimated that 20 percent of pregnancies were unplanned in the 60s. And implications of conception control for the composition of society are far-reaching, because historically there has been a strong association between conception control and socioeconomic status or religion. These associations are now decreasing.

Choosing to have a child probably has many implications, but the prime one is emotional. Voluntary parenthood could be much different from accidental parenthood, especially for women. W. B. Miller (1978) found, for instance, that fully intended pregnancies result in fully wanted children at six months of age, also that women with unplanned pregnancies did not adopt a new identity based on pregnancy. Landis (1952) noted greater emotional upset in the first trimester for women with unplanned pregnancies compared to women who had intended to conceive. An unwanted pregnancy can also be reflected in the mother having a negative perception of the child (Arasteh, 1971; Forssman & Thuwe, 1966). On the other hand, Williams et al. (n.d.) found that whether or not the pregnancy was planned (ascertained in a prepartum questionnaire) was not related to postpartum experiences with, and feelings toward, the new baby, suggesting that many women may adjust quickly after the birth.

Postponement of pregnancy until a couple is ready may have consequences for the father as well as the mother and for marital satisfaction in addition (Christensen, 1968). Older, more-affluent parents may experience less financial stress than younger, impecunious ones. On the other hand, it may be harder for couples who have been married for some time to adjust their routines to accommodate an infant. Steffensmeier (1982), for example, found that greater planning of pregnancy plus higher levels of education of parents led to lower parental gratification. Planning could increase perceived competency, financial security, and the like, but it also may reflect doubts or hesitancy about effects of children on marriage.

Why people become parents

People seem to reach a point in their lives where they confront, explicitly or implicitly, the possibility of having a child (Rapoport, Rapoport, & Strelitz, 1977). Parenting is a major channel that people use to give meaning and purpose to their lives. For some, the decision to parent, like a career decision, may be left to "just happen" (Feldman & Feldman, 1975). For others, it may be planned and scheduled, as a career in its own right or to dovetail with one or both of the couple's occupational careers. For still others, the decision may have an expedient character—it may make women eligible for housing or transfer payments.

Some people become parents because they wish to have someone with whom to develop strong affectional bonds. Unwed adolescent parents from disadvantaged homes often cite this reason. Needs for companionship may be increasingly compelling in a society with close to 50 percent of its marriages failing (Weed, 1980). Parent-child commitments provide anchors in an otherwise shifting social system. Divorced men and women with children still have families and living companions, even if no mate. Over the long term, in fact, the psychological need for children may be greater in many people's lives than the need for a relationship with a person of the opposite sex. Children find it almost as hard to "divorce" parents as parents find it to "divorce" children. Additionally, children provide parents with strong links to other kin, even those of the divorced mate (Cherlin, 1978).

Socialization of parents to new roles

As a topic for research, adult socialization into parental roles has been markedly neglected in favor of adult socialization into occupational roles (see, for example, Cohn, 1978; Kohn, 1971; Kohn & Carroll, 1960; Mortimer & Simmons, 1978).

Fortunately, a few recent studies have actually begun to explore processes related to the socialization of new parents. From an interview study of couples having a first child, Entwisle and Doering (1981) developed models of sociopsychological processes to explain early parenting behavior in terms of psychological and social factors acting during pregnancy and during the parents' birth experience. The models, examined separately for 60 middle- and 60 working-class couples, appear to be substantially different for the two classes in that in the first few weeks following delivery, the middle-class parents appear to parent independently, while the working-class father follows his wife's lead. In addition, previous experience with young infants actually depressed working-class men's parenting activity.

Reilly (1981) extended this work by developing explicit models of the influence of counterroles on women's sense of competence in the parental role and exploring the social-class differences in such effects. He found that there was a significant decrease from before the birth to after in *all* women's views of their own maternal competence— mothering was more difficult than most women anticipated. He also found that middle-class women's self-concepts as mothers remained relatively stable over the period of the birth event, but working-class women's self-concepts did not. (Entwisle, 1983, notes the same interaction between social class and stability of role patterns for men.) However, by the end of the first postpartum year, middle-class women's self-concepts had changed, suggesting that they took longer to make the same role adjustments to parenthood that the working-class women made almost immediately. Working-class parents apparently saw parenting as a stereotyped role and jumped into it with little reflection or negotiation. The middle-class parents, on the other hand, adopted the new role much more slowly, perhaps because they fashioned for themselves an individualized role that took time to formulate. These ideas are consistent with Kohn's (1969) and Bernstein's (1971) theories about social-class differences in family roles and family functioning and also with Steffensmeier's (1982) recent findings about social-class role conceptions of parents.

Furstenberg's (1976) sample of 404 teenagers was much lower in socioeconomic status than respondents in either the Grossman et al. (1980) or Entwisle and Doering (1981) study. He interviewed adolescent mothers during pregnancy, one year after delivery, three years after delivery, and five years after. The last interview tapped the mother's evaluation of her style of parenting in terms of warmth, communicativeness, patience, demandingness, confidence, and control. Furstenberg then related this measure of maternal self-perception to several aspects of the woman's life condition, among which was how the father performed the paternal role. Three levels of participation in the paternal role were considered: father does not live with the mother and has irregular interaction with the child; father does not live with the mother, but has regular interaction with the child; father lives with the mother. The presence of the father in the home apparently made little difference for the mother's adaptation to parenthood. In this respect, Furstenberg's findings are similar to Reilly's (1981), for he found that husband involvement in child care did not affect women's role evaluation in the first few weeks after delivery, and at one year there was a borderline *negative* effect for the working-class women—the more the husband participated in child care, the lower the woman's sense of maternal competence.

In a study of 47 women having a first child, begun in the first trimester and ending six months postpartum, Gerson (1973) and Shaver (1973) found significant zero-order correlations between women's confidence in the maternal role and temperamental characteristics of the child. Further, Shereshefsky, Liebenberg, and Lockman (1973) using the same sample, found that a factor called "woman's confidence" (composed of confidence in maternal role, reaction to pregnancy fears, and perception of being mothered) correlated with the husband's responsiveness to the parental role. Shereshefsky and Yarrow (1973) looked at the effects of the father and infant on woman's evaluation of self in the parental role, but did not attempt to integrate these variables into a single model which would allow the decomposition of their zero-order correlations into direct, indirect, and spurious effects. These authors also did not consider the possibility of social-class differences in the structure of such relationships.

Consequences of parenthood

It is easy to underestimate the stress incurred by the arrival of a couple's first child. Although not all social scientists are willing to label the period as one of crisis (Lamb, 1978) and the view that early parenthood is a strain on marriage is not always supported (Fawcett, 1978; Hobbs, 1965, 1968; Hobbs & Cole, 1976; Hoffman & Manis, 1978), childbirth and the early weeks of an infant's life call for a couple to make drastic adjustments. New behavior patterns are called for as soon as the birth occurs.

A number of studies indicate parents' responses to babies reflect attitudes present before the baby is born or even conceived. Shereshefsky et al. (1973), for example, found that prenatally expressed interest in children predicted maternal adaptation later on, and similar findings are reported by Moss (1967) and Moss and Jones (1977), especially for middle-class mothers. Actual rehearsal of the parent role as babysitter, close relative, or paid parent surrogate is not very common, however, although empirical data are scarce. Entwisle and Doering (1981) found that 57 percent of the women in their sample (interviewed between 1973 and 1976) had *no* experience at caring for a child under six weeks of age. Only 30 percent of the women had had "full charge" experience with a baby six weeks of age or younger. Working-class women were almost twice as likely as middle-class to have had such experience. Dyer (1963) earlier found over a third of the wives and half of the husbands in his sample lacking in "course work" *or* experience with younger siblings, let alone infants. This lack of relevant experience undoubtedly leads to unrealistic expectations that trigger later disappointments. For example, in the Entwisle and Doering sample, over half the women expected the baby to sleep through the night before it was eight weeks of age. Along similar lines, Breen (1975) comments that "the most striking feature amongst the women who experienced most difficulties was the split between a very idealized picture of what they felt a mother should be like . . . and the way in which they saw themselves" (p. 192) after birth of the baby.

The early sociological literature defined the arrival of the first child as a family crisis (Hill, 1951; Waller, 1938), and many studies of the transition to parenthood focus mainly on stress: on whether the transition is of crisis proportions and on identifying the correlates of the degree of crisis experienced by the new parents (Dyer, 1963; Hobbs, 1965, 1968; Hobbs & Cole, 1976; Hobbs & Wimbish, 1977; Jacoby, 1969; Larsen, 1966; LeMasters, 1957; Meyerowitz & Feldman, 1966; Russell, 1974). With the exception of LeMasters and Dyer, the sole criterion for evaluating the "crisis" of becoming a parent apparently was the 23-item checklist Hobbs developed in 1965. As LaRossa and LaRossa (1981, p. 20) point out, parents are *not* asked in this checklist whether there has been any interruption of routine or whether their sex life has changed. Instead they are asked to "indicate the extent to which each one [of the items] has bothered them," with options of "not at all," "somewhat," and "very much," scored 0, 1, and 2, respectively. Thus, if a husband or wife marks "not at all" for "decreased sexual responsiveness of spouse," it is unclear whether there has been no change in the couple's sexual pattern or whether there has been a change but they are not bothered by it. The emphasis of the checklist is not on patterns of interaction but on the coping abilities of the individual parents. Russell (1974) is apparently the only investigator who allowed for more positive reactions by adding a 12-item checklist asking "new parents what things they enjoyed about their newly acquired role" (p. 295).

Earlier research thus concentrated upon the "crisis" character of the transition and not upon the activities or household routines that new parents actually experienced, although some writers mentioned parenting problems. LeMasters (1957), for example, reported that in 38 of 46 couples he observed, a crisis was precipitated because the couples romanticized parenthood. Likewise, Hubert (1974) observed: "[Not] all first pregnancies are a nightmare. . . . But [parents'] ideas and expectations are very confused, and their experience as a result is often surprised and unpleasant" (p. 55). There is now more-ready admission of the heavy burden that children can place on parents (Rapoport et al., 1977; Skolnick, 1973), however, and the costs of parenthood are being increasingly discussed. But the day-to-day consequences of becoming a parent are largely unresearched (LaRossa, 1983), and as Grossman et al. (1980, p. 254) note, the myth of parenthood still survives and tyrannizes many new parents.

The social and geographical isolation of modern families creates great strain, particularly for mothers. Care of a new baby is physically exhausting, and parents must somehow adjust work schedules to needs of caring for infants. A child interferes with a couple's privacy. Young adults seldom anticipate any medical problems with a first birth, although an appreciable number of children are stillborn, others have serious birth defects, many are preterm and require extensive hospitalization, and up to 20 percent of families experience a cesarean birth (Consensus, 1981). In Entwisle and Doering's (1981) sample of 120 women, 2 had to be rehospitalized with thrombophlebitis soon after delivery, one baby had a cleft palate, and another had a serious leg deformity. The average woman in that study saw the birth event in retrospect as being considerably more stressful in physical terms than she had thought it would be beforehand. In addition, 81 percent of the women reported depression at some time in the first few weeks after childbirth, a figure that is fairly typical (Breen, 1975; Yalom, 1968).

The rest of this section is organized as follows: effects of parenthood on the mother, the father, and the marital dyad. These effects are clearly interdependent, although women and men take different views of sexual functioning (Grossman, 1980, p. 128) and the demands of parenting are different.

Effects on mothers.   Hoffman (1978) found that in most cases, children interfered with women's activities to about the degree expected or less. They interfered mainly with social and recreational activities (around 40 percent) and much less with job commitments (about 12 percent). The unexpectedly low level of work interference reported may stem partly from some women's opinion that withdrawal from the labor force is a positive event. Hoffman's analysis of opportunity costs to women of a first child are contrary to intuition: First-time mothers report that children interfere substantially less than childless women estimate. The view that first children carry high opportunity costs for women is thus not supported. Hoffman also finds decreases in women's commitment to work and in women's status achievement through work but increases in traditional ideas about sex roles and power, as well as behaviors consistent with these notions.

Birth of a first child is *generally* reported to move women's views in traditional directions, especially for the less-highly educated (see Rapoport et al., 1977). Over 40 percent of those with a high school education or less in Hoffman's (1978) sample agreed that the "husband should have the main say-so," compared to 18 percent of those with more education. These percentages were closely paralleled by answers to other questions regarding relative husband-wife power. Among full-time working nonmothers, 45 percent reported the husband regularly helped with housework versus 17 percent of nonworking mothers. This differential remained constant across educational levels.

Other research documents severe changes in the daily lives of some mothers. The principal difficulties women experience are lack of help in caring for the baby and the home and a curtailment of personal freedom. Entwisle and Doering (1981) report that the first two to three weeks home from the hospital found a large majority of wives continually tired. At two to three weeks of age, the average infant was crying over one and one-half hours daily. And Williams et al. (n.d.) found that 36 percent of mothers at one month postpartum were going out with their babies only once a week or less and going out even less often *without* their babies. Of these mothers, 75 percent had not been out with their husbands *without* the babies by one month postpartum.

Glass (1983), on the other hand, found few major changes in mothers' attitudes when their prepartum feelings about babies being pleasurable or the reverse were inquired about afterward. She did find, however, that parents reported crying they had actually experienced to be a more aversive experience than expected and that parents were more positive about the need for scheduling infants' demands than they had been previously.

Not surprisingly, women see more overall life change and more change in their personal lives than men (Harriman, 1983; Hobbs & Cole, 1976; Miller & Sollie, 1980). Rindfuss and St. John (1983) emphasize that a woman's first birth often excludes further education and career-building, and the earlier a first birth, the greater the expected quantity and pace of subsequent childbearing. They find that education is the most-important predictor of age at first birth, but both race and religion interact with age. Blacks have first births about four fifths of a year younger than whites, and Catholics have first births about nine months later than non-Catholics.

Married women tend to be in poorer mental health than married men (Gove, 1972), especially if not in the labor force, and children are suspected of directly undermining mental health. Unemployed married women attend to the many demands of children in the household (Gove & Geerken, 1977) and are thereby prevented from interactions with other adults and from using their instrumental skills. Both factors are associated with poorer mental health status, and are especially in evidence when a first birth occurs.

American society has been moving toward less-stereotyped sex roles for women (see Thornton & Freedman, 1979), and broader sex role conceptions encourage women to work outside the home as well as delegate care of young children. The available research indicates that women find it difficult, however, and more difficult than most imagine, to assume the parent role, let alone juggle a full-time job simultaneously. More research is called for on these important topics.

Effects on fathers.   The transition to parenthood is thought to be less problematic for men than for women from several perspectives. They do not undergo the physical experiences of pregnancy, the birth, and possible lactation. In addition to experiencing fewer physical demands, they are spared much of the role conflict between the work role and the parent role that women can experience. If women have outside employment, they are usually the ones who bear the ultimate responsibility for child-care arrangements. But pregnancy and childbirth are psychologically stressful for husbands as well as wives (Arnstein, 1972). The psychiatric literature mentions a few fathers who could not handle the stress, reporting extreme reactions such as sexual acting out and serious psychological problems (Curtis, 1955; Freeman, 1951; Hartman & Nicolay, 1966; Lacoursiere, 1972; Towne & Afterman, 1955). Very little is actually known, however, about stress the average father faces either before or after childbirth, how that stress affects his well-being, or how his reactions to stress may affect his wife's or his child's well-being.

The other side to these issues is that men may experience less stress than their wives at the time of a first birth, but they have less role flexibility—they can seldom take on a full-time nurturing role instead of a provider role even if they want to. The financial obligations that come along with a child can weigh heavily upon men. In Entwisle and Doering's (1981) sample, men frequently mentioned money as a problem, but it was rarely alluded to by women. Men may also feel deprived because their physical ties to the infant are biologically less salient. Rossi (1977) speculates that women may be biologically superior to men in their ability to invest themselves emotionally in offspring. Whatever the case, as men have become increasingly "liberated"— in the sense of taking on expressive and nurturant roles with neonates and infants and in terms of opting for something less than a full-time lifelong career of paid employment—their parenting behavior, by becoming more complex, has become more problematic. Most men lack role models because they have come from families where fathers did not participate in care of young infants. While committed to egalitarian values in marriage and childrearing, men find neither social institutions nor the social climate that make it easy for them to nurture young infants. How can they devote themselves to baby care during the day when there are competing demands from employers or their profession?

Liberation of men is still on the social frontier. Most men are still not able to choose freely whether or not to devote themselves to full-time money-making jobs. Most cannot choose full-time child care easily (see Fein, 1978). Some of the blurring of *men's* sex role obligations in the domain of parenting makes assumption of the parent role more difficult for women as well.

It is a curious fact that until around 1970, fathers in the United States were almost completely shut out from the birth event and the period of early infancy. We have no data on what U.S. fathers themselves really thought about their role in childbirth prior to about 1965 (see Nash, 1976).

The sex role ideas learned early in life by the men who are now young adults have not prepared them either in practical or in emotional terms for the husband and father roles that their wives and much of society now expect them to play (Fein, 1978; Harlow, 1975). Pleck (1981) notes that the basic American value centering upon the importance of the family and the well-being of children has now been extended to include men, but deep-lying sex role ideology of both sexes conflicts with men's active family participation. Only a minority of persons believe men should do more family work, and women hold to this belief as little or less than do men.

The couples in the Entwisle and Doering (1981) panel expressed opinions congruent with Pleck's (1981) views: Both husbands and wives expected to have relatively few children (an average of just over two), and many wives planned to return to work. The division of labor within households before the arrival of the first child was fairly liberal, but the arrival of a child led more to rearrangement of wives' commitments than to change in husbands' commitments.

On the other hand, the men in the Entwisle and Doering (1981) study, irrespective of social class, expressed opinions consistent with an active father role: 78 percent of the young fathers said before the birth that men are just as interested in their children when they are babies as when they are older. Fathers who participated in delivery viewed the experience very positively. According to many reports, new fathers are heavily invested in their newborns (Entwisle & Doering; Fein, 1978; Greenberg & Morris, 1974).

Sex ideology aside, the mere fact that many more women, particularly more mothers of young children, are in the labor force now than a generation ago has implications for men in their home roles. With wives at work, household tasks must be dealt with at night or on weekends. Conflicting pressures may build upon women as a consequence of strain between work and home roles, and some of this pressure is displaced on husbands (see Pleck, 1981). So, in addition to assuming a parent role, many men today must adjust to a part-time or full-time work role for the mother along with parenthood. This adjustment greatly complicates the allocation of time and other resources for both parents.

Effects on marriage.   Much of the early research on effects of a first birth on the marriage relationship is based on retrospective assessments, asking parents to evaluate change in their lives that occurred in the past (Dyer, 1963; Hobbs, 1965, 1968; LeMasters, 1957; Russell, 1974). Fortunately, a few early longitudinal studies, including Meyerowitz and Feldman (1966) and Ryder (1973), supplement more-recent longitudinal research (Belsky, Spanier, & Rovine, 1983; Miller & Sollie, 1980). In addition, Entwisle and Doering (1981), Entwisle (1983), and Grossman et al. (1980) examine issues closely linked to marital satisfaction in their longitudinal studies directed at the parental transition. These issues include spouses' views of each other, the amount of marital quarreling, frequency of sexual intercourse, and the like.

The overall findings concerning effects of a first birth on marital satisfaction are negative on balance. Meyerowitz and Feldman's (1966) study, suggesting slight improvement in marital satisfaction at one month and five months postpartum compared to prepartum, is the main exception. In a cross-sectional sample of 800 couples, both husbands and wives reported a drop in general marital satisfaction with arrival of a first child (Feldman, 1971). Likewise, a longitudinal study also by Feldman (1979) found drops in marital satisfaction and companionship, as well as decreases in frequency and level of communication when couples with a child were compared to the childless. Miller and Sollie (1980) found no change for fathers and an increase in marital stress (i.e., negative change) for mothers at both one and eight months postpartum. At two months postpartum, Grossman et al.'s (1980, p. 201) clinical judgment was "increases in stress and strain in the marriage" reflected in lower marital adjustment scores. Belsky et al.'s (1983) study, which included 41 parents of firstborns, concluded that there were "modest but significant changes in the marital relationship which most would regard as somewhat unfavorable" (p. 578). There was a steady decline in self-reported marital quality from the last trimester of pregnancy to points three and nine months postpartum, with wives' appraisals of their marriages declining dramatically. Additionally, birth of a first child can lead spouses to find each other less sexually responsive (Harriman, 1983).

In most of the longitudinal research, except that by Feldman and his colleagues, parents are compared with themselves before having children, rather than with childless couples. It is thus impossible to rule out secular effects, such as the commonly noted decrease in marital satisfaction over time. In the most-complete design to date, Feldman (1979) assembled a sample of 44 childless couples, carefully screened to be intentionally rather than temporarily childless, and compared them with a sample of 42 couples questioned before and after birth of a first child. In all cases, both members of a couple were queried, and replies within couples were comparable. There were no differences between groups in marital satisfaction or in the frequency of their negative feelings about marriage. Groups did differ, however, in that the childless had significantly more positive marital interactions (including sexual relations) than the parents. Feldman suggests that lowered interaction of parents may stem from the child actually interfering with the process of communication between spouses. The parents also had more traditional ideas toward women.

As Feldman notes, the fact that earlier studies of marital satisfaction found more decreases in marital quality associated with having a child than have more recent studies, could be a cohort-historical type of effect. His most-recent study dealt with couples who chose parenthood, who delayed marriage and parenthood, and who, if they became parents, really wanted parenthood. There is also greater willingness these days for people to acknowledge marital conflict and the costs of having children.

Why would arrival of an infant be expected to have a negative impact on marriage? There are two answers, one emphasizing the psychodynamics of family relationships and the other emphasizing the tasks and responsibilities an infant brings. These parallel the decrease in the expressive nature of a marriage and the increase in its instrumental focus accompanying a first birth.

In terms of psychodynamics, Lacoursiere (1972) emphasized unresolved dependency needs of husbands. Deutsch (1945) sees motherliness as a sublimation of sexuality. Closeness with the infant may interfere with closeness to husband. Displacement of the husband by the infant as a source of affection and gratification for the wife apparently does occur. Baxter (1974), for example, found women who breastfed had lower frequency of sexual intercourse and orgasm in the early postpartum months. Likewise, Grossman et al. (1980) note that for most of the men in their study as well as the women, the marriage appeared to be displaced as a focal source of gratification with the birth of a child. At one year, "the marriage had regained its place in the women's lives as important, but it never seemed to regain the absolute centrality that it had before the first child was born" (p. 247). And couples' sex lives almost—but not quite—approached what they had been before (p. 196).

A disenchantment phenomenon is also part of a psychodynamic explanation: The marriage becomes less engrossing as time passes and as environmental pressures accumulate. Marital duration generally has negative effects on quality of marriage, even for childless couples. Blood and Wolfe (1960), for example, found that newly married childless couples were more satisfied than were the longer married in rating spouse as provider and companion.

The second line of explanation for children's negative effects on marriage is the instrumental one. The tasks of child care and couples' responses to neonates' demands, for a time at least, dominate activities of the marital pair. Although there are few explicit data on the demands couples experience or how these demands are met, marital concerns per se are displaced. LaRossa (1983) describes this vividly. When parents were asked how their lives had changed since their babies were born, "They consistently talk about time. . . . New fathers and mothers report that sleep time, television time, communication time, sex time, and even bathroom time are all in short supply, thanks to their newborns. Paradoxically, they also say that they are more often bored" (p. 579).

A first pregnancy and birth usually lead to a shift toward a more-traditional division of household labor (Arbeit, 1975; Entwisle & Doering, 1981; Grossman et al., 1980; Shereshefsky & Yarrow, 1973). Cowan, Cowan, Coie, and Coie (1978) found that the shift was most marked in household tasks, next in family decision-making roles, and least in baby-care items and that the shift occurred irrespective of how egalitarian the structure of roles was before the birth. But there are also consistencies in behavior. Entwisle and Doering (1981) found that men who helped more around the house during pregnancy were those who diapered and held the baby more often and that division of household labor during pregnancy was associated with measures of the father's later interest in the baby. Also, the degree of the man's interest in pregnancy was correlated with how much he held the baby in the first six weeks, with whether he picked up the baby when it cried.

Arrival of a first child challenges the marital dyad, but questions of causality are complex for several reasons. First, the birth is only one event in a series. Arrival of the child follows a nine-month pregnancy. The arrival itself may be uneventful, but sometimes it is traumatic in terms of the mother's or infant's health. Other events occur simultaneously, such as mother's resignation from the work force and a temporary suspension of sexual activities. Grossman et al. (1980, p. 112) found that postpartum marital adjustment reflected many of the stresses experienced in the preceding months of pregnancy and how well the couple resolved these stresses. They also found that men whose wives had a more-difficult psychological experience of labor and delivery were less satisfied than other men were with their marriages at two months postpartum (p. 179).

Second, the child's birth may *interact* with the quality of the marriage. Marriages with an egalitarian division of labor may be better suited to handle the heavy load of child-care chores that comes with a new baby. Grossman et al. (1980) found that marital style (traditional versus egalitarian) predicted marital satisfaction at one year (p. 129), also that men of higher social status reestablished better relationships with their wives after the birth (p. 179). Along similar lines, a marriage of long duration may promote rigidity in self-concepts or marital roles that impedes incorporation of the new baby into the family system. Entwisle (1982) reports an increase in quarreling over the first year *only* for middle-class couples, not working-class couples. The slower integration of the baby into the family system in middle-class as compared to working-class couples is thought to create friction between the spouses.

Third, there is the question of when the marriage is evaluated. Many authors (e.g., Entwisle & Doering, 1981; Feldman as cited by Hobbs, 1965) refer to a "honeymoon phase" in the first few postpartum weeks. In fact, the marriage relationship may not "settle down" for as long as a year after birth of a first child.

Fourth, as already mentioned, marriages evolve and change irrespective of children's arrival. To compare the quality of marriage after birth of a child with its quality before is insufficient if, as appears to be true, marital satisfaction declines with time even in childless couples.

Last, and perhaps most important, dynamic relationships are involved. Children may place a strain on the marital relationship, but marital relationships may stress the child and set in motion a negative pattern. An unsatisfactory marriage could lead to difficulties in parenting that erode marital bonds. Grossman et al. (1980, p. 242) report that the only predictors of babies' motor development at one year were the mother's and father's sexual activity and satisfaction. Babies who were "alert, curious, relaxed, and happy" had parents who were "comfortable with their marriage." Furthermore, babies with higher Bayley MDI scores had parents who were more satisfied with their marriage.

Limiting consideration of the effects of children on marriage to the dimension defined as "marital satisfaction" may lead to a distorted picture of the marital relationship as a whole. Couples apparently learn to relate to each other in new terms. First-time fathers report a sense of "being more of a family," and mothers report "overall life satisfaction seemed to increase" (Grossman et al., 1980, pp. 132, 200). Couples feel a baby enhances their marital relationship even though it creates more stresses in it (Grossman et al., 1980; Meyerowitz & Feldman, 1966). Likewise, Belsky et al. (1983) found that a "romance" score decreased but a "partnership score" increased, and Steffensmeier (1982) reports that one dimension characterizing the transition to parenthood involved "gratifications."

Finally, causal relationships can point in both directions. Here we have emphasized the effects of a first child on the parents' marriage, but clearly the quality of the marriage affects the adjustment to parenthood and parent-infant relations (Westbrook, 1978), as discussed elsewhere in this *Handbook*.

CONCLUSION

Many writers have commented upon the difficulties in assuming the parent role, and there may be no way to prepare people entirely for their new responsibilities as parents. On the other hand, the psychological and physical distances that now separate couples from their own parents must make it especially hard for kin to help new parents.

Preparation for parenthood is blocked on several fronts. Large families, where older siblings routinely care for younger ones, are now less common. The severe age segregation in present-day America causes young marrieds to live in apartments or subdivisions populated mostly by others like themselves. It also causes teenagers to be locked into an adolescent society, away from very young children and away from places where they could watch young adults care for babies.

Today's childrearing patterns are biased against preparation for parenthood, but neither the structure of society nor people's socialization for parenthood are likely to change in the near future.

REFERENCES

Affonso, D. D., & Stichler, J. F. Cesarean birth: Women's reactions. *American Journal of Nursing,* 1980, *80,* 468–470.

Arasteh, J. D. Parenthood—some antecedents and consequences: A review of the mental health literature. *Journal of Genetic Psychology,* 1971, *118,* 179–202.

Arbeit, S. A. *A study of women during their first pregnancy.* Unpublished doctoral dissertation, Yale University, 1975.

Arnstein, H. S. The crisis of becoming a father. *Sexual Behavior,* 1972, *2,* 42–47.

Baxter, S. Labor and orgasm in primiparae. *Journal of Psychosomatic Research,* 1974, *18,* 209–216.

Belsky, J., Spanier, G. B., & Rovine, M. Stability and change in marriage across the transition to parenthood. *Journal of Marriage and the Family,* 1983, *45,* 567–577.

Bernstein, B. *Class, codes and control.* London: Routledge & Kegan Paul, 1971.

Blood, R. D., & Wolfe, D. M. *Husbands and wives.* New York: Free Press, 1960.

Bott, E. *Family and social network.* London: Tavistock Publications, 1957.

Bowlby, J. *Attachment and loss* (Vol. I): *Attachment.* London: Hogarth, 1969.

Bradley, C. F., Ross, S. E., & Warnyea, J. A prospective study of mothers' attitudes and feelings following cesarean and vaginal births. *Births,* 1983, *10,* 79–83.

Breen, D. *The birth of a first child.* London: Tavistock Publications, 1975.

Cherlin, A. J. Remarriage as an incomplete institution. *American Journal of Sociology,* 1978, *84,* 634–650.

Christensen, H. T. Children in the family: Relationship of number and spacing to marital success. *Journal of Marriage and the Family,* 1968, *30,* 283–289.

Cohn, R. M. The effect of employment status change on self-attitudes. *Social Psychology,* 1978, *41,* 81–93.

Consensus Development Conference. *Cesarean childbirth* (NIH Publication No. 82-2067), Bethesda, Md.: National Institutes of Health, 1981.

Corea, G. *The hidden malpractice.* New York: Morrow, 1977.

Cowan, C. P., Cowan, P. A., Coie, L., & Coie, J. D. Becoming a family: The impact of a first child's birth on the couple's relationship. In W. B. Miller and L. F. Newman (Eds.), *The first child and family formation.* Chapel Hill, N.C.: Carolina Population Center, 1978.

Croghan, N., Connors, K., & Franz, W. *Vaginal vs. C-section delivery: Effects on neonatal behavior and mother-infant interaction.* Paper presented at the International Conference on Infant Studies, New Haven, Conn.: April, 1980.

Curtis, J. L. A psychiatric study of 55 expectant fathers. *U.S. Armed Forces Medical Journal,* 1955, *6,* 937–950.

Deutsch, H. *Psychology of women* (Vol. 2). New York: Grune & Stratton, 1945.

Doering, S. G., Entwisle, D. R., & Quinlan, D. Modeling the quality of women's birth experience. *Journal of Health and Social Behavior,* 1980, *21,* 12–21.

Dyer, E. D. Parenthood as crisis: A re-study. *Marriage and Family Living,* 1963, *25,* 196–201.

Entwisle, D. R. *Cesarean sections: Social and psychological factors* (Final Report, Grant HD13103). Johns Hopkins University, 1982. (Mimeo.)

Entwisle, D. R. *Behavioral effects of cesarean delivery in early postpartum on both parents.* Proceedings of the G. Stanley Hall Conference, Baltimore, Md.: Johns Hopkins Press, in press.

Entwisle, D. R., & Doering, S. G. *The first birth: A family turning point.* Baltimore: The Johns Hopkins Press, 1981.

Entwisle, D. R., & Doering, S. G., & Reilly, T. W. *Postpartum maternal-infant contact and the mother's early use of negative sanctions.* Unpublished manuscript, 1983.

Fawcett, J. T. The value and cost of the first child. In W. B. Miller & L. F. Newman (Eds.), *The first child and family formation.* Chapel Hill, N.C.: Carolina Population Center, 1978.

Fein, R. A. Consideration of men's experiences and the birth of a first child. In W. B. Miller & L. F. Newman (Eds.), *The first child and family formation.* Chapel Hill, N.C.: Carolina Population Center, 1978.

Feldman, H. The effects of children on the family. In A. Michel (Ed.), *Family issues of employed women in Europe and America.* Leiden, Netherlands: Brill, 1971.

Feldman, H. *A comparison of intentional parents and intentionally childless couples.* Cornell University, Department of Human Development and Family Studies, 1979. (Mimeo.)

Feldman, H., & Feldman, M. The family life cycle: Some suggestions for recycling. *Journal of Marriage and the Family,* 1975, *37,* 277–284.

Field, T. M., & Widmayer, S. M. Developmental follow-up of infants delivered by cesarean section and general anesthesia. *Infant Behavior and Development,* 1980, *3,* 253–264.

Forssman, H., & Thuwe, L. 120 children born after application for therapeutic abortion refused: Their mental health, social adjustment, and educational level up to age 21. *Acta Psychiatrica Scandinavia,* 1966, *42,* 71–88.

Foundation for Child Development, *National survey of children: Summary of preliminary results.* New York: Foundation for Child Development, 1977.

Freeman, T. Pregnancy as a precipitant of mental illness in men. *British Journal of Medical Psychology,* 1951, *24,* 49–54.

Furstenberg, F. F., Jr. *Unplanned parenthood.* New York: Free Press, 1976.

Gerson, F. F. Dimensions of infant behavior in the first half year of life. In P. M. Shereshefsky & L. J. Yarrow (Eds.), *Psychological aspects of a first pregnancy and early postnatal adaptation.* New York: Raven Press, 1973.

Gibbons, L. K. *Analysis of the rise in C-sections in Baltimore.* Unpublished doctoral dissertation, Johns Hopkins School of Hygiene and Public Health, 1976.

Glass, J. Prebirth attitudes and adjustment to parenthood: When preparing for the worst helps. *Family Relations,* 1983, *32,* 377–386.

Gove, W. R. The relationship between sex roles, marital status, and mental illness. *Social Forces,* 1972, *51,* 34–44.

Gove, W. R., & Geerken, M. R. The effect of children and employment on the mental health of married men and women. *Social Forces,* 1977, *56,* 66–76.

Greenberg, M., & Morris, N. Engrossment: The newborn's impact upon the father. *American Journal of Orthopsychiatry,* 1974, *44,* 520–531.

Grossman, F. K., Eichler, L. S., & Winikoff, S. A. *Pregnancy, birth and parenthood.* San Francisco: Jossey-Bass, 1980.

Harlow, N. *Sharing the children.* New York: Harper & Row, 1975.

Harriman, L. C. Personal and marital changes accompanying parenthood. *Family Relations,* 1983, *32,* 387–394.

Hartman, A. A., & Nicolay, R. C. Sexually deviant behavior in expectant fathers. *Journal of Abnormal and Social Psychology,* 1966, *71,* 232–234.

Hess, R. D. Class and ethnic influence upon socialization. In P. H. Mussen (Ed.), *Carmichael's manual of child psychology.* New York: John Wiley & Sons, 1970.

Hill, R. *The family: A dynamic interpretation* (2d ed.). Hinsdale, Ill.: Dryden Press, 1951.

Hill, R. Psychosocial consequences of the first birth: A discussion. In W. B. Miller & L. F. Newman (Eds.), *The first child and family formation.* Chapel Hill, N.C.: Carolina Population Center, 1978.

Hill, R., & Aldous, J. Socialization for marriage and parenthood. In D. Goslin (Ed.), *Handbook of socialization theory and research.* Skokie, Ill.: Rand McNally, 1969.

Hobbs, D. F. Parenthood as crisis: A third study. *Journal of Marriage and the Family,* 1965, *27,* 367–372.

Hobbs, D. F. Transition to parenthood: A replication and extension. *Journal of Marriage and the Family,* 1968, *30,* 413–416.

Hobbs, D. F., & Cole, S. P. Transition to parenthood: A decade replication. *Journal of Marriage and the Family,* 1976, *38,* 723–731.

Hobbs, D. R., Jr., & Wimbish, J. M. Transition to parenthood by black couples. *Journal of Marriage and the Family,* 1977, *39,* 677–689.

Hofferth, S. L. Childbearing decision making and family well-being: A dynamic sequential model. *American Sociological Review,* 1983, *83,* 533–545.

Hoffman, L. W. Effects of the first child on the woman's role. In W. B. Miller & L. F. Newman (Eds.), *The first child and family formation.* Chapel Hill, N.C.: Carolina Population Center, 1978.

Hoffman, L. W., & Manis, J. D. Influences of children on marital interaction and parental satisfactions and dissatisfactions. In R. M. Lerner & G. B. Spanier (Eds.), *Child influences on marital and family interaction.* New York: Academic Press, 1978.

Hogan, D. P. *Transitions and social change: The early lives of American men.* New York: Academic Press, 1981.

Hubert, J. Social factors in pregnancy and childbirth. In M. P. M. Richards (Ed.), *The integration of a child into a social world.* London: Cambridge University Press, 1974.

Jacoby, A. P. Transition to parenthood: A reassessment. *Journal of Marriage and the Family,* 1969, *31,* 720–727.

Kessler, R. C., & Cleary, P. D. Social class and psychological distress. *American Sociological Review,* 1980, *45,* 463–478.

Kilbride, H. W., Johnson, D. L., & Streissguth, A. P. Social class, birth order, and newborn experience. *Child Development,* 1977, *48,* 1686–1688.

Klaus, M. H., & Kennell, J. H. *Maternal-infant bonding.* St. Louis: C. V. Mosby, 1976.

Klein, R. P., & Gist, N. F. *Antecedents of unanticipated cesarean deliveries.* Paper presented at the Southeastern Conference on Human Development, Baltimore, April 1982.

Kohn, M. L. *Class and conformity.* Homewood, Ill.: Dorsey Press, 1969.

Kohn, M. L., Bureaucratic man: A portrait and an interpretation. *American Sociological Review,* 1971, *36,* 461–474.

Kohn, M. L., & Carroll, E. E. Social class and the allocation of parental responsibilities. *Sociometry,* 1960, *23,* 372–92.

Lacoursiere, R. Fatherhood and mental illness: A review and new material. *Psychiatric Quarterly,* 1972, *46,* 105–124.

Lamb, M. E. Father-infant and mother-infant interaction in the first year of life. *Child Development,* 1977, *48,* 167–181.

Lamb, M. E. Influence of the child on marital quality and family interaction during the prenatal, perinatal, and infancy periods. In R. M. Lerner & G. B. Spanier (Eds.), *Child influences on marital and family interaction.* New York: Academic Press, 1978.

Landis, J. T. Intent toward conception and the pregnancy experience. *American Sociological Review,* 1952, *17,* 616–620.

LaRossa, R. The transition to parenthood and the social reality of time. *Journal of Marriage and the Family,* 1983, *45,* 579–589.

LaRossa, R., & LaRossa, M. M. *Transition to parenthood.* Beverly Hills, Calif.: Sage Publications, 1981.

Larsen, V. L. Stresses of the childbearing year. *American Journal of Public Health,* 1966, *56,* 32–36.

Leifer, A. D., Leiderman, P. H., Barnett, C. R., & Williams, J. F. Effects of mother-infant separation on maternal attachment behavior. *Child Development,* 1972, *43,* 1203–1218.

Leifer, M. *Psychological effects of motherhood.* New York: Praeger Publishers, 1980.

LeMasters, E. E. Parenthood as crisis. *Marriage and Family Living,* 1957, *19,* 352–355.

Marieskind, H. I. *An evaluation of cesarean section in the United States* (Final Report to Dept. HEW), Seattle, Wash.: 1979.

Marut, J. S., & Mercer, R. T. Comparison of primiparas' perceptions of vaginal and cesarean births. *Nursing Research,* 1979, *28,* 260–266.

McClellan, M. S., & Cabianca, W. A. Effects of early mother-infant contact following cesarean birth. *Obstetrics and Gynecology,* 1980, *56,* 52–55.

Mehl, L. E. The outcome of home delivery research in the United States. In S. Kitzinger & J. A. Davis (Eds.), *The place of birth.* New York: Oxford, 1978.

Meyerowitz, J., & Feldman, H. Transition to parenthood. *Psychiatric Research Reports,* 1966, *20,* 78–84.

Miller, B. C., & Sollie, D. L. Normal stresses during the transition to parenthood. *Family Relations,* 1980, *29,* 459–465.

Miller, C. A. *Cohort variations in the transition to adulthood for urban American women.* Paper presented at American Sociological Association meetings, San Francisco, August, 1982.

Miller, W. B. The intendedness and wantedness of the first child. In W. B. Miller & L. F. Newman (Eds.), *The first child and family formation*. Chapel Hill, N.C.: Carolina Population Center, 1978.

Mortimer, J. T., & Simmons, R. G. Adult socialization. *Annual Review of Sociology*, 1978, *4*, 421–454.

Moss, H. A. Sex, age, and state as determinants of mother-infant interaction. *Merrill-Palmer Quarterly*, 1967, *13*, 19–36.

Moss, H. A., & Jones, S. J. Relations between maternal attitudes and maternal behavior as a function of social class. In P. Leiderman, S. Tulkin, & H. Rosenfeld (Eds.), *Culture and infancy*. New York: Academic Press, 1977.

Nash, J. Historical and social change in the perception of the role of the father. In M. E. Lamb (Ed.), *The role of the father in child development*. New York: John Wiley & Sons, 1976.

Norr, K. L., Block, C. R., Charles, A., Meyering, S., & Meyers, E. Explaining pain and enjoyment in childbirth. *Journal of Health and Social Behavior*, 1977, *18*, 260–275.

Nye, F. I. *Role structure and analysis of the family*. Beverly Hills, Calif.: Sage Publications, 1976.

Pedersen, F. A., Zaslow, M. J., Cain, R. L., & Anderson, B. J. Cesarean childbirth: Psychological implications for mothers and fathers. *Infant Mental Health Journal*, 1981, *2*, 257–163.

Pleck, J. H. Husbands, paid work and family roles. In H. Z. Lopata (Ed.), *Research on the interweave of social roles: Women and men* (Vol. 3). Greenwich, Conn.: JAI Press, 1981.

Querec, L. J. *Characteristics of births* (Series 21, No. 30, Department of Health, Education, and Welfare No. PHS 78–1908). Washington, D.C.: Government Printing Office, 1978.

Rapoport, R. Normal crises, family structure and mental health. *Family Process*, 1963, *2*, 68–80.

Rapoport, R., Rapoport, R. N., & Strelitz, Z. *Fathers, mothers and society*. New York: Basic Books, 1977.

Reilly, T. W. *Modeling the development of women's self-evaluations in parental role*. Unpublished doctoral dissertation, Johns Hopkins University, 1981.

Rindfuss, R. R., & St. John, C. Social determinants of age at first birth. *Journal of Marriage and the Family*, 1983, *45*, 553–565.

Robson, K. S. The role of eye-to-eye contact in maternal-infant attachment. *Journal of Child Psychology and Child Psychiatry and Allied Disciplines*, 1967, *8*, 13–25.

Rossi, A. S. Transition to parenthood. *Journal of Marriage and the Family*, 1968, *30*, 26–39.

Rossi, A. S. A biosocial perspective on parenting. *Daedalus*, 1977, *106*, 1–32.

Russell, C. S. Transition to parenthood: Problems and gratifications. *Journal of Marriage and the Family*, 1974, *36*, 294–302.

Russo, N. F. Overview: Sex roles, fertility, and the motherhood mandate. *Psychology of Women*, 1979, *4*, 7–15.

Ryder, R. G. Longitudinal data relating marriage satisfaction and having a child. *Journal of Marriage and the Family*, 1973, *35*, 604–607.

Seashore, M., Leifer, A., Barnett, C., & Leiderman, P. The effects of denial of early mother-infant interaction on maternal self-confidence. *Journal of Personality and Social Psychology,* 1973, *25,* 369–378.

Shaver, B. A. Maternal personality and early adaptation as related to infantile colic. In P. M. Shereshefsky & L. J. Yarrow (Eds.), *Psychological aspects of a first pregnancy and early postnatal adaptation.* New York: Raven Press, 1973.

Shereshefsky, P. M., Liebenberg, B., & Lockman, R. F. Maternal adaptation. In P. M. Shereshefsky and L. J. Yarrow (Eds.), *Psychological aspects of a first pregnancy and early postnatal adaptation.* New York: Raven Press, 1973.

Shereshefsky, P. M., & Yarrow, L. J. *Psychological aspects of a first pregnancy and early postnatal adaptation.* New York: Raven Press, 1973.

Simmel, G. *The sociology of George Simmel* (K. Wolff, Ed.). New York: Free Press, 1950.

Skolnick, A. *The intimate environment: Exploring marriage and the family.* Boston: Little, Brown, 1973.

Steffensmeier, R. H. A role model of the transition to parenthood. *Journal of Marriage and the Family,* 1982, *44,* 319–334.

Stryker, S. The interactional and situational approaches. In H. T. Christensent (Ed.), *Handbook of marriage and the family.* Skokie, Ill.: Rand McNally, 1964.

Thornton, A., & Freedman, D. *Consistency of sex role attitudes of women, 1962–1977.* Ann Arbor, Mich.: Institute for Social Research, 1979.

Towne, R. D., & Afterman, J. Psychosis in males related to childbirth. *Bulletin of Menninger Clinic,* 1955, *19,* 19–26.

U.S. Bureau of the Census. *Patterns of aggregate and individual changes in contraceptive practice: United States 1965–1975* (National Center for Health Statistics, Series 3, No. 17, Department of Health, Education, & Welfare Publication No. PHS 79–1401), Washington, D.C.: Government Printing Office, 1979.

U.S. National Center for Health Statistics. Monthly vital statistics report. *Advance report of final natality statistics 1978,* 29(1). U.S. Department of Health and Human Services, Washington, D.C.: Government Printing Office, 1980.

Vietze, P. M., MacTurk, R. H., McCarthy, M. E., Klein, R. P., & Yarrow, L. J. *Impact of mode of delivery on father- and mother-infant interaction at 6 and 12 months.* Paper presented at the Second International Conference on Infant Studies, New Haven, Conn., April 1980.

Waller, W. W. *The family: A dynamic interpretation.* Hinsdale, Ill.: Dryden Press, 1938.

Watson, J. Who attends prepared childbirth classes? A demographic study of CEA classes in Rhode Island. *Journal of Obstetric, Gynecologic and Neonatal Nursing,* 1977, *6,* 36–39.

Weed, J. A. National estimates of marriage dissolution and survivorship: United States. *Vital and Health Statistics* (Analytical studies, Series 3, No. 19, Department of Health & Human Services Publication No. PHS 81–1403). Hyattsville, Md.: National Center for Health Statistics; Public Health Service, U.S. Department of Health & Human Services, 1980.

Westbrook, M. T. The reactions to child-bearing and early maternal experience of women with differing marital relationships. *British Journal of Medical Psychology,* 1978, *51,* 191–199.

Westoff, C. F. Marriage and fertility in the developed countries. *Scientific American,* 1978, *239,* 51–57.

Williams, T. M., Davidson, S. M., Joy, L. A., & Painter, S. L. *Parent-infant program* (Final Report). School of Nursing, University of British Columbia, n.d.

Yalom, I. D. Postpartum blues syndrome, *Archives of General Psychiatry,* 1968, *28,* 16–27.

Chapter 20

Parent-Child Interaction

WILLIAM S. POLLACK
FRANCES K. GROSSMAN

During the last 20 years, psychologists have discovered the family. Until recently, the mainstream in child development emphasized the child's separateness (Kessen, 1979); to find out how the child develops, his or her personality or cognitive abilities were looked at in the laboratory in isolation from the natural environment. Next, the importance of looking at the child with its mother was discovered (e.g., Ainsworth & Bell, 1969; Ainsworth, Bell, & Stayton, 1971). Maybe who the child was could be seen best in the context of that seemingly very important relationship with the person most involved in the child's caretaking. Yet it was only the child's capacity for separation from the mother that was seen and studied as representative of it's important attachments. Most recently, we are acknowledging that children grow up not just as separate beings or in dyads with their mothers but also with their fathers and in families. In fact, even very young children are born with capabilities to relate responsively to a variety of individuals from birth onward.

In our review, we report many of the creative efforts to grapple with the complex and intricate issues of family psychology from a perspective of parent-child interaction within a family system. In particular, we focus on what we consider the most important American family interaction studies published in the last 10 years. To meet our criteria, they must include at least dyadic interactional data from both mothers and fathers with their children. We focus particularly on the apparent effect on child development rather than, for example, aspects of adult development related to parenting. Given the constraints of space, we have limited ourselves to studies of normal families.

In choosing between a focus on method and a focus on content, we have selected the latter (with only occasional comments on method when it seemed particularly germane). In general, we do not present studies we view as so methodologically flawed as to be invalid. This stance is consistent with our view that knowledge comes to the field of family psychology from the repetition of findings from a variety of studies using different samples and methodologies and having, inevitably, a variety of strengths and weaknesses. Also, the samples for most of these studies are Caucasian, broadly speaking middle-class, normal families from relatively traditional households—i.e., families in which the mother is the primary caretaker and the father the primary wage earner. Only when the population differs markedly from these parameters do we mention it.

The chapter begins with a brief review of antecedents to the current development of the field. Following that, we review what we understand to be some of the major topics: attachment studies, language, behavioral approaches, and sex role socialization. Then we move on to important research groups in the field today. Within each section, the order of studies presented is chronological. We conclude with a summary and implications for research and clinical interventions.

HISTORICAL REVIEW

Until recently, such family interaction research as we describe in this chapter would have been unthinkable. Several important changes in the way psychologists and others view both children and the study of development needed to take place before the current style of family research could occur.

Until quite recently, most of the study of children took place in highly controlled laboratory settings, and the children were studied alone—i.e., with the researcher, who was a stranger to them. The implicit view of the child was of a separate, autonomous being who carried it's personality and other characteristics around with it, to be reproduced on demand for researchers (see Kessen, 1979). Bronfenbrener (1974) was able to say, as late as 1974, "Much of American developmental psychology is the science of the behavior of children in strange situations with strange adults" (p. 3).

Bronfenbrener was one of the first to argue for the importance of studying children and their development in their natural settings, including in the home with their families (e.g., Bronfenbrenner, 1979). Most family researchers today agree that at least much, if not all, of the study of children must occur in its natural context.

A second major focus of change involved the naming of the most important "players" in a child's life. At first, early experimental developmental psychologists as well as psychoanalysts looked at children in a vacuum. Later, others such as Mahler (1968), Bowlby (1969), and Ainsworth and Bell (1969) began to focus on the mother-infant relationship as the most significant tie in the child's life. Yet, virtually no attention was paid to the role of the father. Pedersen (1980) has suggested that several important cultural shifts had to occur before the infant and child researchers could begin to appreciate the importance of the father to child development: The cultural view of what are appropriate roles for men and women in families had to broaden; psychological theories of development needed to be expanded beyond the mother-infant dyad; theories linking aspects of the marital relationship to parenting needed to be developed; and the infant needed to be seen in all its considerable complexity and competence. These shifts have begun to occur, and recent research has demonstrated compellingly that American fathers are significantly involved with the parenting of young children, are capable of highly competent, responsive interactions, and indeed are very important to their children. (See reviews of this literature in Belsky, 1981; Grossman, Eichler, & Winickoff with Anzalone, Gofseyeff, & Sargent, 1980; Lamb, 1976e, 1980; Pedersen, 1980, 1981.)

These several changes have led to the current emphasis on more flexible and complex views of parent-child interaction, with a growing awareness of the importance of studying (at the very least) three-way, mother-father-child interactions, observed naturalistically within the home setting. Along with these shifts has come a new awareness of the role of time, including the realization that what parents do with their child during a brief, defined observation period may tell what they are capable of doing but certainly does not describe what they usually do in the course of their daily lives. Thus, the importance of the ecological validity of time and also the need for a longitudinal component in these studies of the child in his or her family have been increasingly adopted by researchers in the field.

The recent three-way interactional studies have highlighted the importance of indirect, or "second-order," effects (Bronfenbrenner, 1974). These are effects that occur in complex systems like the family—instances in which one member of a group may have an important influence on another member, but indirectly. For example, a family member not directly involved in an interaction may affect its outcome. Within such a complex systemic approach, issues of the relationships among role functions (e.g., being a father and being a husband) and of so-called bidirectional effects (children influencing parents as well as parents influencing children) become central.

Our initial approach to the family interaction literature informed us that, while much is recent, the total number of studies of families is very large and indigestible in a single review chapter. Fortunately, Jacob (1975) performed a major service by critically reviewing most of the family interaction studies published by June 1973. Because of the thoroughness of Jacob's and others' reviews (see also Riskin & Faunce, 1972), we have chosen not to cover the ground they did, but instead to begin where Jacob left off, in the middle of 1973, and to cover the 10-year span to mid-1983.

ATTACHMENT STUDIES

One of the earliest sets of family interaction studies was the extension of the study of infant-mother separation research to include father within the Ainsworth stranger paradigm (Ainsworth et al., 1971). This research is reviewed very briefly as one important forerunner of current family interaction research.

Kotelchuck and his colleagues (Kotelchuck, 1973, 1976; Lester, Kotelchuck, Spelke, Sellers, & Klein, 1974; Ross, Kagan, Zelazo, & Kotelchuck, 1975; Spelke, Zelazo, Kagan, & Kotelchuck, 1973) studied separation protest through the child's reactions as mother, father, and stranger left the room for brief periods of time.

Kotelchuck (1976) found that there is a bond between father and child, as well as between mother and child, and a threshold level of paternal caretaking necessary for a relationship between infant and father to exist. Ban and Lewis (1974) observed attachment behavior in the laboratory and found that both girls and boys sought closeness and physical contact significantly more with mothers than with fathers. Fathers reported an average of 15 to 20 minutes a day of contact with their children at home. Cohen and Campos (1974) found that fathers elicited more attachment behavior than did a stranger, yet were second to mothers at all age levels. Feldman and Ingham (1975) saw few significant differences in attachment between fathers and mothers for both one- and two-year-olds.

Willemsen, Flaherty, Heaton, and Ritchey (1974) found that the more attached girls were to either parent, the less exploration they did, while there was no relationship for boys between attachment and exploration. And while Lamb (1978c) discovered that the security of the child's attachment to either parent predicted significantly to the nature of the relationship with the other parent, Main and Weston (1981) argued that those attachments were quite independent.

It is not surprising that researchers have found that fathers are more important to their children than strangers and have a different relationship with their children than their mothers do. It is perhaps more surprising how similar children's relationships with their mothers and fathers appear in these studies. Although important gender differences were discovered, the methodology has several inherent limitations. Laboratory contexts demonstrate young children's responses to stress quite well, but give us no idea of their general day-to-day experience. Also, one has to note the oddity of psychologists initially choosing to study normal attachments by looking only at separation.

LANGUAGE AS A MEASURE OF FAMILY INTERACTION

The family interaction studies focused on language tend to distinguish themselves from the rest of the literature by their focus on discrete observable behaviors and by their exclusive cross-sectional designs. The research reviewed in this section tends to be concise and is deliberately limited in scope in contrast to the longitudinal studies, which tend to be global and inclusive.

Gleason and Greif

Gleason and Greif studied verbal exchanges between parents and young children as a socialization paradigm. They began with 24 relatively traditional families, each with a preschool girl or boy. They collected data both in dyadic laboratory situations and by means of an installed tape recorder set at home around the dinner table.

In one study of the ways parents teach politeness routines to their preschool children (Greif & Gleason, 1980), the parents typically prompted their children to respond politely (to say hi, thank you, and good-bye) with no differences in the number of girls and boys prompted, nor in the age of the children prompted. When told to "say . . .", which was virtually the invariant form of the prompt, 86 percent of the children complied. Significantly more mothers than fathers themselves said thank you and good-bye.

These findings highlight the extremely narrowly specified rules parents follow in socializing children to politeness routines and also suggest that while in some circumstances there are no sex differences in what parents say to children about politeness, there might well be differences in their own use of politeness routines.

Using 14 of these families, Masur and Gleason (1980) looked at the differences in verbal behavior of mothers and fathers helping their child play with a rather complex toy car. Fathers were much more likely to use the actual names of car parts and also more often asked the child for names and functions of car parts. The parents' styles showed greater differences in their interactions with daughters than with sons; mothers were least likely to ask their daughters information about the names of parts of the car. Masur and Gleason interpret their results as indicating that fathers provide more complex verbal information to their children and require more complex verbal interaction back than do mothers. And while fathers tended to treat boys and girls the same, mothers were (at least in this context) less demanding of their daughters in this play. It would have been interesting to see if these findings were different with a stereotypically female toy in contrast to interactions around the car, which is so stereotypically masculine.

Greif, Alvarez, and Ullman (1981), in a study of parents' communication with their young children about emotions, found that the largest amount of conversation about feelings was between fathers and daughters and the smallest amount between fathers and sons.

In looking at the dinner table conversations of 14 of these families, Greif (1980a, 1980b) reports somewhat surprising results. All three family members talked approximately the same amount, but there were significant differences in how much individuals interrupted each other. Fathers interrupted daughters most, while mothers interrupted sons least. Overall, fathers interrupted all others significantly more than did anyone else. Fathers and mothers actively attempted to socialize their children to good table manners during these conversations, and there were no differences between parents in the frequency of their efforts, nor in whether the efforts were directed at sons or daughters. The content of these conversations tended to focus on what the child had done during the course of the day. Greif notes that the child *never* initiated that topic; the parents always had to ask. Mothers also often described what they had done during the day, but fathers rarely volunteered such information. In fact, in several instances in their transcripts, children actively attempted to find out what their fathers had done during the day, and fathers resisted describing their activities. Not surprisingly, the parents' conversation often excluded the child.

In another study, Gleason and Greif (1981) found that mothers and fathers simplify their speech when they talk to young children, but only mothers' length of utterances was related to the child's age. Fathers produced significantly more imperatives and teasing names, especially to the sons (e.g., "Anthony, stay out of there before I break your head! Don't go in there again or I'll break your head!"). The authors' interpretation of these findings is that they are consistent with the culturally accepted role of fathers, which is as an authority figure who is not required to be totally sensitive to the needs of the child.

Gleason and Greif (1981) conclude that fathers and mothers provide substantially different linguistic and cognitive input to children. Fathers are more like the outside world in that they are less accepting and empathic and children have to work harder to communicate effectively. Mothers' speech, in contrast, is precisely tuned to young children's needs. Their speech tends to be warmly empathic and accepting of the child's productions, linguistic or otherwise. It is also clear that a great deal of gender role socialization is conveyed linguistically, both in the content of what is said (for example, its complexity) and in its form (for example, who interrupts whom). The differences in fathers' and mothers' speech is much greater at home (for example, around the dinner table) than it is in the psychological laboratory.

These studies are unusually convincing because they focus on naturally occurring but (relatively easily) measurable behaviors between parents and children, and the aspects of the behavior quantified are clearly meaningful in relation to several important psychological issues such as gender role socialization and family interaction patterns. The researchers' data allow them to compare these linguistic interaction patterns between relatively undistorted home contexts and laboratory contexts and also between dyadic parent-child interactions and three-way family interactions.

Other studies of language

Vandell (1979) examined videotapes of six boy toddlers' social interactions with their mothers and fathers. There were no parent gender differences in the basic structure of behaviors in interaction. However, there were gender differences in what Vandell calls the content of the interactions. Mothers used significantly more vocal comments, labels, and routines and showed more positive affect, while fathers used more one-word imperatives. Toddlers did not respond differently to the mothers than to the fathers. Vandell speculates that the structural characteristics of interactions with toddlers, shared by fathers and mothers, teach children the basic structure of interactions. The content differences may facilitate gender-identity development.

Golinkoff and Ames (1979) examined the verbal exchanges of 12 sets of parents with their 19-month-old firstborn children in a laboratory setting. They found no child gender effects but significant parent gender effects. Mothers appeared to "take charge" when the three of them were together—but there were no differences between mothers' and fathers' verbal behavior when alone with the child. Parents of boys talked in shorter sentences and more frequently than did parents of girls.

Golinkoff and Ames (1979) emphasize how few differences appear between the ways mothers and fathers talk to young children, despite the enormous day-to-day differences in the amount of time mothers, in contrast to fathers, spend with children. They interpret the difference in conversational pace as meaning that both mothers and fathers expect girls to be able to pay attention to a longer speech than boys, at this age.

Perhaps the most impressive aspect of these and other studies (e.g., McLaughlin, Schutz, & White, 1980; Stoneman & Brody, 1981) was the researchers' foresight and creativity in looking at language as an important key to family interaction. With this approach, each of the studies reported differences by gender in parent-child conversations, with greater differences in parent behavior than in child behavior. Their findings also make clear that parents respond differently in dyadic and triadic groups. Many of the differences found in these studies seem consistent with sex roles assumed by males and females in this culture. In any case, it seems apparent to us (as each of these authors argues) that these discrete, verbal differences have far-reaching implications for the sex role socialization of children in this culture and consequently have effects upon the entire family system.

BEHAVIORAL/LEARNING THEORY STUDIES

In an intersting application of behavioral approaches to normal family interactions, Wahl, Johnson, Johansson, and Martin (1974) designed a study to examine unplanned interactive contingencies in naturalistically observed family life in 33 normal families with at least several children, including a 4-to-6-year-old target child. These children produced an average of one deviant (i.e., annoying to parent) behavior every 3.17 minutes, representing 3.8 percent of the total child behaviors. Parents tended to respond positively to a child's behavior, whether it was deviant or nondeviant, but did respond negatively to deviant behaviors proportionately more of the time than to nondeviant ones. There were no differences between mothers and fathers in the consequences they provided.

Wahl et al. (1974) suggest that the fact that parents often respond to deviant behavior with a positive response may be one important way in which adult-child interactions are different from child-child interactions. Also, they suggest that their findings support the view that social interactions are reciprocal. Finally, as a caveat, they suggest that their methodology, which required parents and child to be in the same room for an extended period of time, probably increased the total amount of interaction substantially.

Another study of family interaction that has a behavioral theoretical basis is Baskett and Johnson's (1982) study of young children's interactions with parents compared with their interactions with siblings. They studied 47 low-income families, all with two or three children. The identified child of the study was between four and eight years old, with a sibling two or four years older. The authors note few effects of the target child's age or gender on its behaviors. Girls interacted slightly more than boys overall. Of the behaviors emitted toward parents, approximately half were seen by the parents as undesirable, including noncompliance with commands, whining, tantruming, destructiveness, and demanding attention. "With their parents, the target children seemed more likely to alternate between positive social interactions and attention-demanding behaviors, and with their siblings, between quiet play and arguing" (p. 646). Clearly the aversive, coersive behaviors described by Patterson were very much present in the children in this study, and the parents were much more the target than even the siblings.

Loeb and his associates (Loeb, 1975; Loeb, Horst, & Horton, 1980) reach an important conclusion drawn from their data: Identical behaviors on the part of mothers and fathers have differential effects on their children, in part depending upon the gender of the child.

The studies in this section as well as the development of some creative theory in the field (e.g., Patterson, 1971, 1980), although deliberately focused on discrete and measurable behavior, have far-reaching implications for the family system. In particular, they explore the all-too-frequent, naturally occurring aversive interactions between parents and children.

INDEPENDENT STUDIES

Jacob (1974) assessed how a child's age and the family social class interact with each other. He studied 44 middle- and lower-class families with an 11- to 16-year-old boy, using a structured laboratory task. Among his findings were greater initial disagreements among lower-class than middle-class families and among families with a younger, compared with families with an older, boy. In particular, father-son initial agreement was greater with an older, compared to a younger, boy. Middle-class families talked more and successfully interrupted each other more than did lower-class families, and both parents interrupted more in the presence of an older than a younger boy. Older sons had more influence than younger sons. In middle-class families, son's gain in influence—from age 11 to 16—was at the expense of the mother's dominance. In lower-class families, the father had relatively less influence as sons matured. This is one of the few family studies to focus on the meaning of social-class differences for family organization.

Brody, Stoneman, and Sanders (1980) were concerned with the impact of television viewing on family interactions. Fathers', but not mothers', behavior toward their preschool child was greatly affected by the presence of television. Fathers paid less attention to the child and talked less to him or her when in the presence of a television program, while mothers were unaffected in the nature or amount of their interactions with their spouse or child. The authors suggest that "in triadic family interactions, mothers assume a managerial or over-seer role while fathers assume a playmate role" (p. 219). Although for the families the amount of orienting toward one another and conversation with one another was diminished during television viewing, the amount of physical touching was greatly increased, suggesting a system compensation to maintain preferred interpersonal closeness.

Using a competing cognitive task, Zussman (1980) studied 20 mothers and fathers in a laboratory setting, each with two of their children, a preschooler and a toddler. Parents interacted more briefly with their children when they were engaged in a cognitive task (an anagram) but not less often. During the task phase, the fathers and mothers were less responsive to efforts to interact from the preschoolers but not from the toddler. Both mothers and fathers were more curt and abrupt, especially with the younger children, during the task phase. There were no differences between mothers and fathers on the dimensions Zussman measured.

This study seems important because it simulates an ever-present phenomenon in the lives of parents and children, which is parent-child interactions occurring around and through parental involvement in other, competing activities.

Stuckey, McGhee, and Bell (1982) studied 40 rural New Mexican middle- and upper-class families with preschool girls and boys, 20 with employed mothers and 20 with nonemployed mothers. Their data came from both home observations and parent questionnaires. They conclude that parental role specialization is not altered by women's employment and that employment status and attitudes toward this employment together have a stronger impact on parental behaviors than either alone. They raise the possibility that the difference in the amount of attention paid to girls and boys may be elicited by the child and that girls, finding themselves in a family where they have less ready access to attention because of the employment of their mother, seek out and receive more attention from their parents, whereas boys tend not to seek it out.

The studies in this section highlight important variables in the study of family systems. Social class, gender similarity and difference between parents and children, changes in interactions with competing activities (television, a task), and the role of maternal employment all emerge as salient dimensions in the study of family interactions.

SEX ROLE SOCIALIZATION

Space does not permit a review of the recent family interaction studies that have particular implications for sex role socialization (e.g., Bell, Johnson, McGillicuddy-DeLisi, & Siegal, 1981; Fagot, 1974; Field,

1978, 1981; Margolin & Patterson, 1975; Power, 1981; Tauber, 1979; Weinraub & Frankel, 1977).

Power (1981), in his summary of findings concerning sex typing in infancy and gender differentiation, makes note of the fact that fathers tend to engage in differential treatment of the sexes throughout the first 18 months of life, while most studies show mothers responding differently to boys and girls much less during this early period. Fathers tend to actively encourage the development of manipulative and visual spatial capacities in boys, while encouraging the development of verbal ability in the girls. After 18 months of age, mothers and fathers both appear to play an important role in gender or sex stereotyping.

Gender has a powerful effect on both child development and family functioning. The research underlines that people's stated views are often—one might even say usually—quite different from their actual behaviors. Any valid study of sex typing by parents and its effects upon child development must therefore include both observational data of usual interactions *and* measures of the parents' stated attitudes; the discrepancy between these may well constitute an important indirect effect in family functioning.

LONGITUDINAL GROUPS

Brazelton and Yogman

Brazelton and his research group (Brazelton, Koslowski, & Main, 1974; Brazelton, Yogman, Als, & Tronick, 1979) have been interested in understanding the infant's early affective regulatory interactions with caretaking adults. They (Yogman, Dixon, Tronick, Adamson, Als, & Brazelton, 1976; Yogman, Dixon, Tronick, Als, Adamson, Lester, & Brazelton, 1977) have studied in microanalytic detail by means of videotaped interactions the cyclical patterns of such interaction between very young infant, mother, and (most recently) father.

Using this method, Yogman (Yogman et al., 1977) has studied similarities and differences in father-infant and mother-infant interactions. Mothers appear to engage in more structuring, interactive, vocal behaviors, creating what Yogman describes as an "envelope" for the dyad, whereas fathers appear to create a "base" for play. Mothers spend more time with their infants playing verbal games, while fathers and infants engage in more physical play.

Such findings allowed this research group to conclude that "interactions with fathers can be characterized as heightened and playful while the interactions with mothers appear more smoothly modulated and contained" (Brazelton et al., 1979, p. 40). In addition, these studies have made clear to the researchers the importance from birth onward of the infant's need for both connected, attentional phases and disconnected, nonattentional phases. They suggest that the differences in the way mothers and fathers play provide an early opportunity for the development of differential relationships. The triadic family allows for novel but regular forms of interaction for the young infant and leads to a capacity to learn about varying forms of mutual interaction from birth onward. The father's role in very early infant development is seen from this perspective as particularly important.

In another study, Yogman (1981) found that mothers and infants played slightly fewer games than fathers and infants, and visual games were most common in mother-infant play. Yogman suggests that the visual games of the mother appear to "represent a more distal attention-maintaining form of interactive play" (p. 247), while father's play is more proximal, idiosyncratic, and more sharply arousing. Consequently, he suggests that mother's·type of play may lead to the "establishment and consolidation of rules of interchange which are both basic social skills and facilitate later language development" (p. 248), while father's play may develop interests in novel stimuli and alternative forms of social playing.

While most of Brazelton's work (on early mother-infant interactions) falls outside the purview of this chapter, the ingenious extension of his methods by his colleagues allows us to study the earliest experiences of the infant within the three-way setting.

Lamb

Lamb has focused on the widening scope of the infant's social attachments. Although he has published his findings over an extended period of time, and from a number of different perspectives Lamb's (1976a–f, 1977a–d, 1978a–c, 1980, 1981a, 1981b) basic research has consisted of data from two intersecting longitudinal studies plus a number of discrete cross-sectional and laboratory investigations. The first longitudinal study involved naturalistic observations of 20 mother-infant and father-infant girl and boy dyads during the infants' first year of life.

During their first year, the infants in this study showed no preference for either parent in attachment behaviors, and they clearly preferred either parent to a stranger. Affiliative behaviors were more-often shown towards fathers, possibly because fathers played with the babies more. With the youngest infants (seven to eight months), fathers' style of play was noticeably different from mothers'. It was more likely to be idiosyncratic, rough and tumble, and less predictable. These differences diminished as the babies in the study grew older, but the children continued to respond more positively to father-infant play than to play with their mothers. Also, mothers were more likely to hold infants for caretaking, while fathers were more likely to hold their children to play or in response to a direct request.

In a follow-up of this study into the second year of life (Lamb, 1977a, 1977b, 1977d, 1980), fathers were consistently preferred by the boy toddlers in both attachment and affiliative behaviors, while girls showed no preference between the parents in attachment. In addition, fathers vocalized more towards boys than towards girls during that second year, while mothers' vocalizing was essentially the same towards both girls and boys. Indeed, in analyzing parental preferences during the first two years of life, Lamb (1977d) suggests that "between one and two years of age . . . fathers make themselves particularly salient to their sons" (p. 75).

In an attempt at replication in a more-stressful laboratory situation, the preferences for fathers, which had appeared so strongly in the naturalistic setting, dropped out (Lamb, 1976a, 1976f, 1978a, 1980).

Serendipitously, Lamb (1976a) found that when the infants were observed with each parent alone, there was more parent-child interaction with each than when both parents were present, although the same relative preferences emerged. Thus a clear second-order effect emerged when the three-way situation was examined.

In an attempt at cross-cultural replication of American findings, Lamb and his colleagues (Lamb, Frodi, Frodi, & Hwang, 1982; Lamb, Frodi, Hwang, Frodi, & Steinberg, 1982(a) & 1982(b)) turned to Sweden, where there are fathers who, for short periods of time, become the primary caretaker. In the findings from a study of 51 firstborn eight-month-olds and their parents, mothers (whether they were the primary or secondary caretakers) were more likely than were fathers to hold, tend to, and display affection towards the young infants. Fathers showed no significant differences on any parenting behavior based upon whether they were primary or secondary caretakers. There was some evidence that the fathers who were secondary caretakers in Sweden tended to play more with children, like fathers in American families, while fathers who functioned more in the "maternal" role tended to play less.

Although these cross-cultural studies may raise more questions than they answer, they do begin to address the question of whether the significant findings of father-child attachment from earliest infancy onward and the differential effects of mothers and fathers in the interaction with their babies are a culturally bound phenomenon or, indeed, the manifestation and expression of deeply rooted, genetic gender differences. Lamb and his colleagues (Lamb, Chase-Lansdale, & Owen, 1979) as well as Pedersen's group (Pedersen, Cain, & Zaslow, 1982) have begun to address the salience of these differential effects, observing alternative lifestyles within the American culture, particularly in dual-worker families.

Clarke-Stewart

Clarke-Stewart has recently focused on the possible consequences of differential interactions with mothers and fathers on the child's social and cognitive capacities.

The study described here was based upon a small longitudinal sample of 14 families with toddlers, both firstborn and second-born girl or boy toddlers, which was carried out in the families' homes during 1972 and 1973 (Clarke-Stewart, 1978, 1980). As Clarke-Stewart herself has pointed out, the extremely small sample size for such a complex, multimeasure study raises serious questions about replicability, and we share these concerns. We present it here briefly for its creative and heuristic effect.

The results are intriguing. She found no differences in the child's attachment to the mother or father, but children were more responsive to play initiated by the father than to play initiated by the mother. In the natural observational setting, mothers played with the children much more than fathers did. Boys chose to play with father when both parents were present, but girls approached mother more when she was the only parent available. Even during the times when fathers were at home, mothers interacted much more with the child than fathers did. Play with the father was brief in duration, more likely to be physically involving, and less likely to be toy mediated. Over time, as the child grew from infancy to toddlerhood, the father became the more-frequent playmate, and the mother's role as care giver diminished, reducing the discrepancy in their time involvement.

The amount of positive and responsive talk by the mother toward the child was significantly less when the father was home compared with when he wasn't, and it was diminished still more when the father was actually in the room.

For both boys and girls, the children's intellectual competence was most highly and consistently related to the extent that the mother provided intellectual stimulation and expression of positive emotion. Boys were more socially competent if their parents were warm towards them; but for girls, the greater the parental warmth, the lower their social competence.

An oft cited finding of Clarke-Stewart's is her hypothesis, based on a cross-lag analysis, of directionality of effects from mother to father and from child to father. Although an intriguing concept, we have grave concerns about its validity due to the small sample size.

In discussing these results, Clarke-Stewart suggests that the apparent preference for fathers in play can best be understood from the perspective of father's more "engaging style of interaction," which involves physical proximity, directions, and praise for the child, and it is social and physical rather than intellectual or object mediated. In her study, the fathers who played most with their children physically were married to mothers who talked most with their children and engaged them in play with objects. The spouses appeared reciprocally to balance one another in this case. Clarke-Stewart argues for biologically based and culturally supported interactive styles, with the masculine style involving physical play and the feminine style involving care giving, verbal interaction, and object mediation. She emphasizes, however, that similarities outweigh differences in men's and women's interactions with their young children.

Despite her small sample size, Clarke-Stewart has provided beginning empirical support for the fact that daddy makes more than three, he makes for a complex social system of parent/child interaction.

Parke, Sawin, and others

A related and important series of studies is that of Parke, Sawin, and their associates (Parke, 1979; Parke & O'Leary, 1976; Parke, O'Leary, & West, 1972; Parke & Sawin, 1976, 1980; Parke & Tinsley, 1981; Phillips & Parke, 1981; Sawin & Parke, 1979). In the context of their triadic model of family interactions (Sawin & Parke), they conceptualize direct effects of parents on infants, indirect effects of fathers through mothers to infants, and bidirectional effects, in recognition of the infant's role in determining the parental behavior (see Bell & Harper, 1977). From their series of studies of newborns and their parents, Parke and Sawin conclude that fathers engage in more social interactions with infants around feeding than mothers do, while mothers spend more time directly in caretaking. Fathers are clearly competent to engage in the tasks, such as bottle-feeding a young infant, but do not always perform them. Father's presence increases mother's interest in the baby and so performs a very important second-order function. They suggest that mothers smile more at baby than fathers do, but in relation to awareness of infant needs, they found no important differences between mothers and fathers.

In a short-term longitudinal study, Parke and Sawin (1980) followed 40 girl and boy infants, half firstborn and half later-born, and their mothers and fathers for the first three months of the infants' life. Mothers spent more time with the children in routine care giving than did the fathers, while fathers engaged in significantly more social stimulation. While there was little difference in parents' routine care giving towards sons and daughters, they were more affectionate with opposite-sex infants, while attending and stimulating was more frequent with same-sex infants. Fathers were markedly more involved with later-borns and mothers more involved with firstborns.

In summing up the results of their research, Parke and Sawin (1980) suggest that mothers and fathers have both similar and distinctive roles in early infancy. The gender of the infant appears to lead to some differences in the behavior of mothers and fathers. They also note a clear lack of continuity in interaction patterns from the newborn period to three months. In addition to this being reflective of the infant's rapid changes, it may also have something to do with a molecular versus molar means of observing the data. Parke, Sawin, and their colleagues have added to our knowledge of the earliest period of a child's entry into the family system and of the effects of this change upon the members.

Lewis and his colleagues

Lewis, Feiring, and Weinraub (1981), on the basis of numerous studies, have proposed what they call a "social network model" to explain recent evidence about fathers' role in the family. This is a model that suggests that the child is born into a set of interconnected relationships which function as a system. Within this system are subsystems, there is nonadditivity (meaning that knowing about independent discrete events within the system or about two-way interactions cannot add up to a three-way interaction), and there is interdependence among the subsystems. Interactions are not the same as relationships, and dynamic patterns of balancing for a "steady state" or equilibrium within the system are ongoing. (Feiring & Lewis, 1978; Lewis & Feiring, 1979; Lewis & Rosenblum, 1979; Lewis & Weinraub, 1976). They propose, then, a transactional model of interaction in which the child has social ties of significance as well as social and emotional needs which must be met, and these all exist within a matrix of relationships. Within such a structural arrangement, aspects of development over time, family structure, number of siblings, situation (e.g., dinnertime versus playtime), and cultural roles must all be taken into account. Children may acquire knowledge through both direct and indirect interactions with the network. Lewis, Weinraub, and Feiring suggest that this is particularly significant in the father's role, as there is much experimental evidence to suggest that fathers have important effects upon both child and mother in *indirect* ways. (see Brooks-Gunn & Lewis, 1979; Lewis et al., 1981). Lewis and his colleagues argue that the evidence of indirect effects allows for a phenomenon they call "transitivity," which is the relationship of one person to another, indirectly, mediated by a third.

In an attempt to understand parental differential interaction within the social network system, Lewis and Feiring (1982) created a pilot study looking at 15 three-year-old children and their parents during dinner. In their findings, both mothers and fathers performed "expressive" functions (that is, nurturing and care-giving) as well as instrumental or information-seeking functions when dealing with the child, and the differences between parents in the amounts of these behaviors were small. On the other hand, children were more likely to seek information from the mother than from the father, even though there were no differences in the mother's and father's information-seeking behavior toward the child. Thus, differences in children's behavior toward their parents may not necessarily reflect parental differences.

Looking at spousal interactions, fathers were more likely to seek information from mothers, while mothers were likely to nurture fathers. So although parents may not show role specialization of these functions toward the child, they do indeed model it in relation to each other. Thus, children may learn about traditional role expectations for male and female behavior not only directly from their parents' interactions with them but *indirectly* from the observation of their parents as a marital couple. As Lewis and Feiring (1982) point out, learning about social behavior by observation rather than direct interaction or relationship is a form of indirect influence, but may be a central aspect of socialization that has remained unstudied in former research projects.

In summarizing their groups' work over the last 10 years, Lewis and his colleagues emphasize the necessity of conceptualizing the child's social network. Thus far, little research has been done on the child's relationship to peers, grandparents, friends, etc., and only a beginning has occurred on the study of three-way systems with fathers from a social network perspective—including bidirectionality, subsystems, and indirect as well as direct effects. They remind us that data have shown that fathers affect the quality as well as quantity of maternal behavior (e.g., Clarke-Stewart, 1978), and since fathers appear to spend more time naturally in interaction in three-person settings than in two-person settings, the role of fathers may (even more significantly than mothers) point to the importance of indirect and systems effects (e.g., Pedersen, 1980). Lewis and his research group express the hope that their attempts at creating a better conceptual model of the social network will allow for a broader-based set of hypotheses and research studies to understand the role of the father in the child's life from the perspective of a complex interactional system. Such attempts will require not only creative conceptualization but also new statistical and analytical approaches to understand the data gathering within these new, creative conceptual models.

Belsky group

The creative work of Belsky and his colleagues is reviewed extensively in another chapter in this *Handbook* (see Chapter 18). Consequently, we do not review this important family interaction research in any depth. However, several of his findings are central to the view of family interaction presented in this chapter and are mentioned here only briefly (Belsky, 1979, 1980, 1981; Belsky, Gilstrap, & Rovine, 1984; Belsky, Spanier, & Rovine, 1983).

Belsky is one of the few researchers to analyze his data from the perspective of what he calls family styles—i.e., combining mother and father styles within each family—in addition to contrasting mothers and fathers. This perspective sheds an entirely different light on family functioning and, in our view, is a fruitful line of future research.

Another point Belsky emphasizes is the distinction between competence, or potential capacity, and actuality. He has shown that when fathers are asked in a laboratory to be competent with their children, they often "look much like mothers," but within the naturalistic setting of the home, they rarely do this on a routine basis.

Belsky has begun to provide compelling empirical evidence supporting his theoretical arguments that a developmental psychology can only provide a truly comprehensive and usable analysis of the entire family system if it is based upon bidirectional triadic interactional studies (in the home), taking into account the complex dynamic interface between husband and wife—both as a marital couple and as parents—with their infants over a longitudinal period of change.

Pedersen group

Pedersen and his various colleagues were among the first to conceptualize and study the role of the father in the developmental infancy-family context as a part of an "interactive system" (Pedersen, 1975; Pedersen & Robson, 1969). Indeed, Pedersen's research has continued to be a seminal and innovative point for all other workers in this field. Belsky's studies, for example, are based partly upon Pedersen's theoretical and observational methods (see Belsky, 1980).

In 1975, Pedersen, Anderson, and Cain (1980) began an important study on parent-infant and husband-wife interactions observed at the baby's five-month birthday. They asked the families in their studies to keep records of how time was spent together in the course of their everyday lives. In traditional families, the most characteristic context for the mother with the infant was a two-person interaction, while for the father with the infant, it was usually a threesome of mother, father, and infant. Once focused upon the mother-father-infant triad, the authors became aware of the importance of the interplay of the couple unit and parent-infant interactions. The sample for the study was comprised of 41 middle-class white families with a firstborn five-month-old infant. Data were collected in four home visits. They found no main effects for gender of the infant. Mothers performed 3 out of 12 parental variables (verbalization to baby, smiling, and feeding liquids) significantly more often than fathers. Importantly, mothers and fathers were not different in their rate of vocalization or "baby talk," nor in their rate of vigorous tactile-kinesthetic stimulation, nor object-mediated play, nor focused social play. This last is especially noteworthy, since play has been a major differentiation for other parent-infant interactional studies. Pedersen and his group concluded that fathers are engaged in a wide variety of roles with their infants (Pedersen et al., 1980; Pedersen & Robson, 1969).

Although there were very few differences between mothers and fathers in general, whether the group was a twosome or threesome had a very strong impact on parental behavior. Mother and fathers carried out a number of parental behaviors more often when alone with the child. Similarly, the infants looked at their mother's or father's face and smiled and vocalized more in the dyad versus the triad. These findings are extremely important, since in traditional families, fathers tend to interact with their infants with mothers present. Consequently, even though parental behaviors may be similar, one may expect that the infant will have dramatically different interactions with mother and father.

In relation to couple interaction, there was some husband-wife communication 51 percent of the time that the triad was studied. When all three family members were together, greater role specialization for mothers and fathers was found, with fathers now providing more tactile-kinesthetic stimulation than mothers.

Mothers and fathers responded somewhat differently to the threesome. In the three-way setting, mothers were more affected by communication with their spouse in their interactions with their child. They appeared more responsive to the interpersonal demands of both husband and child. All measures of the infant's social behavior were well coordinated with changes of the parental behavior. Pedersen and his colleagues conclude:

> In fact the infant at only five months of age shows the ability to engage in a complex intermeshing of behavior with both parents that is also coordinated with their behavior to each other. This suggests that the three-person group, which typically the presence of the father creates, may provide unique learning opportunities for the infant and may contribute to its expanded repertoire of behavior. (Pedersen, et al. 1980, p. 83)

Applying Belsky's (1979) analyses to the data from this study, Pedersen (1980) found that husband-wife communication about the baby did seem to improve the father-child relationship, but this was not true for the mother.

Pedersen argues for the need for a more complex analytic model, one that can view fathers in a family context yet also look at different *patterns* of maternal and paternal behavior in pairs, rather than unitary analyses of mothers or fathers alone. Pedersen also suggests that it may be the role of the father to expand the infant's environment and to promote an awareness of the interesting responses of people beyond the mother-child bond. Indeed, this may be an important cognitive and social developmental factor for the infant, moving the baby beyond symbiosis into the larger, more complex social world of human development (Pedersen, 1981; Pedersen, Yarrow, Anderson, & Cain, 1979).

Reiss

Another very different approach to studying families is that of Reiss (1981) and his colleagues. He utilized a method for observing family styles of interaction around problem solving that involved strictly controlling the nature of the communication between family members. On the basis of such tasks with a variety of families, some "normal" and some with a diagnosed family member, Reiss has developed an intriguing system for conceptualizing family interactions and typing families according to that conception. A basic formulation is that a family's approach to a laboratory task reflects the underlying constructs the family shares about the world, and those constructs regulate a family's responses to the world. Families can be typed in terms of their styles of information processing. Secondly, he argues that family crisis is central in bringing about change—both positive and negative— in family life and that change is reflected in the family's shared conception of the world. Lastly, Reiss suggests that the medium for preserving the shared family view is enduring family interaction patterns.

While his approach to data collection more resembles the family research styles of the 50s than of the 70s and 80s, his conceptual formulation seems to us to have substantial relevance for all researchers attempting to link family interaction research and clinical understandings of family functioning.

Lytton

One of the most methodologically impressive family interaction studies is that of Lytton (1980). His particular interest was to describe socialization techniques of parents with young children and to begin to determine the direction of causality of behaviors of parents and their toddlers. He studied 46 same-sex male twin sets, 44 male singletons (all between two and three years of age), and their parents. His data collection sources included both home observations and a laboratory session with each toddler and mother. In the final analysis, he discovered that the laboratory data had the least heuristic value in predicting child outcome variables.

Looking first at attachment behaviors, much more was directed towards mothers than fathers, even controlling for the amount of time each parent spent with the children. Neither mother nor father was able to ignore attachment approaches by their toddler; both were responsive nearly all the time. Thus the child seemed to control attachment interactions to a large extent. Interestingly, a disproportionate number of twins were more attached to their fathers, and these father-attached children were less mature and had mothers who displayed fewer positive qualities. Primary attachment to the father over the mother by the two-year-olds was apparently due to an unavailability of the mother, as in families with twins, or less responsiveness and attractiveness of the mothers.

Lytton (1980) found, as others have, that rough and tumble play was disproportionately associated with the father. However, he often found it impossible to judge who initiated such play. Several interesting findings emerged about responsiveness. Parents were very similar to one another in their degree of responsiveness. They tended to attend to their toddler's needs and wishes and to comply. Mothers' responsiveness was less variable than fathers. Generally parents' positive responses predominated over negative, while for the toddler, negative responses predominated.

In contrast to the area of attachment behavior, where the toddler seemed to call the shots, child compliance was greatly influenced by parental actions. In turn, child compliance or noncompliance had relatively little impact on the parent's subsequent behavior. Parental smiling and praising accompanying verbal commands increased the likelihood of the commands being obeyed, whereas physical control and criticism decreased the likelihood and compliance. In an interesting second-order effect, father's presence reduced the number of efforts on the mother's part to control the two-year-old and increased her effectiveness.

Looking at parent-child conversation, parents talked more than the child, and parents responded more to the toddler's speech than the two-year-old responded to theirs. A triadic family system of communication existed, reflected, for example, in the high correlations of amount of speech among all three family members. Lytton (1980) found that when both parents were with the toddler, there was more total speech to the child, but each parent talked somewhat less than when alone with the child. The total amount of speech generated by the parents, the emotional climate of family interactions, the level of cognitive stimulation, and mother's sensitivity in responding were all conducive to high language development.

An intuitively important sequence of interactions was related to mother's disapproval and criticism and child's attention seeking. When the mother was critical, the child tended more often to seek her attention and help, which in turn led her to be more negative. Children of noncollege-educated mothers were significantly more active overall, were more restless, and talked less than children of college-educated mothers. In laboratory situations, college-educated mothers exerted significantly more pressure on the child to comply than noncollege-educated mothers. Interestingly, these groups were not different in responsiveness to the child's needs and wishes.

Activity level decreased with age and was also related to nonverbal attachment behavior. Thus, Lytton (1980) suggested that activity level was closely related to immaturity. In this study, activity level also went with a "happy, less-dysphoric mood" (p. 248). The strongest predictors of activity level were mother's lower educational level and the amount of father's play with the child. Lytton concluded that "while the child shapes his own immediate environment to some extent, he has little power to mold his parents' enduring characteristics" (p. 282). He thus suggests some important limits in the impact of at least a toddler on the family interactions. However, Lytton's own data make clear that in some domains of interaction, even two-year-olds have a substantial effect, while in others, parents are relatively unresponsive to particulars of the child's behavior. And as Rowe (1981) suggested in his review of Lytton's work, possibly this balance of power may shift more to the child as the child grows older.

Boston University Pregnancy and Parenthood Project

Several studies of family interaction have come out of the Boston University Pregnancy and Parenthood Project. (The findings from pregnancy to the child's first birthday are described in Grossman, Eichler, & Winickoff, with Anzalone, Gofseyeff, & Sargent, 1980). Interactional data were collected at both the two- and five-year follow-ups of this longitudinal study. Initially, 100 women and 90 of their husbands were seen when the women were near the beginning of pregnancy. Approximately half were pregnant with their first child; the rest had one to three children. The families were seen again periodically up to the child's fifth birthday. By the time of the two-year follow-up, 52 mother-father-toddler units remained in the sample. Data were from home visits and came from naturalistic and structured observations, interviews, paper and pencil scales, and child testing.

Varrin (1979), using data from this project, attempted to study the temperamental styles of parents and children, both from paper and pencil measures and from observational ratings of temperament from the interactions. She found some support for her hypothesis that a greater temperament difference between parents and child would relate to less-healthy adaptation of the child. Fathers and sons were more likely to be different in mood than fathers and daughters, and mothers and fathers were more different in mood during the observation when the child was a boy than when the child was a girl. Overall, however, parents and their children tended to be similar to each other in mood and energy level. It is an interesting aside that parents generally did not perceive this similarity; their ratings of their own and their child's moods were essentially unrelated on questionnaires.

Vojdany-Noah (1983) applied a microanalytic measure of synchrony, based on work by Brazelton and others (Brazelton et al., 1974; Brazelton et al., 1979), to videotapes of the interactions between the two-year-olds and their mothers and fathers separately. Neither synchrony (which is an empirical measure of the extent of agreement of affective involvement between parent and child) nor the frequency of successful interactions related to whether the child was a firstborn or later-born, but there was an intriguing gender effect. On the one hand, boys and their parents had significantly more synchronous interactions than did girls and their parents. On the other hand, girls and their parents had a significantly higher frequency of successful interactions than did boys and their parents. Vojdany-Noah's interpretation is that the higher synchrony seen in interactions with toddler boys relates to the persistence of young boys about their demands, also noted by Martin (1981). Two-year-olds who had more synchronous interactions with their parents were doing less well in their lives. Vojdany-Noah suggests that while high synchrony may be optimal in responsively parenting a newborn, it might well represent enmeshment with a toddler, who requires a constantly fluctuating degree of closeness and autonomy. Finally, both mothers and fathers had more successful interactions with their daughters than with their sons, and this was more true for fathers than for mothers.

An ambitious effort to measure aspects of the families' interactions more directly, rather than inferentially, was conducted by Michael (1980), also using the 52 families in the longitudinal study for the two-year follow-up. Based primarily on Kantor and Lehr's (1975) formulation of the importance of modes of family distance regulation, Michael developed measures of five modes—physical, temporal, and emotional proximity and two aspects of boundary functioning within a family. The measures were from observation, from interviews with each parent individually, and from paper and pencil scales completed by each parent.

In addition to an effort to validate measures of family relationships around closeness and distance, the study was designed to test the hypothesis that a curvilinear relationship exists between degrees of family proximity and aspects of parent and child adaptation. Some intriguing findings appeared. The closer the parents and the two-year-olds, the less well the child was doing on a variety of measures. Mothers of firstborns were significantly closer to their two-year-olds and spent much more time alone with them than did mothers of later-born children in the study; and the longer a couple had been married, the less their observed physical and temporal closeness! Families with boys indicated a greater wish for more shared family time than did families with girls; and not surprisingly, the more mothers worked, the more time fathers spent with their two-year-olds.

In his interpretation of his findings, Michael (1980) suggests that less adapted, or less mature, two-year-olds require and elicit greater proximity from their parents as a response to their immaturity. The alternative explanation, of course, is that greater parental involvement *causes* less-adaptive functioning on the part of the two-year-old. His measures hold promise as a way of operationalizing family systems concepts that go beyond dyadic interactions.

Grossman (1981b) focused on some surprising second-order effects in predictions from aspects of parent functioning to child adaptation at the two-year follow-up. For firstborn children, the better the mother was doing psychologically in the early postpartum period both individually and as a mother, the better her child was doing at age two. For later-born children, in surprising contrast, the opposite picture tended to hold: the *less* depressed the mother at two months postpartum, the higher her psychological adaptation, and the more adequate the quality of her mothering, the less well her child was doing at age two. These apparently paradoxical results were more strongly and consistently true for boys, but somewhat true for the total group of later-born children in the study. Other data made clear that when the mother was doing less well in a variety of ways in the early postpartum period, the fathers in this sample were spending more time with the child. It was specifically the quantity and not the quality of their fathering that was affected, and these husbands of depressed and anxious women continued to spend more time at the two-year follow-up.

There was some suggestion in the data that for firstborn girls and boys and for later-born girls, the more time their fathers spent with them, the *less* well they were doing at two years. For later-born boys only, the more time their father spent with them, the *better* they were doing at two years.

Thus, in generally well functioning family units such as participated in this study, a complementarity of functioning holds sway such that when a mother is able to care responsively for her young children, she in fact does the largest proportion of that caretaking; but when she is unable to do that (because she is anxious or depressed or otherwise insufficiently responsive to an infant), her husband steps in and spends more discretionary time with the child. For firstborns, who in general are so tied to their mothers psychologically (see Grossman, Eichler, & Winickoff, with Anzelone, Gofseyeff, & Sargent, Winickoff, 1980), father's involvement is not sufficient to eliminate the negative impact of the mother's malaise. Later-born girls also appear to be negatively affected, perhaps because the gender similarity with mother makes her more salient for the daughter. However, it appears to be so valuable to later-born sons to have their fathers more involved in their lives that they are positively benefited by difficulties of their mothers that result in the father's stepping in to a greater extent!

The study suggests several tentative conclusions. Father's time involvement with his young children is responsive to such reality factors as the hours of his wife's employment (Grossman, 1981a) as well as other psychological variables. This data suggests that father's time involvement is also strongly dependent on the family system's need for him to step in. However, for the child, the consequences of greater father involvement and lesser mother involvement are different depending on whether the child is firstborn or later-born and whether the child is a girl or a boy.

At the fifth year of the study, the sample consisted of 43 families from the original longitudinal group plus 14 cross-sectional additions for a total of 57 husband and wife pairs, each with a five-year-old child. Pollack (1982a), utilizing 33 of the families from the five-year follow-up, attempted to study empirically several seminal concepts of modern psychoanalysis. He argued that recent psychoanalytically informed research on infant-mother interaction was beginning to yield a concept of child development quite different from Mahler's single-axis lines of individuation, (Mahler, 1968) and more akin to Kohut's dual parallel lines for development of the emergence of the self (Kohut, 1971, 1977). Borrowing from the theoretical works of Stechler and Kaplan (1980) and Klein (1976), Pollack hypothesized that children with parents who could foster their capacities both for autonomy *and* for affiliation (called *"I"ness* and *"We"ness*) would be healthier than those children whose parents were competent at either one of these tasks alone (see also Balser, 1980).

As expected, the child's healthy adaptation was related to high levels of I-ness and We-ness in parents. However, I-ness and We-ness together were better predictors than either parental capacity alone. Spouses' capacity to support *autonomy* in their children was related, while their capacities for *affiliation* were not. If the child did well with mother, he or she was likely to do well with father as well. Surprisingly, however, father's affiliative and autonomy-enhancing functions powerfully related to his child's healthy functioning with mother as well as to the child's adaptation with him. This was a significant indirect, or second-order, effect that did not occur for mother and child.

Unlike mother's, father's affiliative and autonomous components appeared to be more independent of both age and financial circumstances. Father's affiliative aspects appeared most distinct from his wife's psychological constellation, but they continued to exert a strong effect, both direct and indirect, on the child's development. A serendipitous finding was gender disparity in the actual components of I-ness and We-ness (see also Hoffman, 1977, on gender differences in empathy).

Relating the significance of these findings to researching the family as a system (1982b), Pollack argues that self-psychology and the concept of an internalized representational world (Atwood & Stolorow, 1980) allowed psychoanalytic metapsychology to come closer into line with a general psychology: with both a clinical systems theory of family functioning and the burgeoning developmental evidence of three-way parent-child interactional studies. Specifically, he argues that his findings support the need for recognizing the complex interactive bidirectional and systematic phenomena present in parent-child interactions and, consequently, in family functioning.

Pollack (1982b), argues that the integration of self-psychology and family interaction data gives promise of yielding a new research paradigm. This model may explain the internalization of significant interpersonal memories and their intergenerational transmission within a family system—creating a bridge between the *internal* and *external*. In turn, psychoanalytic theory can enrich our understanding of family interaction data.

Golding (1983) attempted to systematically study five-year-old children's cognitive understanding of affects and their expression of affects within the context of parent-child interaction. She found systematic relationships between aspects of parenting and expressive affective measures. The more support for closeness and autonomy the mothers and fathers provided, the more positive was the child's affect quality in the interaction. A significant gender difference was also found in that father's *affiliative* quality was more important in influencing children's affect quality with him, while mother's *autonomy*-enhancing qualities were more important in facilitating children's affect quality with her. Whether the direction of these effects, however, is from parent to child or from child to parent remains in question.

In an interactional study still in progress, Kauffman (1982, 1983) observed a subsample of 40 of the five-year follow-up families from the perspective of parental control speech and its relationship to child adaptation. In preliminary results, no significant differences have been found to exist between the frequencies of different attempts at control speech for mothers versus fathers. While maternal control was not related to the gender of the child, it was affected by whether the child was a firstborn or later-born; mothers gave more directives and fewer indirect control statements to later-born children. The greater the amount of maternal *non*control talk, the better the child's adaptation. With brighter children, mothers tended to speak more and fathers less. And, intriguingly, the more children in the family, the more direct control statements from *both* mothers and fathers, with socioeconomic status controlled.

Grossman (1983) utilized data from pregnancy to predict later child adaptation with the families from the longitudinal sample. In relation to firstborns, mothers who were feeling and doing better in a variety of ways during pregnancy had children also doing well at five years. Similarly, the better adapted the father was to pregnancy, the better the mood of the firstborn child in interaction with him at five years.

Striking differences were found in the predictors of later-born adaptation. The more anxious and depressed the mother in pregnancy, the better the child was doing in a number of ways. Most of the significant predictors from pregnancy to the five-year-old were for later-borns and not firstborns, and the majority were indirect effects. In addition, when looking at interaction scores, some apparently positive parental characteristics during pregnancy predicted negatively to the laterborn's interactive adaptation. Fedele (1983) elaborates upon these parenting and gender effects from the parental perspective.

In some situations, reciprocity between parents was apparent, such as later-born five-year-olds with more anxious mothers showing more positive affect with their fathers. Grossman, Winickoff, and Eichler (1980) have argued that when mothers are less able to provide an adequate holding environment (most especially with later-borns), fathers may step in and play a more salient role and, in consequence, have a more-potent effect.

The unique significance of this longitudinal study and of the papers based on its findings derives from several factors. The perspective informing the design, measures, and interpretations is both clinical and developmental. It is one of the few studies to focus on families with their first child and families with a second or later offspring. As a result of these two factors, some of the studies' findings are unique. Whether they will ultimately prove to be enduring will only be clear when other studies undertake similarly multimodel, multiperspective, wholistic approaches to the family.

CONCLUSION

American developmental psychology has moved irrevocably beyond atomistic or dyadic laboratory-based investigation into new frontiers of ecologically representative, naturalistically oriented, and family-based interactional research. The studies reviewed in this chapter represent some of the most-creative efforts of the past decade to investigate parent-child interaction within the developing family system.

When fathers were added to the classical mother-child developmental paradigms, daddies appeared (to paraphrase Clarke-Stewart) to make more than just three—they added an entirely new dimension to observation and outcome. Now, the narrowness and the shallowness of the scope of our previous research methods have become woefully obvious. We are forced to acknowledge that the isolated two-dimensional study of infant and one parent (invariably the mother) is as accurate a representation of actual human affective and cognitive development as a flat-surfaced picture of the solar system is reflective of the power of the heat of the sun.

The realities of the so-called second-order, or indirect/mediated, effects are a major consequence of this deeper and wider view of the entire family system. Fathers as well as mothers are clearly salient figures of attachment for their children, from birth onward. In their roles as husbands and wives, parents also represent a significant marital family subsystem, with indirect effects upon their own functioning as parents as well as direct influences upon their children's developing attitudes, behavior, and personalities. In turn, children may reciprocally influence their parents' marital satisfaction and thereby indirectly influence their own parenting environment! The implications are awesome and demand the type of sophisticated behavioral analyses and methodological creativity that many of the research groups described in this chapter bring to their studies.

The phenomena of bidirectionality of effects between parents and children, the reciprocity of the spousal/parental functions, and the mounting evidence of indirect (second-order) influences point us in several new directions. First, studies that claim to describe actual children or actual parenting must acknowledge the reality and importance of the three-way or greater family system. Data collection cannot rest with measures of attitudes concerning parent-child interactions. Data analyses may need to move beyond more classical linear models, encompassing new techniques to capture the geometrical expansion of knowledge.

Yet, in the midst of all these dynamic new approaches, the majority of the studies also show that the similarities between parents of both sexes far outnumber any significant differences. And though fathers show on demand, many *potential* competencies with their children, most fall far short of these expectations in real child care in the *actual* setting of the home.

Turning now to several important and often-repeated sets of findings: Although a large number of family interaction studies report few or no differences in child behavior by the gender of the child, an increasing number of studies have found differential effects of parent-child interactions depending upon the gender of the parent and, most complexly, the gender matching between parent and child. A summary of these effects would include nearly every study we have described. A few general points can be made. Mothers and fathers tend to be similar in their dyadic interactions with young children, although some differences in language and in style of play do appear consistently. In three-person groups, more differences appear. As we have noted, the changes in parent-child interactions from the dyad to the triad are particularly important because many American fathers spend a large proportion of the time with their young children in groups of three (or more) persons.

Virtually all of the studies that have data to examine parent and child gender interactions find them. Many studies show what appears to be a greater affinity, or comfort, between like-sexed pairs. In areas related to cultural sex typing—such as achievement, assertiveness, and emotionality—mothers and fathers tend to respond differently to girls and boys, with fathers generally fostering what appears to be more stereotypically sex-typed behaviors in their young children. When birth order is added to gender of parent and child, the interaction effects increase geometrically.

Despite the richness and sophistication of so many of the studies we described, few family interaction researchers have yet dealt explicitly with the importance of birth order. Some have mixed firstborn and later-born children, with no effort at separate analyses; many more have samples of families with their firstborns only. In a number of projects, the description of the sample leaves the question of birth order unclear.

Of the studies that have focused on birth order differences, only Grossman and her colleagues have emphasized this dimension as a central characteristic powerfully influencing the interactions between parents and children. Some of the repeated findings from this literature are that parents spend substantially less time with later-borns compared to firstborn children and have a more-directive, controlling style with them. There is some evidence that maternal characteristics that support an optimal context for development of a firstborn have very different effects for a later-born, possibly by means of the effect of the mother's behavior on the father's parenting.

The family surround of later-born children in middle-class American families is substantially different from the ecological niche of firstborns, not the least because of the largely unstudied relationship of the older siblings with the younger. Adequate understanding of development will have to acknowledge that many children are not firstborns, and the factors affecting later-borns' development may well be significantly different.

The studies in this chapter may force us to rethink many of our clinical models of psychopathology as well as our model for therapeutic intervention. Certainly, we must have renewed respect for family therapy as a *primary* modality for emotional change in our patients or clients. Yet, we believe that there are even more far-reaching repercussions for psychodynamic theories of development and illness, as well as consequences for individual modes of psychotherapy.

The accumulating research data contradict the classical clinical view that unresolved symbiosis with the mother in childhood is a primary cause of severe adult psychopathology. Fathers play an important role in the healthy development of even very young children, a fact still unrecognized in many consulting rooms. And normal development does not move in a single line from symbiosis to autonomy. Healthy infants, as healthy adults, have a capacity and a need for both connection and separateness. Approaches to therapy—both individual and family—need to acknowledge the significance of people's *connectedness* as well as their *autonomy*.

REFERENCES

Ainsworth, M. D. S., & Bell, S. M. Some contemporary patterns of mother-infant interaction in the feeding situation. In A. Ambrose (Ed.), *Stimulation in early infancy*. New York: Academic Press, 1969.

Ainsworth, M. D. S., Bell, S. H., & Stayton, J. J. Individual differences in strange situation behavior of one-year-olds. In H. R. Schaffer (Ed.), *The origins of human social relations*. New York: Academic Press, 1971.

Atwood, G. E., & Stolorow, R. D. Psychoanalytic concepts and the representational world. *Psychoanalysis and contemporary thought*, 1980, *3*(1), 267–290.

Balser, R. B. *Parental empathy*. Unpublished doctoral dissertation, New York University, 1980.

Ban, P., & Lewis, M. Mothers and fathers, girls and boys: Attachment behavior in the one-year-old. *Merrill-Palmer Quarterly*, 1974, *20*, 195–204.

Baskett, L. M., & Johnson, S. M. The young child's interactions with parents versus siblings: A behavioral analysis. *Child Development*, 1982, *53*, 643–650.

Bell, R. Q. & Harper, L. V. (Eds.) *Child Effects on Adults*. Lincoln, Nebraska: University of Nebraska Press, 1977.

Bell, C. S., Johnson, J. E., McGillicuddy-DeLisi, A. & Siegel, I. E. The effect of family constellation and child gender on parental use of evaluative feedback. *Child Development*, 1981, *52*, 701–704.

Belsky, J. Mother-father-infant interaction in a naturalistic observational study. *Developmental Psychology*, 1979, *15*, 601–607.

Belsky, J. A family analysis of parental influence on infant exploratory competence. In F. A. Pedersen (Ed.), *The father-infant relationship: Observational studies in a family setting*. New York: Praeger Publishers, 1980.

Belsky, J. Early human experiences: a family perspective. *Developmental Psychology*, 1981, *17*(1), 3–23.

Belsky, J., Gilstrap, B., & Rovine, M. The Pennsylvania Infant and Family Development Project, I: Stability and change in mother-infant and father-infant interaction in a family setting at one, three, and nine months. *Child Development*, 1984, *55*(3), 692–705.

Belsky, J., Spanier, G., & Rovine, M. Stability and change in marriage across the transition to parenthood. *Journal of Marriage and the Family*, 1983, *45*, 553–566.

Bowlby, J. *Attachment and loss* (Vol. 2). New York: Basic Books, 1969.

Brazelton, T. B., Koslowski, B., & Main, M. The origins of reciprocity: The early mother-infant interaction. In M. Lewis and L. A. Rosenblum (Eds.), *The effect of the infant on its caregiver*. New York: John Wiley & Sons, 1974.

Brazelton, T. B., Yogman, M. W., Als, H., & Tronick, E. The infant as a focus for family reciprocity. In M. Lewis & L. A. Rosenblum (Eds.), *The child and its family: The genesis of behavior* (Vol. 2). New York: Plenum Press, 1979.

Brody, G. H., Stoneman, Z., & Sanders, A. K. The effect of television viewing on family interactions: An observational study. *Family Relations: Journal of Applied Family and Child Studies*, 1980, *29*, 216–220.

Bronfenbrenner, U. Developmental research, public policy and the ecology of childhood. *Child Development*, 1974, *45*, 1–5.

Bronfenbrenner, U. *The ecology of human development*. Cambridge, Mass.: Harvard University Press, 1979.

Brooks-Gunn, J., & Lewis, M. Why mama and papa? The development of social labels. *Child Development*, 1979, *50*, 1203–1206.

Clarke-Stewart, K. A. And daddy makes three: The father's impact on the mother and young child. *Child Development*, 1978, *49*, 466–478.

Clarke-Stewart, K. A. The father's contribution to children's cognitive and social development in early childhood. In F. A. Pedersen (Ed.), *The father-infant relationship: Observational studies in a family setting*. New York: Praeger Publishers, 1980.

Cohen, L. T., & Campos, J. J. Father, mother and stranger as elicitors of attachment behaviors in infancy. *Developmental Psychology*, 1974, *10*, 146–154.

Fagot, B. I. Sex differences in toddlers' behavior and parental reaction. *Developmental Psychology*, 1974, *10*, 554–558.

Fedele, N. *The developing parent: life span development and dimensions of parenting*. Unpublished doctoral dissertation, Boston University, 1983.

Feiring, C., & Lewis, M. The child as a member of the family system. *Behavioral Science*, 1978, *23*, 225–233.

Feldman, S. S., & Ingham, M. Attachment behavior: A validation study in two age groups. *Child Development*, 1975, *46*, 319–330.

Field, T. Interaction behaviors of primary versus secondary caretaker fathers. *Developmental Psychology*, 1978, *14*, 183–184.

Field, T. Fathers' interactions with their high-risk infants. *Infant Mental Health Journal,* 1981, *2,* 249–256.

Gleason, J. B., & Greif, E. B. Men's speech to young children. In B. Thorne, N. Henley, & C. Kramerae (Eds.), *Language and sex: Difference and dominance.* Royley, Mass.: Newbury House, 1981.

Golding, E. R. Affective development in five year old children. Unpublished doctoral dissertation, Boston University, 1983.

Golinkoff, R. M., & Ames, G. J. A comparison of fathers' and mothers' speech with their young children. *Child Development,* 1979, *50*(1), 28–32.

Grief, E. B. *Parent-child conversations.* Paper presented at the meeting of the American Psychological Association, Montreal, September 1980. (a)

Greif, E. B. Sex differences in parent-child conversation. *Women's Studies International Quarterly,* 1980, *3,* 253–258. (b)

Greif, E. B., Alvarez, M., & Ullman, K. *Recognizing emotions in other people: Sex differences in socialization.* Paper presented at the Society for Research in Child Development, Boston, April 1981.

Greif, R. B., & Gleason, J. B. Hi, thanks and goodbye: More routine information. *Language in Society,* 1980, *9,* 159–166.

Grossman, F. K. *Fathers and toddlers: Predicting the quality and quantity of fathering.* Unpublished manuscript, 1981. (a)

Grossman, F. K. *A longitudinal focus on fathers: Predicting toddler adaptation.* Paper presented at the Society for Research in Child Development, Boston, April 1981. (b)

Grossman, F. K. *A look at two and five year olds: Longitudinal predictions from pregnancy.* Paper presented at the Society for Research in Child Development, Detroit, April 1983.

Grossman, F. K., Eichler, L. S., Winickoff, S. A., with Anzalone, M. K., Gofseyeff, M. H., & Sargent, S. P. *Pregnancy, Birth and parenthood.* San Francisco: Jossey-Bass, 1980.

Grossman, F. K., Winickoff, S. A., & Eichler, L. S. *Psychological sequelae to caesarean delivery.* Paper presented at the International Conference on Infants. New Haven, Conn., April 1980

Hoffman, M. L. Empathy, its development and prosocial implications. *Nebraska Symposium on Motivation.* Lincoln: University of Nebraska Press, 1977.

Jacob, I. Patterns of family conflict and dominance as a function of child age and social class. *Developmental Psychology,* 1974, *10,* 1–12.

Jacob, T. Family interaction in disturbed and normal families: A methodological and substantive review. *Psychological Bulletin,* 1975, *82*(1), 33–65.

Kantor, D., & Lehr, W. *Inside the family.* San Francisco: Jossey-Bass, 1975.

Kauffman, C. *Control as an aspect of family process.* Paper presented at the meeting of the Massachusetts Psychological Association, Boston, June 1982.

Kauffman, C. Mothers' and fathers' control speech to their five year old boys and girls. Paper presented at the Society for Research in Child Development, Detroit, April 1983.

Kessen, W. The American child and other cultural inventions. *American Psychologist,* 1979, *34*(10), 815–820.

Klein, G. S. *Psychoanalytic theory—an exploration of essentials.* New York: International Universities Press, 1976.

Kohut, H. *The analysis of the self.* New York: International Universities Press, 1971.

Kohut, H. *The restoration of the self.* New York: International Universities Press, 1977.

Kotelchuck, M. *The nature of the infant's tie to his father.* Paper presented at Society for Research in Child Development, Philadelphia, April 1973.

Kotelchuck, M. The infant's relationship to the father: Experimental evidence. In M. E. Lamb (Ed.), *The role of the father in child development.* New York: John Wiley & Sons, 1976.

Lamb, M. E. Effects of stress and cohort on mother- and father-infant interaction. *Developmental Psychology,* 1976, *12,* 453–443. (a)

Lamb, M. E. Interactions between eight-month-old children and their fathers and mothers. In M. E. Lamb (Ed.), *The role of the father in child development.* New York: John Wiley & Sons, 1976. (b)

Lamb, M. E. Interactions between two year olds and their mothers and fathers. *Psychological Report,* 1976, *38,* 347–350. (c)

Lamb, M. E. The role of the father. In M. E. Lamb (Ed.), *The role of the father in child development.* New York: John Wiley & Sons, 1976. (d)

Lamb, M. E. *The role of the father in child development.* New York: John Wiley & Sons, 1976. (e)

Lamb, M. E. Twelve-month-olds and their parents: Interaction in a laboratory playroom. *Developmental Psychology,* 1976, *12,* 237–244. (f)

Lamb, M. E. The development of mother-infant and father-infant attachment in the second year of life. *Developmental Psychology,* 1977, *13,* 637–648. (a)

Lamb, M. E. The development of parental preferences in the first two years of life. *Sex Roles: A Journal of Research,* 1977, *3*(5), 495–497. (b)

Lamb, M. E. Father-infant and mother-infant interaction in the first year of life. *Child Development,* 1977, *48,* 167–181. (c)

Lamb, M. E. A re-examination of the infant's social world. *Human Development,* 1977, *20,* 65–85. (d)

Lamb, M. E. Infant social cognitive and "second order" effects. *Infant Behavior and Development,* 1978, *1,* 1–10. (a)

Lamb, M. E. Influence of the child on marital quality and family interaction during the prenatal, perinatal and infancy periods. In M. Lerner & G. B. Spanier (Eds.), *Child influences on marital and family interaction: A life span perspective.* New York: Academic Press, 1978. (b)

Lamb, M. E. Qualitative aspects of mother and father infant attachments. *Infant Behavior and Development,* 1978, *1,* 265–275. (c)

Lamb, M. E. The development of parent-infant attachments in the first two years of life. In F. A. Pedersen (Ed.), *The father-infant relationship: Observational studies in the family setting.* New York: Praeger Publishers, 1980.

Lamb, M. E. The development of father-infant relationships. In M. E. Lamb (Ed.), *The role of the father in child development* (2d ed.). New York: John Wiley & Sons, 1981. (a)

Lamb, M. E. Father and child development: An integrative overview. In M. E. Lamb (Ed.), *The role of the father in child development (2d ed.). New York: John Wiley & Sons, 1981. (b)*

Lamb, M. E., Chase-Lansdale, L., & Owen, M. T. The changing American family and its implications for infant social development: The sample case of maternal employment. In M. Lewis & L. Rosenblum (Eds.), *The child and its family,* New York: Plenum Press, 1979.

Lamb, M. E., Frodi, A. M., Frodi, M., & Hwang, C–P. Characteristics of maternal and paternal behavior in traditional and nontraditional Swedish families. *International Journal of Behavioral Development,* 1982, *5,* 131–141.

Lamb, M. E., Frodi, A. M., Hwang, C–P, Frodi, M., & Steinberg, J. Effect of gender and caretaking role on parent-infant interaction. In R. N. Emde & R. J. Harmon (Eds.), *The development of attachment and affiliative systems.* New York: Plenum Press, 1982. (a)

Lamb, M. E., Frodi, A. M., Hwang, C–P, Frodi, M., & Steinberg, J. Mother- and father-infant interaction involving play and holding in traditional and nontraditional Swedish families. *Developmental Psychology,* 1982, *18,* 215–221. (b)

Lester, B. M., Kotelchuck, M., Spelke, E., Sellers, J. J., & Klein, R. E. Separation protest in Guatamalan infants: Cross-cultural and cognitive findings. *Developmental Psychology,* 1974, *10,* 79–85.

Lewis, M., & Feiring, C. The child's social network: Social object, social function and their relationships. In M. Lewis & L. Rosenblum (Eds.), *The child and its family: The genesis of behavior* (Vol. 2). New York: Plenum Press, 1979.

Lewis, M., & Feiring, C. Some American families at dinner. In L. Laosa & I. E. Siegel (Eds.), *Families as learning environments for their children.* New York: Plenum Press, 1982.

Lewis, M., Feiring, C., & Weinraub, M. The father as a member of the child's social network. In M. E. Lamb (Ed.), *The role of the father in child development* (2d ed.). New York: John Wiley & Sons, 1981.

Lewis, M., & Rosenblum, L. (Eds.). *The child and its family.* New York: Plenum Press, 1979.

Lewis, M., & Weinraub, M. The father's role in the child's social network. In M. E. Lamb (Ed.), *The role of the father in child development.* New York: John Wiley & Sons, 1976.

Loeb, R. C. Concomitants of boys' locus of control examined in parent-child interactions. *Developmental Psychology,* 1975, *11*(3), 353–358.

Loeb, R. C., Horst, L., & Horton, P. J. Family interaction patterns associated with self-esteem in preadolescent girls and boys. *Merrill-Palmer Quarterly,* 1980, *26*(3), 205–219.

Lytton, H. *Parent-child interaction: The socialization process observed in twin and singleton families.* New York: Plenum Press, 1980.

Mahler, M. S. *On human symbiosis and the vicissitudes of individuation.* New York: International Universities Press, 1968.

Main, M., & Weston, D. R. The quality of the toddler's relationship to mother and to father: Related to conflict behavior and the readiness to establish new relationships. *Child Development,* 1981, *52,* 932–940.

Margolin, G., & Patterson, G. Differential consequences provided by mothers and fathers for their sons and daughters. *Developmental Psychology,* 1975, *11,* 537–538.

Martin, J. A. A longitudinal study of the consequences of early mother-infant interaction: A microanalytic approach. *Monographs of the Society for Research in Child Development,* 1981, *46*(3), (Serial No. 190).

Masur, E. F., & Gleason, J. B. Parent-child interaction and the acquisition of lexical information during play. *Developmental Psychology,* 1980, *16,* 440–409.

McLaughlin, B., Schutz, C., & White, D. Parental speech to five-year-old children in a game-playing situation. *Child Development,* 1980, *51,* 580–582.

Michael, R. G. *Family distance regulation modes and styles: Implications for adaptation.* Unpublished doctoral dissertation, Boston University, 1980.

Parke, R. D. Perspectives on father-infant interaction. In J. D. Osofsky (Ed.), *Handbook of infant development.* New York: John Wiley & Sons, 1979.

Parke, R. D., & O'Leary, S. E. Father-mother-infant interaction in the newborn period: Some findings, some observations and some unsolved issues. In L. Riegal & J. Menacham (Eds.), *The developing individual in a changing world.* The Hague: Mouton, 1976.

Parke, R. D., O'Leary, S. E., & West, S. Mother-father-newborn interaction: Effects of maternal medication, labor and sex of infant. *Proceedings of the American Psychological Association,* 1972, 85–86.

Parke, R. D., & Sawin, S. E. Perspectives on father-infant interactions. *Family Coordinator,* 1976, *25*(4), 365–371.

Parke, R. D., & Sawin, S. E. The family in early infancy: Social interactional and attitudinal analyses. In F. A. Pedersen (Ed.), *The father-infant relationship: Observational studies in the family setting.* New York: Praeger Publishers, 1980.

Parke, R. D., & Tinsley, B. R. The father's role in infancy: Determinants of involvement in caregiving and play. In M. E. Lamb (Ed.), *The role of the father in child development* (2d ed.). New York: John Wiley & Sons, 1981.

Patterson, G. R. *Families: Applications of social learning to family life.* Champaign, Ill.: Research Press, 1971.

Patterson, G. R. Mothers: The unacknowledged victims. *Monographs of the Society for Research in Child Development,* 1980, *45*(5).

Pedersen, F. A. Mother, father, and infant as an interactive system. Paper presented at the meeting of the American Psychological Association, Chicago, August 1975.

Pedersen, F. A. (Ed.). *The father-infant relationship: Observational studies in the family setting.* New York: Praeger Publishers, 1980.

Pedersen, F. A. Father influences viewed in a family context. In M. E. Lamb (Ed.), *The role of the father in child development* (2d ed.). New York: John Wiley & Sons, 1981.

Pedersen, F. A., Anderson, B. J., & Cain, R. L., Jr. Parent-infant and husband-wife interactions observed at age 5 months. In F. A. Pedersen (Ed.), *The father-infant relationship: Observational studies in the family setting.* New York: Praeger Publishers, 1980.

Pedersen, F. A., Cain, R. L., Jr., Zaslow, M. J., & Anderson, B. J. Variation in infant experience as associated with alternative family roles. In L. M. Laosa & I. E. Sigal (Eds.), *Families as Learning Environments for Children,* New York: Plenum Press, 1982, 203–221.

Pedersen, F. A., & Robson, K. S. Father participation in infancy. *American Journal of Orthopsychiatry,* 1969, *39,* 466–472.

Pedersen, F. A., Yarrow, L. J., Anderson, B. J., & Cain, R. L. Conceptualization of father influences in the infancy period. In M. Lewis & L. Rosenblum (Eds.), *The child and its family: The genesis of behavior* (Vol. 2). New York: Plenum Press, 1979.

Phillips, S. V. & Parke, R. D. Father and mother speech to prelanguage child. Unpublished manuscript, University of Illinois, 1981.

Pollack, W. S. *"I"ness and "We"ness: Parallel lines of development.* Unpublished doctoral dissertation, Boston University, 1982. (a)

Pollack, W. S. Family as process: Researching the system—a psychoanalytic perspective. Paper presented at the meeting of the Massachusetts Psychological Association, Boston, June, 1982. (b)

Power, T. G. Sex-typing in infancy: The role of the father. *Infant Mental Health Journal,* 1981, *2,* 226–240.

Reiss, D. *The family's construction of reality.* Cambridge, Mass.: Harvard University Press, 1981.

Riskin, J. M., & Faunce, E. E. An evaluative review of family interaction research. *Family Process,* 1972, *11*(4), 365–456.

Ross, G., Kagan, J., Zelazo, P., & Kotelchuck, M. Separation protest in infants in home and laboratory. *Developmental Psychology,* 1975, *11, 256*–257.

Rowe, D. C. Who controls parent-child interaction? (Review of *Parent-child interaction: The socialization process observed in twin and singleton families* by H. Lytton). *Contemporary Psychology,* 1981, *26*(10), 744–745.

Sawin, D. B., & Parke, R. D. Father's affectionate stimulation and caregiving behaviors with newborn infants. *Family Coordinator,* 1979, *28*(4), 509–513.

Spelke, E., Zelazo, P., Kagan, J., & Kotelchuck, M. Father interaction and separation protest. *Developmental Psychology,* 1973, *9,* 83–90.

Stechler, G., & Kaplan, S. The development of the self—a psychoanalytic perspective. *The Psychoanalytic Study of the Child,* 1980, *35,* 85–106.

Stoneman, Z., & Brody, G. H. Two's company, three makes a difference: An examination of mothers' and fathers' speech to their young children. *Child Development,* 1981, *52,* 705–707.

Stuckey, M. F., McGhee, P. E., & Bell, N. J. Parent-child interaction: The influence of maternal employment. *Developmental Psychology,* 1982, *18*(4), 635–644.

Tauber, M. A. Sex differences in parent-child interaction styles during a free play session. *Child Development,* 1979, *50*(4), 981–988.

Tronick, E., Als, H., & Brazelton, T. B. The structure of face to face interaction and its developmental sequence. Paper presented at the Society for Research in Child Development, New Orleans, March 1977.

Vandell, D. L. A microanalysis of toddlers' social interaction with mothers and fathers. *Journal of Genetic Psychology,* 1979, *134,* 299–312.

Varrin, P. H. The temperamental styles of child and parent in relation to early childhood adjustment. Unpublished doctoral dissertation, Boston University, 1979.

Vojdany-Noah, S. V. Patterns of parent-child interaction: The effects of parental anxiety and marital adjustment. Unpublished doctoral dissertation, Boston University, 1983.

Wahl, G., Johnson, S. M., Johansson, S., & Martin, S. An operant analysis of child-family interaction. *Behavioral Therapy,* 1974, *5,* 64–78.

Weinraub, M., & Frankel, J. Sex differences in parent-infant interaction during free play, departure, and separation. *Child Development,* 1977, *48,* 1240–1249.

Willemsen, E., Flaherty, D., Heaton, C., & Ritchey, G. Attachment behavior of one-year-olds as a function of mothers versus fathers, sex of child, session and toys. *Genetic Psychology Monographs,* 1974, *90,* 305–324.

Yogman, M. W. Games fathers and mothers play with their infants. *Infant Mental Health Journal,* 1981, *2*(4), 241–248.

Yogman, M. W., Dixon, S., Tronick, E., Adamson, I., Als, H., & Brazelton, T. B. Development of infant social interaction with fathers. Paper presented to Eastern Psychological Association, New York, 1976.

Yogman, M. W., Dixon, S., Tronick, E., Als, H., Adamson, I., Lester, B., & Brazelton, T. B. The goals and structure of face-to-face interaction between infants and fathers. Paper presented at society for Research in Child Development, New Orleans, March 1977.

Zussman, J. V. Situational determinants of parent behavior: Effects of competing cognitive activity. *Child Development,* 1980, *51,* 792–800.

Chapter 21

Teenage Parenting, Delayed Parenting, and Childlessness*

MARK W. ROOSA
HIRAM E. FITZGERALD
MARY CRAWFORD

INTRODUCTION

Originating in the 15th and 16th centuries, the modern concept of the family achieved institutional status by the 18th century (Aries, 1962). The Enlightenment philosopher Rousseau (1712–1778) described the family as the oldest of all societies and "the only one that is natural." Today, Rousseau's "natural" family is the traditional nuclear family, consisting of a married man and woman and their offspring (Murdock, 1960). Indeed, the Enlightenment helped to solidify the notion that the family's *raison d'être* was to bear and rear children. For example, Reiss's (1980) concept of the family system supposes that nuturance of the newborn is *the* crucial and central function of the family. If rearing of children is a natural (and obligatory) function of the "natural" family, then a childless "family" by definition is against nature. To be sure, stereotypes of childless married women in our culture include such attributions as selfishness, irresponsibility, immorality, unhappiness, and lack of femininity (Blake, 1979; Calhoun & Shelby, 1980). The chorus of women in Euripides' (484–406 B.C.) *Medea* speaks to a decisively minority audience in modern society:

> And amongst mortals I do assert that they who are wholly without experience and have never had children far surpass in happiness those who

* During preparation of this chapter, Hiram Fitzgerald was supported, in part, by a grant from the Spencer Foundation, and Mary Crawford was supported by NIMH Post-doctoral Fellowship T32 MH–14622–07.

are parents. The childless, because they have never proved whether children grow up to be a blessing or curse to men who are removed from all share in many troubles; whilst those who have a sweet race of children growing up in their houses do wear away, as I perceive, their whole life through; first with the thought how they may train them up in virtue, next how they shall leave their sons the means to live; and after all this 'tis far from clear whether on good or bad children they bestow their toil.

While the overwhelming majority of the U.S. population follows traditional pathways to family formation, significant numbers of people follow less-traditional pathways. This is especially true for teenage women, many of whom would be excluded from current definitions of the family despite the fact that teenage women account for almost 20 percent of all births in the United States. It is also true of couples who delay parenthood, voluntarily postponing childbearing until age 30 or older, many of whom eventually decide to remain childless. Other couples are unable to bear children, but desire a parenting role. Society provides several ways for such couples to fulfill their desire to parent, but what society does not always provide is a sense of being a family until the couple does have children to rear.

In this chapter, we will explore the processes and consequences, as far as they are known, for less-common modes of family formation: teenage parenting, delayed parenting, voluntary childlessness, and involuntary childlessness. Because the extant literature provides few examples of transactional research in the areas of concern, we present several heuristic models in an effort to stimulate investigators to adopt multivariate-systems approaches to research and to eschew univariate and bivariate approaches. Moreover, the very inclusion of this chapter in a handbook on family psychology challenges theoreticians to examine anew contemporary definitions of family.

EARLY CHILDBEARING: TEENAGE FAMILY FORMATION

Teenage family formation generally follows a different order of events than does nonteen family formation. For instance, 72 percent of the first births to teenage women in 1978 were premaritally conceived (Alan Guttmacher Institute, 1981). Although 26 percent of pregnant teenagers marry between conception and the birth of the child, almost half of the first births to teenagers in 1978 occurred out of wedlock. In fact, the increase in out-of-wedlock births to teenagers since 1960 is probably one major reason for increased public attention to early childbearing (Sklar & Berkov, 1981).

Researchers have given comparatively little attention to the study of teenagers who marry prior to conception, despite the fact that 28 percent of first births to teens are conceived after marriage (Alan Gutt-macher Institute, 1981). These couples generally receive parental and/or community support for their marriages (Aug & Bright, 1970; DeLissovoy, 1973). Other than their possible immaturity and higher divorce rate (Cromwell, 1974), there is little to differentiate these couples from older ones. Unfortunately, what little research exists in this area is confounded by a failure to clearly distinguish teen couples married prior to conception, teen couples married prior to birth, and either premaritally pregnant teens (DeLissovoy, 1973; Inselberg, 1961) or married older couples (see Aug & Bright, 1970).

Antecedents of teenage pregnancy

A significant aspect of the search for ways to reduce the rate of teenage pregnancy is a concerted effort to identify causal factors leading to conception during adolescence. With few exceptions, this research focuses on the individual teenage girl, looking for a flaw in personality or character that would explain the occurrence of a pregnancy. The underlying assumption of much of this research is that there must be a motivating factor, conscious or unconscious, that leads to teenage pregnancy (Furstenberg, 1976). However, the search for causes within the individual has not been very productive. In summarizing his detailed review of this literature, Quay (1981) notes that "few, if any differences can be demonstrated in either intelligence, personality, or psychopathology when unmarried pregnant girls are compared using appropriate methodologies to their nonpregnant peers. It appears that the more rigorous was the investigation, the fewer the differences which emerged" (pp. 88–89).

Several researchers have taken a somewhat broader and more-complex perspective on teenage pregnancy. Their research on the antecedents of adolescent pregnancy can be categorized into three topical areas: studies involving aspects of family structure, studies of the relationship of the adolescent couple, and studies of the relationship of the adolescent with her/his family.

Family structure. Although some investigators have not found causal relationships between family structure and teenage pregnancy (Burchinal, 1959) or between family conflict and age at first pregnancy (Uddenberg, 1976), the weight of the evidence suggests that these factors are related to teenage sexuality/teenage pregnancy. Hetherington (1972) notes that daughters in father-absent homes or in homes marked by marital conflict often have problems establishing intimate ties with men. Several studies link father absence or family conflict to the age at which daughters begin sexual activity (Akpom, Akpom,

& Davis, 1976; Hetherington; Kantner & Zelnik, 1973). Others report that the loss or threatened loss of a family member through divorce or separation is correlated with premarital teenage pregnancy (Babikian & Goldman, 1971; Coddington, 1979; Dame, Finck, Mayos, Reiner, & Smith, 1966; Kantner & Zelnik; LaBarre, 1980; Reiner & Edwards, 1974). Finally, data from the national longitudinal study of the labor market experiences of young women (Moore & Hofferth, 1978) suggest that being reared in an intact family has a direct, positive effect on the age of family formation.

Despite such documentation of the correlation between female teenagers' sexuality/probability of pregnancy and family structure, very little is known about the underlying causal factors mediating teenage sexuality and family structure. One possibility is that intact families may provide closer supervision of the teen than single parents can (Moore & Hofferth, 1978). If so, intact families may provide the resources and environmental support that encourage higher levels of educational attainment and indirectly discourage early sexual activity and/or pregnancy. Another possibility is that teenagers in single-parent families may be exposed to the sexual activity of that parent, thus legitimizing nonmarital sex (Fox, 1978; Hetherington, 1972). Verification of these possible causal chains and the mediating effect of the parent-adolescent relationship in either intact or broken homes awaits further systematic examination.

Adolescent males do not seem to be influenced in the same way as adolescent females by family structure or conflict. In fact, one of the few studies that focused on males involved in teenage pregnancies, reported that black teen fathers were more likely to come from large, intact families than from broken homes (Hendricks, 1980). Unfortunately, there are no obvious reasons to explain why adolescent males and females may be affected so differently by similar family structures. Certainly one suspects that different developmental needs and resources of teen males and females as well as the nature of parent-son versus parent-daughter relationships are involved. Furthermore, since not all teenage girls in broken or conflict-ridden homes become sexually active or pregnant at early ages, it is important to identify differences between the homes of girls who are affected and those who are not.

Relationship of the adolescent couple. Although there is general agreement that the one commonality among all pregnant teenagers is unprotected or inadequately protected coitus, very little research examines the nature of the relationship in which this sexual activity takes place. Apparently, teenage sexual intercourse and pregnancy are more likely to result from relatively long-term, stable relationships as opposed to promiscuous relationships (Cobliner, 1974; DeAmicis, Klerman, Hess, & McAnarney, 1981; Furstenberg, Gorid, & Markowitz, 1969). Furstenberg (1976) noted that "frequent dating over a long period of time is eventually accompanied by sexual activity, and few adolescents are able to remain sexually active for long before pregnancy occurs" (p. 42). Furthermore, many of these relationships continue throughout pregnancy and beyond, even if the couple does not marry in response to the pregnancy (Earls & Siegel, 1980; LaBarre, 1980; Panzarine & Elster, 1982; Presser, 1980). This suggests that there is a certain level of commitment to the relationship or to each other, as opposed to casual sexual activity (LaBarre).

A study by Jorgenson, King, and Torrey (1980) that focused on the relationship of the sexually active adolescent couple supports and broadens Furstenberg's analysis. For their sample of 147 adolescents attending family planning clinics, Jorgensen et al. reported that perceived mutual love in the relationship is positively related to sexual permissiveness. In fact, the nature of the couple's relationship was more strongly associated with risk for pregnancy than were peer or family relationships. Satisfaction with the relationship was found to be positively related to both the frequency of sexual intercourse and the regularity of effective contraceptive use. However, the relative power of the female in the dyadic relationships, especially with regard to sexual matters, was inversely correlated with the frequency of sexual intercourse. (It should be noted that Jorgenson et al. gathered their "couple" data from an exclusively female sample and that there is no indication as to what portion of the sample subsequently experienced a teenage pregnancy.)

Other data suggest that adolescent users of the contraceptive pill, compared with noncontraceptors, have longer relationships with their partners, engage in more frequent sexual intercourse, and are more trusting of their partners (Cvetkovich & Grote, 1981). Contraceptors also were older at the initiation of sexual intercourse, were more negative towards premarital pregnancy, and perceived the risks of unprotected intercourse as greater than did noncontraceptors. This same study reported that when the condom was used for contraception, sexually active women were more likely than noncontraceptors to discuss their sexual debut with the partner beforehand. Furthermore, compared to noncontraceptors, those protected by the condom were described as having better role-taking skills, more discussions with male friends about a variety of topics, and, incongruously, less-negative attitudes about becoming premaritally pregnant. Although these data were obtained from an all-female sample and the focus was upon the individual, again there is evidence that characteristics of the couple's relationship were related to the decision of whether or not to contracept and to the type of contraception to use.

Relationship with the family. Evidence suggests that parent-child communication about sex may play an important role in the child's developing sexuality (Fox, 1978; Furstenberg, 1971, 1976). After a thorough review of research concerning parent-child communication about sex, Fox concluded that relatively little communication about sex takes place in the home; when sex information is communicated, it almost always involves the mother-daughter dyad; and parental communication about sex, even if vague or incorrect, seems to be related to more-effective contraceptive practices. Fox also reports that the absence of a strong affiliative bond between mother and daughter is related to the age of initiating coitus, the level of sexual activity, and the probability of pregnancy. Apparently, by explicitly acknowledging the possibility that the daughter is sexually active, the mother allows her daughter to acknowledge her own sexuality and to take an important step toward assuming responsibility for her sexual activity. On the other hand, a disturbed mother-daughter relationship seems to interfere with the daughter's ability to integrate and use her knowledge of sexuality and contraception (Hertz, 1977).

The temporal nature of the couple's relationship is another important determinant of the family's influence on the couple's contraceptive experience. For example, Furstenberg (1971, 1976) reported that there was negligible family influence on contraceptive use in temporary relationships. The family was more influential in longer-term relationships.

Families also influence their daughters' sexual relationships through their attitudes regarding premarital or nonmarital sexual activity. In families that strongly condemn nonmarital sexual activity, it can be extremely difficult for mothers to admit the possibility of their daughters' sexuality. This may be especially true if the mother herself was pregnant as a teenager (Faigel, 1982). In such families, mothers are not likely to discuss sex at all (Fox, 1978). The path of least resistance for the daughter is to cooperate with the mother's unrealistic view. Thus, mother and daughter enter into an unspoken conspiracy in which they jointly refuse to acknowledge the daughter's sexual activity. In this climate, intercourse tends to be an unexpected, spontaneous event, and use of contraception by the daughter is unlikely. Both Furstenberg (1976) and Fox suggest that when attitudes toward nonmarital sexual activity are not as condemning, there is a greater likelihood of effective contraception.

Modeling within the family also plays a role in teenage pregnancy. Mothers of teenage mothers often began their own childbearing as teenagers (Furstenberg & Crawford, 1978). Furthermore, teenage pregnancy seems to be more common among girls whose sisters or other relatives were teenage mothers (Aug & Bright, 1970; Furstenberg & Crawford; Goldfarb, Mumford, Schum, Smith, Flowers, & Schum, 1977). Girls in such families probably have learned to think of teenage pregnancy as common, acceptable, and perhaps even expected. Furstenberg (1976) notes that the age of dating, and thus sexual activity, is often delayed if the girl has high educational goals (usually a function of family modeling and values). However, it is not known whether this is due to the behavior of the girl with boys, the type of boys selected as dates, or parental restrictions. Nor do we know if there is a similar process operating for adolescent males.

Summary

Although a vast literature exists detailing the sexual behavior and attitudes of individual adolescents, results of these studies have been inconclusive or contradictory with respect to antecedents of adolescent pregnancy. Conversely, research has been rare concerning the effects of family structure variables and interpersonal relationship variables on teenagers' sexual behavior and susceptibility to pregnancy. Nevertheless, it is precisely the latter research approach that is most promising for the generation of realistic and practical models of the determinants of adolescent pregnancy. Such transactional or systems models must recognize that the teenager's knowledge and attitudes about sexuality and sexual behavior are shaped and sustained by a variety of forces including those emanating from the family, peer group, local culture (ethnic community, neighborhood), general culture, and the dyadic teen relationship itself.

Some teenage couples delay sexual intercourse, and some sexually active couples use effective contraception. How are these couples different from their sexually active or noncontracepting peers? Recent research suggests that cognitive factors common to adolescent development—such as figurative thinking (reacting primarily to sensory input) (Cobliner, 1974), the imaginary audience (preparation for sexual intercourse is admitting to the world that one is sexually active), and the personal fable (pregnancy won't happen to me)—contribute to the ineffective use of contraception (Dembo & Lundell, 1979; LaBarre, 1980; Nadelson, Notman, & Gillon, 1980; Rogel, Zuehlke, Peterson, Tobin-Richards, & Shelton, 1980; Schinke, Blythe, & Gilchrist, 1981). However, we do not know how such individual cognitive factors manifest themselves in couples. What types of parent-child transactions structure individual cognitions and values with respect to sexual behavior? How do family process variables and cultural values influence adolescent sexual behavior? These are only a few questions that must be studied if the determinants of adolescent pregnancy are to be specified beyond simple descriptions of teenagers' attitudes and behaviors.

Research into the causes of teenage pregnancy has suffered from a variety of methodological problems, the most significant of which is reliance on univariate and bivariate causal models. A second major problem has been the near-exclusion of the male or the couple from these studies. As a result, research concerning the antecedents of teenage pregnancy has been dominated by the hypothesis that teen pregnancy is "caused" by a psychological flaw within the individual (female).

Greater emphasis must be given to specification of the various developmental pathways that lead to parenthood or nonparenthood during adolescence. Because so many variables may influence adolescent sexual behavior, we advocate application of causal modeling techniques (Asher, 1976) to explore reciprocal linkages among the variables contributing to teenage pregnancy. Insofar as the antecedents of adolescent pregnancy are concerned, current literature suggests that at least five sources of variance should be taken into account when developing structural causal models of teen pregnancy. These five sources, shown in Figure 1, are: family characteristics, individual characteristics, couple characteristics, teen peer group characteristics, and environmental characteristics.

Premarital teen pregnancy

Few teenage pregnancies are planned (Furstenberg, 1976). Therefore, how the couple and their families react to the pregnancy disclosure and how they approach decision making with respect to pregnancy outcome and marital status are important issues affecting teenage family formation.

Reactions to the pregnancy. The most-common responses to teenage pregnancy are astonishment and despair (Furstenberg, 1976; LaBarre, 1980; Smith, Nenny, Weinman, & Mumford, 1982). Although they perceived few negative social consequences associated with premarital teenage pregnancy (Smith, Weinman, & Mumford, 1982), by early in the pregnancy, most teen mothers became quite unhappy about the prospects of motherhood. More than half of Furstenberg's (1976) sample did not tell their parents about the pregnancy for several months; often they simply waited for their parents to discover the pregnancy for themselves. Upon learning of the pregnancy most parents were upset and felt disappointed, hurt, and angry.

Nevertheless, most teens and their families gradually accept the inevitable reality of the impending birth and develop more-positive

Figure 1

Heuristic model for examining teenagers' transitions to parenthood

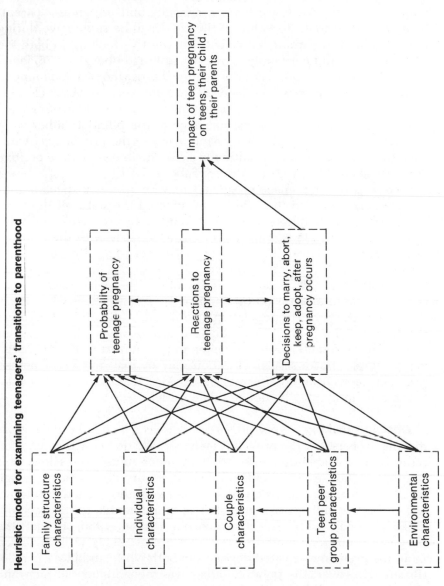

feelings about it (LaBarre, 1980). For example, Smith (1975) found that as the birth neared, prospective grandparents became active participants in the pregnancy and looked forward to the birth as a joyous event. Marital status plays an important role in structuring the pregnant teen's attitudes toward her pregnancy and impending parenthood. Knowing that the father of the child will be supportive during the pregnancy apparently contributes to positive feelings in both the pregnant teen and her family. However, in Furstenberg's (1976) longitudinal study of teen pregnancy, only those teens who married immediately after conception was verified (20 percent) were "unambivalently" positive about the prospect of becoming a parent. Even unmarried teens who anticipated eventual marriage to the putative father were more likely to develop positive feelings early in the pregnancy. Assurance that education can be continued also contributes to more positive attitudes about the pregnancy (Furstenberg, 1976).

One response to teenage pregnancy may be quite unexpected. Furstenberg (1976) found that pregnancy affected the status of the teenager within the family unit. In most families in his study, the status of the pregnant teen was elevated to near-equality with the status of her mother. Moreover, the level of social exchange often increased, resulting in an improved emotional climate in the family. However, this aspect of teen pregnancy must be interpreted with caution. Furstenberg's sample consisted predominately of individuals who closely resembled the poverty population as defined by the 1970 Bureau of the Census. Thus, status elevation to near-equality with the mother may be an extremely positive reaction in the context of Furstenberg's study sample, but a similar elevation may or may not occur among pregnant teens from other ecological settings, where the mother's status in the family may be defined differently.

Decision making.   Very little research has examined the decision-making processes of the pregnant teenager. We do know that abortion often is not a viable option, since many teens refuse to disclose their pregnancies for several months. When disclosure occurs early enough in the pregnancy, the pregnant teenager's mother and the putative father are the individuals most likely to be influential in the decision-making process with respect to abortion (Rosen, 1980). In fact, the pregnant teenager's mother is the person most likely to be involved in all the pregnancy-related decisions in both white and black families (Rosen). However, the putative father was more influential for white girls, but not for black girls, who chose to keep the baby. As Presser (1980) noted, when the putative father was involved in the decision-making process, he rarely encouraged abortion or adoption. Furstenberg (1976) reported that mothers were quite influential in the decision of whether or not to marry; however, the teenager's education level and aspirations along with her perception of the male's ability to support a family were also important considerations.

The means by which parental influence is communicated to the pregnant teenager has received some attention as well. Rosen, Benson, and Stack (1982) reported that indirect pressure (anticipation that resources may be used as a weapon) was most common among those who chose abortion, and indirect influence (parental modeling) was most common among those who chose to marry and keep the child. Direct pressure and direct influence, as defined by Rosen et al., either were used less often or were not clearly dominant in the decisions regarding abortion, adoption, keeping the child, and marrying.

The children of teenage parents

In a recent, thorough review of the literature, Roosa, Fitzgerald, and Carlson (1982c) noted that researchers have consistently reported that children of teenage mothers are more likely than other children to experience any of a variety of developmental problems. Although the authors reviewed strong evidence that the teenage mothers' socioeconomic status (SES) accounted for most of the reported developmental deficits, they found little information about possible specific causal mechanisms. Some of the variables that were identified as potentially related to the reported developmental deficits were the poor obstetric performance of teenage mothers, negative maternal attitudes of teenage mothers, less-stimulating home environments provided by teenage mothers, and the quality of child care provided by teenage mothers. However, as Roosa et al. (1982c) reported, most of the studies of teenage parenting attitudes and behavior had serious design flaws, such as relying on subjective evaluations and not using comparison groups.

Studies that have used more objective measurement instruments and appropriate control groups have yielded somewhat different results. In general, these studies have reported finding more similarities than differences between the parenting characteristics of teenage and older mothers (Roosa, Fitzgerald, & Carlson, 1982a; 1982b; Roosa & Vaughan, in press; Rothenberg & Varga, 1982). Based on theoretical relationships suggested from their review of the literature (Roosa et al., 1982c), Roosa and his colleagues constructed the research design shown in Figure 2 (Roosa et al., 1982a). The model posits two causal chains for examining the effects of maternal age on child development. Briefly, the model indicates that maternal age has an effect on prenatal preparation, behavioral status of the infant at birth, physical status of the infant at birth, maternal attitudes, and the quality of mother-infant interaction patterns. Similarly, SES is hypothesized to have an

Figure 2

Model for examining the effect of maternal age upon child development

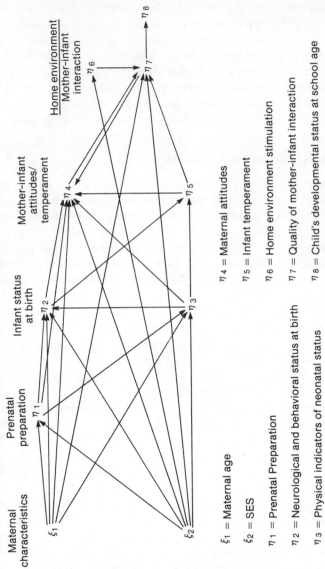

ξ_1 = Maternal age

ξ_2 = SES

η_1 = Prenatal Preparation

η_2 = Neurological and behavioral status at birth

η_3 = Physical indicators of neonatal status

η_4 = Maternal attitudes

η_5 = Infant temperament

η_6 = Home environment stimulation

η_7 = Quality of mother-infant interaction

η_8 = Child's developmental status at school age

Source: Roosa, M. W., Fitzgerald, H. E., and Carlson, N. A., "A Comparison of Teenage and Older Mothers: A Systems Analysis," *Journal of Marriage and the Family* 44 (1982), pp. 367–77.

effect upon the same variables as maternal age but, in addition, is thought to affect the quality of the home environment. Expected causal linkages among the remaining variables also are specified, including a reciprocal linkage between maternal attitudes and the quality of mother-infant interaction.

The model shown in Figure 2 was evaluated as a system of linear equations, using data obtained from a sample of 62 women (15 to 32 years old) and their firstborn infants. The two most important findings were that SES was the strongest influence upon each variable in the model and that the influence of maternal age consistently was in the opposite direction to that of SES. The fact that SES and maternal age had causal effects in opposite directions is discrepant with much of what has been reported about teenage parenting. The data suggest that the negative effects of adolescent childbearing upon child development are not due to maternal age, but instead can be attributed to the correlates of early childbearing. Such correlates include truncated education, limited job opportunities, and reduced earning power for the mother and her male companion.

Roosa et al. (1982a) suggest that discrepancies between extant theory and the results of their study can be attributed to the greater degree of complexity represented in their structural model in contrast to models used in previous research. For example, consider that in every case in which SES was a causal variable, Roosa et al. found that it had a larger impact than any other variable entered in the equation. If the effect of SES had been controlled methodologically, it would have distorted the causal realities of the variables analyzed. Thus, when bivariate analyses control for the effect of one or more variables, they risk distortion of the transactions that in fact are often the causes of behavior.

Other aspects of the structural analysis suggest that teenage mothers do provide less-optimal home environments, less verbal stimulation, and less contingent responsiveness to their infants than do older mothers (Roosa et al., 1982a). In addition, teen mothers may be less knowledgeable about child development and may have less positive attitudes toward their preschool children than do older mothers (Roosa & Vaughan, in press). Each of these differences could contribute to poorer care-giving, which (when interactive with low SES) would position children of teenage mothers on the at-risk side of the continuum of care-giving casualty (Sameroff & Chandler, 1975).

Summary

Interestingly enough, research into the various aspects of teenage family formation typically has not had a family focus. Instead, researchers have focused attention on individual characteristics, especially those of the pregnant teenage girl. Males involved in teenage pregnancies are regularly ignored, and the families of the involved couple tend to be treated as static entities. The dynamics of the interpersonal interactions surrounding teenage pregnancy have only begun to be examined. Furthermore, most research attention on teen pregnancy has been directed to the study of low-income, inner-city, black teens despite the fact that the majority of pregnant/parenting teenagers are white and all social classes are involved.

All available evidence suggests that teenagers, in general, probably have poorer parenting skills than older mothers. However, the methodological problems common to studies of teenage parenting, the choice of simple cause-effect research designs, and the circumstantial nature of other evidence presented (see Roosa et al., 1982c) suggest that we are a long way from an accurate description of teenage parenting in the United States. Study of the effects of teenage parenting on child development must progress beyond the descriptive and correlational approaches that have been favored in the past. Researchers need to develop complex, multivariate models that can take into account the independent and interactive causal linkages of the relevant variables. As indicated by the Roosa et al. (1982a) study, use of complex causal models is likely to produce a decidedly different and ultimately more realistic perspective on teen pregnancy and parenting than the more commonly used approaches.

DELAYED CHILDBEARING

Delayed childbearing refers to initiating childbearing after the normative age for such behavior. Although delayed childbearing is not a new phenomenon, it recently has received attention from the popular media, policymakers, and researchers for at least two reasons. First, the number of women or couples who are choosing this option to family formation is growing at an unprecedented rate (Alden, 1981; Daniels & Weingarten, 1982). Second, the pattern of delayed childbearing is changing as a growing number of women are combining successful professional careers with childbearing and childrearing (Alden; Daniels & Weingarten, 1982; Wilkie, 1981).

It is well established that there is an inverse relationship between education level or female employment and fertility (see Alden, 1981; Clifford & Tobin, 1977; Wilkie, 1981). As increasing numbers of women receive college degrees, there is an increasing trend toward smaller families (Alden). Moreover, as the quality and quantity of career options for women increase, more choose either to remain childless (voluntary childlessness) or to establish themselves in their chosen careers before beginning to have children (delayed childbearing). At least some career women may avoid the motherhood option or may postpone parenting, because their careers are intrinsically rewarding and/or because they have developed equality-based camaraderie with their husbands (Colman, 1978).

These trends become clear when we examine recent childbirth data. Women over 25 now account for over one third of first births in the United States (Wilkie, 1981). Nearly 50 percent of college-educated women between 25 and 29, as well as 17 percent of those 30 to 34, were childless in 1978 (Alden, 1981). For women with graduate training, over 60 percent between 25 and 29 were childless, as were 32 percent of those 30 to 34. Finally, in 1978, almost one fourth of all first births to female college graduates occurred between ages 30 and 40, compared to just 10 percent in 1970 (Alden; Wilkie). As these figures suggest, while there is an increase in childlessness among college-educated women, many are having children—although at later ages than in the past.

Decision making

Deciding to delay childbearing is probably a complex and difficult process. Such decision making involves the weighing of both spouses' values, backgrounds, and family situations (Alden, 1981). The wife's commitment to work (part-time or full-time) also is a factor. Additionally, Alden identifies several "triggers" of the desire to parent that may influence decision making. These triggers include: (1) myths and images of the obstetric problems of delayed childbearing that become particularly salient upon turning 30, (2) the norm of childbearing/childlessness and the age of childbearing among a couples' peers, (3) boredom with a career, (4) psychological readiness to guarantee the survival of one's genes, and (5) pressure from the husband or grandparents that increases with age. Although a logical case can be made for each of these triggers, the amount of empirical evidence to support them varies greatly. Moreover, we know little about the relative importance of any one of these factors or the interrelationships among them with respect to delayed childbearing.

In addition to suggesting triggers, Alden (1981) identified three types of women who may make the decision to delay childbearing. She labels these the *deliberates,* the *nondeliberates,* and the most-prevalent group, the *deliberators.* The deliberates are those who have consciously coordinated their professional and parenting careers. Women in this group have chosen to establish themselves in their careers and begin their advancement up the corporate ladder or to wait until their husbands reach certain career goals before beginning childbearing. Nondeliberates are those who delay because of unforeseen circumstances, not because of consciously made timing plans. Divorce, unplanned work-related separation, illness, death of a spouse, or unplanned late marriage makes it difficult or impossible for such couples to have children while in their 20s. Finally, deliberators are those who constantly agonize over the decision of how to combine children and a career. This group is less certain of their personal and professional goals. The decision to delay may, in fact, reflect an inability to decide; the decision to have children may be a reaction to "time running out." There are few clues as to the role of the husband in this decision process or as to the relative effect of the various triggers on each group.

Daniels and Weingarten (1980, 1982) referred to the strategy of those who purposely delay childbearing (Alden's deliberates) as programmatic postponement—the putting off of parenthood until personal and professional goals are reached. In contrast to Alden's findings, programmatic postponers (deliberates) were the largest group of delayers in Daniel's and Weingarten's study. Daniels and Weingarten identified three major and sometimes overlapping reasons for purposely delaying parenthood:

1. Psychological readiness: A delay is needed while individual and couple relationships are formed.
2. Intimacy: A delay is needed to find the right partner and create a strong marriage.
3. Career: A delay is needed to complete education programs, begin a career, and reach career goals for either or both spouses.

For delayers, according to Daniels and Weingarten:

> The decision to become parents frequently signals the end of a period of identity experimentation, a reflective and emotionally unthreatening distance from or identification with one's own parents, and a sanguine stance toward one's own childhood, all of which adds up to a readiness to risk taking responsibility for the childhood of one's own children. (1982, p. 65)

Delayed childbirth, marriage, and career

One reason many women give for delayed childbirth is their desire to establish themselves in their careers, to build a power base, so that their careers won't suffer from short maternity leaves (80 percent take less than three months) (Alden, 1981). However, upon becoming pregnant, many career women agonize over perceived conflicts between parenting and career.

Although research suggests that most couples experience a decline in marital satisfaction with the arrival of the first child, it is not known if this finding applies to delayers. Since couples who delay childbearing are often well set financially and more mature psychologically when the child arrives (Wilkie, 1981), they may be better able to handle the stresses associated with family formation than are other couples. Furthermore, because of the intimacy with which these older couples share the delivery and early postpartum experiences, positive changes in the marital relationships may occur, at least in the short run (Colman, 1978). On the other hand, delayers may have developed and experienced a particular lifestyle for so long that the addition of a child produces more stress into the marriage than is the case for younger couples. Although there is some evidence that the addition of the parent role does appear to complicate the life situation of delayers and make the pursuit of dual careers difficult (Daniels & Weingarten, 1982; Holahan & Gilbert, 1979), we can only speculate as to how marital happiness or satisfaction is affected. Rapoport and Rapoport (1971) did report that continuously working career women/mothers had lower levels of marital happiness than noncontinuous workers; however, the nature of their study did not permit them to determine whether marital happiness was a cause or an effect of the chosen lifestyle.

There is evidence to suggest that delayed childbirth occurs most often in highly egalitarian marriages with both spouses having high priorities for careers (Daniels & Weingarten, 1982; Holahan & Gilbert, 1979). In these families, the spouses tend to be very supportive of each other's career goals. Although they probably share in home management and child care to some extent, the bulk of the child-care tasks continue to fall to the wife regardless of work commitments (Alden, 1981).

Professional women may be uniquely qualified for handling the stress of the conflicting demands of a career and children. Holahan and Gilbert (1979) report that professional women are more likely than other women to have masculine or androgynous sex role identities. Thus, they may be more effective and efficient at managing multiple roles than are other women. Nevertheless, professional women do perceive more conflict between work and home maintenance than do men (Daniels & Weingarten, 1982; Holahan & Gilbert). This conflict may be exacerbated as childbearing leads them to reevaluate the importance of their careers and their willingness to put in the long hours needed for career success (Alden, 1981; Daniels & Weingarten, 1980, 1982).

With regard to child care, older mothers are reported to be more flexible and warmer (Mercer, Hackley, & Bostrom, 1982; Sears, Maccoby, & Levin, 1957) less likely to use physical punishment or ridicule, and more likely to use withdrawal of privileges for discipline than younger mothers (Sears et al.). Furthermore, older couples are more likely to agree on childrearing policies than younger couples. However, some of these behavior differences attributed to maternal age may be explained by the social-class differences between younger and older mothers. Additionally, there is disagreement as to whether older mothers derive more (Ragozin, Basham, Arnie, Greenberg, & Robinson, 1982) or less (Mercer et al.) satisfaction from parenting than do younger mothers.

There is very little direct evidence of the impact of delayed childbearing upon the children involved. Since delayed childbearers are generally middle class or upper middle class by virtue of both their income and education, one would expect that the developmental prognosis for their children would be good. However, the hours that delaying mothers spend away from home, combined with increased father participation in child care and with the age of the parents, raise some interesting questions regarding sex role development, long-term psychological development, and the development of social skills. Research in these areas is sorely needed.

Summary

There is growing evidence that delayed childbearing accompanied by full-time employment and career is an increasingly popular family formation choice. Although a relatively new field of study, delayed childbearing apparently has received considerable attention from those interested in the demographic and economic consequences of this choice. Unfortunately, researchers have not been as quick to examine the consequences of this option on marital happiness, family interaction, and child development. Much of the extant research on delayed parenting has been exploratory in nature, using small samples and open-ended interviews. Furthermore, what research there is on these topics tends to focus on either dual-career couples of any age or delayed childbearers who leave the labor force during childbearing and initial childrearing. Delayers in dual-career families who are continuously employed would appear to be an important group for further study, and they may be quite different from younger dual-career couples or other delayers. Finally, more information is needed regarding the husband's role in deciding to delay, in eventually deciding to have children, and in the dynamics of dual parenting among delayers.

Figure 3 contains a model that summarizes or extends many of the relationships discussed above. To date, much of the literature on delayed childbearing has been descriptive or speculative. To be sure that we understand this phenomenon and that our results are applicable to a variety of groups, we must eventually move toward larger samples and more-stringent analyses. Models such as the one in Figure 3 would allow the testing of the findings and speculations of the pioneering studies in this area.

VOLUNTARY CHILDLESSNESS

Couples who choose to remain childless elect a family style that not only is nontraditional but also is likely to be viewed as deviant. In contrast to cultural stereotypes, however, voluntarily childless couples seem to have fewer health problems, happier and more-equalitarian marriages, higher educational attainment, and stronger career orientations than do couples with children (Chester, 1972; Houseknecht, 1979a). Although the desire for children was nearly universal among American women in 1960 (Westoff & Westoff, 1968), more-recent studies suggest that the desire for children is less pervasive (Hastings & Robinson, 1974; Poston & Gotard, 1977), at least among white women less than 30 years of age (Grindstaff, 1976; G. Shapiro, 1980). Using a path analysis of childlessness rates from 1940 to 1974, DeJong and Sell (1973, 1978) identified three factors that account for 69 percent of the cohort change in childlessness: age of first marriage, change in student status, and change in the labor force. Thus, as the average age of first marriage increases, educational attainment increases, and women find a more receptive labor market, the likelihood of voluntary childlessness increases.

Definitions of voluntary childlessness vary but tend to include a decision not to have children, the use of contraception to prevent pregnancy or abortion to terminate pregnancy, the absence of physical problems that would prevent pregnancy, and no interest in adoption (Pohlman, 1970; Poston, 1976). Houseknecht (1979b) distinguishes two pathways to voluntary childlessness. The first begins early in life, before marriage (early articulators). The second occurs after marriage, when women choose a lifestyle that precludes children (postponers). In a retrospective study of early articulators and postponers, Houseknecht tested a social psychological model of voluntary childlessness and the prediction that three factors account for the major proportion of variance associated with voluntary childlessness: family background, self-other attitudes, and reference groups. Early articulators reported greater psychological distance from their parents, less family warmth, more achievement demands, less parental authority, and less encouragement for assertive autonomy during adolescence than did postponers. The two groups differed little in their use of reference groups, although postponers tended to consult more reference groups when making their decision to remain voluntarily childless. The fact that

Figure 3

Heuristic model for examining delayers' transition to parenthood or nonparenthood

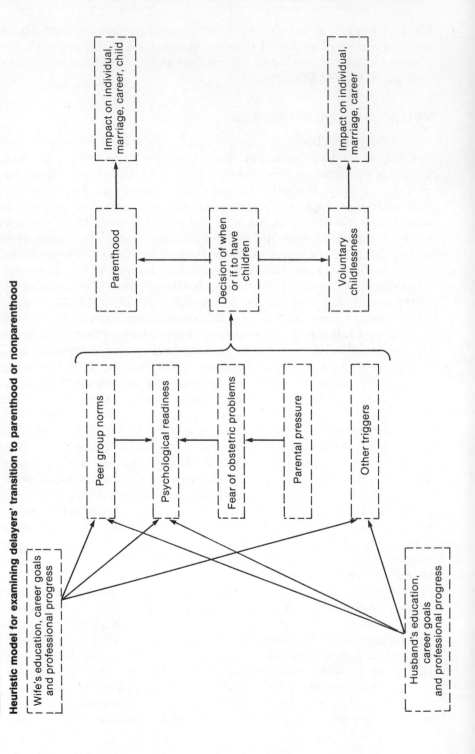

significantly more early articulators (74 percent) than postponers (31 percent) were voluntarily sterilized suggested a stronger commitment to childlessness on their part.

Veevers (1973) has described a four-step process characterizing the transition from delayed parenthood to postponer to nonchildbearer: The childless couple first decides to postpone childbearing for some fixed period of time (delay). As delayed parenthood continues, the time for childbearing becomes less definitive (postponers). The couple now begins to consider the possibility of remaining childless, and finally arrives at the conclusion that they will not have children (nonchild-bearer). During the first three to four years of marriage, external pressures on the couple to become parents are greatest. After five or six years, however, other family members slacken pressure or give up completely as they begin to realize that the couple is not going to procreate or adopt children.

As previously noted, the general public views childlessness from the perspective of a strong negative stereotype (Veevers, 1975). Childless husbands are perceived to have higher psychological disturbance than are fathers (Calhoun & Shelby, 1980). Peterson (1980) found that college students who intended to remain childless scored high in psychopathology as measured by the MMPI. Conversely, the same students also tended to be bright, achievement oriented, and academically successful. Students perceive both voluntarily childless men and women negatively, but childless men are rated even less favorably than are childless women (Jamison, Franzini, & Kaplan, 1979). On the other hand, ethnographic comparisons suggest that women are blamed for childlessness in an overwhelming number of societies (Rosenblatt, Peterson, Portner, Cleveland, Mykkanen, Foster, Holm, Joel, Reisch, Kreuscher, & Phillips, 1973). Silka and Kiesler (1977) reported that the decision to remain childless appears to be made jointly in most cases. However, when childlessness was not jointly determined, it was more likely to be the wife's decision. Interestingly enough, nearly half of the husbands volunteered that they would change their minds about having children if their wives so desired. It is conceivable, therefore, that negative attributions about childless fathers are in part tied to beliefs that men should be assertive in dictating the couple's decision regarding childbearing. This suggests that culturally determined stereotypes about masculinity may bias perceptions about the psychological stability of childless fathers.

Pronatalism certainly is the mainstream view in American society. Blake's (1979) multivariate analysis of survey data from 1,600 respondents indicated that people who are more pronatalist tend to be less educated, older, male, Catholic or Jewish, believers in God, and more strongly committed to social striving than are those who are less pronatalist. The strongest predictors for pronatalism were gender, education, and marital status. Members of the National Organization of Non-Parents report that the most frequent pronatalist arguments to which they are exposed focus on issues related to personal selfishness (52 percent), unhappiness in old age (no grandchildren) (47 percent), responsibilities to one's country (to bear children) (35 percent), and fulfillment as a man or woman (30 percent) (Barnett & MacDonald, 1976). Only a handful of voluntarily childless couples' parents approved of their decision not to have children.

While no current theory can account for such strong pronatalist views and such negative perceptions of voluntarily childless couples, certainly there is a pervasive assumption that childlessness is somehow contrary to nature. Recall Reiss's (1980) assertion that the family's primary function is to provide for the nurturance of the newborn. What evidence exists to support this procreative-instinct theory? Apparently, very little. Veenhoven (1974) found no support for any hypothesis derived from procreative-instinct theory. Parents and nonparents did not differ in happiness, incidence of psychosomatic complaints, physical health, doubts about the meaning of life, or concerns about the quality of their future. Respondents who were pregnant when participating in the study were, in fact, less happy than nonpregnant married female respondents.

Given such strong social and parental pressures to bear children, why do couples elect childlessness? There is no simple answer to this question. Reasons for childlessness include: concerns about population control, just do not want children, health (of wife), career time commitments, interference with marital relationship, too old to begin family, restriction of personal independence, dislike of children, responsibilities of childrearing, economic costs, fear of pregnancy, and world conditions (Barnett & MacDonald, 1976; Baurn & Cope, 1980; Gustavus & Henley, 1971; Silka & Kiesler, 1977).

Voluntarily childless couples do seem to have stronger interpersonal relationships than do parents. For example, childless couples tend to talk more about work, health, feelings, mutual friends, politics, and sexual relations, whereas parents tend to talk more about children (Feldman, 1981). Indeed, studies comparing parent communication styles with and without children present find that child presence suppresses parent communication (Rosenblatt et al., 1973). Childless couples also score higher in cohesiveness on such issues as leisure time interests, household tasks, and career decisions (Houseknecht, 1979a). In short, childless couples tend to have happier marriages than do couples with children. Within childless-couple samples, the happiest marriages are those in which the wife is neither a mother nor working outside the home. Moreover, there appears to be little empirical support for popular notions that childlessness is related to marital instability and divorce (Chester, 1972). In fact, divorce statistics suggest that divorcees have higher fertility rates than nondivorcees (Gibson, 1980).

Summary

Voluntary childlessness is a type of family formation chosen by about 4 percent of married couples. Although studies of voluntary childlessness do tend to use multivariate analyses, they generally involve population demographics and surveys. Relatively few studies have been directed to questions related to developmental precursors of voluntary childlessness. Nevertheless, the proclivity of researchers to use path models establishes a strong base for generation of causal systems models which, if added to prospective designs, would probably make study of voluntary childlessness exemplary in the area of family formation. In any event, the extant literature—as opposed to the extant stereotype—suggests that voluntarily childless couples differ little from couples with children with respect to family stability, family harmony, and family health. Where differences do occur, they tend to reflect positively on the voluntarily childless couple.

Regardless of whether one is an early articulator or a postponer, it is the case that many childless couples eventually decide to parent, either by bearing or by adopting children. It is also the case that many childless couples are so because of their inability to bear children. It is to these two forms of childlessness that we now turn as we consider issues of infertility and adoption.

INVOLUNTARY CHILDLESSNESS

Infertility

Infertility, defined as the inability to conceive a pregnancy after a year or more of regular sexual relations, affects about 15 percent of all married couples in their childbearing years (Houghton, 1977; C. H. Shapiro, 1982; Zimmerman, 1982). In 10 to 40 percent of infertile couples, male factors are responsible (C. H. Shapiro). Infertility in males may be related to premature ejaculation or an inability to maintain an erection or to produce sperm. In females, infertility has been linked to ovulatory disorder, anatomic anomaly, painful intercourse, or genetic dysfunction. Although approximately 50 percent of infertile couples eventually become fertile (Zimmerman), the other 50 percent must choose another pathway to family formation. They may elect to remain childless, to adopt, or to use a reproductive alternative such as artificial insemination.

Reactions to infertility. For many couples, the discovery of infertility is stressful. Their reactions often mirror the grieving process that has been described for those suffering the loss of a loved one (C. H. Shapiro, 1982). Thus, they must resolve issues dealing with denial, anger, guilt, bitterness, and grief before they are able to accept the reality of their infertility (Kraft, Palumbo, Mitchell, Dean, Meyers, & Schmidt, 1980; Menning, 1977). Because many couples assume that conceiving and bearing a child is "natural," they deny the possibility that they could be infertile. Thus, they often avoid seeking medical help or may go from physician to physician in an effort to confirm their normalcy.

Anger follows denial as couples begin to realize that they are powerless to control their reproductive choices. Anger may affect their sexual relationship and cause marital tension. The anger may be directed at the infertile spouse or turned inward, resulting in depression and emotional isolation. Guilt reactions may surface as a result of their inability to bear the child they and the rest of society expect them to have.

Grief involves a sense of loss over children not to be born and parental roles not to be fulfilled through one's biological offspring. Intense grief occurs as the individual and the couple begin to perceive the loss of the potential for biological parenting and the loss of new dimensions in the marriage through the incorporation of one's "own" children. The crisis of infertility goes counter to the strong belief in the commonplaceness of childbearing. Working through the grief process often leads to an awareness of universal but generally unacknowledged beliefs about marriage and the value of children. For example, Payne (1978) found that infertile couples express their desires for children more clearly than do fertile couples. While both sexes put a high premium on children, women are more likely than men to feel they will miss out of a major life goal if they are unable to bear children. This raises the possibility that voluntarily and involuntarily childless women differ markedly in their motivation for parenthood, though no direct test of this hypothesis has been made to date.

Acceptance of infertility is the final stage in the mourning process. Not all couples or individuals achieve acceptance, particularly when no cause of infertility can be established. In such cases, couples persist in the hope that they might yet conceive (C. H. Shapiro, 1982). Once infertility is accepted, however, the future is viewed more positively, and alternatives to childbearing are considered. Individuals feel renewed energy and enthusiasm, hope instead of despair (Menning, 1977). Adoption agencies consider the acceptance of infertility as an important qualification in infertile couples if they are to be able to develop the parenting attitudes necessary for a healthy adoptive relationship (Kraft et al., 1980).

Infertility and marital relationship. Infertility is a crisis that stresses marriage (Ledward, Crawford, & Symonds, 1979). Most people view children not only as a consequence of marriage, but as an integral part of it (Payne, 1978). In the desperate attempt to procreate, the couple may severely impair their sexual relationship. Evaluation and treatment of infertility involves substantial regulation of sexual activity, fitting sexual intercourse to the woman's fertile periods. The lack of sexual spontaneity interferes with the pleasure of sex as couples avoid intercourse except on the proscribed days. Depression follows when the all-consuming effort to conceive proves unsuccessful (C. H. Shapiro, 1982). Under such circumstances, many marriages fail, although the negative impact of infertility is lessened when the initial relationship is a strong one (Kraft et al., 1980). Much depends on patterns of communication between spouses as couples face decisions about fertility treatments and alternatives to childbearing if the treatments fail.

At least one researcher has reported that infertile couples deemed eligible to adopt appear to be more compatible than couples with children (Humphrey, 1975). Unfortunately, Humphrey's study focused on infertile couples who successfully negotiated the screening programs of adoption agencies. The selection process is likely to weed out couples who were less compatible and, thus, judged to be greater risks as adoptive parents. This highlights a basic problem with the literature on infertility. All too often, research involves the description of experiences of infertile couples seen in infertility clinics, at adoption agencies, or in psychiatric clinical practice. Clearly, infertility is a severe life crisis for these couples. But what about couples who are aware of the problem, yet do nothing to resolve it? There are no estimates of how large the latter group may be. Until studies include such people, one cannot safely make generalizations about the effects of infertility on individuals and marriages. Moreover, there are no studies examining family relationships and child development in the 50 percent of infertile couples who eventually conceive as a result of medical intervention.

Adoption

Characteristics of adopting families. For involuntarily childless couples, adoption has historically been the dominant, if not the only, approach to family formation. Data collected by the National Center for Social Statistics (Bonham, 1977) indicate that there is broad support for adoption as a way of increasing family size, and about 4 percent of American women have adopted a child by the time they are 45 years of age. Infertile couples are more likely to adopt than are fertile couples or couples with children. Average maternal age at the time of first adoption is about 30 years, considerably older than other first-time mothers. This is not surprising, since infertility is generally diagnosed about the same time other couples are having their first baby and often is followed by a rather lengthy medical evaluation and course of treatment.

The modal adopting couple is white (though adoptions occur for all ethnic/racial groups), highly educated, and middle class. On average, they adopt one or two children, most of whom are white, below one year of age, and born to unwed mothers. Since 1970, the number of adoptions has declined due to a combination of falling white unmarried birth rates and an increasing tendency for single mothers to keep their children. As a result, more infants of other races and nationalities are being adopted (Bonham, 1977) as are so-called hard-to-place older and/or handicapped children (Brockhaus & Brockhaus, 1982; Hockey, 1980).

Aside from the fact that the children are not the biological offspring of their parents, do families formed by adoption differ from families with biological children? Are adoptive parents satisfied with their role as parents? Are adopted children similar to their nonadopted peers? Although these questions have been addressed in the literature on adoption, most studies are based on clinical data, fail to use appropriate groups, or vary greatly in how successful parenting and successful child adjustment are defined and measured. Nevertheless, the literature does provide some insight into the dynamics of adoptive families.

During the first half of this century, the supply of babies in need of adoption exceeded the demand. Prospective adopting parents searched for the "perfect baby," and adoption agencies tried to comply. Today, the supply-demand ratio has reversed, and the emphasis has switched from "perfect baby" to "perfect home" (Kim, Hong, & Kim, 1979). Formerly, it was assumed that the baby would automatically fulfill the adoptive couple's desire for a happy home life, although this assumption has never been empirically verified. Today, research focuses on the adoptees. What little is known about parents comes from studies of their impact on the child, not directly from studies of parental behavior and attitudes or as a result of parent-child transactions.

Descriptions of the family life of adoptees indicate that there is a great variety among adoptive families, just as in natural families (Triseliotis, 1973). Many adoptees (and their parents) describe a happy home life when they were growing up; however, adoptive families do seem vulnerable to the secret of adoption. Many parents either do not freely reveal information about their child's adoption or do so in a cursory fashion. This suggests that once the adoption is complete, many adoptive parents would prefer to forget about it and behave as if they were a biologically completed family. However, adult adoptees often report awareness of, and concern about, their adoption whether or not their adoptive parents confronted the issue. Currently, adoptive parents are counseled to tell their children of the adoption before age five. It is not known if early disclosure makes the fact of adoption less problematic for children, although Triseliotis found that adoptees told before age 11 had fewer emotional problems.

Not only do the attitudes of adoptive parents toward the adoption affect the child, but the attitudes of extended-family members also have an impact. Descriptive studies indicate that acceptance by grandparents and other relatives has a positive effect on family adjustment (Wolters, 1980). Conversely, comparing the adjustment of black and white children in white families, Silverman and Feigelman (1981) found that extended-family disapproval of the adoption had a negative effect on the children's adjustment.

Studies of clinical populations suggest an overrepresentation of adopted children compared to children raised in their biological families (Simon & Senturia, 1966). Several authors have suggested that in addition to the fact of adoption and problematic emotional responses to it, adopted children are referred more often to psychiatric clinics because their parents are more anxious and less knowledgeable about normal behavior. Austad and Simmons (1978) could find no striking trend that distinguished adopted from nonadopted children seen in their mental health clinic. However, they suggested that parents of the adopted children were motivated to bring their children to the clinic because children were not living up to parental expectations and were presenting problems that the parents were not able to solve. Although they did not use a matched control group of nonadopted children, Austad and Simmons suggest that adoption can create ongoing difficulties in interpersonal relationships and can interfere with parent-child attachment even when the children are adopted at an early age.

A greater incidence of problems in adopted children has also been reported in nonclinic samples. When adopted children have been compared to their nonadopted peers, they have been found to have a greater frequency of behavior disorders according to teachers' reports. Lindholm and Touliatos (1980) examined the records of 3,032 school children and found that the adopted children exceeded nonadopted children in conduct problems, personality problems, and socialized delinquency. The incidence of such problems increased from kindergarten through eighth grade for the adoptees, but not for nonadopted children, and was greater for boys than for girls. An epidemiological study examining psychiatric illness in adults adopted as infants found a significantly higher frequency of personality disorders and substance abuse among male and female adoptees compared to nonadopted controls (Bohman & von Knorring, 1979). Males also had a greater incidence of neuroses, though females did not. Despite significant findings, it is important to note that the overall number of adopted children with behavior problems is small relative to the total number of adopted children.

It may be inappropriate to restrict comparisons of adopted children to those growing up in their biological families. Some unwanted children are not adopted but remain in institutions or are raised by foster parents. Other unwanted children are not placed for adoption but remain with their biological parent(s). A prospective study of 624 Swedish children who were candidates for adoption at the time of their birth, examined child functioning at 11 and 15 years of age (Bohman & Sigvardsson, 1980). The group was divided into children who were adopted, those who remained with their biological mothers despite the initial request for adoption, and those who were raised in foster homes. Children in the target groups were compared with same-sex classmates. At age 11, all three groups of children put up for adoption fared more poorly than did their classroom controls. By age 15, differences between adopted children and their controls had all but disappeared.

Interestingly enough, children who remained with their biological mothers and those who were fostered had poorer grades and a greater variety of behavior and adjustment problems than adopted children or classmates. Despite adoptive parents' worries about the development of their children, adopted children were behaving in a manner similar to their nonadopted peers by age 15. The fact that adopted children fared better than fostered children or unwanted children reared by their biological parents suggests that adoption can have positive effects on child development.

Transracial adoptions have increased in recent years. Placing black infants in white families seems to answer a pressing need for both infants and adopting couples, yet serious objections have been voiced on the grounds that transracially adopted children presumably will suffer identity problems and loss of ethnic heritage. In fact, transracially adopted children have been found to be comparable to their nonadopted peers in social adjustment, intellectual development, and racial attitudes (Womak & Fulton, 1981). Silverman and Feigelman (1981) found that the adjustment of transracially adopted children was similar to that of other adopted children when age at placement was taken into consideration. They argue that earlier placement is critical for the sound adjustment of black children in white families. Early placement (before age six months) has also been found to benefit children going to families of the same race (Bohman & Sigvardsson, 1980).

Several characteristics of adoptive parents have been found to predict better adjustment in adopted children. Using number of behavior problems described by the parent as the dependent variable, Kraus (1978a) found that adopted children fared better when the father was in a professional/skilled occupation, when family income was high, and when parents had achieved at least a high school education. In addition, children of younger mothers (below 30) tended to have fewer problems. Finally, Kraus (1978b) found that birth of a biological child, born after a previously childless couple adopted, is associated with serious behavioral dysfunction in the adopted child. In light of major methodological criticisms of Kraus's study (Goda, 1979), his recommendation that prospective adoptive parents be refused a child when parental and family structure characteristics are adverse should be viewed with great caution, or perhaps ignored, until additional evidence is compiled.

Alternatives in human reproduction

Problems associated with adoption lead some infertile couples to seek other means to bring children into the family. Thus, many couples are choosing artificial insemination either by husband (AIH) or by donor (AID), AIH being far less common than AID. This method is only available to couples whose fertility problem is male- rather than female-related. Couples choose AID instead of adoption for a variety of reasons, including long waiting lists and/or nonavailability of babies, lack of eligibility for adoption, preference for a child with some family resemblance, the stress of the adoption procedure, the vulnerability of adopting parents before the courts, and anticipated difficulty accepting an adopted child (Ledward et al., 1979). Other reasons for choosing AID over adoption are the desire to experience pregnancy and birth, to conceal male infertility, or to have a socially acceptable inconspicuous child (Snowden & Mitchell, 1981; Waltzer, 1982). It is obvious that the criteria for eligibility for AID differ from those required for adoption. Generally, selection of AID couples and donors is at the discretion of the AID practitioners (Snowden & Mitchell).

AID is a controversial approach to childbearing and family formation and, thus, is often shrouded in secrecy. First, there are legal questions about the legitimacy of the AID child. Additionally, few religious organizations completely approve of AID, and some oppose it entirely. Therefore, most couples tell no one of their AID experience, and the mother's husband often is listed on the birth certificate as the child's father.

The few interview studies that have been done suggest that AID can be psychologically stressful for couples. Many women who fail to conceive report adverse psychological effects which they attribute to

AID (Reading, Sledmere, & Cox, 1982). Women sometimes feel guilty for conceiving; men are often ambivalent in their feelings about having their wife impregnated with another's sperm. Whereas AID sometimes compounds a couple's problems, it gives most couples a sense of hope (Snowden & Mitchell, 1981). Several investigators report that the marital relationship often is consolidated before treatment, presumably when the couple considers the decision to request AID, and that going through the process draws the couple even closer together (Kraus & Quinn, 1977; Ledward, Symonds, & Eynon, 1982). If the treatment is successful and a child is born, the marital relationship is further strengthened (David & Avidan, 1976), and parents often request a second AID child (Czyba & Chevret, 1980).

Children born of the AID procedure seem to be physically and psychologically sound. A study conducted in Japan found no adverse physical or intellectual effects in AID children compared to a control group of children conceived the natural way (Iizuka, Sawada, Nishina, & Ohi, 1968). Kraus and Quinn (1977) reported that AID children are above average in physical, mental, and motor development. However, issues of identity may be more serious for AID children than for adopted children because they are generally denied any information about their origin (Kraus & Quinn).

Although most of the research is favorable to AID, it must be pointed out that self-selection is a major confounding factor in current studies. The relatively few couples willing to participate in these studies are likely those with the most favorable experiences. Secrecy and self-selection pose formidable barriers to valid and generalizable developmental research on AID children or families.

The advantage of AID over adoption is that the child is genetically related to one of its parents—the mother. In surrogate parenting, on the other hand, it is the wife rather than the husband who is sterile. Thus, through surrogate parenting, the infertile couple can have a child who is biologically related to at least one parent—the father. A woman other than the wife agrees to be impregnated by the husband's sperm, carry the baby, and then give the child to the infertile couple. This is such a recent phenomenon that virtually no research on its effects has been done. One psychiatric study reported no overt psychopathology in women applying to be surrogate mothers (Franks, 1981). Similarly, research on the newest medical techniques for fertilization, such as in-vitro fertilization or ovum transfer, has yet to begin.

CONCLUSION

In this chapter, we have examined four of the less-common types of families: teenage childbearers, delayed childbearers, voluntarily childless couples, and involuntarily childless couples. Unfortunately, research on these families has been dominated by bivariate analyses. Research on early childbearing and voluntary childlessness appears to be the most advanced in the use of multivariate models, although there is considerable room for improvement in the research on all four of these family types. Only rarely have researchers on these types of families used transactional models to represent the complexity of interactions between the individuals involved and between these individuals and their environments.

One of the consistent shortcomings in the research on these four types of families is the singular focus on the female and the near-exclusion of the male. Each of the family types examined above is confronted by a myriad of questions regarding family formation (When, if, or how to have children as a couple or as a single parent? How will child care be handled or shared?) It is hard to imagine the males involved being simply neutral observers. Yet rarely are males included in studies of these families in more than a superficial way. Since the major differences between traditional family formation and nontraditional family formation lie in the nature of the decisions that *couples* make, researchers must focus on the dynamics of decision making in couples, not in individuals.

Taken together, the four types of families examined above represent a significant proportion of all families in the United States. However, because of the simplicity of the models used and the nearly exclusive focus on females, it can be argued that we have an unrealistic picture of the dynamics involved in these less-common types of family formation. If we are to make significant strides in understanding these families, researchers must (1) treat families as systems of interacting individuals; (2) use transactional models that reflect the complexity of family interactions and decision making; and (3) use prospective research designs.

REFERENCES

Akpom, A. C., Akpom, L. K., & Davis, M. Prior sexual behavior of teenagers attending rap sessions for the first time. *Family Planning Perspectives,* 1976, *8*(4), 203–206.

Alan Guttmacher Institute. *Teenage pregnancy: The problem that hasn't gone away.* New York: Author, 1981.

Alden, A. *Delayed childbearing: Issues and implications.* Unpublished doctoral dissertation, Harvard University, 1981.

Aries, P. *Centuries of childhood: A social history of family life.* New York: Vintage Books, 1962.

Asher, H. B. *Causal modeling.* Beverly Hills, Calif.: Sage Publications, 1976.

Aug, H. G., & Bright, T. P. A study of wed and unwed motherhood in adolescents and young adults. *Journal of the American Academy of Child Psychiatry*, 1970, *9*, 577–594.

Austad, C. C., & Simmons, T. L. Symptoms of adopted children presenting to a large mental health clinic. *Child Psychiatry and Human Development*, 1978, *9*, 20–27.

Babikian, H. M., & Goldman, A. A study of unwanted pregnancy. *American Journal of Psychiatry*, 1971, *128*, 755–760.

Barnett, L. D., & MacDonald, R. H. A study of the membership of the National Organization for Non-Parents. *Social Biology*, 1976, *23*, 297–310.

Baurn, F., & Cope, D. R. Some characteristics of intentionally childless wives in Britain. *Journal of Biosocial Science*, 1980, *12*, 287–299.

Blake, J. Is zero preferred? American attitudes toward childlessness in the 1970's. *Journal of Marriage and the Family*, 1979, *41*, 245–257.

Bohman, M., & Sigvardsson, S. A prospective, longitudinal study of children registered for adoption. *Acta Psychiatrica Scandinavica*, 1980, *61*, 339–355.

Bohman, M., & von Knorring, A. L. Psychiatric illness among adults adopted as infants. *Acta Psychiatrica Scandinavica*, 1979, *60*, 106–112.

Bonham, G. S. Who adopts: The relationship of adoption and social-demographic characteristics of women. *Journal of Marriage and the Family*, 1977, *39*, 295–306.

Brockhaus, J. P. D., & Brockhaus, R. H. Adopting an older child—the emotional process. *American Journal of Nursing*, 1982, *82*, 288–291.

Burchinal, L. G. Adolescent role deprivation and high school age marriage. *Marriage and Family Living*, 1959, *21*, 378–384.

Calhoun, L. C., & Shelby, W. Voluntary childlessness, involuntary childlessness and having children: A study of social perceptions. *Family Relations*, 1980, *29*, 181–183.

Chester, R. Is there a relationship between childlessness and marriage breakdown? *Journal of Biosocial Science*, 1972, *4*, 443–454.

Clifford, W. B., & Tobin, P. L. Labor force participation of working mothers and family formation: Some further evidence. *Demography*, 1977, *14*(3), 273–284.

Cobliner, W. G. Pregnancy in the single adolescent girl: The role of cognitive functions. *Journal of Youth and Adolescence*, 1974, *3*(1), 17–29.

Coddington, R. D. Life events associated with adolescent pregnancies. *Journal of Clinical Psychiatry*, 1979, *40*, 180–185.

Colman, L. *Delayed childbearing: A descriptive study of pregnancy and the postpartum in twelve primiparous women over thirty years old.* Unpublished doctoral dissertation. Wright Institute, 1978.

Cromwell, R. E. A social action program directed to single pregnant girls and adolescent parents. *Family Coordinator*, 1974, *23*(1), 61–66.

Cvetkovich, G., & Grote, B. Psychosocial maturity and teenage contraceptive use: An investigation of decision-making and communication skills. *Population and Environment*, 1981, *4*(4), 211–226.

Czyba, J. C., & Chevret, M. Psychological reactions of couples to artificial insemination with donor sperm. *International Journal of Fertility*, 1980, *24*, 240–245.

Dame, N. G., Finck, G. H., Mayos, R. G., Reiner, B. S., & Smith, B. O. Conflict in marriage following premarital pregnancy. *American Journal of Orthopsychiatry*, 1966, *36*, 468–475.

Daniels, P., & Weingarten, K. Postponing parenthood. *Savvy,* May 1980, pp. 55–60.

Daniels, P., & Weingarten, K. *Sooner or later: The timing of parenthood in adult lives.* New York: W. W. Norton, 1982.

David, A., & Avidan, D. Artificial insemination donor: Clinical and psychological aspects. *Fertility and Sterility,* 1976, *27,* 528–532.

DeAmicis, L. A., Klerman, R., Hess, D. W., & McAnarney, E. R. A comparison of unwed pregnant teenagers and nulligravid sexually active adolescents seeking contraception. *Adolescence,* 1981, *16*(61), 11–20.

DeLissovoy, V. High school marriages: A longitudinal study. *Journal of Marriage and the Family,* 1973, *35*(2), 245–255.

DeJong, G. F., & Sell, R. R. Changes in childlessness in the U.S.: A demographic path analysis. *Population Studies,* 1973, *31,* 129–142.

DeJong, G. F., & Sell, R. R. Changes in childlessness for all women in the U.S.: A reply to Spencer. *Population Studies,* 1978, *32,* 196–198.

Dembo, M. H., & Lundell, B. Factors affecting adolescent contraception practices: Implications for sex education. *Adolescence,* 1979, *14*(56), 657–664.

Earls, F., & Siegel, B. Precocious fathers. *American Journal of Orthopsychiatry,* 1980, *50*(3), 169–480.

Faigel, H. C. Late social and psychological aftereffect of pregnancy in adolescence. *Journal of Adolescent Health Care,* 1982, *2,* 209–212.

Feldman, H. A comparison of intentional parents and intentionally childless couples. *Journal of Marriage and the Family,* 1981, *43,* 593–600.

Fox, G. L. *The family's role in adolescent sexual behavior.* Washington, D.C.: Family Impact Seminar, 1978.

Franks, D. D. Psychiatric evaluation of women in a surrogate mother program. *American Journal of Psychiatry,* 1981, *138,* 1378–1379.

Furstenberg, F. F., Jr. Birth Control experiences among pregnant adolescents: The process of unplanned parenthood. *Social Problems,* 1971, *19,* 192–203.

Furstenberg, F. F., Jr. *Unplanned parenthood: The social consequences of teenage childbearing.* New York: Free Press, 1976.

Furstenberg, F. F., Jr., & Crawford, A. G. Family support: Helping teenage mothers to cope. *Family Planning Perspectives,* 1978, *15*(6), 322–333.

Furstenberg, F. F., Jr., Gordis, L., & Markowitz, M. Birth control knowledge and attitudes among unmarried pregnant adolescents: A preliminary report. *Journal of Marriage and the Family,* 1969, *31*(1), 34–42.

Gibson, C. Childlessness and marital instability: A reexamination of the evidence. *Journal of Biosocial Science,* 1980, *12,* 121–132.

Goda, D. F. A comment on "Family structure as a factor in the adjustment of adopted children." *British Journal of Social Work,* 1979, *9,* 233–235.

Goldfarb, J. L., Mumford, D. M., Schum, D. A., Smith, P. G., Flowers, C., & Schum, C. An attempt to detect "pregnancy susceptibility" in indigent adolescent girls. *Journal of Youth and Adolescence,* 1977, *6*(2), 127–144.

Grindstaff, C. F. Trends and incidence of childlessness by race: Indicators of black progress over three decades. *Sociological Focus*, 1976, *9*, 265–284.

Gustavus, S. O., & Henley, J. R., Jr. Correlates of voluntary childlessness in a select population. *Social Biology*, 1971, *18*, 277–284.

Hastings, D. W., & Robinson, J. G. Incidence of childlessness for U.S. women, cohorts born 1891–1945. *Social Biology*, 1974, *21*, 178–184.

Hendricks, L. E. Unmarried adolescent fathers: Problems and support systems. In W. T. Hall and C. L. Young (Eds.), *Proceedings: Integrating tertiary care into community health services*, Pittsburgh, Pa., June 22–25, 1980, pp. 124–132.

Hertz, D. G. Psychological implications of adolescent pregnancy: Patterns of family interaction in adolescent mothers-to-be. *Psychosomatics*, 1977, *18*, 13–16.

Hetherington, M. E. Effects of father absence on personality development in adolescent daughters. *Developmental Psychology*, 1972, *2*(3), 313–326.

Hockey, A. Evaluation of adoption of the intellectually handicapped: A retrospective analysis of 137 cases. *Journal of Mental Deficiency Research*, 1980, *24*, 187–202.

Holahan, C. K., & Gilbert, L. A. Conflict between major life roles: Women and men in dual career couples. *Human Relations*, 1979, *32*(6), 451–467.

Houghton, P. Childless, no choice. *New Society*, 1977, *40*, 227–228.

Houseknecht, S. K. Childlessness and marital adjustment. *Journal of Marriage and the Family*, 1979, *41*, 259–265. (a)

Houseknecht, S. K. Timing of the decision to remain voluntarily childless: Evidence for continuous socialization. *Psychology of Women Quarterly*, 1979, *4*, 81–96. (b)

Humphrey, M. The effect of children upon the marriage relationship. *British Journal of Medical Psychology*, 1975, *48*, 273–279.

Iizuka, R., Sawada, Y., Nishina, N., & Ohi, M. The physical and mental development of children born following artificial insemination. *International Journal of Fertility*, 1968, *13*, 24–32.

Inselberg, R. M. Social and psychological factors associated with high school marriages. *Journal of Home Economics*, 1961, *53*, 766–772.

Jamison, P. H., Franzini, L. R., & Kaplan, R. M. Some assumed characteristics of voluntarily child free women and men. *Psychology of Women Quarterly*, 1979, *4*, 266; 273.

Jorgensen, S. R., King, S. L., & Torrey, B. A. Dyadic and social network influences on adolescent exposure to pregnancy risk. *Journal of Marriage and the Family*, 1980, *42*(1), 141–155.

Kantner, J. F., & Zelnik, M. Contraception and pregnancy: Experience of young unmarried women in the United States. *Family Planning Perspectives*, 1973, *5*(1), 11–25.

Kim, S. P., Hong, S., & Kim, B. S. Adoption of Korean children by New York area couples: A preliminary study. *Child Welfare*, 1979, *58*, 419–427.

Kraft, A. D., Palumbo, J., Mitchell, D., Dean, D., Meyers, S., & Schmidt, A. W. The psychological dimensions of infertility. *American Journal of Orthopsychiatry*, 1980, *50*, 618–628.

Kraus, J. Adjustment of adopted children and demographic profile of adoptive parents. *Australian and New Zealand Journal of Psychiatry*, 1978, *12*, 181–187. (a)

Kraus, J. Family structure as a factor in the adjustment of adopted children. *British Journal of Social Work*, 1978, *8*, 327–337. (b)

Kraus, J., & Quinn, P. E. Human artificial insemination. *Medical Journal of Australia*, 1977, *1*, 710–713.

LaBarre, M. Emotional crisis of school-age girls during pregnancy and early motherhood. *American Journal of Orthopsychiatry*, 1980, *50*, 537–557.

Ledward, R. S., Crawford, L., & Symonds, E. M. Social factors in patients for artificial insemination by donor (AID). *Journal of Biosocial Science*, 1979, *11*, 473–479.

Ledward, R. S., Symonds, E. M., & Eynon, S. Social and environmental factors as criteria for success in artificial insemination by donor (AID). *Journal of Biosocial Science*, 1982, *14*, 263–275.

Lindholm, B. W., & Touliatos, J. Psychological adjustment of adopted and nonadopted children. *Psychological Reports*, 1980, *46*, 307–310.

Menning, B. E. *Infertility: A guide for the childless couple*. Englewood Cliffs, N.J.: Prentice-Hall, 1977.

Mercer, R. T., Hackley, K. C., & Bostrom, A. Factors having an impact on maternal role attainment the first year of motherhood (Final Report, Department of Health and Human Services). Washington, D.C.: National Technical Information Service, 1982.

Moore, A., & Hofferth, L. *Factors affecting early family formation: A path model*. Washington, D.C.: Urban Institute, 1978.

Murdock, G. P. The universality of the nuclear family. In N. W. Bell & E. F. Vogel (Eds.), *A modern introduction to the family*. New York: Free Press, 1960.

Nadelson, C. C., Notman, M. I., & Gillon, J. W. Sexual knowledge and attitudes of adolescents: Relationship to contraceptive use. *Obstetrics and Gynecology*, 1980, *55*(3), 340–345.

Panzarine, S., & Elster, A. B. Prospective adolescent fathers: Stresses during pregnancy and implications for nursing interventions. *Journal of Pediatric Nursing and Mental Health Services*, 1982, *20*(7), 21–24.

Payne, J. Talking about children: An examination of accounts about reproduction and family life. *Journal of Biosocial Science*, 1978, *10*, 367–374.

Peterson, R. A. Intended childlessness in late adolescence: Personality and psychopathology. *Journal of Youth and Adolescence*, 1980, *9*, 439–447.

Pohlman, E. Childlessness, intentional and unintentional. *Journal of Nervous and Mental Disease*, 1970, *151*, 2–12.

Poston, D. L., Jr. Characteristics of voluntary and involuntary childless wives. *Social Biology*, 1976, *23*, 198–209.

Poston, D. L., Jr., & Gotard, E. Trends in childlessness in the U.S.: 1910–1975. *Social Biology*, 1977, *24*, 212–224.

Prosser, H. B. Sally's corner: Coping with unmarried motherhood. *Journal of Social Issues*, 1980, *36*(1), 107–129.

Quay, H. C. Psychological factors in teenage pregnancy. In K. G. Scott, T. Field, & E. Robertson (Eds.), *Teenage parents and their offspring*. New York: Grune & Stratton, 1981.

Ragozin, A. S., Basham, R. B., Arnie, K. A., Greenberg, M. T., & Robinson, N. M. Effects of maternal age on parenting role. *Developmental Psychology*, 1982, *18*(2), 627–634.

Rapoport, R., & Rapoport, R. N. Early and later experiences as determinants of adult behavior: Married women's family and career patterns. *British Journal of Sociology,* 1971, *22*(1), 16–30.

Reading, A. E., Sledmere, C. M., & Cox, D. N. A survey of patient attitudes towards artificial insemination by donor. *Journal of Psychosomatic Research,* 1982, *26,* 429–433.

Reiner, B. S., & Edwards, R. L. Adolescent marriage: Social or therapeutic problem? *Family Coordinator,* 1974, *23,* 383–390.

Reiss, I. L. *Family systems in America* (3d ed.). New York: Holt, Rinehart & Winston, 1980.

Rogel, M. J., Zuehlke, M. E., Peterson, A. C., Tobin-Richards, M., & Shelton, M. Contraceptive behavior in adolescence: A decision-making perspective. *Journal of Youth and Adolescence,* 1980, *9*(6), 491–506.

Roosa, M. W., Fitzgerald, H. E., & Carlson, N. A. A comparison of teenage and older mothers: A systems analysis. *Journal of Marriage and the Family,* 1982, *44,* 367–377. (a)

Roosa, M. W., Fitzgerald, H. E., & Carlson, N. A. Teenage and older mothers and their infants: Descriptive results. *Adolescence,* 1982, *17*(65), 1–17. (b)

Roosa, M. W., Fitzgerald, H. E., & Carlson, N. A. Teenage parenting and child development: A literature review. *Infant Mental Health Journal,* 1982, *3,* 4–18. (c)

Roosa, M. W., & Vaughan, L. A comparison of teenage and older mothers with preschool children. *Family Relations,* in press.

Rosen, R. H. Adolescent pregnancy decision-making: Are parents important? *Adolescence,* 1980, *15*(57), 43–54.

Rosen, R. H., Benson, T., & Stack, J. M. Help or hindrance: Parental impact on pregnant teenagers' resolution decisions. *Family Relations,* 1982, *31,* 271–280.

Rosenblatt, P. C., Peterson, P., Portner, J., Cleveland, M., Mykkanen, A., Foster, R., Holm, G., Joel, B., Reisch, H., Kreuscher, C., & Phillips, R. A cross cultural study of responses to childlessness. *Behavior Science Notes,* 1973, *8,* 221–231.

Rothenberg, P. B., & Varga, P. E. The relationship between age of mother and child health and development. *American Journal of Public Health,* 1981, *71*(8), 810–817.

Sameroff, A. J., & Chandler, M. J. Reproductive risk and the continuum of caretaking casualty. In Frances Dugan Horowitz (Ed.), *Review of child development research* (Vol. 4). Chicago: University of Chicago Press, 1975. Pp. 187–244.

Schinke, S. P., Blythe, B. J., & Gilchrist, L. D. Cognitive-behavioral prevention of adolescent pregnancy. *Journal of Counseling Psychology,* 1981, *28*(5), 451–454.

Sears, R. R., Maccoby, E., & Levin, H. *Patterns of child rearing.* Evanston, Ill.: Row & Peterson, 1957.

Shapiro, C. H. The impact of infertility on the marital relationship. *Social Casework,* 1982, *63,* 387–393.

Shapiro, G. Predicting the course of voluntary childlessness in the 21st century. *Journal of Clinical Child Psychology,* 1980, *9,* 155–157.

Silka, L., & Kiesler, S. Couples who choose to remain childless. *Family Planning Perspectives,* 1977, *9,* 16–25.

Silverman, A. R., & Feigelman, W. The adjustment of black children adopted by white families. *Social Casework,* 1981, *62,* 529–536.

Simon, N. M., & Senturia, A. G. Adoption and psychiatric illness. *American Journal of Psychiatry,* 1966, *122,* 858–867.

Sklar, J., & Berkov, B. Teenage family formation in postwar America. In F. F. Furstenberg, Jr., R. Lincoln, & J. Menken (Eds.), *Teenage sexuality, pregnancy, and childbearing.* Philadelphia: University of Pennsylvania Press, 1981.

Smith, E. W. The role of the grandmother in adolescent pregnancy and parenting. *Journal of School Health,* 1975, *45*(5), 278–283.

Smith, P. B., Nenney, S. W., Weinman, M. L., & Mumford, D. M. Factors affecting perception of pregnancy risk in the adolescent. *Journal of Youth and Adolescence,* 1982, *11*(3), 207–215.

Smith, P. B., Weinman, M. L., & Mumford, D. M. Social and affective factors associated with adolescent pregnancy. *Journal of School Health,* February 1982, pp. 90–93.

Snowden, R., & Mitchell, S. *The artificial family: A consideration of artificial insemination by donor.* Winchester, Mass.: Allen & Unwin, 1981.

Sorosky, A. D., Baran, A., & Pannor, R. *The adoption triangle: The effects of the sealed record on adoptees, birth parents, and adoptive parents.* Garden City, N.J.: Anchor Press/Doubleday, 1978.

Triseliotis, J. *In search of origins: The experiences of adopted people.* Boston: Beacon Press, 1973.

Uddenberg, N. Mother-father and daughter-male relationships: A comparison. *Archives of Sexual Behavior,* 1976, *5*(1), 69–79.

Veenhoven, R. Is there an innate need for children? *European Journal of Social Psychology,* 1974, *4,* 495–501.

Veevers, J. E. Voluntarily childless wives: An exploratory study. *Sociology and Social Research,* 1973, *57,* 356–366.

Veevers, J. E. The moral careers of voluntarily childless wives: Notes on the defense of a variant world view. *Family Coordinator,* 1975, *24,* 473–487.

Waltzer, H. Psychological and legal aspects of artificial insemination (AID): An overview. *American Journal of Psychotherapy,* 1982, *36,* 91–102.

Westoff, L. A., & Westoff, C. F. *From now to zero: Fertility, contraception, and abortion in America.* Boston; Little, Brown, 1968.

Wilkie, J. R. The trend toward delayed parenthood. *Journal of Marriage and the Family,* 1981, *43*(3), 583–591.

Wolters, W. H. G. Psychosocial problems in young foreign adopted children. *Acta Paedopsychiatrica,* 1980, *46,* 67–81.

Womack, W. M., & Fulton, W. Transracial adoption and the black preschool child. *Journal of the American Academy of Child Psychiatry,* 1981, *20,* 712–724.

Zimmerman, S. L. Alternatives in human production for involuntary childless couples. *Family Relations,* 1982, *31*(2), 233–241.

Name Index

A

Abbott, D., 760, 761, *779*
Abel, E. L., 305
Abel, R., 1259, *1273*
Abelson, R., 973, 987
Aberle, D. F., 508, *518*
Abernathy, S. R., 761, *780*
Abernathy, V., 545, *549, 695*
Abrahams, J. P., 286, *314*
Abrahams, R. B., 342, 346, *351*
Abramovitch, R., 190, 200, 201, 203, *210*
Abramovitz, R. S., 503, *518*
Abramowitz, S. I., 449, *521*
Abramson, L. Y., 1066, *1068*
Abramson, P. R., 446, *463*
Abroms, E., 1283, *1309*
Achenbach, T. M., 996, 1000, 1082, 1102, 1352, *1376*
Ackerman, N., 52, *71,* 1281, *1309,* 1318, 1341
Ackerman, N. W., 18, *35*
Acock, A. C., 514, *518,* 1220, 1241
Adams, B. N., 182, 186, 191, 200, 202, 204, *210,* 323, *381*
Adams, D. L., 293 F, *311,* 407, *429*
Adams, G. R., 229, *247*
Adamson, I., 596, *622*
Adcock, S., 864, *870*
Addison, S., *779*

Adelson, E., 914, *931*
Adelson, J., 160, 216, 217, 221, 222, 223, 224, 225, 227, 228, 239, 240, 242, *247, 249*
Adler, A., 154, 197, *213,* 1138, 1148
Adler, K., 414, *422*
Adler, M., 178, 189, *210*
Adler, P. T., 232, 234, *247*
Adorno, T. W., 448, *462*
Affonso, D. D., 562, *579*
Afterman, J., 572, *584*
Agrawal, K. C., 691, *696*
Ahrens, A., 112, 113, 114, *129*
Aiello, J. R., 1223, 1243
Aiken, L. R., 289, *311*
Aikins, F. R., 1436
Ainsworth, M., 528, *549, 550*
Ainsworth, M. D., 186, 187, *210,* 524, *549*
Ainsworth, M. D. S., 586, 587, 589, *615*
Ajzen, I., 347, 348, *353*
Akers, R. L., 233, *247*
Akins, D. L., 1436
Akpom, A. C., 625, *653*
Akpom, L. K., 625, *653*
Alabiso, F., 1158, 1169, *1175*
Albert, R. S., 784, *807*
Alberti, R. E., 1042, 1068
Albrecht, S. L., 703, 707, *733*
Alden, A., 636, 637, 638, *653*

Note: Pages 1–660 are in Volume I; pages 661–1457 are in Volume II. Italic numbers indicate reference citations.

Aldous, J., 157, 164, 165, *174*, 261, *281*, 449, 510, 515, *518*, 519, *520*, 564, *581*, 698, 699, *733*, 755, *773*
Alexander, J. A., 1320, 1321, 1324, 1325, 1327, 1328, 1332, 1335, 1336, 1338, 1341, 1342, 1343
Alexander, J. B., 1228, 1241
Alexander, J. F., 127, *129*, 234, 235, 236, 243, 245, *247*, 366, *375*, 813, 821, 823, 826, 827, 831, *840*, *841*, *842*, 967, 986, 996, *1000*, 1076, 1078, 1079, 1080, 1084, 1086, 1091, 1102, 1346, 1355, 1372, 1375, *1376*
Alexander, J. W., 539, *552*
Al-Issa, I., 849, *868*
Allan, G., 192, *210*
Allen, C. M., 998, 1000
Allen, G., 158, *171*
Allen, W., 663, 664, 666, 671, 689, *695*
Allman, C. R., 1129, *1148*
Allport, F., 6, *35*
Allport, G. W., 102, *129*
Allred, M., 1292, 1303, *1309*
Alpert, J. L., 508, *518*
Als, H., 596, *616*, *621*, *622*
Altman, I., 362, 364, 366, 367, 368, *373*, *374*, *375*, 411, 412, 418, *422*, *427*, 1220, 1245
Altsteen, H., 1397, *1412*
Alvarez, M., 591, *617*
Alverez, M. D., 106, *132*
Amatea, E., 1256, *1273*, 1292, *1309*
American Bar Association, 1394, *1409*
American Psychological Association, 1249, 1255, 1257, 1258, 1261, *1273*
Ames, G. J., 592, *617*
Amish, P., 908, 909, *933*, *936*
Ammons, P., 308, *311*
Amster, L. E., 299, *311*
Anaquost, E., 888, *896*
Ancher, K. N., 1346, 1358, *1376*
Anderson, B. J., 562, *583*, 603, 605, *620*
Anderson, C., 467, *493*
Anderson, C. W., 449, *518*
Anderson, D., 1048, 1071
Anderson, L., 1111, *1125*, 1256, *1273*, 1292, *1309*
Anderson, R., 74, *98*
Anderson, S. A., 117, *138*, 993, 1000, 1001
Anderson, S. H., 1227, 1241
Andolfi, M., 1161, *1175*, 1288, 1291, *1309*
Andrulis, D. P., 857, *868*
Andry, R. G., 231, *247*
Angelo, C., 1161, *1175*
Angst, J., 126, *131*

Angyal, A., 1288, *1309*
Annis, H. M., 233, 234, *247*
Annon, J., 1108, 1124
Anolik, S. A., 232, *247*
Anthony, E. J., 825, *840*, 865, *868*, 1270, 1280
Anthony, J., *247*
Antill, J. K., 117, 118, *129*
Antrobus, J., 1155, 1159, 1173, *1177*
Anzalone, M. K., 588, 607, 610, *617*
Apfel-Savitz, R., 414, *426*
Aponte, H., 744, *773*
Appel, W., 832, *840*
Applebaum, A. S., 447, *462*
Applebaum, M., 1081, 1082, 1103
Aptheker, H., 667, 674, *695*
Araoz, D. C., 791, *807*
Arasteh, J. D., 566, *579*
Arbeit, S. A., 576, *579*
Ardrey, R., 1222, 1241
Arel, B., 1301, *1309*
Arendt, H., 170, *171*
Arias, I., 1061, 1071
Aries, P., 623, *653*
Arieti, S., 852, *868*
Arkin, R., 1422, 1433
Arling, G., 293, *311*, 326, 342, *351*
Arling, G. L., 902, 912, *934*
Armin, R., 474, *494*
Arnie, K. A., 640, *657*
Arnstein, H. S., 572, *579*
Aronovich, J., 1282, *1309*
Aronowitz, S., 161, *171*
Aronson, E., 125, *129*
Arrington, A., 965, 975, 984
Ashby, W. K., 14, *35*
Ashe, M. L., 761, *780*
Asher, H. B., 630, *653*
Asher, S. J., 328, *352*, 1035, 1068
Ashton, G. C., 221, *254*
Atchley, R., 193, *214*
Atchley, R. C., 284, 285, 286, 287, 288, 289, 291, 292, 296, *311*, *319*
Athanasiou, R., 432, *434*, *462*, 466, *492*
Atkinson, J. R., 305, *318*
Atkinson, J. W., 808
Attneave, C., 18, *37*, 744, *773*, 1271, 1273, 1279
Atwood, G. E., 611, *615*
Auerback, H. H., 1060, 1068
Auerswald, E., 157, *171*
Aug, H. G., 539, *552*
Aug, R. G., 625, 629, *654*
Ault, M. H., 982, 984
Austad, C. C., 649, *654*

Note: Pages 1–660 are in Volume I; pages 661–1457 are in Volume II. Italic numbers indicate reference citations.

Averett, C., 419, *423*
Averill, J. R., 1419, 1420, 1421, 1433
Avery, A., 258, *282*
Avery, A. W., 1187, 1204, 1207, 1208, 1209, *1215*
Avidan, D., 652, *655*
Axelrod, M., 335, 336, 337, *355*
Axline, V., 1153, *1175*
Ayllon, T., 1141, *1148*, 1153, *1175*
Azrin, N. H., 995, *1000*, 1041, 1043, 1064, 1068

B

Babchuk, N., 277, *280*
Babikian, H. M., 626, *654*
Bach, G., 417, 418, *422*
Bach, G. R., 893, *896*, 1237, 1241
Back, K., 124, *131*
Backman, J., 1153, 1175
Bacon, M., 233, *247*
Bader, E., 1182, 1187, *1209*
Baer, D. M., 982, 983, 1351, *1376*
Bagarozzi, D. A., 111, *129*, 893, 897, 991 n, 993, 995, 996, 996 n, 997, 998, 1000, 1282, 1293, 1296, *1309*
Bahr, H. M., 117, 118, *129*, 703, 707, *733*
Bahr, S. J., 1394, *1409*
Bailey, D., 747, 773
Bailey, K. G., 1225, 1243
Bailyn, L., 717, 718, 725, *733*
Bakeman, R., 975, 977, 983, 984, 1081, 1082, 1103
Baker, E., 1257, 1278, 1294, 1295, *1313*
Baker, G., 1135, 1139, *1149*
Baker, L., 392, *403*, 793, 794, *808*, 1080, 1105, 1260, 1278
Baldwin, A. L., 538, *549*
Baldwin, B. A., 1040, 1049, 1052, 1054, 1055, 1070
Baldwin, C. T., 538, *549*
Baldwin, J. A., 904, 910, 916, 922, *928*
Baldwin, W. P., 860, *868*
Bales, R. F., 87, 88, 90, 93, 96, 98, 99, 1129, *1150*
Balkwell, C., 298, 299, *311*, 419, *422*
Balkwell, J., 419, *422*
Ball, J., 309, *311*
Ball, O., 309, *311*
Ball, P. G., 886, *897*
Ball, R. E., 687, *695*
Balser, R. B., 610, *615*
Balswick, J., 418, 419, *422*, 1129, *1148*
Balswick, J. O., 279, *282*
Balswick, J. O., Jr., 386, 389, *401*

Baltes, P., 157, 160, 163, 164, *171*
Bambreck, A., 1269, *1275*, 1291, 1292, 1293, 1298, *1311*
Bamewalt, D., 703, 718, *737*
Ban, P., 531, 532, 533, *549*, *550*, 589, *615*
Bandler, R., 1076, 1103
Bandura, A., 232, 234, *247*, 544, *549*, 912, 914, *929*, 1302, 1309
Bane, M. J., 810, 843
Bank, B. J., 218, *247*
Bank, S., 116, 131, 995, 1002
Bank, S. P., 181, 182, 187, 188, 190, 194, 195, 196, 204, 205, 206, 207, *210*
Bankoff, E. A., *311*, 342, 346, 351
Bannister, D., 7, *35*
Barahal, R. M., 912, *929*
Baratz, J. C., 691, *695*
Baratz, S. S., 691, *695*
Barbach, L. G., 1108, 1119, 1124
Barbarin, O. A., 688, *696*
Barbe, W., B., 782, 783, *809*
Barber, C., 146, *171*
Bard, M., 882, *897*
Bardill, D., 1301, 1302, *1309*
Bardwick, J. M., 122, *129*
Barker, D., 155 n, *171*, *172*, 514, *518*, 1220, 1241
Barker, R., 155 n, *171*, *172*, 514, *518*
Barkley, R., 1154, 1157, 1165, 1166, 1169, 1170, *1175*, *1178*
Barnes, G., 305, *311*
Barnes, G. M., 232, 234, *247*
Barnes, H., 234, *254*, 732, *738*
Barnett, C., 561, *584*
Barnett, C. R., 119, *138*, 561, *582*
Barnett, L. D., 644, *654*
Barnett, R. C., 723, 726, *733*
Barrett, C., 911, 912, 925, 926, *930*
Barrett, C. J., 297, 298, *311*
Barrett, J., 1225, 1243
Barrett-Lennard, G. T., 1042, *1068*
Barry, W. A., 80, *100*, 367, *375*, 1116, 1126, 1129, *1148*, 1250, 1279
Bartko, J., 938, 940, 941, 942, 943, 950, 957
Bartlett, W., 1297, *1309*
Bartolome, F., 729, *735*
Barton, C., 127, *129*, 236, 243, 245, *247*, 996, 1000, 1001, 1076, 1079, 1083, 1091, 1102, 1103, 1228, 1241, 1320, 1321, 1324, 1325, 1327, 1328, 1335, 1336, 1338, 1341, 1342, 1343, 1346, 1375, *1376*
Barton, K., 117, 118, 120, 121, *129*, *131*, 544, *552*

Note: Pages 1–660 are in Volume I; pages 661–1457 are in Volume II. Italic numbers indicate reference citations.

Baruch, D. W., 1063, *1068*
Baruch, G. K., 514, *518*
Barwick, J. M., 505, 506, *518*
Barzun, J., 1288, *1309*
Basham, R. B., 344, *352*, 640, *657*
Baskett, L. M., 593, *615*
Bastiaans, J., 394, *402*
Bates, A., 259, 262, 277, *280*
Bates, A. P., 259, 262, 277, *280*
Bates, E. E., 1387, *1409*
Bates, J., 543, *549*
Bateson, G., 13, 15, 16, 18, 19, 28, 33, 34, *35*, *36*, 53, 57, *71*, 851, 860, *868*, 961, 984, 992, 1001, 1078, 1103, 1136, *1148*, 1251, 1252, 1260, 1282, 1288, 1289, *1309, 1315*
Baucom, D. H., 1044, 1047, 1048, 1051, 1052, 1055, 1059, 1064, 1068, 1071
Bauer, R., 1253, 1258
Bauer, W. D., 902, 905, *929*
Baum, C. G., 974, 984
Bauman, K. E., 432, *434*, 436, 439, 453, *462, 464*
Baumrind, D., 531, 532, 533, *549, 550*
Baurn, F., 644, *654*
Bausano, M., 823, 826, *844*
Baxter, J. C., 1221, 1223, 1241, 1242
Baxter, S., 576, *579*
Bayer, A. E., 324, *352*
Bayley, H., 751, 757, *775*
Bayley, N., 531, *550*
Beach, S. R. H., 1063, 1066, 1068
Beam, L., 476, *493*
Beavers, W. R., 84, 91, 92, 96, *99*, 756, 765, *778*, 793, 805, *808*, 991, *1003*, 1016, 1030, 1226, 1230, 1235, 1238, 1242, 1244, 1270, 1277, 1324, 1327, 1342
Beavin, J. H., 14, 33, *36*, 793, *809*, 992, 1004, 1086, 1106
Bebbington, A. C., 721, *733*
Beck, A. T., 303 n, 311, 992, 1001, 1135, 1137, *1148*
Beck, D., 1256, 1258, 1436
Becker, H., 179, *210*
Becker, J., 965, 984
Becker, M. R., 119, 121, *130*
Becker, W. C., 449, *518*, 542, *550*, 757, 773, 996, *1001*, 1154, *1175*
Beckham, K., 293, 299, *313*
Beckman, L. J., 292, 294, *311*
Beckman, P. J., 751, *774*
Beckwith, L., 526, *551*
Bee, H. L., 1234, 1242
Beeghly, M., 185, *210*

Beels, C. C., 1251, 1273, 1291, 1315
Beels, C. E., 852, *868*
Begun, A., 180, 190, 191, 193, 207, *210, 213*
Behrens, M. I., 940, 948, *955*
Beier, E. G., 1340, 1342
Beisser, A. R., 1035, 1068
Bell, C. S., 595, *615*
Bell, D. C., 230, *247*
Bell, G. C., 1009, 1029
Bell, L. G., 230, *247*
Bell, N., 547, *556*, 1226, *1280*, 1282, *1315*
Bell, N. J., 230, *247*, 595, *621*
Bell, R. Q., 449, *518*, 524, 526, *550*, 600, *615*, 748, 757, 760, *774*, 918, *929*, 991, *1003*
Bell, R. R., 466, *493*
Bell, S. H., 586, 589, *615*
Bell, S. M., 528, 549, 550, 586, 587, 588, *615*
Bellack, A. S., 1064, 1071
Belle, D. E., 546, *550*
Belloti v. *Baird*, 1396, *1409*
Bellugill, 68, *71*
Belmaker, R., 391, *403*
Belsky, J., *523*, 524, 527, 528, 529, 536, 537, 538, 543, 544, 545, 546, 549, *550*, 574, 575, 578, *579*, 588, 603, 605, *616*, 912, 925, *929*
Bene, F., *247*
Benedek, T., 499, 508, 509, *518*
Benegas, J. E., 999, 1004
Beneson, H., 699, *733*
Benett, W. H., 455, *462*
Bengston, V. L., 220, *247*, 309, *311*, 510, 511, 514, *518, 519*
Benigas, J. E., 117, *138*
Benjamin, L. S., 10, *36*
Bennett, I., 232, 233, *247*
Bennie, E. H., 904, 923, 924, *929*
Bensman, J., 155 n, *176*
Benson, T., 633, *658*
Bentovim, A., 1266, 1269, 1275
Bentzen, F., 1153, *1175*
Berardo, F. M., 449, *519*
Berbaum, M. L., 126, *130*
Berenson, B., 1294, *1314*
Berezin, M. A., 192, *210*
Berg, P., *493*, 1110, 1124
Berger, A. M., 900, 901, 902, 904, 913, 914, 915, 925, *929, 933*
Berger, A. S., 436, *464*
Berger, B., 837, *840*
Berger, J., 1291, *1313*

Note: Pages 1–660 are in Volume I; pages 661–1457 are in Volume II. Italic numbers indicate reference citations.

Bolstad, O. D., 974, 976, 979, 980, 981, 982, 985
Bolton, C. D., 262, 264, *280*
Bolton, F. G., 907, *929*
Bond, C. A., 1431, 1433
Bonham, G. S., 647, 648, *654*
Boning, R., 1169, *1175*
Boney, M. B., 231, *241*
Booraem, C. D., 1225, 1242
Booth, A., 466, 483, 487, *493*, 723, 727, 728, *734, 740*
Borduin, C. M., 963, 985
Borgotta, E. F., 432, *434*, 436, *464*
Boriskin, J. A., 916, 917, *931*
Borke, H., 185, *210*
Borkevec, T. D., 1057, 1071
Borman, K. M., 702, *734*
Bornstein, P. H., 1060, 1068
Bosco, A., 309, *311*
Bosco, J., 1155, 1156, 1158, 1159, 1168, 1170, *1177*
Boscolo, C., 991, *1004*, 1105, 1136, 1137, *1150*, 1264, 1269, 1279, 1284, 1286, 1287, 1293, 1301, 1302, *1310, 1315*
Boss, P. O., 1228, 1242
Bossard, J. H. S., 179, 196, 198, 200, *210*
Bostrom, A., 639, 640, *657*
Boszormenyi-Nagy, I., 62, *71*, 75, 93, 96, *99*, 308, *311*, 408, *423*, 507, *519*, 904, 924, *929*, 1008, 1029, 1229, 1236, 1242, 1258
Bothwell, J., 1136, *1149*
Bott, E., 166, *172*, 277, *280*, 562, *579*, 744, *774*, 847, *868*
Botwinick, J., 302, 303, *312*
Boulding, E., 733, *734*
Bousha, D. M., 902, 919, 921, *929*
Bousswain, J., 271, *280*
Bowen, M., 13, *35*, 159, *172*, 240, *248*, 414, *423*, 743, 756, *774*, 793, *807*, 1078, 1103, 1157, *1175*, 1293, *1310*
Bower, K. S., 1427, 1433
Bowerman, C. E., 185, *210*
Bowlby, J., 113, *130*, 186, 187, 210, 336, 431, 434, 467, 486, *493*, 561, *579*, 588, *616*, 1109, 1114, 1118, 1124, 1231, 1232, 1242
Bowman, P. J., 687, *696*
Boyack, V. L., 309, *311*
Boylton, M., 1300, *1310*
Bradley, C. F., 562, *579*
Bradley, F., 1285, *1311*
Bradley, R., 526, *551, 552*, 1285, *1314*
Bradlyn, D., 1166, *1178*
Bradshaw, R. V., 791, *807*

Brady, C., 548, *556*
Brady, E. M., 192, *231*
Braiker, H. B., 1116, 1124
Brakarsh, D., 232, *248*
Branch, J. D., 691, *696*
Brandsma, J., 1136, *1149*
Brannigan, G. G., 447, 454, *463*
Brassard, J., 546, *551*
Brassard, M. R., *841*
Braucht, G. N., 232, 233, *248*
Brazelton, T. B., 596, 597, 608, 616, 621, 622
Breedlove, J., 117, 118, *135*
Brehony, K., 1166, *1178*
Breitenbucher, M., 917, 925, 926, 930
Bretherton, I., 185, *210*
Breunlin, D. C., 1078, 1103, 1267, *1269*
Brewster, F., 1298, 1303,*1304, *1315*
Brien, D., 569, *570, 579*
Bright, T. P., 546, *549*, 625, 629, *654*
Brim, O., 160, *171*
Bristol, M., 156, *172*, 749, 751, 752, 757, 761, 768, 771, *774*
Britt, B. C., 477, *494*
Brock, G., 1193, 1194, *1210*
Brock, T. C., 908, *929*
Brockhaus, J. P. D., 648, *654*
Brockhaus, R. H., 648, *654*
Broderick, C. B., 259, 261, *280*
Broderick, J. E., 1062, 1063, 1068, 1069
Brodsky, A. M., 1328, 1342
Brodsley, S. L., 1408, *1409*
Brody, E., 860, *868*
Brody, E. M., 285, 292, 295, 300, 310, *312, 315*
Brody, G. H., 593, 594, *621*, 760, 761, 764, 773, *774*, 1345, 1356, *1378*
Broedel, J., 415, *424*
Brokowski, A., 1264, 1277
Brolchain, M., 414, 415, *423, 424*
Bromberg, E. M., 293, 294, *312*
Bromley, D. G., 234, 248
Bronfenbrenner, U., 54, 63, *72*, 157, 160, 163, *172*, 219, 241, *246*, 546, 547, *551*, 587, 588, *616, 695*, 861, *868*
Bronfenbrenner, V., 699, *734*
Bronner, A., 231, *251*
Bronzaft, A. L., 783, *808*
Brooks-Gunn, J., 601, *616*
Brophy, K. M., 1397, *1409*
Broscart, K. R., 718, *734*
Broskowski,˙ H., 306, *313*
Brotherson, M. J., 742, 746, 762, 771, 773, 779, 780
Brown, A. H., 111, *130*

Note: Pages 1–660 are in Volume I; pages 661–1457 are in Volume II. Italic numbers indicate reference citations.

Note: Pages 1–660 are in Volume I; pages 661–1457 are in Volume II. Italic numbers indicate reference citations.

Note: Pages 1–660 are in Volume I; pages 661–1457 are in Volume II. Italic numbers indicate reference citations.

Cleary, E. W., 1389, *1409*
Cleary, P. D., 562, *581*
Cleghorn, J., 1286, 1291, 1292, 1298, 1299, *1310*
Cleveland, D., 762, 763, *775*
Cleveland, M., 643, *658*
Cleveland, S. E., 1222, 1243
Clifford, W. B., 636, *654*
Cline, V. B., 1325, 1336, 1342
Clinebell, C., 405, *423*
Clinebell, H., 405, *423*
Clingempeel, W. G., 123, *130*, 1402, *1409*
Clore, G. L., 362
Cobb, J. A., 970, 974, 986, 987, 1355, *1378*
Cobb, S., 163, 258, *280*, 343, 350, *352*, 700, *735*
Cobliner, W. G., 627, 629, *654*
Cochran, M., 546, *551*
Cochrane, C., 1259, 1279
Coddington, R. D., 626, *654*
Coffins, P., 813, *841*
Cohen, B. H., 755, *779*
Cohen, C., 852, *868*
Cohen, D., 299, *313*
Cohen, F., 700, 701, 702, 720, *734*
Cohen, J., 821, 822, 823, 827, 828, 830, 834, *841*, *842*, 980, 984, 1021, 1022, 1024, 1025, 1026, 1029
Cohen, L. T., 589, *616*
Cohen, M. B., 1135, 1139, *1149*
Cohen, M. I., 904, 910, 916, *930*
Cohen, M. W., 1207, *1310*
Cohen, R. A., 1135, 1139, *1149*
Cohen, R. S., 980, 984
Cohen, S. E., 526, *551*
Cohen, S. L., 856, *869*
Cohen, S. P., 88, *99*
Cohen, S. Z., 286, 297, 312
Cohler, B. J., 84, 86, *99*, 299, 300, *312*, 372, *374*, 864, *870*, 1236, 1237, 1242
Cohn, P. M., 437, 439, 448, 455, *463*
Cohn, R. M., 567, *579*
Coho, A., 342, *352*
Coie, J. D., 576, *579*
Coie, L., 576, *579*
Colapinto, J., 1263
Colarusso, C. A., 786, *807*
Cole, A. L., 472, *493*, 494
Cole, C. M., 467, *493*, 1119, 1120, 1125
Cole, J. O., 1128, *1149*, 1325, 1336, 1342
Cole, R. E., 538, *549*
Cole, S. P., 569, 572, *581*
Coleman, J., 225, 240, 246, *248*, 511, *519*
Coleman, K. H., 887, 893, *897*
Coleman, M., 120, *130*

Coles, R., 822, *841*
Colletta, N. C., 279, *280*, 538, *551*
Colletti, G., 762, *775*
Collins, A. M., 1328, 1342
Collins, J., 288, *319*, 1130, *1149*, 1203, *1210*
Collmer, C., 536, 538, 549, *554*
Collmer, C. W., 900, 903, 904, 924, 925, *934*
Colman, L., 637, 639, *654*
Combrink-Graham, L., 167, 168, *172*
Comly, H., 1156, *1176*
Condran, J. G., 703, 714, *734*
Cone, J. D., 971, 974, 985
Conger, J. J., x, xi, xii, 218, 224, 226, 229, 239, *248*, 254, 449, *521*
Conger, R. D., 911, 918, 919, 925, 926, *930*
Conger, R. E., 996, 1003, 1346, 1355, 1356, *1378*
Connell, M. J., 1391, *1410*
Connolly, P. R., 1223, 1241
Connors, C., 1164, 1165, *1175*
Connors, K., 563, *579*
Conrad, P., 1155, 1158, 1175
Conrad, W., 1156, *1175*
Consensus Development Conference, 562, *571*
Constantine, J., *359*, *374*
Constantine, J. A., 1078, 1103, 1269, *1274*
Constantine, L., 359, *374*, 1285, 1287, 1288, 1293, *1310*
Conway, D., 119, *135*
Cook, J. J., 757, *775*
Cook, N., 548, *556*
Cook, T. D., 1081, 1099, 1103
Cookerly, J. R., 1056, 1069
Coombs, R., 259, 277, *280*
Cooper, A., 1250, 1268
Cooper, K. J., 864, *868*
Coopersmith, S., 533, *551*
Cope, D. R., 641, *654*
Copitch, D., 920, *936*
Corea, G., 560, *579*
Corigliano, A., 1161, *1175*
Cormican, E. J., 285, 301, *312*
Cornblatt, B., 865, *869*
Cornelison, A., 13, *36*
Cornelison, A. R., 852, *872*, 1080, 1105
Corrales, R. G., 755, 765, 773, *775*
Corter, C., 190, *210*
Coser, R. L., 731, *734*
Costa, L. A., 1196, *1210*
Cotter, P. R., 292, 294, *313*
Cottrell, L. S., 19, *35*
Coufal, J., 1192, 1193, 1194, *1210*, *1212*

Note: Pages 1–660 are in Volume I; pages 661–1457 are in Volume II. Italic numbers indicate reference citations.

Council on Battered Women, 892, *897*
Coutts, R., 405, *423*
Covis, L., 861, *868*
Covitz, F., 526, *556*
Cowan, C. P., 576, *579*
Cowan, P. A., 576, *579*
Cox, D. N., 652, *658*
Cox, M., 1262, 1276, 1402, *1410*
Cox, R., 1262, 1276, 1402, *1410*
Coyne, J. C., 1137, 1138, *1149, 1150*
Cozby, P., 418, *423*
Cozby, P. C., 349
Craig, R. R., 95, *99*
Crandall, V. J., 531, *551*
Crane, D. R., 117, *133*, 923, *930*
Crane, R., 1303, *1313*
Crawford, A. G., 629, *655*
Crawford, L., 647, *657*
Crawford, M., 277, *280*, 623
Creson, D. L., 1119, 1120, 1125
Cresse, D., 234, 245, *256*
Crichton, L., 906, *930*
Crisci, R., 120, *130*
Crits-Cristoph, P., 726, *738*
Crnic, R. A., 344, *352*
Crockenberg, S., 191, 207, *210*
Crockenberg, S. B., 345, *352*, 528, *552*
Croghan, N., 563, *579*
Cromwell, R. E., 242, *248*, 967, 984, 989,
    997, 1001, 1266, 1267, 1268, 1269
Cronbach, L. J., 11, *36*, 1090, 1103
Cronbach, L. S., 971, 984
Cronen, V., 1283, 1284, *1314*
Croog, S. H., 324, 340, *352*
Croske, J. W., 832, *841*
Cross, H. J., 119, 121, *130*, 444, 445, 448,
    458, 459, *462, 463*
Crouch, R. E., 1404, *1410*
Crouter, A. C., 546, 547, *551, 552*
Crowe, J. C., 339, *353*
Crowe, M. J., 1040, 1041, 1042, 1043, 1055,
    1056, 1057, 1063, 1069
Cruickshank, W., 1153, *1175*
Csikszentmihalyi, M., 95, *99*, 217, *248*,
    270, *281*, 358, 368, *374*
Cuber, J., 21, *35*
Cuber, J. F., 470, 471, 473, 475, 481, 482,
    494
Cuisenier, J., 146, *172*
Cumming, E., 296, 297, *312*
Cummings, S. T., 751, 757, 758, *775*
Cunningham, J., 413, *423*
Cunningham, M., 413, *426*
Cunningham, M. R., 1226, 1229 n, 1245
Cunningham, O. E., 759, 761, *775*

Curtis, J., 1436
Curtis, J. L., 572, *579*
Cushman, D. P., 95, *99*
Cutrona, C. E., 345, *353*
Cvetkovich, G., 627, *654*
Czyba, J. C., 652, *654*

D

Dabbs, J. M., 1223, 1224, 1241
Dahms, A., 405, *423*
Dallas, M., 1059, 1070
Dalton, M. J., 189, *213*
Dame, N. G., 626, *654*
Dammann, C., 240 n, *249*, 1296, 1298,
    1300, 1302, *1309*
Dan, A. M., 506, *519*
Dancy, B. L., 232, *249*
Daniel, J. H., 925, *930*
Daniels, J., 234, *255*
Daniels, L. R., 110, *130*
Daniels, P., 636, 638, 639, *655*
Dannefer, E., 166, *173*
Darling, R., 749, *750,* 752, 768, 769, 771,
    775
Darrow, C., 77, *174*
Darrow, C. N., 449, *520*
D'Ary, E., 754, *775*
Dasen, P. R., 866, *868*
Dasser, D. A., 386, *401*
Datan, N., 160, 163, *172*
Datta, L. E., 784, 807
D'Augelli, A. R., 458, 459, *462*, 1206, *1210*
D'Augelli, J. F., 444, 445, 448, 458, 459,
    462
D'Aulaine, E., 144 n, *172*
D'Aulaine, I., 144 n, *172*
Davey, A. J., 334, *353*
David, A., 652, *655*
David, H. P., 860, *868*
Davidson, J. L., 294, *312*
Davidson, S. M., 563, *585*
Davidson, T., 877, 884, 887, 889, *897*
Davidson, W. B., 292, *313*
Davis, D., 117, 119, *130*
Davis, D. M., 861, *868*
Davis, D. R., 767, *775*
Davis, J., 419, *423*
Davis, K. E., 104, 116, 117, 119, *130, 133,*
    261, 275, *280*
Davis, L. G., 1436
Davis, M., 411, 412, *423*
Davis, S. A., *493*
Day, D., 225, *251*
Day, J., 18, *37*

Note: Pages 1–660 are in Volume I; pages 661–1457 are in Volume II. Italic numbers indicate reference citations.

Note: Pages 1–660 are in Volume I; pages 661–1457 are in Volume II. Italic numbers indicate reference citations.

Erickson, P. E., 339, *353*
Ericson, P. M., 911 n, 1002
Eriksen, J., 166, *173*
Erikson, E., 149, 157, 159, 160, 161, 162,
    166, 167, *172*, 406, 407, *424*, 528, 529,
    533, 534, *552*
Erikson, E. H., 75, 79, 80, *99*, 219, 231,
    238, *249*, 359, 360, *374*
Erkut, S., 716, 717, *735*
Erlanger, H. S., 925, *931*
Erlenmeyer-Kimling, L., 865, *869*
Ernst, C., 126, *131*, 305, *311*
Eron, L. D., 912, *933*
Eskew, R., 84, *101*, 366, *376*
Essman, C. S., 203, *211*
Evans, E. M., 908, 914, 920, 927, *930*
Evans, L., 287, *320*
Evans, P. A. L., 729, *735*
Evans, R. R., 432, *434*, 436, *464*
Everett, B. A., 1402, *1411*
Everett, C., 1298, *1311*
Everett, C. A., 244, *249*
Eyberg, S. M., 962, 985, 1346, 1367, *1376*
Eynon, S., 652, *677*
Eysenck, H. J., 433, *434*, 435, *462*, 477,
    494

F

Fagan, J., 1109, 1125, 1258, *1274*
Fagot, B. I., 541, *552*, 595, *616*
Faheem, A. D., 848, *869*
Faigel, H. C., 628, *655*
Falbo, T., 326, *353*
Falicov, C., 1078, 1103, 1269, 1274, 1291,
    1292, 1297, 1298, *1311*
Faling, V., 367, *374*
Falloon, I., 1261, 1274
Fandetti, D. V., 857, *868*
Faranoff, A., 916, *931*
Farber, A., 538, *552*
Farber, B., 745, 750, 751, 753, 754, 755,
    756, 763, 767, *775*
Farberow, N. L., 1035, 1071
Farel, A. N., 547, *552*
Farkas, G., 703, 705, *735*
Farley, F. A., 415, *494*
Farley, J., 415, *424*
Farley, J. E., 1226, 1229 n, 1242
Farr, L., 1240, 1244
Farrelly, F., 1136, *1149*
Farrington, D. P., 1348, 1349, 1350, *1379*
Farris, J. A., 372, *376*
Fast, I., 415, *424*
Fasteau, M., 421, *424*

Faulk, M., 887, *897*
Faulstich, G., 761, *780*
Faunce, E. E., 124, *137*, 589, *621*, 966,
    978, 987
Faunce, E. F., 852, *873*
Favazza, A. R., 848, *869*
Fawcett, J. T., 506, *519*, 569, *580*
Feather, N. T., 225, 227, *249*
Fedele, N., 612, *616*
Feffer, M., 229, 234, *249*
Feigelman, W., 649, 650, *658*
Fein, R. A., 342, *353*, 573, 574, *580*
Feingold, B. F., 1153, *1175*
Feiring, C., 601, 602, *616*, *619*, 849, *869*
Fejer, D., 233, 236, *255*
Feld, T., 1256, 1275
Feldman, H., 569, 574, 575, 577, 578, *580*,
    582
Feldman, H. A., 566, *580*, 644, *655*
Feldman, L., 416, 417, *424*
Feldman, L. B., 388, *401*, 1132, 1133, 1134,
    1143, *1149*, 1237, 1242
Feldman, M., 566, *580*
Feldman, S. S., 589, *616*
Feldman-Rotman, S., 197, *213*
Felker, D. W., 174, *214*
Ferber, A., 1228, 1242, 1251, 1273, 1291,
    1292, 1300, 1301, 1302, *1311*, *1313*
Ferber, H., 1346, 1367, *1376*
Ferber, M., 731, *735*
Ferguson, C. R., 1286, 1293, *1311*
Fergusson, L., 965, 986
Fernandez Pol, B., 859, *869*
Ferndeg, P., 758, *777*
Fernell, D., 1277, *1278*, 1291, 1295, *1314*
Ferraresc, M., 866, *870*
Ferree, M. M., 725, 726
Ferreira, A., 249, *250*, *257*
Ferriera, A. J., 969, 978, 985, 993, 1002,
    1166, *1175*, 1263, 1280
Feshbach, N., 905, *931*
Feshbach, N. D., 389, *403*, 533, 552
Feshbach, S., 533, *552*, 905, *931*
Feshback, S., 34, 35
Festinger, L., 124, *131*
Fetterman, D., 1264, 1274
Ficher, I. V., 474, 489, 492, *494*
Field, T., 595, *616*, *617*, 1419, 1433
Field, T. M., 562, 563, *580*
Fields, J. D., 716, 717, *735*
Fielgelman, W., 649, 650, *658*
Figley, C., 1189, *1211*
Fillenbaum, G. G., 286, *317*
Fincham, F., 128, *131*, 1046, 1061, 1071
Finck, C. H., 616, *654*

Note: Pages 1–660 are in Volume I; pages 661–1457 are in Volume II. Italic numbers indicate reference citations.

Frazier, E. F., 665, 666, 667, 671, 672, 674, 675, 676, 677, 678, 679, 680, 682, 694, *695*
Frazier, S. H., 1128, *1149*
Fredericksen, N., 927, *931*
Freed, D. J., 1390, 1391, 1392, 1393, 1399, 1400, 1403, 1404, *1410*
Freedman, D., 572, *584*
Freeman, T., 572, *580*
Freeston, B. M., 753, *776*
Freiderich, W. L., 750, 754, *776*
French, J. R. P., 700, *735*
Frenkel-Brunswick, E., 448, *462*
Frenken, J., 1041, 1069
Freud, A., 185, *210*, 219, 238, *250*, 1230, 1243, 1398, 1402, *1410*
Freud, S., 8, 54, 72, 80, 154, 467, *493*, 524, 847, 850, 851, *869*
Freud, S. A., 533, *552*
Frey, J., 387, *402*, 415, 417, 418, 419, *424*, *425*
Frey, J., III, 1424, 1434
Fried, M., 862, *869*
Fried, M. H., 153, *173*
Fried, M. N., 153, *173*
Friedeman, J. S., 289, *313*
Friedenberg, E., 157, 160, *173*
Friederich, W. N., 750, 751, 754, *776*, 916, 917, *937*
Friedlander, S., 75, *99*, 360, 361, *374*
Friedman, A. S., 1134, 1136, *1149*
Friedman, E., 150, *173*
Friedman, E. H., 215, 216, *250*
Friedman, H., *395*, 401, *402*
Friedman, J., 414, *424*
Friedman, L. C., 379, *404*
Friedman, S. B., 904, 917, 921, 922, 931, *933*
Friest, W. P., 1187, *1214*
Frieze, I. H., 103, 111, *139*, 449, *519*
Friis, H., 294, *318*
Frodi, A. M., 598, *619*, 905, 916, 920, *929*, *931*
Frodi, M., 598, *619*
Fromm, E., 188, *212*, 407, 417, *424*
Frommer, E., 539, *552*
Fromm-Reichmann, F., 17, *35*, 961, 985, 1135, 1139, *1149*
Fruchtman, L. A., 885, *898*
Fulcomer, M. C., 310, *312*
Fulmer, R. H., 244, *250*
Fulton, W., 650, *659*
Furlong, M. J., 510, *519*
Furniss, T., 1266, 1269, 1275

Furstenberg, F. F., 816, *842*
Furstenberg, F. F., Jr., 183, *212*, 568, 580

G

Gabrielson, P., 1363, *1377*
Gadlin, H., 289, *312*, 405, *424*
Gaensbauer, T. J., 917, *931*
Gagnon, J. H., 436, *464*
Gaind, R., 401, *402*
Gaines, R., 902, 904, 907, 910, 916, 923, 924, *931*
Gaines, T., 1291, *1315*
Galbraith, R. C., 126, *132*
Galdston, R., 904, 907, 908, 918, 923, *931*
Galinsky, E., 153, *173*
Gallagher, B. J., 511, *519*
Gallagher, D. E., 303, *313*
Gallagher, J., 156, *172*, 749, 952, 757, 761, 771, *774*
Gallant, D., 864, *870*
Galligan, R. J., 1074, 1104
Gallimore, R., 204, *214*
Gallope, R. A., 1009, 1015, 1016, 1029
Ganahl, G. F., 1198, 1211, 1250, 1270, 1271, 1275
Ganong, L., 120, *130*
Gans, B. M., 286, 297, *312*
Gantman, C., 236, *250*
Garbarino, J., 901, 925, 926, *931*
Gardner, R. A., 1401, 1402, *1410*
Garduque, L., 533, *555*
Garfield, R., 1291, *1311*
Garfield, S., 1295, *1311*, 1340, *1342*
Garland, T. N., 716, 717, 718, 731, *738*
Garlington, W., 1257, 1274
Garmezy, N., 851, 864, 865, 866, *869*, *870*
Garner, A., 759, *780*
Garooglan, A., 1437
Garrigan, J., 1269, *1275*, 1291, 1292, 1293, 1298, *1311*
Garrison, H. H., 702, 716, *737*
Garrison, V., 853, *870*
Garvey, C. S., 839, *842*
Gassner, S., 1260, 1275
Gath, A., 754, 755, 762, 763, *776*
Gatz, M., 11, *37*
Gear, G., 782, *807*
Geeds, V., 94, *99*
Geerken, M. R., 572, *581*
Geiser, R. L., 902, *931*
Geiss, S. K., 1048, 1069
Gelfand, D. E., 292, 294, *313*
Gelfand, D. L., 857, *869*, 1082, *1104*
Geller, J. D., 75, *99*, 360, 361, *374*

Note: Pages 1–660 are in Volume I; pages 661–1457 are in Volume II. Italic numbers indicate reference citations.

Gelles, R. J., 324, *353*, 878, 881, 882, *897*, 901, 903, 904, 907, 910, 913, 914, 923, 924, 925, 926, *931, 932*, 1387, *1412*
Genovese, R. J., 1195, *1211*
George, C., 917, *932*
George, L. K., 286, 294, 297, 298 n, 299, *313, 317*
George, R., 511, *519*
Gerard, D. L., 851, *870*
Gergen, K. J., 112, 115, *131, 132*
Gershenson, C., 816, *842*
Gersick, K. E., 539, *552*
Gerson, F. F., 568, *580*
Gerstel, N. R., 729, 730, *735*
Gersten, J. C., 860, *871*
Gerth, H., 157, *173*
Geschwender, J. A., *211*
Gevitz, J. L., 1231, 1243
Gewirtz, J. L., 187, *212*
Geyer, S., 1236, 1237, 1242
Gibaud-Wallston, R. B., 548, *552*
Gibbons, L. K., 562, *580*
Giblin, P. R., 1028, 1029
Gibson, C., 645, *655*
Gibson, D. M., 975, 984
Gibson, G., 332, 338, *353*
Gibson, W. F., 1225, 1243
Giddings, C. W., 893, *897*, 995, 996 n, 997, 998, 1001
Gideonse, S., 702, *734*
Giele, J. Z., 75, 94, *99*
Gil, D. G., 901, 904, 907, 910, 911, 920, 922, 925, 927, *932*
Gilbert, L. A., 502, *519*, 639, *656*, 718, 722, 723, 731, *734*, 735
Gilbert, R., 978, 980, *985*
Gilbert, S., 416, *424*
Gilbert, S. J., 366, *374*
Gilchrist, L. D., 629, *658*
Giles-Sims, J., 895, *897*
Gilligan, C., 165, *173*, 221, 229, *250*
Gillon, J. W., 629, *657*
Gilmore, J. V., 1255, *1275*
Gilmore, S. K., 1357, *1379*
Gilner, F. H., 386, *404*
Gilstrap, B., 544, *550*
Gilutz, G., 197, *213*
Gilstrap, B., 603, *616*
Ginsberg, B. G., 1192, 1206, *1211*
Ginsberg, L., 160, 163, *172*
Giordano, G. O., 853, *870*
Giordano, J., 853, 857, *870*
Giordano, J. A., 300, 304, 308, 309, *311, 313, 314*

Giordano, N. H., 299, 300, 304, 305, 308, 309, *313, 314*
Gist, N. F., 561, *582*
Glaser, R., 941, *956*
Glass, G. V., 1038, 1039, *1069*, 1099, *1104*
Glass, J., 571, *580*
Glass, S. P., 466, *493*
Glasser, L. N., 294, *313*
Glasser, N., 1035, *1068*
Glasser, P., 360, 371, *374*
Glasser, P. H., 294, *314*
Glatt, M. M., 305, *318*
Glazer, N., 506, *519*
Gleason, J. B., 590, 591, *617, 620*
Glenn, N. D., 292, *314*, 326, 328, 330, *353*, 432, *434*, 439, 451, 455, *462*
Gleser, G. C., 971, *984*, 1090, *1103*
Glick, I. D., *1437*
Glick, I. O., 298, *314*
Glick, J., 1155, 1159, 1173, *1177*
Glick, M., 1422, 1434
Glick, P. C., 94, *99*, 165, *173, 314*, 324, *354*, 1056, 1072
Glick, P. G., 687, *695*, 810, *842*, 1035, 1069
Globetti, G., 455, *462*
Gluck, N., 166, *173*
Glueck, E., 231, 232, 233, 244, *250*
Glueck, S., 231, 232, 233, *250*
Glynn, S., 1192, *1212*
Glynn, T. J., 232, *250*
Goda, D. F., 651, *655*
Goddard, H. C., 146, *173*
Goddard, H. H., 782, *807*
Goetz, K. M., 884, 894, *899*
Goff, J. A., 860, *871*
Goffman, I., 741, 767, *776*
Gofseyeff, M. H., 588, 607, 610, *617*
Goglia, L., 1025, 1029
Goldberg, E. M., 391, *401*
Goldberg, H., 421, *424*, 884, 887, 894, 895, *897*, 1290, *1311*
Goldberg, I., 1290, *1311*
Goldberg, S., 527, *554*
Goldberg, W., 509, *521*
Golden, M., 997, 1004
Golden, R. P., 1009, 1013, 1015, 1016, 1029
Golden, S., 703, *736*
Goldenberg, H., 1336, 1342
Goldenberg, I., 1291, 1301, 1302, *1315*, 1336, 1342
Goldfarb, J. L., 629, *655*
Golding, E. R., 611, *617*
Golding, S. L., 166, *134*
Goldman, A., 626, *654*
Goldsmith, J., 1237, 1243

Note: Pages 1–660 are in Volume I; pages 661–1457 are in Volume II. Italic numbers indicate reference citations.

Note: Pages 1–660 are in Volume I; pages 661–1457 are in Volume II. Italic numbers indicate reference citations.

Note: Pages 1–660 are in Volume I; pages 661–1457 are in Volume II. Italic
numbers indicate reference citations.

Harrell, J. E., 995, *1003*, 1187, 1204, 1207, *1212, 1214, 1215*
Harriman, L. C., 572, 575, *581*
Harrington, D. M., 544, *550*
Harris, D., 159 n
Harris, G., 548, *556*
Harris, I. D., 507, 508, 514, *519*
Harris, L., 285, 309, *314*
Harris, M., 164, *174*
Harris, S., 533, *554*
Harris, S. L., 761, 762, *775*
Harris, T., 414, *423*, 539, *551*, 861, *870*, 926, *929*, 1143, *1149*
Harrison, A. O., *735*
Harrison, D., 419, *425*
Harrison, D. E., 455, *462*
Harter, S., 1420, 1433
Hartik, L. M., 884, *897*
Hartman, A. A., 572, *581*
Hartman, L. M., 1112, 1113, 1125
Hartmann, D. P., 980, 985, 1038, 1039, 1072, 1082
Hartnett, J. J., 1225, 1243
Hartup, W., 42, *72*
Hartup, W. W., 179, 187, *212*
Harvey, C. D., 117, 118, *129*
Harvey, D., 1263, 1278
Harvey, G. H., 215, *251*
Harvey, J. H., 104, 106, 128, *130,* 1109, 1126
Harvey, O. J., 1022, 1029
Harvey, R. B., 1118, 1125
Hassan, S., 941, 942, *956*
Hastings, D. W., 641, *656*
Hastings, J., 1165, *1175*
Hatfield, E., 108, 109, 110, 111, *132,* 370, *376,* 411, 412, 416, *424, 426*
Hauenstein, L. S., 728, *736*
Havighurst, R. J., 285, *317,* 811, *842*
Hawes, L. C., 1092, 1104
Hawkins, J. L., 388, *402*
Hawkins, N., 1345, 1355, 1356, *1378*
Hawkins, R. P., 1345, 1355, *1377*
Hay, R. A., 1099, 1101, 1105
Hayes, R. F., 783, *808*
Haynes-Clements, L. A., 1187, 1207, *1215*
Hays, W. C., 1088, 1090, 1091, 1092, 1104
Hazzard, A., 971, 972, 973, 974, 984, 996, 1002
Healy, W., 231, *251*
Heath, A., 1297, 1300, 1301, 1302
Heath, D. H., 471, 474, 478, 479, *494,* 538, 547, *553*
Heaton, C., 589, *622*
Hechtman, L., 1169, *1176*

Hediger, H., 1222, 1243
Hegrenes, J., 758, *778*
Heider, F., 104, *133,* 261
Heilbrun, A. B., 850, 852, *870*
Heilman, A. E., 751, *777*
Heiman, J., 476, 482, *494,* 1108, 1119, 1125
Heinecke, C. M., 538, *553*
Heinrich, A., 1301, *1314*
Heisenberg, W., 20, *35*
Heiss, J., 419, *424*
Helfer, R. E., 908, 910, 911, 924, 925, *932*
Heller, J., 40, 43, 47, 53, 55, 56, 58, 64, 65, 66, 67, 69, *71, 72*
Helmersen, P., 1424, 1433
Henderson, D. J., 902, *932*
Henderson, S., 864, *870*
Hendrick, C., 127, 129, *133*
Hendrick, S. S., 117, 118, *133*
Hendricks, C. D., 284, 289, *314*
Hendricks, J., 284, 289, *314*
Hendricks, L. E., 626, *656*
Henggeler, S. W., 220, 221, 223, 226, 241 n, *251,* 963, 985
Henker, B., 1155, *1178*
Henley, H. C., 889, *898*
Henley, J. R., Jr., 644, *656*
Hennessey, E. F., 1387, *1410*
Henry, J., 1219, 1243
Henry, W., 296, 297, *312*
Herceg-Baron, R. L., 1130, 1134, *1150*
Herjanic, B. L., 233, *255*
Herman, B., 941, 953, *956*
Herman, J. B., 722, *736*
Herold, E. S., 442, 444, 450, 452, 455, 456, 459, *462*
Herrenkohl, E. C., 916, 922, *932*
Hersch, P. D., 447, *462*
Hershenberg, B., 1206, *1210*
Herskovits, M. J., 674, 683, *696*
Herson, J. H., 860, *871*
Hertel, R. K., 80, 100, 367, *375,* 1116, 1126, 1250, 1279
Hertz, D. G., 628, *656*
Hertzig, M. E., 1234, 1243
Herzberger, S. D., 915, *932*
Herzog, C., 813, *842*
Herzog, E., 233, *251*
Heshka, S., 1223, 1224, 1243
Heslin, R., 1220, 1243
Hess, B. B., 288, 292, 310, *314*
Hess, D. W., 627, *655*
Hess, R. D., 562, *581,* 860, *870,* 1225, 1226, 1243
Hesse, S. J., 698, *736*

Note: Pages 1–660 are in Volume I; pages 661–1457 are in Volume II. Italic numbers indicate reference citations.

Note: Pages 1–660 are in Volume I; pages 661–1457 are in Volume II. Italic numbers indicate reference citations.

Horall, B. M., 787, *808*
Horn, D., 1251, 1267, 1291, *1310*
Horn, J. M., 120, *135*
Hornung, C. A., 725, *736*
Horowitz, M. J., 303 n, *314*, 1222, 1225, 1243
Horst, L., 594, *619*
Horst, P., 474, *494*
Horton, P. J., 594, *619*
Hosford, R., 1263, 1264, 1276, 1288, 1294, *1312*
Houghton, P., 645, *656*
House, A. E., 1354, *1379*
House, J. S., 325, 344, *354*
Houseknecht, S. K., 641, 644, *656*, 728, *736*
Hovestadt, A., 1271, *1278*, 1291, 1295, *1314, 1316*
Howard, A., 232, *253*
Howard, J., 97, *99*, 357, 359, *374, 777*
Howard, K. I., 238, *254*
Howells, J. G., 850, 853, *871*
Howells, J. J., 1231, 1243, 1441
Howenstine, R. A., 75, *99*, 360, 361, *374*
Hoyer, W. J., 286, *314*
Hsu, J., 221, *254*
Hubbard, R. W., 305, *315*
Huber, J., 713, 731, *735, 736*
Hubert, J., 570, *581*
Hudgins, W., 233, *252*
Huesmann, L. R., 108, 114, 115, *133, 135*, 302, *374*
Huges, S., 168, *174*
Hughes, M. C., 1422, 1433
Hughes, S. F., 740, 745, *777*
Hughsten, C. A., 307, *315*
Humphrey, M., 647, *656*
Hunt, D. E., 1022, 1023, 1029
Hunt, D. G., 233, *252*
Hunt, J., 526, *556*
Hunt, J. G., 727, *736*
Hunt, L. L., 727, *736*
Hunt, M., 483, 484, 489, *494*
Hunter, R. S., 904, 908, 910, 912, 916, 923, 924, *932*
Hunter, W. W., 309, *315*
Huntington, D. S., 1233, 1243
Hurley, D. J., 688, *696*
Hurley, J. R., 904, *933*
Hurvitz, N., 1258, 1276
Huser, W. R., 723, *736*
Huston, T. L., 107, 111, 112, 113, 116, 128, *133, 134, 135*, 179, *212*, 258, 266, 270, 272, 276, *281, 282*, 1109, 1126
Hutton, S. P., 1020, 1021, 1024, 1029
Huygen, F., 1250, 1276

Hwang, C-P, 598, *619*
Hyde, J. S., 289, *315*
Hyer, W. J., 286, *314*
Hyman, C. A., 918, *932*
Hyman, H. K., 297, 301, *318*

I

Ickes, W. J., 104, *132*
Idol-Maestas, L., 1156, *1176*
Ihinger, M., 179, 181, 182, 183, 191, 203, 206, 207, *212*
Iizuka, R., 652, *656*
Inazu, J. K., 122, 123, *131*
Ingham, M., 589, *616*
Insel, J., 1156, *1175*
Inselberg, R. M., 625, *656*
Irving, H. H., 333, *354, 1410*
Itil, T. M., 863, *871*
Ivey, A., 1292, 1294, *1311*
Iwakani, E., 965, 984

J

Jablonsky, A., 864, *874*
Jacklin, C. M., 513, *521*
Jacklin, C. N., 1233, 1234, 1244
Jackson, D., 961, 984, 1078, 1086, 1103, 1106, 1251, 1260, 1265, 1276, 1318, 1342
Jackson, D. D., 12, 13, 14, 18, 19, 33, *35, 36*, 111, 122, *133, 134*, 473, 474, 476, 488, 494, 793, *809*, 992, 1104, 1117, 1125, 1136, 1148, 1236, 1245
Jackson, E., 1040, 1042, 1043, 1050, 1052, 1053, 1059, 1069
Jackson, J. A., 122, *133*
Jackson, J. S., 684, 687, *696*
Jackson, R., 759, *780*
Jacob, T., 123, *132*, 223, 225, 231, 239, 243, *252, 257*, 589, 594, *617*, 852, *871*, 939, 956, 961, 964, 971, 978, 985, 1276
Jacobsen, R. B., 730, *737*
Jacobson, N. S., 995, 1002, 1045, 1053, 1057, 1059, 1061, 1064, 1065, 1070, 1187, 1212
Jacobson, R., 987, 995
Jacobstein, J. M., 1381, 1382, *1410*
Jacoby, A. P., 569, *581*
Jaffe, D., 360, *374*
Jaffe, D. T., 823, *842*, 1129, 1148
James, W. H., 470, 471, 475, 481, *493*
Jameson, J. D., 860, *871*
Jamison, P. H., 643, *656*
Janoff-Bulman, R., 106, *135*

Note: Pages 1–660 are in Volume I; pages 661–1457 are in Volume II. Italic numbers indicate reference citations.

Jarvik, L. F., 303, *315*
Jedlicka, D., 432, *434, 436*, 438, *464*
Jeffries, V., 548, *555*
Jellison, J., 1422, 1433
Jenkins, R. L., 232, *252*
Jenne, W., 763, *775*
Jensen, G. O., 229, *247*
Jerdee, T. H., 720, *739*
Jessee, E., 415, *424, 425*
Jessee, E. H., 1023, 1024, 1029, 1128, 1137, 1143, 1146, 1149, 1291, 1292, 1295
Jesser, C. J., 454, *463*
Jessop, D. J., 223, *252*
Jessop, D. L., 510, *520*
Jessor, R., 232, 233, 234, 236, *252*
Jessor, S. L., 232, 233, 234, *252*
Joel, B., 643, *658*
Joffe, J. M., 1431, 1433
Johansson, S., 593, *621*
John-Parsons, D. S., 730, *736*
Johnson, A., 16, 18, *36*
Johnson, A. M., 232, *252*
Johnson, B., 904, 910, 916, 917, 918, 922, 923, 924, *932*
Johnson, C. L., 182, 195, 202, 207, 208, *212*, 707, 723, 730, *736*
Johnson, D. L., 562, *582*
Johnson, E. S., 94, *99*, 292, 295, 306, 309, *315*
Johnson, F. A., 707, 723, 730, *736*, 1108, 1126
Johnson, J. E., 593, 595, *615*
Johnson, J. H., 447, *462*
Johnson, J. S., 386, 387, 393, *403*
Johnson, K. W., 123, *131*
Johnson, L. B., 447, 454, *462*, 663, 664, 665, *696*
Johnson, M., 513, 514, *520*
Johnson, M. P., 117, 119, *133*, 270, 271, 272, 273, 275, 277, 278, 279, *281*, 341, *354*
Johnson, N., 315, 1156, *1177*
Johnson, P., 1297, *1312*
Johnson, P. B., 388, *401*, 449, *520*
Johnson, P. T., 310, *312*
Johnson, S., 545, *553*, 1258, 1260, 1277
Johnson, S. J., 1354, *1377*
Johnson, S. M., 593, *615, 621*, 962, 970, 974, 976, 979, 980, 981, 982, 985, 1064, 1070, 1345, 1346, 1367, 1376
Johnson, V., 289, *316*
Johnson, V. E., 465, 477, 479, 481, 486, 488, 491, *494*, 1108, 1115, 1118, 1123, 1126
Johnston, J., 1298, *1316*

Joint Commission on the Mental Health of Children, 1258, *1276*
Jones, E. E., 104, 106, *133*
Jones, F. H., 866, *869*
Jones, J., 970
Jones, J. E., 939, 941, 942, 945, 947, 949, 953, *956*
Jones, J. M., 258, *280*, 344, 350, *352*
Jones, L. M., 266, *281*
Jones, M., 1256, 1258
Jones, M. B., 232, 233, 234, *247*
Jones, R., 995, 1000, 1041, 1043, 1064, 1068, 1153, 1169, 1176
Jones, R. G., 997, 1002
Jones, R. M., 229, *247*
Jones, R. R., 973, 996, 1003, 1096, 1104, 1346, 1355, 1356
Jones, S. E., 1223, 1243
Jones, S. G., 234, *255*
Jones, S. J., 569, *583*
Jorgensen, B. W., 117, 118, *135*
Jorgenson, S., 156, *174*
Jorgenson, S. R., 627, *656*, 1204, 1207, *1215*
Jourard, S., 75, *100*, 411, *425*
Jourard, S. M., 369, *374*, 443, 470, 490, 491, *494*
Joy, L. A., 563, *585*
Judah, J. S., 819, *842*
Judson, H., 158, *174*
Jurich, A. P., 448, 449, *463*
Jurich, J. A., 448, 449, *463*
Jurkovic, G., 157, 160, *172*, 228, 235, 246, *247, 252*
Jurkovic, G. J., 749, *774*
Justice, B., 911, 925, *932*
Justice, R., 911, 925, *932*

K

Kacerguis, M., 407, *425*
Kaffman, M., 863, *871*
Kafka, J. S., 259, *282*
Kagan, J., 526, 527, 531, *553, 556*
Kagan, L., 218, *254*, 341, *355*
Kagan, N., 1295, 1296, 1297, 1298, 1303, 1304, *1312*
Kagen, J., 449, 503, 507, *520, 521*, 589, *621*
Kahn, A. J., 1187, *1212*, 1402, *1411*
Kahn, M., 380, 382, *402*
Kahn, M. D., 181, 182, 187, 188, 189, 190, 194, 195, 196, 204, 205, 206, 207, *210*
Kakar, S., 149, *174*
Kalisch, B. J., 1437

Note: Pages 1–660 are in Volume I; pages 661–1457 are in Volume II. Italic numbers indicate reference citations.

Note: Pages 1–660 are in Volume I; pages 661–1457 are in Volume II. Italic numbers indicate reference citations.

Note: Pages 1–660 are in Volume I; pages 661–1457 are in Volume II. Italic numbers indicate reference citations.

Note: Pages 1–660 are in Volume I; pages 661–1457 are in Volume II. Italic numbers indicate reference citations.

Lickona, K., 363, 364, *375*
Liddle, H., 167, 168, *174*
Liddle, H. A., 1251, 1253, 1261, 1265, 1267, 1269, *1277*, 1283, 1284, 1286, 1287, *1290*, 1291, 1294, 1295, 1296, 1297, 1298, 1300, 1301, 1305, *1313*, *1316*
Lidz, T., 13, *36*, 397, *402*, 852, *872*, 940, *957*, 1080, *1105*
Liebenberg, B., 568, *584*
Lieber, D. J., 953, *956*
Liebman, R., 392, *403*, 1259, *1278*, 1291, *1314*
Liem, J. H., 945, *956*
Lifton, R. J., 506, *520*
Light, R., 546, *553*
Lillenfeld, A. M., 755, *779*
Lillie, F., 1261, 1274
Lindbergh, C., 544, *555*
Lindenthal, J. J., 1130, *1150*
Linder, D., 125, *129*
Lindholm, B. W., 649, *657*
Lipetz, M. E., 261, *280*
Lipman, R. S., 861, *868*
Lipman-Blumen, J., 511, 514, *520*
Lipset, D., 19, *36*
Lipsitt, L., 157, *171*
Lipson, A., 340, *352*
Lipton, M. A., 302, 303, *316*
Lisiecki, J., 1136, *1150*
Litman, R. E., 1035, *1071*
Littenberg, H., 1265, *1277*
Little, K. B., 1222, 1223, *1244*
Litwak, E., 293, *316*
Litz, T., 1236, *1244*
Livingston, D. D., 361, *376*
Livingston, K. R., 361, 366, *375*
Lo, T., 864, *872*
Lo, W., 864, *872*
Lobitz, C. K., 1064, *1070*
Lobitz, G., 545, *553*
Lobitz, G. K., 970, *974*, *986*, 1258, 1260, *1277*, 1354, *1377*
Locke, H., 381, 402
Locke, H. J., 754, *778*, 963, 972, *986*, 1044, 1045, 1046, 1047, 1048, 1051, 1056, 1063, *1070*, 1266, *1277*
Lockman, R. F., 568, *584*
Locksley, A., 728, *737*
Loda, F., 904, 908, 910, 912, 916, 923, 924, *932*
Loda, F. A., 545, *554*
Loeb, R. C., 594, *619*
Loeber, R., 1354, 1372, *1377*, 1423, *1434*
Loehlin, J. C., 120, 121, *135*

Loether, H. J., 298, *316*
Loevinger, J., 79, 80, *100*
Loganbell, C., 1295, 1296, 1297, 1298, *1313*
London, J., 702, 719, 720, *737*
Loney, J., 1154, 1156, 1157, *1176*, 1177
Long, L., 157, *174*
Longfellow, C., 544, *556*
Looff, D., 391, *402*
Lopata, H. Z., 289, 291, 297, 298, 301, *316*, 703, 710, 718, *737*
LoPiccolo, J., 476, 482, *494*, 1061, *1071*, 1108, 1110, 1119, *1125*, *1126*
LoPiccolo, L., 1119, *1125*
Lorber, J., 506, *519*
Lord, D. A., 244, *250*
Lotecka, L., 234, 237, *247*
Lott, B., 119, 122, *135*
Lourie, R. S., 911, *935*
Louy, V. E., 916, *931*
Love, H., 753, *778*
Loveland, N., 940, *956*, 970, *986*
Lowell, E. L., *808*
Lowenthal, M., 157, 160, 163, 165, *175*, 413, *425*
Lowenthal, M. F., 277, *282*, 287, 289, *316*, *520*
Lu, E., 981, *986*
Lu, Y., 1236, *1244*
Luborsky, L., 1060, *1068*, 1118, *1125*, 1332, *1342*
Luby, L. W., 787, *808*
Luchterhand, E., 222, *256*
Luckmann, T., 64, *71*
Lumsden, B. D., 309, *316*
Lundell, B., 629, *655*
Luria, Z., 540, *555*
Lurie, E. E., 288, *316*
Luthman, S. G., 1291, *1313*
Lynch, J. J., 371, *375*
Lynch, M. A., 907, 916, *933*
Lynn, D. B., 503, 513, 514, *520*, 521, 1221, *1244*
Lystad, M., *1437*
Lytton, H., 119, 122, *135*, 605, 606, *619*

M

Maas, H. S., 289, 310, *316*
MacBride, A., 232, *253*, 345, *356*
Macchitelli, F., 1136, *1150*
Maccoby, E., 121, *138*, 513, *521*, 542, 544, *554*, *555*, 639, *658*
Maccoby, E. E., 912, *935*, 1233, 1234, *1244*, 1350, *1379*, 1402, *1411*

Note: Pages 1–660 are in Volume I; pages 661–1457 are in Volume II. Italic numbers indicate reference citations.

McCarrick, A. K., 116, 119, *135*
McCarthy, B. W., 1108, 1126
McCarthy, M. E., 563, *584*
McCarty v. McCarty, 1393, *1411*
McCaslin, T. L., *1438*
McCleary, R., 1099, 1101, 1105
McClellan, M. S., 561, *582*
McClelland, D. C., 117, 119, 121, *135, 139,* 786, *808*
McClintock, E., 117, *138,* 1109, 1126
McClintock, M., 506, *519*
McColley, S., 1259, 1278, 1294, 1295, *1313*
McCord, J., 231, 232, *253, 254,* 1349, *1377*
McCord, W., 231, 232, *253, 254*
McCormick, N., 447, 454, *463*
McCrady, B. S., 110, *136*
McCubbin, H. I., 234, *254,* 732, *738,* 1166, *1176*
McCullough, B. C., 725, *736*
McCunney, N., 1187, 1207, *1215*
McCutchen, M. B., 999, 1004
McCutcheon, M. B., 117, *138*
McDaniel, S., 1287, *1313*
McDermott, J. F., 221, *254*
McDonald, M. G., 111, *136*
McDowall, D., 1101, 1105
McElrath, D., 413, 414, *427*
McGhee, P., 547, *556*
McGhee, P. E., 595, *621*
McGillicuddy-DeLisi, A., 595, *615*
McGoldrick, M., 165, 167, *172,* 241, *248,* 743, 744, 745, 775, 857, *872,* 1165, *1175,* 1280, 1290, *1310*
McGratta, C., 117, *130*
McHale, S. M., 116, *135,* 762, 763, 773, *779*
McHenry, S., 1196, 1198, 1199, *1213*
McKee, B., 77, 157, *174,* 449, *520*
McKeever, J., 1287, *1313*
McKenney, M., 1438
McKeon, D., 1271, *1278,* 1291, 1295, *1314*
McKinley, D., 547, *554*
McLanahan, S., 292, *314,* 326, *353*
McLaughlin, B., 593, *620*
McLean, M., 167, *173,* 742, 746, 761, 767, 771, *776*
McLeer, S. V., 881, 892, *898*
McLemore, C. W., 9, *36*
McMahon, R., 1153, *1176*
McNamara, J. R., 976, 987
McNatt, V., 1027, 1030
McNeal, S., 1345, 1355, 1356, *1378*
McNemar, Q., 1088, 1105
McPherson, S., 970, 985
McRae, J. A., 723, 724, 727, *736*

Mead, D. E., 236, *254*
Mead, E., 1303, *1313*
Mead, G. H., 9, 17, 23, 24, 26, 32, *36*
Meadows, L., 544, *555*
Medalie, J., 244, *250*
Medinnus, G. R., 232, *254*
Mednick, S., 864, 865, *872*
Meehl, P. E., 965, 986
Mehl, L. E., 560, *582*
Mehm, J. G., 915, 933
Mehrabian, A., 229, *254,* 1224, 1244
Meidinger, E. E., 1101, 1105
Meisels, M., 218, *254*
Meissner, W. W., 232, *254,* 474, *494*
Mejia, J. A., 1325, 1336, 1342
Melko, M., 330, 331, *352*
Melman, S. K., 1048, 1071
Melnick, B., 904, *933*
Melson, G. F., 699, 700, 701, *737*
Melton, M. B., 1399, *1411*
Mendelsohn, J., 1291, 1300, 1301, 1302, *1311, 1313*
Mendelsohn, M. J., 303, *311,* 439, 442, 445, *463*
Mendelsohn, N., 1156, *1177*
Mendelsohn, W., 1156, *1177*
Mendelwicz, J., 303, *316*
Mendes, H., 539, *554*
Mendez, O. A., 1234, 1243
Menghi, P., 1161, *1175,* 1291, *1309*
Menning, B. E., 646, *657*
Menolascino, F., 742, *780*
Mercer, G. W., 437, 439, 448, 455, *463*
Mercer, R. T., 562, *582,* 639, 640, *657*
Mercy, J. A., 126, *138*
Meredith, D., 232, *247*
Merkel, W., 1263, 1278
Merlin, M. M., 218, *247*
Mersky, R. M., 1381, 1382, *1410*
Merton, R., 681, 682, *696*
Messerly, L., 379, *404,* 548, *556*
Messersmith, C. E., *494,* 1109, 1126
Metzen, E. J., 703, 706, 716, *737*
Meyer, J. P., 117, 118, *136*
Meyering, S., 560, *583*
Meyerowitz, J., 569, 574, 578, *582,* 753, 768, *778*
Meyers, E., 560, *583*
Meyers, S., 646, *656*
Meyerstein, I., 1166, *1177,* 1291, 1294, 1300, 1301, 1302, *1314*
Michael, R. G., 608, 609, *620*
Michael, S. T., 538, *553*
Michaels, G. Y., 509, *521*
Michalson, L., 1418, 1419, 1420, 1428

Note: Pages 1–660 are in Volume I; pages 661–1457 are in Volume II. Italic numbers indicate reference citations.

Micheal, S. T., 856, *874*
Michela, J. L., 106, *136*
Michelson, L., 1153, *1177*
Mickey, R., 812, *843*
Milardo, R. M., 258, 267, 268, 270, 271, 273, 274, 275, 277, 278, 279, *281,* 311, *354*
Milden, J. W., 1438
Milea, K., 166, 173
Miley, C. H., 177, *213, 214*
Milgram, J. I., 189, 190, 192, 193, 194, *206*
Milhoj, P., 294, *318*
Miller, B., 156, 157, *174*
Miller, B. C., 572, 574, *582*
Miller, C. A., 557, *582*
Miller, D. A., 304, *316*
Miller, D. C., 440, *464*
Miller, D. R., 3, 29, *36,* 228, *254*
Miller, J., 156, 161, *175,* 702, 716, *737*
Miller, N., 3, 762, 763, 775
Miller, N. E., 1323, 1342
Miller, S., 193, *214,* 309, *317,* 1199, 1200, 1201, 1205, *1213, 1214*
Miller, S. J., 286, *319*
Miller, P. L., 305, *318*
Miller, T. W., 120, 122, *136*
Miller, W. B., 566, *583*
Miller, W. R., 1187, 1196, *1212*
Milliones, J., 543, *554*
Mills, C. W., 143, 157, 161, 164, 169, *173, 175*
Mills, J., 112, 113, 123, *130,* 354
Milman, L., 392, *403*
Milner, J. S., 903, 904, *933*
Minde, K. K., 758, 761, *778,* 1156, *1177*
Mindel, C. H., 293, 300, *316*
Miniturn, L., 504, *521,* 818, *843*
Mintz, M., 857, *875*
Mintz, N. L., 862, *872*
Minuchin, S., 42, *72,* 168, *175,* 181, 182, 202, *213,* 230, 241, 392, *403,* 743, 744, 745, *778,* 793, 794, *808,* 1008, 1030, 1076, 1078, 1079, 1080, 1105, 1166, *1177,* 1251, 1260, 1261, 1266, 1278, 1320, 1326, 1328, 1335, 1343
Mirande, A. M., 449, *463*
Miranna, A. C., 234, *256*
Mischel, W., 965, 968, 986, 1250, *1278*
Mischler, E. G., 103, *138,* 396, 397, *403,* 852, *872,* 941, 953, *956,* 978, 986, 1078, 1105, 1132, *1150,* 1282, *1314*
Mitchell, C., 128, *137*
Mitchell, D., 646, *656*
Mitchell, K. M., 1331, 1335, 1343
Mitchell, P., 413, *427*

Mitchell, R. E., 688, *696*
Mitchell, S., 651, 652, *659*
Mitler, D. C., *464*
Miyoshi, N., 1258, 1259, 1278
Mnookin, R. H., 1394, *1411*
Mock, J. E., 303 n, 311
Model, D., 703, 714, *737*
Modigliani, K., 888, *896*
Mohammed, Z., 1303, *1314*
Moles, O. C., 117, *135, 136*
Monahan, T. P., 232, *254*
Montagu, A., 848, *872,* 1118, 1126
Montalvo, B., 793, 794, *808,* 1166, *1177,* 1300, *1314*
Montgomery, J., 284, 288, *319*
Montgomery, R. L., 716, 717, 722, *736*
Moore, A., 626, *657*
Moore, B. M., 220, *254*
Moore, C., 84, 86, 96, *101,* 368, *376*
Moore, D., *494*
Moore, D. M., 720, *737,* 882, *898*
Moore, K. A., 724, *737*
Moos, B. S., 999, 1003
Moos, R. H., 999, 1001, 1003, 1266, 1267, 1278
Moran, M. A., 767, *779*
Moreland, R. L., 126, *130*
Moreno, J. L., 17, 18, *36*
Morgan, A. G., 1204, 1207, *1215*
Morgan, K. L., 692, 693, *696*
Morgan, L. A., 298, *316*
Morgan, S. M., 896, *898*
Moroney, B., 720, *736*
Moroney, R., 771, *779*
Morris, D., 465, *494*
Morris, G., 940, *957*
Morris, J. E., 117, *138,* 999, 1004, 1154, 1156, *1177*
Morris, M. G., 924, *933*
Morris, N., 561, 574, 575, *581*
Morris, N. M., 436, 453, *464*
Morris, P., 468, *494*
Morris, W. N., 825, *842*
Morrison, D. C., 75, *99,* 360, 361, *374,* 1355, *1379*
Morrison, R. L., 1064, 1071
Morrow, W. R., 535, *554*
Morse, C. W., 904, 917, 921, 922, 931, *933*
Morse, H. A., 904, 911, 916, 917, 918, 922, 923, 924, *932*
Mortimer, J. T., 567, *583,* 702, 716, 719, 720, *737*
Morton, D. R., 123, *131*
Morton, T., 412, 418, *426*
Morton, T. L., 111, 136, 366, *375*

Note: Pages 1–660 are in Volume I; pages 661–1457 are in Volume II. Italic numbers indicate reference citations.

Mosatche, H. S., 192, 213
Mosher, D. L., 437, 439, 442, 444, 445, 446, *463*
Mosher, L. R., 854, *871*
Moss, H. A., 531, *553*, 569, *583*
Moss, M. S., 299, *316*
Moss, N. E., 449, 507, 508, 512, 514, *521*
Moss, S. Z., 299, 316
Most, R., 1206, 1208, *1214*
Most, R. K., 527, *550*
Mousaw, P., 367, *374*
Moynihan, D. P., 680, 682, *696*
Mozdzierz, G., 1136, *1150*
Mueller, C. B., *493*
Mulhern, R. K., 920, *934*
Mulvey, E. P., 1406, *1411*
Mumford, D. M., 629, 630, *655, 659*
Mungo, R., 820, *843*
Munley, A., 287, *320*
Munns, M., 218, *254*
Munson, P., 1292, *1309*
Munson, T., 1256
Murdock, G. P., 623, *657*
Murillo-Rhode, I., 858, *872*
Murphy, G., xi, xii
Murphy, H. B. M., 847, 853, 867, *872*
Murphy, J. M., 853, *872*
Murray, E., 1260, 1275
Murray-Parkes, C., 1232, 1244
Murstein, B. I., 111, 113, 117, 118, *136,* 348, *351,* 360, *375,* 469, 481, 492, *494*
Mussen, P. H., 218, 219, 225, 229, *254,* 449, *521,* 533, *554*
Musser, L. M., 180, *212*
Muten, M., 235, *254*
Muxen, M., 732, *738*
Myers, J. K., 847, *872,* 1130, *1150*
Myers, M. A., 290, 291, *319*
Mykkanen, A., 643, *658*

N

Nadelman, L., 180, 190, 191, 193, 207, *213*
Nadelson, C. C., 629, *657*
Naegele, K. D., 508, *518*
Nagel, E., 5, 7, 9, 20, *36*
Naisbitt, J., 86, 94, *100,* 359, *375*
Naka, S., 867, *872*
Nakamura, C. Y., 120, 121, *138*
Nanda, H., 971, 984, 1090, 1103
Nangle, G. N., 731, *739*
Napier, A. Y., 755, 756, *779,* 1228, 1229 n, 1244, 1269, *1278,* 1320, 1343
Narus, L. R., Jr., 390, *403*
Nash, J., 573, *583*

Naster, B. J., 995, 1000, 1041, 1043, 1064, 1068
National Conference of Commissioners on Uniform State Laws, *1411*
Navarre, E., 360, 371, *374*
Navran, L., 972, 986
Naylor, A. K., 861, *872*
Neale, J., 1156, *1175*
Neeb, M., 492, *493*
Neighbors, H. W., 687, *696*
Neill, J., 432, 433, *434,* 485, *494,* 1116, 1126, 1260, 1278
Nelson, B., 1130, *1149*
Nelson, D. D., 526, 534, *554*
Nelson, G. M., 111, *136*
Nelson, K., 526, *554*
Nelson, M., 111, *136*
Nelson, R. C., 1187, *1214*
Nelson, Y., 1223, 1224, 1243
Nenny, S. W., 630, 639, *659*
Nettles, E. J., 84, *100,* 363, *375*
Neugarten, B. L., 285, 297, 298, 301, *317*
Nevaldine, A., 413, *426*
Newberger, G. H., 925, *930*
Newcomb, T., 449, *463, 464*
Newcomb, T. M., 125, *136*
Newman, B. M., 217, 222, 228, 230, *254*
Newman, C. J., 791, *808*
Newman, H. M., 107, *136*
Newman, P. R., 217, 222, 228, 230, *254*
Newton, N., 506, *519*
Neysmith, S. M., 310, *317*
Nichols, E., 413, *426*
Nichols, M. P., 396, *403*
Nichols, W., 1290, 1297, 1300, 1303, *1314*
Nickols, S. Y., 703, 706, 716, *737*
Nicolay, R. C., 572, *581*
Nijhawan, H. K., 120, 122, *136*
Nikelly, G., 863, *869*
Niles, F. S., 220, *254*
Nisbett, R. E., 104, 106, *133,* 1322, 1323, 1343
Nishina, N., 652, *656*
Noberini, M. R., 192, *213*
Noble, S., 904, 916, 923, 924, 925, *935*
Nobles, W., 683, *696*
Noel, C., 301, 304, *313*
Noller, P., 116, 117, 118, *136,* 380, 381, 382, 383, 385, *403,* 541, *554*
Nordstrom, L., 866, *870*
Norman, R. D., 515, *521,* 788, *808*
Norr, K., 703, 718, *737*
Norr, K. L., 560, *583*
North, J. D., 1354, *1376*
Norton, A. J., 324, *354,* 1035, 1069

Note: Pages 1–660 are in Volume I; pages 661–1457 are in Volume II. Italic numbers indicate reference citations.

Note: Pages 1–660 are in Volume I; pages 661–1457 are in Volume II. Italic numbers indicate reference citations.

Parker, C., 470, *494*
Parkes, C. M., 297, 298, *314, 317*
Parks, M. E., 258, 260, 277, 278, 279, *282*
Parks, S. H., 350, 351, *355*
Parloff, M. B., 784, *807,* 1057, 1064, *1071,* 1268, *1280*
Parmelee, A. H., 526, *551*
Parson, B. V., 995, *1000,* 1076, *1102,* 1320, 1325, 1332, 1335, 1336, 1341, 1342, 1346, 1355, 1372, 1375, *1376*
Parsons, A., 862, *873*
Parsons, B., 1086, *1102,* 1292, 1293, 1303, *1309*
Parsons, J. E., 388, *401*
Parsons, T., *323,* 1129, *1150*
Pascarelli, E. F., 305, *317*
Pascoe, J. M., 545, *555*
Passer, M. W., 106, *136*
Passman, R. H., 920, *934*
Pastushak, R., 1253, 1265, *1277*
Paternite, C., 1154, 1156, 1157, *1177*
Paterson, J. A., 367, *375*
Patterson, G., 596, *619*
Patterson, G. R., 334, *356,* 594, 596, *620,* 970, 971, 973, 974, 985, 986, 987, 995, 996, *1003,* 1041, 1043, 1044, 1045, 1047, 1059, 1070, 1071, *1072,* 1073, 1078, 1106, 1344, 1345, 1346, 1347, 1348, 1349, 1350, 1351, 1354, 1355, 1356, 1357, 1358, 1363, 1365, 1366, 1367, 1369, 1370, 1371, 1373, 1374, *1376, 1377,* 1423, *1434*
Patterson, J., 1166, *1176*
Patterson, M. J., 1220, *1243*
Patterson, R. D., 303, *317*
Paul, G., 1263, *1278*
Paul, J. S., 973, *987*
Paulhus, D., 126, *137*
Paulson, M. J., 911, *934*
Pawlby, S., 539, *553*
Paykel, E., 414, *423*
Paykel, E. S., 344, *355,* 538, *556,* 1130, 1134, *1150, 1151, 1157*
Payne, B., 367, *375*
Payne, H., 753, *780*
Payne, J., 646, 647, *657*
Pearce, K. J., 857, *872*
Pearce, W., 1283, 1284, *1314*
Pearl, A., 830, 834, *843*
Pearlin, L. E., 95, *100,* 359, 370, 372, *375*
Pearson, J., 1394, *1411*
Peck, A. L., 902, *932*
Peck, D. G., 305, *317*
Peck, T. P., *1438*
Pedersen, F., 527, 529, *555, 556*

Pedersen, F. A., 562, 563, 588, 598, 602, 603, 605, *620*
Pedhazur, E. J., 1098, *1104*
Peed, S., 1346, 1374, *1378*
Peek, C., 418, *423*
Peek, C. W., 389, 401
Peele, S., 9, *36*
Pelfrey, M. C., 234, *256*
Pelton, J. H., 925, *934*
Pendergast, E., 993, *1002*
Pendleton, B. F., 716, 717, 718, 731, *738*
Pengelley, E. J., 290, *317*
Penn, P., 993, *1003,* 1269, *1278*
Pepitone, A., 6, 10, 23, *36,* 102, 117, *137*
Peplau, L., 279, *281*
Peplau, L. A., 128, *134,* 350, 355, 419, *426,* 432, *434,* 437, 440, 453, 454, 456, *464,* 1109, 1114, 1118, 1124, *1126*
Pepler, D., 190, *210*
Pepper, M. P., 1130, *1150*
Pepper, S., 117, 118, *136*
Peres, Y., 467, *494*
Perlman, D., 349, *355*
Perlman, T., 1169, *1176*
Perlmutter, M., 416, *426*
Perls, F., 1141, *1150*
Perrucci, C. C., 703, 704, *738*
Person, T. M., 863, *871*
Pervin, L. A., 1419, 1420, 1428, *1434*
Pesses, D. I., 975, *984*
Peters, M. F., 691, *696*
Peterson, A. C., 629, *658*
Peterson, C., 723, 724, *735*
Peterson, C. C., 515, *521*
Peterson, D. R., 128, *134,* 270, *282,* 962, 987, 1109, *1126*
Peterson, G., 1266, *1268,* 1285, *1314*
Peterson, G. W., 242, 248
Peterson, J. L., 515, *521*
Peterson, P., 629, *658*
Peterson, R. A., 643, *657*
Peterson, R. F., 982, *984,* 1345, 1355, *1377, 1379*
Pettis, E., 769, 770, 771, *776*
Pfeiffer, E., 289, 300, 302, 303, 309, *312, 317*
Pfouts, J. H., 191, 194, *213*
Phelps, R., 1263, *1278,* 1345, 1355, 1356, *1378*
Phillips, R., 643, *658*
Phillips, R. A., Jr., 832, 838, 840, *842*
Phillips, S. L., 333, *353*
Phillips, S. V., 600, *621*
Phillips, V. A., 84, *100,* 756, 765, 766, *778,*

Note: Pages 1–660 are in Volume I; pages 661–1457 are in Volume II. Italic numbers indicate reference citations.

Radin, N., 531, *555*
Radke-Yanow, M., 1350, *1378*
Radloff, L., 723, *738*
Ragozin, A. S., 344, *352*, 640, *657*
Rahe, R. H., 1035, 1070, 1166, *1176*
Raimy, V. C., 1264, *1279*
Rainwater, L., 506, *521*, 684, 685, *696*
Rajaratnam, N., 971, 984, 1090, *1103*
Ralston, E. J., *1438*
Ramey, J. W., 405, *426*, 817, *843*
Rampage, C., 1250, *1268*
Randall, T. M., 119, *120*
Rands, M., 272, *282*, 421, *425*
Ransom, D., 1256, *1279*
Raphael, B., 344, *355*
Raphling, D. L., 904, 910, 916, *930*
Rapoport, R., 161, 165, 167, *175*, 557, 566,
    570, 571, *583*, 639, *657*, 699, 718, *738*
Rapoport, R. N., 165, *175*, 566, *583*, 639,
    657, 699, 718, *738*
Rappaport, A., 995, *1003*
Raskind, C. L., 286, *314*
Rassaby, E. S., 344, *355*
Rathbone-McCuan, E., 307, *317*
Ratzeburg, F., 1153, *1175*
Raush, H. L., 80, 96, *100*, 112, *137*, 358,
    367, 368, *375*, 1116, 1126, 1250, 1279
Ravitch, R. A., 969, 987
Rawnsley, K., 753, *780*
Ray, D. W., 388, *402*
Ray, R. S., 970, 987, 1355, *1378*
Reading, A. E., 652, *658*
Redlich, F. C., 855, 867, *870*
Reed, L., 105, *139*
Reed, R. B., 925, *930*
Reedy, M. N., 367, *375*
Rees, R., 758, *780*
Reese, II., 157, 160, 163, *171*, *176*
Regula, R. R., 1195, *1214*
Rehberg, R., 535, *555*
Reichardt, C. S., 1081, 1103
Reichler, M., 544, 547, *553*
Reid, J. B., 918, 920, 921, *934*, 973, 981,
    986, 987, 995, 996, 1003, 1344, 1346,
    1347, 1349, 1354, 1355, 1356, 1357,
    1358, 1361, 1365, 1366, 1367, 1369,
    1374, *1376*, *1378*, 1423, 1434
Reid, W. J., 308, *317*, *318*
Reidy, T. J., 918, *934*
Reifman, A., 854, *871*
Reilly, T. W., 561, 562, 563, 567, 568, *580*,
    583
Reiner, B. S., 626, *654*, *658*
Reisch, H., 643, *658*

Reiss, D., 50, 55, 64, 65, *72*, 159, 166, *175*,
    243, *255*, 605, *621*, 741, 752, 756, *779*,
    855, *873*, 1157, 1158, 1171, *1177*,
    1221, 1227, 1245, 1266, 1268, 1279
Reiss, E., 1020, 1030
Reiss, I. L., 360, *375*, 440, 442, 443, 445,
    449, *464*, 623, 644, *658*
Reissman, F., 830, 834, *843*
Rennie, T. A. C., 856, *874*
Renshaw, D. C., 902, *934*
Renshaw, R. H., 902, *934*
Repetti, R. L., 728, *738*
Repucci, N. D., 1402, *1409*
Resnick, J. L., 515, *521*
Resnikoff, R., 1269, 1279, 1292, *1314*
Rest, S., 105, *139*
Reuler, E., 759, 761, *775*
Reuter, M. W., 539, *555*
Reuveni, U., 1271, 1279
Revenstorf, C., 1047, 1050, 1052, 1054,
    1059, 1060, *1070*
Rey, L. D., 123, *131*
Rhamey, R., 125, *130*
Rhi, B. Y., 862, *871*
Rhoads, D. L., 703, 704, *788*
Ricci, J., 940, *957*
Rice, D. G., 1297, *1314*
Richardson, J. G., 725, *738*
Richardson, M. S., 342, *355*, 509, *521*
Richardson, R. A., 524, *551*
Rickard, H., 1263, 1265, 1279, 1289, *1314*
Rickels, K., 861, *868*
Rickert, V., 1300, 1301, *1315*
Ridberg, E., 237, *251*
Riddle, R., 1182, 1187, *1209*
Ridley, C., 258, *282*
Ridley, C. A., 728, *739*, 1187, 1204, 1207,
    1208, *1209*, *1215*
Ric, H., 751, 757, *775*
Riegel, K., 75, *100*, 163, 164, *175*
Rigler, D., 904, 911, 924, 925, *935*
Rimon, J., 788, *809*
Rimon, R., 371, 391, *403*
Rindfuss, R. R., 572, *583*
Rioch, M., 1270, 1279, 1288, *1315*
Riskin, J., 124, *137*, 852, *873*, 966, 978,
    987, 1235, 1245
Riskin, J. M., 589, *621*
Risley, T. R., 982, 983
Ritchey, G., 589, *622*
Ritvo, E. R., 855, *873*
Ritz, M., 1301, *1314*
Ritzler, B., 942, 947, *956*
Roberge, L., 902, *935*
Roberts, B. H., 847, *872*

Note: Pages 1–660 are in Volume I; pages 661–1457 are in Volume II. Italic
numbers indicate reference citations.

Roberts, F. J., 386, *402,* 1129, 1130, 1131, 1132, 1134, 1142, *1149*
Roberts, J., 342, *352,* 907, 915, *933*
Roberts, M., 1346, 1374, *1378*
Roberts, R., 820, *845*
Robertson, J. F., 93, *100,* 296, 297, *318, 320,* 371, 372, *375*
Robey, A., 883, *898,* 1408, *1409*
Robillard, A. B., 221, *254*
Robin, A. L., 1187, *1215*
Robin, S., 1155, 1156, 1158, 1159, 1168, 1170, *1177*
Robins, E., 270, *282*
Robins, L. N., 179, *212,* 233, *255*
Robinson, B., 287, *316*
Robinson, J. G., 641, *656*
Robinson, J. N., 709, *739*
Robinson, N. M., 344, *352,* 640, *657*
Robinson, P. A., 232, *255*
Robison, E., 722, *739*
Robison, I. E., 432, *434,* 436, 438, *464*
Robson, K. S., 561, *583,* 603, 604, *620*
Rocheford, E. B., 811, *843*
Rockwell, R. C., 117, 118, *137*
Rodgers, R., 165, 166, 167, *175,* 284, *314*
Rodgers, W., 700, *735*
Rodick, J. D., 963, 985
Rodman, H., 998, 1003
Rodnick, E., 231, *250*
Rodnick, E. H., 399, *401,* 851, 852, *870,* 939, 946, 949, 952, *956,* 970
Roe v. Wade, 1395, *1411*
Roff, J. E., 850, 864, *873*
Roffe, M. W., 474, *494*
Rogel, M. J., 629, *658*
Rogers, C. H., 1320, 1335, 1336, 1343
Rogers, L. E., 991 n, 1002, 1003
Rogers, M. F., 998, 1004
Rohde, P. D., 401, *402*
Rohrbaugh, M., 1137, *1150,* 1282, *1315*
Rohrbeck, C. A., 909, 936
Rokeach, M., 225, *255*
Rokoff, G., 731, *734*
Rolf, J., 1270, 1280
Rollins, B. C., 288, 318
Romano, J., 865, *873*
Ronald, L., 234, *253*
Rook, K. S., 348, 349, 350, *355*
Roosa, M. W., 623, 633, 634, 635, 636, *658*
Rose, R. J., 123, *136*
Rose, S. E., 562, *579*
Rosen, B., 720, *739*
Rosen, J., 1136, *1150*
Rosen, L. A., 466, *493*
Rosen, R. H., 632, 633, *658*

Rosenbaum, I., 1291, *1315*
Rosenbaum, R. M., 105, *139*
Rosenberg, B. C., 178, 180, 182, 197, 201, 202, 207, *214,* 371, *376*
Rosenberg, D., 917, 925, 926, *930*
Rosenblatt, P., 413, *426*
Rosenblatt, P. C., 95, *100,* 117, 118, *137,* 643, 644, *658,* 1226, 1229 n, 1245
Rosenblum, L., 601, *619*
Rosenfeld, H., 1224, 1245
Rosenmayr, L., 293, *318*
Rosenthal, A. J., 940, 948, *955*
Rosenthal, M., 1346, 1358, 1359, *1377*
Rosenthal, R., 389, *403*
Rosenwald, R., 883, *898*
Rosin, A. J., 305, *318*
Rosman, B., 157, 167, *175*
Rosman, B. L., 392, *403,* 793, 794, *808,* 940, *957,* 1080, 1105, 1166, *1177,* 1260, *1278*
Rosow, I., 286, *318,* 340, *355*
Ross, D., 912, *929*
Ross, D. J., 117, 118, *137*
Ross, E. R., 1204, *1215*
Ross, G., 589, *621*
Ross, H. G., 189, 190, 192, 193, 194, 206, *213*
Ross, J., 1303, *1312*
Ross, J. A., 117, 120, *137*
Ross, L. D., 106, *136*
Ross, N. W., 832, 835, *843*
Ross, S. A., 912, *929*
Ross, S. E., 562, *579*
Rossi, A., 506, *519*
Rossi, A. S., 506, 508, 509, 513, 515, *521,* 558, 564, 573, *583,* 729, *739*
Roszak, T., 832, 838, *843*
Rothenberg, P. B., 633, *658*
Rotheram, M. J., 722, 725, *739*
Rothschild, N., 183, *212*
Ro-Trock, L., 755, 765, 773, *775*
Rotter, J., 1223, 1245
Rotter, J. B., 447, *464,* 1022, 1023, 1030
Rounsaville, B. J., 894, *898,* 1130, 1134, *1150*
Routh, D., 1164, *1177*
Routh, D. K., 509, *522*
Rovine, M., 528, 544, *550,* 574, *579,* 603, *616*
Rowe, D. C., 607, *621*
Rowe, G., 259, 261, *280*
Roy, M., 879, 882, *898*
Royce, J., 1256, 1279
Royce, J. E., 305, *318*
Rozella, R. M., 1221, 1241

Note: Pages 1–660 are in Volume I; pages 661–1457 are in Volume II. Italic numbers indicate reference citations.

Saward, Y., 652, *656*
Sawhill, I., 824, *844*
Sawin, M., 1187, *1215*
Sawin, S. E., 600, 601, *620*
Sborofsky, S. C., 1206
Scanzoni, J., *137*
Scarr, S., 122, 123, *132, 137,* 180, 209, *213,* 1421, 1429, 1432, 1434
Scauzoni, J., *739*
Schachar, R., 1154, *1177*
Schachler, F. F., 197, *213*
Schachler, S., 124, *131*
Schaefer, E. S., 996, 1004
Schafer, R. B., 724, *736*
Schaeffer, E. S., 757, *779*
Schaeffer, M., 405, *426*
Schaffer, N. D., 1335, 1336, 1337, 1343
Schaie, K., 163, *175*
Schalock, H. D., 973, 987
Scharff, D. E., 1109, 1118, 1126
Schatzberg, A. F., 1128, *1149*
Schechter, L. F., 1388, *1412*
Schechter, M. D., 902, *935*
Scheer, N. S., 882, *898*
Scheflen, A., 157, 159, *175,* 749, *779,* 1238, 1245
Scheibe, K. E., 3, 37, 447, *462*
Scheiber, B., 769, 770, 771, *776*
Schenk, J., 474, 488, *494*
Scheper-Hughes, N. M., 861, *874*
Scherer, S., 233, *255*
Scherf, G. W. H., 117, 118, *138*
Scherz, F. H., 300, *318*
Schetter, C., 419, *426*
Schiavo, R. S., 1325, 1335, 1336, 1341, 1346, 1375, *1376*
Schiff, N. R., 309, *318*
Schilz, B., 432, *434*
Schindler, L., 1047, 1050, 1052, 1054, 1059, 1060, 1070
Schinke, S. P., 629, *658*
Schlein, S., 1206, *1215*
Schlenker, B. R., 1422, 1434
Schlesinger, B., 1438
Schmidt, A. W., 646, *656*
Schmidt, G., 432, *434, 495*
Schneider, I., 357, *376*
Schneidman, E. S., 785, *809,* 1035, 1071
Schneyer, L. C., 788, 789, *809*
Schnieder, S. J., 286, *319*
Schnieder, W., 1323, 1327, 1343
Schofield, M., *464*
Schoggen, D., 155 n, *171*
Schonfeld, L., 306, *313*
Schonnel, F. J., 750, *779*

Schooler, C., 177, *213*
Schopler, E., 1259, 1279, 1291, *1315*
Schopler, J. H., 889, *898*
Schover, L., 1061, 1071
Schover, L. R., 1126
Schratz, P. R., 235, *255*
Schreibman, L., 762, *779*
Schroder, H. M., 1022, 1029
Schroeder, C., 1164, *1177*
Schubert, D. S. P., 178, *214*
Schubert, H. J. P., 178, *214*
Schuckit, M. A., 305, 306, *318*
Schulman, J., 1400, 1401, *1412*
Schulman, J. B., 1439
Schulsinger, R., 864, *874*
Schultz, L. A., 1346, 1347, 1358, 1367, 1372, *1376*
Schultz, L. G., 883, *898*
Schultz, W., 1289, *1315*
Schultz, W. C., 1041, 1071
Schulz, B., 436, 450, 455, *464*
Schum, C., 629, *655*
Schum, D. A., 629, *655*
Schumer, F., 793, 794, *808,* 1166, *1177*
Schumm, W. R., 117, *138,* 999, 1004
Schutz, C., 593, *620*
Schvaneveldt, J. D., 179, 181, 182, 183, 203, 206, 207, *213,* 229, *247*
Schwartz, A. N., 294, *318*
Schwartz, C., 769, 771, *779*
Schwartz, D., 1343
Schwartz, D. T., 862, *872*
Schwartz, R., 1171, *1178,* 1267
Schwartzman, J., 859, *874,* 1235, 1236, 1245
Schweid, E., 1345, *1377*
Sclare, A. B., 904, 923, 924, *929*
Scoresby, L., 991, 1004
Scott, R., 864, *870*
Scott, W. J., 904, 911, *935*
Sears, P. S., 785, *809*
Sears, R., 60, *72,* 544, *555*
Sears, R. R., 121, *138,* 639, 640, *658,* 912, *935,* 1233, 1245, 1350, *1379*
Seashore, M., 561, *584*
Seashore, M. J., 119, 120, *138*
Secord, P. F., 8, *36,* 443
Sedge, S., 301, *312*
Sedlacek, W. E., 1328, 1342
Seelbach, W. C., 284, 300, *318*
Segal, J., 858, *874*
Segal, L., 1161, *1176*
Segraves, R. T., 477, *495,* 1109, 1115, 1116, 1126
Seiden, A. M., 1328, 1343

Note: Pages 1–660 are in Volume I; pages 661–1457 are in Volume II. Italic numbers indicate reference citations.

Note: Pages 1–660 are in Volume I; pages 661–1457 are in Volume II. Italic numbers indicate reference citations.

Singer, M. T., 851, 852, 855, 865, *874,* 937, 938, 939, 940, 941, 942, 943, 944, 946, 947, 948, 950, *956, 957, 958,* 970, 986, 1166, *1178*
Singh, B. K., 452, 453, 455, *464*
Sinha, B. P., 120, *137*
Sinkford, S. M., 916, *931*
Sinnott, J. D., 300, 304, *311, 313*
Siomopoulos, U., 1424, 1427, 1434
Skinner, E. A., 540, *554*
Sklar, J., 624, *659*
Skolnick, A., 570, *584*
Skrtic, T. M., 762, *779*
Skynner, A. C. R., 1040, 1041, 1064, 1072
Skynner, P., 1281, 1304, *1315*
Skynner, R., 1281, 1304, *1315*
Slater, P., 271, 275, *282*
Slaughter, H., 758, *780*
Sledmere, C. M., 652, *658*
Sloan, S., 405, *425,* 1422, 1423, 1425 n, 1434
Sloane, H., 1345, *1379*
Sloane, S. Z., 1189, *1213*
Slovenko, R., 1400, *1412*
Smalley, R. E., 190, *213*
Smart, R. G., 233, 234, *255*
Smelser, N. J., 75, *100,* 359, *376*
Smith, A., 1154, *1177*
Smith, B., 755, 765, 773, *775*
Smith, B. O., 626, *654*
Smith, C. U., 663, *696*
Smith, D., 1255, 1279
Smith, D. K., 1027, 1030
Smith, E. W., 632, *659*
Smith, H., 149, *175*
Smith, J., 187, 188, *214*
Smith, K., 1165, *1177*
Smith, M. B., 229, *251*
Smith, M. O., 508, *521*
Smith, P. B., 630, *659*
Smith, P. G., *655*
Smith, S. M., 904, 907, 908, 911, 914, 916, 922, 924, 925, *935*
Smith-Blackmer, D., 508, *521*
Smith-Rosenberg, C., 504, *521*
Smyer, M. A., 341, *353*
Snell, J. E., 883, *898*
Snoek, J. D., 117, *135*
Snowden, R., 651, 652, *659*
Snyder, D. K., 882, 885, *898,* 1059, 1072, 1110, 1124
Snyder, E. E., 726, *739*
Snyder, J. J., 970, 977, *987*
Snyder, P. K., 306, *318, 493*
Snyder, W., 1368, *1379*

Sokal, R. R., 927, *935*
Sokolovsky, J., 852, *868*
Sollie, D. L., 572, 574, 575, *582*
Solnit, A. J., 1398, 1402, *1410*
Solvberg, H., 941, *957*
Sommer, R., 968, 987, 1222, 1223, 1245
Sommers, A. A., 116, *134*
Soper, P., 1018, 1030
Sorell, G. J., 540, *554*
Sorrentino, B., 411, *427*
Soucy, G., 1250, 1268
South, G. R., 218, *250*
Spanier, G., 155, 156, 163, 166, *176,* 546, *550, 552,* 603, *616*
Spanier, G. B., 183, *212,* 216, 217, 218, 227, 230, 241, 243, *253,* 261, *282,* 464, 465, *495,* 574, *579,* 724, 728, *739,* 963, 987, 1056, 1063, 1072
Spark, C. M., 75, 93, 96, *99*
Spark, G. M., 507, *519,* 904, 924, 929, 1008, 1029, 1229, 1236, 1242
Sparling, J. J., 689, *696*
Speck, R., 18, *37,* 1271, 1279
Speer, D., 32, *37*
Speer, D. C., 969, 972, 987
Spelke, E., 589, *619, 621*
Spence, D. L., 309, *315*
Spenner, K. I., 123, *131*
Spicer, J. W., 341, *355*
Spiegel, J., 143, 144, 157, 158, 159, 164, *176,* 241, *255,* 749, *779,* 858, 873, 1259, 1266, 1279, 1282, 1315
Spiegel, N. H., 395, *404*
Spinetta, J. J., 904, 911, 924, 925, *935*
Spinks, S. H., 995, 1001
Spitze, G., 713, *736*
Spivack, G., 1166, 1169, *1178*
Spooner, S., 405, *426*
Spreitzer, E., 726, *739*
Sprenkle, D., 51, *72,* 93, 1020, 1030, 1226, 1244, 1245, 1266, 1278, 1320, 1324, 1343
Sprenkle, D. H., 230, 255, 474, *495*
Srole, L., 856, *874*
Sroufe, L. A., 528, *555,* 691, *696,* 902, 930
Stabenau, J., 941, *957,* 978, 987
Stabenau, J. R., 236, *255*
Stachkowiak, J., 764, *779*
Stack, C., 684, 685, 687, *696*
Stack, J. M., 633, *658*
Stahl, J. M., 715, *739*
Staines, G. L., 719, 725, *738, 739*
Stambaugh, E. E., 1354, *1379*
Stan, C. M., 258, 260, 277, 278, 279, *282*
Stan, S., 1303, *1312*

Note: **Pages 1–660 are in Volume I; pages 661–1457 are in Volume II.** Italic numbers indicate reference citations.

Note: Pages 1–660 are in Volume I; pages 661–1457 are in Volume II. Italic numbers indicate reference citations.

Note: Pages 1–660 are in Volume I; pages 661–1457 are in Volume II. Italic numbers indicate reference citations.

Varga, P. E., 633, *658*
Varrin, P. H., 608, *621*
Vasta, R., 920, *936*
Vaughan, L., 633, 635, *658*
Vaughan, P. W., 386, 402
Vaughn, B., 916, *930*
Vaughn, C., 398, 400, *402, 403*
Vaughn, C. E., 953, *957,* 1260, 1261, 1274, 1280, 1418, 1419, 1428, 1434
Vaux, A., 217, *251,* 533, *555*
Veenhoven, R., 644, *659*
Veevers, J. E., 506, *522,* 643, *659*
Vellerman, J. O., 232, *253*
Verbrugge, L. M., 326, 327, 328, 330, *356*
Verevoedt, A., 289, 302, *313, 317*
Verling, L., 1399, *1410*
Verma, P., 120, 122, *136*
Veroff, J., 328, 339, *356,* 1256, 1275
Viano, E. C., 300, *320*
Vicks, T. D., 715, *739*
Vidich, A., 155 n, *176*
Vierra, A., 721, *740*
Vietze, P. M., 563, *584,* 761, *780*
Vincent, C., 1270, 1280
Vincent, J., 995, 1005
Vincent, J. P., 116, *130,* 334, *352,* 379, 399, *403*
Vincent, P., 548, *556*
Vincent, S. P., 970, 984
Vinsel, A., 368, *376*
Viveros-Long, A., 703, 712, 719, *734*
Vockell, E. L., 177, *214*
Voeller, M. N., 84, 91, 96, *99,* 1324, 1342
Vogelsong, E., 1189, 1192, 1193, 1206, *1211, 1212, 1216*
Vojdany-Noah, S. V., 608, *621*
von Bertalanffy, L., *72*
Vondra, J., 523
Von Knorring, A. L., 650, *654*
von Trommel, M., 1281, 1291, *1316*
Voos, O., 916, *932*
Voyles, B., 307, *317*
Voysey, M., 749, *780*
Vygotsky, L., 9, *37*

W

Wachs, T., 526, 529, *556*
Wachtel, P. L., 1361, *1379*
Wackman, D. B., 309, *317,* 1199, 1200, 1201, 1205, *1214*
Wackwitz, J. H., 234, *256*
Wagner, G., 1109 n, 1126
Wagner, M. E., 178, *214*

Wagner, V., 419, 422, *425,* 1018, 1019, 1026, 1027, 1028, 1030, 1342, 1424, 1425 n, 1428, 1434
Wahl, G., 593, *621*
Wahler, R. G., 1157, 1158, 1165, *1178,* 1346, 1354, 1355, 1375, 1379, 1423, 1434
Wain, J., 146, *176*
Waisbren, S. E., 754, 755, *780*
Waites, E. A., 883, *899*
Wakeley, R. P., 862, *875*
Walberg, H. G., 178, 214
Walberg, H. J., 178, *214*
Walbridge, R. H., 102, *138*
Walder, L. O., 912, *933*
Waldron, H., 509, *522,* 1290, 1292, *1309,* 1320, 1321, 1324, 1327, 1335, 2338, 1341
Walizer, M. M., 1087, 1088, 1106
Walker, A. J., 333, 336, 337, *356*
Walker, H., 1166, *1178*
Walker, K. N., 345, *356*
Walker, L., 1388, 1389, *1412*
Walker, L. E., 885, 888, 890, 893, 895, *899*
Wall, S., 528, *549*
Wallace, D., 467, 491, *494*
Wallace, D. H., 467, 475, 486, *495,* 1118, 1127
Wallace, K., 381, *402*
Wallace, K. M., 754, *778,* 963, 972, 986, 1044, 1045, 1046, 1047, 1048, 1051, 1056, 1063, 1070, 1266, 1277
Wallace, W. L., 694, *696*
Waller, W., 260, 261, 252, *283,* 995, 996, 1004
Waller, W. W., 569, *584*
Wallerstein, R., 1300, *1311*
Wallin, P., 471, 472, 473, 483, *495*
Wallston, B. S., 702, 716, 717, 719, 720, *735, 739, 740*
Walsh, F., *780,* 1236, 1245, 1263, 1270, 1280, 1282, *1316*
Walshok, M., 718, *740*
Walster, E., 108, 109, *138,* 348, *356,* 360, 361, 362, 363, 364, 367, 368, 370, 371, *377,* 411, *427,* 460, *464*
Walster, E. H., 361, 362, 363, 367, 370, *374*
Walster, G. W., 348, *356,* 360, 361, 362, 363, 364, 367, 368, 370, 371, *377,* 411, *427,* 460, *464*
Walster, W., 108, 109, *138*
Walter, H. I., 1357, *1379*
Walter, R. G., 481, *495*
Walters, D. R., 902, 911, 925, 927, *936*

Note: Pages 1–660 are in Volume I; pages 661–1457 are in Volume II. Italic numbers indicate reference citations.

Walters, J., 230, 232, 243, 253, 256, 372, *376,* 449, 506, *522*
Walters, L. H., 180, *214,* 449, 506, *522*
Walters, R., 544, *549*
Walters, R. H., 234, *247*
Walton, M., 1304, *1316*
Waltz, M., 1298, *1316*
Waltzer, H., 651, *659*
Wampler, K. S., 1183, 1199, 1201, 1214, *1216*
Wampold, B. E., 379, 384, *403*
Wandersman, L. P., 548, *522*
Wang, H. S., 289, *317*
Ward, C., 303 n, *311*
Waring, E. M., 391, *404,* 474, 488, 490, 491, *495*
Waring, J. M., 288, 292, 310, *314*
Warkentin, J., 482, *495*
Warnyea, J. A., 562, *579*
Warren, N. J., 386, *403*
Warren, S. F., 1431, 1435
Warshak, R., 544, *555*
Waskow, I., 1268, 1280
Wasli, E., 414, *427*
Wasserman, S., 904, 908, *936*
Wasserman, T., 120, *138*
Waterman, J., 912, *929*
Waters, E., 528, *549*
Watson, J., 559, *584*
Watt, N., 1270, 1280
Watts, B. H., 750, *779*
Watzlawick, P., 14, 33, *36,* 793, 794, 795, *809,* 969, 988, 992, 997, 1004, 1041, 1072, 1078, 1086, 1106, 1109, 1117, 1127
Waxler, C. Z., 977, 978, 988
Waxler, N. E., 103, *138,* 396, 397, *403,* 852, 862, *872,* 875, 941, 944, 953, *956, 957,* 978, 986, 1078, 1105, 1132, *1150,* 1282, 1314
Waxler, P. H., 1220, 1245
Way, A., 306, *318*
Weakland, J. H., 13, 18, *35, 37,* 391, *404,* 961, 984, 1041, 1072, 1078, 1103, 1109, 1117, 1127, 1136, 1137, *1148,* 1161, *1176,* 1236, 1245
Weakland, K., 851, 860, *868*
Weary, G., 104, *132*
Weaver, C. N., 432, *434*
Webber, P. L., 122, *137*
Weber, T., 1287, *1313*
Wechsler, D., 1164, *1178*
Wechsler, H., 232, *256*
Wedderburn, D., 294, *318*
Weed, J. A., 567, *584*

Weeks, G., xi, xii, 1136, 1137, 1138, *1150,* 1172, 1178, 1187, *1213*
Weeks, K., 720, *736*
Weiber, J. D., 823, 824, 825, 844
Weick, K. E., 103, *138,* 967, 988
Weigert, E. B., 1135, 1139, *1149*
Weiman, R. J., 1203, *1216*
Weinberg, R. A., 122, 123, *132, 137*
Weinberg, S. L., 509, *522*
Weiner, B., 104, 105, 106, *133, 139*
Weiner, I. B., 223, 227, 242, 244, 245, *249, 256*
Weiner, M. F., 361, 364, *377*
Weiner, N., 722, 725, *739*
Weingarten, H., 117, 119, *134*
Weingarten, K., 635, 638, 639, *655,* 702, 706, *740*
Weinman, M. L., 630, *659*
Weinraub, M., 596, 601, *619, 622*
Weinrott, M. R., 762, *780,* 1349, 1374, *1378*
Weinstein, K., 296, 297, *317*
Weinstock, C. S., 449, *522*
Weintraub, S., 1156, *1175,* 1269, *1274*
Weir, T., 411, 419, *423,* 724, 725, 727, 728, *734*
Weis, D. L., 474, *495*
Weisberg, C., 388, *402*
Weisberg, D. K., 360, *374,* 823, *842*
Weishaus, S., 287, *320*
Weisner, T. S., 182, 204, *214,* 812, 813, 816, 818, 819, 822, 823, 824, 825, 826, 827, 828, *842, 843, 844*
Weiss, D. J., 981, 988
Weiss, G., 1169, *1175,* 1156, *1177*
Weiss, J. L., 864, *870*
Weiss, L., 413, *425*
Weiss, R. L., 116, *130,* 334, *352, 356,* 379, *404,* 768, 780, 970, 984, 985, 995, 997, 1003, 1005, 1041, 1043, 1044, 1045, 1047, 1059, 1070, 1072, 1078, 1106
Weiss, R. S., 298, *314,* 1399, 1400, *1412*
Weissman, M., 414, *423*
Weissman, M. M., 538, *556,* 1130, 1134, 1136, *1149, 1150, 1151*
Weisz, G., 414, *427*
Weithorn, L. A., 1399, *1413*
Weitz, S., 1219, 1245
Weitzman, J., 894, 895, *899*
Weitzman, L. J., 1380, 1387, 1391, 1400, *1413*
Welch, S., 723, 727, *740*
Weller, L., 222, *256*
Wellish, D. K., 830, 831, *844*
Wells, G. L., 106, *132*

Note: Pages 1–660 are in Volume I; pages 661–1457 are in Volume II. Italic numbers indicate reference citations.

Subject Index

Note: Pages 1–660 are in Volume I; pages 661–1457 are in Volume II. Italic
numbers indicate reference citations.

Note: Pages 1–660 are in Volume I; pages 661–1457 are in Volume II. Italic
numbers indicate reference citations.

Note: Pages 1–660 are in Volume I; pages 661–1457 are in Volume II. Italic numbers indicate reference citations.

Note: Pages 1–660 are in Volume I; pages 661–1457 are in Volume II. Italic numbers indicate reference citations.

Note: Pages 1–660 are in Volume I; pages 661–1457 are in Volume II. Italic
numbers indicate reference citations.

This book has been set VideoComp in 10 and 9 point Gael, leaded 2 points. Section numbers are set in 18 point Spectra Extra Bold, section titles in 18 point Spectra. Chapter numbers are 24 point Spectra Extra Bold, and chapter titles are 18 point Spectra. The size of the type page is 27 by 46 picas.

Note: Pages 1–660 are in Volume I; pages 661–1457 are in Volume II. Italic numbers indicate reference citations.